OPERA IN CHICAGO

Books by RONALD L. DAVIS

A HISTORY OF OPERA IN THE AMERICAN WEST

OPERA IN CHICAGO

OPERA IN CHICAGO

by RONALD L. DAVIS

ILLUSTRATED

APPLETON-CENTURY New York

First edition

Library of Congress Catalog Card Number: 65-23018

MANUFACTURED IN THE UNITED STATES OF AMERICA FOR MEREDITH PRESS

VAN REES PRESS • NEW YORK

For STEVE–

both of them

FOREWORD

Opera in Chicago tries to deal with more than just the great moments of a rich operatic history. Hopefully, the book attempts to catch something of the social flavor surrounding each opera season. More important, the author ties the story of opera in Chicago into the history of the city and the nation. The opera house has served as a specialized test tube in which American intellectual and social trends may be observed. At the same time effort has been made not to slight the musical side of the story, and much of the color which Mary Garden, Rosa Raisa, Amelita Galli-Curci, Maria Callas, Renata Tebaldi, and a host of other notables have brought to Chicago has been included. Still, *Opera in Chicago* is written not as a music critic would write it, but as an American social and cultural historian would, with an eye always on the larger picture.

The list of persons to whom I am indebted for assistance is lengthy. Special thanks, however, must be extended to Carol Fox, Lawrence Kelly, and Danny Newman for their insights into recent Chicago operatic history. Conversations with Tito Gobbi, Edith Mason, May Higgins (former secretary to Claudia Muzio), and Mrs. René Devries (wife of the noted Chicago critic) also proved particularly helpful. Without the willing assistance of the staffs of the Newberry Library, the Chicago Public Library, the Chicago Historical Society, the Michigan State University Library, and the University of Missouri Library, research on the volume could never have been completed. Professors Edward and Alma Homze of the University of Nebraska spent long hours offering valid criticism of the manuscript, as did Steven C. Trimble of Emporia, Kansas. Much of the proofreading was done by Mrs. Paul Trimble, while the entire manuscript was typed by Marilyn B. Davis. Finally, I would like to express my gratitude to Theodore M. Purdy, my editor, for his suggestions and for allowing me to shape the project as I saw fit.

R.L.D.

SOURCES

By far the bulk of the material presented here is drawn from contemporary Chicago newspapers—the *American*, the *Daily Journal*, the *Democrat*, the *Morning News*, the *Chronicle*, the *Dispatch*, the *Record*, the *Evening Post*, the *Herald*, the *Daily News*, the *Inter-Ocean*, the *Sun-Times*, and particularly the *Tribune*. Next in importance are the various musical journals, especially *Musical Courier*, *Musical America*, *Music News*, *Musical Leader*, *Etude*, and *Opera News*. Invaluable are the Auditorium scrapbooks and the Gleason Collection, both located in the Newberry Library in Chicago. Memoirs of musical personalities like Emma Abbott, Clara Louise Kellogg, James Henry Mapleson, Theodore Thomas, Walter Damrosch, Luigi Arditi, Mary Garden, Frances Alda, Marguerite D'Alvarez, and Sergei Prokofieff provide information available nowhere else. Karleton Hackett's *The Beginnings of Grand Opera in Chicago*, George Upton's *Musical Memories*, Edward C. Moore's *Forty Years of Opera in Chicago*, and C. J. Bulliet's *How Grand Opera Came to Chicago* are essential records by men who witnessed much of Chicago's operatic history, as are portions of Arthur Meeker's *Chicago, with Love* and Vincent Sheean's *First and Last Love*. For the Metropolitan's visits to Chicago, Quaintance Eaton's *Opera Caravan* offers a good account.

Among the biographies C. E. Le Massena's *Galli-Curci's Life of Song*, George Jellinek's *Callas: Portrait of a Prima Donna*, Forrest McDonald's *Insull*, Vincent Sheean's *Oscar Hammerstein I*, Joseph Wechsberg's *Red Plush and Black Velvet* (Melba), and Ishbel Ross's *Silhouette in Diamonds* (Mrs. Potter Palmer) are particularly significant to the Chicago Opera story. For material concerning the building of the Auditorium, it is necessary to consult Louis H. Sullivan's *The Autobiography of an Idea* and Dankmar Adler's article in the initial volume of *The Architectural Record* (Vol. 1, No. 4). Scattered but highly valuable information on various aspects of the Chicago operatic scene may be found in articles in *Harper's*, *The Literary Digest*, *The Dial*, *Cosmopolitan*, *Craftsman*, *The Forum*, *The Bookman*, *The New Republic*, *The Nation*, *Arts and Decoration*, *Newsweek*, and *Time*.

For general historical background and interpretation, Louis B. Wright's *Culture on the Moving Frontier*, Walter P. Webb's *The Great Frontier*, Walter Lord's *The Good Years*, and Frederick Lewis Allen's *Only Yesterday* and *Since Yesterday* have proved of special interest. For material on the early history of Chicago, Bessie L. Pierce's *A History of Chicago* is basic. Less complete but highly reliable is Emmett Dedmon's *Fabulous Chicago*. More specialized are Harry Hansen's *Chicago*, Ernest Poole's *Giants Gone*, Alson J. Smith's *Chicago's Left Bank*, and Edgar Lee Masters' *The Tale of Chicago*. Of considerable merit on the city's literary history is Bernard I. Duffey's *The Chicago Renaissance in American Letters*.

Programs for Chicago's resident opera companies may be found, with a few gaps, in the Chicago Public Library.

CONTENTS

ILLUSTRATIONS

(following page 114)

OPERA IN CHICAGO

Chapter 1

A CAT CAME FIDDLING OUT OF A BARN

THE land was a prairie, dotted here and there with clumps of trees, rolling gently until just before it reached the great lake, then leveling into a grassy marsh. The Indian knew the land, cut his trails through it, and hunted there. The buffalo knew it too, grazed on its grasses, and drank from the lake. But this was before the white man came. Then everything changed, everything but the wind and the rain and the cold.

The white man came from beyond the lake, from the direction of the morning sun—first the French, who explored and traded; then the British, who traded and conquered; and finally the Americans, who conquered and stayed. The Americans came because they were concerned about the land, concerned about what the British and the Indians were doing there. By the spring of 1804, American soldiers had built a fort on the land, a log fort with a double stockade. They built it near where the river meets the lake, and they called it Fort Dearborn.

The fort brought other Americans to the land, mostly soldiers, Indian traders, and farmers. By 1812 a little community had sprung up, numbering nearly forty inhabitants, housed in a dozen crude cabins. It was a lonely, monotonous life here in this frontier outpost. Occasionally a traveler would come through, and in the spring the fur traders would stop by for supplies, but there was little contact with the world beyond. What amusement the settlers had they made for themselves. Hunting offered a pleasant diversion in the fall, as well as a change of diet. A foot race might enliven an afternoon now and then, but the dwellers around Fort Dearborn wanted something more. They longed for the pleasures they had known before they came to this untamed country, and they longed for assurance that even here in this primitive wilderness they would not revert to savagery. In short, they yearned for the civilization they had left behind.

Whenever they could, these frontiersmen brought with them the trappings of the civilization they held so dear—partly for their personal pleasure, partly as a protective shield against the barbarities of the frontier. John Kinzie, the first white trader to settle outside Fort Dearborn, brought along his violin. Kinzie's little cabin was located on the north bank of the Chicago River, just across from the fort, and after the labors of the day were over, he used to fiddle there, simply for his own amusement. On warm evenings the soldiers across the river could hear him playing as they fed and watered the stock for the evening, and, when their chores were finished, they were wont to rest themselves a moment outside the barn, sitting on the edge of the watering trough or crouched on their haunches, listening to his tunes in the otherwise still dusk.

But the strains of John Kinzie's violin were soon drowned out by the menacing throbs of the war drum. With the outbreak of the War of 1812 and the accompanying Indian hostilities, the lives of the Dearborn settlers became seriously imperiled. Orders were given for the garrison to be abandoned. On their retreat to safety, just south of the fort, the pioneers were overpowered by an Indian war party, and most of them were massacred.

During the next four years, the land lapsed back into prairie wilderness, and the fort fell into decay. Then, in the summer of 1816, with hostilities over, a second Fort Dearborn was raised. Within a few months news of it spread, and before long American settlers began appearing once more, this time to remain.

Slowly the village of Chicago grew up in the shadows of the new fort. Then, with the completion of the Erie Canal in 1825, the town's embryonic stage was over, as the lake region was now joined by a water highway to the eastern seaboard. Pioneers on their way to make homes on the western prairie began trickling, then pouring, through the town, and merchants and land agents were not long in seeing the opportunities awaiting them there. By 1833 Chicago numbered almost four hundred souls and was one of the fastest-growing boom towns in the West. Buildings appeared virtually overnight, some three stories high! But the settlers came faster than the buildings, and the town's hotels turned away more people than they housed. Temporary shanties were thrown up in an attempt to take care of the overflow, but still more came. By 1837 Chicago's population was a congested, ill-housed four thousand.

Most of these early settlers came from the northeastern United States, primarily from New England and the parts of New York and Pennsylvania settled by New Englanders. But foreigners came too, especially Germans,

Irish, and Norwegians, who sought a refuge from the political unrest and economic instability of their homelands. Men came alone at first, to carve something decent out of this western territory. Even as late as 1834, the complaint was raised that there were only two girls of marriageable age in the whole town. Within two more years, the community boasted a small cluster of refined ladies and supported a larger group of women, amiable, if not genteel.

Yet this pairing of the cultured and the mundane was typical of the Chicago of the 1830's. On the surface at least, the town was raw, coarse, insensitive, violent. A little deeper, however, could be found the same concern for civilization that had caused John Kinzie to bring his violin with him from the East. The new arrivals, like the old, needed the assurance that whatever befell them here in this rustic environment, they would not regress to barbarism. And so amid the muck of the streets, amid the squalor of the surrounding hovels, amid the brothels and saloons, there was always an element of something finer, a reminder that the town, after all, was an appendage of civilization.

As early as 1832, Chicago had a library, set up in connection with the Sunday school of the Presbyterian Church. The first newspaper and the first literary club both appeared in 1833, and that same year Mark Beaubien, who doubled as a ferryman and owner of a public tavern, began playing his fiddle for weekly dances held in the dining room of his establishment. A little later, his brother, Jean-Baptiste Beaubien, imported a piano, and the two played duets for the dancers and an appreciative, though somewhat bewildered, claque of Indians who crowded the doorway. February, 1833, brought what was probably the first professional entertainment Chicago had seen, when a program of "magic, ventriloquism, and stunts" was performed at Dexter Graves's Mansion House.

Miss Wythe opened her music school in 1834, and the Old Settlers Harmonic Society was formed. For the next several years, concerts were held regularly in the Presbyterian Church and were well attended, although it took some doing just to get there. The audience first had to pick its way through an ankle-deep mire and then walk a slippery log across a stretch of swamp. A choir was formed in 1836 at St. James's Episcopal Church, and the town's first organ was installed there. Before long, a number of music societies, like the Mozart Society, the Beethoven Society, and the Apollo Club, were organized, all helping to stimulate an interest in "good" music.

Chicago's first play, *The Stranger*, was given in the dining room of the Sauganash Hotel in 1837. Its success was so impressive that a regular theater was soon opened on the upper floor of a plain wooden building on Dearborn Street. While this Chicago Theater, as it was known, provided amusement for many, it had its share of financial troubles, and the puritanical element of the town's New England population bitterly denounced it as a "nursery of crime" and "grossly demoralizing."

To conclude that Chicagoans in the thirties and forties lived from one concert or play to the next would be obvious folly. The town still loved its gambling and carousing, and a number of popular amusements dominated most of its leisure time. Horse racing and boating became favorite sports in the thirties, and cricket was considered second only to the card table. When the first circus appeared in town in 1836, its tent was crowded for every performance. General Tom Thumb, P. T. Barnum's famous midget, appeared on the scene in 1845 and was given a royal welcome. Minstrel shows were as enthusiastically attended as they were frequent. And, of course, for real excitement there was nothing like a good hanging, the location of which was often chosen for the convenience of gaping spectators. Still, by 1840 Chicago had passed through the wildest of its boom-town days, and serious music and theater had at least made a beginning.

Although this was still primarily a man's world, society—with a capital *S*—had put in a nominal appearance, too. By the late thirties, the fancier dances were called balls. Despite the fact that women were generally transported to these gatherings huddled upon straw in rude carts, one lady in 1839 paid five hundred dollars for her gown. By the forties the ladies were freely indulging in the luxuries of fashion, and merchants found a going business in the sale of imported perfumes, tortoise shell combs, wigs, tooth and nail brushes, and the like. The wealthier citizens lived on the North Side, and William H. Brown's ten-thousand-dollar home set the standard for others. The practice of exchanging cards, calls, and dinner parties gradually became accepted social behavior as Chicagoans began to imitate what the Chicago *American* in 1837 called "all the humbug and frippery of an eastern city." A variety of delicacies could now be found in the shops: rare fruits, spices, nuts, imported wines. And the barber shops of the thirties gave way in the forties to "Hair Dressers and Tonsors," places where a gentleman could have his "beard taken off with . . . ease and grace."

Chicago's population in the forties doubled and redoubled, totaling over twenty thousand in 1848. Improvements in transportation, particularly the westward extension of the railroad, brought in ever-increasing numbers of settlers from the East. While the native American population continued to predominate, vast scores of Germans and Irish also came, drawn by the demand for labor and by the low fares charged by the railroads. By 1850 more than 17 per cent of Chicago's population was German. Although most of the new arrivals, both native and foreign, were workers, the nucleus of wealthy citizens increased proportionately as the town grew. Successful men in commerce, industry, finance, and real estate generally became social as well as economic leaders. And yet the social lines were never as sharply drawn here as in the East. Society in early Chicago was made up of wealthy men—and their wives, of course—who had worked their way up by the sweat of their own brows. Conditions simply did not permit their removing themselves very far from those with more modest incomes. Certain class distinctions were always present, but these were not pronounced in Chicago until after the Civil War. Until then, religious differences were much more important than economic considerations in the social cleavage of the town.

Chicago in the late forties, then, was a growing center of trade and industry with a nascent social and cultural awareness, coupled with the remnants of a frontier environment. It was still not uncommon to see bearded hunters riding into town with rifles over their shoulders and knives stuck in their belts. Cattle grazed in Dearborn Park, and streets were still so muddy in bad weather that boards had to be laid across them to afford the multitude passage from one side to the other. The plank sidewalks offered some protection from the slush and slime, but their semiexposed nails seemed to be placed there for the special purpose of snagging women's dresses. Gas-burning lamps lined the main streets, but citizens still felt safer carrying pistols after dark. On the other hand, the town boasted two luxury hotels—the Sherman House, a skyscraper of four stories, and the Tremont House, adorned by thirty-four mantels imported from Italy and a ballroom with a marble floor. And in J. B. Rice's Chicago Theater the city had a playhouse complete with carpet, boxes, and settees.

By the time John Rice arrived on the scene in 1847, Chicagoans had succeeded in getting around the Yankee prejudice against "frivolous entertainment" by building a theater as part of a museum. But it was Rice who really made theatergoing respectable. Rice came to Chicago from Buffalo, where he had been a theatrical manager, and erected a frame structure forty by eighty feet on the corner of Dearborn and Randolph Streets. He designated the second floor of the building as a theater and furnished it comfortably and tastefully. The surroundings were made as sedate as possible in the hope of keeping criticism at a minimum. The boxes were so elegant that, according to the Chicago *Daily Journal*, they rather resembled "a boudoir or private sitting room in a gentleman's house than an apartment in a place of public resort." Rice emphasized respectability even in his advertisements, insisting that women would not be admitted unless "accompanied by gentlemen."

The theater was constructed within a period of six weeks, at a cost of four thousand dollars—a "striking exponent of Western industry and enterprise." It opened on June 28, 1847, with a play entitled *The Four Sisters* and a large audience in attendance. The *Journal* was convinced that "a new era is unquestionably dawning in the theatrical world in this city." Following the opening, a series of Shakespearean tragedies was given, including *Hamlet*, *Romeo and Juliet*, and *Macbeth*. When, still later, a live horse appeared on stage in a production of *Mazeppa*, critics were delighted. Before long the *Journal* reported that "a large number of ladies—the beauty and fashion of the city—are in nightly attendance" at the Rice.

In May, 1848, James H. McVicker appeared at the theater in *My Neighbor's Wife*, and the next month Edwin Forrest assumed the title role of *Othello*. When a cholera epidemic broke out in the city a year later, the theater remained open and did a great deal to prevent spirits from foundering. Neighboring cities that had had theaters for years—Milwaukee, Cincinnati, St. Louis—were inclined to scoff at Rice's but Chicago was proud of its little playhouse and loved it.

On Monday, July 29, 1850, the city bustled with a new excitement, for its first opera troupe was in town. A company of four singers arrived that day by boat from Milwaukee. The singers apparently had constitutions of iron, for despite a rather choppy voyage down Lake Michigan, a performance of Bellini's *La Sonnambula* was announced for that same evening at Rice's Theater. The troupe traveled light, bringing with it neither orchestra nor chorus. But, no matter, the theater band would play the accompaniment, and local singers would undertake the choruses and some of the minor roles. Admission prices ranged from fifty cents in the boxes to twenty-five cents in the pit!

When the curtain rose that night on the first of Chicago's operas, the theater was crowded with the cream of local society. The ladies came dressed in their finest, and members of the "swell set" were apparent by their lorgnettes. Gentlemen were dressed immaculately in evening suits, some with swallowtail coats. As the performance progressed, the leading roles sung by Miss Brienti and Mr. Manvera, the audience became increasingly enthusiastic, but seemed somewhat at a loss as to just how they should go about expressing their enthusiasm. Consequently they managed to applaud in most of the wrong places, and islands of cheers went up here and there as friends and neighbors were recognized among the local singers. At the conclusion one fellow sitting near the front hesitated a moment and then with a laconic "Well, well!" began applauding profusely.

The next day the "opry" was the talk of the town. The *Journal*, however, seemed somewhat tentative in its appraisal of the audience's appreciation: "Whatever may be the taste of the theatre-going public in this city with regard to operas, all must concede that the music was of a high order and executed with admirable grace and skill." Still, the management was encouraged enough to schedule a second performance for July 30.

At the repeat the audience was less numerous, but no less agreeable. The long first act came off quite well, and the ensemble "*O Mio Dolor*," in which Amina pleads her innocence, was soundly applauded. The ovation, however, was not for the soprano or the tenor, but for the villagers—the Chicago chorus—as they tiptoed into the Count's room.

The second act had just begun; Elvino was singing his aria bemoaning his grief. The house was hushed. Then, like an electric shock, cries of "Fire!" rang out from the street below. Suddenly through the windows a reddish glow became discernible. The audience started to panic. But in a moment J. B. Rice stepped from the wings onto the stage and shouted, "Sit down! Sit down! Do you think I would permit a fire to occur in my theater?" So great was the audience's confidence in their man Rice that they calmly resumed their seats. A soft voice was heard from the prompter's box. Rice leaned down to listen, then quickly straightened up, and somewhat sheepishly announced that the theater was indeed on fire.

The house was cleared safely, but not without some mad scampering backward and forward. When everyone was apparently out, a party of visiting English gentlemen missed one of their friends. Thinking he might have been injured, one of the group burst into the theater, bumping into John Rice on his way out carrying a piece of scenery over each shoulder. But there on the front row of the empty house sat the missing Englishman, slightly inebriated, applauding frantically, and declaring that it was the best damn imitation of a fire he had ever seen! He had to be dragged to safety.

The audience was no sooner outside than the rear of the theater was enveloped in flames. In a matter of minutes the entire structure was reduced to a heap of burning rubbish. The curtain, a few fragments of scenery, and most of the private wardrobes of the opera company were saved, but the theater itself, its furniture and fixtures were a total loss. Rice estimated his damages at $7,000, only $1,000 of which was covered by insurance. Though he did not realize it, of course, it was like a rehearsal for the great fire of 1871.

The fire had started in an adjoining stable. Although the alarm had been sounded immediately and firemen had promptly arrived on the scene, the flames had gotten out of control and were not subdued until a half block in one of the most thickly populated sections of the city had been laid in ashes and seven horses and a cow had perished. The fire department, it seems, had not had a hose long enough to reach the blaze, nor did it have suitable hooks and ladders. James H. McVicker, who had acted at Rice's Theater, shared a suite of rooms in the Gurley Building with his family and was compelled by the fire to take a flying leap out a window, leaving two hundred dollars in property behind to burn. All in all, it was one of the worst fires the city had experienced thus far. Over twenty buildings were destroyed, but no one suffered any greater loss than J. B. Rice.

The opera company generously announced they would hold a benefit concert at the City Hall to help recoup some of Rice's losses. The concert was held on August 3, tickets selling for a dollar a head. While the financial assistance was welcome, John Rice seemed little daunted by the destruction of his theater. Within three days after the calamity, he was already making arrangements for the building of a new one, larger and more elegant. It would be erected on the same site as the old and would be built of brick.

Mr. Rice's new theater, like its predecessor, was officially named the Chicago Theater, but it was seldom called that. It measured eighty feet in width, a hundred feet in depth, was lighted with gas, and housed three tiers of boxes and a saloon. Seating capacity was fourteen hundred. Completed in January, 1851, the theater was formally opened on February 3. The cost of construction totaled an eyebrow-raising eleven thousand dollars.

Meanwhile, to fill the gap after the burning of Rice's first theater, in October, 1850, the Tremont House renovated its ballroom, christened it Tremont Hall, and began offering concerts and plays there. It was here at the Tremont in April, 1853, that Chicago first heard Adelina Patti, paired on a somewhat spectacular bill with the famous Norwegian violinist Ole Bull. Patti was then a child of ten, delicate, pale-faced, with two long braids of thick glossy black hair hanging down her back. Dressed in a rose-colored frock, pink stockings, and pantalets, she sang bravura arias as Chicago had never heard them sung before. The girl had been singing professionally since she was seven, but she came from a rugged breed. Her mother, while playing the title role of *Norma* in Madrid, had been taken ill just as the curtain went up on the last act. The next morning little Adelina was born. The child could sing like an angel, and Chicagoans took her to their hearts as they had no one else.

Ole Bull, the other half of the Tremont's program, was giving one of his many farewell tours, a disease which later years seemed to indicate he passed on to Patti. A fascinating rather than a great artist, Ole Bull could work all sorts of magic with his bow, much of it more theatrics than music. Still it was quite a show.

The Patti–Ole Bull recital was interesting for another reason. For the first time in Chicago's theatrical history, numbered tickets and ushers were used. The little city was becoming more sophisticated.

Then in October, 1853, the opera season which the fire had interrupted three years before was continued in Rice's second theater. An Italian opera troupe, with Rose de Vries as prima donna and Luigi Arditi as conductor, was brought in to give two operas, Donizetti's *Lucia di Lammermoor* and Bellini's *Norma.* Within these three years, prices had jumped to the point that top admission fee was now a staggering two dollars. At the opening night of *Lucia* the public was quite exuberant, but the press next day, not quite trusting itself to make a judgment of its own, was cautious. Mme. de Vries, critics conjectured, lived up to the praise she had won in other cities. However, the house was so well packed for the next evening's *Norma* that the company decided to stay over another day and give *Sonnambula* as an encore. Once Bellini was out of the way, the theater was turned over to a troupe of performing monkeys, goats, and dogs, and entertainment returned to normal.

Still, Chicago had at last seen a legitimate, if brief, season of grand opera. Considering that New York had heard its first season a quarter of a century before and New Orleans had been listening to opera regularly for over sixty years, opera's arrival in Chicago may seem somewhat late. Actually, this tardiness is not nearly as provincial as it might seem when it is considered that New York predated Chicago by some 180 years and that New Orleans was a mature city of eighty-five years when Chicago was nothing more than a frontier fort. Neither did Chicago have the ready access to Europe that the eastern and southern coastal cities had, and thus missed most of the European artists on tour. Europeans, whose only knowledge of the West came from James Fenimore Cooper or some equally reliable easterner, were simply wary of going into a land that they believed was teeming with savages, both red and white.

Chicago's retarded operatic development, then, is understandable, as is the five-year lapse between the city's first real season of opera and its second. By then John Rice had retired from the theatrical scene, later to become Chicago's mayor. His place had been taken by James H. McVicker, of window-leaping fame. McVicker in 1857 built what was at that time the most elaborate theater in the West, on Madison Street, west of State. It seated two thousand people and cost over $85,000. This substantial increase in cost (over twenty-one times what Rice had paid for his theater ten years before and almost eight times what he had paid for the later one) reveals two things—first, the sharp rise in prices that had taken place in the past decade and, second, that Chicago's theatrical standards had become significantly higher.

McVicker's theater contained a parquet, boxes, and two galleries, one for whites, the other for Negroes, who, with the Underground Railroad and other recent abolitionist activities, were rapidly increasing. The scenery and props at McVicker's were the finest the town had seen, and so were some of its performers. Edwin Booth, the famous Shakespearean actor, for example, visited the theater in the spring of 1858, playing Brutus and Richard III.

On September 27, 1858, the Durand English Opera Troupe opened a two-week season at McVicker's, bringing an end to a five-year lyric dearth. Advance notices hailed the company as the most extensive to tour the West. Mme. Rosalie Durand herself was the featured soprano, *Miss* Georgia Hodson sang the tenor leads (which must have left much to be desired), and most of the operas were sung in English. After opening with an inevitable *Sonnambula*, the troupe branched out into a diversified repertoire, including Donizetti's *The Daughter of the Regiment*, Auber's *Fra Diavolo*, Balfe's *The Bohemian Girl*, Weber's *Der Freischütz*, and Verdi's *Il Trovatore*.

Chicago by now was a bustling city of 98,000 inhabitants, had grown in the past decade from a little western town with mud streets specked with prairie grass into the throbbing center of the lumber and grain trade of the Midwest, and fancied itself quite mature and worldly-wise. Whereas five years before local critics had been hesitant to voice their views, not exactly trusting their own judgments in matters operatic, by 1858 they were quite outspoken and opinionated. They ridiculed the idea of opera in the vernacular with all the assurance of a veteran connoisseur, and after the presentation of *Il Trovatore*, with Mme. Durand as Leonora and Miss Hodson as Manrico, the *Journal* wrote: "To be sure the anvils seemed natural, and the orchestra played something which sounded like the anvil chorus, but otherwise *Il Trovatore* was shrieked, screamed, groaned, and killed. The whole performance was below mediocrity. The properties were miserable, the action tame, the music inharmonious, false, and discordant. *Il Trovatore* is far beyond the capabilities of the troupe, and we trust that they will not again allow the charge of murder to rest upon them."

While Verdi was being slaughtered down at McVicker's, the German element of the city was having a holiday welcoming the noted basso Karl Formes to the Tremont House. The streets outside the hotel were jammed with Formes' countrymen. The various German singing societies serenaded him, while the basso listened from his balcony with all the dignity of a monarch. Then, after addressing his admirers with a few words in German, he retired, the crowd cheering more vigorously than ever. No doubt about it, Formes stole much of the limelight from the English Opera Troupe during the final part of its stay. When he himself gave a concert a few nights later, he won a rousing ovation, especially after Lindpaintner's "Song of the Standard Bearer," which he was supposed to have sung once upon the battlefield. It seems that when his countrymen faltered in the heat of battle, the basso seized the banner, sang the stirring song, and led them to victory. When he repeated the song in Chicago, the largely German audience rallied, and Formes had indeed won a victory.

In 1859 Chicago heard three different opera seasons, presented by three different companies. The most notable of these was given by Maurice Strakosch and his wife, contralto Amalia Patti, Adelina's sister. The Strakosches offered an interesting array of operas, among them Verdi's *La Traviata*, Bellini's *I Puritani*, Flotow's *Martha*, Donizetti's *La Favorita* and *Lucrezia Borgia*, and Mozart's *Don Giovanni*. Society seems to have presented the most dazzling display yet, the high fashion wearing white, red, or orange cloaks with fleecy hoods and carrying feather-tipped fans. According to one observer, the scene was one of "opera glasses, musk, bouquets, frangipannis, alabaster shoulders, small talk, moustaches, diamonds, Valenciennes, and crinolines of St. Paul-domelike extension."

Chicago had reached the point that it felt fairly confident of its opinions. After all, it had been hearing opera for ten years now. It knew good opera from bad, or thought it did, and was perfectly willing to tell the world what it thought. "The orchestra played too loud," the critics thundered. "Why can't the prompter be more quiet and not interfere with the music?" And a city founded primarily by Yankee businessmen certainly knew immorality when it saw it, and *Traviata* and *Don Giovanni* both surely hinted of that. "To be sure," wrote the *Journal*, "we must atone during lent for witnessing *Traviata*... and *Don Juan*, with their lax morals not altogether covered up by the divine music of the masters."

A city in adolescence began to appraise this thing called opera. Were all the frills and frippery really worth the expense? There were those in Chicago who thought not: "Those Italian singing birds which have been hibernating with us a brief three weeks have warbled their last notes and flown—flown with the good wishes of some and the dollars of all." Opera *was* expensive, then as now, and a city brought up in a tradition of frontier pragmatism might well question the return. "We hope," the *Journal* editorialized, "that the opera with its fashionable toilets has not removed the love of the dramatic. The one pleases the sensuous, the other the intellectual; which shall predominate? The high spiced esculents will do now and then, but they hurt the digestion; the plain, everyday dish administers to our nutriment." Chicago, not unlike the young nation as a whole, still very much had its feet in the soil and was practical to the core.

The next few years saw little operatic activity in Chicago, although the concert circuit remained fairly active. Pianist Louis Gottschalk, who had enough charm for a dozen performers, came in December, 1860, accompanied by Carlotta Patti, another of Adelina's sisters. Carlotta was lame, but stunningly attractive, and, according to George Upton, had an even higher range than her more famous sister.

The Sherman House was the scene of some impromptu singing in the early sixties when a young girl named Emma Abbott from Peoria, Illinois, occasionally came to town with her father. The proprietor of the Sherman was an old friend of the Abbott family, who enjoyed encouraging Emma with her singing as much as he could. Whenever the Abbotts came visiting, he would insist that the dining room immediately be cleared for a concert. Hotel guests were escorted in, and little Miss Abbott was given her chance. She would look back on these sessions with great nostalgia in years to come, when she was a reigning prima donna at Covent Garden.

In the spring of 1861, Chicagoans were still arguing the pros and cons of Lincoln's inauguration as President. Fortunately, he was no radical abolitionist, and he was a westerner. But following his election, seven southern states had seceded from the Union, and others were threatening to follow. Then, on the morning of April 12, came the news over the telegraph: Fort Sumter had been fired upon! Three days later, Lincoln called for troops to put down the rebellion, setting off another avalanche of secessionist activity. The tragic drama of the Civil War had begun.

Almost overnight, the character of Chicago, much like that of the whole war-torn nation, was transformed. Patriotism soared to quixotic heights. The town's few southern families suddenly found themselves watched with a suspicious eye. Before long, the courthouse square was dotted with recruiting tents, and Zouaves were parading up and down the streets, while brass bands played and flags were waved. The demands of war hit Chicago only slightly less than they did the cities of the East. Troops had to be fed, clothed, sheltered, armed, and transported. All of this meant drastic increases in industrial output. New factories were quickly commissioned as old ones buckled under the strain, and still more were needed. For Chicago, and the nation, the Civil War saw the sowing of the seeds of modern industry.

Women helped out the war effort by making bandages and by volunteering as nurses. Sewing circles switched from making quilts for daughters' hope chests to sweaters and uniforms. And everyone, men and women, watched the drama in print as it unfolded on the battlefield: Bull Run, Shiloh, Antietam, Fredericksburg–each a hideous nightmare in itself.

But not everyone took the war so seriously, and some even found it useful in advancing their own greed. Gamblers moved into Chicago from the river towns and the West, eager to take advantage of the drifting population which passed through the city daily. Amid the tensions of war came a rogue's gallery of unsavory characters to establish gambling palaces, saloons, and houses of ill repute; and Chicago, at least in part, reverted to a kind of savagery.

The war situation, in one way or another, consumed both the patriot and the barbarian so completely that there was little time for anything else. Neither cared much about going out in the evenings, certainly not to the theater. They much preferred to go down and read the bulletin boards, where the latest news and casualty lists were posted. If they thought of music, it was "The Girl I Left Behind Me" or "Tramp, Tramp, Tramp, the Boys Are Marching" they wanted, not operatic arias. An occasional concert was given in 1861, but these were invariably poorly attended. John Wilkes Booth played Richard III at McVicker's in 1862, but his performance was more significant in retrospect than it was at the time.

In July, 1863, the combined battles of Vicksburg in the West and Gettysburg in the East saw a turning of the tide. The Union now took the offense, and hopes in the North began to rise. Impresario Jacob Grau felt that perhaps the country was sufficiently safe that people might be interested in a little diverting grand opera. He brought a troupe to McVicker's that year, presenting several works Chicago had not yet heard (*Dinorah, Sicilian Vespers, Un Ballo in Maschera, La Juive,* Rossini's *Moses*), but Chicagoans indicated they would still rather go down to the Court House steps and listen to the Lumbards or John Hubbard or Charley Smith sing war songs.

In 1864, while Grant was winning bloody victories in the Wilderness Campaign and Sherman was making his fiery march on Atlanta, three separate opera seasons were given in Chicago. Grau returned for two weeks, giving the city its first performance of Gounod's *Faust.* The following January, Leonard Grover brought in the first real German opera troupe for fifteen performances, among them stagings of Wagner's *Tannhäuser* and Beethoven's *Fidelio.* The city's German population was highly enthusiastic about the Grover productions, but the town as a whole remained fairly passive. Sherman was now in the Carolinas, Grant in Virginia, pressing in upon Richmond. Victory at last seemed within the Union's grasp, but with losses as heavy as those of the past year, few could feel any real jubilation until the end had definitely come.

Fifteen years had passed now since that first small troupe of singers had given *Sonnambula* at Rice's. While a number of more imposing companies had followed, some greeted quite warmly by Chicago audiences, opera in early 1865 was still a long way from being an integral part of the city's cultural life. The normally unassuming social set attended these brief, sporadic seasons with some aplomb, mainly because they thought it the thing to do, but the wealth and fashion, though growing, was not marked enough yet to support such conspicuous leisure for very long, no matter how much it might want to keep pace with its eastern counterparts. Chicago's middle class was not as yet prosperous enough, sophisticated enough, nor sufficiently educated musically to court the opera with much passion, and for the laboring people the whole thing was pretty much out of the question. The Germans, of course, even the workers, made a special effort to get out for Wagner and Beethoven, but this was considered a patriotic obligation and was highly exceptional.

Basically, the town was still too rustic, the frontier legacy of utilitarianism too strong, for opera to find a particularly comfortable home there. An occasional stopover was fine. If times were good, Chicago would likely be a gracious host. Yet any guest can overstay his welcome, particularly one as demanding as grand opera. The Civil War, however, produced the changes in the city's economic and social fiber which would permit the support of opera on a steadier basis. The town had gradually grown in cultural awareness. J. B. Rice had made the theater, including opera, respectable, and James H. McVicker had kept the art before the public eye. What was needed now was someone flamboyant enough to make opera appealing to the developing nouveaux riches, someone to catch the popular imagination. This was the task that fell to Uranus Crosby.

Chapter 2

WHEN THE PIE WAS OPENED, THE BIRDS BEGAN TO SING

ON APRIL 4, 1865, the Chicago *Tribune* carried the news: "Richmond Is Ours." With the Union flag flying over the Confederate capital, the war was all but over. Chicagoans could now loosen up a bit, begin taking stock of just what had been happening to them over the past four years, and come to grips with the fact that their city was no longer a small, rural town. Chicago had become a major city during the war, both in size and power, and its citizens, once they had time to think about it, were anxious to celebrate their recent coming of age.

On hand to host the festivities was Uranus Crosby, a New England distiller, who had come west fifteen years before. Crosby had shrewdly anticipated the wartime tax on liquor, had built up his supply before the tax went into effect, and had made a fortune. His dream now was to build the most elegant opera house in the country, one large enough to serve as a temple for all the arts, the art of business enterprise included. He chose a site on the north side of Washington Street, halfway between State and Dearborn, and began construction. In the spring of 1865, just as the war was drawing to a close, Crosby put the finishing touches on his $700,000 combination opera house, art gallery, and office building. Designed by W. W. Boyington, the architect responsible for the old waterworks tower, the structure consisted of a formal Italian facade surmounted by a mansard roof. The main entrance was enclosed by a high arch, over which stood four statues representing Music, Painting, Sculpture, and Commerce.

By including the statue of Commerce, Crosby indicated that his was going to be a businessman's approach to the arts, and his insistence upon classical lines reflected something of his conscious aspiration to culture and how he felt this could be attained. To a great degree Crosby symbolized the new rich of his time. His money had come suddenly, as a result of the war. He now sought an air of cultivation. So he built what he thought was the most cultivated thing imaginable, an opera house of classic distinction. But in everything he undertook he remained the businessman first, the cultured gentleman second. His main aim was always to make money, and in this respect artistic projects were no different from any other. Therefore he built his opera house and art museum in conjunction with a piano store, a restaurant, and two floors of offices that could be rented out for profit. There was no reason, he felt, why cultural enterprises could not be run on an economically sound basis, if the proper mind were directing things.

Once inside Crosby's Opera House, however, all this talk about business and profit was forgotten. The auditorium occupied the whole rear portion of the building, seated two thousand five hundred people, and consisted of an orchestra, parquet, and dress circle on the main floor, a balcony with fifty-six boxes in the center, and a family circle. On either side of the high proscenium were frescoes of Comedy and Tragedy, and in the ceiling sunken panels contained portraits of composers. The theater was a model of comfort and beauty, the coloring soft and subdued. The boxes were draped in crimson and gold, while most of the furniture was a mild blue, contrasting rather favorably with the glaring reds and yellows of most public halls of the time. The house was lighted by hundreds of gas lamps and reflectors concentrated in the dome above, an arrangement which gave the whole interior a mellow glow, yet removed the lamps from the range of vision. The theater was built with an eye toward safety, too, for exits opened out onto both Washington and State Streets, escape routes from the upper tiers onto adjacent roofs were designated, and automatic steam devices were provided for flooding the stage in case of emergency. Crosby's theater was in fact one of the most elaborate in the United States, far eclipsing anything Chicago had known before.

For his grand opening Crosby secured the services of Maurice Grau's Italian Opera Company from the New York Academy of Music. The inauguration date was set for April 17, just eight days after Lee's surrender to Grant. With victory in sight, a holiday mood permeated Chicago. The city was ready to have a social spree, and the dedication of Crosby's Opera House seemed like an occasion tailor-made for just that. The fashionable set began humming with an excitement it had not felt in years, and the nouveaux riches were eager for an opportunity to show themselves. Overcoming wartime shortages, shops had a heyday selling opera glasses, fans, cloaks, crystal hair pins, ties, gloves, and handkerchiefs. It was going to be the social revel of the decade.

Then, on the morning of April 15, two days before the scheduled opening, the incredible news was received: President Lincoln had been assassinated. The President was dead. He had been shot by that fellow Booth, who had played at McVicker's two or three seasons ago. After all the nation had been through, this was the final blow. Chicago was shocked, then sick with remorse. From the heights of joy the city catapulted to the depths of despair. In deference to the mourning, Crosby's opening was postponed until Thursday, April 20, and all other amusements shut down.

To add to the gloom, on the night the house was finally opened, a severe thunderstorm hit the city. Still, so badly did Chicago want its celebration that neither its sorrow nor the weather succeeded in marring it. Carriages lined up for blocks along Washington and Dearborn Streets, waiting to discharge passengers at the Opera House entrance, while the rain beat down and crashes of thunder pealed across the heavens. Every horse and hack in the city must have been employed that evening.

After an undignified dash through the puddles to get inside, this opening-night audience was much like any other, except a bit more elegantly dressed than usual for Chicago. In the foyer ladies and gentlemen found separate cloak rooms for their wraps, with attendants waiting to receive them. In the auditorium, ticket holders were directed to their seats by a well-drilled corps of ushers apparently above average in appearance and efficiency. The ushers, the *Tribune* was impressed enough to mention, "were dressed neatly and were white kids, but what is better they understood and did their duty well." The audience seems to have been more responsible than most, too, for despite the rain, every seat in the house was taken before the performance started.

Just before curtain time, loud shouts went up throughout the house, calling "Crosby! Crosby!" After some delay Uranus Crosby stepped before the footlights and was welcomed with a tremendous ovation. Then, following a short round of speeches and the reading of an "Inauguration Ode," the opera, Verdi's *Il Trovatore,* got underway.

Both the performance and the house proved exceptionally agreeable. The theater's acoustics were excellent, and critics professed genuine amazement at the scenery and stage fittings. "We presume there were few in that audience but expected to see trouble in shifting the scenes," wrote the *Tribune.* "There was not an iota. Everything worked as smoothly and with as complete an absence of . . . noise as if the scenes had been trained to run in those grooves for half a century." The only complaint raised against the house was that the ventilation, hailed as unsurpassed by any theater on the continent, was a mite too vigorous, resulting in a rather unpleasant draft.

The performance of *Trovatore* given by the Grau company was heartily received by the public and the critics. All agreed it was one of the finest productions Chicago had heard. The chorus was large and sang "in time and tune," a fact well worth noting. The orchestra was superbly directed. And the noted baritone Bellini revealed himself "one of the most superb artists we have ever seen on the stage." Next day the *Tribune* appraised the situation well: "Thanks to Crosby for such a house, to Grau for such a troupe, to the troupe for such a representation. We at last have opera." Certainly opera had taken a giant step forward in Chicago with the appearance of Crosby's Opera House. And Maurice Grau was unquestionably the most successful impresario of his day, although he himself knew little about music. To Grau opera was purely a business matter, and in this he doubtlessly saw eye to eye with Uranus Crosby. Grau quite frankly admitted that he produced opera not as a luxury for others or for the musical elevation of the public, but to win profits for himself and his stockholders. He was once asked which of the arts he felt was the most noble. Replied Grau, "I think it's the art to make money, and the higher the bank account, the higher the art." Uranus Crosby himself could have spoken the words.

But, while opera might be a business with Grau, he nonetheless gave fairly good performances, and, like Crosby, he had a way of selling his product. For his second evening in Chicago, the impresario prepared to unveil his featured attraction, Clara Louise Kellogg, the first American prima donna to have won international fame. The opera was supposed to be Donizetti's *Linda di Chamounix*, but when on the day of the performance word came that the tenor was stranded en route somewhere in Michigan, the bill was quickly changed to *Lucia di Lammermoor*. Mme. Kellogg had not sung the role in two years, but agreed to go on if the proper costumes could be rounded up. This produced some frantic scurrying among the wardrobe people, and the whole company spent a frantic afternoon. Kellogg and her Edgardo had never sung together before, and both went into the performance without a rehearsal. "It was like entertaining a score of unexpected visitors on cold dinner day," the *Tribune* sympathized. "But how magnificently all these difficulties were met and conquered." And surely there was no greater victor than Clara Kellogg herself: "In all the elements of the true artist Kellogg takes the front rank. Finely formed with an impressive stage presence, graceful and majestic in her gait and gesture, her dramatic qualities polished, and her appreciation of dramatic requirement keen and accurate, she is a consummate actress. . . . Her trills are bird-like."

Much of Chicago's sorrow over Lincoln's death had turned to rage, then vindictiveness, as the search for the assassins continued. Stores struck up a profitable business selling photographs of John Wilkes Booth. "Every loyal person should have a picture of BOOTH the Assassin!" read one advertisement. In an atmosphere of growing hatred and cynicism, the opera season continued. Donizetti's *Poliuto* was given for the first time in the city, amid lusty shouts of *bravo!* Said the *Tribune*, "Throughout, the opera was exceptional, and performed as near to perfection as we ever expect to see." A production of *Lucrezia Borgia* was lauded as the closest thing to an absolute lyric paragon the city had witnessed. Kellogg sang *Martha* and Marguerite in *Faust*, receiving baskets of flowers and impassioned ovations after each performance.

On May 1 and 2, there was no opera, for Lincoln's body, on the way to its final resting place in Springfield, lay in state. The funeral train, black blankets with silver stars draped over its boilers, had at last brought the President's remains back home to Illinois. The casket was taken in slow procession to the Court House, while three dozen high school girls scattered flowers before it. Along the way windows and doorways were bordered with black crepe. At the Court House thousands of people filed by the funeral bier, some having waited in line all night for the opportunity to pay their respects to the man they had known as "Abe." Business had halted. There was not a wheel turning in the streets, nothing to break the solemn stillness. From her windows at the Sherman House, overlooking the Court House grounds, Clara Kellogg watched the scene, and years later it haunted her still. "From sunset to sunrise," she writes in her autobiography, "the grounds were packed with a silent multitude. The only sound to be heard was the shuffling echo of feet as one person after another went quietly into the Court House, shuffle, shuffle, shuffle—I can hear it yet. There was not a word uttered. There was no other sound than the sound of the passing feet."

After the funeral in Springfield, the opera season at Crosby's was resumed, with the same success it had had earlier. Donizetti's *Don Sebastiano*, rare in any repertory anywhere, was given, employing 150 supernumeraries. Never had Chicago seen such a spectacle. Kellogg sang Elvira in *I Puritani* and Zerlina in *Don Giovanni*. And baritone Bellini was an absolute sensation in the buffo role of the Count in Auber's *Fra Diavolo*, the audience almost screaming with laughter. "Restless as a globule of mercury, he ran, sang, danced, whirled, and flew about more like an animated streak of lightning than like Bellini," the *Tribune* declared. "Applause fairly rained upon him."

By this time the opera had caused so much of a stir in the city that word of it filtered down to the common people. More and more, as the season progressed, members of the working class could be seen in the family circle, and announcements were made that certain portions of the upper balcony had been "set apart for respectable colored persons" and that ushers would "be in attendance to show them the designated divisions." With the opera becoming mass entertainment, gentlemen, especially those escorting ladies, were encouraged to purchase their tickets in advance to avoid the mob at the ticket office.

About halfway through the season, some enterprising soul dreamed up the idea of assembling imitation librettos to sell, forcing the Opera House management to suggest, "Visitors are requested for their own interest and satisfaction not to purchase books elsewhere." A short time later, a batch of tickets was stolen from the printer's office, and patrons were asked not to purchase tickets outside the regular box office, as holders of the stolen ones would not be admitted.

On Saturday, May 20, the Grau company gave a gala farewell matinee, celebrating the conclusion of a highly successful four-week season. The performance consisted of *La Sonnambula*, followed by the "Mad Scene" from *Lucia di Lammermoor*. All tickets sold for one dollar, and the house was positively crammed. Uranus Crosby, with no little help from Maurice Grau and his artists, had caught the imagination of the Chicago public, socialites and commoners as well, as no one else had. Partly because of the holiday mood following the end of the war, Chicago's opera had been injected with the spark which had previously been lacking. That intangible ingredient which produces theatrical excitement was there, and for the first time the city felt some of the thrill of grand opera. The Chicago *Tribune* gave the credit to Grau: "His magnificent company, the finest upon the continent, have more than answered the expectations of their most sanguine and ardent admirers, constituting as they have the most perfect ensemble that Chicago has ever witnessed." Clara Louise Kellogg felt "the end of the war had made the nation a little drunk with excitement and [therefore] our performances went with a whirl." But whatever the reason, the success was so great that Grau announced his troupe would return to Crosby's the following month.

Sure enough, on June 5, Grau was back for a brief, ten-night stand, opening with Kellogg in *Faust*. Most of the operas given on this visit were repeats of what had been done earlier, but there were one or two new items. Verdi's *La Forza del Destino* was staged for the first time in Chicago, just four months after its American premiere at the Academy of Music in New York, and Donizetti's *The Daughter of the Regiment* was heard all done up as a military gala.

The idea of giving the *Daughter* had first occurred to the company during the war, when practically no one had much interest in attending any opera. With its military setting and its light, happy music, it was felt that the Donizetti piece might go over when nothing else apparently would. Every possible ounce of martial spirit was put into the production. Clara Kellogg, who sang the title role, learned to play the drum, and all sorts of military and patriotic business was added—bugle calls, American national airs, and real Zouaves as supernumeraries. Served up in a package like this, the opera could hardly fail, catching as it did the popular sentiment of the moment. The only casualty in the operation was poor Donizetti, who somehow just seemed to get in the way.

Now it was learned that on the night of June 12, Generals Grant and Sherman would be in Chicago and planned to spend the evening at Crosby's Opera House. Both Crosby and Grau agreed that a special performance was in order. The wartime version of *The Daughter of the Regiment* seemed like just the thing. The house was decorated with flags and flowers, and the generals were given stage boxes, one on either side of the house. The large audience came early that night, filling the aisles and every inch of standing room. Special precautions were taken to alleviate some of the congestion of carriages waiting to approach the theater entrance. Hack drivers were instructed by the police captain to enter Washington Street from Dearborn only and, after setting down their passengers, pass out through State Street. No carriages would be allowed to enter from State.

Clara Kellogg was backstage in her dressing room still putting on her makeup when she heard the orchestra strike up "See, the Conquering Hero Comes," and the roof nearly came off with people cheering. She was told that General Grant had just entered his box. As the audience applauded, shouted, whistled, waved flags, and fluttered handkerchiefs, backstage the scene was a different type of chaos, the singers and stage crew crowding around the edges of the curtain in an effort to get a glimpse of the show out front. Grant acknowledged his ovation in his customary quiet manner and sat down.

When the performance began, General Sherman had still not arrived. Early in the first act he came in, and the music had to stop while the house cheered him. The General, who could out-theater most professionals and adored being lionized, was effusive in his recognition. He stood in his box, surrounded by his staff, bowing and smiling, as the audience yelled its head off. The more Sherman bowed, the more the house cheered; and the more it cheered, the more he bowed. After this somewhat sticky public romance, Donizetti—or what remained of him—was resumed.

Neither of the generals seemed particularly moved by the opera until Susini, the basso, dressed in a military uniform, made an entrance, walked to the footlights at stage center, and saluted one general after another with military precision. Both guests seemed delighted with this, and the house broke loose in another storm of applause. Later, in the "Rataplan," Kellogg, accompanying herself on a drum as she sang, directed her drum first toward one box and then the other as she gave the rolling salute. Again the house went wild, and the orchestra had to stop.

Between acts the officers paid their respects backstage. Upon meeting Mme. Kellogg, Grant apologized for not shaking hands. "You have had an accident to your hand!" the singer exclaimed. "Not exactly an accident," replied the General. Then, holding out a swollen and inflamed hand, he explained that he had shaken hands with so many people since the war that he could not use his right arm for a while. Sherman, however, seemed to be holding up extremely well.

With the departure of Grant and Sherman, the atmosphere around Crosby's became a little more relaxed. Grau finished up his season there a few nights later, and the theater was turned over to a troupe of actors, who interspersed Shakespeare with morality plays. During the next few months concerts and lectures were heard regularly at the Opera House, minstrel shows were occasionally held there, but opera was not seen again until November, when Maurice Grau and company put in its third appearance for the year. The popular operatic favorites were then given another round, and Donizetti's *L'Elisir d'Amore* was introduced to the city, although not with any particular success. "Donizetti's opera of the 'Elixir of Love' was given last evening for the first time in Chicago," reported the *Tribune*, "and so far as music is concerned, we shall not miss it much if it is the last time."

In May, 1866, Ghioni and Susini's Grand Italian Opera Company, under the direction of Max Strakosch, paid Crosby's a short visit. The company opened with *Lucrezia Borgia*, Amalia Patti Strakosch singing the role of Orsini, and a few evenings later gave Chicago its first chance to hear the Riccis' *Crispino e la Comare*. In June the Grau troupe was back again, giving, among other things, the city's initial production of Meyerbeer's *L'Africaine*.

But Uranus Crosby was smiling less now, for it was becoming apparent that much of Chicago's interest in opera was on the wane. The holiday mood brought on by Appomattox was over, supplanted by the vengeful hate of the Reconstruction debacle. Talk had turned from "victory," "the blessed end," and "preserving the Union" to angry demands of "make the South pay," and "teach the rebels a lesson." Now that Chicago had had its operatic holiday, it was ready to settle down to the more serious things in life, at the moment "reconstructing" the South and stoking the fire under a legion of developing industries. The new rich had had its social coming-out party, and it was ready now to get back to work. Times were booming as never before, and those with an eye to the future had no intention of being caught in the opera house resting on their laurels.

While opera in 1866 could still bring out a fair portion of the established social set on its sporadic appearances, the middle class and the working people attended infrequently at best. Even the wealthy grew weary if the season was too long. The artificialities of the opera were still basically too inconsistent with the pragmatism of the Chicago culture pattern for the art to remain comfortable in the city for very long. European æsthetics were not so easily transplanted to an America still busy cleaning the soil of the frontier from its boots, and Chicago was no exception.

By summer, 1866, it had become obvious that Crosby had seriously miscalculated the demand for opera and the cost of producing it. More and more he was forced to rent the house out to acts like Professor Herrmann's Magic Show and the Buislay Family's Aerialist Exhibition just to bolster the box office. Still, the expenses were tremendous. By the end of the year, Crosby bordered on bankruptcy. His opera house was known and acclaimed the country over, but gradually the owner had come to realize that his temple of the arts had turned into a pecuniary white elephant.

To pull himself out of these financial doldrums, Crosby dreamed up one of the most fantastic schemes in entertainment history. He would hold a lottery! The opera house itself would be the first prize. In addition, to stimulate the sale of tickets, a number of valuable oil paintings from the opera house museum would be given as subsidiary prizes, and everyone who purchased a ticket would be given an engraving as a bonus. To lend even more of a cultural air to the proceedings, art catalogues would be used in place of regular lottery tickets, so that even those violently opposed to gambling could hardly object too strenuously. If he preferred, the purchaser could feel he was buying an engraving, not a lottery ticket. Crosby maneuvered one of the most intensive advertising campaigns the city had ever seen, and managed to keep the suspense building for nearly seven months. The results were phenomenal. Orders poured in from all over the country. Chances sold for $5 each, but most people bought more than one. Pools were formed, buying from $100 to $1,500 worth of tickets. Some buyers preferred to register under assumed names, with the result that the roster of ticket holders became flecked with such entries as Dead Broke, Kiss Me Quick, Ladies' Friend, Bottom Dollar, and Bloody Tub.

The drawing was finally held on January 21, 1867, in Crosby's Opera House. For days before trains had been bringing ticket holders into town. Hotels were bursting at the seams, but most of those who could not find rooms were content to wait it out in a saloon. The night before the drawing the excitement hit such a fever pitch that most ticket holders were unable to sleep. Lotteries and give-away games in general were very much in vogue at this time, but for some reason the idea of owning an opera house had struck the popular mind as just about the grandest thing imaginable. For weeks people had been strolling by the place with a proprietary air.

Early on the morning of the drawing a long line formed outside the Opera House doors. Business practically came to a standstill that day. At eleven o'clock the doors were thrown open, and an extra police force was needed to keep the surging mob in check. In a matter of minutes the house was filled. Those lucky enough to get inside waited for the drawing to start indelicately crunching on candy and peanuts. A number of seats in the orchestra had been cleared for tables for newspapermen, and on stage were two wooden wheels, one containing the tickets, the other the prizes.

Around noon it was announced that some 25,593 tickets were still unsold. These Crosby would hold for himself. As the drawing began, the spirits of the crowd rose higher and higher. When a painting entitled "Strawberries" was given away, the audience sportingly called for cream. When "Chickens" was awarded to another winner, the house yelled, "Fowl play." After about a third of the paintings had been given away, the ticket for the number one prize, the Opera House, was called. From the other wheel was drawn the winning number—58,600. The house sat hushed, waiting for the winner to come forward. No one did. The audience demanded the winner's name be read, but the judges went on with the other prizes.

At the end of the drawing the new owner of the Opera House was still a mystery. Some of the losers were furious, but most took the whole thing goodnaturedly. Rumors concerning the winner's identity shortly began to spread, amid laughter and humorous quips. Some said he was a convict who still had a year to serve. Others heard it was a well-known hack driver called "Shanghai." A group of men found "Shanghai" and took him to "Bock" Meyer's saloon to celebrate. So joyous was the occasion that they persuaded the bartender to stand drinks for the whole crowd. Seven kegs of beer later, the owner appeared and threw them all out.

The Chicago *Tribune*, which had opposed the lottery from the beginning, immediately sensed that all was not quite on the level. It was known that Crosby himself had held the tickets for the three most valuable paintings. Was it possible that he also held the one for the Opera House?

"If this proves the biggest swindle of the season," the *Tribune* warned, "no one will pity the victims."

A short time later, it was announced that the lucky ticket holder was one Abraham H. Lee of Prairie du Rocher, Illinois, a small farming community down in Randolph County. No one seemed to know anything more about him. Since the little town had no telegraph and only one dirt road led into it, it was practically impossible to reach him. For days the announced winner remained cloaked in mystery. Then word came that Lee's wife was ill, and he could not leave her side. He had received the notice of his good fortune, he wrote, just after he "had undressed and was sitting in [his] long-tailed nightshirt." He was very pleased over his winning, but, it was soon learned, the Opera House was for sale.

By January 25, Mrs. Lee's condition had improved enough for her husband to make a trip to Chicago. He came quietly, without any publicity, for he wanted to "transact [his] business with Mr. Crosby without becoming the object of unpleasant notoriety." The purpose of the trip was revealed later in a letter Lee wrote to the editor of the Chicago *Republican:* "Feeling that the opera house should properly be owned by Mr. Crosby, I made him the offer to sell it to him for $200,000 and the offer was accepted in a spirit which was most gratifying and the money promptly paid me."

At this point the *Tribune* flew into a rage. Crosby had sold more than $900,000 worth of chances, retaining approximately one-seventh of them for himself. He had given away about three hundred paintings, but most of these were close to worthless. The most expensive ones he himself had "won." He now paid Abraham Lee, so it was said, $200,000 for the Opera House. Even if the money really had been paid, which was doubtful, this still left Crosby with profits of $700,000 (give or take a few paintings) plus the Opera House!

For months the city buzzed with talk of Crosby's "swindle," finally becoming so heated that the promoter found it advantageous to retire to New England. The Opera House he left in the hands of his uncle, Albert Crosby.

Under Albert's direction, the theater continued operating, but saw more minstrel shows and brass bands than grand opera. In 1867 the city became highly indignant when Max Maretzek, a noted New York impresario, canceled his opera engagement at Crosby's, maintaining that advance subscription was too slight to merit the expense of transporting his troupe clear out to Illinois. "We need hardly say the excuse is a very flimsy one," fumed the *Tribune*. "We have only to chronicle the fact and inform Mr. Maretzek of New York that if he can do without Chicago,

Chicago can do without him." The statement indicated rather clearly the city's growing indifference toward opera.

In the summer of 1868 Crosby's theater was the scene of the Republican national convention, witnessing the nomination of General U. S. Grant for the presidency. With Grant's election in November, the country entered upon a new era. The years ahead were prosperous, gay, morally lax. South of the Potomac the tragedy of radical reconstruction was still being enacted, but in the North there was a vitality, a sureness, and an exuberance that mirrored the growing economic strength. But with the new materialism came a new word for the American vocabulary—"Grantism," symbolizing the wholesale corruption which beset both business and government. And with "Grantism" came a gluttonous sensuality. Drunkenness, gambling, and prostitution were in evidence as never before. A nation bent on business prosperity by day seemed equally dedicated to a leisure of vice and frivolity.

Reflecting the conviviality of the times was the arrival of opéra bouffe on the scene. This light, comic opera was imported from France in the late sixties and before long had almost pushed its older, more serious sister, grand opera, out of the picture. All over America, wherever opera was given, the old favorites of Bellini, Donizetti, and Verdi were forced to yield to the gay, lighthearted music of composers like Jacques Offenbach. Chicago first met opéra bouffe on April 13, 1868, in Crosby's Opera House and immediately fell in love with it. They were introduced by a company headed by Aline Lambele, "a dainty little soubrette, with all the pretty little ways, graceful movements, and fetching costumes of the Frenchwoman." Three of Offenbach's operettas were given by the troupe, *La Belle Hélène, La Grande Duchesse de Gérolstein,* and *Orphée aux Enfers.* Here was something fresh and vivacious. In an era doting on superficial pleasures, Chicago, like the rest of the nation, was charmed.

Before long other troupes began coming over from France. Tostee, the most reckless of all the Parisian opéra bouffe queens, came to Chicago the following September. As George Upton remembered her, "She dressed alluringly, glittered with jewels, contorted vulgarly, sang as raucously as a raven, and skated over very thin ice." Alice Oates arrived about three years later. She was small and "frisked about like a kitten," managing to monopolize the stage whenever she appeared. Her voice was only fair, but her acting saved the day. All that glittered might not be musical gold in these light operas, but in a love affair like this, Chicago, like the cities of the East, could be blind to a few of milady's faults.

None of the opéra bouffe artists, however, created half the sensation that Lydia Thompson and her British Blondes did. The Blondes were large-limbed, beefy types, who gave America its first real look at burlesque.

They opened a three-week run at Crosby's Opera House in November, 1869, with a piece entitled *Sinbad the Sailor*. Lydia herself was the sailor, as male parts were her specialty. Audiences, mostly men, were enthralled by the girls' kicking and dancing, clad in revealing black tights. But newspapers criticized them as lewd and indecent: "Bawds at the Opera House! Where's the police?" Ministers joined in, denouncing the Blondes as painted Jezebels. As the shouts of "lascivious capering" and "gross indecencies" continued, ticket sales steadily rose. Before long the impact of the English Blondes was all too evident: Chicago women were peroxiding their hair! What was the world coming to? Even the staid society circle had taken up the waltz!

After giving Chicago about four months to simmer down, Lydia Thompson and her girls returned early in 1870, more saucy than before. Once again the furor was set off, led by the Chicago *Times*. The storm in fact became so violent that Lydia stopped advertising with the *Times* and publicly called its editor, Wilbur F. Story, a "liar and coward." But the *Times* continued its war. On February 24, a bitter assault was published against the Blondes in general, but against Lydia in particular. This, she said, was too much. A carriage was ordered. Lydia, one of her biggest Blondes, her manager, and press agent boarded it, asking to be driven south on Wabash Avenue. There they waited for editor Story to pass by on his way to the office. When he appeared, accompanied by Mrs. Story, the attack was on! Lydia rushed at the newspaperman, striking him several times with a buggy whip. When he tried to defend himself, he was held in check by the manager and the press agent. A nearby policeman finally broke up the ambush, but not until Lydia had thrashed her assailant rather soundly. The women were ordered to appear in court the next day before Judge Augustus Banyon, who fined them one hundred dollars for disorderly conduct. The fine was later suspended.

None of the adverse criticism levied at Lydia Thompson and her British Blondes had done much to raise the prestige of Crosby's Opera House. And certainly under Albert Crosby's management the offerings had gone farther and farther afield, with the result that the theater's reputation had become seriously cheapened. The statue of Commerce standing over the entrance might be smiling, but those of Music, Painting, and Sculpture were wearing distinct frowns these days. The Lydia Thompson episode brought the matter to a head. Which was Crosby running, a respectable theater or a common burlesque house? He could not do both. After thinking it over, he decided on a return to the arts—the arts in the more classical sense, that is. Shortly a program of serious music was implemented.

Early in 1871, soprano Christine Nilsson appeared in a concert at Crosby's, creating something of an uproar herself while she was in town. It seems that one of the diva's admirers, a Jerome Meyer, not only had fallen madly in love with her, but was determined the lady should marry him. He waited for hours in the Sherman House lobby just to get a glimpse of her and followed her carriage wherever it went. One day he showed up outside the Sherman House entrance with a coach and four horses, resolute that the singer would elope with him. The scene which followed was so frenzied that the police had to be called to remove the eager suitor.

That summer the Opera House was closed for redecoration, a part of the manager's plan for returning the theater to respectability. The summer was a long, hot one, with practically no rain at all, but the rejuvenation of the Opera House went on. Crosby promised the city "something rich and strange" by fall. Carpets and upholstery were specially ordered from France. The interior was repainted, and costly frescoes and mirrors added—all to the tune of $80,000. The new bronze statuary alone cost $5,000. The grand reopening was scheduled for the evening of October 9. Conductor Theodore Thomas, later the founder of the Chicago Symphony, was coming for the event with an orchestra of sixty musicians, and a series of ten concerts was planned.

Less than twenty-four hours before the scheduled opening, Albert Crosby was standing on the Opera House stage discussing the setting up of chairs for Thomas' concert. One of the stage crew happened to mention that the theater's carpenter had been burned out of his home by a fire over in the Irish district of the city. A cow owned by a Mrs. Patrick O'Leary, it was said, had kicked over a lantern and had set off quite a blaze. The fire department was still trying to put it out. Someone commented that it certainly would be a calamity if the Opera House were to burn. "Oh, it will not," said Crosby, laughing. "I have studied the statistics of theater fires, and they occur on an average of once in five years. We had a fire two years ago, so we are immune for three more." Eight hours later Crosby's Opera House was in ashes.

The fire started by Mrs. O'Leary's cow destroyed the whole city. From the west it spread toward the lake, consuming the business district as it went—the Sherman House, the Tremont, McVicker's Theater, the Palmer House, Crosby's Opera House, everything. It reached Crosby's about 5 A.M. Critic George Upton was standing a few feet away when the theater burst into flames. "The beautiful structure seemed to melt away," he wrote. "It did not seem to catch fire at any particular point. It was as if a huge wave of fire swept over and devoured it."

All around people were scurrying this way and that, not knowing quite what to do. Some loaded up as many of their possessions as they could and fled. Others stayed, variously weeping, praying, and looting amid the rain of burning embers. Horses ran loose in the streets, and dogs raced about in search of their masters. One woman knelt in the street holding a crucifix before her, while the hem of her skirt began to burn as she prayed. For seventeen hours the fire burned on. When it was over, nearly three hundred were known dead, ninety thousand were homeless, more than seventeen thousand buildings were destroyed, and an estimated $200,000,000 worth of damage had been done.

Conductor Theodore Thomas heard the news as his train neared the city early in the morning of October 9. He sat paralyzed as he was told that Chicago was burning and that the Opera House had already perished. The train was turned back as it approached Twenty-second Street.

The city lay in ashes. As one walked among the smoking rubble, thoughts turned to the past and to the progress which had been so quickly undone. The great mistress of western commerce had been reduced to a heap of cinders in a matter of hours. An economic empire had literally gone up in smoke. Before the debris that yesterday had been Crosby's Opera House, young men, just making a start in life, remembered how a few years before they had ushered at the theater because they could not afford to hear operas and concerts any other way. Now both the Opera House and their start in life were gone.

But Chicago and most of the individual fortunes recovered from the fire, even if Crosby's Opera House did not. In a short time the city had regained most of what it had lost and had become more dynamic than ever. Her strategic position as a terminal point for lake, canal, and railroad transportation in a rich farming region made it inevitable that the city should again become a vital commercial center. Before long names like Philip Armour, Gustavus Swift, George Pullman, Cyrus McCormick, and Marshall Field had become significant not only in Chicago's business and industry, but in the nation's as well. The city's grain trade shortly hit a new record. With advances in industry, workers began flocking to Chicago for jobs. Some came from surrounding rural communities, as farming became more mechanized and the farmer began to battle the problem of overproduction. Others came from Europe, still led by the Germans, but followed by increasing numbers of Czechs, Poles, and other southern and eastern Europeans.

As Chicago grew back, its society was noticeably more mature, its outlook more urbane. Women were now almost as numerous as men, and the social circle soon took on an opulence the pre-fire years had never known. Mansions bordering on the palatial began to appear on the North Shore. Ladies' clubs and formal dinner parties dwarfed all earlier attempts. The hired girl was superseded by a downstairs maid, and wealthier families hired a butler, too. With business humming as it was, Papa could no longer come home at noon for dinner. The main meal was now served in the evening, when the head of the house could do the carving.

As Chicago society settled down into a new way of life, more thought could be turned toward music and the arts. In the seventies the city, more affluent and adult than before, began taking culture somewhat seriously. "In the ante-fire period there was no decided musical culture," George Upton wrote for *Harper's*. "Music was pursued as a recreation in the midst of the serious work of developing the material resources of the city and laying the foundations of its industrial and commercial future. There was neither time nor opportunity for musical culture." Chicago in the seventies was still busy, its business still developing, but by the eighties the city's economic foundations were laid, its prospects for the future fairly secure. It was then possible for music to become more than mere popular entertainment. In the years following the fire, the socioeconomic milieu necessary to support the development of serious art in the city was growing. The frontier atmosphere was gradually passing so that the idea of art for art's sake could begin to take root. The maturing of the seedlings would not come for nearly forty years, but the ground was being readied. The growing period would be long and arduous, requiring both money and patience. But the fruit was worth waiting for.

Chicago's first musical fling after the fire looked backward rather than forward in its degree of sophistication. That was the Chicago Jubilee of 1873, planned to celebrate the city's rebuilding. The festivities were held in the new Lake Shore Railroad station, with some forty thousand in attendance. The featured attraction of the Jubilee was the favorite musical personality of the day, Pat Gilmore, who conducted a band of three hundred and a chorus of a thousand in "The Hallelujah Chorus" and the "Anvil Chorus." For the latter Gilmore augmented his band with every available anvil on the South Side. The city's ears rang for days.

Light opera continued to be highly popular for the next two decades, still usurping much of the limelight from grand opera. Aimée, one of the best of the opéra bouffe stars and certainly the most refined, came almost every year during the seventies. Emily Soldene, one of the few light opera artists who could really sing, came with a troupe to Chicago in 1875. Most of these operettas were held in Hooley's Opera House, opened in 1872 on the site now occupied by the Sherman House's Celtic Lounge.

Chicago, however, did manage to have some real opera during those years. Colonel James Mapleson, the great English impresario, brought his company to the city in 1878. For opening night he chose Mozart's *The Marriage of Figaro*. Marie Rôze, Mapleson's wife, was to be Susanna, and Minnie Hauk Cherubino. Both, it seems, intended to have the prima donna's dressing room. Hauk arrived at the theater early on the afternoon of the performance, arranging her trunks and costumes to her liking in the star's quarters. An hour after she had gone, Rôze's maid and husband appeared on the scene, moving Hauk's things out and putting Mme. Rôze's in. About five thirty Hauk's agent appeared backstage to check on arrangements and discovered the switch. He did some rearranging of his own, putting his client's things back where he thought they belonged and padlocking the door when he was finished. That evening Rôze arrived at the theater first. She immediately ordered a locksmith, had the dressing room unlocked, and Hauk's things tossed out. When Hauk arrived and saw her rival sitting in *her* dressing room, she was so furious she stormed back to her suite at the Palmer House, refusing to sing. Since it was too late to change operas, *Figaro* began without Cherubino. Mapleson, meanwhile, went over to the Palmer House to try to soothe the Hauk temper. He finally convinced her to return to the theater, and about midway through the performance she joined the cast on stage, glaring at Susanna the whole time.

Emma Abbott, the Illinois girl who used to sing concerts at the Sherman House, returned to the city in 1879, now a full-fledged prima donna. She sang *Mignon* at Hooley's Opera House on January 6, and Chicago gave its first real operatic discovery a sincere welcome home.

About 1879 a phenomenon known as "Pinafore fever" broke out in Chicago and all over the United States. All of Gilbert and Sullivan's works had become immensely popular, but *H.M.S. Pinafore* was particularly so. "It was not only a success, but a frenzy," wrote George Upton, driving "everything else out of the field." By 1880 no less than thirty troupes were touring at one time, all doing a land-office business. The operetta was given by church choirs, amateur groups, and schools. For five or six years *Pinafore* engrossed the public mind, the fever subsiding around 1885.

By the start of the eighties Chicago had had a decade to recuperate from the fire. The urbanizing process had made enormous advances, but was still far from complete. The population was now roughly a half million. The city's economy had withstood the national depression of the seventies and was breathing easier. Society had grown more sophisticated on the one hand, more ostentatious on the other. Cyrus McCormick's Late Renaissance–style house had required five years to build and contained forty-five rooms.

When Mrs. Marshall Field gave a ball for her son on his seventeenth birthday, her house was transformed into a miniature Japanese village. Sherry's of New York catered the affair, requiring two railway cars to bring the linen, silver, and food out from the East. The party is supposed to have cost seventy-five thousand dollars.

The current fad was to own a gilt milking stool or spinning wheel. Businessmen wore massive rings in the form of their company's seal. Children of the wealthy now went to dancing school. Their mothers had club meetings, where they could be seen, gossip, and discuss "cultural and intellectual" topics. Competition for public attention was becoming downright ruthless, and of special importance was the caliber of carriage and horses one owned. For the social aspirant an impressive rig drawn by gorgeous horses was an absolute necessity. Those who could afford one had an English coachman.

Reigning over this social circle was Mrs. Potter Palmer, whose husband had made millions in his retail business and from cotton speculation during the Civil War. He was now proprietor of the fashionable Palmer House. Mrs. Palmer, much younger than her husband, was as charming as she was beautiful, her skin as white as a jasmine flower, her hair and eyes dark. From her English Gothic "castle" overlooking the lake on the North Side, she ruled over the city's society with all the majesty of a European monarch. If Mrs. Palmer wore a particular style of dress, that style became the ultimate. If Mrs. Palmer took an interest in the arts, the fashionable set became interested too. And fortunately for Chicago, the lady was *very* interested in the arts.

Musically, the city still preferred light opera to grand, Lily Langtry to the more plentiful divas of grand opera. But by the middle eighties some of the operetta's charm was wearing off. She was growing older now and often did not age well. The coquette, once so vivacious and appealing, was somehow losing her bloom. Suddenly the temptress was middle-aged and looked it, adding too much make-up, wearing too many frills, laughing too loudly to cover up her faded innocence. As light opera's years began to show, Chicago started looking at grand opera—older, yes, but bearing age more gracefully—with renewed interest. By the mid-eighties the city was taking both opera and itself more seriously.

Still, Chicago had a certain provincial snobbishness and a superficial sense of morality to overcome before it could accept opera, and the theater, fully. This was clearly revealed in 1881, when Sarah Bernhardt made her first American tour. French literature and art were highly suspect at the time and, it was imagined, naughty by definition. When the announcement was made that Mme. Bernhardt would appear in the rebuilt McVicker Theater, preachers were loud in their denunciation of the actress. The annual reception of the Chicago Club was held on the night of her opening, but Bernhardt was not invited. It would have been a scandal for anyone from the stage to appear at such a refined gathering. She opened with *Adrienne Lecouvreur*, in French, playing to a number of empty seats. Madame might be the greatest actress of the day, but the language barrier plus the moral question were enough to make Chicago skeptical to the point of iciness. The city's puritanical attitude toward the theater was still there; all one had to do was scratch the surface. As the Bernhardt performances continued—*Phèdre, Camille,* and others—the city began to loosen up a bit, and some of the society ladies even went to view some of the actress' paintings. But the notion prevailed that there was something terribly risqué in the whole business. A reporter on hand at the art gallery where Bernhardt's work was being shown observed, "There was no small room for amusement in watching the effect upon the ladies who came when they found themselves actually in the same room with the Naughty Sarah against whose skirts they were liable to be swept at any moment by the almost resistless human eddy which surged around the room." For the most part, he felt, the women seemed to look upon her as "an interesting but highly dangerous beast."

Chicago's revived interest in opera, however, was evident as early as the 1883–84 season, when the city heard the two leading companies of the day, Henry Abbey's and Colonel James Mapleson's, almost simultaneously. Abbey and Mapleson were bitter rivals, had battled each other tooth and nail in New York, and were now meeting for the first time on tour. Abbey had the benefit of both Christine Nilsson and Marcella Sembrich, but Mapleson had stolen from him the grandest prize of all, Adelina Patti, and had Etelka Gerster besides. Patti, who as a child had sung concerts at the Tremont House over thirty years before, was now by all standards the reigning queen of opera.

Abbey arrived in Chicago first, having the field alone for one week. Sembrich scored personal successes in *Lucia* and *Faust,* but Abbey's productions on the whole left much to be desired. His presentation of *Lohengrin* had been anticipated with much excitement, and, despite dismal weather on the night of the performance, the house was filled to capacity. But aside from an excellent Elsa from Christine Nilsson, the production fell far short of success. "A worse butchery cannot be imagined," wrote George Upton. "In La Scala or other Italian theatres, the chorus and orchestra would be mobbed if they dared to treat a popular work in the same brutal manner." The rendering may have been brutal for the most part, but the last act contained more than its share of humor. Elsa was singing of her love for Lohengrin from a couch. When her lover sat down beside her, the couch tipped, much to tenor Italo Campanini's surprise. The situation was so amusing that Nilsson lost her composure and broke out laughing. She shortly contained herself and went on with the scene, but Campanini, who had not been feeling well all evening, was so irritated by the episode that he refused to continue. The final scene had to be omitted.

Particularly weak in Abbey's productions were the scenery and physical props. Like most impresarios who toured the country at that time, Abbey relied on the sets of local theaters. Transporting the ones he used in New York was expensive business, and besides they generally would not fit the smaller stages found on tour. This paring down of the visual picture may account for some of the shoddiness of Abbey's performances. At least this was the excuse he gave. "In all Chicago," Abbey told a reporter, "there does not exist an opera house. In my company are eighty choristers, twenty-two ballet dancers, twenty-five in the military band, besides the supers, so that there may be 150 to 250 performers on stage at one time. You cannot do this in Chicago. So tonight thirty of my singers, twelve of my ballet, and twenty of my military band are walking the streets of Chicago with nothing to do." Critics seemed little impressed with Abbey's explanation and bombarded the stage picture unmercifully. To hear them tell it, except for a few of the principals, the whole bunch might as well have been out walking the streets. Certainly, most of the performances were listless at best.

Nor did it help Abbey's frame of mind any to pick up the newspaper and read that Mapleson's advance sale was breaking records and that eager crowds had become almost unmanageable waiting to buy tickets.

The Colonel, meanwhile, had not only his battle with Abbey to worry about, but a raging civil war as well. His two prima donnas were mortally jealous of one another. In Baltimore the week before, Gerster had become so enraged by the audience's preference for Patti that she packed up and left for New York. Mapleson had managed to calm her enough that she eventually agreed to return and was scheduled to sing in Chicago. But the peace was an uneasy one. The Colonel tended to make matters worse by showing Patti special favors, like sending her flowers after a performance. One day Gerster noticed a poster on which Patti's name was printed larger and blacker than hers. The lady became so furious that she disappeared for two or three days, giving Mapleson no idea where she might be reached. Patti maintained that Gerster had an evil eye. Gerster, on the other hand, took delight in striking Patti where it hurt most, reminding her that she was no longer a young woman. When the Governor of Missouri kissed Patti in Gerster's presence, the younger woman observed that there was absolutely nothing wrong with a man's kissing a woman practically the age of his mother. From then on the singers spoke no more and traveled in separate cars. Whenever Gerster's name was mentioned, Patti would cross herself to avert evil.

As if Mapleson and Abbey did not already have enough problems, both companies were housed in the same hotel in Chicago. This meant seven prima donnas housed under one roof. As a matter of fact, they all occupied the same corridor. Certainly this did nothing to ease anybody's tensions.

On Monday, January 28, the competition on stage began. Abbey gave his biggest novelty of the year, *La Gioconda*, with Nilsson in the title role. Mapleson presented Patti in *Crispino e la Comare*, a work heard earlier at Crosby's. The next night Gerster was paired against Sembrich. But by the third evening Mapleson's victory was obvious. Abbey's *Mignon* paled before the Colonel's *Les Huguenots*, boasting Patti and Gerster in the same cast. "Chicago's flower of fashion and cream of chivalry" turned out for the occasion. A little later, when Abbey turned to Meyerbeer's *Robert le Diable*, his box-office take was only $1,015. Even Mapleson's second string could beat that.

There was no doubt that Mapleson held the high ace in Adelina Patti. She could fill the house with anything she sang. But Gerster had also been well received. Although the Colonel's productions were no paragon, particularly the ensembles, they were probably a notch above Abbey's. Both, however, could stand to do some polishing, and Chicago critics were quick to point this out. As the *Tribune* put it, "It is about time that an earnest protest were entered against the policy of using names as a cover for shabbily mounted and carelessly produced wornout operas."

Yet, while the companies had each had their weaknesses, the thrill of the competition between them and the glamour that came with having Patti, Gerster, Nilsson, and Sembrich all in town at the same time had stimulated more of an interest in opera than the city had known for many a year, reminding Chicagoans that an opera season can be pretty exciting business.

A year later the Metropolitan in New York temporarily abandoned Italian opera, and the Damroschs' German opera company took over the house. Leopold Damrosch had been appointed the new Met head, but on February 15, 1885, he died. His Metropolitan duties were taken over by his twenty-three-year-old son, Walter. A few days later, February 23, the company was scheduled to open an engagement in Chicago.

When the audience began filing into the Columbia Theater that evening for Wagner's *Tannhäuser*, the troupe, which was supposed to have arrived the day before, was still not in town. A notice in the lobby informed Chicagoans that "On account of a snow blockade which may retard the company, the audience is asked to excuse a possible delay in the raising of the curtain." The troupe, it seems, had decided to save two hundred dollars by taking a cheaper—and slower—railroad. Their train finally arrived a little past the eight-o'clock curtain time. Meanwhile the audience sat goodnaturedly chatting and gossiping and apparently enjoying itself immensely. In their boxes were the Potter Palmers, the Marshall Fields, and other society notables. Shortly before nine, the doors at the back of the auditorium were thrown open and, as necks craned, young Damrosch and his prima donna, Amalia Materna, entered and hurried down the aisle, wearing heavy coats and carrying their traveling gear. They mounted the stage, bowed in response to applause, and then disappeared behind the curtain. Mayor Harrison shortly appeared, announced that the company had been traveling for forty-nine hours, had not eaten their dinner yet, but would begin the performance as soon as their trunks arrived.

Behind the scenes all was confusion. The trunks containing the wigs were nowhere to be found, nor those with the footwear. About ten o'clock Damrosch began the overture. Then, after another twenty-minute wait, the curtain went up at last. The trunk with Materna's costumes was not located until just before her entrance in the second act, and Tannhäuser and the other citizens of Wartburg appeared dressed in a motley combination of medieval and contemporary dress. But none of this seemed to matter. The audience yelled itself hoarse. The "Evening Star" had to be sung three times. When the performance came to an end at one thirty in the morning, the audience stayed on to cheer.

Damrosch's whole season was a distinct success, so much so that it was extended an extra week. The city was given a rather thorough sampling of Wagner and during the added week heard a real novelty when the young conductor produced Boieldieu's *La Dame Blanche* (in German, of course) for the first time. Part of the season's success may have stemmed from Chicago's great personal admiration for the young man who had so heroically stepped in to perform his father's duties. More important was the consistent high quality of his productions. Damrosch's "non-star" policy resulted in a more finely integrated ensemble than the city had heard. The scenery was still from the local warehouse, resulting in such visual atrocities as a portrait of Mayor Harrison in the supposedly seventeenth-century interior of *Der Freischütz*. But the musical preparation was generally superb.

Another tremendous factor in the success of Damrosch's season was the enthusiastic support of Chicago's German element. This was consistently the case with German opera in the city throughout the nineteenth century. The Germans, of course, made up a goodly percentage of the city's population, over 15 per cent in 1890. A definite loyalty to their homeland pervaded these immigrants, leading them to prefer German goods, German foods, and German pastimes. When they heard the news of the Prussian defeat of France in 1871, thirty thousand of Chicago's

German-Americans marched in a victory procession ten miles long. While they were not the wealthiest members of the community, they were far from the poorest. Occasional Germans had indeed made fortunes, particularly in the brewing and distilling industries. German laborers generally proved excellent workers, and consequently they usually found better than average employment.

Musically, the Germans could always be counted on to attend works of their countrymen, with Wagner a particular favorite. Even Henry Abbey had been able to pack the house with his production of *Lohengrin*, disappointment though it may have been. But patriotism alone did not bring the Germans to the opera; they knew their music. Opera was an integral part of their European heritage, something the native population never quite understood. The immigrants had grown up with opera, understood it, and enjoyed it. To them it was a medium of real entertainment, and even the workers could be found at a Wagner performance in abundance, well versed and highly critical. If the opera was good, no one could be more exuberant, but heaven help the performers of an inferior production. Walter Damrosch's performances *were* good, as any Chicago German would tell you.

The city heard more German opera the next year, and during the 1888–89 season viewed for the first time a complete cycle of Wagner's *Ring*. Italian and French opera, however, were not forgotten during those years. Colonel Mapleson returned with his company in 1886, presenting, among other things, Minnie Hauk as Carmen. The performance was a little more passionate than usual, especially in the third act. The Italian tenor Ravelli, singing Don José, was about to hit a high note when Hauk for some reason suddenly rushed toward him and embraced him around the middle. The high note was ruined, with Ravelli none the happier for it. He gave Hauk a shove meant to send her into the orchestra, but she held tight to his waist until every button on his vest popped off. Then she quickly withdrew to the side of the stage, Ravelli rushing after her shouting with rage. The audience thought the anger was all part of the drama and applauded in noisy approval.

By the late eighties Chicago's renewed flirtation with grand opera was becoming somewhat serious, and from time to time the city found itself absolutely infatuated with the art. Touring companies were coming more regularly now, and the social and economic development of the community was advancing to the point that it could play host to them. The city's musical education was growing, although still rather shallowly spread. One of the most serious limitations in this growth was the lack of a house suitable for presenting opera in an artful manner. Since the burning of Crosby's, Chicago had had no real opera house, and the

Hooley, the Haverly, the Columbia, and even the new McVicker simply were not of the necessary proportions. The stages of those theaters were too small; their scenery not elaborate enough. What was needed more than anything else was an opera house that could match in elegance and equipment Chicago's increasing musical awareness. In the famous Auditorium the city would have just that.

Chapter 3

AND THERE HE KEPT HER VERY WELL

By the dawn of the nineties Chicago had become established as the transfer point of the nation. Its railway connections with the East, the South, and the West brought in elements of all three sections, causing Chicago to grow into a kind of microcosm of the whole country. The city began to mirror much of the nation's growing diversity, reflecting the American character perhaps better than any other. In her attitude toward industry and commerce, in her sharpening conflict between labor and management, in her transition from rural ways to urban, and in her attitude toward education and the arts, Chicago symbolized the development of modern America. More and more the city, like the nation, paused to take stock of itself, to consider just where it was going. There was increasing talk of the emergence of a native American culture, something which had sprung from within the country itself, and nowhere was the blossoming of this native culture any more apparent than in Chicago.

The eighties had seen the architecture of the country move away from the earlier Gothic revival and other European adaptations, running rampant with stained-glass windows, towers, balconies, cupolas, and jigsaw wooden ornament, to the sturdy dignity of the American Romanesque, the simplicity of which was more in keeping with the American culture pattern. Literary figures tended to shift from earlier romantic themes to more realistic ones, and writers like William Dean Howells, Mark Twain, and Henry James were bent upon portraying American life as it really was. Painters continued this trend toward realism, and a fairly distinctive American school of art began to appear. A native music was slower coming, and even more slowly recognized, but the way was being prepared even here.

Accompanying the appearance of this more singular American culture was a general intellectual awakening throughout the country, with Chicago one of the leading centers. Creative forces which had been stirring in the city for some time were almost suddenly unleashed. The Art Institute, organized in 1882, was making remarkable progress, having as one of its ardent supporters Mrs. Potter Palmer. It was Mrs. Palmer who waged a heroic crusade to gain acceptance in the city for French Impressionism. Her private collection was outstanding. The Chicago Symphony Orchestra was founded in 1891, under the direction of the renowned Theodore Thomas. The University of Chicago was established that same year and opened its doors to students the next. Literary figures such as Hamlin Garland were frequenting the city more often, and Chicago architects, particularly John Root and Louis Sullivan, were doing exciting new things, pioneering the development of the functional style.

Amid this burst of cultural expression, it was natural for Chicago to begin giving serious thought to a permanent home for music in the city. Throughout the eighties the project was much discussed. One of its leading spokesmen was Ferdinand W. Peck, a noted Chicago capitalist and son of the founder of the city's fire department. Peck, schooled in the frontier tradition of democracy, dreamed of a place where "the people" could gather for all sorts of cultural enterprises, opera included. But his main concern was acoustics, for he understood that success here was more or less chance. Early in 1885 Peck sought out architect Dankmar Adler, who had something of a reputation for building theaters and was considered an expert on the subject of acoustics. German-born Adler had come to this country during the ante bellum years and had served as an artilleryman with Sherman during the Civil War. He supposedly had designed the bridges which Sherman hastily threw up on his march to the sea. After discussing the auditorium project with Peck, Adler called in his young partner, Louis Sullivan, who was rapidly winning international acclaim with his theory that function should determine architectural style. After some consultation Adler and Sullivan suggested an experiment to prove to Peck that they knew their business. Their proposal was to recondition the interior of the old Exposition Building, turn it into a temporary theater, and see what the acoustics were like.

Peck agreed, and in April Colonel Mapleson's company was brought in for a two-week season of opera. Adelina Patti still headed the troupe, her chief competition now coming from the American soprano Emma Nevada. Luigi Arditi, composer of "Il Bacio," conducted. One of the more interesting performances given during the visit was Patti's singing of Verdi's

Aida, although the part was hardly her forte. By the end of the engagement, Adler and Sullivan had made their point. They knew acoustics.

Plans for the new auditorium now became definite. Peck presented the project to the Commercial Club and had little difficulty in selling the stock necessary to raise funds. Before long Adler and Sullivan were given the nod to go ahead. For four years the two architects worked on the building, the strain shortening Adler's life and bringing Sullivan close to a breakdown. During the early planning period a young man named Frank Lloyd Wright learned that Sullivan was looking for someone to work on some drawings for the auditorium project. He approached Sullivan and was offered a job at twenty-five dollars a week. Since that was more than three times what he had been making, he accepted. His contact with Sullivan would prove invaluable to his later career.

Actual construction on the building began on June 1, 1887, with Adler supervising the acoustics, Sullivan in charge of design, and young Wright presiding over the drawing boards. Although far from complete, the theater was the scene of the Republican convention in 1888, witnessing the nomination of Benjamin Harrison for President and Levi P. Morton for Vice-President. By the fall of the next year the building was finished, a marvel to both eye and ear.

Ferdinand Peck, like Uranus Crosby, was a businessman whose second nature led him to think in terms of profits. To make his home for the arts economically practical, he had suggested that the theater be constructed in connection with an office building and a hotel. Peck's theory, like Crosby's, was that the income from the building as a whole would make the theater self-supporting. When finished, the theater proper became known simply as the Auditorium, the theater plus the offices and hotel, the Auditorium Building. As Dankmar Adler wrote for *The Architectural Record,* "The Auditorium Building illustrates how the versatile Western American can combine sentiment with thrift, and demonstrates how he can endeavor to cultivate the service of Mammon simultaneously with an effort to attain his higher artistic ideals."

The building is essentially American Romanesque in design, somewhat heavy and fortress-like in appearance, the crowning achievement of Louis Sullivan's so-called masonry period. Ten stories high, it is built of granite, and is located on Michigan Avenue, about one thousand feet from the lake front. The structure is no skyscraper, for its walls are not hung on a steel frame, nor do they rest on steel pillars. Its foundation is a raft of stone and concrete, which grows wider at the bottom and is sunk in the ground. The twelve-story tower, which alone weighs thirty million tons, has its own foundation of steel and concrete, designed to withstand the frequent shifts in Chicago's sandy subsoil. This underground loam had always posed a problem for builders, and skeptics fully expected to find Sullivan's tower sinking clear into the ground. The tower was designed primarily as a means of indicating and accentuating the main entrance, but it too was originally filled with offices. As a matter of fact, every foot of the building facing the street served some commercial purpose.

Inside, the floors of the lobby and the foyers were of the most expensive marble obtainable, laid in intricate mosaics, taking thousands of man-hours to fashion.* Leading up from the main lobby to the grand foyer was a broad marble staircase with bronze balusters. The whole interior was painted ivory and gold, accented with marble, onyx, and fine woods. Off the corridors was a series of cloak rooms and lounges.

The auditorium itself was characterized by its vast sweep and expansiveness, determined largely for acoustical effects. The house was low, flaring outward and upward from the stage. The surface of the ceiling was broken by a series of concentric elliptical arches, lined with electric light bulbs. The floor rose more sharply than was necessary for the audience's vision in order to aid the acoustics. Practically every line in the house was curved, and there were virtually no corners. Even the capitals of columns were rounded, helping to make the house echo-free. This low roundness offered the sound little interference and at the same time made the interior seem less vast than it was.

The normal seating capacity of the theater was 4,250, although this could be increased for conventions and other large gatherings to 7,000 by continuing the parquet seating into the main foyer, reseating the boxes, and employing the use of risers on the stage. Boxes were found only at the sides of the parquet and were only forty in number, arranged in two tiers. The lower tier formed an arcade of arches, leaving the boxes quite open. The upper boxes were partitioned one from the other, but not enclosed. Peck regarded boxes as distinctly undemocratic and insisted that they be kept open and at a minimum. He wanted the Auditorium, he said, to represent "the future and not the corrupt past." Besides the parquet and boxes, there were a main balcony and two upper galleries, the latter of which could be closed off from the rest of the house simply by lowering a hinged steel curtain.

Over the proscenium was an allegorical mural painted by Charles Holloway, executed on a background of gold and depicting the various influences of music upon the human mind. On either side of the stage was a

* The interior of the Auditorium is described here in the past tense, although it still exists in a dilapidated state. The building is now owned by Roosevelt University, but the theater itself is in such shambles that it is not open to the public. Plans are currently afoot to restore the theater as soon as possible to a facsimile of its original condition. The problem, of course, is funds, over three million dollars.

quotation from Louis Sullivan's essay on "Inspiration": "O soft melodious spring, first born of life and love" and "A great life has passed into the tomb and there awaits the requiem of winter snows." In the years to come, more than one person, waiting for a performance to begin, would puzzle over those lines. The stage itself was 70 by 110 feet. Its height from floor to loft was 95 feet. The stage floor was divided into sections, each section movable. By merely throwing a series of switches to raise or lower these sections, hills, caves, rocks, terraces, steps, and other effects could be produced. Portions of the stage could also be made to simulate a rocking motion. All in all, the stage was as highly mechanized as any of its day.

The adjoining hotel, the Auditorium Annex (later known as the Congress Hotel), was connected to the Auditorium by an underground passageway and soon became recognized as one of the most luxurious in the country. Its palatial bar became one of the most fashionable in the city. Sullivan himself shortly became a regular patron, making the bar a sort of evening headquarters. The office building, however, was never the success Peck had envisioned, and it was never able to defray the expenses of the theater, as he had hoped.

The Auditorium reflected both Chicago's aspiration to cultural significance and the maturation of the city's wealth and power. Such a building could only have been erected in a city effusive with great fortunes. At the time of its completion it was the largest and most complex structure in Chicago, built at a cost of eight million dollars. The theater was larger than the New York's Metropolitan, the acoustics better. "Its erection," says journalist Emmett Dedmon, "symbolized to Chicagoans the beginning of an era when they might add to the pleasures of accumulating a fortune the satisfaction of indulging in the pleasures it could buy."

Musicians shortly pronounced the Auditorium an acoustical dream. Mary Garden tells of singers' admiration for the theater in her autobiography: "We were always in complete communication with the three thousand people sitting there. And they, in turn, always felt they were very near to us." She says she once asked Jean de Reszke, the famous tenor, what he considered the finest theater in the world for acoustics. Without hesitation he answered, "The Auditorium in Chicago."

On Monday, December 9, 1889, the Auditorium was scheduled for dedication with a special program of speeches and music. Both President Benjamin Harrison and Vice-President Levi Morton, who had been nominated for their offices in the theater the year before, were to be present, and Adelina Patti was to sing. The next evening the Italian Grand Opera Company, co-managed by Henry Abbey and Maurice Grau, was contracted to take over the theater for a four-week season of opera. Patti, their star, was billed to sing most of her famous roles, and excitement in the city was running high.

Patti, now nearly forty-seven years old, was still the undisputed queen of opera. She made her home nowadays in a castle in southern Wales, complete with its own private theater. She traveled with all the pomp and ceremony of the reigning monarch she was. When Abbey and Grau's train pulled into Chicago, it contained twelve cars—four baggage cars filled with costumes for the eighteen operas to be given, a diner, Pullmans, sleeping cars, and a coach. Bringing up the rear was an ornate palace on wheels with "Adelina Patti" written across it. This was the star's private car, furnished her by the management. Its curtains were made of heavy damask silk, its walls and ceiling of gilded leather tapestry. The carpet was velvet, the lamps gold, most of the ornaments silver. A hand-carved grand piano alone cost $2,500. Paintings, estimated worth $2,000, adorned the walls. Ship springs had been added to keep the car in constant balance.

Patti arrived in Chicago with her entourage of maids, secretaries, butlers, and a personal chef—all supplied at Abbey and Grau's expense. Her stage luggage alone consisted of forty-four trunks; the *Traviata* gowns themselves cost one thousand pounds. The diva was still girlish in manner—her personal charm as magnetic, her figure as trim as ever. Yet she maintained an air of dignity and refinement and always seemed in complete self-control. Probably no singer of her day understood the public better than she. Certainly she knew the value of publicity and somehow never failed to receive her share. The 1889–90 season in Chicago was no exception. Most newsworthy of all, she arrived this season a blonde! Tongues were wagging the moment reporters saw her depart from her coach, her black eyes dancing with delight at the sensation she was obviously causing.

While traveling with Mapleson, Patti had competed with Gerster and Nevada, and although her opposition had been formidable, she had managed to hold the limelight. Her chief competitor in the Abbey and Grau company was Lillian Nordica. Nordica, a legend herself, apparently was prepared to give Patti a run for her money both visually and vocally, for it was reported that she had just spent two thousand pounds in London for new costumes. One Chicago newspaper sarcastically, and rather unfairly, commented, "Patti is bringing her voice, and Nordica her wardrobe." Supposedly Nordica was quite unhappy at not having a railroad coach of her own. According to the rumor, Abbey had explained to her that she could have a whole train if she were willing to pay for it.

On the night of the dedication, eight thousand people somehow crowded into the Auditorium, and an estimated thirty thousand more milled about outside in the streets trying to catch a glimpse of the celebrities. The line of spectators had begun forming at seven thirty that morning. By evening the city dignitaries had to pick their way across the street through lines of carriages and a pushing, shoving mob, kept only partially in check by policemen. "Whether the cream of society or only its boiled milk," the Chicago *Tribune* wrote, "all had to pass through the serried ranks of upturned, swaying, laughing, gibing, hooting faces." As they fought their way through the crowd, a gentle rain fell upon the ladies' high-piled coiffures and onto their wraps.

Inside the theater, the stage had been cleared for a few temporary boxes at the sides, while almost a thousand musicians were placed bleacher-fashion in the center. Every seat in the house was taken, and an additional fifteen hundred people stood shoulder to shoulder in the outer foyer. The house represented a conglomeration of the city's elite and the curious. One observer described it as "a well-dressed mob." This was to be one of the great nights in Chicago's history, and the city's commoners as well as its wealth and fashion intended to take part in it, fulfilling Peck's hope for a theater embodying the democratic spirit.

The house was dimly lighted. The chorus on stage and the ladies in the boxes were waving their fans gently, waiting for the festivities to begin. A little past eight o'clock, Vice-President Levi Morton came in and quietly took his seat in one of the stage boxes. The crowd greeted him with hearty applause. There was a brief pause, and then a short, chunky man appeared at the right. The audience recognized him as President Benjamin Harrison. As the *Tribune* described it, "Before the electric light had run a fiery course across the ceiling and the hall was glittering and blazing in every corner, 'His Excellency Benjamin Harrison,' as the program called him, was bowing to a cheer that started musically up on the stage with the singers and ran up to the roof, where the galleries got it and fired it back again." In a moment the lights flashed on, and the band struck up the familiar strains of "Hail to the Chief."

Now that they had the President, the crowd waited for Patti, not altogether patiently. They applauded Théodore Dubois' "Triumphal Fantasy" for organ and orchestra and then checked the program to see how many numbers before Patti. Four more! They cheered Mayor Cregier when he spoke, and Ferdinand Peck, then asked how long before Patti. Frederick Grant Gleason's Auditorium cantata, sung by a chorus of five hundred voices, was graciously received, but the comment was heard, "Beautiful, but it isn't Patti." The last speaker, John S. Runnels, gave the special address, in which he compared the Parthenon, the Pyramids, and the Acropolis with the Auditorium and found the ancient marvels paling before the new. The excitement was reaching its peak. The ladies fidgeted, while the men rolled and unrolled their programs. On stage the musicians began looking anxiously toward the north wing. The violinists made ready their bows, and the audience broke into a spasm of applause. It was Adelina Patti at last!

The diva wore a black-and-white-striped satin gown with a train over a white petticoat. The front of the bodice was trimmed with silver droplets and jet beads. Her long black gloves reached above the elbow, and around her neck she wore a blazing diamond necklace. She had chosen to wear black and white because she was still in half-mourning for her sister Carlotta, who had died the previous June. The singer's reception was one of the greatest of her career. As she walked down to the lights, the house rose to its feet. Ladies waved their handkerchiefs, while gentlemen cheered and whistled until their welcome surpassed even that given the President. "How soft she is," wrote the *Tribune* the next day, "how caressingly inviting; how essentially feminine! No wonder she bewitches the people."

Patti sang "Home, Sweet Home." As the *Herald* reported it, "The mellow notes of a flute came with delicious sweetness. A harp, played by a woman's hand, joined in. . . . Then came the song, beginning so faintly yet so clearly that it sounded like the warble of a bird concealed among the flowers on the stage. . . . Afterward, there was only a blushing, bright-eyed woman, bowing with crossed arms." At the conclusion of the song President Harrison jumped to his feet, leading the house in a grand ovation. As an encore Patti sang the "Swiss Echo Song" by Eckert, but although the house applauded and applauded, she declined to sing another. For her two short songs, the soprano was paid four thousand dollars. One commercially minded observer figured that when Patti trilled, each vibration cost approximately thirty cents.

President Harrison wrote his name in gold lettering on the lobby wall, and the ceremonies were over. When the wealthy went outside to call for their carriages, they faced a real traffic jam. Chaos reigned for an hour, as drivers tried to edge their vehicles up to the front entrance of the Auditorium. One reporter commented, "Big as Chicago is, it is not big enough to grapple with the conundrum presented when 1,200 rigs appear at one hall on a single night and all expect to be assigned to one place, and that directly in the front of the main entrance."

The following evening the first opera was heard in the Auditorium, Gounod's *Romeo and Juliet,* with Adelina Patti in the soprano role. The audience was made up mostly of the society circle, and most of the city's prominent citizens were present. Everyone came in full dress, opera cloaks, décolleté gowns, and ostrich feather fans—these being in particularly high fashion. Most people agreed it was the most brilliant audience that had gathered in Chicago to date.

Patti herself appeared more striking and gayer than the night before. She had put aside her half-mourning habit and as Juliet appeared wearing décolleté costumes. All four of her gowns for the opera were new, and each had been carefully chosen to display the Patti charms. For the first-act ball she wore white satin with pink ribbons and pearls, while the marriage scene found her in gray and pink, the shade of pink so new that no name had yet been given to it. For the bedroom scene she changed into a white gauze tunic worn over a deep blue. And Juliet's death was played wearing white satin embroidered with orange blossoms, silver, and diamonds. Through all five acts Patti was the center of attention, and after every aria she was generously applauded. Each time she paused to bow her acknowledgment before continuing. At the end of her first solo, she carried with her from the stage a huge bouquet, smiling and curtsying as she went. Vocally, however, the soprano was not what she had been a decade or so before. But only the critics seemed to notice; the audience could hardly have been warmer.

Aside from Patti and her costumes, the most dazzling aspect of the production was the sets, the likes of which Chicago had never seen before. It was still the practice for the local theater, not the opera company, to supply all scenery, and the Auditorium's was far above average.

In an interview in her suite at the Richelieu Hotel a few days later, Patti said she thought the Auditorium was "the most perfect hall in the world." Her rooms at the Richelieu were filled with baskets of flowers, making the air heavy with perfume. The diva herself, although dressed all in black, was "charming, affable, and gay." As she talked with reporters, her jeweled hands caressed a tiny dog which she held in her lap, a gift from the wife of the President of Mexico. Why had she bleached her hair? She had lightened it for Juliet when she sang the role in Paris. How much did she receive for each performance? Her usual fee was $3,500 plus 10 per cent of the box office receipts over $5,000. "Patti the divine!" the reporter for the *Tribune* exclaimed. "She is here. Just the same superb Patti the world has been worshipping no one cares to remember how many years."

But as the season wore on, it became obvious that she was not the "same superb Patti" she had once been. Her voice was found increasingly disappointing. Her high notes came with such difficulty that she generally permitted an understudy to take them for her. Even then, her arias were transposed more often than not. In ensembles she frequently remained silent, saving her voice for the solos. Her acting, of course, had always been conventional and superficial. "The engagement of Mme. Patti was a sound operation commercially," the Chicago *Morning News* fumed, "but it nearly ruined the musical record of the season. For several reasons it would be well not to keep up longer the amiable fiction of the pre-eminence of this once great singer." To the public, however, she was still their beloved Adelina, and the soprano packed the Auditorium every time she sang. It mattered little whether the role was Juliet, Lucia, Semiramide, Harriet, Violetta, Amina, or Rosina; she always left the stage carrying roses. The audience came to hear Patti, and she was always just that, no matter the role.

Attendance was consistently high throughout the season, and rarely did the company play to a house of less than three thousand. Financially, it was the brightest yet. Patti, of course, had stimulated much of the interest, but there were other enticements too. Nordica gave a thrilling *Aida*, and Francesco Tamagno made his American debut in Rossini's *William Tell*. Tamagno, well proportioned and standing over six feet tall, brought down the house with his performances, critics pronouncing him an unqualified sensation. Toward the close of the season the tenor gave Chicago its first chance to hear Verdi's *Otello*. The role of the Moor was Tamagno's best, a part he had created in Milan two years before. Verdi himself had coached the singer for the role, and he had just the voice for it, capable of trumpeting out high notes with little effort. Tamagno was the only member of the cast who had sung his part before, and some of the others were rather tentative in their approach. Del Puente, the baritone, wore a moustache as Iago, because, he said, he was "not in the habit of taking buffo parts." Still, most critics found *Otello* the crowning event of the season.

Abbey and Grau's engagement not only set new attendance records, but full dress prevailed to an unprecedented degree. Chicagoans seemed to feel that in a house as elegant as the Auditorium only the most formal wear would be fitting. The chicquest thing the ladies could wear that year was the décolleté gown, although it was still considered rather daring. A survey of Chicago's social notables was taken during the season to see just where they stood regarding the controversial décolleté. The results indicated the city was about equally divided on the subject. To Mrs. Marshall Field the subject was "one which every woman must decide for herself. I never wear a low-necked gown myself and hold that a slender woman's appearance is vastly improved by the Bernhardt style of dress. Of course it is all right for women who have handsome necklaces to cut the dress low enough to display them. But as I never wear jewelry of that kind myself I always have the necks of my dresses cut high." Mrs. John W. Jewett felt that "for the years between 16 and 28 when the neck is plump and full and the skin like satin a dress cut modestly low is not in my opinion inappropriate provided the wearer has exceptionally robust health, but after that. . . ." She let a gesture of her hand finish the sentence.

The bustle was quite pronounced that year, and bodices fitted the figure as closely as possible to emphasize the wasp waist. If the gown had no sleeves, it was fashionable to add puffs of ribbon to the shoulders. White gloves were considered essential for formal wear, and the more diamonds one wore the better. The upper tier of boxes was considered the most elegant place to sit at that time, but sophisticates from all over the house would gather in the foyer to promenade between acts.

Just as Grau had captured the imagination of the general public during his dedicatory season at Crosby's Opera House, he and Abbey now managed to catch temporarily at least the attention of the common man as well as the wealthy elite. For a brief moment opera-going became popular entertainment. "All the world, his wife, his sons, and his daughters," wrote the *Tribune*, "have taken to opera-going, to the neglect of pretty nearly everything else of a social nature. Not to have been seen at least several times at the Auditorium is to argue oneself out of the swim." Those who had no carriage of their own or who could not afford to rent a hack at fifty cents to a dollar an hour, came to the opera by horsecar, the horse-pulled cable cars operating on the city's main streets.

Late in the season Chicago was hit with the influenza wave—"la grippe," as it was known then—which struck all over the country that year. Most of the opera troupe fell ill. Tamagno lay in his hotel room under a mountain of blankets, his neck wound in red flannel. At the Richelieu Nordica was in bed, nursing a sore throat and a bad cough. Most of the rest of the company were in similar condition. "Only myself and Patti are left," said Milward Adams, the Auditorium manager, "and I am not feeling any too well." With most of its artists down, the management began to panic. Would Patti agree to sing as a replacement?

When a group from the Auditorium appeared in Patti's hotel suite, they found her sitting in her parlor, warming her feet over a coal fire and eating marshmallows, which she claimed were good for the throat.

"You are well, are you not?" asked Milward Adams.

"Perfectly," replied Patti.

"Then you can sing tonight?"

"For four thousand dollars."

The committee returned to the Auditorium in despair. Abbey, his hands in his pockets, paced up and down angrily. Peck just sat with his head in his hands and moaned. Adams was so ill-tempered he kicked a man for asking for a free pass. At the last minute Emma Albani agreed to step in for an ailing colleague. The opera was changed from *Otello* to *Les Huguenots,* and the day, or rather evening, was saved.

The largest house of the season was the last, when Adelina Patti sang a matinee performance of *The Barber of Seville*. The ladies particularly turned out for the event. At one o'clock carriages began rolling up to the Congress Street entrance of the theater and from then until halfway through the first act the street was choked with rigs and attractive women dressed in stunning matinee attire. Six thousand people crammed into the Auditorium that afternoon. At ten minutes before two, hundreds of women were roosting on the gallery steps, while others tiptoed past rows of men in the foyer to catch a peek at the gold curtain or the orchestra below it. People were still pouring in through every entrance when the performance began, and ushers were vainly trying to seat a tenth of those who waved coupons in their direction.

Patti, as Rosina, was unusually attractive that day, and she seemed to catch the high spirit of the audience, turning out what was probably her best performance of the season. In the "Lesson Scene" she interpolated the "Shadow Song" from *Dinorah.* The storm of applause that followed caused Figaro to put his fingers in his ears in mock terror. As the tumult continued, Patti seemed to hesitate. Then she stepped forward and curtsied, her hand on her heart. The applause ceased for a moment, but broke forth again when the violins began the introduction to "Home, Sweet Home." Then all was silent. "Patti's first nightingale notes rippled over the footlights in an unbroken breathless silence," the *Tribune* reported. "The great house was hushed. Not the slightest rustle of a skirt broke the fairness of the melody." But when it was over, the crowd went wild. All rose to their feet and cheered. As the diva bowed and smiled, the balconies showered the pit with programs and handkerchiefs. Try as she did to charm the house into silence with her smiles, the tumult refused to stop. Finally, she bent down and whispered something to conductor Luigi Arditi. In a moment the orchestra struck up Arditi's own "Il Bacio." The audience recognized it and cheered all the more.

The end of the opera brought on another ovation. The next day the company was leaving for Mexico. Who knew when the city would see its beloved Adelina again, maybe never. It could not let her go without a farewell encore. At last she stepped to the footlights, and again the violins were heard in the introductory strains of "Home, Sweet Home." She sang it as if she meant it.

The season had been by all accounts Chicago's most successful, creating more genuine excitement than any in the city's history. The Abbey and Grau company had had its artistic weaknesses, to be sure, but these had not eclipsed its strengths. The Auditorium's scenery, without doubt, was the most magnificent the city had viewed, and Nordica and Tamagno had given sterling performances. If Patti's divinity had slipped a bit, it could not be denied that the singer had a way of kindling more popular interest in opera than the rest of the company put together.

The Auditorium itself had proved all, and more, than Ferdinand Peck had hoped. Its acoustics were close to perfect. There was no echo, no reverberation, and even the faintest pianissimo could be heard in the top gallery. The house was indeed one of the finest halls for opera in the country. Only the Metropolitan and the French Opera House in New Orleans could approach it, and from the acoustical point of view the Auditorium outdistanced them both.

Chicago need not have worried about never hearing Adelina Patti again. She would be singing when she was seventy. In 1890 she had not even begun her progression of farewell appearances yet. She was back at the Auditorium that March, again with Abbey and Grau's Italian Opera Company. She added *Linda di Chamounix* and *Lakmé* to her previous performances, but was in distinctly worse voice than she had been three months before. And, it was noticed, she repeatedly had to be prompted from the wings. Nordica and Tamagno were still with the company, offering Chicago their combined talents in a production of Meyerbeer's *L'Africaine*. But much of the winter's enthusiasm for opera had worn thin by spring, and the number of empty seats became increasingly numerous.

Walter Damrosch and his German opera troupe first visited the Auditorium a month later. They opened with Wagner's *Tannhäuser*, featuring Lilli Lehmann as Elizabeth. In certain respects this night was like most opening nights. The house was nearly filled. A double line of carriages rolled down the cobblestone street to the Auditorium entrance, as boys could be heard calling, "books of de oprer." The parquet and boxes, according to the *Tribune*, were "a banquet of white shoulders and roses and diamonds." Still, a night at the German opera was far different from one at the Italian. "When Patti sings," commented the *Tribune*, "the enthusiasm bubbles up in an irresponsible sort of way; people clap and cheer, and very young men cry 'Bravo!' At the German opera the enthusiasm accumulates in silence; then, of a sudden, it is thrown out in great, solid Teutonic chunks. It is the difference between pelting an artist with roses and presenting him with a house and lot."

The opening was a success, and everyone seemed to enjoy himself immensely—everyone, that is, except one poor fellow who had chosen to wear a lilac-colored coat and brown trousers. He looked as if the performance would never be over. For the city's German-Americans this was opera as it should be sung. Others, however, found Wagner's music too advanced. As the crowd was leaving, one young fellow was heard to comment that while the music was of the future, he felt the singers were definitely of the past.

Lilli Lehmann remained a focal point of Damrosch's season, singing *A Masked Ball*, *Fidelio*, and *Norma* within a single week. *Die Meistersinger*, *Lohengrin*, and *The Flying Dutchman* rounded out the German offering, and Cornelius' *The Barber of Bagdad* constituted the major novelty. Ticket prices during the engagement ranged from $2.50 to $0.75, somewhat less than what Abbey and Grau charged.

The Auditorium's use was by no means restricted to opera. Concerts of all sorts were held in the house regularly, along with melodramas and operettas. John Philip Sousa led the United States Marine Band there on several occasions, and Colonel Robert Ingersoll, who was then leading the fight against religious fundamentalism, came to give his famous lecture, "Why Am I an Agnostic?" From October 16, 1891, when its first concert was given, until the dedication of Orchestra Hall in 1904, the Auditorium was the home of Theodore Thomas' Chicago Symphony.

But opera was offered there almost every year. The Abbey and Grau company returned on November 8, 1891. Adelina Patti was no longer with the troupe, but opening night saw the American debuts of three operatic immortals: tenor Jean de Reszke, basso Edouard de Reszke, and soprano Emma Eames. The opera was *Lohengrin,* sung—much to the horror of the Germans—in Italian. The audience acclaimed the de Reszke brothers at once, but remained fairly passive toward Eames. Critics called her a "charming, but not a great artist."

Outside, another drama was enacted, as Chicago began to learn more about traffic problems. It rained like fury that night, and carriages jammed the streets surrounding the Auditorium and were stacked up beyond for blocks. One rabid patron wrote to the *Tribune:* "As this city is no longer a country village, the taking care of 3,000 or 5,000 people, a large proportion of whom were ladies, and in full evening dress, in the midst of a driving northeast rainstorm, should be beyond that of a huskingbee in a country town, and it is time steps should be taken to remedy such discomfort as most of the patrons of opera suffered last night. When the overture began, the entire audience was seated, but the seats of about one-half were their carriages, which reached from Adams to Twelfth street." The situation was no better when the opera was over. At 1:30 A.M. most of the audience was waiting in the foyer, while the ushers were running about in the mud and rain, yelling themselves hoarse in an effort to locate individual carriages.

When Jean de Reszke and Emma Eames teamed for *Romeo and Juliet* a few nights later, critics confirmed their high opinion of de Reszke. He was tall and good-looking, possessing a refined acting style and a thrilling voice. He was every inch the matinee idol, and American women were not long in recognizing him as just that. On the subject of Mme. Eames, Chicago critics now admitted they had made a sad mistake. She *was* charming, as they had first thought, and gorgeous too. But she was also a magnificent artist.

For the next two and a half years, the Auditorium saw no opera. During those seasons Chicago was too busy getting ready for and recuperating from the great Columbian Exposition of 1893 to concern itself much with the music of the masters. It was while the World's Fair was going on, however, that the fabulous Australian soprano Nellie Melba was heard in the United States for the first time. She sang a concert in the Auditorium, although newspapers paid more attention to her dress than her singing. But this was a time when people expected to be dazzled. The fair's buildings saw a momentary return to classical architectural styles, so that the grounds created the illusion that ancient Rome lived again. Landscape architect Frederick Law Olmsted turned Jackson Park into a fairyland of islands, lagoons, and flowers. And, after watching the gyrations of belly dancer "Little Egypt" for several days, reporters were understandably more sensitive to Melba's state of dress than usual.

The year of the exposition also brought a depression to the country, the effects of which would linger for several years. Yet, despite the economic hard times, Abbey and Grau returned to the Auditorium in March, 1894. The box office receipts during this four-week season broke the decade's record for the company. The troupe opened on March 12, with *Faust.* Jean de Reszke sang the title role, his brother, Edouard, was Mephistopheles, and Emma Eames was Marguerite. "Such a volume of applause," reported the *Tribune*, "has not been heard since President Cleveland opened the Fair." Although the principals were superb, the playing of the orchestra was far from satisfactory, and the chorus was even worse.

This was an age when opera managers concentrated on stars. It seemed to be felt that the chorus and orchestra were simply necessary fillers. Ticket sales, after all, responded to the caliber of stars the company offered, not the quality of its string section. And if it was stars the public wanted, it was stars Abbey and Grau intended to give.

While the company boasted the de Reszkes, Eames, and Nordica, the attraction of attractions in 1894 was Nellie Melba, who was making her first American tour in opera. She made her Chicago operatic debut in *Lucia di Lammermoor*, the *Tribune* proclaiming her "second only to Patti."

It was also during this 1894 season that Emma Calvé gave her first *Carmen* in the city. Her interpretation of the role, of course, set the standard for many years. She was as much an actress as she was a singer, and in an era when most operatic creations were shallow and inconsequential, she kept audiences entranced with her freedom of action. Her first-act entrance was made with a rush and a bound, and her facial features throughout reflected the mood of the drama, so intense that the effect registered in the response of her fellow artists. "She watches Don

José," the *Tribune* recounted, "from under half-closed eyelids with an expression in which curiosity, pity, and contempt mingle with coquetry. Curiosity as to how long it will take him to succumb, pity because of his ultimate surrender, and contempt that that surrender must come so soon and with from her so little effort."

High society was a rather consistent patron of the Abbey and Grau productions that year, and despite the financial panic, the social whirl surrounding the opera seemed gayer than usual. It was fashionable then to hold dinners before the opera and suppers after. Over the dinner table the ladies discussed the current dog show, in which most of them had entries, while the men discussed the hard times of business and the growing difficulties with labor. Gompers and the unions were discussed, and Altgeld, the ultraliberal governor of the state. By the last course it was agreed that somehow the western Silverites had to be stopped. "The economy can't stand the inflationary measures suggested by those maniacs!" the host insisted. And they all nodded in approval.

There was no time for dessert. They barely had time to grab their wraps, the ladies their bouquets, and board the carriages for the Auditorium.

"What's playing tonight?" the conversation continued.

"I do hope it isn't Mozart," said one.

"Yes, he's such a bore," another agreed.

Following the Pullman strike that summer, the problem with labor increased, and by the spring of 1895 Abbey and Grau's troubles had increased too. Ticket prices now ranged from $3.50 to $1.50, representing an increase over the previous year of approximately 17 per cent. The result was a drop in attendance and a decrease in revenue. But there were other difficulties, mainly involving shabby productions only partially held together by a few name artists. The opening night performance of *Les Huguenots* is a case in point. The cast included both de Reszkes, Melba, Nordica, and Pol Plançon. What music there was that evening came from these five. The orchestra played abominably, and the chorus sang as poorly. The stage picture was absolute chaos. In the banquet scene papier-mâché roasts fell to the floor with an unappetizing thud, and goblets supposedly full of wine were tipped over without spilling a drop. The throne on which Melba sat was so rickety that the singer looked distinctly uneasy, while the stool on which Nordica rested was no better. During Melba's solo in the second act, the props under the stage balcony broke, and down came a Duchess all clad in red satin. She fell about a dozen feet, hitting a Marchioness full force. Fortunately for the Duchess, her human cushion was of ample proportions, and she was not hurt. The production, however, was damaged irreparably. "In short," the *Tribune* concluded, "the mechanical features, the chorus, and the ballet—the right foot of the latter not knowing what the left was doing—spoiled in a marked degree the excellent work of the principals."

The second-night *Otello*, which saw the return of Francesco Tamagno to the city, went considerably better, but no one much noticed. The audience spent most of the evening with their opera glasses trained on the Nawab of Bhopal, Prince Imad Nawaz Jung Babadun of India and his Princess, who happened to be visiting the city at the time. The Nawab was dressed in oriental costume, complete with red fez, while the Princess, a remarkably attractive woman, wore a sari ablaze with gems. So complete was the sensation caused by the visiting royalty that poor Tamagno and his Desdemona, Lillian Nordica, came out a distinct second best.

The singers, however, had their way in a later *Trovatore*, with not altogether artistic results. The audience was small, but dedicated. When Nordica made her entrance, the applause drowned out her singing for several seconds, and Tamagno was no less enthusiastically received. His "*Di quella pira*" had to be repeated. After seven more curtain calls, it was sung again. The "Tower Scene" was cheered so exuberantly that the closing portion had to be repeated, and following that bunches of roses and lilies were tossed across the footlights to Mme. Nordica. The "Prison Scene" saw another outburst as the audience yelled, "Encore! Encore!" None was given, for it did seem a bit too much to ask three of the principals to die all over again. Still, it was evident that the great age of the star system had arrived, and in an era paying homage to rugged individualism, it was definitely the individual artist that counted, not the integrity of the opera.

A promenader between acts in the Auditorium foyer would now find that the décolleté gown was outnumbered two to one by the high-necked waist. Big, puffy sleeves, "beloved of women and scoffed at by men," were much in vogue, and more concern was being paid to color. Audiences had learned that it was considered stylish to come late, and in this respect, as in others, Chicago's operagoers were becoming increasingly stylish. More people from the surrounding communities were coming into the city for the opera, particularly when Melba or Jean de Reszke sang, and some were coming from considerable distances.

Although style and fashion and the star system predominated during Abbey and Grau's Italian opera season in March, the reverse side of the current operatic coin was exhibited in April, when Walter Damrosch's German Opera Company came to town. Opening night of the German season, as usual, brought out a vastly different crowd than had come to the Abbey and Grau opening, a crowd dominated by Germans, who, moved largely by a pride of patriotism, were both highly sympathetic with the music and the nationalistic overtones of the opera, Wagner's *Die Walküre*. The *Tribune* reported, "If one did not read the faces of the throng in the lobby, one had but to listen and the tongue of the Fatherland told that there were many who were paying tribute to the achievement of a compatriot." This was an audience that came to hear the music for music's sake. A number of them even came with the score of the opera under their arm. When Max Alvary made his entrance as Siegmund, those schooled in Italian opera began to applaud, but were quickly silenced by hisses for quiet. Throughout the rest of the performance respect for the music was shown, applause being held until the end of the acts. "The care with which things were held together," the *Tribune*'s report continued, "and the concentration displayed by all engaged made the first performance of the German season decidedly unlike the generality of such events as established by custom."

The second night of Damrosch's season found *Lohengrin* on the boards, an opera which the city had come to know rather well, although chiefly in its Italianate form. The audience on this occasion, while still dominated by the German element, was more cosmopolitan and fashion-oriented. The society people occupied most of the upper boxes, and city notables could be spotted all over the near-capacity house. "The fame of Walter Damrosch as a conductor," explained the *Tribune*, "had something to do with this, but the chief reason, aside from pure admiration for the opera itself, was to be found in the general desire to compare the production by the German singers in their native tongue with that given in Italian by the Abbey-Grau company a few weeks ago."

On April 17, 1895, the Damrosch forces gave Chicago its first chance to hear Wagner's *Tristan und Isolde*. In the title roles were Max Alvary and Rosa Sucher. The audience was again made up mainly of serious operagoers, mostly Germans. The fashionable set was conspicuously absent. "It was an audience attentive to the point of absolute concentration of eye, ear, and mind," wrote the *Tribune*.

Most of the company's soprano roles were shared by Frau Sucher and Johanna Gadski. During the week's engagement Gadski sang four roles, each a feat in itself: Sieglinde on Monday, Elsa on Tuesday, Elizabeth on Friday, and Eva on Saturday—enough to cause a modern prima donna to run for tranquilizers.

The German opera season closed amid a sea of applause. Musically, Damrosch's productions had caught the spirit of Wagner, often emerging as genuine poetry. The performances had contained none of the star excesses, none of the pandemonium which had characterized the Abbey and Grau productions. "The stage management," the *Tribune* declared, "has throughout the week been in the manner of a revelation after the various phases of grotesqueness which recent opera seasons have brought to view." The audiences seemed interested in the music, irrespective of opera and cast.

But when Abbey and Grau returned a year later, they showed no inclination toward reforming either their production policies or their stars. And the Italian opera season remained, for the most part, a modestly attended social spectacle. "Grease the axles of all sorts of carriages," heralded the *Chronicle*, "dust the cushions, curl the plumes on your bonnets and crimp your hair with both lead and iron, for there is to be grand opera in town."

The company's train arrived late one evening, greeted by one of Chicago's famous March gales. The Auditorium management was there in full force to welcome the bundles of furs, mufflers, ear laps, wristlets, and leggings which debarked. Calvé, clasping the arm of Maurice Grau, was swept by an icy gust as she stepped from the coach, shrilling an unmusical "*Mon Dieu!*" Melba, despite a hat crowned with purple and green plumes, could hardly be seen for her luggage. Mario Ancona, sporting a light beard, stumbled over a satchel as he scurried along, slowing down just long enough to emit, "*Al diavolo!*" Then came the de Reszkes, both muffled to the ears, also grumbling about the beastly weather.

The season opened the next evening with the de Reszkes and Melba in *Faust*. Melba was given another of those boorish floral displays which had become so common in non-German opera. Immediately after the "Jewel Song," right in the middle of the third act, two ushers rushed down the aisles carrying a huge basket and several bunches of roses. The conductor handed them across the footlights, but Melba, looking somewhat embarrassed, quickly placed them in as inconspicuous a corner of the stage as she could and continued the scene. "So serious an interruption," said the *Tribune*, "cannot be recalled since Signor Tamagno forced the lifeless Santuzza down to the footlights to bow her acknowledgements."

While Abbey and Grau had not altered their policies for the better, the Auditorium had improved its handling of the growing traffic problem. Carriages coming from the north and west were now instructed to stop at the Wabash Avenue entrance, while those from the south were asked to use the Congress Street door. The first were given red carriage checks, the second blue ones, in order to prevent delays when the opera was over. As a result the capacity house encountered few of the vexations coming or going so typical of former seasons.

Double bills were then very much in vogue in the Italian camp, some seeming rather unusual today. During this 1896 season *Lucia di Lammermoor*, ending with the "Mad Scene," was paired with *Cavalleria Rusticana*. Acts one, two and four of *Traviata* were given with *Cavalleria*, and

Trovatore, ending with the "Tower Scene," was coupled with Massenet's *La Navarraise*, the biggest novelty of the year. Aided by the acting of Emma Calvé, *Navarraise* was well received by Chicagoans, who found its theme rather timely. The horrors and atrocities of war, particularly against the Spanish, had been much discussed of late, what with the Venezuela boundary dispute and the revolution in Cuba. And Massenet's vivid, thrilling picture of war fell upon the sympathetic ears of a public whose martial temper was slowly being aroused. *Il Trovatore*, on the other hand, was found old-fashioned and sterile. The *Tribune* speculated it was "probably sung at the dedication of the Egyptian pyramids."

The situation in Cuba seemed to be growing worse daily, and newspapers in this country were already beginning to suggest that the Spaniards were butchers at heart. As tales of terrorism in Cuba became more frequent, American passions began to soar. And we were becoming pretty frenzied about something else, too, the crusade for free and unlimited coinage of silver. Farmers, who had been having a bad time of it since the Civil War, and to a less fervent extent the eastern workers, combined with the western mining interests demanding that the economy be expanded by the government's purchase and coinage of unlimited silver. Illinois' governor, John Peter Altgeld, was ardent in his defense of the movement; the nation's business interests, however, could hardly have been more condemning.

Between the talk of bloodshed in Cuba and the squabble over the money question, tensions were running high in Chicago during that spring of 1896, as indeed they were all over the country. It was in this atmosphere of apprehension that the most sensational episode of Abbey and Grau's 1896 Chicago season took place. Jean de Reszke and Melba were singing *Romeo and Juliet*. The "Balcony Scene" had just opened, and the audience was engrossed in de Reszke's solo, which preceded the appearance of Melba. Suddenly, from out of nowhere, it seemed, a man rushed down the aisle, forced his way through the orchestra, threw his hat and coat upon the stage, and climbed up after them. De Reszke was standing with his back to the audience, gazing up at the balcony on which Melba was to appear. Nearly every eye in the house was following his gaze and waiting expectantly for Juliet's entrance, so few saw the man at first. No one made a sound as the attention of the audience gradually shifted from de Reszke to the foreign figure on stage. "Put down your arm, Romeo," the man said to de Reszke, who had now turned toward him. "I want to make a speech." Then, facing the bewildered and frightened audience, he advanced toward the footlights. Stage manager Perry had now appeared on the scene and was trying to get the man to withdraw. "You may think I am crazy, but I am not," the man spoke to the audience. "I am going to make a speech that will prove I am not." A number of stagehands could be seen hesitating in the wings, but no one liked the idea of grabbing the determined speech-maker. "Ring down the curtain," shouted de Reszke, and the curtain came down, shutting the man off from the stage. In another moment two stagehands, in shirt sleeves, came out from the wings and seized him. He resisted only momentarily, then was led behind the scenes.

The man's name was Robert Richard Rothmann, and, it was shortly discovered, he was suffering from religious dementia. As he brushed past one of the ushers in the lobby, he had been heard to say, "I have killed my wife, and now I'll kill myself." In the patrol wagon that took him to the Harrison Street Police Station, Rothmann kept muttering, "I am to be hanged at 3 o'clock tomorrow—at 3 o'clock sharp." And at the police station he said, "I am a bona-fide Messiah, and by the plan divinely ordained these police will hang me at 3 o'clock tomorrow. They will have to do it and can't help themselves. Then the world will be free. Tomorrow night every man in Chicago will believe in God." It was later found that twenty-three-year-old Rothmann had been spiritually converted at a YMCA meeting two weeks before. A speaker at the meeting had said that ignorance was responsible for most of the world's evil. Rothmann had taken as his personal mission to free the world of ignorance. "I went to the Auditorium tonight," he told police, "to announce myself. I had to do it, and I want them all to know who I am. I have got the biggest brain in the world, and I can look at a man and tell just what he is thinking about. I have read political economy all my life, and I know what everybody has thought and written."

Meanwhile, the Auditorium was left in a state of shock. Stage manager Perry said that his first thought was that the man had a bomb and that the Spanish disasters were going to be repeated in Chicago. De Reszke, who remained calm throughout the whole affair, had suspected much the same thing. He said he had shouted for the curtain to be rung down, hoping that it would fall between Rothmann and the audience.* Nellie Melba, however, was so shaken by these events that she could hardly continue with the performance. Even after Rothmann had been carted off and the "Balcony Scene" resumed, Melba was hesitant to appear. "It's all right, Melba," de Reszke whispered to her, "everything is quiet." And

* Despite numerous accounts to the contrary, Rothmann did not aim a gun at de Reszke. As a matter of fact, he was not even carrying one. This is sheer legend which has somehow crept into the operatic literature, one which contemporary newspapers do not substantiate. Neither did de Reszke pin Rothmann against the wall with Romeo's sword, as a number of chroniclers have stated. The tenor did have his hand on his sword, and he did pull it a few inches from its scabbard, but he did not use it.

with that, somewhat to the tenor's own surprise, she came out, looking meek as a lamb.

After the Rothmann episode, the season remained rather placid, much too placid at the box office. The only other real excitement that year was caused by Nellie Melba herself, when she decided to learn to ride a bicycle, the current fad. The thought of Melba on a bicycle in bloomers in Grant Park gave Chicago the best chuckle of the spring.

But after all, the opera folks were a pretty regular bunch—at least "Buck" Taylor, a former Indian scout who was staying at the Auditorium Annex that year thought so. Taylor had become almost a local institution during the winter months and could be found practically any time in the hotel lobby telling stories of his days on the plains. He was there when the opera company arrived, and that is where he remained throughout most of the season, spinning yarns to fascinated groups of singers. Before long the troupe had become thoroughly enamored with him. What did the old plainsman think of the opera people? "Well, I tell you," said Buck, "on the deal, they are not so bad as you might think. Some of them are game clear through. Drink whisky? Well, I wonder. Some of them fellows can hold their own with any of the old boys of the plains." Did he find a group of foreigners hard to get along with? Not in the least, but they did present some problems which he had never had to tackle on the frontier. "Some of the crowd," Buck explained, "have tried to teach me French and for a few days I was making good progress, when along comes one of those Italians and he tells me to drop it and he will teach me his lingo. And between the two I have got my English mixed so that I am not sure how to call for a drink nowadays." How about the women, what were they like? "I don't know anything about them," Buck replied. "They may be all right for some of the high-collared boys, but not for me."

Although Buck Taylor added his share of color to Abbey and Grau's season, the financial record added considerably more—all red. The season in fact was as poorly attended as any on record. The haphazard quality of many of the productions undoubtedly explained much of Chicago's lack of enthusiasm, but the high price of tickets necessitated by the star system made it impossible for the bulk of the city's population to attend, even if it had wanted to. The social set appeared now and then, as it was the fashionable thing to do. But after they had been seen at the Auditorium a time or two, their support dwindled. Those who really knew and loved opera itself either could not afford to go or became so disgusted with the company's indifference to musical values that they simply stayed home. New Yorkers tended to explain this lack of interest by implying that Chicago was really nothing more than a hick town, forgetting apparently that critics in the East had not been any kinder to the Abbey and Grau productions. They too had blasted the star system generally and had editorialized on corruption in opera, mismanagement, and overpaid singers. New Yorkers, however, seemed to expect Chicago to accept with open arms operatic performances which they themselves had declared unworthy.

At any rate the company's 1896 season in Chicago was so poorly attended that Grau was forced to collect about thirty thousand dollars from individual artists just to get his troupe back to New York. Jean de Reszke, who had received some fairly lukewarm reviews during the season, left the city claiming he would never sing there again, as he did not consider its public appreciative. Of course he did return—the very next year.

Henry Abbey died in the fall of 1896, leaving Maurice Grau to manage their company alone. Artistically, the picture changed very little. When the company played Chicago the next spring, the results on stage and at the box office were much as they had been the year before. Opening night, of course, brought out an almost full house, fashionable if not enthusiastic. But once society had shown its gowns and seen the others, it went elsewhere. The second night the theater was practically empty. "How little genuine regard society has for grand opera was sadly proved at the Auditorium last night," wrote the *Tribune*. "Of the boxes something less than half were occupied intermittently during the evening. The parquet was a vast wilderness of empty seats with an oasis of devoted but rather disconsolate music lovers in the center."

Several things complicated Grau's problem that year. First, the country was still in the throes of an economic depression, and opera was one expense most people could easily do without. Second, the season began on the eve of Lent, and this kept the pious away. Third, while the men in the company remained fairly strong, including the de Reszkes, Plançon, and Ancona, the women were decidedly weak. Conspicuously lacking were Melba, Nordica, and Eames; Emma Calvé in fact was about the only big name Grau had that year.

Other explanations concerning just what the trouble was were as plentiful as patrons were few. The Italian members of the chorus were inclined to say that the company had the evil eye on it. Some mysterious nemesis, they felt, was on their trail, bringing ill fortune. "Et es da evil eye, all righta, we can tella," said one of the Italians. "No mistaka, da evil eye on us." The French members, on the other hand, did not hold with this evil-eye business at all. The predicament, they said, was inevitable after what happened at rehearsal soon after the company came to town. During a rehearsal of *Carmen*, just as the chorus came to the first forte passage, a big black cat which had been snoozing in an out-of-the-way dust box jumped out and ran across the stage twice. After a thing like that, how could the company expect anything but trouble?

Some felt Chicago had never really calmed down after the excitement of the 1893 World's Fair. A member of the *Tribune* staff felt the arrangement of the boxes at the Auditorium was at fault. "Society cannot be expected," he wrote, "to sit in compartments arranged like the berths in sleeping cars, and about as hot and stuffy, and be supposed to amuse itself." Nothing less than a complete revamping of the boxes, he maintained, could solve the problems at hand. Another *Tribune* writer felt the fault was less the Auditorium's and more Maurice Grau's. "The repertoires have remained limited and monotonous in color," he insisted, "the ensemble work is all bad, chorus not to be mentioned, and stage management farcical."

As the season progressed, things went from bad to worse. During a performance of *Il Trovatore* the audience was so small as to be almost comical. Rows of seats were empty, and practically all the boxes were unoccupied. In one of the boxes closest to the stage sat Edouard de Reszke, beating his fist against his hand as he stared at the half-dozen other occupants in that tier. With a glance he took in the handful of people sitting on the main floor. The box-office cash drawer was equally barren, containing only "a few lone dollars rattling about in the corners." One attendant said, "The receipts would hardly pay for the fiddle strings used by the members of the orchestra."

The Chicago season was scheduled to run four weeks, but after the disasters of the first, there was talk of its being shortened to two. Perhaps dates for an engagement in another city, maybe St. Louis, could be arranged to fill out the remaining two weeks. When this proved futile, Grau said, "We will remain the four weeks and perform our duty by the public whatever may be the outcome of the engagement." Ticket prices, however, were lowered for the last week. Formerly prices had ranged from $3.50 to $1.50, the reduced scale was from $2.00 to $0.75. With the reduction in prices, coupled with a fairly heavy emphasis on the German repertoire, business picked up appreciably. Also, Mrs. Potter Palmer returned to Chicago from Washington late in the season and helped the company out by appearing regularly in her box at the Auditorium.

When *Lohengrin* was given during that last week at prices they could afford, the city's Germans were much in evidence. A number of society people were there too, producing a rather interesting contrast. As the Chicago *Dispatch* told it: "Enthusiastic Teutons with score books in their laps and the sacred scars of Heidelberg glowing from their beards or creeping into their hair sat beside queer-looking Americans with bronzed faces and red hands and puzzled eyes or sweet-faced matrons in new silks and cloth gloves and continually performing opera glasses. It was the first legitimate night for curious philistines to come in contact with enthusiasts." At the intermissions each group analyzed the other with a mixture of curiosity and suspicion.

When Jean de Reszke sang *Siegfried* a few nights later, the performance drew the largest crowd of the season. Critics hailed it as the best production of the year. Even the staging was complimented, something rare indeed at this time. At the end of the opera a wreath of laurels and roses was passed over the footlights, while the audience cheered its hearty approval. That same week Massenet's *Le Cid* was heard for the first time in Chicago and was unusually well received. According to the *Tribune,* "*Le Cid* awakened an enthusiasm such as no first night has yet aroused in the Auditorium." While these later productions may have been a shade better than the earlier ones, it could hardly be denied that the lowering of ticket prices had much to do with the city's renewed interest in opera.

And to a great degree this was the basic problem with opera, particularly Italian, in the later nineties—it had become too expensive and aristocratic. It was a fashionable fad, a fad which wore off after a few nights. There was little or no attempt to reach the average American, to encourage him to take an interest in opera. Instead the art had become a rich man's toy, starving—artistically and financially—in its exclusiveness. Even the attitude toward supernumeraries seemed to reflect something of the management's basic snobbishness. Instead of paying supers to carry spears or shields, or whatever needed carrying, in his productions, Grau made the supers pay for the privilege of appearing on stage. Most of the company's supers were recruited from the ranks of University of Chicago students or from wealthy young people. The humble youth who might love opera and wanted to serve as a super just to get a closer look at the company in action was told to go home, unless he had fifty cents and either a certificate from one of his professors or a letter of recommendation from a well-known business leader. "We don't want you unless you have the wherewithal," the super captain shouted out the stage door to a group of waiting prospects. "We are getting fifty cents a head from university students, and when I lose my temper I don't get slugged. So you who haven't the half are out of it." Despite much groaning and complaining from the disappointed applicants, the management remained firm.

Girls frequently asked to super, but were always refused. They would get stage fright, the management maintained, if they were required to appear in tights. For the boys serving as supers to flirt with chorus girls was absolutely against the rules. And if the girls wanted to keep their jobs, they knew better than to encourage this. After the performance, on their own time, fraternizing with the young men was one thing—although the management frowned on that too—but during a performance there would be no monkey business! A sign backstage read, "All mail will be found at stage door." Someone had taken a pencil and added a heavy *s* after the word *mail.*

While the engagement had been rather dull except for the last week, it had seen another of those quasiviolent episodes which seemed to plague the Auditorium toward the end of the nineteenth century. It had occurred on opening night, just after the final curtain had fallen on *Carmen.* The large audience was pouring out of the main entrance about 11:30 P.M. when two revolver shots were heard, followed by the sound of running feet. In a moment a policeman ran through the crowd, pistol in hand, in hot pursuit of a hold-up man. "Hey, there!" the policeman yelled. "Hey, there! Stop, or I'll shoot!" The frightened crowd was not sure what to do, whether to go back inside the Auditorium or run for their carriages. When it was obvious the chase had passed, most of the opera patrons climbed into their rigs, giving instructions to their drivers to speed away as quickly as possible. Others could not resist the temptation to investigate just what had happened. They found that Levi's Drug Store, a block away from the Auditorium, had been robbed.

A year later, amid growing concern over the situation in Cuba, Walter Damrosch brought a company to Chicago for two weeks, headed by Melba, Gadski, and Nordica, and presented a series of French, German, and Italian operas. The season was highly successful both artistically and financially. Society seemed fairly enthusiastic, and debutantes, beautifully gowned, wearing bunches of violets on their wrists and wielding lace fans, could be found in regular attendance, their young escorts standing behind their chairs. "This is such a pretty opera season!" one socialite was heard to proclaim. At the end of the engagement Melba departed to sing in San Francisco, while Harry Oberstella, who had been head usher at the Auditorium for years, took off to hunt for gold in the Klondike.

Grau's season the following November was better, although far from good. The Spanish-American War had been fought and won, and times were more relaxed. The company came in the fall rather than spring, hoping to improve attendance by avoiding the Lenten season. It now came to Chicago before going to New York. The opening *Lohengrin* was most notable as the occasion for the American debut of Ernestine Schumann-Heink. Eames was Elsa, Andreas Dippel Lohengrin, and Schumann-Heink Ortrud. It was Schumann-Heink's evening from beginning to end. "Never before in Chicago," the *Tribune* said, "have we heard a contralto with such splendid vocal gifts combined with such dramatic power."

Marcella Sembrich was another sensation that year. When she sang Violetta, critics pulled out every superlative in the book. "Sembrich!" *Musical Courier* sighed. "How satisfactory! What an artistic balm, what a contrast! Without a doubt she is the greatest living singer.... Imagine a Patti with a soul, a Melba with brain and temperament, a Nordica thawed and inspired, a Calvé spiritualized, a Gadski treated to a platonic transmigration of soul, wherein such a voice and style could inhabit the right animal, and you have Sembrich."

But the old weaknesses of the Grau productions were still there. Even some aspects of the successful *Lohengrin* had caused critics to wince. The principals' singing in German, while the chorus sang in Italian, was especially distasteful. *Faust* was mutilated in much the same way, the principals then singing in French. Many of the company's other limitations, *Musical Courier* held, stemmed from the fact that the Chicago performances "are viewed more in the light of rehearsals and preparations for the regular New York season."

Whatever the reason for the mediocre productions, they played again to half-empty houses. After a performance of *Romeo and Juliet*, one observer remarked that there had been more people on stage than in the audience. Realizing that unless attendance picked up, the Grau forces might very well strike Chicago off their tour, newspapers encouraged attendance: "So come to the front, Chicagoans, and be courteous to the strangers within your gates." But the urging was halfhearted at best. When the troupe was gone, *Musical Courier* said that "few among the musical people will regret the departure of the Grau company, not from a musical sense, but from the undoubtedly disturbing influence it exercises on all musical events here." It almost seems that Chicagoans felt the opera season had merely disrupted the concert series, which they patronized with gusto.

As yet virtually nothing had been done to make opera intelligible or appealing to the working people. Consequently, opera's base of support continued to be exceptionally limited. It is doubtful that most impresarios would have wanted it any other way. The thought of the rabble dominating their audiences most certainly would have been unpleasant for them. While they wanted their performances well attended, they insisted that the major portion of their clientele come from the upper social strata, and their ticket prices made this wish a reality. The common people were often curious about the opera, wondered just what went on there, were intrigued by the air of elegance which surrounded it, but found it too expensive and artificial for their liking. Students, of course, who had had some exposure to good music, came when they could, but for the average worker, who made up the bulk of Chicago's population, opera remained a socialite's paradise enveloped in a sea of mystery and misunderstanding, something which they simply could not take seriously.

During the Grau season of 1898, one of the many shop girls flocking into Chicago now by the hundreds from neighboring communities was asked by her steady boyfriend to attend a performance of *Lohengrin.* The girl's name was Jen, a strawberry blonde who sold neckties in a store on State Street. Her steady, Mr. Stubbs, worked in the shoe department. Jen's comments about the opera at lunch the next day to the other girls in the shop are revealing. "My land, girls," she told them, "you needn't expect a body to tell you about the op'ra. If your gentlemen friends can't cop the dough for tickets you won't never realize nothing about the op'ra." But after putting on a few airs, she could stand being coy no longer and told them what she really thought of it all. "I may just as well tell you girls, to begin with, the singin's no earthly good. You have to buy a book just to find out what it's all about. And the acting is just a farce.... And then, anyway, Loengreen is such a chump." By the end of the second act Jen was so bewildered, she said, that she asked Mr. Stubbs if he would please buy her a libretto "to see what they was yawpin about." He came back with a libretto and a box of chocolates. "I purty near wisht we'd gone to vaudeville," Jen told him. "So do I," said Stubbs. "And then," Jen told the girls, "we went over to the variety and saw a better show in five minets than we saw at the other place by the hour. At least the people that was in love with each other didn't simplee stand off and wave their arms around. Still, at the grand op'ra you do see good clothes, only they are made funny." And so it was with thousands of Jens and Mr. Stubbses, who in an age before the phonograph and radio had no experience with the world of opera and therefore found it incomprehensible. Without them, opera at the Auditorium, or anywhere else, was doomed to meager attendance.

Thus, while Grau's seasons at best managed to cover expenses, vaudeville theaters did a roaring business the year around. Musical productions of the Lily Langtry–Lillian Russell variety usually brought out their share of the hoi polloi, and for those with fewer moral scruples, there were always pleasures to be found down at the Levee. But opera, at least as Maurice Grau conceived it, remained pitched at the leisure class, and Chicago's leisured group was simply not big enough to make it successful. Not only was it not large enough, but the wealthy in Chicago were characterized by a continuing air of striving and aggressiveness, which left little time for the nonutilitarian pleasures of life. Opera on opening night was fine. The kings and queens of Chicago society—packers, real-estate dealers, owners of transfer companies, railroad magnates, retailers, big industrialists, and the rest—could generally be counted on to be there in grand style. More numerous and hardly less imposing were the city's lawyers, doctors, and politicians, who also made a habit of attending an opening. After all, it was good to meet one's associates in a social atmosphere. But the Chicago business scene was simply too dynamic to leave much time for such things, particularly when most of its leaders, like those of the East, had only a tentative appreciation of the art anyway. The common people had even less time and considerably fewer resources. One rarely worked twelve hours a day, as was common, only to squander that day's pay on the opera. Occasionally a poor relative might be seen in the rear of a box, the guest of a cousin or a sister. And from time to time a worker might come just because he was curious, but this was usually a once-in-a-lifetime affair. The opera house in the latter part of the nineteenth century represented one of the least democratic aspects of American life—an infrequently used playground for the privileged, but barred to the general public by the dollar sign on the ticket stub. Before Chicago could hope to have a permanent opera company of its own, this picture would have to change. And already changes were taking place in the nation's political and economic structure which would make this possible. For just as the common man was discovered politically and economically, he was discovered in the opera house as well.

In sharp contrast with Grau's experience, two events occurred early in 1899 which indicated that Chicago was not as indifferent to opera as some had thought. First, in March the French Opera Company from New Orleans visited the city for one week, playing at popular prices ranging from $1.50 to $0.50. Its success was nothing short of astonishing. The company's performances were excellent, its repertoire varied, its prices within the reach of the general public. By the second night's *La Juive*, the French Opera Company had conquered the town. *Musical Courier* could hardly restrain its enthusiasm: "We realized opera as it should be—an almost perfect ensemble, with remarkable artists in the principle [sic] roles. It became the talk of the musicians and public generally, the result being that the Auditorium . . . at the first production of Gounod's *Reine de Saba* housed an audience numbering thousands. Opera lived again in Chicago!" Two extra performances were added, and more would have been, but the company had a previous commitment in St. Louis. The New Orleans troupe had shown that Chicago's interest in opera was not nearly as limited as its financial resources and that a company offering well-balanced performances could count on the solid support of the city's music lovers.

This was pointed out again a month later, when Henry W. Savage's

Castle Square Opera Company opened a rather lengthy season in Studebaker Hall. The more popular grand operas were given (*Faust, Cavalleria, Pagliacci, Gioconda, Lohengrin, Carmen*), as well as a number of light operas. Most of the company's singers were Americans, its productions were all sung in English, and its prices were scaled from a dollar to twenty-five cents for evening performances and even less for matinees. The idea of opera in English really caught the fancy of the people, and many of the wealthy seemed to feel that there was an easy chance to find out what opera was all about. The house was nearly full for every performance, and at matinees there was barely standing room. The company offered no great singers, just good all-round productions. Its repertoire consisted mainly of the old-time standards with occasional ventures into light opera. There were weaknesses, of course. The orchestra was small, the sets uninspired. But Savage's success was great enough that his company almost became a resident institution in Chicago, giving the city a season of several months for nearly a decade. His role in building an operatic public, in whetting the city's appetite for opera, is immeasurable.

Maurice Grau, however, was not so fortunate when he returned in 1899. His season got off to a bad start when both Van Dyck, the tenor, and Ternina, soprano, scheduled to sing the opening *Tannhäuser*, canceled due to illness, much to the disappointment and disgust of the patrons. As a result, even the first-night audience was small. Proportionally, more young people seemed to be attending the opera than ever before, particularly the debutante group, or "rosebuds," as they were constantly called. One observer noted that in the upper regions of the house, where the real music lovers generally sat, men predominated, while in the boxes and orchestra women outnumbered men three to one.

Grau's problems did not end with opening night, and attendance throughout the season remained low. Only sixty-five season seats were sold for the three-week engagement. Backstage, there were other difficulties. A disagreement between conductor Mancinelli and the local orchestra that Grau used, made up mainly of musicians from the Chicago Symphony, broke out over whether rehearsals would be held in the morning or afternoon. When Mancinelli insisted on the afternoon, the orchestra got even by playing badly, making mocking sounds with their instruments, and eventually walking out. Both conductor and singers were furious. Ten days later, the supernumeraries, disgusted with having to pay rather than being paid, threatened to disrupt the performance by breaking into ragtime songs unless they were compensated for their services. The ticket sellers also seemed to have troubles that year, aside from not having many customers.

"Did my lady friend leave a ticket for me?" inquired one kindly matron.

"What is the name, please?" the attendant asked.

"Why, didn't she tell you?"

And the ushers had theirs:

"Please, did you see my husband come in?" asked one lady just when the entering crowd was thickest.

Even the ventilation failed to work properly that year, and from the sound of the critics it was needed.

Grau's productions were found less satisfying than ever. Society was a shade more attentive than it had been, and Mrs. Potter Palmer went out of her way to add a touch of color to the season by holding dinner parties regularly. Still, the season was one of the company's worst. Grau was so disgusted that he made it clear he would not be back the following year. "My philosophy, so far as Chicago is concerned," the manager said, "has reached its limit. This is the third consecutive season that I have come here and lost money. Chicago must in the future, I fear, be placed on a par with the interior cities so far as musical appreciation is concerned." The city's critics, on the other hand, were just as disgusted with Grau and the pedestrian quality of his productions. "Faugh!" exclaimed *Musical Courier*. "How bald and uninteresting it all becomes—the same scene year after year, and they call it appreciation for art."

The character of Grau's productions may not have changed over the past few years, but noises and sights around the Auditorium entrance certainly had. Standing just inside the door, one could hear the closing of carriage doors and the patter of horses' feet as one rig was driven away to make room for the next. But every so often the clang of an automobile gong could be heard now, causing people to peer out the door in amazement. With the revolution in transportation came a change in dress. Women, needing something to hold their hair in place and yet not wanting to risk ruining their best headgear, wore golf hats, which they took off as they approached the theater entrance. Dusters were frequently worn by both sexes, and these too had to be shed before making the grand entrance.

The company was still in Chicago during Thanksgiving, and for a number of the singers this was their first experience with either the American holiday or its related festivities. Certainly few of them were prepared for an onslaught of American college students celebrating a winning football game. On this particular Thanksgiving Day Wisconsin defeated Michigan. Shortly after the game, Wisconsin rooters poured into the lobby and bar of the Auditorium Annex, yelling themselves hoarse. Most of the singers thought some sort of riot must be going on or that some disgruntled band of Indians had taken to the warpath. During a brief lull in the cheering, one of the elevators stopped on the main floor, and out stepped Marcella Sembrich and her husband. They were about to descend into the tunnel leading to the Auditorium when a dozen or more students directly below broke into another gridiron salute. The singer stopped, looked at her husband with a start, and listened:

"U'rah 'rah Wis-con-sin
U'rah 'rah Wis-con-sin
U'rah 'rah Wis-con-sin. 'Rah-h-h."

As the last "Rah-h-h" died away, the soprano turned pale and ran back to the elevator. As she did, another crowd of students nearby recognized a group of friends, and pandemonium broke loose. The young men slapped one another on the back, threw their arms about each other, and danced up and down. Mme. Sembrich, greatly alarmed, ordered the operator to take her back to her suite immediately.

In her apartment an American colleague explained that the noise was nothing to worry about. It was only a new American grand opera company, he told her, that had just arrived at the hotel. What she had heard were the members of the orchestra rehearsing *Die Walküre* on a new instrument called the megaphone. Sembrich listened a moment and then realized he was jesting. "You are making a joke, what you call in this countree—a josh." When the real cause of the commotion was revealed, Sembrich laughed and laughed. After a time she asked to be taken down again for another look at the students. The Polish prima donna stood in the lobby shaking her head. "If that is what is called fun—pleasure—in America, I can see why the Spanish do not win the war in Cuba. If this is fun, what must the war be like? It is—what you call it?—fee-rocious. What a noise, it shatter the nerve, make the heart go thump, thump."

Although Grau did not return in 1900, the French Opera Company from New Orelans did, increasing its season to three weeks. Chicago was again quite receptive, particularly to the novelties in the repertoire. The city seemed hungry for a varied operatic diet, and this, of course, Grau had not given. "Novelties we require and novelties the French Opera Company provides," wrote *Musical Courier*. Equally impressive was the support given the Castle Square group when it resumed activities at the Studebaker on a semipermanent basis. Considerably improved and expanded over what it had been the year before, Savage's company was shortly embraced as a city institution. Said *Musical Courier*, "So English opera can go merrily on in this city of goths and vandals, as a noted foreigner [Grau] calls Chicago."

By 1902 the Castle Square company was offering *Lohengrin* one night, Ponchielli's *La Gioconda* the next, and *The Mikado* the next, all in English. "There was no expensive star engaged at the rate of $50 per minute," wrote *Musical Courier*, "and thus relieved from the necessity of watching one extravagant luxury, the audience could observe the general features of the opera and understand its value as a whole."

Grau had returned in 1901, giving the city its first chance to hear Puccini's *Tosca*, and came again in 1902. His success was still fairly modest, but was colossal compared with that of Pietro Mascagni when he came to the city that year. The whole American tour of this noted composer of *Cavalleria Rusticana* was a distinct fiasco, and his Chicago visit was no exception. He had been more widely heralded than any operatic personality since Jenny Lind. But unlike Lind, Mascagni did not have P. T. Barnum to help with public relations once he got here. The composer had little understanding of America and thought of it as a land inhabited by savages. "Shall we see any Indians in New York?" Mascagni asked a friend before sailing. The first savages he found were the critics, who scalped him royally. One southern newspaper suggested, "Mascagni knew now where to look for villains for his future operas."

In April, 1903, Maurice Grau staged his last season in Chicago. After dominating the nation's operatic scene for over forty years, he had made the decision to retire. He opened his "farewell season" in Chicago with a double bill of *The Daughter of the Regiment* and *I Pagliacci*. Sembrich was Marie, the Daughter, "pert, impulsive, lovable." The first-nighters found the performance delightful, a welcome change from the heavy themes of most grand operas. "Taste has changed," wrote the *Tribune*, "and the charming works that made attending a season of opera a thing of pleasure rather than of exhaustive work, and enabled young vocalists to fit themselves to become finished singers rather than declaimers who are soon finished, have gone out of style." *Pagliacci*, on the other hand, was found "ugly and mean... but undeniably effective." The *Tribune* went on to question why the evening had not opened with the tragedy rather than closing with it, suggesting a reaction to the whole realistic and naturalistic tradition permeating both European and American cultural development at the time. The verism in opera, which *Pagliacci* represented, was beginning to have its counterpart in most dramatic enterprises of the day, much to the disgust of romantics. The *Tribune* reviewer concluded that "it seems to be the fashion nowadays to send amusement seekers home with their souls harrowed up and their minds depressed—they are not supposed properly to have enjoyed themselves if they leave in any other state."

The house was not sold out on opening night, but fewer seats remained empty than usual, and society was considerably better represented than had been the case in the past. Fashion had changed somewhat by now. Although the gowns were as beautiful as ever, there was almost an absence of jewels. Tiaras were definitely out, while diamond necklaces and ropes of pearls were rare.

The social set made only a slight pretense of attending the remainder of the season, but the general interest seemed appreciably more widespread than it had been, partly because Grau chose to emphasize German opera that year. By now Chicago had a larger German population than all but two or three of the major cities in Germany. On the nights Wagnerian opera was given, the boxes and main floor were generally sparsely filled, while the galleries were near capacity. The French and Italian works fared less well. After a poorly attended performance of *Un Ballo in Maschera*, the *Tribune* declared, "It is Italian opera in the old-time manner, and we of today have outgrown that manner." The critic went on to explain, "The change in our manner of singing has had much to do with our losing taste for these old-time works—we have forgotten how to sing them, and when we give them in our present day declamatory manner they fail, of course, in effect."

With Grau's retirement as general manager of the Metropolitan, the company's direction was taken over by Heinrich Conried. In his initial season Conried indicated that he was not going to be the spendthrift on stars that his predecessor had been. By 1905 he was able to give Chicago the best season of opera it had heard in years. Opening night set the pace. The house was at capacity, eager to hear Sembrich and a new tenor named Enrico Caruso sing *Lucia di Lammermoor*. Lucia completed her first aria, took her bows, sang her few words to her attendant, who then departed. There was a momentary pause as an air of expectancy swept over the house. "An instant later," the *Tribune* reported, "there came into sight a short stocky figure, undeniably stout, yet moving with an ease and a certain grace that quickly caused forgetfulness of the stoutness." It was Caruso, dressed all in black, except for a white collar and white cuffs, both bordered with lace. He wore a long sword, enclosed in a scabbard of dull red. When he tossed aside his hat, long curling auburn hair was revealed, but the inky black moustache made it obvious that these reddish locks were the wigmaker's doing. The audience burst into applause the moment the tenor came into sight, drowning out his first several notes. "He began his evening amid applause," said the *Tribune*. "He ended it amid applause. The audience welcomed him heartily. It acclaimed him in everything he did before the performance was concluded."

The sextet was scarcely over before the house broke into a tumult. The applause continued as the singers bowed again and again. Sembrich and Caruso looked at each other, but Caruso seemed reluctant to repeat the number. Therefore, conductor Vigna gave the signal for the performance to continue. As the men drew their swords, the audience thought a repeat was forthcoming. When it discovered its mistake, a new din broke out. Sembrich and Caruso again looked at each other, but now it was Sembrich who seemed doubtful. Finally she smiled; Caruso seemed amused. Coming down to the footlights, he motioned for Vigna to repeat the number. The applause, which had continued all through these deliberations, suddenly stopped as the sextet was heard again.

For once Sembrich had an Edgardo worthy of her. Proof of this was that the audience did not rush away after the "Mad Scene," as usual. Everyone stayed to hear Caruso's last scene.

The tenor enhanced his success a few nights later as Canio, drawing an audience of almost three thousand, considered quite substantial in those days. When he sang Enzo in *Gioconda* still later in the week, every seat in the house was sold before noon, and an estimated thousand were turned away at the box office. Late-comers were offering as much as twenty dollars for a ticket.

Wagner's *Parsifal*, given to celebrate the Lenten season, was another success that week, attended by a capacity house even more fashionable than the one on opening night. The performance started at five o'clock in the afternoon. At the conclusion of the first act, about seven, a two-hour break was taken for dinner. The house was completely emptied during the long intermission and the doors locked. A number of hotels in the vicinity served a special "Parsifal Dinner," and there was not a restaurant in six blocks that was not crowded with customers. Special tables were put up in the Auditorium Annex to take care of the overflow there. Some of the more fashion-conscious members of the audience wore afternoon garb for the first act and returned two hours later in evening dress. Most patrons were less meticulous.

During that one week the company took in over eighty thousand dollars, at that time the largest box-office gross for opera in the city's history and rumored to be the largest for any operatic organization anywhere in the world in a single week.

The Metropolitan forces, first under Conried and then under Giulio Gatti-Casazza, returned during each of the next five seasons, introducing Chicago to Geraldine Farrar's Butterfly, Antonio Scotti's Falstaff, and Leo Slezak's Otello. On opening night, 1909, both Emmy Destinn and Arturo Toscanini were heard in their local debuts. *Aida* was the opera. Destinn's success was considerable, the *Tribune* declaring that "it is not risking one's reputation as a prophet to venture the opinion that Mme. Destinn... will become a distinct favorite with the American public."

But the real glory for that performance went to conductor Toscanini. For the first time since the Metropolitan had been visiting Chicago, the company's orchestra was brought in its entirety, and never had the city heard such marvels from the pit. The Met now brought its own scenery, too.

The audience that night was as large as the recently passed fire laws would permit. Society leaders were there, but did not predominate. Many of them now sat in the parquet rather than in boxes, sitting shoulder to shoulder with people who were not of the social elite. Even Mrs. Marshall Field, although a box holder, sat in an inconspicuous seat on the main floor, as she was in mourning for her sister. Throughout the intermissions she remained in her chair, next to her French maid, training her glasses on friends in the boxes. "It was . . . an audience attentive, appreciative, and enthusiastic," wrote the *Tribune*.

In the half-dozen years since Grau retired, Chicago's operatic tastes had changed drastically. In 1903 the Italian operas had played to practically empty houses, while Wagnerian productions could pack the galleries if not the parquet and boxes. The situation by 1909 was just the reverse. Perhaps Caruso, Farrar, Scotti, Destinn, and Slezak, combined with Toscanini's direction, had raised Italian opera to a higher level than had been the case during the heyday of the star system. Perhaps the city's German population by now had become more acculturated into the mainstream of American life and was less enthusiastic about works by their native composers. Perhaps in the chauvinistic conflict that was presently raging between Germany and France, American sentiment was already largely with France. Certainly we had decided very sharply against the German claims in the Moroccan settlement at Algeciras early in 1906. Perhaps this sentiment was reflected in American operatic tastes. Perhaps the German cycle in opera had simply run its course. Whatever the reason, both *Die Walküre* and *Die Meistersinger* played to relatively slight houses in 1909, causing the *Tribune* to conclude: "Public interest seems just at present to center more in the operas of the Italian school than in the Wagnerian music drama."

Yet while Chicago's German element might be less active than it had once been, the city as a whole seemed to be developing a taste for opera so far unprecedented. The more highly integrated productions given by the Metropolitan under Conried's and Gatti-Casazza's management undoubtedly stimulated this in part, but probably more important was the work of the less auspicious Castle Square Opera Company. Between 1899 and 1908, that company presented eighty-eight different musical works at the Studebaker Theatre—twenty-eight grand operas, forty light operas, and twenty musical comedies. The works were given in English, at prices the average person could afford, thus attracting large audiences and serving to educate the public for more serious lyric productions. By the time the excesses of the star system were eliminated from the Metropolitan, Chicago's appetite for opera had become fairly substantial. The Conried and Gatti-Casazza performances served as sort of a finishing course in the city's operatic schooling. When Chicago's resident company appeared on the scene, the groundwork was laid.

Chapter 4

HE CALLED FOR HIS FIDDLERS THREE

NINETEEN-TEN was the year Woodrow Wilson was elected governor of New Jersey; he would be chosen President two years later. William Howard Taft was in the White House at the time, but political progressives were claiming he was carrying out Teddy Roosevelt's liberal policies "on a stretcher." Roosevelt himself spent the early part of the year hunting lions in Africa, but had returned by fall. Many were hoping he would take another try at the Presidency. The Panama Canal was still under construction, and revolution was brewing in northern Mexico. The Anti-Saloon League was as active as ever; so were the suffragettes. Western states were already giving women the right to vote, and eastern males were enjoying what they sensed was their last hour of political supremacy. The Model T Ford was coming into its own; the floor-length skirt was on its way up.

In Chicago a more cosmopolitan way of life was emerging. Homes with wide lawns, one of the most sacred heritages of what had once been fondly known as the "Garden City," were rapidly giving way to new apartment houses. The economic picture all over the country was brighter than it had been in years, and Chicago was no exception. Most of the produce from the prairie states was being funneled through the city's granaries and stockyards on its way east. Culturally, Chicago's prospects were better than ever. Since the turn of the century, young writers like Carl Sandburg had been pouring into the city, attracted by its vigor and its tolerant attitude toward new artistic ideas. While its public might not be as informed as that of the East, neither was it as traditional in its literary views. For a brief time Chicago played host to one of the most significant literary colonies of the day.

Theatrical activities were booming too, many of them independent of New York. About one-fifth of the movies produced at that time were being made in Chicago. The city's symphony was now two decades old and was widely renowned. Its founder, Theodore Thomas, had died in 1905, just a few months after the move to Orchestra Hall, but Frederick Stock, Thomas' assistant, had taken over its direction with superb results.

The city had heard opera every season but two since the dedication of the Auditorium. Although most of these performances had been of the barnstorming variety, many of the city's music lovers had come to feel that there was nothing wrong with Chicago's operatic climate that having a resident company could not cure. The Auditorium was lauded the world over as one of the great halls for opera. Certainly any deficiencies the touring productions might have had could not be excused on the grounds of inadequate housing. The Auditorium had been a gracious host, even if the visitors had sometimes proved disappointing guests. "Some day," Chicagoans were beginning to say, "we will have our own opera company."

One of the earliest advocates of a resident company for Chicago was Karleton Hackett, music critic for the Chicago *Evening Post*, who, spurred largely by Boston's example, began an active campaign early in 1909, aiming his appeal largely at civic pride. Before long he had won his publisher, John C. Shaffer, over to his point of view, and Shaffer began talking with city leaders over the luncheon table and at club meetings. Harold F. McCormick, a head of the International Harvester Company and son of the famous reaper king, and Charles G. Dawes, a leading Chicago financier and later Vice-President of the United States, shortly became two of his staunchest converts. Schaffer, McCormick, and Dawes, along with forty-seven other wealthy devotees of the opera, each contributed $5,000 to a subscription fund. This meant a nest egg of $250,000 for the Chicago Grand Opera Company once it was formed. The papers of incorporation were drawn up on December 9, 1909, and a year-around lease on the Auditorium was purchased.

Meanwhile things were happening in New York which would affect Chicago's lyric destiny immeasurably. Former cigar maker Oscar Hammerstein had erected the Manhattan Opera House in 1906 with the frank purpose of driving the Metropolitan out of business. Hammerstein, dynamic and formidably aggressive, was a showman through and through. It was said he had the only tongue quicker than Mary Garden's. Nellie Melba, who once sang for him, claimed he was "the most American of Americans, and the only man who ever made me change my mind." One thing was sure: wherever his silk top hat went, reporters were sure to follow. He could always be counted on for a story and felt it was a bad day if he failed to make the front page. His approach to opera was as flamboyant as his life. "Opera," he once said, "is not a business but a disease."

Oscar Hammerstein never did anything in a small way. His battle with the Metropolitan was to the death, and the Met management was well aware of it. For four glorious seasons, 1906–10, Hammerstein gave the Met the only real competition it has ever had. He fought against tremendous odds, but Hammerstein was never one to play it safe. Behind the Metropolitan stood the Vanderbilts, the Astors, the Morgans, and a horde of Wall Street financiers. But Hammerstein had the backing of the press, which idolized him. Almost as sympathetic was the public, who found the breezy Oscar a refreshing change from the staid Metropolitan. Then, too, Americans have characteristically been partial to the underdog, and Hammerstein was certainly that.

Artistically, the Met had Caruso, Chaliapin, Farrar, Scotti, Toscanini, and Mahler–formidable all. But Hammerstein had Mary Garden, Luisa Tetrazzini, John McCormack, and conductor Cleofonte Campanini. Even more important, he gave a new look to the New York operatic scene by emphasizing the French repertoire. Debussy's *Pelléas et Mélisande*, Charpentier's *Louise*, Massenet's *Le Jongleur de Notre Dame* and *Thaïs*, and Strauss's *Elektra* (German, but sung in French) are just a few of the works to receive their American premiere at the Manhattan. The Metropolitan at this time had practically no French wing, emphasizing Italian and to a lesser extent German opera. As Hammerstein's war with the Met continued, each side stimulated the other, giving New York a chance to hear some of the best opera in its history. But in the end the Met's superior financial backing proved the winning card. Hammerstein was forced to the edge of bankruptcy. In April, 1910, he signed an agreement with the Met not to enter the American operatic scene for a period of ten years, receiving in exchange a cash settlement of $1,200,000. In addition the Met took over all of the Manhattan's scenery, costumes, and orchestral scores, along with rights to several operas Hammerstein had given and contracts with several of the Manhattan artists.

Hammerstein, some say, had scared the Metropolitan into this cash settlement by appearing in Chicago one day, surrounded by newspaper men, apparently with the purpose of looking over logical building sites. Was he considering building an opera house in Chicago? No one ever really knew. But the Metropolitan was only slightly happier about having Hammerstein in Chicago than it was with having him in New York. Therefore, the Met management negotiated to buy him out. With Hammerstein out of business, the Metropolitan was breathing easier, but it still had problems. It had a warehouse full of expensive sets, costumes, and scores which it simply did not need. The Met therefore quickly began discussions with the Shaffer–McCormick–Dawes group in Chicago, offering to lend a helping hand. A resident Chicago company would be too inexperienced to offer the Met any real competition, it was felt, and besides would need scenery and costumes and scores, which the Metropolitan could sell or rent just then.

When the Chicago Grand Opera Company was formed, Metropolitan support was much in evidence. Harold McCormick was chosen president of the organization, and Charles Dawes first vice-president. But Otto Kahn, president of the Metropolitan, was a second vice-president of the Chicago company. Philip M. Lydig, secretary of the company, was another New Yorker, and Clarence H. Mackay, chairman of executive directors, was another. The Metropolitan backers also helped underwrite the Chicago project, Otto Kahn himself subscribing fifty thousand dollars. Andreas Dippel, one-time tenor and later assistant to Gatti-Casazza at the Metropolitan, was released from his duties in New York to become the general manager of the Chicago company. An arrangement was worked out whereby Chicago acquired most of Hammerstein's scenery, costumes, copyrights, and artists.

The musical director and principal conductor of the new Chicago Grand Opera Company was Cleofonte Campanini, who had been brought to this country by Hammerstein to conduct at the Manhattan. He was the younger brother of tenor Italo Campanini, who had sung in Chicago in the eighties, and was also the brother-in-law of the great coloratura soprano Luisa Tetrazzini. Campanini conducted his operas from a piano score, and rumor had it that he could read no other. While he was a good rather than a great conductor, he had a definite feel for both phrasing and dramatic effect. His presence in the pit was excellent. He threw himself into his conducting, and by the last act the dye he used in his moustache used to run down the corners of his mouth. He was tremendously superstitious and geared his life and business affairs accordingly. He never lost his faith in the magical power of old nails, invariably stopping to pick one up if he saw it. It was not unusual for him to carry a half pound of nails around in his pocket. Playful members of the company used to delight in strewing the tunnel from the Auditorium Annex to the Auditorium with the rustiest nails available just to see the rheumatic Campanini bend over to pick them up.

Although temperamental, he was generally easy to work with. Throughout his life he shared Hammerstein's hatred for the Metropolitan. One of his constant ambitions was to get Mary Garden and a group of the other old-timers together and renew the war which Hammerstein had begun. Campanini's relationship with General Manager Andreas Dippel was never the best. Dippel had been the Met's stand-by tenor for years. He knew almost every opera in the repertoire and could step into practically any role on a moment's notice. While he was far from a great singer, neither was he a poor one. When he later became managing director of the Metropolitan, in charge of the German wing there, he frequently battled with Gatti-Casazza. Dippel had been chosen artistic head of the Chicago company largely because Otto Kahn had insisted upon it. He was more or less to represent the Metropolitan's interests. Dippel and Campanini held views on artistic matters, particularly repertoire, that were often far apart. They would work together only three seasons.

The stage manager of the Chicago company was Joseph C. Engel, who had worked for Hammerstein all through the Manhattan years and would essentially recreate in Chicago the Hammerstein production style. One of his assistants was Carlo Muzio, whose young daughter Claudia would soon become an internationally acclaimed prima donna and one of the Chicago company's brightest stars.

Singers began arriving for the company's first season around the middle of October, 1910, and rehearsals began in the refurbished Auditorium. Most of the artists stayed at the Auditorium Annex, which by now had certain rooms set aside as rehearsal areas. The press covered practically every move the company made. One reporter said he was ashamed to take the money for writing stories about the opera people. "It's too easy," he explained. "It's like grabbing stick candy away from the babies in their little go-carts in Lincoln Park. . . . The stories just make themselves around this grand opera outfit."

Backstage, customs officials could be seen going through the trunks of prima donnas. Supposedly an aged mother of one soprano had been so torn with remorse at the thought of her only child crossing the ocean by herself that she hid in a trunk and traveled that way to Chicago. As the customs inspector opened the trunk, out jumped Mamma!

Meanwhile the Auditorium foyer was stacked high with trunks, boxes, dog crates, and miscellaneous luggage. Owners were rummaging through them trying to find items that had been packed away weeks before. Mingling with the clamor of Italian, French, and German that filled the lobby came the strains of an opera in rehearsal on stage.

On Saturday, October 29, Mary Garden arrived in town. And for the next twenty years she would dominate the Chicago opera scene. The soprano was born in Scotland in 1877, was brought to America at age six, and by 1888 was living in Chicago, where at sixteen she took part in an amateur production of Gilbert and Sullivan's *Trial by Jury*. She was shortly discovered by Mrs. David Mayer, a devotee of the arts and wife of a local clothing-store owner. Mrs. Mayer agreed to finance the young singer for two years' study in Europe. Garden arrived in Paris in 1897. Three years later she was sitting in the audience at the Opéra Comique, listening to a performance of *Louise*. During the intermission following the second act, she was called backstage. The soprano singing the title role had collapsed. Could she take over? Mary Garden, twenty-three years old, sang the last two acts without a single rehearsal and became the toast of the town. She made her American debut at the Manhattan Opera House seven years later in Massenet's *Thaïs* and sang with Hammerstein during his last three seasons. Modern French music was her specialty. She was as noted for her acting as for her singing and was often called the "Sarah Bernhardt of the operatic stage." Like Hammerstein, she knew how to make the headlines and was always good for a statement on something. She was gracious and charming, but above all things, brainy. While singing for Hammerstein, she was invited to a fashionable dinner party, where she was placed next to Chauncey Depew, the New York lawyer and politician. All through the dinner Depew kept staring at Garden's low-cut gown, until finally Mary asked him what entranced him so. "I am wondering, Miss Garden," Depew answered, "what keeps that gown up." Without hesitation, Mary gave him one of her famous smiles and replied, "Two things, Mr. Depew—your age and my discretion."

Now, after being away fourteen years, Mary Garden was returning to Chicago. She came with a foreign accent, a French maid, a valet, a monocle, and a diamond ring from a Turkish pasha—to whom she was supposedly engaged. When she arrived at the railroad station, it was as if some royal dignitary were appearing, so thick was the mob of reporters, photographers, and sketch artists that gathered around her. She was generous with interviews, telling reporters that only two subjects were banned—wrinkles and Oscar Hammerstein. One was a scourge, she said, the other an impresario. "Neither of them, to my mind, has any right to be in evidence. Therefore, I refuse to act as press-agent for either of them." Though she had gotten along well with Hammerstein and liked him, she once claimed that he "treated me worse than a chorus girl."

Her favorite topic seemed to be *Salome*, the Richard Strauss opera, which she was scheduled to sing early in the season. "Chicago's just going to love *Salome*," she declared. "I know what the girl was. I know as nobody else knows. I just get right into her skin when I sing the part." She denied that she was going to marry the Turkish pasha, but swore that one day she would wear a pair of Turkish trousers up Michigan Avenue.

Next day she held a press conference in her Blackstone Hotel suite.

As one observer described the scene, quoted in the Chicago *Inter-Ocean*, "The door of her bedroom jerked back as though there had been sudden application of the hind end of a strong mule, and through the opening whizzed a tornado of choking perfume, shimmering silk, and carrot-red hair." Mary sidled up to the first newsman in sight, grabbed his hand, and shook it as though he were a long-lost friend.

"Oh, I'm just so tickled to see you again!" she bubbled. "I've seen you before, haven't I? Where was it? I'm sure I remember your face."

"Maybe it was down in Macomb. Only other place I've ever been," came the shocked reply.

"Oh, yes!" she effused. "That's where it was. I knew I had seen you before. Macombes—that pretty little villa just outside Paris."

"No, down in Illinois."

At that she spoke a few words of French to her curly-headed valet, smiled faintly, and sank into a chair.

She talked more of *Salome*. "The gown I wear is a peculiar one. I am dressed fully on one side but the other side is draped so as to give a suggestion of nudity." She said she was studying *Carmen*, at the time, her next new role. What about her Turk? "I can tell you I'd be enough for any man, even a Turk," came the response. "But to be serious, he is a fine fellow, handsome and with charming manners. He has auburn hair and he smokes cigarettes." But Mary herself did not care for cigarettes, particularly the smoke. When the room became filled with the stuff, she got up, fanned the air with a diamond-laden hand, and said, "Come right into my bedroom, boys, if you don't mind, and finish your interview." Thereupon she opened the door to her adjoining boudoir, followed by the pack of reporters.

All through the season rumors of the pasha continued to fly. "He is a charming man," Garden said. "No, indeed; he is not one of those old ones; neither is he too young. The man for a good husband should be between thirty and fifty. This one is just about right." It was said that his proposed marriage to the soprano was threatening to break the harem system wide open. Wrote the Chicago *Inter-Ocean*, "The great Oriental institution of marriage, established some thousands of years ago, re-enforced by that sterling advocate of numerous nuptial knots and enemy of race suicide, the well known prophet Mahomet, is trembling on the verge of an annihilating revolution, and all because of a Chicago girl." Garden's pasha was said to have seventy-eight wives, and talk was that they were all on their way to Chicago to plead with Mary not to marry their spouse. "Get the picture?" asked the *Tribune*. "Seventy-eight Turkish ladies in bifurcated hobble skirts parading down Michigan avenue behind a brass band, with big banners reading: 'Mary, do not marry.' "

Needless to say, the wives never showed up. The pasha himself was never heard of again after this season. And, of course, Mary never married anyone.

The Chicago Grand Opera Company launched its career on Thursday, November 3, 1910, with a production of *Aida*. The house was sold out and could have been sold twice again. The spirit of success was much in the air. "The beauty of the costumes displayed in boxes and on the main floor suggested it," wrote the *Tribune*. An additional tier of boxes had been added in the back of the Auditorium, with the recent redecoration, so that a horseshoe was now formed. But in 1910, it was a diamond horseshoe without the diamonds, for the wearing of jewels was still temporarily out of fashion. Besides, most of the women wore too much hair then for tiaras. Mrs. Harold McCormick wore more jewels than most and certainly came up with one of the most unusual hair styles. Her hair was parted in the middle and knotted low in the back. From each ear she wore a diamond pendant reaching well down the neck.

Although it was Harold McCormick who was president of the opera company, it was Mrs. McCormick who really had the greater zeal for opera. Together the McCormicks probably did more than anyone else to make Chicago's company the success it was. Harold McCormick consistently headed the list of guarantors, while his wife, Edith Rockefeller McCormick, daughter of the great oil magnate John D. Rockefeller, lent the same air of social dignity to the opera that Mrs. Potter Palmer had in an earlier era. Mrs. Palmer was absent from the city much of the time these days and therefore had fairly well relinquished her position. To Mrs. McCormick fell the mantle of social leadership. Her attention to protocol was rigid. She was an avowed "dry" and never permitted liquor to be served in her home. She once said this was because of a pledge she had given her father. The McCormicks entertained often at their home on Lake Shore Drive, particularly on opera nights. At pre-opera dinners, it is said Mrs. McCormick sat at one end of the table with a clock beside her. She directed the dinner with business efficiency, insisting that a strict time schedule be kept. If someone dallied over his food, he might likely have his plate snatched out from under him when Mrs. McCormick indicated that time for that particular course was up. In her box at the Auditorium she sat straight in her chair, her eyes fixed on the stage. Above everything else, Edith Rockefeller McCormick loved her opera.

But while the Chicago Grand Opera's opening was a dazzling affair, there was a democratic note to the audience. Clarence Mackay, one of the company's New York backers and president of the Postal Telegraph Company, had come out for the occasion and given a hundred of his messenger boys opening-night tickets.

The performance on stage was "all that could be desired." The chorus was younger than usual, the girls prettier, and the triumphal march ended in a flurry of excitement. The real star of the evening was conductor Cleofonte Campanini. "Mr. Campanini," said the *Tribune*, "possessed that rare and vital artistic requisite, personality. He has the faculty to project himself in the impalpable medium of tone across the footlights and into the minds and hearts of his hearers. . . . The opera, its cast and complicated mechanism is a unit to Campanini." *Aida* has opened many a Chicago opera season, but none more spectacularly than this one. Next day Felix Borowski, critic for the *Record-Herald*, wrote, "The success of Chicago opera means the success of all culture in this city [and] the establishment of a finer standard of art than has ever been known here before."

On Saturday, November 5, Chicago heard both *Pelléas et Mélisande* and Mary Garden for the first time. "If Miss Garden puzzled the audience at first," reported the *Tribune*, "Debussy's opera proved a riddle that was almost unsolvable." Here was a form of music-drama that the city had never experienced before—moody, impressionistic, quiet. The public was simply unprepared for what it heard. In their bewilderment the audience talked through most of the orchestral passages, making the music almost inaudible. Critics, however, were enthusiastic. The *Inter-Ocean* found it "a production of haunting charm." The *Tribune* said it was the "most perfectly proportioned performance of opera that Chicago has ever witnessed." While the public was confused, at the same time it was intrigued. And after a few more hearings, the *Tribune* pronounced it "the success of the season."

Mary Garden had created the role of Mélisande when the opera was first produced in 1902 at the Opéra Comique and repeated the role six years later when the work had its American premiere at the Manhattan Opera House. Debussy himself had coached her for the part, and her interpretation is legendary, so quiet and still. After her first appearance in Chicago the *Tribune* claimed, "Almost everything that we have heard about this great artist was contradicted. We have been told that she is a remarkable actress, but that she cannot sing. She can act wonderfully, but there was none of the hysterical display that one expects when the acting of a singer is praised. And her voice is as wonderful as her acting so far as its power to reach the sympathy of her hearers is concerned."

The second big novelty of the year was another Garden specialty, *Louise*. The audience found Charpentier more comprehensible than it had Debussy, but was still rather tentative in its approval. Critics were again delighted. "*Louise* is the city of Paris set to music," said the *Tribune*. "It is the song of youth and enthusiasm, of hope and courage." And of Mary

Garden it wrote, "Every tone of her voice, every subtle inflection she imparted to the grateful vocal part, every gesture was eloquent of youth."

By now Chicago had learned something of this artistic phenomenon known as Mary Garden. In an era when most singers were still merely automatons on stage, Garden stood out for the depth of her dramatic characterization. She could suggest almost any situation simply by walking across the stage. She could convey more with one intoned word than most prima donnas could in a whole opera. With Garden every movement counted. She could use her arms with more effect than anyone else in the business. Once during a performance of *Thaïs*, she was having trouble hitting high notes. She came to one she knew better than to attempt, and rather than try it, she simply raised her arm, rattled her bracelets, and literally bewitched her audience into thinking they had heard it. On stage she lost herself in the role she was playing. "I never learned to act," she once said, "acting came naturally." But she did practice poses. At her villa in Monte Carlo she had a room with mirrors covering the walls at one end. Here she would spend hours perfecting her gestures for a new role. She stood only five feet four inches, but she looked much taller on stage. Her command of costuming and make-up was fantastic. And even late in her career she could transform her appearance into that of an adolescent girl with a few skillfully applied touches. She always worked as part of the ensemble, and the operas she sang were consistently well prepared, particularly in staging. She saw to that. Almost everyone agreed that her acting was magnificent, but critics often made a habit of slighting her singing. It was a standard cliché that "Garden's wonderful but she can't sing." Her vocal abilities remained a controversial point all through her career, and opera buffs argue it still. But more than a singer, even more than an actress, Mary Garden was a showman. Her stagemanship was second nature with her, and she gave everything she had to each performance.

She once said she felt *Louise* more acutely than any other role she sang. "By the time I have finished the opera," she told reporters, "I'm as limp as a rag—and as for my face—well, I just wish you could see that. Oh! no, I don't either! I wouldn't let anyone see my face under those conditions. I'm a sight—quite an old, old woman. I always throw a veil over my face passing from the stage to my dressing room, I'm such an unholy spectacle." She was exhausted after every performance, so deeply did she live whatever role she sang. "Upon finishing my performance," she writes in her autobiography, "I went home, took a hot bath, and drank down a large glass of hot milk, with ten drops of iodine in it."

On November 25, Garden sang her third role in Chicago, *Salome*, setting off a barrage of fireworks that rocked the city to its moral foundation. It had taken the soprano two years to master the role, one of the most difficult in the entire repertoire. She had sung it in Paris and for Hammerstein in New York, and it was one she dearly loved. The Chicago production was carefully prepared under Campanini's direction, receiving twenty-seven orchestra rehearsals before it was deemed ready, a record which the company never equaled. The normal orchestra of 80 members was expanded to 106. The top ticket price was raised to $7.00, "possibly based on the number of veils worn by Mary Garden," mused *Musical Courier*. At the first performance the house was jammed.

With her great flair for the dramatic, Mary Garden threw herself into the role of Salome with all the realism she could muster. She sang the part in French, using the original Oscar Wilde text virtually intact. Her Salome was young, wild with sensuality, unrestrained in her perversion. "She is a fabulous she-thing," wrote Percy Hammond, drama critic for the *Tribune*, "playing with love and death—loathsome, mysterious, poisonous, slaking her slimy passion in the blood of her victim." Her "Dance of the Seven Veils," which became one of the more controversial aspects of the opera, was designed to further the Strauss drama. "It wasn't a hoochi-koochi dance at all," Garden insists in her autobiography. "Everything was glorious and nude and suggestive, but not coarse. . . . I saw them dance the hoochi-koochi once in Algiers, stomachs all bared and rolling. My stomach wasn't bare in *Salome* and I never rolled it." Her veils were pale pink, and she ran with them flowing through the air. "Then when I finished my dance," the soprano continues, "I put on my dress, a very short dress that went just under my knees, and made of a thick gold mesh covered with jewels, and, oh, those emeralds and diamonds and rubies, how they sparkled and laughed in the light!" When the soldiers brought her the head of John the Baptist, she lifted it over her head and then brought it down quickly and kissed it. "When I was completely *épuisée*, I fell on the head, and Herod, that monster of vice and sensuality, even he couldn't bear the sight of it and he shouted, 'Kill that woman!' "

The audience left the Auditorium silent and shocked. It was impressed, but there was little indication of either appreciation or approval. According to the *Tribune*, patrons "were oppressed and horrified. But of any real enjoyment there was little or no evidence." The newspaper's music critic found *Salome*, already banned in New York, "the most artistic piece of indecency known to the operatic or any other stage."

The next morning Chicago awoke to find itself in the throes of a squabble over the nature of art and morals. Even before the performance Arthur Farwell, head of the city's Law and Order League, had received protests about the opera, and he had sent Chicago's police chief, Leroy T.

Steward, to see the show to find out just what it was all about. Steward reported, "It was disgusting. Miss Garden wallowed around like a cat in a bed of catnip. There was no art in her dance that I could see. If the same show were produced on Halsted street the people would call it cheap, but over at the Auditorium they say it's art. Black art, if art at all. I would not call it immoral. I would say it is disgusting." What about the music? Said Steward, "There is no music to it. What they call music is simply crash after crash made by the great big orchestra." The chief said he was in the process of seeing to it that the opera was closed. Mary Garden's response to the "catnip" statement was, "I always bow down to the ignorant and try to make them understand, but I ignore the illiterate."

Arthur Farwell himself denounced the opera, calling Mary Garden "a great degenator [sic]" of public morals, but he never saw it. He was given a ticket, but refused to go. "I am a normal man, but I would not trust myself to see a performance of *Salome*," he said. "I wish Miss Garden would come to see me; I should like to reform her." The singer replied that she didn't think he could do her much good.

Before long practically every newspaper, clergyman, and neighborhood philosopher in the city had taken a stand. Poems were written on the subject. Everybody talked about *seeing Salome;* no one mentioned *hearing* it. "It was like a session with the vivisectionist," wrote one *Tribune* reporter. Archbishop G. S. Messmer denounced the opera, maintaining that "All the pleas put forth in the name of art cannot overrule the demands of sound morality and Christian principle." One editorial held that "Wilde has written no such drama as Mary Garden plays. . . . His *Salome* is indeed a princess, who impresses one instantly as haughty and restive, struggling to free herself from the orgies of the tetrarch's court. There is not a suggestion of dignity in Mary Garden's impersonation." The Old Settlers Club took up the debate. How did the dance of Salome compare with the historic Indian dances performed by maidens dressed in scanty costumes? But when the society leaders were asked their opinion of the performance, it was hard to find anyone who was there. Judging from responses, one would have thought the Auditorium had been empty that night. One clergyman whose name had been listed as one of the dignitaries present at the opera, later said, "I would not endanger my standing among my friends by going to such an opera." When Mayor Busse was asked his impression of *Salome*, he replied, "Let's see, *Salome*, oh, yes, that's the name of an opera at the Auditorium theater. I saw something in the newspapers about it, and that is the extent of my knowledge of the matter."

While talk of closing the opera continued, a second performance was given. The Chicago *News* said that if "curiosity caused the fall of man, it also led to the progress of the race and it continues a duality of service

. . . it also produced the best crowd of the season." The controversy became more intense than ever. What offended most people was the realism with which Garden portrayed Salome's lust for the prophet John and particularly her perverted ecstasy with the head. In an era when Victorian ideals were still much in evidence, this was considered shocking. London had found it so; so had New York. Police Chief Steward finally offered to abandon the idea of closing the opera if Garden would compromise by toning down the business with the head. But Mary held firm. "If there is any more of this twaddle about immorality," she said, "I shall leave Chicago and go to Philadelphia or some place where art is appreciated and viewed as art."

Then, in the face of growing opposition, the opera company itself suddenly ended the fight, when its board of directors canceled a scheduled third performance. "We want no controversy among the people of Chicago over the merits of grand opera," a company spokesman said. Some claimed that Edith Rockefeller McCormick had ordered the performance canceled, but it seems more probable that the directors were simply trying to shield the young company from unfavorable criticism. After all, a controversy like this one, so early in the company's career, could easily have jeopardized the whole project.

A number of the artists were furious at the action. Tenor Charles Dalmorès, who had sung the role of Herod, exclaimed, "It is horrible. Chicago will be the laughingstock of Europe. It puts you back artistically fifty years. . . . Why, in Europe we talk about America as the land of the free. You are not." And to another reporter he said, "Berlin and Vienna will laugh when they hear this. They will say: 'The great Chicago! What is it? Still a manufacturing city without the true love of art.' " When Oscar Hammerstein heard the news in New York, he laughed and said, "I don't know just what could be done to 'tone down' *Salome*, especially the head scene, unless, maybe they'd give the head a shave and a haircut. . . . If they'd put some flannel petticoats and things on Miss Garden that might help tone things, too. Mary really ought to be petticoated, I think, considering Chicago's climate. You know, when she worked for me, she had a deadly fear when singing *Salome* of getting cold feet."

Salome's dance may have ended in Chicago, but its vibrations lingered on in Milwaukee, where the company had a performance of the opera scheduled for Friday, December 9, ten days after it was closed in Chicago. Two special trains were chartered to take Chicagoans who had missed the performances at the Auditorium up to the neighboring city. The audience there numbered over five thousand. Chicago's Old Settlers Club was still very much interested in the subject of Garden's dance, and after being taken backstage at the Auditorium to view the costume she wore in the opera, the members decided they could solve nothing until they had seen the veils in action. They would journey to Milwaukee, they said, and then render their verdict. As time for the trip drew near, the old-timers found that somehow they had unofficially been sanctioned to decide, once and for all, the question of *Salome*'s morality. As the eyes of the city began to focus on them, the Old Settlers grew nervous.

"You know anything about opera?" one septuagenarian asked another.

"I got a niece that sings in the school choir."

On the evening of the performance, one member of the club had to be out of town. Another was not feeling too well. And the rest decided to postpone their visit to Milwaukee until another time.

There were no dressing rooms in the hall where *Salome* was given, so makeshift papier-mâché rooms had been built for the principals. Mary Garden arrived early for the performance and was dressed and wigged long before curtain time. She was waiting in her papier-mâché dressing room when she thought she heard someone trying to poke his fingers through the wall. She got up, waited a moment, then heard it again. When she opened the door, she found a big, red-faced Irish policeman standing outside.

"What are you doing, poking your finger in my dressing room?" asked Mary.

"I'm looking for Mary Garden," said the policeman shyly.

"I am Mary Garden. What do you want?"

"But you're dressed, Madame," he said with surprise.

"Certainly, I'm dressed. What did you expect?"

"Is that the way you sang *Salome* in Chicago?"

"Most decidedly it was!"

"Well, what are those blankety-blank fellows in Chicago making such a fuss about?"

Actually Milwaukee took *Salome* without a whimper. The Milwaukee press was loud in its praise of both the score and the performance, and the public gave the artists a string of curtain calls at the conclusion. Present for the performance were two full-blooded Indians. One of them, Eagle Horse, was asked what he thought of the "Dance of the Seven Veils." He drew himself up proudly, smiled, and replied, "Ugh!" The Milwaukee mayor did not attend. Neither did the police chief, but the chief said he was not worried about *Salome*. Besides, he said, he had never seen a cat wallow around in a bed of catnip, so he could hardly be expected to know whether the opera was immoral or not.

Why had Chicago raised such a commotion about *Salome* and Milwaukee taken it so calmly? Several factors contributed. First, Chicago at the moment was in the midst of an evangelistic crusade, and this had caused parts of the city to wear its morality on its sleeve. Second, Farwell's Law and Order League had been waging a steady attack since 1907 on public gambling, saloons, houses of ill-repute, payroll stuffing, and so forth. A few months before the *Salome* episode, Farwell had led a group into Freiberg's dance hall, one of the wildest saloons in the city, with the purpose of cleaning it up. As manager Ike Bloom told it, "I order the drinks all around—lemonade; and when they ask for the center of the floor to kneel down and pray and sing 'Washed in the Blood of the Lamb,' I give it to 'em. I give 'em my jazz band, too, which plays their accompaniment." The closing of *Salome* was simply a part of a general clean-up of the city's theaters. On the same day the opera was dropped, all other Chicago theaters were notified that any suggestive material must be eliminated. Certain lines from *The Nigger*, the current play at McVicker's, were ordered cut. At the American Music Hall *The Trials of a German Servant Girl* was suppressed by police until its script was greatly altered. That evening a squad of police censors made a round of all theaters to see if any of the other productions contained profane language or material otherwise objectionable. Third, the closing of *Salome* was simply a reflection of the city's—and, for that matter, the nation's—irrational, dualistic standard of morality. Chicago could and did tolerate one of the greatest centers of vice in the whole country, housed one of the bawdiest red-light districts and probably more "peep" shows than any other American city. Around the turn of the century one correspondent wrote the London *Daily Mail*, Chicago "makes a more amazingly open display of evil than any other city known to me. Other places hide their blackness out of sight; Chicago treasures it in the heart of the business quarter and gives it a veneer." But somehow Mary Garden's dance and head-kissing episode was thought too much. Primarily this stemmed from the fact that the opera was considered society entertainment, and society entertainment, it was felt, should be above reproach. The subtleties of art and bawdiness for bawdiness' sake were, of course, lost in the whole discussion. Chicago had always had a puritanical element, and many of the city's social leaders had inherited more than just a streak of this puritanism. They could turn their back on the vice of State Street because it was farther from home. Farwell's attacks here did not affect them. But when their own entertainment was challenged, when their own virtue was indirectly being questioned, the city leaders could no longer remain passive to Farwell's charges. When the chips were down, they felt they had no choice but to vote nay. Milwaukee, on the other hand, largely *because* of the furor touched off in Chicago, was determined to show its superior sophistication by accepting the opera, come what may.

Less controversial, although still causing an occasional raised eyebrow, was Massenet's *Thaïs*, shortly to become one of the staples of Mary Garden's Chicago repertoire. She made a dramatic first-act entrance scattering roses, and never before had she seemed so beautiful. Many felt the role suited her voice better than any other part she sang. "This music," wrote the *Tribune*'s Glenn Dillard Gunn, "must be sung, not declaimed, and she proved that she can sing with an unfailing sympathy of tone that is so variedly expressive that it compensated for a frequent lack of purity." Mary's explanation for why Chicagoans preferred her *Thaïs* was: "They like me best in *Thaïs* because I wear fewer clothes in that opera." Actually, she wore gorgeous costumes, with lots of veils and pearls. One dress, as the soprano describes it in her autobiography, "was made of crepe de chine, and there was nothing to it. The dress stuck to my flesh, and because it was of the palest pink it made me look as if I were naked." Garden was often at her best playing scarlet women, and *Thaïs* was definitely one of the finest things she did. "Thaïs was a courtesan who knew her profession thoroughly," the diva once said. And Mary Garden was a singing actress who knew how to play such women more convincingly than anyone else on the operatic stage.

Garden also sang *Faust* in 1910, but this was considered her least successful effort. Critics seemed to feel that the role was vocally too much for her, and there seems little doubt that the music of the modern composers suited her abilities much better.

Aside from the Mary Garden roles, the opera to receive most attention that year was Puccini's *The Girl of the Golden West*. The opera was given in Chicago just fifteen days after its world premiere at the Metropolitan. Tito Ricordi, head of the Italian publishing house, came to Chicago to supervise the production, while Puccini himself directed preparations in New York. Rumor had circulated early in the season that Mary Garden would sing the title role in Chicago, but she later declined, maintaining that her command of Italian was not sufficient for the part. The role went to Carolina White, an attractive young Bostonian who definitely looked the part and sang it well. Everyone connected with the production seemed enthusiastic about it, and it was hoped the opera would prove the most notable success of the season. "The whole thing is simply glorious," Carolina White told reporters. "There are several passages that are unusually exquisite. One of these is where 'The Girl' tells all the boys at the Polka good-bye. There is so much feeling and pathos in the music here that I am afraid my throat will close up when I go to sing it." The public and critics, however, received the opera only politely. The *Tribune* felt the music "was inspirationally underdone and . . . our rugged frontier spirit found no harmonious expression in the soft vocables of the Italian translation." The production was greeted somewhat more enthusiastically later in the season when Caruso, who had created the part in New York, came out as a "guest artist" from the Metropolitan to sing Dick Johnson.

There were other "guests" that year too. Melba visited the city for the first time in six years for a *Bohème*. Said the *Tribune*, "The voice that set the standards of bel canto for a former generation still is as faultless, as pure, as limpid, as it was in the days when the older Italian operas represented the ideals of the art." Geraldine Farrar, on loan from the Metropolitan, gave a fine *Madama Butterfly* and teamed with Antonio Scotti for an exciting *Tosca*. Farrar's interpretation departed widely from the tradition established by Sarah Bernhardt in the Sardou play. Bernhardt had played the heroine as a mature woman of the world, quite sure of herself, cold and deliberate in her actions. Farrar presented her as a young girl, timid and hesitant. Her slaying of Scarpia was committed as if she were in a dream.

The Chicago season closed on January 18, 1911, after running approximately ten weeks. Sixty-three performances of twenty-one operas were given. Two-thirds of the repertoire had consisted of Italian operas, the remaining one-third of French. Gross receipts totaled $400,407, resulting in a net loss of some $10,000. Since the season in Chicago was not long enough to permit the company to produce the caliber of opera it sought to produce, and attract the artists it wanted to attract, a plan was worked out with Philadelphia whereby the company would give a follow-up season there nearly as long as that in Chicago. For the first three years the organization was more correctly known as the Chicago–Philadelphia Grand Opera Company, since guarantor support came from both cities.

As could be expected, there were a number of criticisms during the season, some of them thoroughly justified. Many complained because there was no German opera (except for *Salome*, which was sung in French). *The Dial* insisted, "This exclusion was deliberate, and did not result from a lack of the requisite forces; it had only the effect of alienating a large section of the opera-going public. . . . We cannot think it far-sighted policy which filled ten weeks with French and Italian works alone, and which drew its entire repertoire from two classes of works—more or less sensational novelties and hackneyed popular favorites." There had been production mistakes too. During the third act of the first *Thaïs*, several stagehands could be seen passing to and fro in the background, pretty well ruining any illusion of an oasis. The electrical department had been consistently weak, and in *The Tales of Hoffmann*, in particular, the spotlight was everywhere except where it should have been. Another frequent criticism was that the stage was so dusty that clouds could be seen wafting up from the boards, while the ladies' costumes became black around the hem. "It seems as though the cleaner's bill would easily pay for a vacuum cleaner for the Auditorium stage," wrote *Musical Courier.*

Still, on the overall, the season had been a distinct success. "I must say," Andreas Dippel told reporters, "that to all of us this season has passed like a dream." Things had gone well primarily for two reasons. First, the company gave good opera. Second, Chicago—socially, economically, and culturally—was ready for its own opera company. The interest in opera which had been growing in the city for the past sixty years was now brought to maturity by the linking of opera with civic devotion. With the formation of the Chicago Grand Opera, attending the opera became a civic duty. For the dedicated opera-lovers, this did not particularly matter; they would attend any opera, so long as it was worth hearing. But the casual operagoer was much more likely to support a resident company than one from out of town. The Chicago Grand Opera became *our* opera. Mary Garden became *our* Mary. And Cleofonte Campanini became *our* Campanini.

The press had helped out by giving the company skillful publicity and lots of it. The artists had done their share both on stage and off by adding a dash of glamour to the proceedings, and Mary Garden especially caught hold of the public mind as no one since Adelina Patti. The novelties offered had been well produced and well advertised. But advertising and publicity alone could not have turned the trick. The company's high standards and freshness, overlaid with a veneer of civic pride, could and did.

Chapter 5

RINGS ON HER FINGERS AND BELLS ON HER TOES

ALTHOUGH the 1910–11 season had gone quite well in Chicago, its success in Philadelphia later in the season had been less effusive. In an attempt to stimulate more of an interest there, it was decided to split the season the next year. The company would open in Philadelphia in the fall, play there about a month, then leave for its ten weeks in Chicago, returning East for another month about the middle of January.

Chicago awaited the second season of its resident company more eagerly than it had the first, for now the city knew what the Campanini forces were capable of. For weeks before the opening, Chicago shops displayed the latest in fashionable opera wear, and in these prosperous years preceding World War I more people than ever before were buying special garments for the trips to the Auditorium. The opulence of the prewar era was nowhere better reflected than on Michigan Avenue on opera night.

The season opened on November 22, 1911, with a lackluster performance of *Samson and Delilah*. The Saint-Saëns work had been given often in Chicago as an oratorio, but never before as an opera. Charles Dalmorès was Samson, Jeanne Gerville-Réache, Delilah. The production was poorly lighted, poorly staged, and the falling temple would scarcely have hurt anybody. Just the same the audience was a glorious one, enthusiastic about what would come later if not about the performance at hand. Some still came to the Auditorium in carriages, but more were now arriving in automobiles. The mingling of the two as they approached the theater entrance was a rather strange manifestation of the passing of one way of life and the coming of a new.

The first real excitement of the season was caused by Luisa Tetrazzini,

Maestro Campanini's famous sister-in-law. Although she had never sung in opera before in Chicago, Tetrazzini possessed the most sensational coloratura voice since Nellie Melba and was internationally acclaimed. She was such a sure thing that the company raised its top prices for her performances to seven dollars, and to no one's surprise she played to capacity houses. She appeared first as Lucia, setting the audience to shouting and applauding. According to the *Tribune*, "From the first, the triumph of the great singer was assured and it went on crescendo until it reached a climax never before witnessed in Chicago." Tetrazzini remained in the city only two weeks, but during that time sang five operas: *Lucia, Traviata, Rigoletto, Barber of Seville*, and *Lakmé*. Her farewell appearance (again as Lucia) brought twelve thousand dollars into the company's coffers and saw over fifteen hundred people turned away. At the conclusion of the performance the tumult was so tremendous that the singer appeared alone on stage and sang "The Last Rose of Summer" in English. Not since the departure of Adelina Patti in 1890 had an operatic parting been so nostalgic.

After Tetrazzini left town, the coloratura assignments fell to young Jenny Dufau, a situation which brought many a headache to the company's wardrobe department, since the petite Dufau was about half the size of the substantial Tetrazzini. Dufau's first *Lakmé* was well received, but the composition of the audience brought protests. A number of artists had been making a practice of giving free passes instead of tips, with the result that the parquet was often fairly evenly divided between society members and maids and colored waiters from nearby hotels. The social and racial prejudices of the day were not long in revealing themselves. "The artists to whom seats are given," insisted *Musical Courier*, "should distribute their complimentaries to more representative people than colored waiters, who are very nice in their place, but not in a $5 stall, especially when sitting next to a lady who had paid for her seat."

Another new star for the company that year was little Maggie Teyte, who received almost as great an ovation for her Cherubino in *The Marriage of Figaro* as Tetrazzini had for *Lucia*. Teyte was English and was a tiny thing, but her voice was as big as she was small.

Mary Garden returned a trifle slenderer, her hair a shade darker than the year before. At her suite in the Blackstone Hotel she held another of her famous press conferences. As usual, she brought with her trunk upon trunk of gowns, and during the interview she modeled some of these for reporters. The first one was made of thousands of little steel disks put together in overlapping rows like the scales of a fish. She looked something like a mermaid with it on.

"But I can't wear it long," Mary said. "You see, it is just like chain mail and it weighs twelve pounds. . . . I think it is a becoming gown for crowned heads because it's bullet proof."

"What would you do if it ripped?" one of the reporters inquired. "Could you pin it up?"

"Hardly. Instead of a dressmaker, I'd have to find a blacksmith."

Then Mary came out in a black dress all of fringe. "All of my gowns are clinging," she said. "I don't wear corsets, you know."

Her first opera was one of the season's novelties, Massenet's *Cendrillon,* based on the Cinderella story. Garden sang the Prince, opposite Maggie Teyte's Cinderella. "Garden," wrote *Musical Courier,* "is to the French contingent of the opera what Tetrazzini is to the Italian element–the supreme star, and her position has not in any way been endangered by the newcomers among the French singers." Both Massenet's score and the physical production came in for a round of applause. According to the *Tribune,* "The scenic display was the most attractive and pretentious ever shown in opera in Chicago."

Garden also did Massenet's *Le Jongleur de Notre Dame* that year for the first time in Chicago, and it shortly proved one of her very best roles. The part was originally written for a tenor, but had been rearranged especially for Mary Garden. She played a young boy, a juggler, in the opera, and for the part her voice became clear and almost sexless. Dramatically her portrayal was masterly, every movement intense and realistic. She speaks fondly of the role of the *Jongleur* in her autobiography, saying, "I danced my country dances. I played my fiddle. I juggled the three balls, and sometimes I used to let one go and make the people of the village laugh. It made them happier to think I was such a bad juggler. But I was always the boy, excited and awkward and adoring."

A group of jealous singers once claimed that Garden had trained the donkey which followed the young juggler in the opera to prick up his ears whenever she sang and to feign boredom while her associates were performing. The audiences used to get highly amused when the little animal showed such great interest in Garden's singing, but looked so totally indifferent when anyone else did. It was almost worth the price of admission.

Carmen was another new role for Garden in 1911. She sang it for the first time in her career in Philadelphia early in November. Her first Chicago *Carmen* had to be canceled because of an ulcerated tooth, but when she finally got around to doing the part, many thought she made the best Carmen they had ever seen. As always, she worked as part of the ensemble, remaining simply an important part of the total picture. In later years, however, Carmen would become one of the more controversial roles in the Garden repertoire.

The Chicago forces dreamed of discovering and producing the first great American opera. They thought they had found it in Victor Herbert's *Natoma*. Herbert, of course, was an adopted American, but his music contained much of the American idiom. His opera was given by the company first in Philadelphia, then in Chicago. The story was laid in Spanish California and revolves around the love of an Indian maiden, Natoma, played by Mary Garden, for an American naval officer. Although the work was sung in English, most of the cast was French. The mixture of the two often produced some pretty laughable results. As Mary Garden recalled it, "I remember one day I went to rehearsal. As I came in I heard those Frenchmen trying to pronounce some of the English lines. I just lay on the piano in hysterics."

Before the first Chicago performance of *Natoma*, Garden sent a message to Victor Herbert which suggests much of the company's optimism regarding the future of American opera. "All hail, Victor Herbert," she wrote, "the first writer of American grand opera! May it be the beginning of this great art which America does not yet hold! It is not America's fault—great, energetic country! But man's. They are too busy giving their brains to the making of this new world; giving [it] its turn to be the glory of the universe, and grand opera would naturally be the last thought! So lift up your glass to its glory in the next century!"

Chicago gave *Natoma* as great a reception as anyone could have wanted. The first act was followed by ten curtain calls and the last one by even more. At the end Mary Garden tossed a wreath of flowers over the neck of Victor Herbert and tried to do the same to Campanini, but missed. The critics were only slightly less enthusiastic than the public. The *Tribune* found it a "worthy work in many and in some moments a great work." The two high points were Mary Garden's "Dagger Dance" and her invocation to Manitou, which was filled with sincerity and pathos.

The company's first honest-to-goodness American premiere staged in Chicago was given about a month later. The opera was Wolf-Ferrari's *The Jewels of the Madonna*, given in Chicago just a few weeks after its world premiere in Berlin. The composer himself came over to conduct, and the production received over twenty orchestra rehearsals. Everyone went out of his way to make the opera a success, and that it certainly was. Carolina White headed the cast. The audience, as was becoming the custom in Chicago when a new work was given, was highly demonstrative, insisting on several encores. Floral tributes were given to practically everybody—the principals, conductor, general manager, and stage manager. In his excitement Wolf-Ferrari forgot himself, gave Campanini an exuberant kiss, then looked embarrassed. *The Jewels of the Madonna* was probably the greatest find of Campanini's career, and it remained a staple in the Chicago repertoire for many years.

Wolf-Ferrari's one-act *The Secret of Suzanne* was also given that year for the first time in Chicago. (The company had staged its American premiere while on tour in New York the preceding spring.) Since the story involves a young bride trying to hide her cigarette habit from her husband, Carolina White, who sang the title role, was required to smoke several cigarettes on stage. Most everyone was delighted by the goings-on —everyone, that is, except Lucy Page Gaston, the president of the local Anti-Cigarette League. Miss Gaston stalked out after the third cigarette, exclaiming, "Horrible. Horrible. One after another. I saw her with my own eyes. It is enough to turn one forever against grand opera."

A little later Carolina White did some stalking out of her own. For a brief time she went on strike, claiming that Andreas Dippel was a slave driver. Dippel's reply was, "The prima donnas do not work too much; they eat too much." If this applied to White, a handsome woman, it certainly did not show.

Still another "first" for Chicago that year was Nouguès' five-act *Quo Vadis,* based on the Sienkiewicz novel. Maggie Teyte sang the role of Lygie. The production's musical values were probably its least interesting aspect, although none of it was particularly exciting. Practically the whole company was required to stage the work, and several miles of painted canvas were needed for the scenery. The burning of Rome, the gladiatorial games, and the palace of Nero were all there, but were not quite as thrilling as the press build-up had led many to expect. The conflagration scene would scarcely have warmed one's hands. The costumes were lavish, but by midnight even these had become a bore. The opera was never given again after this one season, though the company took it to New York for a single performance at the Metropolitan.

The first German opera was presented by the company that year: *Die Walküre* with Olive Fremstad as Brünnhilde and Ernestine Schumann-Heink as Fricka, *Lohengrin* with Carolina White, and *Tristan und Isolde* with Fremstad and Dalmorès. The *Walküre* particularly was a smash hit, representing the best ensemble the company had achieved yet. The sets and lighting were both outstanding, and the magic fire scene in the last act was so realistic that the whole Auditorium stage appeared to be in flames. A number of women in fact fled from the theater, thinking a disaster had occurred.

On the whole manager Dippel seemed unusually successful in guessing what the operatic public wanted. "One feature of the past ten weeks stands out most prominently," Dippel said at the close of the Chicago season. "It is that nearly all of the novelties have met with immediate success." Seventy-eight performances of twenty-four operas were given that year. Thirty-six of these performances were in French, twenty in Italian, the rest in German or English. Box office receipts totaled $452,536, an increase over the year before of over $70,000. Receipts and expenses just about balanced one another.

Society smiled on the opera all through the season, appearing consistently night after night. Receptions and suppers, usually given in a downtown hotel by one of the wealthier operagoers for the artists, critics, and guarantors, were quite fashionable at the time, adding an air of spectacle to the proceedings. Saturday nights were reserved for a popular-price series, and this was the time most of the workers and not-so-wealthy visited the opera. The Auditorium was usually full then, but on other occasions, except for the Tetrazzini evenings and the first night of new productions, the upper regions of the house were often only sparsely filled. To alter this, midway through the season ticket prices for some fifteen hundred seats in the galleries were lowered. This meant that the highest gallery ticket now sold for $2.00, the cheapest for $0.50. As a result, attendance, particularly for the German performances, picked up appreciably.

In the fall of 1912, Ethel Barrymore was playing at the Palace in Chicago, Eva Tanguay at the Majestic, and Sarah Bernhardt was making her first appearance in vaudeville. Two plays by David Belasco were in town, *Years of Discretion* at the Powers and *The Return of Peter Grimm* at the Blackstone. The Grand Opera House had George M. Cohan's latest musical farce, *The Little Millionaire. Little Women* was playing at McVicker's, and the Ginger Girls were the rage at the Columbia, a local burlesque house. At the Auditorium preparations were underway for the Chicago Grand Opera's third season, which was scheduled to open with the Chicago premiere of Puccini's *Manon Lescaut.*

The singers arrived from abroad a little nervous that year, the *Titanic* disaster still fresh in their minds. Audiences were appreciative, but more critical than they had been. "During the first seasons," explained the *Tribune,* "there was a determined effort to be extravagantly pleased with everything. The audiences were cordial because that is our custom toward newcomers. Also they were set upon making a success of the venture. Finally, they were a little uncertain of their own judgment."

Carolina White made a hit of *Manon Lescaut,* and Tetrazzini returned, adding *Crispino e la Comare* to her Chicago roles. But the big news that year was made when baritone Titta Ruffo first appeared on the scene. At his debut, as Rigoletto, Ruffo was received with such ardent enthusiasm that the *Tribune* claimed "even Mme. Tetrazzini's triumphs of last season seemed dim in comparison." His Rigoletto was acclaimed as a masterpiece of tragedy. He was unable to finish a single aria without an interruption. In the great recitative in the second act Ruffo hit a high *E*, beautifully colored. The house broke into cheers, but then the artist went on to sing a *G*. Somewhat embarrassed at their mistake, the audience burst into renewed applause, only to hear the baritone go on to a high *A* flat, free and effortless. Of his singing the *Tribune* said, "It is truly great. It is the expression of a sincere musician and a splendid actor, possessed of a noble sense of beauty and one of the great voices of the present."

Ruffo's second appearance was in Thomas' *Hamlet*. Although the opera is a mere shadow of Shakespeare's play, the title role served as a good vehicle for the singer. More rewarding was Tonio in *Pagliacci*, which Ruffo turned into a tremendous thing. According to the *Tribune*, he was "the first to show us the half-witted clown as he might appear in person."

German opera came in for another round that season. Nordica appeared as Isolde opposite Schumann-Heink's Brangäne, both of them coming as guest artists. Schumann-Heink also sang the Witch in Humperdinck's *Hänsel und Gretel* in a special New Year's Day matinee. She disguised her voice and played up all the traditional deformities of the role, causing the children in the audience to squeal with delight. For Mme. Schumann-Heink that was reward in itself.

Mary Garden was delayed that year in Paris, and on her way to Chicago she stopped in Boston for a few performances, including *Tosca* opposite Vanni Marcoux. According to the rumors, the mayor of Boston threatened to revoke the license of the Boston Opera Company if the stage business in the second act were not toned down. She repeated the role in Chicago, singing in French, except for "*Vissi d'arte*," while the rest of the cast sang in Italian. The language situation sometimes became fairly ludicrous, but it was still one of Garden's most thrilling roles.

A big novelty of the season was Goldmark's *The Cricket on the Hearth*, based on a story by Charles Dickens. It was sung in English with Maggie Teyte in the lead and proved a delight. "Goldmark's little opera," ran the *Tribune*'s appraisal, "should achieve a permanent place in the repertory. It is not a work of great inspiration, but its music is dainty, charming, gracious, the perfect symbol of the Dickens story." Despite its success, it had only one performance and was never revived.

Noël, an opera by Baron Frédéric d'Erlanger, was given its American premiere by the company, but met with modest acclaim. The best the critics could muster was that it was the best music ever written by a baron. It was a hopelessly sentimental piece about a desperate mother who contemplates throwing herself into a river, but is prevented by thoughts of her child. Inside a church, she prays to the Virgin, then places her baby in the cradle, taking the stone figure of the Christ-child with her. A sacristan discovers the live child and announces that a miracle has taken place. In the end the statue of Christ is found at the bedside of the dying mother.

Riccardo Zandonai's *Conchita*, on the other hand, revealed that Victorian moral standards still prevailed in the city. The story tells of a Carmen-like worker in a cigar factory in Seville, who breaks the monotony of her life by singing and dancing. A suitor seeks her favor by bribing her mother. Most Chicagoans found it coarse and shocking. "The libretto," said the *Tribune*, "is concerned with the detailed study in carnal psychology, and must, therefore, be distasteful to Anglo-Saxons who resent the union of brutality and art. The work is devoid of all nobility, an element which alone can justify such a subject for artistic treatment.... Furthermore, there is no occasion to intrude vulgarity, however true to life, into opera, and those who feel a craving for such cheap sensationalism as is represented by Conchita's dance may satisfy their coarse appetites without going so far south as Spain."

Far less objectionable, although based on the Salome theme, was Massenet's *Hérodiade*, considered by many the most brilliant premiere of the season. Carolina White sang the role of Salome, and the stage picture was rich and colorful. The *Tribune* found the score "innocent and appealing and sympathetic." Massenet's approach to the subject, of course, is quite different from that of Strauss. In his version Salome's love for John the Baptist is much nobler. Rather than dancing for his head out of lust, she tries to save him from execution.

Old-timers were beginning to complain that opera-going had lost its glamour, for few tiaras or ropes of pearls were being worn, nor were heavy satins and velvets in vogue, as had once been the case. Instead the ladies were wearing headdresses of feathers and plumes and occasionally drapes of crystals or pearls across the forehead. The most fashionable corsage a lady could wear then was a bunch of violets, selling for two dollars a hundred. Orchids were next best and sold for a dollar each. A corsage of gardenias or sweet peas, also popular, cost fifty cents.

More people were attending the opera than ever before, probably with greater understanding. But there were still indications that not everyone was quite aware of just what was going on. At a performance of *The Secret of Suzanne* early in 1913, one lady was extravagant in her admiration for the singing of tenor Charles Dalmorès that night. He was not in the cast. "But I do wish he would sing the 'Toreador Song,'" she added. "Yes," replied her companion, "dear Mme. Schumann-Heink has taught us to love that song." During a staging of *Die Walküre* slightly earlier, a lady dropped a bottle of smelling salts at the very moment Sieglinde handed Siegmund the horn of mead. "That must be a strong drink," exclaimed one neighbor. "You can smell it way out here."

Critics were still disturbed by the preeminence of the star system, which, although seldom in the excess that plagued Abbey and Grau's productions in the nineties, has habitually dominated American operatic performances. In 1913 the Chicago *Tribune* wrote, "The American public long since has adopted the Latin viewpoint as to opera. We are less concerned with the work to be performed than with the singers who are to assist in its presentation. To the average American opera means the 'star'; and while our public welcomes novelties in the repertory, is not averse to a beautiful orchestra, an adequate chorus, a great conductor, intelligent stage management, and effective scenic settings, these things are merely incidents to the display of great voices."

That spring, just as Woodrow Wilson was being inaugurated President of the United States and promising the nation something called the "New Freedom," the Chicago Grand Opera Company made its first tour west. After first visiting New York, it headed down to Dallas, then out to the Pacific Coast, and back by way of Salt Lake City, Denver, Omaha, Kansas City, and St. Louis. Financially, the tour was a great success, showing a profit of $68,000. But the company was seething with internal discord. No sooner had it returned home than General Manager Andreas Dippel suddenly resigned. He was paid $25,000, the full amount of his next year's salary, in return for an agreement not to reenter the operatic field for a period of three years. Campanini was elevated to general director, taking charge of both the artistic and business affairs of the organization.

There had been friction between Dippel and Campanini from the beginning. They had disagreed on many things, but the production of *Conchita* had been sort of the proverbial last straw. Campanini had agreed to stage the opera long before Dippel was consulted about it. Rehearsals for the production were long and expensive, costing the company over $25,000. The opera was a failure. What particularly infuriated Dippel was that *Conchita* had been given at the expense of the later Wagner productions, which were always his personal preference and had drawn well.

Aside from purely artistic considerations, Dippel tended to represent the New York backers of the company, while Campanini had become identified with the McCormick-Dawes group. The alliance with the East had never been as cordial as had been hoped, and Campanini for one—with his great hatred of the Metropolitan—dreamed of the day when the organization would be run exclusively by Chicagoans. The McCormicks gradually came to share his sentiment, growing eager to convert the company into a strictly Chicago concern. It was really at the McCormicks' insistence that Campanini was made general director.

With the ousting of Dippel, New York support dropped to a minimum. Only Otto Kahn remained on the board of directors. A number of the Chicago backers, mainly fearing that Campanini was something of a spendthrift, resigned from the board. During the Dippel years a reasonably tight budget had been kept. The first season resulted in a slight deficit; the second just about broke even; and the third saw a slight profit. Campanini's seasons would indeed produce greater expenditures.

By fall it was announced that Harold McCormick had purchased all stock remaining in eastern hands, reimbursing owners the price they had originally paid. This cleared the way for the Chicago Grand Opera to concentrate its activities in Illinois and the West. Said one unidentified director, "The eastern engagements did not pay. On the other hand our western tour showed a book profit last year." McCormick's holdings were now far larger than anyone else's, so much larger in fact that his wish pretty well became company law. It was his decree that Campanini be given a blank check in artistic matters, and under the new arrangement not even the board of directors had the authority to challenge Campanini's decisions.

But these were affluent years. The opulence of the prewar era had reached a zenith. The buxom Gibson girl had now given way to the slinky look, and the big, billowy hats so popular a few years before had shrunk because of the automobile. Irving Berlin's "Alexander's Ragtime Band" was the current rage, popularizing a new style of jazz, and *The Chocolate Soldier* was the big hit on Broadway. The one-step and tango were taking the place of the two-step and waltz, while the turkey trot was fascinating the young and disgusting the old.

In literature the big sensation of the year was Willa Cather's *O Pioneers!* and young writers were still gathering at Chicago's Cliff Dwellers' Club, which Hamlin Garland had established in a penthouse atop Orchestra Hall, to discuss recent developments in the arts. Theodore Dreiser and Edna Ferber, after spending considerable time in the city, were producing books that were causing people to take notice, and a magazine called *Poetry*, established in 1912 by Harriet Monroe, was beginning to publish poems by Edgar Lee Masters and the early works of Carl Sandburg. There was a great deal of stir around the Art Institute these days, as Chicago was hosting a new generation of talented young artists.

At the Auditorium Campanini caught the economic and intellectual richness of the times, producing thirty different operas within the first six weeks of the company's 1913–14 season, something of a record. Opening night found Mary Garden on stage as Tosca. Her Scarpia was Vanni Marcoux, making his first appearance with the company. Although Chicagoans did not find the performance as shocking as Boston had the year before, they were intrigued with the brutal ruthlessness of Vanni Marcoux's interpretation and the drama which he and Garden injected into the second act.

Lucien Muratore made his debut with the company that year as Faust, a handsome figure with a good French singing style. He was the matinee-idol type and had begun his stage career as an actor, playing opposite Bernhardt. His bride, Lina Cavalieri, alleged to be the most beautiful woman in the world, was also scheduled for two operas, but she never sang. Some said her husband was so jealous that he would not permit her to make love to other men on stage. Others said the soprano, another of Hammerstein's former stars, had become afflicted with stage fright.

Toward the end of the first week, a rather momentous *Aida* took place —momentous because it had Cyrena Van Gordon as Amneris and, even more important, Rosa Raisa in the title role. Both artists were being heard for the first time with the company, Raisa for the first time in the United States. The soprano would remain the backbone of the Chicago Opera's dramatic wing for over twenty years. She possessed a voice matched by no other in volume or intensity. Born in Poland, Raisa had begun her singing career in Italy, had become a favorite in Latin America, and once, while traveling from Mexico City to El Paso, Texas, had sung for the revolutionary bandit Pancho Villa when he accosted her train. She was a woman of majestic beauty, and according to Mary Garden, "a lady of great charm."

Although Raisa was well received from the start, she remained somewhat in the background during her first season with the company. She was not at all the flamboyant type, and of course, was very young at the time. Campanini himself said, "I know she is young now and not fully developed artistically, but mark my word, one of these days she will be known all over the world as one of the greatest dramatic sopranos."

Following her success in *Aida*, she sang Minnie in a revival of *The Girl of the Golden West*. Although Raisa herself received standing ovations after the second act, the opera, mildly applauded three years before, was now held in contempt. The *Tribune* spoke of "the pronounced dislike of the public for this unfortunate Puccini opera," and implied that it was a disservice to the composer to present it. When Franchetti's *Cristoforo Colombo* was given its American premiere later in the season, Raisa sang the role of Isabella of Aragon, opposite Titta Ruffo's Columbus. The work had met some success in Italy, but Chicagoans found it only of passing interest. "It is a historic pageant with incidental music," observed the *Tribune*. The music must not all have been incidental, however, for in the first act the queen is said to have prayed for fifteen minutes in the upper soprano register before giving Columbus her jewels.

Another new opera was Kienzl's *Ranz des Vaches*, a tale of the French Revolution, sung in French. The *Tribune* praised its old-fashioned theme: "The plot turns upon a virtue we are not sufficiently advanced to despise—the love of home." The reviewer went on to say, "Such words as decadent, degenerate, neurotic, perverse, cacophonous, discordant, uncouth, and ugly, may be given a well earned rest, while it is attempted to praise in old-fashioned phrase the homely virtues of romance and sentiment and graceful song."

Leoncavallo's *Gli Zingari*, despite the composer's presence in the pit, was given only a lukewarm reception—Chicago finding the tale of a wounded tenor who lures his soprano wife and her baritone boyfriend into a barn and then sets fire to the place a bit too much. Ruffo sang the first *Don Giovanni* the city had heard in fourteen years, but Mozart was never his element. Wagner's *Parsifal* was produced, after fifteen full orchestra rehearsals, with Charles Dalmorès in the title role. Frances Alda made her debut with the company in *Bohème*, not with any particular acclaim, and Florence Macbeth made hers in *The Barber of Seville*. Macbeth would soon become one of the regulars of the Chicago forces, but she suffered during her first season from too much advance publicity.

Mary Garden added several new roles to her local repertoire that season, among them Massenet's *Manon*, which she sang with Muratore, one of the few tenors who could compete with her on equal footing. She and Vanni Marcoux teamed for the Chicago premiere of *Don Quichotte*, Massenet's last opera, both singers winning more acclaim than the opera itself. Vanni Marcoux was tall and lank and turned the role of the Don into a personal tour de force. Mary Garden meanwhile surprised even her most ardent admirers by singing a difficult coloratura role divinely. "Her song disclosed unsuspected elements of brilliancy," wrote the *Tribune*, "it cascaded through dazzling cadenzas of coloratura, trilled and fluted in the canzonette, which she sings to the accompaniment of her guitar; and in the scene wherein Dulcinée discloses her true nature to the Don, it expanded to include every interpretative resource of the lieder singer, to discover accents of refinement and of beauty rarely heard in opera."

Winning a more permanent place in the Chicago repertoire, largely because it was such an excellent vehicle for displaying Garden's special talents, was Fevrier's *Monna Vanna*. It was really more drama than opera, but Mary Garden played it for all it was worth, aided in the premiere by both Muratore and Vanni Marcoux. Before the performance there had been some apprehension over what Garden might *not* wear in the part, but no one was particularly shocked. Everyone agreed that the music was pretty thin, but Chicagoans welcomed the work more cordially than any new opera since *The Jewels of the Madonna.*

Campanini always tried to stage new or unpopular operas with established, favorite singers and to use popular operas to introduce new artists. This helped the box office to some extent, but the director was never as skillful in his handling of finances as many of the guarantors would have liked. The deficit at the end of the 1913–14 season was a startling $250,000, and this, at a time when a slight economic recession had set in, produced much grumbling among a number of the company's backers. Some complained about what they considered Campanini's mismanagement; others resented Harold McCormick's domination of the company. Before long a number of subscribers withdrew their support, among them John Shaffer.

Just as this crisis reached its peak, the European war broke out, offering a convenient way out of a fairly knotty situation. The heavy deficit plus the drop in guarantor support had forced the company into something of an economic bind, and the internal turmoil was no less damaging. It was therefore decided not to give a season in the fall of 1914. But problems remained. The company now had contractual obligations with a number of artists and no season to fulfill them. It seemed the only way out was to declare the organization bankrupt and permit it to pass into the hands of a receiver. This was done, Harold McCormick purchasing the company's scenery, costumes, and properties for $75,000. With that, the first of Chicago's various opera companies came to an abrupt end.

Then, in the spring of 1915, it was announced that a new company, the Chicago Opera Association, had been formed, and that a guarantee fund of $110,000 a year for the next two years was pledged. Harold McCormick would again be president of the company, Charles G. Dawes vice-president. Campanini was reinstated as general director. Otto Kahn, the last vestige of eastern support, was no longer a member of the board of directors, but appearing on the list of guarantors for the first time was Samuel Insull, the utilities king who would later head the city's opera.

From now until the breakup of the company in 1922, the Harold McCormicks, despite growing reports that their marriage was foundering, would run the Chicago Opera much as if it were their private entertainment. Their domination was almost complete, but in return they underwrote an increasing portion of the company's annual deficit. The opera produced was sumptuous and well rehearsed, for money was scarcely an object. Operas were often given once, then never heard of again, the sets and costumes simply tucked away in the warehouse. The McCormicks probably gave Chicago the best opera the city has ever seen, supporting it in a manner reminiscent of the royal courts of eighteenth-century Europe.

Chapter 6

ONE FOR MY MASTER, ONE FOR MY DAME

By the fall of 1915 America's initial shock over the outbreak of war in Europe had given way to a feeling of relief. It was comforting to know that an ocean separated us from the hostilities. The sinking of the *Lusitania* the preceding spring had already indicated that even the great Atlantic was less of a barrier than we would have liked, but President Wilson was still telling us to remain neutral in thought and deed. Throughout that summer and fall there were increasing reports of ships being sunk on the high seas, making Wilson's ideal of neutrality difficult to realize.

And there were other problems. Pancho Villa was claiming, "I can lick the United States," and even then there was talk of American intervention in Mexico. The economy was still somewhat depressed, and in 1915 there was considerable concern over feeding Chicago's poor and hungry.

Since the new opera company was not organized until March, little time was left for putting a season together. New contracts had to be drawn up with artists, and many of the former Chicago stars had either been made unavailable by the war or already had previous commitments by the time Campanini was able to make them a definite offer. Mary Garden had engagements in Paris. Rosa Raisa and Titta Ruffo were busy in Italy. And Carolina White was making a tour of the vaudeville circuits. Therefore Campanini had to settle for a number of singers unknown to Chicago audiences—singers who in some cases proved distinctly second-rate.

The season opened with Emmy Destinn in *La Gioconda*. The audience in most respects was more dazzling than the opera, and *Gioconda* was given only a modest reception. Fashion now dictated that the gowns be cut low, with tight-fitting bodices. Girdles outlined the waist, and skirts were full and off the ground. Sleeves, if they were worn at all, were filmy and scarflike.

Lucien Muratore, one of the few company regulars to return that year, won ovations as Romeo and Werther and did all he could for the American premiere of Saint-Saëns' *Déjanire*. The opera is based on a story from Greek mythology, and Muratore played the role of Hercules. "From the theatrical angle," said the *Tribune*, "it is about as dead in human interest as one of Lord Bacon's essays." The audience was hardly enthusiastic, finding the work cold and aloof. "Its score," continued the *Tribune*, "has no throb for the audience that loves its emotions raw and bleeding."

Equally unsuccessful was the American premiere of Massenet's *Cléopâtre*. Maria Kuznietsov, hailed as Campanini's latest "find," sang the title role, gowned so that "voice teachers could assure themselves of her perfect diaphragm action." Kuznietsov was able to make but little of the opera, mainly because there was so little to make. The *Tribune* called it "a naked opera . . . both as to musical worth and as to costuming." Mary Garden would be able to do a little more with it later, but even she was working against tremendous odds.

The season was disappointing backstage too. Quite a stir was created when a dapper young professional claqueur named Nathan Arlock was exposed by the local press. Arlock, it seems, had negotiated with several of the leading singers, promising them ovations for a fee of fifty dollars each. On at least one occasion, he had even referred the artist to Maestro Campanini himself, saying that the director would vouch for his abilities. Apparently Arlock had even gotten free tickets for the members of his claque from one of the company officials.

Still, the season had its positive side. Helping to fill the gaps in the Chicago Opera Association's initial roster were a number of guest artists: Melba, Fremstad, Farrar, among others. Farrar had just made a couple of movies, and some critics claimed they had ruined her acting. After her *Carmen*, however, the *Tribune* insisted, "If the 'movies' inspired this characterization, by every token let us insist that all singers be put through the same routine before their debuts."

Since so many of the French and Italian singers Campanini usually employed were unavailable that year, the director decided to emphasize the German repertoire, despite the war in Europe. The German wing had always been slighted by the company, and even when German operas had been staged, they suffered from inadequate rehearsals and some rather wild stage direction. Campanini sought to rectify this in 1915–16. He staged *Tristan und Isolde*, *Parsifal*, *Tannhäuser*, and the first complete

Ring the city had heard in over twenty-five years. One part of the epic was given on each of four successive Sunday afternoons. The performances were well staged, well sung, and well rehearsed, and, despite the anti-German sentiment building in the country, the public response was excellent. After the *Rheingold* performance, the *Tribune* wrote that the audience "sat rapt before the stately unfolding of this epic music drama. No such tribute to any performance here has been paid within our memory."

But as the summer of 1916 wore on, it became obvious to many Americans that we could not afford to ignore the war much longer. The Chicago *Tribune*, one of the first newspapers in the country to recognize that American destiny was irretrievably linked with Europe's, warned that we could not stand by and allow the British navy to be destroyed. Our own foreign policy was too dependent on the British supremacy of the seas. The *Tribune* even editorialized that we should form an immediate alliance with Great Britain, and if necessary, enter the war in her behalf. There could be little doubt that American public opinion was becoming more sharply anti-German.

Proof of this was that Campanini's repeat of Wagner's *Ring* in 1916–17 was almost a total fiasco. Again each of the epic's four components was staged on successive Sunday afternoons. But what had been hailed as the triumph of the year before, playing then to near-capacity houses, now brought letters of protest pouring into the management and the press. One writer was shocked that anything so immoral as *Die Walküre*, with its incestuous relationship between Siegmund and Sieglinde, would be staged on the Sabbath. Wagner's music was condemned as barbaric, and attendance fell to practically nothing. Apparently even the city's Germans, always so reliable before in their attendance of Wagner, stayed away—perhaps because they had been absorbed by the main stream of American life by this time, but more probably because they feared being condemned as un-American. Campanini staged nine German operas that year, the most he ever gave in any one season, and seemed little disturbed by their slight attendance. "When the day comes," he wrote, "that art is so impersonal that it is not touched by nationality, then we shall have a thinner, more meager art; we shall have a purely technical art." American neutrality was obviously a shallow one, and, as Campanini put it, "As music is the most emotional of all arts it stands to reason that it must be the least neutral. We can no more in these complicated war days expect the Germans to applaud French music or the French to hold German music on the boards, the English to enjoy Hungarian dances, and the Russians to appreciate Austrian opera than we can expect any of the nationalities to meet whole-heartedly to appreciate the accomplishment of the other. . . . War itself is no more emotional than music."

But, if the German offering resulted in something of a disappointment, the French and Italian fared far better than it had the year before, largely because the artists were superior. Raisa was back, opening with *Aida* and later giving the city its first opportunity to hear Giordano's *Andrea Chénier*. Zandonai's *Francesca da Rimini* was mounted especially for her, and although it showed her voice to good advantage, the opera itself was judged somewhat pedestrian. The baritone appearing with her in each of these productions, as well as in a staging of Verdi's *Falstaff*, was Giacomo Rimini, later Raisa's husband.

Mary Garden returned, too, repeating several of her earlier successes and adding Massenet's *Grisélidis* to her gallery of Chicago portrayals. The opera was set in the time of the Crusades, and the *Tribune* found it "one of the most interesting of the numerous pieces imported by her from the modern French repertoire." Muratore scored his great triumph that year as Canio, while Geraldine Farrar won hers in Humperdinck's *Die Königskinder*, aided by a whole flock of squawking geese.

The event which turned the 1916–17 season into a sensation, however, was very quietly revealed on Saturday afternoon, November 18. Almost everyone who entered the Auditorium that day expected just another performance of Verdi's *Rigoletto*. So far as anyone knew, the most exciting thing about it was that Giacomo Rimini was singing the title role. His Gilda was to be a new soprano named Amelita Galli-Curci. Nobody had ever heard of her before they saw her name on the program. For the first quarter hour, the performance was little better than routine. Then a slim, dark-skinned young woman with a prominent nose and only slight physical beauty appeared on stage. She sang "*Caro nome*" more entrancingly than the city had ever heard it. At its close she slowly climbed the flight of stairs, candle in hand, to Gilda's room, holding a final *E* of consummate purity for several moments. As the tone died away, the audience broke into perhaps the most spontaneous burst of applause since the beginning of the city's own opera. What had earlier been a calm, suave, sophisticated gathering now began to shout and stamp its delight with the new singer, some even standing on their seats the better to cheer. Certainly nothing like Galli-Curci had ever been heard before. One man arrived late, and as he entered the Auditorium lobby, he heard the tumult inside. When he asked what the noise was all about, he was told, "It's a new singer, name's Galli-Something-or-Other, and she's got them crazy."

It was later learned that Campanini had rather casually arranged for the singer to come to Chicago for two performances—the matinee *Rigoletto,* sung, incidentally, on her twenty-seventh birthday, and a *Lucia di Lammermoor* the next week. She had agreed to sing for a slight $300 a performance. The understanding was that any further engagements would depend upon her reception in these two. Fortunately Campanini had sat in on the *Rigoletto* rehearsals, and after hearing her "*Caro nome*," he rushed backstage to the soprano's dressing room, offering her a contract for the rest of the season at $1,000 a performance. She accepted, but Campanini decided to withhold any advance publicity, allowing Chicago to discover her for itself.

The reception surpassed even Campanini's wildest dreams. During the intermissions of *Rigoletto* people rioted in the lobby trying to buy tickets for her *Lucia* three days later, and the house was sold out before the afternoon was over. Frederick Donaghey, the *Tribune* critic covering the performance, rushed into his newspaper's office shortly after the opera in a high state of excitement and persuaded his editors that the integrity of their next issue hung upon the insertion of a column about Galli-Curci. The edition was held up, while a piece was written. "Galli-Curci," ran the review, "if Saturday's performance be a reasonable measure of her quality, is the greatest coloratura since Sembrich. . . . There was brain in all she did in *Rigoletto* from her singing of '*Caro nome*' to the manner in which she took her calls."

The artist had begun her career as a pianist, but had switched to singing at the suggestion of composer Pietro Mascagni. She was reputedly self-taught, claiming never to have had a teacher. Following modest success in Italy, she had sung with Caruso in Buenos Aires the summer before her United States debut at the Auditorium. Her acclaim in Chicago made her an international celebrity. Her vocalism was not something that bore rational analysis, for certainly it was no paragon of technical perfection. Its charm was partly her ability to sing the most artificial aria in a simple, straightforward manner, comprehensible even to the unsophisticated listener. "I have lived so close to the language of the earth," Galli-Curci once said, "and I have looked with such admiration upon the distance of the stars and the great expanse of the sky, that I have had no time to enter into the complication of spectacular feeling. Music above all things is song, and song is the voice of aspiring human beings. Singing is from the heart, and not from the vanities or intellectuality of thought."

Whatever the secret of her magic was, she could project it as no one of her day. Newspapers called her the feminine counterpart of Caruso. Chicago's Herman Devries held that "in thirty years, I, veteran operagoer, have never heard such matchless, flawless beauty of tone, so satiny

Crosby's Opera House.
Chicago Historical Society

Auditorium and Hotel, 1889.
Chicago Historical Society

Outside the Auditorium, circa 1909.
Chicago Historical Society

Auditorium—Stage (*Lohengrin*, Act I). *Chicago Historical Society*

Civic Opera Building, 1930.
Chicago Historical Society

Civic Opera, Interior.
Chicago Historical Society

Samuel Insull.
Chicago Historical Society

Cleofonte Campanini.
Chicago Historical Society

Harold McCormick, with Mary Garden, 1921. *Chicago Historical Society*

Giorgio Polacco. *Opera News.*

Nellie Melba as Juliette. *Opera News*

Adelina Patti. *Opera News*

Lina Cavalieri and Lucien Muratore, 1913.
Chicago Historical Society

Mr. and Mrs. Enrico Caruso, 1919.
Chicago Historical Society

Mary Garden in *Le Jongleur de Notre-Dame. Aimée Dupont*

Amelita Galli-Curci in *Dinorah. Matzene–Q. Eaton*

1921-22

Grand Opera Season

MARY GARDEN, General Director

THURSDAY NIGHT, JANUARY 5, AT 8.

The Love for Three Oranges

A Fantastic Opera in Four Acts and Ten Scenes, with a Prologue.

Words and Music by Serge Prokofieff, after the Fairy Tale by Carlo Cozzi.

The King of Trifle, king of an imaginary kingdom..Edouard Cotreuil
The Prince, his son..........Jose Mojica
The Princess Clarice, niece of the King..........Irene Pavloska
Leandre, Prime Minister..........William Beck
Trouffaldino..........Octave Dua
Pantalon..........Desire Defrere
The Magician Tchelio..........Hector Dufranne
Fata Morgana, a witch..........Nina Koshetz
The Devil Farfarello..........James Wolf
Smeraldine..........Jeanne Schneider
The Creonte..........Constantin Nicolay
The Master of Ceremonies..........Lodovico Oliviero
Ninetta, Nicoletta, Violetta — the Princesses.......... Jeanne Dusseau, Frances Paperte, Philine Falco
The Herald..........Jerome Uhl

Ridicules, Comiques, Lyriques, Tragiques, Empty Heads, Devils, Doctors.

Incidental Dances by Corps de Ballet.

Orchestra Under the Direction of Alexander Smallens.
Mise-en-Scene Established and Staged by Jacques Coini.

Scenery, costumes and properties especially designed and executed for this production by Boris Anisfeld.

Mason & Hamlin Piano Used Exclusively.

In the interest of the art, encores are not permitted.

Program for a World Premiere, 1922.
Chicago Historical Society

Edith Mason as Mimi in *La Bohème*.
De Gueldre–Q. Eaton

Rosa Raisa as Norma.
Daguerre–Q. Eaton

Claudia Muzio in *Il Trovatore*.
Opera News

Tito Schipa in *La Traviata*.
Opera News

Maria Callas
David H. Fishman

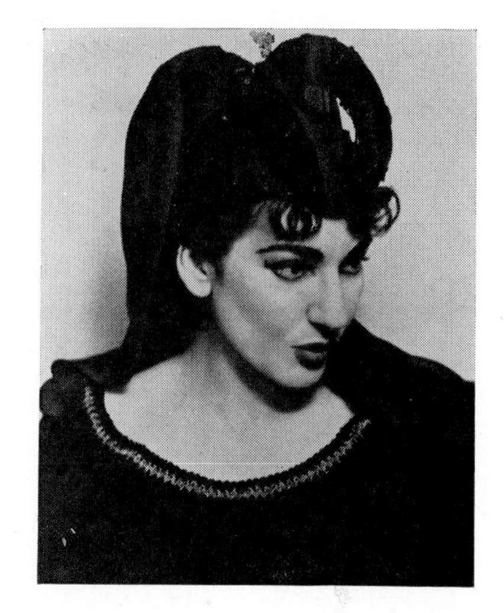

Carol Fox. *Opera News*

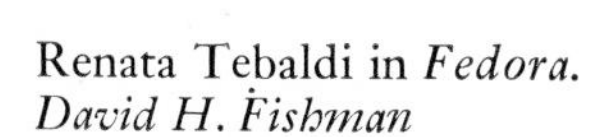

Renata Tebaldi in *Fedora.*
David H. Fishman

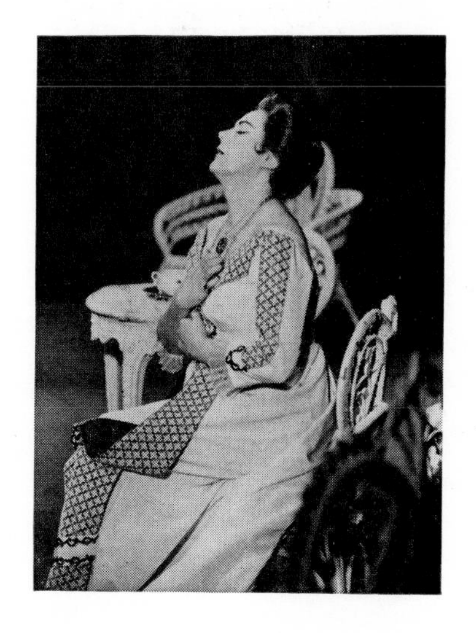

Callas and Rossi-Lemeni in *Norma*.
Chicago Historical Society

Tito Gobbi and Nicolai Ghiaurov in *Don Carlos*.
Opera News–David H. Fishman

Christoff, Arova, Nureyev and Danon (*Prince Igor*).
Nancy Sorenson

a timbre, such delicately lovely phrasing, such innate God-given talent and feeling for the true bel-canto." It had been said that the age of coloratura was dead, that modern audiences could no longer be carried away by anything so mechanical and impersonal. But Galli-Curci proved the supposition wrong in a single afternoon. "Just think," wrote Karleton Hackett, "in these days, of people awaiting with bated breath and other evidences of emotional excitement for a performance of *Lucia!* Well, such is a fact. It may be that the old-timers will come in for another inning and that once again the coloratura soprano, which the wise ones have been telling was a species as extinct as the dodo, should be the reigning favorite."

Her Lucia was every bit the sensation her Gilda had been. The "Mad Scene" was followed by twenty curtain calls and then had to be repeated. Between acts Campanini was heard to say, "What a find! What an asset! What a tone! What an art! Great coloraturas average one to a generation, and this is Galli-Curci's generation."

She was heard that season in fifteen performances of five operas. When she sang *Romeo and Juliet,* an extra row of seats was placed in the pit, but still hundreds were turned away. Prices were raised, so that the box-office receipts for a single performance totaled $14,000. Her performances of *La Traviata* and *The Barber* were all sell-outs. Chicagoans found her personally a quiet, amiable woman who dressed so tastefully that one forgot she was not beautiful. When she sang, her vocal beauty was such that she even took on an odd physical charm that she lacked offstage.

Campanini waged a campaign that season to improve the stage picture, particularly striving to add more color. "In the opera we have sought practically every other art as a hand-maiden to music," the director wrote for *Craftsman.* "We have the greatest singers, the greatest dancers, drama, literature; but we have forgotten that the big gift of Nature is color, and we have either filled out stages with neutral tones, or we have left them bare; we have either killed the imagination of our audience, or we have overworked it; and we have not realized that emotions can be stimulated almost as powerfully through color as through music or drama." The new productions that fall began a trend toward greater brilliance of design.

Economically, times were still hard, and as the financial squeeze became greater, the American labor scene became more restless. On December 10, just before a performance of *Die Götterdämmerung,* the Chicago Opera's male chorus went on strike. The choristers had been paid twenty-four dollars a week, with two dollars extra for Sunday matinees. They now sought five dollars for the Sunday work. Campanini maintained that their demands were unreasonable and refused the raise. While the strikers discussed their strategy in the stage alley, *Götterdämmerung* was given with supernumeraries standing in for them and Octave Dua and Désiré Defrère, the tenor and baritone, filling in the choral vocalism. *Die Königskinder* and *Manon* were staged with only the female chorus, and *Rigoletto* was given with a few soloists subbing for the strikers. The strike was eventually broken, but not until Campanini threatened to bring in a new chorus from New York unless the present one returned to the job. When the strikers came around, they blamed the agitation on two Russians in the group. Russia at the time was on the verge of its Bolshevik revolution. Since Bolshevism was highly suspect in this country, it was becoming even then a convenient scapegoat for explaining labor unrest here.

The first two seasons of the Chicago Opera Association, it will be remembered, had been covered by guarantors against an annual deficit of $110,000. The losses both seasons were just slightly in excess of this. In the winter of 1916, Vice-President Charles Dawes announced that patronage of $100,000 a year had been pledged for another five years. The Harold McCormicks generously promised to make up any deficit not covered by this amount.

The company closed its second season on January 21, 1917. Ten days later the German government announced its resumption of a policy of unrestricted submarine warfare. Slightly over two months after that, the United States entered the war on the side of England, France, and Italy. We went into the fight with high hopes. As President Wilson put it, we were going to see that the world was made "safe for democracy." Although few American boys were overseas yet, more than one Chicago woman spent the better part of that summer making socks and sweaters.

As fall approached, it was speculated that the feeling of wartime humility would stifle the usual gaiety that surrounded the opera season, making it a somber, almost dutiful, occasion. Theatrical activity in the city generally had fallen off, and it was expected the opera would follow suit. Opening night, however, found practically a carnival air permeating the Auditorium, making it the happiest opening in the seven-year history of Chicago's own opera. The *Tribune* claimed, "Nobody even knitted." The opera was Mascagni's *Isabeau*, staged now for the first time in America, with Rosa Raisa in the lead. After the first act, Campanini asked the audience to stand while the cast led the singing of "The Star-Spangled Banner," the evening's only concession to the war effort. As the anthem was sung, someone in the house was heard to comment, "If the Italians could only fight as well as they sing—oh, boy!"

Isabeau was based on the Lady Godiva legend. The famous ride takes place early in the second act, and rumor had it that it was going to make Salome's dance look like a nursery rhyme. For once everyone was in his seat promptly, waiting for the curtain to go up. Raisa put everything she had into the scene, and when she threw off her cloak and ran off the stage, the house gasped, thinking she was actually naked. As she rode by on her horse later, she was practically covered by the hair of her long wig, but it was obvious she was wearing flesh-colored silk tights. One reviewer called it the "Ride of the Valkyraisa."

The ladies may not have knitted on opening night, but they certainly did during performances later on, and intermissions found "four-minute men" giving speeches telling of the necessity of the war to "stop the Hun." There was no German opera that year, of course, for the repressive attitude in evidence the year before now bordered on fanaticism. As the pressure grew, German-born Frederick Stock, the honored conductor of the Chicago Symphony, resigned his post rather than embarrass his sponsors. He was not rehired until after the war.

Although most Americans felt fairly secure knowing that there was still an ocean between them and the fighting in Europe, a certain tension and anxiety could nevertheless be sensed. This was reflected one night during a performance of *Dinorah*. Galli-Curci, who was singing the title role for the first time in the city, had just left the stage after her first aria. Suddenly Campanini, conducting that evening, heard a hissing sound and smelled a peculiar stench. Someone had bought a seat on the right-hand center aisle, placed a bomb under it, and left. Campanini quickly stopped the opera, struck up "The Star-Spangled Banner," and ordered Galli-Curci before the footlights. "Sing, madame," he commanded, and sing she did—a whole octave high. Meanwhile, a fireman sitting nearby rushed to the empty seat, wrapped the bomb in his coat, and carried it outside. It all happened so fast that the audience scarcely had time to panic, although one man is supposed to have jumped over the orchestra rail and hidden behind a cello. Fortunately, the bomb turned out to be a dud. It was a crude, homemade job, nothing more than a gas pipe filled with .22 cartridges. The person who left it was later picked up by the police, but his name was never revealed. In an atmosphere of wartime suspicion, it was hard to convince many that the whole thing was not part of a German plot.

During the war subscribers who found they would not be able to use their tickets agreed to leave them at the box office so they might be given free to a soldier or sailor who wanted them. The company itself gave away unsold seats to military personnel, no questions asked. Vincent Sheean, then a member of the Student's Army Training Corps at the University of Chicago, remembers how he was given tickets even as a student: "We lined up in the lobby of the Auditorium at an appointed desk and were given our tickets well before curtain time. And they were very often among the very best seats to be had. . . . There were plenty for all: I never got a bad one and was never turned away."

Galli-Curci continued to be the company's number one sensation, rarely playing to anything less than a sold-out house. Raisa sang *The Jewels of the Madonna* for the first time and made it even more of a success than it had been before. Mary Garden was delayed in Paris until the last three weeks of the season, and in her absence most of the French soprano roles were taken by Geneviève Vix, who was making her initial appearances with the company. Other newcomers were Georges Baklanoff, a fine Scarpia, and Anna Fitziu, who sang, among other things, the world premiere of Henry Hadley's *Azora*. Azora was the daughter of the Aztec emperor Montezuma, and the opera was sort of an American version of *Aida*. It had all of the pomp and ceremony of the Verdi opera, but unfortunately not the music. "If there be a worse libretto than that of *Azora*," remarked the *Tribune*, "it is not readily accessible." The first two performances of the opera played to full houses, but a good percentage of these people were there on passes. Campanini claimed that aside from the regular subscribers, only five persons had actually bought seats on the main floor for the second performance.

Another premiere was Arthur Nevin's *A Daughter of the Forest*, a tale of the American Civil War. The composer himself, musical director at Camp Grant at the time, showed up in khaki uniform to conduct. The opera was given one performance and then never heard from again. *Le Sauteriot* by Silvio Lazzari, telling of life among the peasants of Lithuania, was also given a sole performance. With the McCormick millions backing the project, there was no financial barrier to experimenting with new items, and experiment the company did. If it failed, the management could always hope for better luck next time.

The war ended on November 11, 1918. President Wilson said that "everything for which America fought has been accomplished," and Americans were joyous. The flu epidemic was abating, and by the end of the month even the Fuel Administration's edict for lightless and heatless days had been revoked.

The Chicago opera season opened a week after the Armistice, with Galli-Curci singing *Traviata*. The note of victory was dominant. "The smiles and beckonings of a glad, triumphant people," wrote the *Tribune*, "made the night shine." The Auditorium was ablaze with the banners of the allied nations "to keep in mind the men of many lands who had fought and won beside our own in the khaki and the blue." The house was crowded with people from all walks of life, from the Italian street sweeper in the last row of the top gallery to the society leaders in their boxes. After the second intermission a trumpet called the audience back to their seats before the intermission was five minutes gone. Campanini left his box and led three of the company's conductors to the pit. The curtain was drawn back, revealing the whole chorus on stage. Then entered Auguste Bouilliez, one of the season's new baritones, wearing the beige dress of a Belgian soldier and carrying the colors of his native land. The house cheered and then grew quiet as he sang his country's national anthem. Next came Riccardo Stracciari, the evening's elder Germont, to sing the Garibaldi Hymn of Italy. Muratore appeared, wearing the uniform of a French soldier, and sang the "Marseillaise," evoking quite a demonstration from the audience. Then little Tamaki Miura, the Japanese soprano who would sing *Madama Butterfly* later in the week, toddled out in a kimono and looking for all the world like a doll out of a Tokyo curio shop. She carried her country's flag and sang its slow, subdued national hymn. Cyrena Van Gordon followed, appearing to many to resemble the image of Britannia on the posters that had so recently adorned the nation. She sang "God Save the King," the audience joining her. Only a few zealous patriots made the mistake of singing the words to "America." Campanini took the baton, calling out, "The United States all the time!" With that the house cheered until the walls seemed to wobble. Galli-Curci herself, escorted on stage by the ballet, led the singing of "The Star-Spangled Banner." She said "night" for "flight," but nobody much cared. According to the *Tribune*'s Frederick Donaghey, "There was a volume of voiced patriotism surpassing in definite punch any other public venture with 'O, say' in my hearing." Max Pam, one of the company's vice-presidents, made a plea for contributions to the war chest drive, and *Traviata* was resumed.

That performance introduced to the city Giorgio Polacco, later the company's musical director, but then on contract for only one year. Campanini's health had been none too good the past two seasons, and doctors had ordered him to slow down. He was advised to give up most of his conducting duties, so Polacco was invited in temporarily to fill the gap. A native of Venice, Polacco had begun his career playing with an operatic orchestra in London directed by Luigi Arditi, and by the time he came to Chicago he had conducted in most of the famous opera houses in Europe and South America. He had worked with Toscanini at the Metropolitan, remaining there several years after Toscanini left. Like Campanini, he was a man of the theater and had a special flair for the dramatic. As one Chicago lady recalled nearly a half century later, "When Polacco conducted, it was just as if the music were coming out of the end of his baton."

Mary Garden sang two new roles that year, both painstakingly rehearsed, as all of the Garden operas were. Yet the two of them together were given a total of three performances that season. The first was the world premiere of Février's *Ghismonda.* Some found the opera more tuneful than the composer's *Monna Vanna,* and almost everyone agreed it was a good part for Garden. "She found, as she went along," wrote the *Tribune,* "unsuspected places for delectable didos with which she has fertilized many a sterile libretto in other seasons; and she came through." Just the same, the work was hardly a lasting success. Her other new role was Massenet's *Cléopâtre,* staged earlier by the company with Maria Kuznietsov, but which somehow seemed like a better opera than it really was now that Garden was singing the lead. The *Tribune* said she wore "costumes that are gorgeous so far as they go" and "no one can seduct [sic] better than she."

Loreley (planned for Raisa, but staged with Anna Fitziu when Raisa was forced into an emergency appendectomy) was given its first American performance by the company, as was Xavier Leroux's *Le Chemineau.* The first would be more successful in a revival later with Claudia Muzio, while the second was received far better by the critics than the public. The soprano in *Chemineau* was a newcomer named Yvonne Gall, a fine addition to the French wing.

After her stint in the hospital, Raisa sang *Tosca, Trovatore,* and *William Tell,* while Galli-Curci added *Linda di Chamounix, Crispino e la Comare,* and *La Bohème* to her Chicago repertoire. Her Mimi was sung opposite the Rodolfo of Irish tenor John McCormack, who had momentarily deserted the concert stage for what was by then a rare appearance in opera.

It was about this time that a funny incident was rumored about Marcel Journet, the French basso. It was said that he had been caught snatching pigeons off the ledge outside his hotel window, eating them, and stuffing the feathers and remains down the toilet. According to the report, a pipe leading to his bathroom had been reported clogged. When the plumber checked it, he found it full of feathers.

There was still no German opera in the repertoire, just as there was none at the Metropolitan. The Met was talking about returning Wagner to the boards as soon as possible, but the proposal had touched off quite a controversy. The *Tribune*'s Frederick Donaghey, writing on December 15, 1918, had some thoughts on this: "The thing to be done with Wagner's operas when put back on the American stage, is to use English text, to cut them into humane lengths, and to prevent German singers from messing them up. The Germans among us, of course, will not go to hear the operas after such revision; but the Germans among us never went to hear the operas when they were given in German, uncut, by German singers.... Wagner, rightly edited, could easily be made as popular as Puccini; such editing would put away all the traditions and practices when his operas are restaged. Also, a fair one-third of the music could profitably be cut out and placed in a museum for preservation. As to the performers, most of the good Wagner singers have not been Germans. . . . The four parts of *The Ring* and two or three of the other operas are good, in the best conditions, for one performance a season in Chicago." The war, it seems, was still too fresh in our minds to permit either our musical values or our interpretation of history to wrest itself free of prejudice. Even Donaghey's suggestion that Wagner should be given at all brought letters of protest pouring into the *Tribune* office.

A week before the 1918–19 opera season closed in Chicago the Peace Conference got underway in Paris—its aim to tie up the loose ends of the war. President Wilson decided to attend the meeting himself. All through that spring and into the summer the Allied heads haggled over the objectives of the war, and by the end of the proceedings Wilsonian ideals had melted into a sea of cynicism. More and more Americans were beginning to ask, "What did *we* get out of the war?"

One thing we had learned from the war was aggressiveness, striking down what we hated. We had hated the Germans, and Germany had been put in her place. We now hated Bolshevism, which we feared was spreading to our own country, and the Bolsheviks would have to be put in their place. With the war, prices had risen sharply, while wages remained literally too constant for comfort. Released from the feeling of patriotic duty by the Armistice, labor began to strike, only to find itself denounced as a part of the Bolshevik conspiracy.

The months following the close of the war found vast numbers of Negroes moving into Chicago from the southern portions of the United States, hoping to find there some degree of social and economic equality. In the summer of 1919 Chicago experienced its first real race riot, resulting from the alleged stoning of a Negro boy swimming in Lake Michigan.

The younger generation was causing concern among the older ones, for never had the young people seemed so restless, aggressive, and independent. The more established order tended to retaliate by building high walls around the most cherished clubs and social institutions. Mme. X, who for years had been writing a society column for the *Tribune*, wrote on the day the 1919–20 opera season opened, "The youth of the day is terrifying in its tendency utterly to ignore anything but itself, its desires, aspirations, and tastes. 'Heaven protect us,' it seems to cry, 'from association with the stodgy folk who have run the world up to now!' It's the same cry each generation, say you? Yes, but never, perhaps, quite so piercing and shrill as now."

Chicagoans went to the Auditorium that fall amid a growing sense of uneasiness and disillusionment. Already there was a tendency to look back on the victory celebration which had opened the season before, and the optimism it represented, with bitter cynicism. "We didn't know much then," wrote the *Tribune* in November, 1919; "we all thought peace was at hand, and rejoiced accordingly." A popular song of the day was "I'm Always Chasing Rainbows," its sentiment pretty well summing up the frustration at hand.

The wealthier people were practically all coming to the Auditorium in automobiles now. Anyone who lingered too long over dinner or in the bathtub, ran the risk of being fined for speeding if his dash down Michigan Avenue was too hurried. The law permitted fifteen miles an hour in the residential districts, but no more than ten in the downtown sections.

On the way to the theater, talk might well turn to the coming of prohibition. The Eighteenth Amendment had already been ratified, but would not go into effect until the first of the new year. This obligingly gave people almost a full year to stock up on their liquor. Hostesses were already indicating whether a party would be wet or dry. One Chicago socialite was heard to comment that fall, "I'm afraid that I can't have the so-and-so's again to dinner. He lapped up a whole bottle of my precious Scotch. My supply won't stand such a strain." And another said, "I'm awfully sorry that I have to leave out those nice B——'s, but, you know, they've laid up nothing—not a bottle!"

As the first-nighters alighted from their automobiles in front of the Auditorium entrance, it was obvious that there had been other changes in the past year. Skirts were now six inches above the ground, and there was talk that they would become even shorter. Vivid colors were more in evidence than before, and women were again permitting their ears to show. For the past several seasons ears had been completely covered by the coiffure. While hair was still long, fashion had at last decreed that the tips or even the whole ear ought to be displayed. One, of course, could not go to the opera with naked ears, so earrings were back in vogue. And with the return of earrings came jewels in general. Out came the tiaras, dog collars, necklaces, and gems that had been in hiding for nearly two decades. Most women were wearing powder these days, but rouge was still generally frowned upon.

Still another noticeable difference between this opening-night audience and those of former years was the number of young people present. The season's debutantes were much in evidence, but the young married set was even more so. The foyer was more brilliantly lighted than ever before, for between acts moving-picture cameras filmed the social notables as they promenaded.

The opera that night was Montemezzi's *La Nave*, being staged for the first time in America just a year after its world premiere at La Scala. The cast was headed by Rosa Raisa, Alessandro Dolci, and Giacomo Rimini, while the composer conducted. It was said that this was Montemezzi's first occasion to conduct any opera in public. *La Nave* was set in early Venice. Norman Bel Geddes designed the scenery, which cost a staggering $60,000. It was some of the heaviest and bulkiest the company ever used, a virtual nightmare for the stagehands. The stage was so cluttered that at no time was it possible to make an entrance from stage center. Critics found the stage picture "impressive" (particularly the scene showing the launching of the great ship) and remarked about the compelling use of color. Raisa sang the role of an avenging daughter who turns seductress, but most people agreed that the enchantress bit was a little out of her element. Still, as novelties went then, the opera had a fairly lengthy run—two performances.

Another new work that year was De Koven's *Rip Van Winkle*, which Campanini had commissioned especially for the Chicago Opera. The work was given only six orchestra rehearsals, and this was thought so shameful at the time that Louis Hasselmans refused to conduct the performance, maintaining he wanted no part of a production so poorly prepared. Nevertheless young Evelyn Herbert had a success as the leading soprano. More successful was Puccini's *Trittico*, the Chicago performance trailing the world premiere at the Metropolitan by a year, but considerably better sung and staged. Ravel's *L'Heure Espagnole*, staged with Yvonne Gall in the lead, and André Messager's *Madame Chrysanthème*, a sort of warmed-over *Madama Butterfly* story, prepared as a vehicle for Tamaki Miura, were each given their first American staging.

Mary Garden sang Montemezzi's *L'Amore dei Tre Re* for the first time in her career during the season, and it proved one of her very best roles. It was the only opera she ever sang in Italian. The *Tribune* called it, "the climax of the opera season," pronouncing Montemezzi's score "the most beautiful opera any modern Italian has given the world." The second act was particularly marvelous. The part of the blind old king was sung by Virgilio Lazzari, and the excitement he and Garden could build into the strangling scene was positively thrilling. The two used to fight it out as though they really meant business. In her autobiography Mary Garden tells how Lazzari used to come to her after a performance and say, "Mary, look at my hands!" They were covered with scratches from her nails. "How I used to fight for my life in that opera!" she writes. "Lazzari killed me, but what a struggle it was, and how I loved and adored it! I lived and died every minute of it. What a scrap that was, so real you'd have thought he had really killed me! Then Lazzari would pick me up, throw me on his back, and carry me off the stage." A few seasons later he flung her over his shoulder into something of an awkward position, hurting her back rather seriously. As she lay dangling in the air, she was forced to move her head and whisper, "Lazzari, for God's sake, change my position! I'm dying of pain." The basso apparently did not hear, for he changed nothing. She wanted to scream, but of course was supposed to be dead. When the curtain finally fell, she had wrenched her back so badly that she was unable to take her curtain calls.

Raisa became identified with a significant new role that year too, Bellini's *Norma*, staged for the first time in Chicago since Lilli Lehmann had sung it twenty-five years before. Raisa had done the role first in Mexico City the previous summer, where the Mexicans demanded seventeen performances of it. It became one of her great, though seldom-given, operas in Chicago. She made the headlines in 1920 for one performance of *Norma* she refused to sing. The Juvenile Protective Association threatened to prevent a five-year-old child from appearing with her on stage. Raisa balked, and the performance had to be canceled.

Galli-Curci acquired not only a new opera, but a new singing partner as well. The opera was *La Sonnambula*, one of the finest things she ever did. Her partner was Tito Schipa, who appeared on the Chicago scene as an unknown. He indulged in some Italian excesses at first, but as soon as these were toned down, he became one of the company's featured attractions. Another newcomer, one who would sing with the Chicago forces only three seasons, was Edward Johnson, the Canadian tenor who later became general manager of the Metropolitan. His Chicago debut was as Loris in Giordano's *Fedora*, and his "*Amor Ti Vieta*" literally stopped the show.

The overwhelming event of that 1919–20 season, however, was the sudden death of Cleofonte Campanini. He had arrived in Chicago that fall suffering from a bad cold, but had gone about his duties doggedly. Although he was conducting very little these days, he and Mrs. Campanini never missed a performance—the director at times sitting with his wife in their box, but more frequently lending a hand backstage. One night the Campaninis failed to appear. As the performance began, word spread among the cast that their director had been taken from his suite at the Congress Hotel to St. Luke's Hospital. His cold had turned to pneumonia. Early in the morning of Friday, December 19, Chicago's beloved Campanini was dead.

The following Sunday the coffin bearing his body was brought to the Auditorium, where the company gave him a farewell as theatrical as his life had been. The casket was placed in the center of the stage, surrounded by masses of flowers and the sets of the "Transformation Scene" from *Parsifal.* At either end of the coffin was a burning wax candle, while on a stand nearby was his baton and one of his scores. The company paid their respects in a musical service, the Chicago public paid theirs filing by the bier for three full hours, and then, as Mary Garden tells it, "the curtain came down slowly, and that was the last we saw of Cleofonte Campanini." His body was placed in a vault at Calvary Cemetery, but removed the following spring and taken to his home in Parma, Italy.

With Campanini's death some of the disillusionment and pessimism which was sweeping the country penetrated the Chicago Opera. Gino Marinuzzi, who had been brought in that year to carry most of the conducting load, took over the direction of the company on a temporary basis, but things ran far from smoothly. As critic Edward Moore wrote for the *Tribune* a decade later, "After his [Campanini's] death there was a time of stress. At times it did not seem possible that the Chicago Opera could continue. Worse, a good part of the public began to believe that it could [not] continue."

All at once there seemed to be a general disintegration within the organization. The artists became too independent for the general good, and there was a growing concern about the opera's future financially. The McCormicks were still underwriting a lion's share of the deficit, as they had promised when they agreed to cover any loss over $100,000. But three of the promised five years had passed, during which time Chicago had seen some of the lushest opera in its history, with as varied a repertoire as has ever been seen this side of the Atlantic. Shortly after Campanini's death, Harold McCormick reconfirmed his pledge for two more years of support. "What we're trying to do," he explained, "is to make the opera company an attractive proposition for the guarantors who will have to relieve us at the end of two years." But would there be guarantors then willing to finance the company in the manner to which it was accustomed? There were doubts, serious ones. One businessman, admittedly no devotee of the opera, estimated in the spring of 1920 that the company was worth a million dollars in advertising to the city and five million in actual monetary profit to hotels, restaurants, clubs, theaters, and so forth. Yet he warned, "It is likely to slip away just so long as its maintenance is dependent solely upon the mood and inclination of a single individual." Now that Campanini was dead, it seemed to many that it could slip away all the easier.

As if these problems were not enough, the company was roasted by critics that spring on its New York tour. "One thing is certain," one critic wrote. "Not even the Chicago Opera Company, which has apparently thrown to the winds most of its earlier pretensions to fine art, can continue to live by noise alone." According to Mary Garden, "New York critics are all dried-up old men. They have no 'modern sap' in the veins." This might be, but their carping hurt just the same.

The company's future looked bleaker than it had since its beginning. Its director was dead; its patrons were due to retire in only two more years; and its artistic standards appeared to be slipping. While there were still glorious years ahead, there could be little doubt that with the passing of Campanini a great era in the history of Chicago Opera had come to an abrupt close.

Chapter 7

MISTRESS MARY, HOW DOES YOUR GARDEN GROW?

The early twenties ushered in the age of the flivver and the flapper, the Charleston and the raccoon coat, Babe Ruth and Bobby Jones, the Ziegfeld Follies and George White's Scandals. The movies were rapidly gaining in popularity, and in 1920 Norma Talmadge and Wallace Reid were voted America's favorite stars. Skirts were now nine inches above the ground. Cosmetics were becoming universal, and the corset was on its way out. More and more supposedly "nice" girls were admitting they smoked cigarettes. Prohibition made its entrance, followed by the rum-runner, the speakeasy, and the racketeer. The economic scene after 1921 began to show a marked improvement, and business was better than ever.

But the intellectual and cultural environment so pronounced in Chicago before the war had largely evaporated. The great literary renaissance which had flowered in the city at the turn of the century was over. Frank Norris, Theodore Dreiser, Upton Sinclair, Carl Sandburg and the rest had lingered in the city, then moved on. In their place came the jazz musicians up from New Orleans. The skyscraper was blazing new trails architecturally, but even it reflected the extent to which American culture had become commercial. As it entered the new age, Chicago, as much of the rest of the nation, discovered that literature and the arts, at least momentarily, had been reduced to riding in the rumble seat.

The change in atmosphere was keenly felt by the Chicago Opera during the 1920–21 season, primarily in a sharp drop in attendance. One wealthy stockbroker, interviewed by *The Musical Leader*, told a reporter: "Aw, I don't like opera. What's it all about anyway? I've spent fifteen hundred dollars on opera. My wife has to have new dresses all the time, and I've got to dress and hang around at the back of a box, twiddle my thumbs, when I could be at the club having a nice quiet game." A banker, asked why he went to the opera so seldom, replied, "I only go when Mary's there, because you know—hm! ha!—she really is good to gaze upon." A Chicago woman put it this way: "I don't like going Saturday afternoon because there is always a show like the 'Scandals' or 'Follies' in town; my husband doesn't like going out nights, and my husband likes 'Scandals.' " On the basis of this survey, *The Musical Leader,* a Chicago publication, concluded that the city was good for no more than two weeks of opera a year. "The Chicago public knows nothing about art," the journal said; "it is a plain butcher and broker business city. The merchants have no interest in anything save their counter-jumping and the wares upon their shelves; the stockbrokers and grain dealers know nothing except that which pertains to their own individual profits."

Seriously weakened by the recent death of Campanini, the company in many respects was poorly equipped to meet the public's sudden disinterest. Gino Marinuzzi had been appointed artistic director, while Herbert Johnson, the association's former business comptroller, served as executive director. Both positions had been newly created in an effort to cover the duties formerly performed by Campanini as general director. While both men were competent enough, they had more than their share of complications.

The season opened that year with the American premiere of director Marinuzzi's own *Jacquerie,* a tale of a fourteenth-century peasant revolt in France. The sets and costumes alone cost $50,000. Yvonne Gall and Edward Johnson headed the cast, while the composer conducted. It was not a great success.

The new management's preference for Italian opera was obvious in the repertoire it drew up. Only nine French operas were given that year, as compared with twenty-three Italian. No Massenet, at the time one of the city's favorite composers, was heard until the final two weeks, when Muratore and Gall teamed for an excellent *Manon.* Galli-Curci and Florence Macbeth both sang *Lakmé.* Their tenor was Tito Schipa, whose voice, *Musical America* said, was "like a river of sunlight."

Yvonne Gall introduced her Tosca to the city, adding just the right trifles to the performance to make her interpretation a truly remarkable one. When she placed the candles at Scarpia's head, for instance, she did it with her face averted and with a quiver of shrinking. All through the last act she was conscious of Cavaradossi's suffering and danger. Her voice was not as large as others who have sung the part, but few have been so effective. She was once asked how she was able to make *Tosca* so gripping without tearing the roof off. "Ah," she replied, "it is not necessary to shriek to express the emotions of anger and horror that Tosca feels. It is by gesture, by coloring the tone of the voice, by facial expression, that Tosca expresses her emotions. Mere fortissimo singing expresses nothing except lung-power."

Another great performance heard for the first time by the city was Charles Marshall's Otello. The tenor had sung in Europe with some success, but was brought to Chicago as sort of an operatic dark horse. This was another case of advance publicity's being held to a minimum. He sang his debut opposite Raisa's Desdemona and Ruffo's Iago. The final ovation was almost a riot. Not since the appearance of Galli-Curci had a new artist been so enthusiastically acclaimed.

Ruffo sang a role that season written especially for him, *Edipo Re*, Leoncavallo's last opera. The opera was being given for the first time anywhere. Although the score was weak, Ruffo made it a real tour de force, receiving a storm of applause. When he appeared for his curtain calls at the end, his face was still blood-stained, his hands smeared with blood, having just committed Oedipus' final deed on stage.

At a performance of *L'Elisir d'Amore* it was found, much to everybody's surprise, that the curtain would not go up. Upon checking, it was discovered that the electric power was low. Members of the stage crew ran next door to the Congress Hotel, asking that the elevators there be stopped and all unnecessary lights be turned off. Twenty minutes late, the curtain rose.

The question of German opera was still a touchy one. When Mrs. Oscar Hammerstein, the widow of the recently deceased impresario, announced her intention of staging a series of Wagnerian operas in German at the reopened Manhattan Opera House, New York's several American Legion posts threatened to buy the house out, fill it with husky veterans, and break up the performances. The Metropolitan continued to play it safe by giving *Tristan und Isolde* and *Parsifal* in English. The words "IN ENGLISH" were prominently displayed on all posters. The Chicago Opera did much the same. *Lohengrin* and *Die Walküre* were given in 1920–21, but both were sung in English. *Die Walküre*, cut to three hours and a half, was billed as *The Valkyrie*. Even in English, Cyrena Van Gordon made a thrilling Brünnhilde, while Georges Baklanoff was proclaimed by *Musical America* "without doubt the best Wotan that ever stalked the Auditorium stage."

Much was made that year of the fact that eleven American singers were on the roster, reflecting something of our growing chauvinism. "The jingo might burst into glee," wrote Ruth Miller for the *Tribune* shortly after the season began, "over the prevalence of American singers in the casts. Note the preponderance of Anglo-Saxon names on the first popular Saturday night bill." And there were indications of our concern over radical political doctrines. When Giordano's *Andrea Chénier* was given, one *Tribune* reviewer referred to the French revolutionary hero as that "Socialistic and tactless poet." The year before, the Department of Justice had deported some 556 persons, claiming they were political radicals and therefore dangerous to our internal security.

Mary Garden arrived in the city on Christmas Day, more effervescent than ever. She was unhappy that the company was not doing more French opera, but apparently delighted with everything else, including prohibition. "I hope the whole world goes dry," she said. "Prohibition is a good thing for this country, and it will be a good thing for the world. I mean it." She wished everyone at the La Salle Street station a "Merry Christmas," scattered around a handful of silver coins, and departed for her suite at the Blackstone Hotel.

Her first role that year was Erlanger's *Aphrodite*, which she had sung in its American premiere when the company staged the opera ten months before in New York. She sang the part in Chicago first on New Year's Eve. The audience found the music dull; the *Tribune*'s Ruth Miller pronounced it "tedious, stupid, and more or less meaningless." But the opera contained another of those courtesan roles which Mary Garden played so well. She made the part of Chrysis so commanding that the audience could almost overlook the shortcomings of the score. In one scene Garden was clad in transparent rose and a leopard's skin about which she twisted a long blue-green scarf. She so mesmerized her audience with a few simple motions that scarcely anyone was aware of the screams and moans of a slave being crucified a few feet away. "Mary Garden!" wrote the *Tribune*. "A long, slow lift of that white arm and she has portrayed an ecstasy."

But Mary had her temperamental side, and this she revealed one day during an *Aphrodite* rehearsal. The soprano became infuriated with the French conductor Henri Morin. Finally, she walked over to him, twisted the baton out of his hand, and denounced him for knowing nothing about music. Meanwhile the rest of the cast looked on, eyes wide, mouths open.

Following *Aphrodite* she sang *Faust* with Lucien Muratore. It was the first time she had sung the opera in Chicago since her first season there a decade before, confining herself since then almost exclusively to the modern repertoire. To the surprise of many, she proved that conventional singing was not an unknown art with her. "On the contrary," wrote *Musical America*, "she displayed a voice of excellent natural qualifications schooled according to the best canons of art. She was a delight to look upon, a girlish, playful, sensitive, Botticelli figure of a Marguerite."

But the biggest drama that year was not played on the stage. It came as a result of a backstage feud that began with the sudden departure of

Ganna Walska from the city. Walska, whose main ability seems to have been an extraordinary talent for collecting wealthy husbands, unfortunately also fancied she was something of a soprano. Her success was modest at best. When she sang with the Havana Opera Company in 1917, she walked out right after her debut in *Fedora*, amid blistering reviews. She came to Chicago in 1920, having won the confidence and affection of Harold McCormick. At that time she was the wife of Alexander Smith Cochran, multimillionaire sportsman and carpet king; later she would be Mrs. Harold McCormick.

Her Auditorium debut was set for December 21. The opera was to be Leoncavallo's *Zaza*, a part in which Geraldine Farrar had made a personal success at the Metropolitan. The house was sold out long in advance. But rehearsals had not gone well. Gino Marinuzzi and Walska had had words almost from the first over her failure to project beyond the orchestra pit. Finally, in disgust, Marinuzzi turned the production over to Pietro Cimini, telling him to make the best of it. Three days before the scheduled performance, a dress rehearsal was called. After asking Walska several times to sing louder, Cimini at last implored, "Madame, please sing in your natural voice." She glared down at him, then cried out, "Pig, you would ruin my performance." With that she ran off the stage. When she found Marinuzzi and Herbert Johnson in the business office, she supposedly told them, "Gentlemen, I am packing my bags. At the end of this season you will be packing yours." She left the Auditorium, checked out of her suite at the Blackstone Hotel, and departed from Chicago, saying simply "There is a great deal of trouble, and I am tired." She left for Europe shortly thereafter. The only public statement the company made was that *Zaza* was not ready and that the performance was indefinitely postponed.

The sensational debut of the American tenor Charles Marshall seems to have been another source of difficulty, supposedly producing much jealousy among the Italian members of the company. Some said that *Otello* had been given only at the insistence of Herbert Johnson and that the Italians had even tried to stop it. It was also said that an Italian manager of several key artists had his eye on the directorship of the company and that he used the Marshall incident to aggravate national jealousies. Whether this is true or simply represents an attempt to find a convenient scapegoat for executive unrest by playing on the antiforeign sentiment present in the country at the time, is pure conjecture.

At any rate, two weeks after the Walska incident Gino Marinuzzi resigned as artistic director. When he made his statement to the press, he appeared physically exhausted. His face was drawn, his brow furrowed by deep lines. "I could not stand the wrangling of the stars any longer," he said. "They have given me nothing but sleepless nights. Their voices have been in my ears twenty-four hours a day. Each one with a grievance, each one objecting to a role I have assigned to some one else." He agreed to remain with the company as a conductor for the rest of the season.

A week after that, to the surprise of the public, Mary Garden was chosen general director of the Chicago Opera Association, in full charge of the company's artistic and financial affairs. She became the first woman ever to head any opera company, elevated to that post less than five months after American women gained the constitutional right to vote. The same day that Garden's appointment as director was announced, Herbert Johnson's resignation as executive director was made public. Said Johnson, "Miss Garden probably will surround herself with extremely competent people, people more competent than I." When asked if he was glad to be out, he replied, "Yes. Why shouldn't I be? I've been working day and night. If you were here half an hour, you'd be glad to get out too."

Since Garden was scheduled to sing a performance of *Monna Vanna* the day after her appointment, she remained secluded in her hotel suite, unavailable for interviews. Two detectives sat outside her door all day, barring unwelcome visitors. During the second intermission of *Monna Vanna*, however, she held a press conference in her dressing room, looking radiant and obviously overjoyed with her new position. As she sipped a cup of tea, the press fired one question after another at her concerning the changes she would make. "First of all," she said, "this is to be an American company, run from top to bottom by Americans." Her intention, she said, was to make the company "absolutely the best in the world." Would she succeed? "Of course I'll succeed!" came the answer. "I have the directors behind me, I am assured of the loyal support of Mr. and Mrs. Harold McCormick, and of the members of the company, all of whom have signed a letter congratulating me on my appointment."

She said she would give fewer operas and thus better ones. Her aim was to give 50 per cent Italian operas, 35 per cent French, and 15 per cent English. She would like to give German opera, but not until it could be sung in the original language, as she abominated translations. "I have heard Wagner butchered by poor translations," she said. "I want to give opera in English, but it must be American opera, written by Americans, and sung in the language it is written in. I hope we can have at least one new American opera every year." She said she would pay big salaries only to those artists who could draw large audiences. She would pay more attention to the opera than the artist, for she deplored the "star" system. Would she be able to handle the backstage bickering that Marinuzzi had complained about? "I am a fighter. I am an Anglo-Saxon, and we love, by gosh! nothing better than a fight. And count me as a fighter. I am right there in the fray; but the Latin races must be treated with kindness and consideration, and I would pat their cheeks." How would she restore order to the company? "By imposing discipline," was her immediate response. "I know the need, the absolute need, of discipline. Yet in our company the word has lost its meaning." How long would she serve as the company's director? "I am taking this big work for one year, and if they like me we shall go ahead and I shall be happy. If they don't like me, I shall have to say, 'Goodby.' "

There had been talk of Mary Garden's being made director shortly after Campanini's death, but a number of the backers had been fearful that a woman's name might not carry with it the necessary weight and prestige. The summer before her appointment she visited Mrs. Harold McCormick in Europe, and, according to reports, was told then that should any conflict arise the next year, she might be called upon to serve as company head. After Marinuzzi's resignation, Garden was elevated to the position largely because the McCormicks insisted upon it. Mrs. McCormick was in Zurich, Switzerland, at the time, but she sent a cable message to the board of directors a few days before the election, urging the Garden appointment. According to Garden, Harold McCormick approached her, reminding her that his term of patronage had only one more year to go. "We want to go out in a blaze of glory," he told her, "and we need your name." With attendance temporarily off, he undoubtedly felt it would take someone with Mary's flamboyance and understanding of the public to restore the box office to its normal level. When Garden consented, McCormick presented her name to the board of directors, many of whom had strong reservations about the appointment. Even Mary herself admitted that Charles Dawes particularly was quite cool to the idea. But McCormick insisted. Garden was invited to appear before the board and in the interview succeeded in convincing a majority of its members she could handle the job. She would continue as an artist as well as director and would accept no salary for her managerial duties, only for the performances in which she herself starred. And she would accept the position, she told the board, only on condition that "you don't give me a business manager with whiskers."

She assumed her new office curiously determined to make this "an American opera company" run by "American businessmen," as she said time and again. On tour with the company in San Francisco that spring, she told a luncheon group, "Now that we have succeeded after rather a long time in eliminating foreigners from the administration and executive departments of the Chicago Grand Opera Association, it is the intention to make this an exclusively American institution throughout, except behind the scenes. There we must have the foreigners because the best voices and the best musicians are foreigners." She told the San Franciscans that she was pleased to accept the position of director "because the Americanization of this American institution had long been my dream and now it is realized. We mean to carry it out to the end and always maintain this policy." And in New York a month later, she said, "It's going to be an American opera company, too. Young American singers used to knock at the doors of the American opera companies, only to have them opened by foreigners, who would say: 'Not at home.' Now they will be welcomed by an American, and that is as it should be." Interestingly enough, Mary herself was legally still British, not American.

Shortly after becoming director, Garden cabled Giorgio Polacco, asking him to return to the company as principal conductor. Polacco, it will be remembered, had filled this role during the 1918–19 season, but had remained only one year. Although he had won the city's admiration then, the contract for Marinuzzi to fill this post the following year had already been signed when Polacco was approached by the Chicago management. Following his appointment by Garden, Polacco would remain with the company until after the move to the new opera house on Wacker Drive.

Another Garden import was stage manager Jacques Coini, who had been with Hammerstein during the Manhattan days. George M. Spangler, for thirteen years convention manager of the Chicago Association of Commerce, was appointed by the board as the company's new business manager. "In making this appointment," the official statement read, "Mr. Spangler was chosen as the man who by American business methods is best fitted to wipe out the annual deficit of the company, amounting last season to $350,000." It was Spangler's belief that to make opera pay, opera had to be popularized. His approach was not limited to the upper social strata, but aimed at Chicago as a whole. "It's their support, not their dress suits, we want. Even if they wear overalls, they're welcome." It had been Harold McCormick's hope that when his term of patronage came to an end, the Association of Commerce would take up the financial burden. The appointment of Spangler was the first step in this direction. The board's feeling was that if Spangler could reduce the deficit appreciably, the Association of Commerce would then be kindly disposed to serve as the company's principal guarantor.

Following the company's spring tour, director Mary Garden—the "directa," as she insisted upon being called—left for Europe. She spent her summer scouting for talent, trailed by George Spangler, who fruitlessly tried to keep expenses down as low as possible. He was working against impossible odds, however, for thrift had never been one of Mary Garden's virtues. She insisted that Harold McCormick had told her the deficit for the coming season could run as high as $600,000. Therefore, when Spangler balked at an expense, Garden would turn to him and ask, "Have we reached the six hundred thousand dollar mark yet?" Once she signed up a young artist who would gladly have come to Chicago for $200 a performance. "Why two hundred dollars per performance?" the directress asked. "You are worth six hundred dollars!" And $600 it was.

By fall Mme. Directa had signed up the largest array of artists in Chicago's operatic history, promising them fees that were more than generous. The final roster listed seventeen sopranos, nine contraltos and mezzo-sopranos, thirteen tenors, eight baritones, nine bassos, and five conductors. There were just about twice as many singers in each category as the company actually needed or would be able to use. Three days after the season opened, George Spangler was asked by the board of directors to resign. "I will say nothing," was Spangler's only comment. "If anything must be said, Mr. McCormick will say it." McCormick's only explanation was, "The move was for the best interests of the opera. I can say nothing further."

Mary Garden arrived in Chicago that fall carrying a swagger stick and wearing bobbed hair. She cut her hair, she said, "simply to save the time of fixing it every morning." She was also thinner. "I've taken off twelve pounds, and this is how I did it. I swam a mile every day—or almost every day. And, in case anyone may want to know why I wear short skirts, it is to get about more easily and quickly. I will move in streaks until the beginning of our season next week." She later said that Émile Coué, the French psychotherapist, who made "Every day in every way I am getting better and better" proverbial, had cured her of bronchial pneumonia, colds, buzzing in the head, irritability, and depression.

It was Mary's ever-ready comment on any and every subject put to her that had endeared her to most Chicagoans, but there were those who objected to her glibness and objected rather strenuously. She once appeared at the Chicago Stock Exchange to auction off boxes for a charity fund-raising drive. As she stood before the crowd, a "dreadful looking man with long gray hair and shabby clothes" tried to attack her. When the police seized the would-be assassin, the only comment they could get out of him was, "She talks too much."

The season got under way on November 15 with a production of *Samson and Delilah*. Head bands were worn by most smartly dressed women, and pearls were quite the fashion. The Harold McCormicks were both in the audience, but in separate boxes. (They would be granted their divorce later in the season.) Directa Garden, whom the press delighted in calling Mary the First, did not sing but occupied the director's box with her parents. She was dressed in a stunning "velvet gown of jade green, with ropes of pearls and a pearl fillet binding her bobbed auburn hair." The singers were even more numerous offstage than on. Lina Cavalieri was there. So were Cyrena Van Gordon, Edith Mason, and Claire Dux.

The evening's Samson was Lucien Muratore, singing the role for the first time in America. His Delilah was Peruvian contralto Marguerite D'Alvarez. Polacco conducted. The chorus and ballet seemed considerably rejuvenated, the orchestra transformed. The only mishap of the evening came with D'Alvarez' entrance. She was singing her opening phrase, looking straight ahead at Muratore, when she slipped on the temple stairs, skidding almost to the middle of the stage. She raised herself immediately and continued singing, somehow even managing to keep her pitch throughout the incident. The next time she sang the role she put so much rosin on her sandals that the squeak could practically be heard to the lobby of the Congress Hotel.

Lina Cavalieri was supposed to make her Chicago debut the next evening as Tosca, but a week before the performance she canceled, pleading illness as she had in 1913. Although she never sang with the company, she frequently attended performances, particularly on nights when her husband, Muratore, was singing. She was still gorgeous, almost the embodiment of the Platonic idea of beauty. "I saw her really incomparable face and figure quite often and quite close," Vincent Sheean remembers in his *First and Last Love*. "It was a breathtaking apparition."

An exciting newcomer that year was Polacco's wife, Edith Mason, an American soprano who had won a big reputation in Europe, at the Metropolitan, and even at Chicago's own Ravinia Park. She made her debut at the Auditorium in *Madama Butterfly*. "The chief duty in considering the performance," wrote Edward Moore in the *Tribune* next day, "is to sort out a set of superlatives and put them in the proper places. Looking back at it, one has a mild sort of wonder as to whether the opera was ever given in Chicago before." At the end Mason was practically buried behind a mass of flowers, and Moore says he lost count of the number of curtain calls. "There was something rather too exciting going on to indulge in arithmetical exercises," he wrote. "At any rate, when it was finally over, there were several thousand pairs of blistered palms in great need of cooling."

A week later the German soprano Claire Dux was introduced as Mimi in *Bohème*. *Musical America* reported, "A voice of rare sweetness is the gift of Miss Dux, and she used this voice with extraordinary charm. Her pianissimo tones are marvels of purity and grace." When she sang Nedda a little later, the same reporter wrote, "Her acting was the sprightliest and most vivacious seen on the Auditorium stage this season and her singing was beyond reproach." An excellent impression was also made by the

American Mary McCormic when she made her Chicago debut as Micaela in a matinee *Carmen*, the one bright spot in an otherwise routine performance. "If Mary Garden is to be thanked for nothing else," said *Musical America*, "it should be for introducing her to Chicago audiences. She sang with limpid, colorful tones, warm, tender and powerful, with exquisite pianissimo shadings and an effortless swelling to her full voice."

Galli-Curci was now dividing her time between Chicago and the Metropolitan, and Raisa remained the mainstay of the company's dramatic wing. Mary Garden, despite her duties as director, sang sometimes as often as three times a week, doing the roles she enjoyed most: *Carmen*, *Le Jongleur de Notre Dame*, *Louise*, *Monna Vanna*, *Pelléas et Mélisande*, *Thaïs*, and *Salome*.

It had been eleven years now since the Strauss opera had caused its furor at the Auditorium, and it had been a lively topic of conversation off and on ever since. Still, it was felt that in the sophisticated twenties audiences would probably find the work not nearly so shocking as they had a decade before. To be sure, things did go better, although not without commotion. Most critics indicated that their taste in art at least had matured over the years, for a number of those who had opposed the performance in 1910 now found nothing immoral about it. *Musical America* deemed it "weighty, thrilling, majestic." René Devries, writing for *Musical Courier*, said, "No censor, no member of the Baptist Church, or of any other congregation, could, even with field glasses, find anything depraving or even degrading in her [Garden's] Salome." But others still had reservations. "After witnessing *Salome* again last night, with an interval of eleven years," wrote the *Tribune*, "I am divided in my mind whether to be more enraptured over the gorgeousness of Richard Strauss' score or appalled over the frightful insanity of Oscar Wilde's play. There is no question that Strauss wrote the most vivid, the most colorful, the most entrancing score that ever was put into operatic form. In one way Miss Garden and her associates in the Chicago opera have done us a poor service. There can be no further thrills over any music that may come up in the future. *Salome* is the last word." But even an age becoming schooled in Freudian psychology, when such terms as "id" and "ego" and "repression" were becoming a part of a good many people's working vocabulary, was not quite ready to accept the sexual excesses of Salome. "There is no question either," the *Tribune* continued, "that insanity is the one word that will describe what Wilde put into his play, and insanity of a peculiarly repellent, nauseating kind. It is pure psychopathy. You can see the same sort of subjects in an institution for the care of such unfortunates." Said the reviewer, "I confess to have felt a bit squirmy inside for a number of minutes after the curtain went up."

Polacco, who had had a lifetime ambition of conducting *Salome,* worked marvels with the orchestra, and Muratore made a thrilling Herod. But it was Garden's show all the way. "As for Miss Garden herself," the *Tribune* wrote, "there are no words to tell of her savagery, her beauty, the terrifying fascination she throws over her victims and her audience as well. She must be seen to be believed."

Salome played to two sold-out houses, but just as eleven years before, a scheduled third performance was canceled. Company officials declined to give any reason for the cancellation, although some reports again claimed Edith Rockefeller McCormick had ordered the opera suppressed. A number of well-known box holders had turned in their tickets the night of the first performance, and others had refused to attend. Sporadic protests were sounded all over the city, particularly by the militant fundamentalist religious groups. Revivalist Billy Sunday even took up the fight. Although dropped in Chicago, the opera was given by the company in New York and in twelve of the cities on the spring tour.

The first German opera sung in the original language since the war was given in 1921–22: *Tannhäuser*, *Lohengrin*, and *Tristan und Isolde*—none of which were among Wagner's more nationalistic works. The opposition was minimal.

On December 30, the world premiere of Sergei Prokofieff's *The Love for Three Oranges* was given. The work had been especially commissioned for the company by Campanini, and the production, sung in French translation, cost in the neighborhood of $100,000 and was one of the most elaborate the company ever staged. According to the *Tribune,* "Never was paint applied to scene cloth more lavishly or gorgeously." As *The New Republic* described it, "Rose and scarlet, orange and purple, sapphire and gold, backdrops of wild sunset skies, foregrounds of burlesque court furnishings, deserts, mountains, and witches' caverns, all are beautiful beyond reality, and all share the happy overemphasis of the whole production.... No stage sets have ever been more beautiful or more daring than these."

Few Chicagoans understood either the libretto or Prokofieff's advanced music, but most tended to be highly flattered that a world premiere of an opera by an important composer was being staged by their local company. Others found the whole thing impossible, and more than one person in that first-night audience left before the performance was over, muttering "Disaster!" Even the critics disagreed over the merits of the score. "The music, I fear," said the *Tribune*'s Edward Moore, "is too much for this generation. After intense study and close observation at rehearsal and performance, I detected the beginnings of two tunes.... For the rest of it Mr. Prokofieff might well have loaded up a shotgun with several thousand notes of varying lengths and discharged them against the side of a blank wall." *The New Republic*, on the other hand, declared, "Prokofieff's score is a masterpiece of modern descriptive music.... It is true that there is nothing in the entire score which one may whistle as one goes out. It is only an ingrate who would demand sweet melodies; with Mr. Prokofieff's crackling, shimmering miracle in the air, melody seems no more indispensable than a pretty, stupid woman of the eighteen-eighties." *The New Republic* felt that Prokofiev had achieved a perfect unity with his score, the whole production splendidly integrated. "For once," the review concluded, "in a way Truth walks unashamed upon the boards where for generations passion has halted for arias, and death has been obligingly arrested for sextettes. At last Grand Opera, so called, has become a dramatic production."

The opera received only two performances in Chicago, the composer conducting both of them. The work was presented by the company in New York the following February, where critics proved generally hostile. "It was as though a pack of dogs had broken loose and were tearing my trousers to shreds," Prokofieff recalls in his memoirs.

Meanwhile, all was not well backstage at the Auditorium. A feud had been raging practically from the moment the season began. Mary Garden says in her autobiography that she had no sooner taken over the management of the company than she began receiving anonymous letters. Next, she says, "knives would reach me by post, then revolvers, and once I got a box of bullets, and in the box was a letter that said, 'Remember that there should be twelve bullets in this box. Count them. There are only eleven. The twelfth bullet is for you.'" Harold McCormick eventually hired a detective to accompany her wherever she went. Who sent the notes and weapons, no one ever found out. Certainly there were a number of people within the company unhappy with Garden's direction, although there is no evidence that any of them were quite at the bullet-sending stage.

Johanna Gadski, hired to sing Isolde at $1,500 a performance, waited two weeks after coming to the city for rehearsals to begin, but was never even able to get the management to set the dates for her performances. She was eventually handed a check for $7,500, told her services would not be needed, and dismissed. When she inquired into the situation, she was told that the subscribers had voiced opposition to her appearances because of her husband's questionable war record. Gadski brought suit against the company for $500,000 damages on grounds of slander. When *Tristan und Isolde* was finally given, Beatrice Sutter-Kottlar sang the soprano lead.

Next Tito Schipa left the company in a furor, having been called upon to sing only one performance during the first three weeks. Lucien Muratore, signed to star in a number of productions at $2,800 each, refused to sing *Samson and Delilah* again because some performances of the opera were assigned another tenor, Charles Marshall. He insisted his contract gave him exclusive right to the role and threatened never to sing with the company so long as Mary Garden was director. "The trouble with Miss Garden is that she is capricious and uncertain," the tenor said. "She kisses one moment and kicks the next. She treats the artists like children." Garden insisted she would not permit "dictation by foreign artists." As a result of the Muratore episode, *Samson* was dropped from the repertoire. Marguerite D'Alvarez, the Delilah, was paid for the remaining six performances called for in her contract and dismissed.

Before long other artists began finding that they had been hired for more performances than they could ever hope to fill. One singer had been contracted for thirty-five engagements, but sang only about half that many. Edward Johnson and Charles Marshall each sang only one role. Florence Macbeth was not heard at all, although she was in Chicago waiting to sing her assignments. Maria Ivogün was brought all the way from Europe; she sang once. The essential problem was that Garden had contracted too many singers, promising them too many roles. It was simply impossible to work all the performances in, with the result that a goodly number of significant stars were idle the better part of the season. With idleness came bickering, especially since Mary Garden herself was singing two, sometimes three, times a week. "The passing of the first quarter of the season," wrote *Musical America*, "finds many of the members of the company perplexed, others disillusioned, and some in open rebellion." At the end of the fourth week, Edward Moore wrote, "In almost any corner around the Auditorium you may observe baritones gnashing their teeth, sopranos emitting plaintive sounds of distress, tenors wondering whether their chances would be ruined if they took a few days off for a concert engagement."

Garden and Polacco had their difficulties, too. At one performance of *Pelléas et Mélisande*, the audience was exceedingly cold, and Garden returned to her dressing room in an unhappy mood. When Polacco called to pay his respects, she complained that his orchestra was "rotten" and had played too loud. When he informed her that the orchestra was his business and not hers, she pushed him out the door and slammed it in his face. Polacco was quoted as saying Garden was like a floating frog, turning first this way and then that. He refused to conduct her next *Louise* and later complained that Garden had too many spies in the theater for his liking. When he told Mary this, she took him by the shoulders and this time threw him bodily out of her dressing room. Muratore said, "She has treated him abominably all season."

Despite all this, from the artistic standpoint the season was in many ways a success. Productions were probably better rehearsed than at any time in the company's history. As Marguerite D'Alvarez remembered it, "One was given time to become at home with the artists with whom one was singing." Seven weeks deep in the season, the *Tribune* wrote, "There is no question but that the operatic season this year has been more brilliant than ever before." Garden had promised to make each evening a gala event, and she very nearly did it. "It is Chicago's big year in opera," proclaimed Edward Moore. If Harold McCormick's principal concern was going "out in a blaze of glory," he certainly got his wish.

Financially, the story was a different matter. Attendance had picked up over the previous year's decline, but the cost of keeping so much inactive talent around the Auditorium was staggering. Productions were extensively rehearsed, and this too cost money. Garden had asked the French composer Gabriel Grovlez the summer before to write a ballet for the company. He went to work, composed *La Fête à Robinson,* and was brought to Chicago to conduct it. Costumes and sets were made for the production, and a number of rehearsals were held. The ballet was announced for two different occasions, but, while it was given on tour in New York, it was never given in Chicago. Costumes and scenery were also made for *Sniegurotchka,* both quite lavish and costly. When it came time to stage the work, the management discovered it had no orchestral parts. Not a single complete score could be found, so the project was abandoned for the time being.

When the deficit for the year was figured, it totaled $1,100,000, as compared with the previous high of $350,000 for the season before. But Harold and Edith Rockefeller McCormick, true to their promise, paid everything over $100,000 and paid it without a whimper.

Had Mary Garden turned the Chicago Opera Association into a truly American company? Lucien Muratore at least said not. "Miss Garden wrapped herself in the American flag," the tenor stated. "She has been directress for one year and what has she done for American artists? Nothing! All the Americans in the company were engaged before she became directress. The American artists have been sacrificed. Roles were taken away from Americans and given to foreigners. There are but twelve American artists in a company of sixty principals."

After completing its season in Chicago, the company—the "Lake Michigan Minnesingers," as one New York journalist called it—opened a month's engagement at the Manhattan Opera House. New York critics after early enthusiasm had become increasingly hostile to the Chicagoans, and there had been no little conflict with the Metropolitan, which now looked upon Chicago's mid-winter tour as undesirable competition. By June it was decided that hereafter the company would forego the New York part of its tour. "The destiny of the Chicago Grand Opera Company is in Chicago and the Middle West," said Harold McCormick.

Throughout that 1922 spring tour, Mary Garden was asked if she planned to continue as the company's director. "I have been elected but I have not signed yet," she answered. "Who knows what will happen in the meanwhile. I like my job because it is a battle, but I do not like a battle that is conducted in an underhand manner. Intriguing bores me." What had caused all the trouble back in Chicago? Said Mary, "Most of the trouble in the company has been the work of the men. They must be coddled and humored. From the women there has been nothing." Was Polacco leaving the company? "There is no unpleasantness between us," she assured reporters. "He is a dear and I have always liked him immensely. There is absolutely no trouble between us."

But in April, Mary Garden resigned her post as general director. "I am an artist," she declared, "and I have decided that my place is with the artists, not over them." After Samuel Insull became the new Chicago Opera head, he said he thought Garden "had acted in a very gentlemanly manner." Undoubtedly she had given Chicago the most lavish season of opera in its whole history, although squandering a great many McCormick dollars in the process. Says Mary in her autobiography, "If it cost a million dollars, I'm sure it was worth it."

Chapter 8

SING A SONG OF SIXPENCE

WITH the end of Mary Garden's directorship came the end of the McCormicks' era of patronage, and with the end of McCormick patronage came the end of the Chicago Grand Opera Association. In the spring of 1922 the company was reorganized into the Chicago Civic Opera. Although the new company would continue in much the same vein artistically as its predecessor, its financing was revolutionized, a move necessitated by basic changes in the nation's economic pattern. To a large degree the McCormick support of the Chicago Opera represented a last vestige of a dying epoch, a time of giant fortunes relatively unhampered by taxation. With the reforms of the Wilson years, however, the United States had seen its first constitutional income tax enacted, heralding a day when it would be impossible for one individual, or even a small group of individuals, to finance a significant opera company. There were still great fortunes in Chicago, as elsewhere, but the reform legislation of the early twentieth century sealed the doom of unlimited wealth amassed in a few hands. While the general standard of living in the country was steadily advancing, the very wealthy were beginning to feel the pressures, slight though they were at first, brought on by government regulation, particularly the graduated income tax.

With the passing of massive fortunes went the days of great guarantor support for the arts. The burden now had to be spread out over several hundred, eventually several thousand, people. Fortunately for the Chicago Opera, by 1922 a fairly sizable operatic public had been created. Opera had been considerably democratized during the twelve years the city had had a resident company, and the phonograph and, beginning in

1922, the radio helped make opera, or at least operatic selections, available to many who had had only slight acquaintance with it before. Through the years the city's operatic public had been gradually broadened, and as its public grew, so could the guarantor support.

The original plan for financing the Chicago Civic Opera was for 500 guarantors each to pledge $1,000 a year for five years. All through the 1921–22 season a fund drive had been in progress. By January 11 it was announced that half the amount needed had been raised. The new company was then officially incorporated, although it would not actually take over until after Mary Garden's spring tour. By early summer the entire $500,000 a year had been pledged, plus an additional $25,000 for good measure. To secure this amount, however, it had been necessary to accept contributions of $500 and even $100. Rather than the 500 guarantors the company originally envisioned, by the time the goal was reached, the list of patrons numbered 2,200. All of the properties, costumes, scenery for ninety operas, and contracts of the Association were turned over to the new company as a gift from the McCormicks. The new organization began operations without any financial obligation whatsoever.

If anything was more admired in the 1920's than business, it was business efficiency, and the Chicago Civic Opera became an embodiment of this ideal. The company's president was Samuel Insull, who had carved an empire out of public utilities. Insull was born in England, had begun his business career at fourteen as an apprentice clerk at five shillings a week, and had come to this country nine years later as Thomas Edison's private secretary. Proving himself financially precocious, he shortly became Edison's business manager, and in 1892 was placed in charge of the Edison Company in Chicago. With this as a base, he rapidly assimilated his public utilities kingdom.

Although his first love was business, Insull had always been somewhat stage-struck and at an early age became a devotee of the opera. As a working boy in London, he had given up meals to buy a six-penny seat in the upper gallery at Covent Garden. He had attended opera at the Auditorium from his first days in Chicago, eventually buying a box for the season and later serving as a minor guarantor. By 1922 he was firmly established in both the city's business and operatic circles, a logical successor to Harold McCormick. But just as McCormick was representative of the opulent fortunes of his age, Insull was typical of the business efficiency of his. He had built his empire from nothing, had struggled as a young man, and knew the value of a dollar. Thrift was a keynote of his business philosophy, and he saw the Civic Opera as no different from any other business. "I am not in any sense an authority on Grand Opera," he once said, "except as to what it costs." Therefore, he ran the Opera just as though it were one of his utilities companies. "One cannot ignore the dollar without getting into trouble," he declared.

Equally dedicated to a policy of efficiency was Charles G. Dawes, who continued as the Opera's vice-president. Dawes was also heading President Harding's national Bureau of the Budget at the time, where his duty was to scrutinize each governmental expenditure and eliminate every possible waste. His goal was to cut government spending to the minimum. His views on the financing of the Chicago Opera were but a carbon copy of his outlook on the federal budget. Together Dawes and Insull worked out a strict accounting system for the Civic Opera, geared toward cutting out every unnecessary extravagance. "No contract will be signed by any general director or business manager or any other individual from this day on," Insull assured. "Every contract in the future must bear the signature of the chairman of the finance committee and one member of the Board of Directors. We will spend our own money."

Although ticket prices in 1922 were increased slightly, ranging now from six dollars to one dollar, Insull was strong in his belief that opera should be for the people. His biographer, Forrest McDonald, says that "though he grew up to sit with bejeweled ladies in the finest boxes, his heart never left the gallery or the people in it." He therefore set out to democratize the Chicago Opera even further, not particularly endearing himself to the social elite in the process. McDonald even suggests that certain opera performances were purposely set for the same nights as concerts by the Chicago Symphony, so that those with more aristocratic tastes would feel obliged to attend the symphony rather than the opera.

The Civic Opera Company opened its first season on November 13, 1922, with a production of *Aida*. Rosa Raisa and Charles Marshall starred, while Giorgio Polacco, elevated by Insull to the position of musical director, conducted. "Be it announced," wrote the *Tribune*, "that this performance of *Aida* was as good a show as has been seen at the Auditorium since Chicago's name first went on to an opera company.... It would seem that grand opera made safe for democracy, Chicago brand, means grand opera indeed, fine opera, brilliant opera, even grandiose opera." Raisa's voice, according to Edward Moore, was "like silk shot through with gold." With the increase in ticket prices, the box office return was higher than any previous opening night in the city's operatic history, and the audience seemed even gayer than usual. The head bands so stylish the year before were not as much in evidence, but jewels were more so. Particularly fashionable were long pendant earrings, some hanging almost to the shoulders.

Mary Garden continued as one of the company's major artists, receiving even from the expenditure-conscious Insull an appreciable $3,500 a performance. She sang during the first two weeks of the company's 1922–23 season, then left for a six-week concert tour, and returned during the last two. Galli-Curci also sang with the Civic Opera for two seasons, showing considerable interest by then in roles such as Mimi, Madama Butterfly, and Manon, but her success in the lyric realm was never equal to her triumphs in the coloratura.

Puccini's *The Girl of the Golden West* was revived again in 1922 for Raisa, but was still found somewhat humorous. Particularly so was the second-act storm which blew so hard that the footlights flickered for several minutes after the door of the cabin was closed, but did not bother the candle on the table at all. More successful was the first production of Halévy's *La Juive* by Chicago's resident forces. Of Raisa, who sang the role of Rachel, Edward Moore wrote, "I never heard her when she was as glorious as she was last night." So great was the enthusiasm for the opera that during an intermission one ticket holder visited the business office and requested to have his name put down for the following season's subscription list.

Claudia Muzio made her first appearances with the Chicago Opera that year, a sensation in virtually everything she did. She had already sung with the Metropolitan for five seasons and had been widely acclaimed in both Europe and South America. She made her Chicago debut as Aida, proving herself as convincing dramatically as vocally. When she sang *Trovatore* a few nights later, it was discovered that she was also a woman of great physical beauty. A lonely person off stage, Muzio devoted herself almost wholly to her art. It was her custom to show up at the theater two hours before curtain time to prepare herself for the role she was to sing, and so completely did she live her parts that after a highly dramatic opera like *Cavalleria Rusticana* or *Andrea Chénier* she frequently came off the stage in a noticeable daze. May Higgins, her one-time secretary, once asked her how she could stand to make love on stage to a particular tenor whom the whole company considered despicable. "When I'm singing," Muzio replied, "I actually love him." She insisted on realism in her operas, clear down to the wearing of real jewels and the serving of real champagne in *Traviata*. She used to fall over backward on the church steps in *Cavalleria* with such force that unknowing stagehands wondered if she had knocked herself unconscious. Unlike most of her colleagues, she rarely sought publicity and did everything she could to avoid it. "On stage she was like a queen," Miss Higgins says, "but off stage she was like a child." For nearly a decade she was one of the most beloved stars in Chicago's operatic firmament.

Another newcomer was mezzo-soprano Louise Homer, who came to the company in 1922 as a guest artist. She made her debut as Azucena.

Wrote the *Tribune*, "Never in this generation was there such a marvel of a voice."

And there was Feodor Chaliapin, who came for the title role of Boito's *Mefistofele* and left audiences practically gasping for breath. The *Tribune* said flatly, "At last the climax has been reached. Feodor Chaliapin appeared with the Chicago Opera last night." He stood six feet four inches tall, his "muscles rolling and rippling and knotting with every movement he makes, every inch and every ounce of him he-man." He appeared in the first act of *Mefistofele* in the gray robe of a friar, made neither sound nor gesture, walked and looked, but so dominated the scene that Moore claimed in his review that the other singers, good ones, were completely forgotten. He directed the staging of the "Brocken Scene" himself and made it unforgettable—the singer, half-naked, a giant monument of a man, towering over the shrieking chorus as it went about its frenzied diabolical spree. Moore claimed, "It was by all odds the best stage scene I have ever witnessed in opera."

A little earlier Chicagoans had been introduced to *Sniegurotchka* (*Snow Maiden*), the opera that had been planned for the year before but was canceled when no music could be found. "If the Chicago Civic Opera company does nothing else notable for the rest of the season . . . it would still have justified its right to exist from the manner in which it brought out Nicolai Andreyevitch Rimsky-Korsakov's *Sniegurotchka* at the Auditorium last night," Moore said. Edith Mason, who starred in the production, remembered it forty years later as one of the loveliest things the Chicago Opera ever did. The opera was staged six times in 1922–23 and repeated the next year, as compared with the two, or at most three, performances given novelties during the McCormick era.

German opera was only slightly in evidence that season, and what there was, was met by a generally unresponsive public. "The officials of the Civic Opera discovered," commented the *Tribune*, "that if [for] any reason they desired an audience too small to pay the running expense of the day, the way to get it was to put on a Wagner opera." *Parsifal* and *Die Walküre* both played to such poor houses that performances of *Tannhäuser* announced earlier in the season were withdrawn.

Even the French works were considerably deemphasized, leaving the repertoire heavily weighted in favor of the Italian wing. This would consistently be the case with the Civic Opera, although in varying degrees. In 1922–23, eighteen Italian operas, four French, two German, and one English (the world premiere of Theodore Stearns' *Snowbird*) were staged, as contrasted with the thirteen Italian, thirteen French, and three German operas given during the Mary Garden year.

Every effort had been made to adhere as closely as possible to the safe, popular repertoire. Although attendance was generally good, by the end of the season there was much indication that the public was dissatisfied with not seeing more novelties. While there had been slight attendance at the German operas, the public did seem to miss the French. The *Tribune* received one letter stating irately, "We subscribers did not put our money down to hear practically nothing but Italian opera and Italian artists."

There was also some feeling that perhaps the atmosphere around the Auditorium had become too businesslike for the best artistic results. From the beginning a number of the artists were heard to grumble that Insull's business techniques might be all right in his utilities companies, but they were certainly ruining the Chicago Opera. Edward Moore observed, "One finds the prevalent comment about the Auditorium to be: 'See what a fine box office statement we have,' instead of: 'See what a fine performance we are giving to justify a fine box-office statement.' " Summing up the season, the critic felt that the new budget system had definitely limited the artistic resources of the company, creating a number of problems. The tenor section, for instance, was distinctly weak. The corps de ballet had been cut back to the point that the ballet in *La Juive* had to be omitted. Funds for costuming had been so sharply cut that wigs on occasions had to be forgotten. And despite the presence of the great Chaliapin, the basso's finest role, Boris Godunov, could not be staged for him, as the company had no scenery for it and was unwilling to part with the funds to have some made. Still the season ended with a deficit of $350,000 (the same as it had been just prior to the extravagant Garden year), necessitating the calling of 70 per cent of the pledged guaranty.

Disappointment had been so great over the company's failure to stage *Boris Godunov* in 1922–23 that it was decided to open the season with it the following year. It was sung in Italian, save for the leading part, with Chaliapin in the title role, and given with splendid new scenery and 352 new costumes. "What a combination it was!" wrote Edward Moore. "It was color, pageantry, drama, music, and a singing actor in the principal role who started a thrill with every tone and even gesture." The basso made his entrance surrounded by the cheering Russian populace and the sound of pealing bells. He descended the steps of the cathedral, gigantic, sinister, morose, walking with preoccupied steps. His death scene was incomparable. "It may be that one of these days or years," Moore continued in his review, "the Civic Opera company will be able to bring out something mightier, something more magnificent in picture and music. But last night's achievement so far surpassed anything that has been done before that the company has set a difficult record to equal."

Boris opened in a refurbished Auditorium, painted now gray and gold.

For a number of years the interior had been a glowing ruby hue, and everyone seemed rather happy about the return to something approaching the original color scheme. "It looks once more like a shrine place of the arts instead of a grandiose hotel lobby," said the *Tribune*. The stage curtain remained gold, but was also new.

It was decided to open the season on a Thursday night rather than the usual Monday in an attempt to convince the social set that Monday night, the traditional dress night in Chicago, was no longer the only time to attend. Capacity seating at the Auditorium was then 3,650, but somehow 3,700 people were admitted for *Boris*, and more people were turned away from the box office than had ever before been the case for a Chicago opening. "Civic opera, I think," said Samuel Insull, "now has a place of its own in the affections of the mass of our people." So confident of this was Insull that he extended the season from ten to eleven and a half weeks.

The movies had become immensely popular by this time, a formidable competition for all other entertainment forms. Even opera undoubtedly lost a certain number of patrons nightly to Mary Pickford, Lon Chaney, and William S. Hart, yet in absolute numbers attendance at both mediums continued to improve—and this despite the rapid development of radio. More people were becoming entertainment-conscious, and to an extent one entertainment form tended to stimulate the others. It is unlikely that many moviegoers left a William S. Hart Western eager to compare it with Puccini's *The Girl of the Golden West*, but the movies did get people to go out at night, caused them to become more theater-conscious, and therefore indirectly stimulated a greater interest in all entertainment —opera ultimately, if not immediately. With the city's population growing, and with a general increase in the nation's standard of living, Chicago's theatrical enterprises could all look forward to generally good times in the middle twenties.

Businesses in the twenties discovered the power of advertising, employing every device from the singing commercial to the highway billboard. Opera, particularly opera run in the businesslike manner in which Insull ran his, could hardly remain immune. A simple announcement of *Faust*, listing cast and conductor, would no longer do. Instead, a *Tribune* advertisement read:

HE SOLD HIS SOUL
TO BE YOUNG AGAIN

but he had to pay. In the end "Faust"
belonged to The Devil. He took his fill
of the fleshpots of the world and
Mephistopheles took him.

Massenet's *Cléopâtre* was repeated for Mary Garden, given more shockingly than ever before. "After many years of study and thought," wrote Edward Moore the next day, "I have at last learned why they give grand opera in foreign languages. It is so that they may present Massenet's *Cléopâtre*... without danger of police interference." The critic even hesitated to dwell on the details of the performance "in the columns of a newspaper intended for general circulation." One finds them, he said, "in medical works, or perhaps in the unexpurgated Arabian Nights." American producers, the critic felt, had never been known for their lack of daring in presenting scenes that tended to make audiences sit up and take notice. "Yet as far as I know, no American producer has ever had the temerity to present anything as raw as was offered upon the Auditorium stage last night.... Compared to it, the *Salome* of a few years past was a demure and inexperienced young flapper." Aside from the more sensational aspects of the performance, Moore concluded, "there are memories of much scenery, colorful costumes, and the most appalling score that was ever perpetrated. Never did much come nearer to registering absolute zero than in the music of *Cléopâtre*. Mary Garden's voice... could neither help nor harm it."

Claudia Muzio did *La Traviata*, probably her greatest role, in Chicago for the first time that season. She was perfect for the part in practically every respect, and her beautiful, somber eyes reflected all of Violetta's anguish and passion. Wrote *Music News*, "The laughter and sobs tremble on her notes and are drawn from the profoundest depths of herself, thus giving them a persuasive force which is unresistible." Herman Devries, critic for the Chicago *Evening American*, pronounced her "without doubt the greatest Violetta of them all." She also did *Andrea Chénier* in 1923 and got so wrapped up in her role that during one performance she actually fainted in the third act when she was torn from the arms of the condemned Chénier.

Meyerbeer's *L'Africaine*, sung in Italian, was given for the first time by Chicago's own opera company, but despite the presence of Raisa, Marshall, and Macbeth, it somehow seemed old and decrepit. "At present it has an aria that is sometimes used in a tenor song recital," wrote Edward Moore, "but not a tune that has ever reached the distinction of being refurbished into a jazz record." The scenery reflected more of the company's budget-cutting, for it was simply a composite of sets already in the warehouse.

And there were other indications of a continued tightening up on finances. Most obvious perhaps was the need for additional rehearsal. Humperdinck's *Königskinder*, for instance, was flagrantly under-rehearsed, although Claire Dux herself scored quite a personal triumph in the lead. As the *Tribune* described the second act, "The Hellabrunn clock struck the hour of noon, the gates of the city were opened, and there stood a goose girl, golden crown on golden hair, her geese waddling and cackling about her feet, a scene that by its complete simplicity and sincerity was one to touch the heart and live in the memory."

The Chicago Symphony's Frederick Stock conducted for the opera company for the first time. The opera was *Siegfried*, given in a highly shortened—but fairly successful—version. It was the only Wagner in the repertoire that season.

This was Galli-Curci's last year with the company. She and Polacco had gotten into an unfortunate argument before the season began regarding the vehicle for her first Chicago appearance. Galli-Curci preferred *Dinorah*, but the conductor wanted *Lakmé*. She complained about being treated in a "curt, high-handed manner" and appealed to Insull. When Insull stuck by Polacco, she was furious. "I do not hold one of 'Big Tim' Murphy's cards," she fumed, "and I cannot be ordered about like a gas house worker. I will not submit to the steam roller tactics of Mr. Insull." But Insull insisted she had agreed to open in *Lakmé*, then changed her mind. When it became clear that the company's decision would stand, Galli-Curci telegraphed Insull: "I am obliged to accept your decision inasmuch as I am bound to the company for this season. I deem it but fair, however, to inform you at this time... I shall not be with the company next season."

The press took up the controversy, with editorials appearing on both sides. A poll, taken in streetcars, offices, stores, and elevated trains, revealed that the public was solidly behind Galli-Curci. "They'd be crazy to let her get away from Chicago," seemed the general consensus. Insull showed no signs of budging in the argument, but did say he hoped the soprano would exercise a woman's prerogative and change her mind. When Mary Garden was asked what she thought of the situation, she threw back her head, laughed, and said simply, "Oh, they're all crazy."

When Galli-Curci actually appeared on the scene, she sang *Lakmé* and was met by unanimous applause. Her entrance interrupted the performance for several minutes, and it could not continue until she stepped out of character and walked down to the footlights. She sang better than she had in years, and her audiences were at capacity all season long. When she sang Rosina in *The Barber of Seville*, the company's "no encore" rule had to be broken after the "Lesson Scene," one of Galli-Curci's most charming moments. She always interpolated "Home, Sweet Home" in the scene, in place of Rossini's original music, accompanying herself on the spinet. Audiences never seemed to tire of it. Visually, too, the scene was quite thrilling. As the *Tribune* reported it, "Here the brilliant red and yellow of Mme. Galli-Curci's second act costume was given a background of lavender walls and rose curtains, the whole comprising an eruption of color that tended to set the teeth on edge."

The soprano's last appearance with the Civic Opera was as Juliet, and she sang it as she never had before. Her Romeo was Charles Hackett, who had made his debut with the company a little earlier in the season. Fervid applause for the departing singer broke out at every possible place. An adding machine would have been necessary to keep track of the curtain calls which followed every scene, and at the end even the soprano herself had tears in her eyes. Said Edward Moore the next day, "Galli-Curci came to Chicago to be greeted by a blaze of enthusiasm. She went out the same way. Addio, Amelita."

Aside from the loss of one of Chicago's most popular artists, the Galli-Curci farewell illustrates a point that a number of critics were beginning to make. That was that the company had become increasingly addicted to the "star system." "Nowadays, whatever may be the official pronouncement," said the *Tribune*, "the bystander thinks of Chicago opera as being chiefly a matter of stars, and more particularly because the present officials walk a safely conservative path on the matter of repertoire."

The repertoire in 1923–24 was less heavily weighted in favor of the Italian works than had been the case the year before, although they still predominated. The listing showed nineteen Italian operas, twelve French, two English, and two German. Some thought the list too long, which it probably was if each opera were to be rehearsed as it should be. *Music News* objected to the ever present sound of the prompter's voice, but added that this was probably "entirely an unavoidable adjunct to a season where so many operas are presented."

The 1924 spring tour found the company going first to Boston for two weeks, then Cleveland, Pittsburgh, Detroit, Cincinnati, Chattanooga, Tulsa, Houston, Dallas, Los Angeles, San Francisco, Portland, Seattle, Salt Lake City, Denver, Wichita, and finally Kansas City. It traveled some 9,957 miles within eight weeks. A survey of the books reveals that the total income for the year was $1,510,515.86–$861,127.14 coming from the ninety-one performances in Chicago and $64,388.72 from the sixty-one on tour. The season's deficit amounted to $326,759.25, over $23,000 less than the year before. During the Chicago season 50,252 more persons attended the opera this year than last, with an increase in receipts of $143,965.53.

Summertime was a time for building new sets and repairing old, sewing new costumes and mending old. The company had its own warehouse on Wabash Avenue, where scenery was stored and costumes, including wigs, shoes, armor, spears, and battle axes were made. Occasionally sets were painted there, but more frequently this work was done in the Auditorium. A temporary flooring was put down over the downstairs seating circle, so that big canvasses could be spread out and worked on. When the company built a new, larger warehouse a year later at Dearborn and Twenty-sixth Streets, even the most space-consuming work could be done there.

By the fall of 1924 the crossword puzzle had become a national pastime, even more popular than Mah-Jongg. Chicago had been shocked, along with the rest of the nation, at the murder of little Bobby Franks and was awaiting the trial of his accused murderers, Leopold and Loeb. On Tuesday, November 4, Calvin Coolidge was reelected President of the United States in a landslide victory over Democrat John W. Davis. The country's new Vice-President was the Civic Opera's own Charles G. Dawes.

The Chicago opera season opened the day after the election with Rosa Raisa's masterly portrayal of Ponchielli's *La Gioconda.* According to *Music News*, she "sang as one inspired and looked like a goddess." The occasion proved almost a festival in celebration of the Republican victory. "On last Tuesday," reported the *Tribune,* "we all went to the polls, and having accomplished there the highly desirable result, we went with light heart on Wednesday to the opening performance of Chicago's great opera season."

The house was packed. Opening nights usually were, but the company was not taking any chances nowadays. It had a full-time publicity agent, named Charles Isaacson, whose job was to convince more people, particularly those in the suburbs, to attend the opera. Isaacson went about his campaign so energetically that he himself missed the opening performance.

Fashion now decreed that the ladies wear gowns of pastel or black, gleaming with crystal and perhaps caught low on one hip with a puff of ostrich feathers. Most gowns were sleeveless with a V-neckline, likely to be quite low in back. Wraps were either velvet with upstanding collars of fur, metal with a velvet lining, or embroidered, fringed shawls, which were wound about the figure or flung over one shoulder. Hosiery, if the ultimate in stylishness, was of gold or silver, actually woven of metal threads. These sold for fifteen dollars a pair. Bands for the bobbed head now had elastic at the back to make them easy to adjust and were fashioned to give the effect of a rhinestone tiara. These were priced at twenty dollars. Silver or gold tinsel, with an undertone of jade or orchid, was prominent in evening shoes. Gloves were either kid or suede, and, if they were of the approved length, were trimmed with twenty buttons.

Harold McCormick was in Europe now with his new wife, Ganna Walska. The operation he had hoped would rejuvenate him had failed. Edith Rockefeller McCormick was back in Chicago, after having spent some time in Switzerland, and was a regular patron at the Auditorium, lending some of the old social air to the season. Both McCormicks were still members of the company's Board of Trustees.

Mary Garden continued to entrance audiences and amaze critics. A new role, or rather one sung again after many years, was Charlotte in Massenet's *Werther*, a part which suited her very well. "*Werther*, heretofore voted the very dullest of operas," said *Music News*, "proved at this time to be a veritable delight." The *Tribune* insisted that Mary actually looked twenty-five. Particularly effective was the scene in which Charlotte romps with her small brothers and sisters. One of the little girls who played in the scene apparently discovered something about Mary Garden that everyone else had missed. The girl was called upon to give Mary a kiss on stage. When her little friends found out about this, they were quite jealous and asked her to give Mary a kiss for them. "Oh, I don't know," the young actress replied, her face becoming serious. "Miss Garden's terribly shy."

The old Garden roles were still immensely popular. The public flocked to *Thaïs* every time it was staged, although critics were beginning to indicate it was wearing a little thin with them. The role reviewers were taking Garden most to task for was Carmen. Some said she overacted the part; others insisted it just did not suit her. *Le Jongleur de Notre Dame*, however, everyone seemed to like. And *L'Amore dei Tre Re* was another perennial favorite. Mary spent the last twenty minutes of this opera with her head hanging over the end of a bench, playing dead. She always did it herself, refusing to let an understudy take her place. A game which some of the opera circle sometimes played at parties was called: "What Does Mary Garden Think About All the Time She's Lying There Supposedly Dead?"

A tenor with whom Garden was singing frequently these days was José Mojica, sometimes called "the Rudolph Valentino of opera." Mojica was young, Mexican, strikingly handsome, and the possessor of a unique sense of characterization and costume. Commenting on his performance of Pelléas, the Chicago *Evening American* said, "He was at all times a picturesque figure, adolescent, with the halting grace of adolescence, beautifully bewigged and well costumed, acting with ease and considerable personal dignity." Operatic lore has it that he was so gorgeously costumed as Nicias in *Thaïs* that once a couple of infrequent operagoers were astonished when Mary Garden appeared on the scene. They had assumed Mojica was the leading lady. He had a way of turning small parts into important ones, even quite minor roles like the marriage broker in *Madama Butterfly* and Narraboth in *Salome*. He later tried his hand at movies, then eventually went off to Peru to become a Franciscan friar.

An impressive newcomer that season was coloratura Toti Dal Monte, a small, plumpish woman, with beautiful eyes and a winning smile, who made her local debut in *Lucia di Lammermoor*. During a later performance of the opera, Dal Monte disagreed with the tempo of the conductor, waddled down to the footlights, and led the orchestra with a reproachful forefinger.

A young Chicago girl named Gladys Swarthout made her first appearances with the company, singing such roles as Mercedes in *Carmen*, the shepherd in *Tosca*, Myrtale in *Thaïs*, and the Sandman in *Hänsel und Gretel*. She was a radiant, charming girl, beautiful in face and figure. An eager student, she attended virtually every rehearsal, taking in every little detail. Rarely was she seen around the Auditorium without a half dozen different scores under her arm. Reviewing her Siebel in *Faust*, *Music News* wrote, "That Miss Swarthout should so quickly have overcome every trace of amateurishness and that she can, today, appear with such poise and to such splendid advantage even in the most distinguished company afforded by the Chicago Civic Opera is nothing short of marvelous." During rehearsals one day a cry of "Swarthout!" went up. "Where's Swarthout?" It was Mary Garden. Young Swarthout appeared before Mary meek as could be, fearing she had done something dreadfully wrong. Garden threw her shawl to the young mezzo, predicting that she would be the next great Carmen.

Two novelties that year were Meyerbeer's *Le Prophète* and Bizet's *The Pearl Fishers*. Neither was especially successful, the first suffering seriously from haphazard stage direction. Claudia Muzio added *Tosca* to her Chicago repertoire, again proving herself one of the most stage-wise singers around. Edith Mason repeated *Madama Butterfly*, using her own small daughter as the child, Trouble. The little girl almost stole the show, particularly when she was heard to say in loud, clear English, "Mother. Don't cry, Mother."

Americans in the twenties had strong opinions on certain subjects and these the opera reflected. Nowhere was the spirit of the times any more clearly revealed than in the question of opera in English. The argument over the desirability of presenting opera in translation is practically as old as the art itself. It has been debated by every generation, and at present we are no closer to a definitive position than critics were in the 1850's when the English Opera Troupe first set off the controversy in Chicago. But in the 1920's, when Americans were thoroughly disillusioned in foreign affairs and strongly isolationist in sympathy, when we tended to view everything in terms of an exaggerated patriotism, it was inevitable that the age-old dispute over opera in English be magnified into the burning issue facing the American operagoer. The overwhelming foreign element in the opera was simply too incompatible with the nativism of the times for the situation to be otherwise. By 1924 the debate had become heated.

Even better than opera in English, it was felt, would be to concentrate on strictly American-composed opera. But even the most radical on the subject recognized that this might take a while. "Every American opera should be tried out to a finish," wrote *Music News*, "and eventually we should attain a nationalistic repertoire. And meantime, just as rapidly as we can get really good translations (and they are coming) we should insist upon our opera being translated." Why should we insist on our opera being translated? *Music News* gave two reasons: "(1) because we want nationalism in this country, and (2) because we want our own artists here to have at least an equal chance with the artists of other countries." Notice that no mention is made of the possible advantage of understanding the text.

Time and again the complaint was raised to the effect that "the only thing wrong with last night's performance was that it wasn't sung in English." After a production of Auber's *Fra Diavolo*, *Music News* said, "To sit and calmly accept an opera such as this in any other language than our own is certainly the mark of such indifference on our part as almost to label us unintelligent." For several years a column appeared in *Music News* supposedly written by a visitor from a small town in Washington who called himself Uncle Ned. Uncle Ned was presented as a country bumpkin, somewhat overawed by the big city. His questioning of certain practices was supposed to have the same effect on Chicago's musical scene that Montesquieu's *Persian Letters* had had upon eighteenth-century French society. "I wondered," Uncle Ned wrote in mock simplicity, "until the end of the opera why you people of Chicago will sit, night after night, in expensive opera seats and submit to having stories played before you in foreign languages." He later said he was tired of Italians all around him laughing at comic opera and his not understanding a word of what was going on.

Why was opera not given in English? Critic and librettist Charles Henry Meltzer in a letter written to the *Tribune* focused on two reasons. First, he said, American audiences are snobs and think it a mark of sophistication to listen to opera in a foreign language. Second, and more important, the foreign artists refuse to sing in English, are totally "out of sympathy with American aspirations," and are "hungry to protect the virtual monopoly which they have, God knows why, been permitted to possess here." Meltzer confessed that he, like Insull, was British-born. "But," he insisted, "I will fight till I drop for American art in America and for the use of our own tongue in opera."

When the *Tribune's* Edward Moore was brought into the controversy, he at first steered a rather conservative path, stating that he felt most of the public cared far more for tunes and personalities than for the language the opera was sung in. "This department," he wrote, "remains a bit skeptical about anything but big names in opera being enough of a magnet to make opera possible." Immediately after his views were printed, Moore was besieged with letters informing him in no uncertain terms that his "tunes and personalities, not words" thesis (as he later called it) was wrong. One letter even insisted that opera should be translated not into English, but American. The critic's answer to that was that if *Cavalleria Rusticana* were ever translated into American, Alfio's song of the teamster would surely go:

> With differential banging
> And timing gear clanging,
> With three cylinders missing, hurrah!

But even Moore was forced to admit, "That the advocates of translated opera have all the logic on their side is . . . unquestionable."

Whenever an occasional opera was given in English, as *Hänsel und Gretel* was in 1924–25, critics went out of their way to praise the effectiveness of the translation. Greeted no less warmly were appearances by American artists. Whenever singers like Forrest Lamont sang, reviewers seemed compelled to mention that they were Americans. When a Chicago girl named Helen Freund made her debut with the company as Mary Garden's oldest sister in *Werther*, the critics praised everything she did. "One thing for which we must very especially commend her was her refusal to come on to acknowledge applause even though this was continued almost indefinitely," *Music News* asserted. "That is lack of artistic feeling which is often shown by foreigners of the Chicago Opera Company, but one of which no intelligent young American girl should ever be guilty."

Even more exuberantly hailed was Henry G. Weber, a twenty-three-year-old Chicago boy who made his debut with the company conducting a performance of *Tannhäuser*. His success was genuine, and as his later career verified, richly deserved. But *Music News* could not resist editorializing, "This ovation and the interest in Mr. Weber's work throughout were sufficient to prove once and for all time that American audiences (especially Chicago audiences) are more than ready to listen to American artists and that, being given the opportunity, they recognize the merit and are ready to applaud their excellent points."

If for some reason American singers were not treated kindly by the press, there always seemed to be a ready alibi to explain why the artist had not shone brilliantly. When Louise Taylor, for example, sang with the company, critics agreed she had not performed particularly well, but insisted she had been miscast. When Mary McCormic won bad reviews for *Faust*, it was said the fault was not hers, but Chaliapin's. The basso, critics insisted, had monopolized the stage and introduced so much extraneous buffoonery that McCormic did not have a chance.

Many complained that American singers were being sacrificed in favor of the foreigners—foreigners who, in some cases, so it was said, were decidedly inferior. *Music News* pointed a condemning finger at both Toti Dal Monte and Elvira de Hidalgo (later the teacher of Maria Callas), calling them "good routined opera singers, but decidedly passé in both cases and not to be compared with singers who have been neglected because of their engagement." There were even rumors afloat that foreign artists were conspiring against the American singers, and according to *The Musical Leader*, all sorts of foreign intrigue had been going on backstage.

Even the most ardent proponents of opera in English recognized that translations could not be given successfully until singers, native and foreign, were trained to sing English clearly and intelligently. Some said the foreigners could never learn the language well enough to be understood. But *Music News* insisted, "The really fine artists could learn English if they were asked to do it and if the minor artists could (and would) not then they should (and would) be deposed in favor of Americans."

There seemed to be some feeling that the lack of a native school of opera was an anachronism out of keeping with America's present role as a world power. "America is invited today to sit in all international councils, political and business," said *Music News*, "simply because in those lines we are national and characteristically strong. In music we are despised simply because we have not developed a national music and are content to accept French, Italian, and German operas as better than our own and the French, Italian, and German languages as finer than English."

Determined to prove American superiority in every endeavor, we became highly sensitive about our national image, tender to the slightest possible criticism. After viewing a performance of *Madama Butterfly*, Uncle Ned suggested, "I wondered if it was very good loyalty to have these bits [of the "Star-Spangled Banner"] appear as the Pinkerton motif . . . for if Pinkerton was a fair representation of American men, then God help the rest of us!"

But there were other problems facing the Civic Opera and a number of rather serious criticisms, only part of them justified. Almost everyone agreed the company's stage management had become perfunctory at best, except in those cases where a Garden or a Chaliapin had taken charge and impressed their ideas upon the production. At times the stage picture appeared downright slovenly. Complaints were raised that the stage director could often be seen and heard in the wings giving instructions to the people on stage at the top of his voice, swinging his arms to demonstrate his point, and that at other times the chorus master could be seen in the wings with his baton, beating out the time for his singers. Once as the curtain opened on the "Fair Scene" in *Martha,* three stagehands were discovered in the center of the stage hard at work. Their dash out of view was so comical that the audience broke into gales of laughter, and the scene was pretty well spoiled. The ballet was definitely weak, and there were still too many operas given, with too little rehearsal. The French wing was deteriorating badly, and the company was relying even more heavily on popular favorites. The limitations necessitated by the management's rigid bookkeeping system continued to have certain adverse effects and resulted in some rather unusual practices. For a time, for instance, the management offered the same opera on Saturday afternoon and Saturday night to save money on hauling and installing scenery.

Yet even with such a close eye on the budget, the season ended with a deficit of $400,000, a substantial increase over the year before. Although attendance was advancing faster than expenses, there were those who complained that the deficit was too high and the season too long. "This year," said one *Tribune* editorial, "Mr. Samuel Insull prolonged the period to eleven and a half [weeks]. Suffering Rotarians, nearly three months! Mr. Insull is a wizard. He knows how to do it better with gas. Some... may have wished at times he would." To prove just how bad things had gotten, the critic recalled glorious days of the past, remembering them perhaps a bit more gloriously than they actually were: "Here in Chicago the grand days of grand opera were back in the years when the New York company came out for a month with Pol Plançon, the De Reszkes, Melba, Eames, and the rest of the old galaxy. Four weeks was enough. It was a crowded month, but the shopworn citizen could stand it. The wives bought their new wraps. They came in from the neighboring towns and bought them. Business was good along the street and at the box office." The writer objected to the linking of the opera with civic duty, saying that not to attend somehow was "to commit a civic offense and be carried off on a floodtide of wrath from cultural uplifters, friends of opera, city boosters, music-loving aliens, display-loving wives, and all the milliners, jewelers, modistes, etc." He even insisted that the Opera had killed off practically all other theatrical activity in the city, since there was no "civic stuff" backing the rest. "A citizen can't go to the theater if his wife has him at the end of a chain at opera two or three times a week. His cultural cosmos might be widened and made happier in the theater, but evenings find him asleep in the dark on the arm of an opera seat." The lengthening of the opera season had simply made a bad situation worse, the critic said. "The citizen who takes his culture from his wife found himself getting into the harness two or three times a week. The oak leaves were just falling when he began, and when he was released it was about time to look for hepatica. He wore out two sets of harness and a new pair of chains."

The *Tribune* editorial even cast some doubt on Insull's business efficiency, at least as applied to the opera. "If business managed opera as well as it manages baseball, the operatic talent would be thoroughly disciplined, and many communities would be served with the best. Babe Ruth plays in eight cities in the season. The management of his team could sell him, if it were crazy enough to want to, and he'd bring a big price. . . . Mr. Insull lost Galli-Curci, just lost her, and didn't get a penny when New York took her. It's all wrong and Chicago's out $400,000 in a season which never had a chance." In this age of business prosperity, any deficit was suspect, and there seemed to be a feeling that if American ingenuity were really put to it, the whole thing could be wiped out. "Opera, as is," the *Tribune* wrote, "requires a subsidy whether it gets it from mad citizens or mad kings."

The editorial even charged that the Chicago Civic Opera "wasn't civic and it wasn't grand." Critics praised the opera, the indignant writer said, because they dared not do otherwise. "If it is awful, the critic must find an aria to praise. If it is mediocre, he must say it is good, and if it happens to be good, it must be superlative."

That this particular position was extreme there is little doubt, but the fact remains that the 1924–25 season did produce a barrage of criticism, which *Musical America*, *Musical Courier*, *The Literary Digest*, and others felt compelled to report. *Music News* agreed that there had been more complaints from the public than usual, but explained it as "merely an expression of that independent Americanism which has been born and is now growing toward the strength of youth and full stature and which is only a part of the change and the growth of the world in general." Still *Music News*, the most chauvinistic of the music journals, did not agree that the Civic Opera was deteriorating and maintained that any loss of interest the Opera had suffered could be rectified by the greater application of American business principles and by employing more American operas and English translations of the standard repertoire. "There is no reason at all why we should not now have businesslike opera and Americanized opera."

At the end of three seasons, Insull could look back on a number of artistic successes, substantial increases in attendance, and, in a world of rising costs, relatively moderate deficits. While his company had its share of weaknesses, Insull found himself in the uncomfortable position of being attacked from both sides. On the one hand, artists, professional critics, and serious operagoers were saying that his strict fiscal policy was stifling creativity and high production standards. On the other, it was being suggested that the season was too long and the deficits too large, almost un-American. The latter seemed to feel, to wrench a phrase from Al Smith, that the only cure for the ills of American opera was not, in this case, more opera, but greater Americanism. And so it went for another half decade.

Chapter 9

COME, BLOW YOUR HORN!

NOVEMBER, 1925, found Chicago, like the country as a whole, enjoying the greatest prosperity it had ever known. The farmer was still suffering, as he had been since the Civil War, but the stock market broke a ten-year record that month. Automobiles could now be bought for $195 down, the balance "conveniently arranged." As a result of an unprecedented advertising build-up, more people were beginning to think about owning land in Florida, where again easy terms could be arranged. Prohibition had produced the speakeasy, which in turn had produced the racketeer. The younger generation was still causing alarm among the older folk, so much so that a special conference was held that month to discuss the revolt of the youth. Increased attention was being given to psychiatry and personal freedom and the breakdown of moral taboos. The intellectual set was taking great interest in a new magazine called the *American Mercury*, in which H. L. Mencken insisted that the masses were yokels and boobs and that America, their paradise, provided "the only really amusing form of government ever endured by mankind." Sinclair Lewis' *Babbitt* was still widely read, but was being edged off the best-seller list by F. Scott Fitzgerald's *The Great Gatsby*. Jeanne Eagels was in town, starring in *Rain* at the Harris Theater. Vilma Banky's first film, *The Dark Angel*, was playing, and Red Grange was the pride of the Illinois backfield.

The Chicago Opera opened that fall with the local premiere of Richard Strauss's *Der Rosenkavalier*, a dozen years after its first American staging at the Metropolitan. By all accounts it was quite an occasion. "Once more the trumpet blares and the drum rolls; the dulcet strain of the ballyhoo resounds," commented the *Tribune*. Charles Dawes came out from Washington for the event. While most of the city's social leaders were present, there seemed to be more young married couples in the audience than ever before.

Der Rosenkavalier, featuring Rosa Raisa as the Marschallin, Edith Mason as Sophie, Olga Forrai as Octavian, and Alexander Kipnis as Ochs, was given a generally enthusiastic reception. Edward Moore said, "If the Chicago Civic Opera really wants to sell itself to the public, and it has been known to express that desire, it might begin by presenting *Der Rosenkavalier* frequently and often. For opera, the precious, the exotic, the glorious, the glittering, came into our midst again last night." *Music News*, on the other hand, found it no more than "a fragile comedy," insisting that "Octavian is... listed much too young, for to ask us to accept the amours of a thirty-five year old princess with her seventeen year old relative is just too much, and it becomes ridiculous.... The disparity in the story ages is too great to permit anything but its humorous aspect to come to the front."

Everyone agreed, however, that *Rosenkavalier's* stage direction was superior to anything seen at the Auditorium in many a year. Charles Moor, who had won acclaim for his work in England and Germany, had been brought over from Europe to stage this one production, and he turned what easily could have been chaos into almost perfect harmony. "Any one who can put over as smooth and as logical and as attractive a performance as he," the *Tribune* wrote, "ought to be signed up at once for the remainder of his life." He was brought back the next year.

The company's repertoire was still mammoth for the relatively short season, consisting of thirty-two operas. Nineteen of these were Italian, eight French, three German, and two English. Insull was still waging an energetic campaign to make opera popular, employing salesmen and lecturers to help coax the public into attending. His most successful effort was the initiation of a "suburban" series on Sunday afternoons, with four dollars the top price.

Massenet's *Hérodiade* was given a revival that season with Edith Mason as Salome and Cyrena Van Gordon as Herodias. While the ladies may have walked off with most of the singing honors, Herod apparently had his compensations, as he sat "in his own apartment..., surrounded by the most lavish and ostentatious display of female legs and knees that the opera company has yet displayed." The curtain was held on one performance when one of the artists, baritone William Beck, failed to show up. When a search party was sent out to look for him, he was found dead in his hotel room. It was officially stated that he died of a stroke, but there were rumors that he became ill after drinking some wine he had received as a gift. The bottle was taken for examination, but its contents disappeared before the chemist could complete his analysis.

Raisa gave one of her rare performances in *Madama Butterfly*, evoking such heartfelt emotion that people openly wiped their eyes unashamed. *Manon Lescaut* was given, for the first time in fourteen years, with Claudia Muzio. After the performance Edward Moore wrote, "If you can keep your eyes off her when she is in the scene, you can do more than I." Reviewing a production of *Pagliacci*, Moore said, "Claudia Muzio is to all other Neddas as a limousine to a baby carriage."

Louise Homer sang *Samson and Delilah*, and Toti Dal Monte did *The Barber of Seville*. American baritone Richard Bonelli made his local debut as the elder Germont during one of the Sunday-afternoon performances. And Marguerite D'Alvarez returned to the city, after an absence of several years, to sing *Carmen*. In her autobiography Mme. D'Alvarez remembers her days in Chicago fondly and comments on a problem which the city was becoming all too familiar with as the twenties wore on. "I loved Chicago," she writes, "as I think do all artists—the windy city, so evil and interesting, cleansed, I felt, by its mysterious lake and daily hurricanes. It is the rendezvous of most of the American gangsters, and perhaps those winds also help to purify their torpid minds. The lake has been the cemetery of many of their victims, but unlike the seas with her tides, she does not give up her dead."

Mary Garden's entrance into the city, of course, made news. She came with jingling beads and bracelets and smelling of French perfume. She kissed a baby, joked with a porter, and settled down to talk with reporters. She, like a number of other people who would later change their minds, was then quite enthusiastic about Benito Mussolini. "A wonderful man," said Garden. "So aggressive, so cleancut in his wishes and the execution of those wishes. He might be a descendant, or even, the incarnation of Napoleon." She talked much of the Russian "choo-choo" train she had brought along for *Resurrection*, the Alfano opera she was to sing that season. "Mary Garden," the *Tribune* mused, "as difficult of classification as a French verb."

The American premiere of *Resurrection* was staged at the Auditorium on New Year's Eve. The opera, based on a portion of Tolstoi's novel, was written in Italian, but sung by the Civic Opera in French. The part of Katusha, which she sang in Chicago for the first time anywhere, was one of the best of the later Garden roles and one of her favorites. Its dramatic possibilities suited her. Says Mary in her autobiography, "Oh, how I adored that opera! That poor girl's innocence, her disillusionment with men, her crime and imprisonment, and the final resurrection of her soul. Each act was different, each about a different woman, really. . . . Perhaps that fascinated me most of all, how I managed to be so many women and so many voices in one opera."

In the first act Katusha is wooed, won, and seduced by Prince Dimitri (sung in Chicago by Fernand Ansseau). Act II takes place six months later, when Katusha goes to a railroad station hoping to see the prince and explain matters to him. It is here she realizes that she has been nothing more than a plaything for him. The scene included the most realistic snowstorm ever put on the Auditorium stage and the appearance of the Russian "choo-choo" train that everyone was talking so much about. It turned out to be nothing more than a papier-mâché toy, which passed swiftly across the back of the stage.

Act III occurs in the prison at Petrograd. The prince discovers to his shock the drunken degradation into which the girl he had known several years before has fallen. He tries to redeem himself by proposing marriage, but is hysterically rejected by Katusha. As Garden played it, it was quite a scene. "I was never drunk," she writes in her autobiography, "yet there was Katusha . . . , hiding her bottles in her prison bed and getting drunk on vodka. At that moment I *was* drunk. There I lay on the floor when the prince came in, and he left me because he couldn't bear it any more. But before leaving, he put into my hands a photograph of my home when I was a child, and in my stupor I looked up and around like a real drunkard to see if anyone was in the place. Then I took the picture and suddenly I was myself, and in that drunken daze I cried hot tears."

In the last act Katusha is being taken in a train of prisoners to Siberia. The trip is long, and she is forced to submit to all sorts of mistreatment by the guards. The prince is following her, still determined to make amends. But Katusha has learned through her suffering and through her relationship with Simonson, a fellow prisoner, that it will be better for all concerned to let the prince go and link her life with Simonson's.

The scenery and costumes throughout were expertly done, except for the velvet dress and silk stockings which Garden wore in the last act, making it hard to believe that she had spent a month plodding toward Siberia.

A capacity house gave the opera a cordial welcome, declaring that Mary Garden had done it again. As *Music News* told it, "Deluge is the only word to express the applause that swept the theater as the last curtain descended, for artistically and vocally the production was a triumph." Everyone seemed to agree that Garden was in better voice than she had been in some time and that the role suited her beautifully. About Alfano's score, however, critics were more reserved. "The music of *Resurrection* is not, by any means, great music," wrote *Music News*, "but it has a cleverly curious knack of fitting the text with extreme nicety—there are moments of purely orchestral thrill, but the score is mostly uneven and sometimes blatantly common." Edward Moore was a bit more generous: "Alfano has composed some highly effective music of the theater." But even Moore agreed that without someone of Mary Garden's dramatic abilities *Resurrection* would be pretty pale, for certainly it was drama first and music second.* "That *Resurrection* of Alfano's is an acting opera," Garden writes in her autobiography, "and therefore you have to find someone who not only sings but who knows what drama is."

While Chicago's operagoers were spending their New Year's Eve, or at least a part of it, at the Auditorium listening to Mary Garden, the city as a whole was having itself quite a celebration. "Chicago last night had its little drink," the *Tribune* reported, "a considerable nip it was—and a New Year's eve more merry than usual." Every hotel dining room, night club, cabaret, and café in the city was positively crammed, reservations having been filled a week or two in advance. There was drinking in all of them, generally with a couple of prohibition agents in attendance. One of the chief means of getting around the law in the hotels was to reserve several guest rooms upstairs in advance. The liquor supply was kept there. Guests spent their time shuttling between the dinner table, the dance floor, and the upstairs rooms. In the Congress Hotel, next door to the Opera, there were 2,200 people in the dining room and 900 private parties in upstairs rooms. Waiters and bellhops were kept busy supplying ginger ale and ice. Down the street at the Blackstone, there were only 150 reservations downstairs, and a more sedate crowd could hardly be found. But upstairs 400 parties were in progress, and waiters spent the whole evening trotting from floor to floor in a steady stream. In the wee hours of the morning Major R. Q. Merrick, chief enforcement officer, announced with pride that not a single arrest had been made for drinking. "Apparently an army could drink so slyly as not to be caught," the *Tribune* remarked. It was also reported the next morning that one person had been killed and ten others wounded by stray bullets fired by celebrants as the new year came in.

Earlier in the season "Samoots" Amatuma, one of the city's most notorious bootleggers, stopped in a barber shop for a shave, a manicure, and a shoeshine. He was shot on his way out. When they picked him up, four tickets for that evening's opera were found in his pocket.

There was considerable talk around the Auditorium that year that perhaps opera could be made more popular if it were modernized. Some of the critics thought it might be a good idea. After viewing the com-

* Alfano himself considered the opera one of his more immature works. He had just completed the last scene of Puccini's *Turandot*, and at the time Chicago staged *Resurrection*, he was in grave danger of going blind.

pany's production of *Die Walküre*, Edward Moore gave some suggestions for how the Wagner drama might appear in a 1920's setting. "In *Die Walküre* we have Hunding, the perfect type of operatic Babbitt. He believes in one country, one scale of morals, and one wife at a time. In the modernized version, he comes home late in the afternoon to find that Siegmund, whom he has just run out of breath in a butter and egg deal on Main Street, has dropped in for a cup of tea and a cigaret with his wife. The exchange has closed for the day, so Hunding merely warns Siegmund that settlement time will be next morning, and goes to bed. The tea hound and the wife decide to elope." Sieglinde keeps Hunding quiet for the night by giving him "synthetic gin." When Hunding starts out in pursuit the next morning, he is checked by Wotan, "the political boss of the district." Brünnhilde emerges as an "apostle of feminine freedom," while the Valkyries become "a crowd of gossips at a country club."

Largely in response to the growing insistence upon opera in English, the world premieres of three "American" works were planned for the 1925–26 season: Franchetti's *Namiko-San*, Harling's *A Light from St. Agnes*, and Cadman's *A Witch of Salem*. Delays in the preparation of the latter finally forced its postponement until the next year.

Namiko-San barely qualified as an American opera, as its composer, Aldo Franchetti, was naturalized just days before the premiere. Every expedient was exhausted to hasten the completion of the proceedings so that his work might qualify as a native composition. And so it was that an opera set in medieval Japan, written by a naturalized Italian, but sung in English, came to be deemed an American opera.

Franchetti's work was based on a Japanese tragedy so gory that the composer thought it too much even for grand opera audiences. In the original, Namiko-San's head is severed by a machete and later, when she is touched, falls from her body and rolls across the stage. In the Franchetti version the heroine's death became less graphic. The title role was sung by Tamaki Miura, who had not been in Chicago for several seasons.

Advocates of opera in English were delighted with the Franchetti drama. But even *Music News* admitted that no more than 25 per cent of the text could be understood, insisting this would improve with repetition. "The Chicago company proved once and for all," the journal concluded, "that it can present opera in English and do it as well as any opera in Italian or French."

A Light from St. Agnes was more indigenous. The libretto was written by Mrs. Minnie Maddern Fiske and had originally been a one-act play in which Mrs. Fiske had acted. Its composer, W. Franke Harling, was an American song writer and one-time musical director at the United States military academy at West Point. Harling had gone on record as saying he felt jazz to be "the true American folk music," and his score contained a number of jazz effects.

The real heroine of the opera never appears on stage. She is Agnes Devereaux, who spent her life in a small community in Louisiana doing good. Before her death she built a chapel for her patron saint, and during the opera she is lying dead in her coffin in the chapel, its rose window looming over her in the background.

Both of the main characters had a jazz theme which suited his or her nature. "This was good musicianship and good drama," said Edward Moore, "consequently good opera. There was a little bit of saxophone in the orchestra, a smaller bit of xylophone, both of them needed to project the jazz theme." There was also some use of the banjo. "I sincerely believe," Moore continued, "that Mr. Harling has opened up the way for a legitimate and dramatic use of this much despised rhythm. As we say when we are among the best people, he has something. In fact he has a great deal."

The jazz motif had presented something of a problem, since most of the jazz musicians hired to augment the orchestra could not read the score and most of the regular orchestra members threw up their hands at trying to master the jazz technique. The composer conducted the performance.

During one of the curtain calls following the premiere, Raisa flung her arms around Harling's neck and gave him "a smack that sounded too sincere to be operatic." The opera-in-English enthusiasts in the audience decided this was a capital suggestion, and by the time the blushing composer managed to escape from the Auditorium, his wife acting as bodyguard, he had been kissed by admirers an estimated two hundred times. "If kisses measure a composer's success," the *Tribune* insisted, "W. Franke Harling is the most successful because [he is] the most bekissed American who ever wrote a grand opera."

By this time even Edward Moore, fairly conservative on the subject the year before, had been swung over to the idea of opera in English. Said he, "From this time on I shall decline to listen to any argument about the unsingability of English. . . . I know English can be sung plainly and that its sounds are entirely pleasant. I suspected this before, but this season it has been proved." *Music News* by now was giving free advertising space to any program given in Chicago or New York in which all items presented were either written by an American composer or sung in English translation.

The company faced a serious claque problem during the season, a number of singers actually being threatened that if they did not employ the claque, physical violence would result. The business office eventually issued a notice saying, "Ignore cajolery, but if direct threats are made to you, please inform the management."

Artistically, the company's greatest weakness was still the lack of stage direction. Charles Moor had done wonders with *Der Rosenkavalier*, but he had returned to Europe after the one production. Mary Garden had whipped things into shape for *Resurrection*, and Polacco had taken charge of the visual, as well as musical, effects of a splendid *Falstaff*, but with these exceptions most productions just sort of staged themselves and looked it. Lighting effects, traditionally one of the worst features of the Auditorium's productions, failed to operate on cue more times than not, or so it seemed. During one performance of *Hänsel und Gretel* the figure of the witch was supposed to be seen riding through the air. Thanks to some mechanical defect, the ride ended up about six times as long as it was supposed to be, producing gales of laughter from the audience. Critics also complained about the company's understudy system, which was practically nonexistent. Time and again operas had to be changed at the last minute because of the illness of a singer, sometimes quite a minor one.

On December 9, Samuel Insull addressed a group of five hundred businessmen at an Association of Commerce luncheon. It was then that he first bared his plans for the building of a new opera house. He reminded the group that the upcoming 1926–27 season would see the end of the five-year financial guaranty promised in 1922. A new fund drive would have to be launched. Despite the fact that the company had done everything possible to cut costs, unsubsidized opera, Insull said, seemed impossible. Still there was a way, he felt, of putting the Chicago Opera on a self-supporting basis. If an opera house were built on the ground level of a giant skyscraper, the upper regions of the building could be rented out as office space. The rental should eventually be sufficient to cover the inevitable operatic deficit. And so the first plans were laid for the structure that would eventually become 20 North Wacker Drive.

Late in January the company went on tour. Twenty-four baggage cars were needed to transport the scenery, while two special trains were chartered for the personnel. Rail fares for the tour totaled just under $85,000. As always, this cost the Civic Opera nothing, for these expenses were underwritten by the various cities visited.

That summer it was announced that the management had scored a real coup. Charles Moor had been hired as the permanent stage director. The transformation in the company's stage picture was noted as early as the 1926–27 opening. The opera was *Aida*, with Claudia Muzio in the title role. Muzio was great, but critics almost slighted the singers in their enthusiasm for the staging. "Suddenly the strange feature became clear," wrote Edward Moore. "The stage band was hidden from view, and there was not a pair of spectacles or eyeglasses in all the triumph scene, not even among the trumpeters. This was startling. Up to that time many years' attendance upon *Aida* had firmly convinced me that opticians drove a thriving trade in ancient Egypt." As the season progressed, evidences of Moor's accomplishments became even greater. "The good results of his being here are almost too numerous to classify," the *Tribune* wrote, "but bit by bit the situation is being cleared up. The choristers on the stage are now a disciplined group instead of a disorderly mob; spring, summer, and autumn flowers no longer appear together in the same garden scene; graven images have been banished from the home of Eleazar in *The Jewess;* lights answer to their cues. And if a mistake occurs in one performance, it is corrected the next time. In the old days the theory was apparently that a mistake should be continued until it had crystallized into a tradition."

The season had now been expanded to twelve weeks. Vanni Marcoux returned to the company after an absence of several years, and the Chicago *Herald-Examiner* called his *Boris Godunov* the greatest triumph of the season. "Towards the end of the last act," René Devries reported in *Musical Courier*, "just previous to the Czar's death, he had practically an epileptic fit—the entire body shaking, the jaw made stiff, the tongue paralyzed, the eyes dead even though bewildered, the cheeks sagged and we saw a hideous figure, a face tortured with physical and mental ills, a man whose agony was frightful." In *Faust* he threw tradition to the wind by appearing as Mephistopheles without a devil's costume, playing him instead as an elegant gentleman.

Henry Weber continued as Polacco's fair-haired boy on the podium. Toti Dal Monte sang a fine *Sonnambula* with Tito Schipa, and Edith Mason made such a success of Micaela that one critic said *Carmen* ought to be renamed. Cyrena Van Gordon produced rave reviews for everything she did, looking as beautiful as she sang. Giordano's *La Cena delle Beffe* was heard for the first time in the city, Claudia Muzio in the soprano lead. Although the house was packed on the Saturday afternoon of the premiere, a number of critics apologetically said they would have to review a later performance. It seems that the Army-Navy football game was being played at the same time at Soldier's Field, and most of the critics were down there.

New Year's Eve had become a special occasion at the Opera. Either a premiere or a new production of a standard work was almost always given then, with a particularly exciting cast. In 1926 a new production of *Don Giovanni* was unveiled. Vanni Marcoux was the Don, Rosa Raisa the Donna Anna, Edith Mason the Zerlina, and Tito Schipa the Don Ottavio. Polacco conducted. The futuristic, cubistic sets were executed from sketches by Schenck von Trapp of Germany, but were only mildly received by the critics. René Devries also complained that the electrician kept putting spotlights on the principals, giving the production something of a vaudeville aura.

Another gala occasion that season was the night Queen Marie of Romania visited the Opera. When the announcement was made that the Queen would attend, there was a mad scramble for tickets, and the house was sold out almost immediately. On the night of the performance the automobiles of the royal party pulled up outside the Auditorium, escorted by the screeching whistles of a police escort, about twenty minutes past curtain time. The opera, *Aida* with Raisa, had been held. The royal entourage, including Marie's son and daughter, occupied three boxes, Samuel Insull sitting at the Queen's side. Before beginning the performance, Polacco struck up the Romanian national anthem and followed it with "The Star-Spangled Banner." A good portion of the audience spent the evening gaping at the dignitaries. As *Music News* reported it, "the Auditorium was invaded and packed by two factors, the first that great public which loves and appreciates the Aida of Rosa Raisa and the rest that mob of real and make-believe 'society people,' who were there to see the Queen and who, by their monkey-shines, proved in many cases that if given opportunity [they] would have crawled into her box on their hands and knees for the privilege of kissing her hand." The beautiful Queen herself sat reserved and dignified, apparently enjoying the performance.

Mary Garden's big novelty of the season was Honegger's *Judith*, given in Chicago for the first time in America. The opera, based on a story from the Apocrypha, tells of an Assyrian attack on a Jewish city. Judith, a Jewess seductress, gets the Assyrian leader inebriated, cuts off his head, and in the blood-curdling finale rushes from the general's tent with his head in a basket. The music was ultramodern, causing many of the critics to react negatively toward it. René Devries was kinder: "That Honegger writes in various keys all at once, is true; that his idiom is revolutionary, is a fact; but that he wrote a score that has many beautiful moments is also undeniable." There was little doubt that the role allowed Garden to do some of the best acting of the season, and the vocal line suited her well. As the *Tribune* put it, "Because her music lies mostly in the middle part of a mezzo-soprano range, everything that she sang was projected easily and forcefully in her own characteristic Marycantation." Her costuming was more dubious. "Imagine," *Music News* wrote, "Mary Garden going through all of this in silks, laces, and satins, with long trailing robes and a neck and two arms full of jewelry."

She repeated her success in *Resurrection*, although critics were becoming more outspoken in their feeling that musically it was not much of an opera. More and more Mary's age was being brought up, although no one dared mention the subject to her. "It is remarkable," said *Musical Courier*, "that a woman of her age should give the illusion of a young woman, but Garden's artistry is such as to disguise the blemishes of time, as even her hands are so well made up as to blend with her young appearance. Then her elastic walk is an excellent copy of that of a young woman." She still had more stage intelligence than anyone else in the business, as a performance of *L'Amore dei Tre Re* that year revealed. Mary was standing on the balcony in the second act dressed in bright red. When she turned around to greet Avito, she found much to her horror that he was clad in a gorgeous purple which did raucous things to the red. With uncanny cleverness she managed to modify her own dress through the whole scene by holding in her hands a long white scarf, interposing it between the clashing purple and red.

But time had taken its toll. Reviewing Garden's Tosca, René Devries pronounced it the first total disaster of her career. Napoleon, he said, "found his Waterloo in the middle of June, 1815, and Garden, in the beginning of 1927 found her first defeat as Tosca." The production was rather questionable from another angle, too, for linguistically it had been sheer bedlam. Fernand Ansseau, the Cavaradossi, sang in Italian until Garden made her entrance, then shifted to French. Upon her exit, he returned to the original. In the second act Garden sang in French except for the "*Vissi d'Arte*," which she did in Italian. Vanni Marcoux, the Scarpia, was the only consistent member of the triangle, limiting himself to Italian. However, when Garden demanded from him, "*Combien?*" (How much?), and Vanni Marcoux, supposedly echoing her question, responded with "*Quanto?*" the whole thing became pretty laughable.

The world premiere of Cadman's *A Witch of Salem*, postponed from the year before, took place on December 8, 1926. Charles Hackett sang the lead, and Henry Weber conducted. Edward Moore maintained, "With the possible exception of Victor Herbert's *Natoma*, it would seem to be the best of the American operas to date." The opera deals with the witch-hunting craze in seventeenth-century Massachusetts. Its score was dominated by a Puritan hymn which appeared in several variations, but there was also some eerie witchcraft music, a pirate chanty, an Irish tune, and a Puccini-like love duet. The advocates of opera in English were perfectly ecstatic in their praise of the work.

D'Albert's *Tiefland* was given at the Auditorium for the first time anywhere in English. Moore felt that the production left the question of translated opera pretty much where it was. "Those who are for opera in English will be more for it, those who are not will be less so." *Music*

News, which, of course, was very much for it, found the performance "one of the most notable in many years."

Music News was still insisting that if the Civic Opera were really a civic enterprise, it would give all its productions in English. After all, the magazine said, Chicago, not the foreign artists, was paying the bills on the Opera. The value of foreign musicians in our midst was becoming increasingly suspect in the radical camp. "The foreign musicians," Jacob Eisenberg wrote for a special "Americanization Number" of *Music News,* "taught us to believe that Americans are inferior as musicians. They taught us to believe that we were money chasers. They were telling us all this, while at the same time, their own reason for coming to America was to make Americans pay them well for the little they were prepared to, or were capable of, teaching us. They came here to make money but they accused the Americans of being monetary." Eisenberg felt that we were on the verge of developing a truly American musical school. "There is a constant search for music that is distinctly characteristic of America. Some are adopting the native American or Indian music, others are using the Negro population songs, while still others are employing what was originally known as 'popular music.' Only time will tell which will remain fixed in our souls. But that is immaterial. What does matter is that Americans are displaying an American Consciousness."

Although there were a number of protests to the effect that the opera was not as good as it was five years ago, the guaranty fund was renewed without any real trouble. A sum of $520,000 a year was promised for the next five years. Approximately three thousand guarantors made up the total, pledging varying amounts. The new opera house had already become somewhat controversial. Insull, at a company gala at the end of the season, said, "It cannot possibly be purely monumental. It must be commercial—not only self-supporting; it must be profitable." *Music News* objected: "Bless you! No! This opera house is not to be a monument to opera and music in anything like predominant sense—but is, per contra, to be a great commercial enterprise." But Insull insisted the Auditorium was scheduled to be torn down and that it was mandatory that the company move to new quarters.* He announced that the site for the new structure would be in the block bounded by Madison, Market, and Washington Streets and the Chicago River. Again *Music News* was indignant—the idea of an

* Despite recurring threats, the Auditorium was not torn down, of course. After several reprieves, it was scheduled for demolition in 1941, but was saved by the war. Then it became a recreation center for service men, with bowling alleys built on the main floor of the hall. After the war the Auditorium Building became the home of Roosevelt University.

opera house on that "melliferous river"! The complaint about the location was fairly universal. It was ridiculous, many charged, to build an opera house at one side of the Loop in a cramped, noisy section. It should be built on Michigan Avenue. Insull was accused of simply trying to perpetuate his name by building a monument to himself. And if there had to be a new opera house, many asked, why not make it a thing of beauty rather than a utilitarian skyscraper?

Plans for the new house continued all through the summer and into the fall. September brought the Dempsey-Tunney fight. October found Al Jolson singing aloud in *The Jazz Singer*, the first "talkie." And no one who was anyone attended the football games that fall without a raccoon coat. November brought opening night at the Chicago Opera and Claudia Muzio's Violetta.

The *Tribune* insisted that getting to the Opera on opening night was getting to be a more difficult operation every year. Traffic was thicker and moved faster. The somewhat tentative sound of the Model T had given way to the "gentle purr of high powered motor cars," which rolled up to the entrance and discharged their passengers onto a velvet carpet. "You approach the Auditorium," the *Tribune* said, "amid glare and boom through the batteries of photographers who are engaged, and quite unerringly at that, upon the matter of picking out the colonel's lady from the Gold Coast and omitting Judy O'Grady who lives somewhere else. You finally reach the lobby, which is pervaded by a mingled and not unpleasant odor of flashlight powder, smoke, perfumes, and mothballs."

Gowns were now predominantly pastel in color. Gone were the glittering gold and silver of a year or so before, replaced by white velvets, pink crepes, and an occasional black or deep-toned velvet. Whereas it had been the upper boxes that were the more fashionable when the Auditorium was new, it was now the lower ones that held social priority.

The company gave twelve performances in the first ten days of the 1927–28 season, with only one opera repeated. "No wonder the singers spend most of their time staring at the prompter's box," more than one critic said. The two big novelties that year were Massenet's *Sapho*, staged for Garden, and Catalani's *Loreley*, given for Muzio. The latter tells of a beautiful woman who is abandoned by her lover and swears vengeance by becoming a spirit to lure sailors into bad water to their death. According to Edward Moore, it was most notable because "it gave Claudia Muzio the most effective role of her Chicago career." She was absolutely gorgeous in the part, especially dressed in the pale blue chiffon which she wore after becoming a spirit, and sang divinely. "Too bad she has not some real music to sing," Moore said, "for she does so much with what she has."

Sapho was another of those operas which was dramatically good for Garden, but which was close to nil musically. As *Music News* evaluated it, "the music seemed scarcely more than an irritation." The opera was painstakingly staged, particularly the first act orgy. "In and out Miss Garden flashed in gorgeous red hues, bare armed in the second act, bare legged in the first, which classifies as a distinct tactical error." Edward Moore said, "She came close to making the hit of her Chicago career with it." But *Music News* was more reserved: "Miss Garden sang a little, declaimed a great deal, snorted and 'Ha Ha'd' quite as usual and never for a moment let anyone forget that she was present."

Mary Garden had arrived in Chicago fresh from having sung "The Star-Spangled Banner" at Charles A. Lindbergh's reception in Paris. She confessed to reporters that she had to make a fast trip to the library to check on the words before she sang it.

About a month after the season began, Al Capone, who held the distinction of being one of the few Chicago citizens to ride through the streets in a seven-ton bulletproof car, returned to the city after a hunting trip in the north woods and a visit to the West Coast. "Well, if he's back, he's back," the Chicago police chief said philosophically. "That's all there is to it." While out west, Capone had had a chance to do some sightseeing. "I went over some of the movie studios in Hollywood," he announced. "That's a grand racket."

Another "grand racket" was radio, although it took a while for opera to benefit much from it. Experiments with broadcasting had been tried as early as the initial season of the Civic Opera, when Station KYW carried *Rigoletto* with Galli-Curci. The results had been disappointing, with more static than music coming over the airwaves. Besides, most people at that time were more interested in seeing how many different stations they could find than in listening to any one program clear through. The opera broadcasts were later stopped, as it was feared they might cut into attendance at live performances. But it was soon discovered that radio, like records, not only did not hurt opera attendance, it actually stimulated it. Eventually the National Broadcasting Company installed eighteen microphones on and about the Auditorium stage, and broadcasting was resumed, capable of being picked up—with varying reception—on the East Coast, well into Canada, over to the Rocky Mountains, and down as far as south Texas. Just the same, there were problems and prejudices to overcome. In 1925 *Music News* said, "For the life of us . . . we cannot see how anyone could possibly care for 'radioed' opera!" Live audiences, although only the overhanging microphone was visible to them, often complained that performers became so concerned with the effects of the broadcast that they were not heard at their best in the house. Radio audiences objected that microphones hidden in scenery or somewhere else out of sight picked up private conversations of singers, choristers, and stagehands standing in the wings.

In November, 1927, *Music News*' critic became indisposed and decided to listen to a performance of *Faust* on the radio rather than go down to the Auditorium to hear it "live." "What I heard was a caution!" he insisted. "The strings of the orchestra sounded just like three banjos and all the percussions put together sounded like an occasional bang on the bottom of a dishpan. . . . The announcer's voice giving out the story was no more to me than a bowl of mush. Miss Mason's lovely high voice carried reasonably, but her low voice was inaudible and the middle scale a squawk. Mr. Hackett's famous high tone in falsetto sounded like the wail of an infant." The critic concluded that if any of these artists ever heard themselves on the air, they would never sing for a broadcast again.

The company's New Year's Eve gala that year was Johann Strauss's *Die Fledermaus,* its first real experiment with operetta. The performance was sung in English, while the cast included Rosa Raisa, Charles Hackett, Giacomo Rimini, Toti Dal Monte, José Mojica, and Virgilio Lazzari. Henry Weber conducted. Most of the critics agreed that the Auditorium was too large for staging works of such an intimate nature with much success.

Rimsky-Korsakov's *Snow Maiden* was revived, but with only modest success now. It was sung in English, and Edward Moore reviewed the translation quite favorably. Shortly afterward he received a letter from a Mrs. Orpha Hinton Dearbeyne, congratulating him on his stand. "Apropos of your most interesting comment on opera translated into English," Mrs. Dearbeyne wrote, "I say 'Amen,' and please keep on saying it until the high and mighty at the Auditorium get 'hep' to the fact that we really do want just that." By now even Mrs. Rockefeller McCormick was enthusiastic about opera in English.

Time for the move to the new opera house was drawing near. The company's last season in the Auditorium opened on October 31, 1928, with a mildly interesting production of *Carmen,* starring Maria Olszewska. Edith McCormick was present, wearing her famous necklace, which was supposed to be valued at more than a million dollars. She was still the focal point of the diamond horseshoe. The Insulls sat in Campanini's old box, Mrs. Insull wearing flesh-colored beaded tulle. But observers were lingering on the fact that the opera was not the spectacle it once was. "Gone are the tiaras and dog collars of the old days," said the *Tribune,* "the solid ranks of the dowagers have admitted younger society to places within the charmed circle, and the simplicity of 1928 fashions transforms the erstwhile colorful grandeur of the horseshoe into a pale aura of its former gaudiness."

The season as a whole was pretty routine, as almost everyone seemed preoccupied with the coming move. Fourteen new singers were added to the roster, seven of them Americans. The English soprano Eva Turner was introduced as Aida and made fine impressions in *A Masked Ball*, *Il Trovatore*, *Cavalleria Rusticana*, and *The Marriage of Figaro*. Coe Glade, the most successful of the new American artists, was introduced as Amneris and later sang a first-rate *Carmen*. Frida Leider made her local debut as Brünnhilde in *Die Walküre*, opposite Lamont's Siegmund, Turner's Sieglinde, Kipnis' Wotan, and Olszewska's Fricka. Polacco conducted. It was one of the highlights of the season. Olszewska, whose reception in the opening *Carmen* had been lukewarm at best, proved that German opera was really her element, and her Ortrud particularly brought to mind the days of Ernestine Schumann-Heink.

Claudia Muzio canceled her appearances that year because of her mother's illness, but rumors had it that Mussolini might insist she keep her Chicago engagements to avoid possible American prejudice against Italy resulting from the broken contract. Neither Garden nor Raisa arrived in the city until just before Christmas. Raisa sparked the greatest excitement of the year with her New Year's Eve *Norma*, aided by Charles Marshall, Coe Glade, and Virgilio Lazzari. On January 21, Marion Claire, one of the new American singers, who had sung Mimi and Elsa, caused some excitement offstage, when she married conductor Henry Weber.

Already, however, there was a conspicuous cooling off of Chicago's interest in opera. Most of the city's music critics had detected the growing indifference, but few could explain it. "Many people," wrote Edward Moore, "even when they for one reason or another go to opera, frankly admit that they are bored by it. Taste for opera is not growing as fast as it should." But the apathy apparently was not limited to opera. *Music News* said it had gotten letters "ad nauseum" from musicians, managers, teachers, and artists alike, complaining about the "unprecedented hard times." Moore eventually said flatly, "Music is in the doldrums." There was also increasing opposition to the move to the new opera house. "And to think," *Music News* fumed, "that Chicago, now become The Iconoclastic, The Restless, The Inartistic among cities submits tamely to the suspension of its [the Auditorium's] use for our opera!" Traditionally, Chicago always rushed to embrace the new, considering it a sign of progress, but the building of the Civic Opera House was a rather marked exception.

Just why the musical depression had set in, when times were still so prosperous, is not easy to explain. The opera-in-English advocates claimed it was because the opera was dominated by foreigners who refused to sing in a language Americans could understand. Perhaps this was a factor. More important probably was that the frenzied pace of the later twenties had become too fast for anything as conventional as opera to bear up particularly well. There were too many other things to do, too many other thrills to be had, too many quicker ways of fleeing the world of reality. In a mad whirl of a world, living from one sensual pleasure to the next, opera had become outmoded. At the same time the Civic Opera itself had slipped a notch or two, giving generally pedestrian seasons during its last two years at the Auditorium. The company's interest was so taken up with the building of the new house that these seasons sort of muddled through on their own. Besides, it seemed hardly worthwhile to try anything really new or exciting until after the move. Once the new opera house was finished, the management promised, Chicago would see opera as it never had before.

On January 26, 1929, the company gave its final performance in the Auditorium. Gounod's *Romeo and Juliet*, the first opera sung there forty years before, was also the last. For the farewell Edith Mason and Charles Hackett were the Veronese lovers, both singing their finest. Between acts, Polacco struck up "Home, Sweet Home" and "Auld Lang Syne," while the audience rose to its feet and sang. With that, sentimentality was cast aside and attention shifted to the new structure being completed on Wacker Drive—for better or worse, the Chicago Opera's new home.

Chapter 10

HUMPTY DUMPTY HAD A GREAT FALL

IN 1928 there was scarcely a major city in the country where the clatter of riveters could not be heard throughout the business district. Steel girders of apartment houses and office buildings dotted the horizon, becoming as integral a part of the American urban scene as the bootlegger or the financial page. In the midst of this unprecedented building boom, work on Insull's opera house began. In February, buildings were cleared away, and the ground was broken. Four months later the singers of the Civic Opera gave a concert as a publicity stunt in the excavation for the new house. As construction began, curiosity mounted, for only the general plans for the building were made public. The interior was kept a secret even from the company's executive committee.

The nation was entering the last speculative phase of the Coolidge-Hoover prosperity. Al Capone's gang was at its peak, and the speakeasy had become an American institution. Amos and Andy began their radio career in 1929; Rudy Vallee's by then was well underway. A new tune, "Singin' in the Rain," indicated just how good times were, at least on the surface. On September 3, 1929, the Big Bull Market reached its climax. Stock that Samuel Insull had bought a few months before at less than $8 a share was now priced at $115 a share. The opera house at 20 North Wacker Drive was by then practically ready.

When completed, the building stood forty-five stories high, the larger part of the first six set aside for the opera company. Chicago has always been a business city, and it has a long tradition of mingling business with art. Like Uranus Crosby and Ferdinand Peck, Samuel Insull was convinced that opera could be put on a self-supporting basis by combining the opera house with an office building, allowing the office rental to cover the opera deficit. Insull's skyscraper was financed by selling ten million dollars' worth of stock to the city's music lovers and giving the Metropolitan Life Insurance Company a mortgage on the rest. Most of the stock was sold to Insull's own employees and through the agencies handling his companies' stock. The common stock was held in trust for the Chicago Music Foundation, a nonprofit organization which Insull hoped would train local singers and educate the city's musical public. Eventually, it was hoped, this foundation would emerge with a clear title to the building. Insull was convinced the plan was infallible. All that was needed was "reasonable foresight and management such as you would give to any other business." The project began under good omens when Insull himself leased large sections of the office space for his utilities companies. The top floor he chose for his own office, which he lavishly furnished with a grand piano, a directors' table, and plush divans.

There were still those who opposed the whole idea of building a new opera house, and many saw the structure as nothing more than a grand monument to Insull. A number of people objected to moving the opera out of the Auditorium, particularly to a site as unattractive as Wacker Drive was then. Others simply opposed Insull and everything he did. "Insull's throne" some called the new building, and if looked at from the rear, it actually took on the appearance of a giant seat with a huge armrest on either side. "All this was a material expression of the super-man, Insull," wrote Edgar Lee Masters.

Shortly after September 3, 1929, two months before the opera house was scheduled to open, the stock market took a sharp drop. Throughout that month and the early part of the next, it fluctuated unsteadily. Then on Thursday, October 24, some 12,800,000 shares changed hands. The following Tuesday, October 29, the bottom fell out, plunging the country into a financial panic unlike anything in its history. Six days later, November 4, amid talk of business failures and bank closures, the Civic Opera House opened in Chicago.

The day before the opening the city's newspapers were inundated with detailed instructions telling the public just how to get to 20 North Wacker Drive. The house was difficult to reach in those days by public transportation. It was not close to any of the leading hotels, and the city's taxi service was expensive and not altogether effective. Although traffic congestion around the entrance of the house would be a continuous problem later on, opening night seemed to present a minimum of confusion, despite the fact that hundreds of automobiles descended on Wacker Drive and Madison Street at approximately the same time. Pedestrians, on this occasion at least, offered more of a problem, giving the Chicago police force a pretty strenuous workout. An estimated two thousand sightseers congregated around the portico of the house, making it necessary for the audience to force its way through a wall of people to reach the doors. One newspaper photographer was seriously burned on the face when he was pushed against a flashbulb just as it exploded.

Patrolling the city's boulevards and drives leading to the Opera House that evening were eight detective bureau squads, stationed along the route to protect opera patrons against possible robberies. At a time when gangs and mobsters practically ruled the city, it was risky business to wear jewels and furs out at night without special precautions. Twelve plainclothesmen mingled with the crowd outside the opera house, with orders to arrest any suspicious-looking characters. Squad cars were concentrated along Lake Shore Drive, Michigan Avenue, and the Lincoln Park drives, while the Gold Coast area particularly was heavily patrolled.

In the foyer of the Opera House Samuel Insull, just a week shy of his seventieth birthday, personally greeted as many of the opening-night audience as he could. After shaking hundreds of hands, he finally became so flustered at all the praise that for once he became literally speechless and could respond only with smiles. The *Times* said the next day that Insull had done everything to get the house ready except "dust off the seats."

Although it was observed that outside the "rich and poor mingled in the milling mob before the doors of opera gone democratic," the first-night audience itself was composed mostly of the city's business leaders and art lovers. *Music News* claimed that the display of fashion and wealth was beyond anything in recent memory. More men were now wearing starched collars and waistcoats than in former years, and hats and double-breasted suits were more frequent than previously. For women the ideal figure was the straight-up-and-down look, one deemphasizing the hips, waist, and bust as much as possible. Evening dresses were backless and sleeveless, with long trailing skirts. Most gowns were either white, eggshell, or pastel satins, and practically every other woman wore an ermine wrap. The standard hair style was shingled in back, the hair drawn forward over the ears.

Mrs. Rockefeller McCormick was present for the occasion, wearing a white satin gown and her gorgeous diamond necklace, almost an inch wide and reaching practically to her waist. Mrs. Insull wore an eggshell satin trimmed with crystal and jet beads and a flounce of black tulle. A strand of pearls and a wide diamond bracelet constituted her jewelry.

Since the plans of the house had been kept secret, the first-nighters were anxious to see just what Insull had wrought. On the ground level of the building were, and still are, both the Civic Opera House and the smaller Civic Theater. A colonnade of twenty-two pillars lines the edifice along Wacker Drive from Washington to Madison Street. Five doors lead into the outer lobby of the Opera House, where a series of marble columns rises to a vaulted gold ceiling. The auditorium is decorated in rose and gold, the lower walls covered by oak paneling, the upper ones formed by bays which gradually step back, giving greater width to the rear. The house seats 3,471 persons and consists of a main floor, two balconies, and thirty-one boxes.

The stage is 145 feet high, 120 feet wide, and 75 feet deep. Between acts, a steel curtain, 35 by 50 feet, on which is painted a procession of some thirty operatic characters, is brought down over the stage. All in all, it was one of the best-equipped houses in the world at the time it was built, and was one of the three great opera houses in the United States. The others were the Metropolitan and the San Francisco Opera. The total cost of Insull's building was a substantial twenty million dollars.

The theater began filling a full hour before Polacco lifted his baton on the dedicatory opera, *Aida*. At eight fifteen the lights were lowered, and a hush fell over the capacity audience. In a moment the lights were lifted again, and the orchestra struck up "The Star-Spangled Banner." The house rose and sang. Then, after the brief prelude, the curtains parted, revealing the palace at Memphis. Rosa Raisa sang Aida, Charles Marshall Radames, Cyrena Van Gordon Amneris, Cesare Formichi Amonasro, and Virgilio Lazzari Ramfis.

Charles Moor continued as stage director. Since the height of the stage in the new house was nearly twice that of the old, most of the scenery for *Aida* had to be rebuilt, and all of it was repainted. Many of the costumes were also new. Edward Moore claimed in his review that the principals and orchestra had never been better and declared, "The new Civic Opera house is going to be kind to its singers." *Music News*, however, complained about the staging and particularly objected to the "Triumphal Scene": "From the gallery the setting for this scene looked like a cross section of a department store—every color and kind of dry-goods."

Between acts the foyer was crowded with promenaders, while the auditorium itself made a stunning sight. As the *Tribune* recorded it, "The wealth of jewels and shimmering fabrics that graced the women in the boxes and on the main floor glittered in the rose velvet setting like so many animated gems in a giant jewel case."

Insull received congratulatory telegrams from Otto Kahn, Gatti-Casazza, and scores of other operatic notables. But the response of the Chicago public and critics to the new house was divided from the first. Edward Moore was one of the most favorably impressed. "A romantic adventure," he wrote in the *Tribune*, "has culminated in the most beautiful operatic theater that ever eyes fell upon, one that has achieved stateliness and avoided austerity, has attained amiability and dodged gaudiness, is large and looks intimate, possesses comfortable seats, enchanting colors, stimulating acoustics." When Moore wrote his *Forty Years of Opera in Chicago,* published in 1930, he could hardly have been more enthusiastic. "The new opera house," he stated, "is a dream of Mr. Insull's, a dream realized in terms of steel and stonework. In entering it the opera company sloughs off a chrysalis and steps into new and gorgeous trappings. It has taken time, immense amounts of money, prolonged and intense concentration, but Mr. Insull is the kind of a dreamer whose dreams come true, a poet who does not write verse but accomplishes enormous and beautiful things for the betterment of his community and nation." Moore ended his book on a high note of optimism, indicating that the city's operatic future would surely be even more glorious than its past.

Music News found the house beautiful enough, but complained bitterly about the location in its report of the opening: "Through great good fortune nobody fell in the river on last Monday night, opening of the new Chicago Civic Opera House, although the building stretches along that salubrious stream for one block and the lighting in the neighborhood is none of the best.... It would have been hard to find a more ugly environment." And to a large degree *Music News* was right. It was an unattractive site. Standing directly in front of the main entrance was an old spur of the elevated railway, while the whole area was dark and dreary. But Insull maintained the city would grow in that direction, as it has.

Many complained about the strong gusts of wind which blew through the portico, menacing women's hair and skirts. Others felt the acoustics left something to be desired, and old-timers will tell you yet that the sound in the Auditorium was much better than that in the Civic Opera House. An Irish cleaning lady at the Blackstone explained the Auditorium's superior acoustics by saying, "The heavy stone kept the sound in. At the new opera house the walls are too thin." This may not be the most scientific of explanations, but it does suggest something of the popular sentiment.

By all odds, the biggest source of complaint, however, about the new house was the arrangement of the boxes. Insull had insisted from the beginning that opera must be democratized, that its supporters should be found in the telephone directory rather than the social register. As a manifestation of this goal, he reduced the number of boxes in the new house and placed them at the rear. He did not want the fine clothes and jewels of the society people to detract from the performance on stage. Some grumbled that this was simply Insull's most blatant indication of his contempt for the Gold Coast. One observer said that from the main floor the occupants of boxes looked as if they were sitting in bath tubs. "Insull built an opera house without a single prominent box," writes Forrest McDonald. "Bejeweled and befurred ladies and their penguin escorts would have to sit in anonymous, proletarian darkness, just like people in the sixpenny gallery."

When Mary Garden saw the new house, she was not impressed at all. As she tells it in her autobiography, "The opera house that Mr. Insull built had forty-seven rows of seats, with two enormous dark walls on each side and not a single box along them. The only boxes were far off at the end of the rows of seats, and nobody could see anybody else. They just couldn't reach us, and we couldn't reach them. When I looked into that long black hole, I said, 'Oh, no!' " It was no real opera house at all, Garden said, but "more like a convention hall. We had absolutely no communication with the public."

While the social circle bemoaned the loss of the "Golden Horseshoe," there were others who spoke approvingly of the democratic spirit Insull had injected into the house. A number of critics pointed with pride to the fact that the seats in the upper balcony were as comfortably upholstered and as plush as those on the main floor. Others, however, asked if the Opera had really been democratized when only those people who owned private cars could get to the house with any ease.

Through the years the Civic Opera House has remained a source of controversy. One critic remarked that Insull had had architects visit every major opera house in the world and then built one unlike any of them. Arthur Meeker in his *Chicago, With Love* wrote, "Everything about the Chicago Civic Opera House was (and is) exactly wrong . . . ; the interior has always reminded me of a salmon-salad sandwich. This long pink rectangular hall had neither majesty nor intimacy; it was just the wrong shape, made in such a way that the maximum number of persons seemed to be at the maximum distance from the stage." When Meeker heard of the Fox-Kelly-Rescigno plans to revive the Chicago Opera in 1954, he said, "I wish them luck . . . and regret only that . . . they must be saddled with that cheerless and ill-designed barn, the Civic Opera House; it counts two strikes against them from the start."

Still the novelty of the new house stimulated better attendance in 1929–30 than had been the case during the last several seasons at the Auditorium. The subscription sale for the Monday night series was up $150,000, almost 100-per-cent increase over the year before. Each of the other series was up at least 30 per cent, while the total subscription sale exceeded by over a quarter of a million dollars that for the last season in the Auditorium.

The night following the opening brought a rare staging of Mascagni's *Iris,* starring Edith Mason. The work was first given in Rome approximately thirty years before, and most critics agreed it was about on a par with the composer's *L'Amico Fritz.* "A certain number of agreeable melodies," wrote the *Tribune,* "are hedged off from each other by dialogue and orchestral music which for want of better description may be termed dramatic." The reviewer concluded, however, that if *Iris* became a permanent item in the repertoire, it would be because of Edith Mason. "Miss Mason classifies among the company's golden throats, a gold that is close to being twenty-four karats fine."

Claudia Muzio returned to the company that season, singing *La Traviata* and *Il Trovatore* during the first week. The latter, on Saturday evening, November 9, was the first opera broadcast from the Civic Opera House stage. Mary McCormic, who spent most of her time in Paris these days, returned to the company after several years' absence, singing first *Romeo and Juliet.* Rosa Raisa continued to score successes in *Norma, Tosca,* and *Falstaff.* Her husband, Giacomo Rimini, was still singing with the company, making one of the great Sir Johns of all time. "Even his voice sounded fat," the *Tribune* wrote.

Mary Garden came to town in 1929 prone to talk about the freedom of the modern woman and love. The contemporary woman, and especially the American woman, Mary said, was too calculating to love completely. "Women," she insisted, "do not live for love. They work for their living. They do not inspire men, and they do not care whether they do or not." Then with a smile she added, "Still women are not wholly free. I wonder if they ever will be. Perhaps in fifty years they may be. They may not care about love at all then." Pausing a moment, she lifted her chin, and with a flash of her eyes, said, "Oh, I do not like the past! After all, it is fine that women do no longer love as they did. It will be even finer if they can win absolute freedom. Formerly we were under the man's heel. Now just his little toe is on us. Yet how conscious we are of that little toe!"

Garden and Insull had never gotten along. They disagreed on many things, but particularly repertoire. She says in her autobiography that she went to his office one day shortly after he took over the opera. Hanging on the wall opposite his desk was an enormous painting of Adelina Patti. "Mr. Insull," Garden said, "what makes you keep Adelina Patti up there? It's been so many years since she stopped singing." Jokingly she added, "Why don't you put me up there?" Insull looked at her over his rimless glasses and in dead seriousness said, "Miss Garden, I hate modern opera. I like the old things." Mary said she knew then they could never work together well. Insull had little interest in the French works, particularly the newer ones that Garden had made her specialty. "There are," he told her, "four hundred thousand German-Americans in Chicago, and a quarter of a million Italian-Americans, and not a handful of Franco-Americans." He really wanted to stage no more than two French operas a year, although he usually did several, mainly because Garden and her colleagues insisted on it. Mary also objected to Insull's views that an opera company was just another business. "I saw very soon what Mr. Insull had in mind," she writes. "That was to turn the opera into a utility.... You can't do that, of course, without destroying the very spirit of art. Nobody ever did and nobody ever will make a business of grand opera. It's just impossible."

Garden's first appearance in the new opera house was as Fiora in *L'Amore dei Tre Re*. Dramatically, she was all she had ever been. "There was a love scene that would cause hesitation in the mind of any right-minded movie censor," Edward Moore wrote. Her singing by now was something else, and tactful critics simply avoided any mention of it. She also did *Le Jongleur de Notre Dame*, still one of her finest vehicles. From time to time there had been talk that the role should be returned to a tenor and sung as originally written. Moore objected. "No tenor, no matter how talented, could ever be as boyish as Miss Garden. I would rather hear her sing and then cry and mop her eyes and wipe her nose than listen to the finest tenor on earth in the part. When the prior scolds her she twists her body into something that is all knees and elbows, and it is all boy, too."

Charles Marshall repeated his Otello that year. Zandonai's *Conchita* was presented by the company for the first time since 1913, now with Rosa Raisa. Massenet's *Don Quichotte*, not performed in the city in sixteen years, was revived and proved to be one of the biggest successes of the year. Vanni Marcoux was again the Don; Coe Glade was his Dulcinea. The management decided to emphasize Wagner that season, uncut Wagner at that. *Tristan und Isolde* was well staged, with Frida Leider as Isolde, Maria Olszewska as Brangäne, Alexander Kipnis as King Mark, and Theodore Strack, in his local debut, as Tristan. Egon Pollak conducted. These same principals headed the *Die Walküre* cast, plus Eva Turner as Sieglinde.

Although there were complaints about the length of the performances, audiences attended dutifully and remained until the final curtain fell somewhere around one o'clock in the morning. On the evening of the first *Lohengrin* the city was hit by the worst blizzard it had experienced in more than a decade. Still the house was large and appreciative. "Hearing Wagner has become a matter of unsmiling earnestness this year," Edward Moore wrote. "For a number of seasons I have been voicing the opinion that listening to music should be approached in the mood of high, fine entertainment and not of deliberate, laborious uplift. There is reason to believe that the approach will have to be changed." Toward the end of the season, however, Moore did say, "Wagner at full length outside of Germany is a bit long."

The opera-in-English craze was abating, as the spirit of jingoism became less pronounced. "It is evident," Moore said, "that the public greatly prefers its opera in a language it cannot understand and boycotts the box office when any effort is made to use even as much English as can sift across operatic footlights."

By the end of the season the economic crisis that had begun on Wall Street had spread to every artery of the nation's business and fiscal bloodstream. A new popular song assured that "Happy Days Are Here Again," but the words had a distinctly hollow ring. With the depression came a revolution in the American way of life. Tired of talking about sex and moral taboos, tired of ballyhoo and unbridled sensualism, the nation became on the one hand more serious, on the other more romantic. Although the hard times awakened a feeling of social consciousness, they also produced an escapist urge, a desire to flee from an exasperating reality.

Skirts came down with stock prices, and bobbed hair began to lose favor. The corset was coming back in vogue, along with an air of formality. As historian Frederick Lewis Allen tells it, "No longer was it the American woman's dearest ambition to simulate a flat-breasted, spindle-legged, carefree, knowing adolescent in a long waisted child's frock. The red-hot baby had gone out of style."

But still the depression worsened. Unemployment rose. Business and bank failures increased. Bread lines grew. Samuel Insull believed the depression to be of major proportions, but in some respects less acute than many that had preceded it. Particularly favorable, he said, was that the money supply was still plentiful. He was confident that in the utilities field the depression was only temporary, declaring that it would have little effect on the growth of his company. Even Insull later admitted he had been too optimistic.

By the time the 1930–31 opera season opened, the nation was in the depths of total depression. The season began for the first time in several years with a novelty, the American premiere of Ernest Moret's *Lorenzaccio*. Moret, a pupil of Massenet, based his drama on the relationship between Lorenzo de' Medici and his cousin Alessandro de' Medici, Duke of Florence. Lorenzo, at heart a republican, wins the confidence of the Duke, then turns on him, ridding Florence of tyranny. The opera consists of four acts and eleven tableaux, although two scenes were omitted in the Chicago production. "With Massenet as a starting point," *Musical*

America wrote of the score, "there are frequent reminiscences of Wagner, Debussy, and Puccini. The composer's purpose was primarily to underscore the drama. The music never interferes with the play." Vanni Marcoux, who had created the role in Paris ten years before, was Lorenzo, while Charles Hackett sang Alessandro. The production included the interesting debut of the Canadian mezzo-soprano Jennie Tourel, although her role was a minor one.

Most critics agreed that *Lorenzaccio* was not a wise choice for opening night, since it contained little in the way of a melodic vocal line and contained practically no action. What the opera did do was to concentrate on the psychological development of the main character, and in this it gave Vanni Marcoux an almost limitless range of possibilities for dramatic expression. "Superbly costumed," *Musical America* reported, "his progress from effeminate youth, simulating cowardice, to a fanatical murderer was a brilliant tour de force of dramatic art."

The next evening saw one of the most significant American debuts in the history of Chicago Opera, when Lotte Lehmann appeared in *Die Walküre. Musical Courier* said, "Her Sieglinde is perfection itself—perfection of voice and of action." *Musical America* affirmed, "She has one of the loveliest voices ever heard on the Civic Opera stage. It is of a freedom and purity seldom discovered in German singers and employed with an eloquence and artistry that moved the audience to a great demonstration." Her endearment to the public was immediate. She followed Sieglinde with Elizabeth and achieved another success. "Her Elizabeth was a spiritual figure," *Musical America* wrote, "yet infused with reality and the charm of life. Her singing was of a superb order, tonally beautiful, emotionally warm, yet always informed by authoritative musicianship." When the company staged *Die Meistersinger* later in the season for the first time in its history, Lehmann was Eva, and she proved a delight. The management had been planning the production for nearly a decade, but it had been repeatedly postponed. It was given now with splendid results. "We can think of no higher praise," *Musical America* avowed, "than that, at the end, one's thought was not of this or that individual or detail of the performance, but solely of the colossal genius of Richard Wagner, which had been so lucidly and affectionately revealed."

John Charles Thomas made his debut with the company that same year as Tonio in *Pagliacci.* He appeared without fanfare and literally took the house by storm, producing a demonstration unlike anything since Galli-Curci first sang at the Auditorium. His prologue was an absolute marvel, and at the end of the first act shouts for Thomas went up all over the theater. Not even a solo bow by Charles Marshall, the Canio of the evening, could silence the crowd. "Thomas! Thomas!" the audience cried.

Marshall brought out all the members of the cast, but Thomas would not appear alone. Still the audience was not satisfied. They wanted Thomas and spent the whole intermission, even with the house lights up, yelling his name.

Mary McCormic was back, scoring triumphs as Cio-Cio-San and Massenet's Manon. She sang the *Butterfly* in French, while the rest of the cast sang in Italian. But her performance was thrilling. Her interpretation of the role was demure with an undercurrent of humor, as when she kicked Yamadori, her would-be suitor, in the seat of the kimono. Vocally she was best in the soaring moments of the second act, when the lovely quality of her upper register was revealed. *Manon*, to a number of critics, was the best thing she had ever sung in the city. Gorgeous to the eye, stunningly gowned, she was ravishing visually and vocally.

Frida Leider sang Fidelio, Isolde, and the Marschallin, and Vanni Marcoux sang his first Chicago Iago. "He is never the obvious villain," *Musical America* assured. "Only rarely, but with devastating effect, does he permit to be glimpsed the consuming hatred for his chief.... Yet the contrast of suave exterior with the seething, malignant, real self, formed one of the most consummate bits of dramatic art we have ever witnessed." Supported by Tito Schipa's Wilhelm Meister, Coe Glade turned Thomas' *Mignon* into a virtual sensation. "As sheer entertainment," *Musical America* said, "the resident company has done nothing better."

A new role for Claudia Muzio that year was Fiora in *L'Amore dei Tre Re*. "A very intelligent actress," *Musical Courier* said, "she played the part probably as a Sarah Bernhardt or a Duse would have elected to do." *Musical America* found her "a Fiora stately of figure and beautifully costumed, some of whose most effective moments were those when she eschewed all action and depended solely upon the value of significant pose. Vocally it was—as are all of Muzio's performances—quite beyond criticism." She also sang Santuzza in *Cavalleria Rusticana*, a performance which found Jennie Tourel singing the role of Lola. Muzio and Charles Marshall teamed for *La Forza del Destino*, Salvatore Baccaloni, a new buffo from La Scala, making his debut as Melitone.

The big Mary Garden novelty of the season was the world premiere of Hamilton Forrest's *Camille*. Forrest was born and raised in Chicago and at one time had worked as an office boy in Insull's utilities. His composition had been called to the attention of Mary Garden, who encouraged him and said she would try to help get his opera staged. She broached the subject to Insull, reminding him that the composer had once worked in his office. "Is it a good opera?" Insull wanted to know. "I think so," Garden answered. "But I also think we owe it to him as an American composer. They don't get much of a break, you know." Somewhat reluctantly Insull agreed to mount it, with Garden slated to sing the title role. The production was first planned for 1929–30, but was postponed until the next season. When it was finally staged, *Camille* boasted some of the most lavish sets the company ever used, costing in the neighborhood of $42,000.

The score was modern and difficult. Garden says in her autobiography, "I think *Camille* was the hardest music we ever struggled with. It just screeched with modernism. At our first orchestra rehearsal the men put down their instruments and groaned, it was so fearfully difficult. And poor Emil Cooper, who conducted! What a wretched time he had! He put all his soul into it, but he said that never in his life had he conducted anything so difficult." But Mary said she felt there must be progress in music and opera as in everything else. She told reporters, "Opera must be modernized. The days of the 'I lo-o-o-ve you' are gone. No more operas with old kings, queens, princesses.... No more repetitions, but single, direct speech; no more phrases such as, 'Do you know this lady?' to be answered with, 'Yes, I know her,' and then another protagonist adding, 'Yes, he knows her,' to which the two principals answer, 'Yes, we know each other,' and the male chorus then shouting, 'Yes, he knows her' and the ladies singing, 'Yes, she knows him' and the big finale with all singing, 'He knows her,' 'She knows him.' That sort of opera cannot survive, no matter what language it is sung in."

On the night of the premiere the house was filled; the atmosphere was electric. Every box was overflowing, and extra chairs had been wedged in wherever possible. Almost all of the city's prominent opera supporters were there, including Mrs. Charles Forrest, the composer's mother, who was the center of attention for those nearby. According to Miss Anna Morgan, who had been present at the Auditorium when Adelina Patti sang there, this was the most exciting operatic event the city had seen since, not excluding the opening of the new opera house.

The opera consisted of three acts and a prologue. When Mary Garden made her entrance, the house gasped. "We are incapable of proper description of the costume," *Musical America* confessed. "But the most amazing feature of the apparition was a wig that would have shamed a Zulu medicine man." One observer said that Mary "must have put up her hair with an egg-beater." Charles Hackett took the role of Armand, and Coe Glade, Jennie Tourel, and Thelma Votipka were all in the cast. The opera, sung by the Chicago forces in French, contained an occasional jazz motif and a blues number, snappily sung by Coe Glade. However, according to *Musical America,* "The music left no easily describable impression, save that of a wearying monotony.... Only once, at the moment of Camille's collapse in the second act, when the orchestra produced a curious gasping succession of sounds, did there seem to be any discoverable relation between the drama and the music." Although the stage was crowded with people much of the time, the composer failed to write any telling choral parts, and the libretto left as much to be desired. *Musical America* felt it was a good thing the opera was sung in French rather than English. "Had the audience understood the utterly trite dialogue, the enthusiasm might not have swelled to such overflowing heights."

But the audience was enthusiastic indeed. Each act was followed by prolonged applause, and when the composer was brought on stage at the end of Act II, the tumult reached a climax. After taking several bows alone, he was surrounded by the singers and applauded by them. Mary Garden gave him a pat on the cheek, causing the house to cheer all the more. Society writer Mildred Jaklon said in the *Tribune* the next day, "The throngs at the opera house last night . . . witnessed a social, dramatic, and musical thriller such as few members of this generation have experienced."

About the only thing the critics found thrilling about it were the sets, which they all said were exquisite. René Devries claimed the gambling-house scene surpassed "in beauty perhaps anything ever presented on our opera stage." Aside from that the professionals agreed the whole thing had been a grand disappointment—"disappointment," *Musical America* said, "that a young American composer, faced with the teeming variety of modern life, should have reverted to the insipid banalities of the Camille story for a subject; disappointment in the resultant product; disappointment that the resources and immense influence of the Civic Opera should have been exerted to a maximum degree in behalf of a work so utterly lacking in any sort of significance." Edward Moore, one of the kinder reviewers, said simply, "Just at present I am unable to state whether it was good opera or good drama." Almost everyone else said flatly it was a big bore.

Even Mary Garden appeared below her usual level, sparking real excitement only in her death scene and in the telephone incident of the second act. Here the great Garden of the past came through. "I only know," Moore wrote, "that her incredibly savage, raging, blazing outburst was an exciting exhibition of the theater." The role called for little vocal prowess from its star, and any success the opera had was due to her acting ability. Garden herself admitted even before the work was staged, "There are beautiful pages and some very poor ones in *Camille*." But in her autobiography she remembered it as "an absolute flop."

She repeated *Resurrection* that season and sang Anita in Massenet's *Navarraise* for the first time in Chicago, effecting the nervous excitement of the part, if not the powerful voice. The season closed with Garden singing *Le Jongleur de Notre Dame*. She later said that during the opera, while the others were singing, she sat by herself on a bench in one corner of the stage. Before she realized it, she was talking to herself, or rather to the little boy she was playing. "Dear little Jongleur," she said, "you've performed all your little stunts. Everything you had you've given to the Virgin. Now your work is done." Then, turning to herself, she thought, "I, Mary Garden, have given twenty of the best years of my life to my work here in Chicago, and I've given everything to the people as well as I could, and now I think I'll go." When the curtain fell, she went to her dressing room, gathered her things together, returned to her hotel, and without saying good-by to anyone, left the city. When she got back to Paris, she cabled Samuel Insull: "My career in America is done."

And done it was. Garden had caused more excitement on the Chicago operatic scene, off stage and on, than any other singer in the company's history. She began her career in controversy and ended it the same way, remaining a newsmaker to the last. James Gibbons Huneker once said of her, "A condor, an eagle, a peacock, a nightingale, a panther, a society dame, a gallery of moving pictures, a siren, an indomitable fighter, a human woman with a heart as big as a house, a lover of sport, a canny Scotch lassie—a superwoman, that is Mary Garden." During these twenty years, her name had become virtually synonymous with the Chicago Opera, and her departure seemed to foreshadow the dark days ahead. For with the passing of Mary Garden, the great, golden era of Chicago's operatic history was practically spent.

All through that 1930–31 season there had been grumbling about both the opera house and the quality of the opera itself. Much of the glamour and joy of the Opera had vanished. The depressed economic situation had undoubtedly had much to do with this, but even Edward Moore, who had been so ecstatic about the opera house the year before, admitted now that it had had some ill effects. There was still the problem of transportation, and the city's ruling, later rescinded, against taxicabs parking within hailing distance of the entrance made things difficult for many, particularly in bad weather. Moore felt that the long aisles, running from front to back, with few side exits, made visiting between acts difficult and thus discouraged the social air that had been so characteristic of opera at the Auditorium. "Even the lighting," Moore wrote, "is kept in so unbrilliant a scheme that it muffles some of the gaiety."

For whatever reason, a general loss of interest was obvious. Large sections of unsold seats in the rear of the main floor were characteristic all season long, except for a few productions of unusual popular interest. Reviewers later admitted they had been kinder than they should have been, hoping to encourage attendance. The company's cost of operation was now something like $2,500,000 a season, or close to $125,000 a week. Patrons during the thirteen-week season paid an average of $3.99 each for their tickets, receiving in return $8.01 worth of opera. The deficit for the season was $1,079,473, by far the largest since the formation of the Civic Opera. With the marked drop in ticket sales, coupled with this tremendous loss, the guarantor support, which would have to be renewed the next year, was going to be difficult, if not impossible, to raise.

The economic picture all over the country was getting blacker. More people were out of work, and most of those who did work had taken a salary cut. In great sections of the country starvation stalked the land, hovering over park benches and "Hoovervilles" and hundreds of abandoned railway cars. According to a new song, life was just a bowl of cherries, but nobody believed it, the rich no more than the poor. Americans wanted to laugh, and if they could not laugh, they wanted to cry, but they wanted to cry about somebody else's troubles. Capitalizing on this, movies became more popular than ever, partly because the "talkies" had become better technically and partly because they served as a means of escaping a bitter reality. Comedies were popular; so were musicals, particularly Al Jolson's. Marie Dressler, who kept her audiences laughing one moment and crying the next, was another favorite. Also taking an upsurge in popularity was the "horror" film. Boris Karloff had just made his first Frankenstein picture, and Fredric March had just completed *Dr. Jekyll and Mr. Hyde.* Critics were beginning to say that the movies generally were becoming too gruesome, but the public disagreed. In *The Cheat,* released in the fall of 1931, Tallulah Bankhead was shown being branded on the breast with a hot iron. Critics insisted her screams and the wisp of smoke were too much; the public loved it. Escape above everything else was what the public wanted from its entertainment, even if it bordered on sadism.

The Chicago Opera caught something of this escapist sentiment, and during its 1931–32 season entertainment was the keynote. A repertoire was chosen which the management felt would have wide popular appeal. Herbert Witherspoon, the new artistic director, who replaced the ailing Giorgio Polacco, was dedicated to the policy that above everything else opera should be first-class entertainment. The public, he insisted, did not want to be musically educated; it wanted to relax and enjoy a good show. "In developing the plans and repertoire for the season of 1931–32," Witherspoon assured, "we have paid particular attention to the fact that in times like these people need the kind of entertainment that will cheer them up."

For a people looking for flights into fantasy, opera in one sense should have been immensely popular, for certainly it contained the romance, the blood and thunder, even the sadism which the public seemed to find so appealing in the movies. But despite Witherspoon's best efforts, opera attendance remained lax. Americans on the whole have never been able to identify with opera as they have with the motion picture, or television, or even staged drama, largely because they have never become accustomed to the convention of singing. Although they will tolerate screen stories of vampires and mad monsters and beserk gunmen with glee, librettos involving burned up babies and insane sopranos are denounced as ridiculous and implausible. Without defending either, it would seem that the major difference here is the singing. It is an undeniable fact that for most Americans a sung drama is no drama at all, and their reaction to it remains detached, except for an occasional familiar aria. Once the depression hit, casual operagoers, particularly those from the lower-income brackets, thought twice about parting with an admission fee several times that of other entertainment media they enjoyed more and considered less artificial.

Witherspoon had been a Metropolitan basso from 1908–17 and had come to Chicago in 1925 as president of the Chicago Musical College. Later on, for a few weeks before his death in 1935, he was appointed general manager of the Metropolitan, succeeding Gatti-Casazza. When he took over the musical direction of the Chicago Opera in 1931, much was made of the fact that he was an American, an American who could supposedly trace his ancestry back to a signer of the Declaration of Independence. This was somehow construed to mean that he had some special clairvoyance for understanding what the American public wanted in opera. As Karleton Hackett wrote for the Chicago *Evening Post*, "Mr. Witherspoon . . . is an American, not one of the noisy 100 per cent variety, but coming from an old American family; and, having been born and raised in this land, he understands our public and sympathizes with our point of view."

The season opened with a production of *Tosca*, featuring Claudia Muzio, Vanni Marcoux, and Jan Kiepura, the latter making his American debut. Edward Moore called the second act "a struggle of giants." The audience seemed gay enough, and one would hardly have guessed from the looks of it that the country was in the midst of the worst depression in its history. Long, trailing velvet cloaks of deep purple and wine with large sable collars were much in vogue then, while gowns were cut low in back and front. Outside, reported the *Tribune*, there were "more expensive looking automobiles than you are likely to find outside of an automobile show." But still something was missing. That intangible spark, that feeling of excitement, was no longer there. The depression certainly made itself felt psychologically, it not materially, stifling much of the former enthusiasm. Then, as Moore suggested, "One sometimes fears that an animated flow of spirits is a bit checked by the opera house itself." And again he complained about the lighting. "The illumination of the auditorium may be artistic, even comforting, but it is well suppressed, and patrons last night talked in low tones, almost whispers, while the house was being filled."

Although the standard favorites dominated the repertoire more than usual that year, the company did produce its initial *Magic Flute*, the first the city had heard in twenty-three years. Most of the singers were young unknowns, but Moore said they "made the best balanced cast I ever heard." Massenet's *Hérodiade* was revived after an absence of six years, with Mary McCormic singing Salome and John Charles Thomas as Herod. The first *Parsifal* in eight years was heard, every seat in the house being sold five days before the performance—a record for the new house. René Maison was Parsifal, Frida Leider Kundry.

But the two big novelties that season were Leoni's *L'Oracolo* and Schillings' *Mona Lisa.* The first is set in San Francisco's Chinatown and tells of Chim Fen (sung in Chicago by Vanni Marcoux), the keeper of a combination gambling house and opium den, who kidnaps a child, murders the young man who tries to rescue it, and in turn is killed by the young man's father, Win Shee (sung by Virgilio Lazzari). The last scene, at least as Vanni Marcoux and Lazzari played it, was quite thrilling. Chim Fen has been stabbed and strangled by Win Shee, but is held by his murderer in an upright sitting position on a bench, while a policeman strolls by on his beat. When the policeman disappears down the dark alley, Win Shee gets up, lights his pipe, and strolls away, as the body of Chim Fen slowly collapses and falls to the ground. Antonio Scotti had made quite a reputation in the part at the Met, and he had already sung it at Ravinia in 1919. Now *L'Oracolo* was given on a triple bill with the ballet from *Prince Igor* and Puccini's one-act *Gianni Schicchi.* The *Tribune* called it "the most entertaining evening ever presented by the Civic Opera company, a program full of brightness, color, contrast, and general good feeling."

Mona Lisa, sung in German, was set in Renaissance Florence, and Frida Leider played the title role. When the opera opens, the famous Da Vinci portrait is hanging in the lady's home. Her husband is a goldsmith, much older and exceedingly jealous; he is unhappy because his wife rarely smiles in his presence as she does in the portrait. When he discovers her lover hiding in a small, airless treasure vault, the husband slams the door on him and leaves him to suffocate. Mona Lisa discovers the key and opens the door, allowing her lover to escape. When the husband goes in to find out what has happened, she in turn closes the door on him, locks it, her face lighting up in the famous smile of the portrait, shortly turning into a hysterical, shrieking laugh of triumph. Although the music was not nearly as interesting as the drama, Moore called it "stirring entertainment."

Rosa Raisa returned to the company that year, after giving birth to a baby daughter. The rest had rejuvenated her vocally, and she sang better than she had in years. Reviewing *La Juive*, her first performance of the season, *Musical America* said, "The voice has regained its incomparable luster, its prodigious overwhelming power, its inescapable appeal to the emotions. . . . It was a triumph such as one rarely witnesses in the theatre."

Lotte Lehmann returned for *Lohengrin* and *Die Meistersinger*. John Charles Thomas did his first *Rigoletto* with the company. Cyrena Van Gordon and Charles Marshall teamed for *Samson and Delilah*, and Vanni Marcoux again won honors as Boris Godunov. Throughout the whole season critics bent over backward to give the performances good reviews, some of them deserving. Three weeks deep in the season, Moore wrote, "Up to the time this is being written there has been not only no failure but not even a sag. Brilliant performances have been the rule, and their reactions on the audiences have been unmistakable." Even Moore himself later admitted this was laying it on a bit thick.

With the economic squeeze becoming greater, the artists agreed to take a salary cut of from 10 to 20 per cent, just as they had at the Metropolitan. Ticket prices still ranged from six dollars down to one dollar, substantial enough to make attendance impossible for some and difficult for others. Although attendance on the whole dropped, a new element became noticeable, Chicago's numerous Polish-Americans. The debut of their fellow countryman Jan Kiepura on opening night had brought out several, but the tenor's appearance in *Rigoletto* later in the week and subsequent performances produced even greater Polish support.

But the fund-raising campaign had not gone well. If the Civic Opera were to continue, it would be necessary to secure a total pledge of $500,000 a year for the next five years, just as had been done in 1922 and 1927. On January 30, a production of *Martha* was given, and with that the Civic Opera came to an end, its collapse spelling the end of an epoch. On February 16, Mr. Insull announced to the Friends of Opera that only $234,000 of the needed amount had been secured. In times as tight as these, patrons were understandably reluctant to commit themselves to lend financial support to anything, and many found it positively impossible. By the end of the season it was obvious that the funds could not be raised.

Then, adding a sad denouement to an already melancholy tale, Samuel Insull himself met with disaster. In April, 1932, his utilities kingdom collapsed. Companies valued at one time at three billion dollars were forced into bankruptcy. Faced with charges of fraud and embezzlement, Insull fled to Paris and later Athens. "I wish my time on earth had already come," he was quoted as saying. In March, 1934, extradited from Greece, he was arrested in Istanbul by the Turkish government and turned over to the United States. Brought back to Chicago, he was tried three times and each time acquitted. In May, 1934, Insull had said, "What I did, when I did it, was honest; now, through changed conditions, what I did may or may not be called honest. Politics demand, therefore, that I be brought to trial; but what is really being brought to trial is the system I represented." His empire and his great operatic dream were suddenly as dead as the age he embodied. Only the empty "throne" on Wacker Drive remained as Insull's legacy.

Chapter 11

ALL ON A SUMMER'S DAY

ANOTHER dimension to the Chicago Opera story which simply cannot be overlooked is the summertime opera given for nearly two decades at Ravinia Park on Chicago's North Shore, some twenty-five miles up from the Loop. The thirty-seven-acre Ravinia, owned first by the Chicago and Milwaukee Railway and later by a group of local citizens headed by Louis Eckstein, began its career in 1904 as an amusement park, only a little more sedate and tasteful than most. It had the usual bandstand, baseball diamond, carousel, Ferris wheel, and café. Occasionally a band concert was given there, and in 1906 Walter Damrosch came to conduct the first symphony in the park. Later, afternoon and evening concerts by Frederick Stock's Chicago Symphony and other orchestras became a fairly regular feature of Ravinia's summertime entertainment. Gradually these programs were broadened to include dance, drama, and opera. The bandstand was rebuilt so that it became the back wall of a stage projecting west. A large wooden pavilion, open on three sides, was constructed in front of it.

The guiding genius behind these musical presentations, Louis Eckstein, was a leading Chicago businessman. Eckstein was something of a man of mystery. Little is known of his early life or just how he got his start. He first appeared in Milwaukee, where at one time he played second violin in the resident orchestra. His fortune was primarily made in real estate, but by 1932 his name appeared on the boards of directors of some of the largest banks in Chicago. He once said he would be glad to prove that he had been a professional musician by playing the fiddle with the Chicago Symphony at Ravinia if his friend Charles Dawes would join him on the flute. Dawes declined, saying he would just as soon restrict his support to the guarantor fund.

Eckstein was a dedicated opera lover, and as early as 1912 a few operatic selections were presented at Ravinia as a supplement to the orchestral program. Shortly entire acts from operas were given on certain evenings of the week. At first only a few singers were hired, but the number was quickly increased, for Eckstein was convinced that Americans would love opera if they were given more of a chance to hear it. By 1915 a full-fledged opera season was being staged at Ravinia during five of the ten summer weeks. Eckstein's first plan was to give opera in English, feeling that this was the best way of teaching the American public to appreciate the art. When this failed, Eckstein begin hiring some of the great Metropolitan and Chicago Opera artists and switched to opera in the original language. His success was almost immediate, and crowds began flocking to his productions.

Ravinia's setting undoubtedly had something to do with its success, for it was, and is, perfectly beautiful. Describing the scene for *The Etude* in 1932, Glenn Dillard Gunn wrote, "Imagine a park set on the shores of a great inland sea, its lawns verdant, its every vista inviting. Imagine an ancient and weathered pavilion set amid towering elms and maples so that it seems a part of the grove. Picture these trees dark against the sunset glow, black and misty in the moonlight or vaguely etched against the stars. . . . Such is Ravinia."

Summertime in Chicago, as elsewhere, has traditionally been a time of informality, one when social activities are few. Families could go to Ravinia, spread out a blanket in the glade in front of the pavilion, and have a picnic before the performance began. There was none of the pomp and ceremony of the winter opera season at Ravinia, none of the society air and none of the snobbery. Patrons walked and chatted among the trees until the trumpet called them to their places. Once in their seats, audiences seemed more attentive than usual, and conversations during overtures and orchestral interludes were characteristically held to a minimum. Audiences seemed to be caught by the spell of the opera and the surroundings.

The pavilion itself could seat eighteen hundred people, but thousands more could lie on blankets or sit on stools and listen to the music. Smoking was permitted for those who wanted to, and no one objected if the men took off their coats on warm evenings. An occasional pop bottle might roll down under the seats during the performance, or a plane might be heard overhead, but these became part of the charm, as were the periodic showers. Since admission prices were kept reasonable, people from every walk of life attended. Most patrons came from Chicago and Milwaukee, but music lovers from all over the nation made a point of visiting Ravinia if they were in the vicinity. Special trains and trolleys were chartered to bring people out from the neighboring cities, and many came by car.

The acoustics at Ravinia were superb, so good that on a calm evening the music could be heard for more than a mile away. "Its dull brown rafters," Gunn said, "its gabled ceiling of board and shingle, the planks of its floor and the strained timbers of its proscenium are so many parts of a resonant chamber." Critics said this wooden chamber gave the voice a mellow sound. Otto Kahn, who once called Ravinia "the Stradivarius of all theaters," insisted that if it could be picked up and carried to some location in central Europe, people would throng to Ravinia from all over the civilized world. The pavilion itself was strung with Japanese lanterns, lending even more atmosphere to the natural, rustic environment.

Louis Eckstein directed Ravinia with the same executive ability that had earned him his millions, and he did it practically alone. He planned the season, engaged the artists, and arranged the repertoire. He donated his services and in the end paid the bulk of the deficit, which was always substantial. In 1929 the then ten weeks of summer opera showed a loss of $200,000; in 1931 it was $280,000, over two-thirds of which was borne by Eckstein. By 1932 it was estimated that Ravinia had cost its manager over a million dollars in the past twenty years.

By the early 1920's the "opera house in the woods" had become internationally acclaimed. It imported some of the outstanding singers of the operatic world, sometimes long before they sang with the downtown forces, and gave fine performances. Edith Mason, one of the artists whom Chicagoans first heard at Ravinia, made her debut there in 1917—four seasons before she was hired by Mary Garden to sing at the Auditorium. Forty years later, Miss Mason recalled Ravinia with much fondness, insisting that she "loved it there." Claudia Muzio first sang at Ravinia in 1918, two years after her Metropolitan debut, but before she had sung in either South America or with the downtown Chicago company. Eckstein even coaxed Muzio into the French repertoire, and she did roles for him, like Manon and Marguerite, which she rarely did anywhere else.

In 1919 Antonio Scotti appeared at Ravinia in Leoni's *L'Oracolo,* an opera which the baritone had performed successfully at the Metropolitan, but one which Chicago had not heard before and would not hear again until 1931. Scotti returned the next year to sing Scarpia, and Charles Marshall added his name to the roster that same season. Anna Fitziu played Tosca in 1921 to the Cavaradossi of Charles Hackett, while Florence Macbeth sang Gilda. Tito Schipa, who had sung four years with the Chicago

Opera, made his Ravinia debut on opening night 1923 as Alfredo in *Traviata. Musical America* called it "one of the best *Traviata* performances ever given anywhere." It was sold out five days in advance. Lucrezia Bori opened the festival in 1925 as Fiora in *L'Amore dei Tre Re*, and later in the same season Rosa Raisa and Giacomo Rimini made their Ravinia debuts. Through the years some of the greatest names from both the Metropolitan and the Chicago Opera appeared on Ravinia's roster: Yvonne Gall, Edward Johnson, Florence Easton, Mario Chamlee, Elisabeth Rethberg, Giovanni Martinelli, Virgilio Lazzari, to name just a few. The chorus numbered about forty, the orchestra around fifty, and among Ravinia's conductors were Gennaro Papi and Louis Hasselmans.

Eckstein's repertoire was progressive and varied. During the first three weeks of the 1921 season, for instance, fourteen different operas were heard. The following season opened with *Boris Godunov*, a year before the opera was heard at the Auditorium. *The Secret of Suzanne*, *La Navarraise*, and *Zaza* (with Alice Gentle) were all heard that same summer. In 1928 Rabaud's comic *Marouf*, an opera never given by the downtown forces, was staged with Yvonne Gall and Mario Chamlee and proved at Ravinia to be the success it had been in Paris, rather than the failure it had been at the Metropolitan. In 1929 De Falla's *La Vida Breve*, another work never sung by the Chicago Opera, was given at Ravinia with Lucrezia Bori in the lead. Smetana's *The Bartered Bride*, Puccini's *La Rondine* (with Bori), Respighi's *La Campana Sommersa*, and Deems Taylor's *Peter Ibbetson* (sung by Bori, Johnson, and Macbeth) were all big successes at Ravinia. But the old favorites were not forgotten. In later years, for example, Bori sang Manon, Martinelli did Radames and Andrea Chénier, and Rethberg sang Elsa, Aida, and Madeleine.

Besides giving good performances, the artists seemed to enjoy themselves. Once in *La Rondine*, during prohibition, Bori watched with laughing dark eyes while the company lifted their glasses and found them actually filled with expensive champagne. Another time Mario Chamlee echoed the pitch of a train whistle that could be heard in the distance. One exceedingly warm evening Martinelli, singing Faust, came on stage only to break up with laughter when he found Mephistopheles' goatee stuck to his neck.

There were problems, of course, in presenting outdoor opera. The stage was small and therefore permitted little of the spectacle that one customarily found in the productions at the Auditorium, and seldom was any attempted. Since many people came to Ravinia by train, schedules had to be taken into consideration, even though the trains were specials. It was necessary that the opera be over as close to eleven o'clock as possible. Therefore, the longer works had to be given in shortened versions. This was a great handicap—*Carmen* was reduced to three acts, *Lohengrin* to two, and intermissions were held to a minimum.

What was lost in length, however, was gained in intimacy, for really no one in the pavilion was very far from the stage, not nearly as far as in the normal opera house. Comic operas, like *The Barber of Seville*, *L'Elisir d'Amore*, and *Don Pasquale*, particularly benefited from this, although the dramatic works, too, often became more interesting in the smaller confines.

But the depression hit Ravinia just as it did the Civic Opera and everything else. In April, 1932, it was announced that there would be no summer opera that year. "Existing economic conditions prompt this action," Eckstein explained, "not only from the standpoint of the guarantors but from the standpoint of the public." For four seasons Ravinia was not used at all for music, and the opera season there was never resumed.

Summer programs returned to the park in 1936, consisting of a variety of musical events. A modern music shed eventually replaced the old bandstand and pavilion that Eckstein had built, and seating and parking facilities were expanded. An attendance record was established in 1936 when pianist-composer George Gershwin appeared, while Artur Rodzinski made his initial appearance with the Chicago Symphony at Ravinia in July, 1938. Frederick Stock, then retired, conducted the opening concert in 1941, honoring the successful conclusion of the Chicago Symphony's golden-jubilee year. That same summer Sir Thomas Beecham, Pierre Monteux, and Georg Szell were all guest conductors there, and Helen Traubel and Yehudi Menuhin were among the soloists. Great jazz artists like Benny Goodman have appeared there frequently, and a summer program today might well range from Igor Stravinsky to Joan Baez to Dave Brubeck to Elisabeth Schwarzkopf. While its opera belongs to the past, Ravinia remains one of America's finest and most popular summer musical festivals.

Chapter 12

OH! DEAR, WHAT CAN THE MATTER BE?

In the spring of 1932 the depression was nearing rock bottom. Nearly forty Chicago banks had gone under, and Charles Dawes, heading Hoover's Reconstruction Finance Corporation at the time, had to resign his post so that the RFC could authorize a loan of ninety million dollars to save his own First National Bank, one of the hardest hit. That summer both the Republican and the Democratic conventions were held in Chicago. The first rather listlessly renominated Herbert Hoover, while the latter chose New York's governor, Franklin Roosevelt, who energetically promised Americans a "New Deal." Meanwhile the depression wore on.

Fall found Chicago in the depths of cultural, as well as economic, despair. With the collapse of the Civic Opera Company, the new Opera House would remain dark, spelling unemployment for some and musical privation for many more. "The fact is that opera has little real hold upon Americans," the *Christian Science Monitor* explained. "It is a curious, if unpalatable, commentary on the status of music in the United States that the closing of the Chicago Civic Opera will leave just one major and permanent operatic association to serve a population of 120,000,000." But even the Metropolitan had a tough time of it in those years. Its season was cut by a third, and the interest of the public, and particularly society, had dwindled to a minimum. "The Met is old," said one report, "and has committed the crime of outliving the social generation that gave it brilliance and to which it gave a rococo Victorian setting." London's Covent Garden and the Colon Opera in Buenos Aires had it no easier, both coming close to canceling their seasons. The Cincinnati Zoo Opera and the

Philadelphia Grand Opera did cancel, and the Chicago Symphony almost went under.

The only local opera Chicago heard in 1932–33 was given by the Chicago Stadium Grand Opera Company, which began a popular-priced series on October 15 with a production of *Aida.* Maurice Frank was the impresario. One end of the Chicago Stadium was designated as a stage by a canvas proscenium arch. A single set was used throughout, augmented with a few movable props. An estimated twelve thousand people, coming from every segment of society and including several thousand school children, attended the opening. The repertoire consisted solely of popular favorites, and, compared to the Civic Opera, production standards were rather amateurish.

Late in the summer of 1933 the Chicago Grand Opera Company was formed, with George Woodruff as its president. Paul Longone, one-time associate of Campanini in the old Chicago Grand Opera Association and later director of the Dal Verme Theater in Milan, became the general manager, while Gennaro Papi was chosen musical director. There was talk for a while that the new company would stage its operas in the Auditorium, but eventually the Civic Opera House was selected, since the scenery, costumes, and properties of the Civic Opera were tied to the new house. Although the Auditorium was still strongly preferred, using it would have meant paying a rental on scenery and costumes in addition to the fee for the Auditorium itself.

The season that winter was planned in about five weeks. Two weeks before the opening decisions on repertoire and casting were still being made. The company operated on a financial shoestring, its weekly outlay averaging from $29,000 to $36,000, as compared with the $125,000 a week spent by the Civic Opera. Ticket prices were scaled from fifty cents to three dollars. Shortly before Christmas, the canvas coverings were taken off the seats at the Civic Opera House. The dust was swept up, and music once more began to resound from its stage.

The five-week season opened on December 26, with the Tosca of Maria Jeritza. Edward Moore was enthusiastic: "The new season went off with a bang. All that the Chicago Grand Opera company has to do now is to keep up the record that it set last night, and there can be little question but that opera will once again be one of the favorite indoor amusements of the Chicago public." Outside it was ten degrees below zero. Inside something approximating the old glamour returned. Tiaras were on almost every head, while gowns tended to be tight-fitting, swirling around the ankles and often ending in a long train. Feathers were adding a feminine touch, worn in the hair, and around shoulders and ankles. Grace and delicacy were still the keynote. The *Tribune* reporter observed that women were even walking more elegantly and seductively than they had a few years before, when the athletic, mannish stride was so fashionable. During intermissions the lobby was filled with promenaders, while dozens hung over the banisters of staircases and over the railing of the upper foyer, watching the scene below. Inside the auditorium, a temporary row of boxes had been added across the main floor, halfway back from the stage.

Among the great triumphs of the season was the first Chicago staging of Puccini's posthumous *Turandot.* Rosa Raisa, who had created the part at La Scala seven years before, sang the title role, repeating one of the triumphs of her career. Gennaro Papi conducted the score entirely from memory, as was his custom with all operas. "The spectacular work," according to *Musical America,* "was staged with a lavishness and generosity which betrayed no hint of depression." Raisa's costumes particularly were positively gorgeous, her train in the second act forty feet long. At the end of the music completed by Puccini, Papi paused, while critic Karleton Hackett came on stage to inform the audience that the composer's death had prevented his finishing the opera and that the work from this point on had been completed from Puccini's sketches by Franco Alfano. At its conclusion the capacity house remained to applaud and cheer long after the final curtain.

The rest of the repertoire consisted of familiar works, sung mostly by favorite artists. Raisa did *Tosca, Aida,* and *Cavalleria Rusticana.* Edith Mason returned, her entrance in *La Bohème* almost stopping the show. She later sang *Faust* and *Madama Butterfly.* Elisabeth Rethberg also did *Butterfly,* and Coe Glade repeated Carmen, a role she had made her hallmark during the Civic Opera days.

Escapism was still the dominant theme in American entertainment. Buster Crabbe was hailed that year as the new Tarzan, while "I'm No Angel" was making Mae West a household word. Walt Disney was delighting audiences that winter with his *Three Little Pigs,* although the porkers' song, "Who's Afraid of the Big Bad Wolf?" had more than romantic meaning for a people who were beginning to feel, despite only slightly improved conditions, that the depression could be overcome. The "hundred days" were now history, but the "New Deal" was still largely enjoying a honeymoon. Huey Long was booed when he assailed President Roosevelt in a speech in Louisiana. The United States was still insisting that Europe would have to get out of its present difficulties without our help—we had our own problems. That we were more confident about solving those problems was also becoming apparent.

The Chicago Grand Opera Company opened its season in the fall of 1934 on an equally optimistic note. Harold F. McCormick had agreed to serve as the honorary chairman of the board, and the season had been extended to six weeks. The top ticket price had been increased to four dollars. The season began with *Turandot*, now with Maria Jeritza as the Chinese princess. "I wish that words could express the magnificence of Mme. Jeritza," Moore wrote in his review, "as she appeared on an enormous staircase, a flight that looked as though it were leading up to the stars, flanked on each side with what looked like thousands, but perhaps might have added up to scores of choristers." Society had been shocked when the company broke precedence and announced the opening for a Saturday night. But the fashionable set showed up just the same, with furs "so much in evidence that one might have thought that ermines and silver foxes were as plentiful as alley cats." After the opera the chief executives and their wives gave a reception on stage for the guarantors and the first-night box holders.

Jeritza sang *Salome* a little later, reviving memories of Mary Garden for a small, but appreciative, audience. Moore felt that "even after a quarter century's hardening process one still finds some slight reason to cavil at what Oscar Wilde put into words and Richard Strauss underlined with one of the most skilful [sic] operatic scores ever composed." The production emphasized Salome's evil through the use of vivid reds. Jeritza's cloak and hair were both scarlet, accentuated by red pillars and a red light shining down on her face. At the moment of the execution she became so excited that she lowered the upper part of her body into the well, only her naked legs remaining visible.

No less exciting was Edith Mason's first *Traviata* on any stage. *Musical America* said, "Miss Mason's delightful voice and exquisite art have never been heard to better advantage," while Edward Moore wrote, "I . . . desire to testify that never before have I heard the role of Violetta sung as Miss Mason sang it, and I have been listening to *La Traviata* ever since Tetrazzini was in her prime." The first-act coloratura was dashed off with almost reckless brilliance, but in the lyrical second act her triumph was even greater.

Lauritz Melchior made his local debut in a Saturday matinee of *Tristan und Isolde*, opposite Elsa Alsen, under the direction of the Chicago Symphony's Frederick Stock. It was the second time that Stock had appeared with the city's opera forces; the first was the *Siegfried* back in 1923. Moore proclaimed Melchior "the best Tristan who had ever appeared in Chicago," but almost everyone agreed the real honors of the afternoon went to Stock. At the end of the performance manager Longone appeared on stage to present the conductor with a floral wreath. That evening Ezio Pinza made his debut in the city as Don Giovanni. As *Musical America* recorded it, "He was suave, dashing, handsome, a consummate actor, everything that a Don Juan should be, and more, a superb singer." It was by all odds the biggest day of the season.

Lotte Lehmann returned to the Civic Opera House for *Lohengrin* and *Tannhäuser*, both conducted by Henry Weber, now the musical director of radio station WGN. Elisabeth Rethberg, Coe Glade, and John Charles Thomas were all back, and Giovanni Martinelli was a sensation in everything he did, particularly *La Forza del Destino*.

A number of slightly known Americans were included on the roster that season, mostly as an economy measure, although this was not admitted at the time. "There is little reason to look to Europe for our stars," Paul Longone had said. "Today the best American singers rank on a par with the best of the foreign groups." He was particularly excited about two youngsters—Franca Somigli, who was called Marion Clark when she lived in New York, and Giuseppe Bentonelli, known by his friends at Oklahoma Agricultural College as Joe Benton. Somigli sang Madeleine in *Andrea Chénier* and Leonora in *Trovatore*, both with Martinelli. Bentonelli did Cavaradossi opposite Maria Jeritza's Tosca. The two Americans were received politely, but little more.

The season closed with a gala potpourri, including a rather pointed burlesque entitled "Syringomyelia," a medical term denoting a chronic progressive disease of the spine. It began with a director's meeting in which Paul Longone was portrayed arguing for an opera season with first-rate casts, one which would cost from fifty to seventy-five thousand dollars, while the directors ordered him to engage Americans that would sing for nothing. With that, largely because of financial reasons, the company suspended operations.

That summer another attempt was made to revive the city's opera when the Chicago City Opera Company was organized, Paul Longone again serving as general manager. Looking to business leaders and civic officials for support, Longone vowed that operating costs would be kept to a minimum and that ticket prices would be held within the reach of as many people as possible. Consequently, there was a return to the three-dollar maximum.

The 1935 season opened with Boito's *Mefistofele*, sung by Ezio Pinza for the first time in the United States. The *Tribune* maintained, "The majesty of the '*Ave Signor*' and the effective pantomine of the scene confirmed his audience in the belief that he is one of the very finest singing actors of the day." Edith Mason was the Marguerite, and Gennaro Papi conducted.

Skirts were now long, way below the knee, and a lady of fashion was paying more attention to her hair. "Sleek, perfectly cut and curled hair isn't enough," said society columnist India Moffett; "to be really chic she must have an ornament in her hair and when she steps from her motor she is apt to be hooded so that not one hair can be displaced by the wind." The opening seemed gayer than it had in some time, because, said the *Tribune*, "every one is in a better frame of mind and feeling a bit more prosperous." New faces were becoming increasingly dominant, as more and more of the old-timers were disappearing. Harold McCormick had been ill and was not present, and right before the season began, critics Karleton Hackett and Edward Moore died within a day of each other. Hackett died in the hospital, following a long illness, while Moore was standing on the station platform at Ravinia when he succumbed to a heart attack.

Yet judging from this opening, Chicago's interest in opera seemed to be as keen as ever. Not only was the Civic Opera House sold out, but the Auditorium, where Fortune Gallo's San Carlo company was giving *Carmen*, also played to a capacity house. Over seven thousand people heard grand opera in Chicago that one evening.

The general picture, however, was less happy, both in attendance and in production standards. The Chicago City Opera operated on a budget cut to the bone. So great was the financial pressure that more than once it was improbable at six o'clock in the evening that the curtain would even go up at eight. As a result, performances were often ragged and under-rehearsed. Many of the singers were grossly unqualified for their roles, as one of Longone's more dubious policies was his practice of allowing wealthy would-be singers to purchase productions, a practice he defended as helping to balance the budget. And there were bizarre attempts to make opera more popular. For instance, night-club entertainers Veloz and Yolanda were borrowed from the Empire Room of the Palmer House to head the ballet in *Carmen.* Shep Fields, the Empire Room's band leader, took the baton for their dances. During this same performance, Micaela lost her hat when Don José fired at her from offstage, causing one gentleman in the audience to emit, "Too bad; they missed her."

Individual artists frequently gave outstanding performances, apparently oblivious to the low-level production standards around them. Marjorie Lawrence sang Brünnhilde opposite Melchior's Siegmund in *Die Walküre*, and Lily Pons, who had scored such a sensation in her Metropolitan debut in 1931, was first heard in Delibes' *Lakmé*. Helen Jepson was introduced to the city in *Thaïs*, supported by John Charles Thomas' Athanael.

Lotte Lehmann sang the Marschallin in *Der Rosenkavalier* for the first time in the city in a generally good production, conducted by Henry Weber and staged by Désiré Defrère, who had sung with the Chicago Opera during the Campanini days. *Turandot* was successfully given for the third consecutive year, again with Raisa. But the unqualified success of the season was the first American staging of Respighi's *La Fiamma*, trailing the world premiere in Rome by one year. "The music," the *Tribune said,* "is hysterical, maddening, torturing, as he [Respighi] marshals all the resources of voice and orchestra and all the accumulated technical devices of three centuries of operatic history to project the horror and savagery of this grisly tale of witch burning and despair and falseness." Rosa Raisa sang the lead, doing "some of the most effective singing and acting of her career." As *Musical America* put it, "In the midst of the chaos and turbulence which have characterized the course of the present opera season came a novelty and a performance which carried Chicagoans back to the best of the good old days for adequate comparison." *Time* agreed that *La Fiamma* had been better than good, but added, "It was not enough to make subscribers forget what they had sat through before."

John Charles Thomas, in addition to *Thaïs* and *Rigoletto*, took part in the world premiere of Ethel Leginska's one-act *Gale*, with Miss Leginska, formerly conductor of the Chicago Women's Symphony, serving in the pit. Friends of Leginska had put up five thousand dollars to see her opera produced, one thousand dollars of which was to cover Thomas' fee. Indicating the extent to which chaos reigned at the Opera House that season, four days before the premiere of *Gale* nothing had been done toward its preparation. The first performance was really nothing more than a public rehearsal, as even Thomas did not know his part. His understudy said that Thomas sang only about half of the correct words that first night.

At the end of what *Time* called "undoubtedly the worst season of opera that a resident Chicago company has ever presented," the deficit was figured at something under $40,000, less than half what it had been the year before. Of this the city paid $15,000, in an effort to keep the company alive. Attendance for the year had been around 60 per cent of capacity.

It was obvious that the Chicago City Opera could not go through another season without somehow securing a firmer economic base. Jason F. Whitney, the company's president, who came to Chicago from Boston eight years before, after retiring as head of a large cheese factory, proposed a "cash-and-carry" plan, whereby one thousand Chicagoans would each give one hundred dollars to the company at the outset of the new season. In return they became life members of the new Opera Club, were given their choice of season's seats, and were "guaranteed" life immunity from further expenditures arising from deficits. By October Whitney announced that his one thousand donors were in sight. In addition those businesses which directly benefited from the opera season—clothing stores, shoe stores, glove stores, cleaning and dyeing establishments, taxi companies, hat shops, hairdressers, hotels, and restaurants—were asked to make cash donations to bolster the Opera's deficit fund.

By 1936 the era of good feeling for the New Deal was over. Franklin Roosevelt was being denounced by some as too liberal, by others as too conservative. The election that fall would measure the people's response to his program of social reform. Americans now realized that there was no easy way out of the depression and had steeled themselves for a long battle against economic ill winds. When the opera season opened—October 31, three days before the Presidential election—a more somber atmosphere pervaded than had been the case a few months back. In keeping with this more serious attitude, tiaras and silk hats were much less in evidence among the first-nighters than was the modest garb of the ordinary music lover. The coming coronation in England, however, had affected headdresses to a point where dozens of women were wearing Prince-of-Wales plumes in their hair. Mrs. Bertha Baur, who was running for Congress herself, wore a corsage of Landon buttons instead of flowers.

The company opened, somewhat desperately, with the big hit of the year before, *La Fiamma*. It was less successful now, and even Raisa herself had vocal difficulties, much of her former ease and opulence of voice seemed missing. Compared with an opening twenty years before, the whole occasion was a pretty tame affair. A veteran ticket-taker, who had been standing at the door of first the Auditorium and then the Civic Opera House, watching opera patrons arrive for forty years, told India Moffett, "It isn't the same, Mrs. Moffett. Are the ones who used to come dead and don't their sons and daughters like opera?" Many of the old-timers were dead, and a number of their sons and daughters did not like opera, but a new age was dawning in the city's operatic history, one less oriented toward the Gold Coast. For India Moffett, "the audience that filled the great Civic Opera house last night was an inspiration, an augury of the splendid future that is ours, a future in which opera, like so many other things, is 'of the people . . . for the people.' " Throughout the season the company urged people to come in business clothes. Dressing formally was no longer expected.

The Chicago City Opera had worked out an arrangement with the Metropolitan which enabled a number of Met artists to participate in the Chicago season, heralding a period when Chicago's productions would virtually look like carbon copies of those given in New York. Martinelli sang *Otello* for the first time in the city that year, ably supported by Edith Mason and Lawrence Tibbett, and also teamed with Elisabeth Rethberg for *Aida*. Helen Jepson sang *Louise* and *Martha*, the latter with Tito Schipa and Giacomo Rimini, and Marjorie Lawrence did Elizabeth in *Tannhäuser*. Louis Gruenberg's *Jack and the Beanstalk* received its world premiere at a Saturday matinee, displaying a score which the *Tribune* said was "clever, apt, rich in surprises, effectively scored." The treatment of the story, however, was somewhat unorthodox at times, including a giant with a falsetto voice, an unbelievable gullibility, and a passion for jazz. The cow was depicted as a bitter defeatist, eager to denounce, in a loud bass voice, the vanity of accomplishment, yet with a sentimental turn which caused her to break easily into tears.

Three ladies sang *La Bohème* that year, each making news. One was a fifteen-year-old Chicago high school junior named Betty Jaynes, who was appearing in opera for the first time. As a matter of fact, *Bohème* was the only opera she knew. She sang opposite Martinelli, following an enthusiastic press build-up. Critics were kind. More impressive was Vivian Della Chiesa, another Chicagoan, who two years before had won a vocal contest conducted by a local radio station. She was so enthusiastically greeted when she made her entrance that it was necessary for her to take a bow before the performance could continue. At the end of Mimi's first aria, the house broke into a storm of applause. A little later in the season she triumphed again in *L'Elisir d'Amore* with Schipa.

But the big news that year was the much discussed return of Galli-Curci. She had not sung in opera in six years because of increasing vocal troubles resulting from goiter. An operation in the summer of 1935, it was said, had returned her voice to its former beauty and given it new weight. She was through with coloratura, Galli-Curci declared, and planned to focus her new career on lyric and dramatic roles. Her return to opera was set for November 24, 1936, twenty years, give or take a week, after her legendary American debut at the Auditorium. She chose *La Bohème* as the opera, and the Civic Opera House was sold out long in advance. The soprano had never sung with any of Longone's singers, was a stranger to the new opera house, but was told there would be no rehearsal.

The audience came that night nervous and afraid, hoping beyond hope that she would be the great Galli-Curci of the past, but fearing disaster. The first twenty minutes of *Bohème* seemed like an eternity. There was no reaction to the preliminary antics of the Bohemians except for an occasional forced giggle. When Galli-Curci came on the scene, the audience overwhelmed her with a seven-minute ovation. As she began to sing, the house realized that she, too, was nervous. "Touched by the vehement friendliness of her reception," the *Tribune* reported, "and realizing the terror of this moment which was to answer the unasked question in these thousands of minds, the great soprano used her voice gingerly." Now and then a tremolo was audible, and she consistently backed away from climaxes, apparently "unwilling to trust her full tones." In the middle register some of the old magic seemed to remain, but on the high notes she seemed to be treading lightly. It was from everyone's viewpoint, the *Tribune* said, "one of the most fearfully nervous evenings in operatic history." During the final curtain calls the audience, almost with a sense of relief, insisted on a whole string of solo bows from the diva, and only then did her stage fright seem to leave her. The critics were gentle. Edward Barry of the *Tribune* wrote, "The answer is neither Yes nor No. It is Probably." But Galli-Curci knew better. She discarded further operatic plans, restricting herself to an occasional concert.

On the whole the 1936 Chicago season had gone better, if not well. Attendance was up about 5 per cent, including at least nine sold-out houses, and the financial picture was considerably improved. To achieve this, however, the company had resorted to some rather incredible measures, including the holding of open houses on Saturday afternoons, where, for fifty cents, opera buffs could watch a rehearsal and pry around backstage. Still the purpose was achieved; the company remained solvent.

Americans had lived with depression now for over seven years, and in most circles subsistence had become a way of life. Music and drama had been hit as hard as anything else, and more than one writer and actor and musician was kept alive through these lean years by WPA support. When the 1936 opera season opened, the WPA's dramatization of Sinclair Lewis' *It Can't Happen Here* was playing at the Blackstone. In December the Great Northern was offering a song-and-dance frolic called "O Say Can you Sing?" also sponsored by WPA funds. After living with their belts tightened for these seven years, most Americans had given up putting on airs. Their pleasures, for the most part, were of the simpler sort—listening to the radio at home, playing cards, or attending an occasional Saturday night movie, especially if the latest Ginger Rogers–Fred Astaire musical or Jean Harlow film was playing. In times like these, opera was destined to know privation, and did. Just as for many individuals, survival for the opera company spelled success.

Only about half of the opening-night audience in 1937 came in formal evening dress. The other half, many of whom sat on the main floor, simply wore street clothes. Furs were only sparsely in evidence. One observer said that the most dressed-up people there were the ticket-takers, who wore black broadcloth opera capes. Another unusual fact was that the audience consisted of people of all ages, including tiny children. The whole event seemed to be more a family affair than a grand social occasion. "The thousands had one thing in common, however," the *Tribune* reported, "every face was eager and expectant as though its owner was thrilled at being there. The Chicago City Opera company already has achieved what the management has hoped for—to have opera of the people."

Aida held the boards for the opening, again with Rethberg and Martinelli. From the beginning there seemed to be more genuine interest in opera than at any time since the collapse of the Insull regime, and the performances certainly were better than they had been. Kirsten Flagstad, who had first appeared at the Metropolitan two years before, caused a sensation when she made her local debut as Isolde, opposite Melchior's Tristan. "Mme. Flagstad's voice rides the long breathed phrases," the *Tribune* said, and "she has a genius for looking epic." The packed house staged a demonstration in her behalf unparalleled in recent years. She repeated her triumph later in *Tannhäuser* with Melchior and again in *Die Walküre*, with Melchior and Helen Traubel.

Traubel had first been heard in the city as Mary in Walter Damrosch's *A Man Without a Country*, the seventy-five-year-old composer conducting. "Here is an American opera," Edward Barry wrote for the *Tribune*, "with the smell of the soil in the first act and the tarry exhilaration of seagoing frigates in the second." The opera had its world premiere at the Metropolitan less than six months before, with much the same cast.

Grace Moore made her Chicago debut in *Manon*. She had been scheduled to sing in 1936, but had had to cancel when a movie she was making ran over schedule. She was well known to Chicagoans through her films and radio appearances long before she actually sang there and was an instant success. Physically beautiful, magnificently gowned, and displaying skillful acting and singing, she was a Manon to reckon with. For the first time since the opening of the Civic Opera House, flowers were thrown across the footlights from the orchestra floor. Still another newcomer was twenty-six-year-old Jussi Bjoerling, making his American debut as the Duke in *Rigoletto*. Well-built and handsome, he was considered at the time something of a boy wonder. "Mr. Bjorling [sic] revealed an excellent tenor that at times betrays immature handling," *Musical America* said, "but he has fine range and volume and an easy stage presence." His Gilda was an eighteen-year-old Chicago schoolgirl named Beverly Lane. Lawrence Tibbett was the Rigoletto.

Lily Pons sang *Lucia di Lammermoor*. Martinelli did *Samson and Delilah*, sharing honors with Ruth Page's ballet. Raisa returned for *La Juive* and *Cavalleria Rusticana*. Helen Jepson made personal successes of *Traviata* and *L'Amore dei Tre Re*. Rose Bampton, another new voice, was heard as Leonora in *Trovatore*, while Gina Cigna was introduced as Norma, in a cast that included Coe Glade, Frederick Jagel, and Ezio Pinza. Lotte Lehmann was back for *Der Rosenkavalier* and *Lohengrin*, and Moniuszko's *Halka* was given in the original Polish, much to the pleasure of the city's sizable Polish population.

The season, which everyone seemed to agree was the best since the pre-depression days, closed with a gala which included the premiere of a ballet by Jerome Moross, entitled *An American Pattern*. It was an interesting piece, reflecting much of the liberal, intellectual questioning of the time. Danced by Ruth Page and her ballet, the story tells of an American wife who grows tired of her businessman husband and attempts to flee the respectability and conventionality of her class. She experiments with gigolos, lovers, exotic religions, and communism, but in the end she is conquered by the figures of three old women symbolizing middle class, conventionality, and respectability.

The Civic Opera House was still the subject of a lively controversy, just as it had been when it was built. Cecil Smith, writing for the *Tribune*, said during the season, "You may despise the garish decorative scheme of our opera house as much as I do, but at least the theater is blessed with infinitely better visibility and far more comfortable seats than the Metropolitan Opera House."

The 1938 season opened on October 29—amid talk of German rule of Hungary and Hitler's ousting the Polish Jews—with Martinelli, Jepson, and Tibbett in *Otello*. Tweeds for the ladies were now in high fashion, along with some of the wildest feather headdresses in captivity. "One young woman," the *Tribune* reported, "was wearing what appeared to be a large red uncurled ostrich feather fan fastened to the side of her head so that her face was completely hidden from that side. Another had three decided question marks above her brow and still another had a swirl of aigrettes like a Fourth of July pinwheel." One old-timer, who had attended many an opening, said in disgust, "There are more clowns here than I've ever seen before; I almost would think it was a fancy dress ball." "Maybe it's because it's Halloween," his companion suggested.

The season was extended that year to seven weeks, with ticket prices ranging from $1.10 to $4.40. *Turandot* again proved a popular success, now with Eva Turner in the title role. Dusolina Giannini and Bruna Castagna were introduced to the city in *Aida*, while James Melton was heard first as Pinkerton. And returning to the American operatic stage, after an absence of six years, was Beniamino Gigli. Forty-eight years old, an international sensation for eighteen years, Gigli had never been heard in opera in Chicago. He came now for *Martha*, with Helen Jepson. The "audience reacted to the double excitement of a long heralded return and a long awaited local operatic debut by putting on a demonstration that all but blew the roof off the Civic Opera house," the *Tribune* reported. After "*M'Appari*" the house broke into one of the most spontaneous, most genuine, ovations the city has ever paid any artist. The opera came to a complete standstill, until finally the no-encore ruling had to be set aside. "Here were tone colorings," the *Tribune* declared, "calculated to mist the eyes of the most hardened operagoers, phrasing of such exquisite delicacy that the audience hardly dared to breathe until a cadence of some sort came along."

That summer disaster again struck Chicago's opera. In August, less than a month before the German invasion of Poland, Paul Longone, the central pillar of the company for the past six years, died in France. He had already worked out the plans for the 1939 season, and these Henry Weber agreed to implement when he took over as musical director.

The season began with *Boris Godunov.* By now France and Great Britain had entered the war. Germany had just signed a non-aggression pact with Russia. Therefore, the *Tribune* felt *Boris* a timely revival, adding prophetically, "We are hearing plenty about Russia these days, and are likely to hear more." Ezio Pinza sang the role of the mad czar, while Elen Longone, the late director's widow, sang the role of Marina. Weber conducted. The opera was considerably shortened, for it was President Jason Whitney's conviction that opera should be as concentrated as possible. His aim, as the *Tribune* interpreted it, was to present the "business man's opera by doing away with long and tedious recitation conducive to slumber. So the *Boris* score had been attacked with an ax, and not permitted to get good men down on the opening night. In the eighteenth century, opera-goers had plenty of time to sleep next day, and a five hour performance was what they were paying for."

The younger set was conspicuously absent from the Opera House these days. One observer on opening night said, "You could count the young marrieds present on your fingers." Women seemed to be rediscovering jewels and furs, and lace mantillas had returned to fashion. But for once the men made a more striking picture than the ladies, wearing swallowtail coats, white bow ties, white kid gloves, and high silk hats. The crowd that gathered outside just to watch the first-nighters arrive had become larger with the years, making "an opera premiere somewhat like a movie preview in Hollywood."

Returning that year, now as a mature artist, was Gladys Swarthout. She sang *Mignon* and her first *Carmen* on a major operatic stage, proving every bit the sensation Mary Garden had predicted she would be. Grace Moore was heard in her first Chicago *Louise* by a house that could have been sold out twice again. Gigli returned for *Andrea Chénier*, and John Charles Thomas did Figaro in *The Barber of Seville*. Giovanni Martinelli added some excitement by singing his first German opera anywhere. "When I am old and gray," Edward Barry wrote, "and full of yarns the luckless tots who will have to listen to tales of the golden age of opera will come to hate the very mention of November 24, 1939." That was the date of Martinelli's first *Tristan und Isolde*, which Barry found "the most sensational . . . I have ever heard." Kirsten Flagstad, the Isolde, "rose to heights of fury and splendor which even she has never exceeded." To *Musical America*, "Martinelli was a Tristan worthy of Mme. Flagstad's Isolde. His youthful appearance in the first act was captivating. Here was the young, daring knight of legendary times." Others felt he was a good, but not a great, Tristan. He never sang it at the Met.

At the end of the season the company was again reorganized, now taking the name Chicago Opera Company. Chauncey McCormick became the new chairman of the board, Walter Kirk was the new president, and Henry Weber was appointed general director. The new board of directors consisted of some of the leading names in the city's industrial, managerial, and social regime—a far more imposing group than had been gathered in several years. During the summer the chorus and ballet were revamped, the orchestra was overhauled, and much of the company's scenery was refurbished. There was much talk about the dawn of a new era in Chicago Opera, and when *Aida* opened the 1940 season, it seemed that perhaps this might be so. "Last night's performance," the *Tribune* said, "revealed something more important even than a new cast, new ballet, new chorus, new direction, and new sets. It revealed in the company a spirit of freshness and youth and hope which seemed to actuate every body concerned with the presentation—from principals and conductor down to the humblest spear toter." Making her local debut in the name part was the Metropolitan's Zinka Milanov, who "turned phrases so eloquently that they became not merely acceptable musical phrases but heart storming expressions of emotion." Giovanni Martinelli was the Rhadames, John Charles Thomas the Amonasro, and Henry Weber the conductor. "I was as skeptical as you about the promised new era of opera in Chicago," Cecil Smith wrote, "until I saw and heard it with my own eyes and ears."

The war in Europe had its effects on the Opera by now, with far fewer artists coming from abroad. Here at home, Congress had enacted our first peacetime draft, and President Roosevelt was asking for an unprecedented third term to "finish his job." On November 5, the nation voted, rejecting Wendell Willkie and giving Roosevelt his wish. At the Opera House that night election returns were posted in the foyer so that patrons could see how things were going during intermissions. The opera was *Traviata*, with Jepson, Melton, and Thomas, an all-American cast.

It was an outstanding season in several respects; most of the productions were polished and well integrated. After a *Trovatore* with Bampton and Martinelli, the *Tribune* said, "Every detail, both musical and histrionic, had evidently been scrupulously and intelligently rehearsed." On the podium there were giants, Artur Rodzinski and Fritz Reiner, both making their Chicago Opera debut. Rodzinski was conductor of the Cleveland

Symphony at the time. He came to Chicago for *Salome*, planned for Marjorie Lawrence. When Lawrence became indisposed, Rose Pauly took over on less than a day's notice. Critics called the performance electrifying. Lawrence sang the role later in the season under the direction of Carl Alwin, proving better vocally, but lacking Pauly's psychological intensity. Fritz Reiner was brought in to conduct *Der Rosenkavalier*, which many felt was the season's pinnacle. Among other things it had the benefit of Risë Stevens' Octavian, the mezzo also making her first appearance with the Chicago Opera. "Miss Stevens," the *Tribune* said, "is the only Octavian we have seen who really looked like a boy."

Italo Montemezzi came that year to conduct his *L'Amore dei Tre Re*, in a production featuring Grace Moore. It was Moore's first Fiora anywhere, and Montemezzi spent a great deal of time coaching her in the part. Looking regally beautiful, she sang the second-act love scene with a "compelling sweep" and an "urgent passion." The *Tribune* wrote, "It was enormously stimulating last night, as on several other memorable occasions this week, to see the public imagination catch fire from the emotional heat of a good opera performance."

Falstaff was given in English with John Charles Thomas in a somewhat modernized version. Rather untraditionally, Thomas' Falstaff was "an obese, amorous, gastronomous, and inebriated fathead who sings and whistles like a bird." Another break from tradition was Marjorie Lawrence's Carmen. Vocally, the *Tribune* said, she "somehow managed to draw an almost complete blank... her voice steadfastly refused to take on color or vanity." Histrionically, "Miss Lawrence gave the impression that the Bizet heroine got her men by main strength and held them because they were too cowed to run away." The work had been restaged by William Wymetal, who emphasized liveliness and realism. "The illogicalities of action, the violations of both the spirit and the letter of the libretto were eradicated in favor of naturalistic, reasonable action," the *Tribune* reported. "There was little or none of the static massing of choristers which used to make everything look cramped and gave a generally soggy and waterlogged impression of our *Carmen* performances of other seasons."

The season played to more critical applause than any in years. After several distinctly mediocre seasons, the company—largely at Henry Weber's insistence—had decided to make one last, almost desperate, attempt at producing gala opera. But with higher standards came a higher deficit, bringing complaints from the guarantors. That summer Weber announced his resignation as general director, saying, "Conditions and circumstances are such that I feel the high excellence maintained last year cannot be repeated."

Fortune Gallo, who for twenty-five years had managed the itinerant San Carlo Opera Company and actually made money, became the new director. Although it was assumed that if anyone could make opera pay, Gallo could, rumors circulated that after the expense of the season before no guarantors could be found to back the company. Gallo assured his board that if they would take care of the boxes, he would take care of the rest of the house. Still, financial support shrank to a minimum, and Gallo began preparations for the 1941 season with little real financial assurance at all. On September 17, it was announced that Giovanni Martinelli would become the company's new artistic director. His appointment, like Mary Garden's twenty years before, was mostly a prestige move. The tenor would continue to sing with the company and with the Metropolitan.

The season was shortened to five weeks, and ticket prices were reduced. Opening night brought a fairly sluggish production of *Ballo in Maschera* with Martinelli, Rethberg, and Thomas. Fortune Gallo was in the lobby, smiling and bowing to the audience as it entered. "It's a swell house," a member of the Opera staff was heard to say. "Every seat taken. Good business; hope it keeps up. But if they'd asked me I'd have had some Klieg lights and some mikes and made the opening a little tonier." The management seems to have had its own ideas for how to create the proper opening-night atmosphere, for perfume, costing ten dollars an ounce, was sent through the ventilating system. It could be smelled near the doors, where fresh air was pouring in, but farther into the house it became almost overpowering. "Individual scents and fresh flower perfumes," the *Tribune* said, "were completely vanquished by the all pervading, penetrating, sickening smell that poured from the ventilators."

Many of the so-called four hundred of Chicago society were conspicuously absent. One society editor said, "There is some doubt as to whether there is any such group today." By now Harold McCormick was dead, and the era in which the list of box holders read like the Social Register had essentially died with him. There were still some gorgeous gowns, many ordinary ones, and others that made their wearers look "like the proverbial circus riders." There were few real jewels, but lots of costume jewelry. One young woman entered in street clothes with a huge box under her arm and changed into an evening gown in the powder room. Dozens of women arrived carrying their corsages in a box.

From the standpoint of attendance this 1941 season was a huge success. Five of the first six operas played to capacity houses. No longer was it possible to go down to the Opera House on the day of the performance and buy two decent tickets. Ever since the breakup of the Civic Opera, the management had been fighting furiously just to attract audiences large enough to take the chill off the house. Even at performances offering all-star casts, great empty blocks of seats had been the general rule. "The main difficulty this year," the *Tribune* declared, "seems to be to find enough tickets to sell. The company is torn between the desire to laugh with delight at its extraordinary record of sold-out performances and to weep with chagrin at the necessity of turning grumbling would-be ticket buyers away from the box office window."

Artistically the season saw an intensification of the star system, and a general drop in production standards. Big-name casts often failed to jell, and most performances were more notable for individual portrayals than for over-all production quality. Licia Albanese was introduced to the city that year as Micaela and later gave a fine Butterfly. Bidu Sayao made her first Chicago appearance as Rosina, while Dorothy Kirsten, who had made her operatic debut with the company the year before, sang Musetta, in a production which featured her mentor, Grace Moore, as Mimi. Kirsten was also heard in *Carmen*, both as Frasquita and Micaela. Moore sang her first Chicago *Tosca*, and Lily Pons made a big success of *The Daughter of the Regiment*, just as she had in San Francisco and at the Metropolitan. Gennaro Papi returned to the company as guest conductor for the *Daughter*, and Armando Agnini, of the San Francisco Opera, was brought in as guest stage director. Helen Jepson, Richard Crooks, and Ezio Pinza combined forces for *Faust*, and Edith Mason emerged from voluntary retirement for Mimi, her first appearance with the company in two years. Although she had some vocal difficulties, the *Tribune* said the house "gave her round after round of cordial applause and tossed her enough flowers to start a shop."

Eighteen operas were given—most of them in Italian, three in French, and one, *Lohengrin*, in German. The attendance record showed sixteen sold-out houses out of a possible twenty-six, with an over-all attendance of 90 per cent.

A week before the season closed, Pearl Harbor was bombed by the Japanese. The next day President Roosevelt asked for a declaration of war, and Congress responded. With the American entry into the war, the question was raised whether it would be appropriate or possible to stage an opera season in 1942. Most people felt that giving one would be good for morale. The company emphasized that it already had the scenery and costumes needed to stage the operas that would be given, so that no materials would be diverted from the war effort.

The season opened on November 7, the night before the Allied landing on North Africa. Lily Pons was scheduled to sing *Lakmé*, but when she came down with laryngitis, *Aida*, with Zinka Milanov, was substituted. The audience seemed cheerful, although a little less glittering than usual. "The women took seriously the advice of periodicals and newspapers to keep up morale by looking their prettiest," the *Tribune* reported, "whether in street clothes enlivened by orchid corsages and well groomed hair, as many were, or in the most formal of evening gowns."

The war seemed to have two major effects on opera audiences. First, there were many army and navy personnel present at performances, and, second, many women were there unescorted. There was no boycotting of Wagner as there had been during World War I, although there were some protests, mainly from nonmusical sources. *Madama Butterfly*, on the other hand, mainly because of the feeling resulting from Japan's surprise attack, was not done. The public showed no vigorous opposition to it, but the management, both in Chicago and at the Metropolitan, simply felt its exclusion the safest path. *Musical America*, nevertheless, concluded, "The American musical public has shown itself in this war a good deal more rational than it did in the last and has scrupulously avoided making a scapegoat of art."

Gallo's production standards still left much to be desired. The Chicago ballet was unionized for the first time in 1942, forcing the management to pay higher salaries. Gallo made up for this by cutting down on rehearsal time. The results were sad indeed. And there were embarrassments resulting from the star system. The first subscription performance, following the forced substitution on opening night, began an hour late, so that Josephine Antoine could fulfill a radio engagement. Ruth Page and her ballet kept the public entertained until the opera, *Rigoletto*, could begin. Gladys Swarthout set off something of a furor when she canceled an afternoon performance of *Carmen*, fearing she would not make her broadcast in New York if she sang it. Gallo said he was willing to begin the opera fifteen minutes early, but he refused to ask his audience "to bring their lunch." Coe Glade sang instead.

Most of the operas that year were popular favorites. The one novelty, *Halka*, was staged in honor of the recently organized Polish Opera Guild under the baton of the Polish-American conductor, Jerzy Bojanowski. Jennie Tourel, now a recognized star, came from New York for the title role of *Mignon* with Richard Crooks. Albanese, Crooks, Thomas, and Nicola Moscona headed the cast of a strong *Faust*, while Antoine, Glade, and Melton sang a considerably "Hollywoodized" version of *Martha* in English. Most of the singers now were Metropolitan stars, with resident singers and members of the San Carlo Opera filling minor roles and occasionally taking major ones. "Our resident opera has become a branch of the Metropolitan in the past ten years," René Devries lamented in *Musical Courier*. "We sometimes . . . feel a nostalgia for the long era when Chicago boasted a company all its own, when singers were honored to call themselves members of the Chicago Opera."

Capacity houses again proved the general rule. The war seemed actually to have stimulated opera attendance, just as it had in New York and San Francisco. The Chicago Symphony also did a booming business that year. Gallo closed his season with a deficit of only $25,000, a new low.

In March, 1943, the Civic Opera building was sold to the General Finance Corporation, which assumed a mortgage of $9,885,000 and paid the Chicago Music Foundation, the principal stockholder, set up by Insull, a settlement of $266,000. The Music Foundation funds were used to pay off previous operatic deficits and to set up a guarantee fund for the city's opera, $25,000 of which could be used annually to cover deficits for ten years. The General Finance Corporation assured the opera company that it could continue using the Civic Opera House under "very favorable terms."

By the time this settlement was worked out, it was late to plan a season that year. Fortune Gallo had resigned as general manager, intending to produce two operettas on Broadway and continue with his San Carlo Opera Company. The chorus had pretty well disintegrated, many of them taking jobs on Broadway, and the war had made transportation exceedingly difficult. Therefore, it was decided there would be no 1943 season. With the yearly $25,000 now available from the Chicago Music Foundation as a lure, plans began immediately for the next season, and a survey was made "to select the best available artistic director." By fall the Chicago Opera Company was reorganized, with Fausto Cleva as artistic director.

The five-week 1944 season opened with *Carmen*, starring Gladys Swarthout and Kurt Baum. Maestro Cleva conducted. Claudia Cassidy said *Carmen* "was neither the big bear of triumph nor the little bear of failure, but rather the middle sized bear of something worth watching and, whenever possible, encouraging." Transportation was still a serious problem for the company and could not be relied upon. The chorus was none too young, the ballet downright makeshift. Staging for the most part was pedestrian, as rehearsals were limited. The strong point of the opening production was Cleva's conducting.

Fashion was considerably less lavish than usual, although orchids and ermine could be found in the boxes and on the main floor. A few men came in black tie, even fewer in full dress, but most of these wore tweed topcoats and felt hats, toning down the picture of elegance. Probably because of the war, there were none of the "crazy costumes and giddy accessories that some openings have brought forth." Mrs. John R. Orndorff, whose custom it was to attend the opening gowned as the leading character, wore a black-lace mantilla draped over a high gold comb in her hair. Two years before, not finding out that Lily Pons was unable to sing *Lakmé* until too late, she wore a blue-and-gold Hindu costume with bare midriff. (Fortunately, *Isabeau* was not done these days.)

The season played to large audiences, several performances sold out far in advance. Metropolitan artists continued to dominate the roster, while the repertoire remained standard. Brazilian soprano Bidu Sayao was heard as a charming *Traviata,* wearing a gown in the first act studded with what were reputed to be diamonds from her family's diamond mines in Brazil. She also sang the first *Pelléas et Mélisande* the city had seen since Garden. Milanov and Baum did *Trovatore,* Leonard Warren and Jan Peerce *Rigoletto,* Della Chiesa *Tosca,* and Traubel and Astrid Varney *Die Walküre.*

A non-Metropolitan artist who made quite a stir that year was movie actress Jeanette MacDonald, making her operatic debut with the company. She was heard first in a Saturday matinee of *Romeo and Juliet,* which set a capacity audience wild. According to the press, she was so nervous over her debut that she had paced the floor most of the night before, singing Juliet over and over in her head. Finally, after raiding the ice box for some cottage cheese and apple sauce, she managed to get a few hours sleep. On stage she looked radiant and serene—"better than in Technicolor," one critic observed. "Her Juliet," according to Claudia Cassidy, "is breath-takingly beautiful to the eye and dulcet to the ear. Her voice is slender, a little reedy, but sweet, and she uses it delicately, with a sensitivity that accents the drama in music drama." After her Marguerite a few days later, Cassidy confirmed, "From where I sat . . . Jeanette MacDonald has turned out to be one of the welcome surprises of the season." Certainly her popular success was considerable.

By the time the 1945 season opened, World War II was over. The *Tribune* said, "More furs, laces, satins, and—yes, top hats—came thru the windswept doors of the Civic Opera house last night" than had been seen since before the war. The opera was a none-too-polished *Manon,* although Bidu Sayao in the title role was "sheer delight, vocally and histrionically." Fausto Cleva conducted.

It was an uneven season filled with troubles, including the appearance of a claque. When Eugene Goossens, scheduled to conduct a performance of *Pelléas,* suddenly became ill, there was no one around to take over except a young prompter named Vittorio Trucco. His major qualification for the job was that he had prompted an earlier performance of the opera. George Szell had been signed for a production of *Parsifal.* He had asked for an augmented orchestra but maintained, when he arrived, that it was not up to specifications. He withdrew from the production, saying he did not feel the performance would be a creditable one. Fritz Stiedry, not even a name to most Chicagoans, was called in at the eleventh hour, and despite too few rehearsals, the small orchestra, and other makeshifts, *Parsifal* turned out to be one of the season's best productions. "True," *Musical America* said, "a phalanx of prompters in the wings incessantly uttered raucous sounds seemingly as confusing to singers as audience, but with it all the essential quality of Wagner's great opera was preserved."

Zinka Milanov sang her first American *Tosca* in Chicago that year. "It was not an unqualified success," *Musical America* held, "as her interpretation lacked the melodramatic flair to give proper pace to the role." *La Forza del Destino*, on the other hand, *was* an unqualified success, made so by conductor Bruno Walter. The cast included Stella Roman, a replacement for Milanov, Warren, Baum, and Moscona. "Mr. Walter's presence," wrote *Musical America*, "acted like magic on singers and orchestra and the performance moved with exhilarating zest throughout the evening." Walter also conducted *The Marriage of Figaro* with Roman, Pinza, John Brownlee, and Jarmila Novotna. Herbert Graf did the staging. Claudia Cassidy said, "At its best, it was opera to renew one's faith in the lyric stage." *Musical America* reported, "Mr. Walter's affection for the beautiful score was apparent in the painstaking care with which he molded every phrase."

Walter's affection for the score, however, had gotten something of a jolt during rehearsals. Things had gotten off rather badly, but at last had settled down. Walter was busily giving his all to a reading of the score, trying to draw from the orchestra and singers every subtle Mozartian nuance. Suddenly the big stage door at the back was thrown open with a bang, and a huge truck came rolling onto the stage to unload the scenery for that evening's performance. Maestro Walter went livid. As a matter of fact, he never conducted any Mozart opera after that in Chicago.

The company's dependence on the Metropolitan had been tolerated during the war because there was no alternative, no possibility of recruiting artists from Europe. Even then there were criticisms. In 1944, when twenty-six of the company's leading singers came from the Met roster, Elsa Borowski wrote for *Musical Courier*, "The hasty borrowing of singers from the Metropolitan for an appearance or two is a system which contains within itself the seeds of decay, as obviously a fine ensemble cannot be achieved by this means. No 'star,' however refulgent, can entirely carry a performance." With the war over, this criticism became even sharper. "Some one said the other night," Claudia Cassidy wrote in one of her reviews in 1945, "that a performance by the Chicago opera was a first rate one for a second rate company. He wasn't trying to be funny. He was stating a fact. It was a pretty good show that struck none of the fire of greatness, a performance Fortune Gallo's San Carlo troupe might have given us years ago at the Auditorium had he been able to raid the resident company's opulent warehouse."

The season now began early in October, so that it would be over shortly after the Metropolitan's began. Singers came to Chicago for sort of a warm-up session before they appeared in New York, often in the same roles. Better performers were badly needed in the smaller parts; Cassidy said mammas and duennas were consistently ludicrous. The chorus, orchestra, and stage direction varied with the conductor or director in charge, but were more often than not weak. "At the moment the Chicago Opera is in no ruin," Cassidy said, "but it is trying to dig its way out of what sometimes seems to be an uncommonly long tunnel with too few glimpses of the sunny operatic sky." The company said it was tired of being compared with "the greatness of the past." As one official put it, "You don't see a sports writer going to a baseball game and comparing what happened yesterday to what happened at a game ten years ago."

The criticism had its effect just the same.

In the summer of 1946 Fausto Cleva made a trip to Europe to scout for fresh talent. He engaged a number of artists Chicago had never heard before, including Ferruccio Tagliavini and Italo Tajo from Italy and Janine Micheau from France. A sincere effort was made in the following season to free the company from its dependence on the Metropolitan and to improve production standards. To a considerable degree this was realized. The chorus, orchestra, and ballet were all more polished. Rehearsal time was more plentiful, and the new singers not only enhanced the quality of productions, but also helped make things more interesting. "We have a few singers," Cassidy wrote early in the 1946 season, "who are not . . . required by booking schedules to hurry in for a performance which finds them exhausted . . . only to hurry out again as soon as the curtain falls." And *Musical Courier* effused, "Important news of the moment is the vastly improved condition of the Chicago Opera Company. . . . The first three weeks, despite a few imperfections, happily disclosed a standard of performance that Chicagoans had long ceased to expect from a local company."

The season had opened with a mildly interesting *Aida*, which featured Milanov, Baum, and Warren. It also introduced Italo Tajo, as Ramfis, whom the *Tribune* called "a high priest head and shoulders higher than his minions, with a voice rich in quality and full of operatic promise." Socially, it was the most brilliant opening the city had seen in many a year. White ties, ermine, and orchids were back in abundance, and a gala atmosphere filled the foyer of the Civic Opera House. Mrs. Orndorff was there dressed as Aida, of course, wearing curled plumes in her hair and on her purse, a gold dress, and gold powder and sequins dusted over her skin. A new generation of operagoers seemed to be growing up. "Many of the old, familiar faces," the *Tribune* reported, "were missing, their places taken by happy, young ones."

Dorothy Kirsten was heard that season as the first Butterfly since Pearl Harbor and later as Mimi, opposite Tagliavini's Rudolfo. His Cavaradossi was considered the personal triumph of the season. Milanov sang *La Gioconda,* Patrice Munsel and Richard Tucker *Lucia di Lammermoor,* and Janine Micheau Micaela and Violetta. Erich Leinsdorf conducted one of the season's finest offerings, *Tristan und Isolde* with Traubel, Set Svanholm, and Blanche Thebom. *Musical America said,* "The music pulsated with exalted emotion, and the enchantment of the drama held even through the long third act, which was given uncut." Breaking the shackles of conservatism, the company offered Menotti's *Amelia Goes to the Ball* and Gruenberg's *Emperor Jones,* with Tibbett in the title role and Leinsdorf conducting. "Discretion may be the better part of valor," Cassidy said, "but too much discretion makes a dull season, and at least the Chicago Opera company had the right idea last night when it ventured out on the limb of an unusual double bill."

While the season was undoubtedly more exciting than any heard in Chicago in years, it was poorly attended. Even superb productions like *Tristan und Isolde* played to scant houses. "We may have to go back to coaxing the customers in," Claudia Cassidy wrote. "It has been a season of pleasures and disappointments, played largely to a new audience, as the once dependable backlog of Chicago opera-goers has been conspicuously absent." The deficit for the six weeks was nearly $150,000, a sum not paid until 1948, when the General Finance Corporation, still owner of the Opera House building, paid it as an outright gift. With this heavy deficit on its shoulders, the Chicago Opera found itself paralyzed. Until this debt was paid, there could be no possibility of future opera. Besides, the company was sure to lose financial support with this large a loss on its record. The funds in the Chicago Music Foundation account remained, but even these were tied up until the present deficit was paid. And so the Chicago Opera Company, at the height of its artistic glory, died a beggar's death.

The next years were frustrating ones for Chicago's opera enthusiasts. There was much talk about reviving the resident company, but little action. A troupe called the Chicago Opera Theatre had been founded in 1946 under the direction of Giovanni Cardelli, but it was short-lived. Its major accomplishment was the American premiere of Benjamin Britten's *The Rape of Lucretia.*

Next a group known as the United States Opera Company planned to open a five-week season at the Civic Opera House on January 6, 1947, with a production of *Turandot,* starring a young, plump, nearsighted unknown named Maria Callas. Under the general direction of Ottavio Scotto, the company planned to make Chicago its headquarters, produce an annual season there, using the old Chicago Opera's sets and costumes, and then go on a nationwide tour. Scotto engaged a number of artists in Europe, most of whom had never sung in the United States. Sergio Failoni was to be the principal conductor, George Sebastian an associate conductor. Among the singers signed were Géori Boué, Mafalda Favero, Max Lorenz, and Nicola Rossi-Lemeni. The company's scheduled repertoire included Italian, French, and German operas. After a number of delays the company arrived in Chicago in February. Mail orders had already been taken for a season which never came off. The group went bankrupt before the curtain ever went up. Its only performance was a benefit concert given to raise funds for getting some of the artists back to Europe. Others, including Maria Callas, were simply stranded here. As a desperation measure to obtain return passage to Europe, Callas signed a contract with E. Richard Bagarozy, giving him sole managerial rights to her career. There was to be a much publicized sequel to her action.

In the fall of 1947 Kirsten Flagstad returned to the United States for her first performances since the war. She sang a benefit performance of *Tristan und Isolde* at the Civic Opera House with Artur Rodzinski and the Chicago Symphony. The top ticket price was fifteen dollars, but the house was filled just the same. "It was as though the fabulous days of Chicago's operatic past had returned," *Musical America* said. "Kirsten Flagstad sang Isolde with all the glory of former years and something more besides. Her voice had the same shining golden splendor, but it seemed that her queenly characterization had more warmth and femininity than ever before."

In 1948 it was decided to use the remainder of the Chicago Music Foundation funds to bring in the New York City Opera Company. It was hoped that some kind of permanent arrangement could be worked out whereby the New York company would visit Chicago each fall, drawing an increasing number of artists from the Chicago locale and eventually belonging equally to both cities. The Chicago Music Foundation money was to help make this possible.

On December 1, 1948, the company opened a three-week season in the Civic Opera House. Among its artists were Brenda Lewis, Winifred Heidt, Ramon Vinay, Frances Yeend, Walter Cassel, and Marguerite Piazza. The repertoire included *Salome, Carmen, La Bohème, Amelia Goes to the Ball, The Old Maid and the Thief, Cavalleria Rusticana, I Pagliacci, Pelléas et Mélisande,* and *Don Giovanni.* The next year the company returned, with Chicagoans then having a hand in selecting and training the chorus, orchestra, and ballet.

Although the New York City Opera continued to come to Chicago, it remained essentially an import, its season brief. For a city that had known operatic greatness, a few weeks of opera by an alien company, no matter how good, would hardly suffice. There was a feeling that some day the Chicago Opera must be revived; some day Chicago must rejoin the operatic capitals of the world. And so a city of music lovers hoped and dreamed and waited.

Chapter 13

RUB-A-DUB-DUB, THREE IN A TUB

CHICAGO was without a resident company for eight years. With each passing year a revival became more difficult. The city had all but gotten out of the opera habit. A new generation had grown up with little or no acquaintance with the art, at least as a live entertainment form, and even many of those who had once been fond of opera were beginning to feel that it belonged to the past. But the prosperous years following World War II found opera enjoying an international renaisssance, aided in Europe by Marshall Plan dollars, stimulated here by the Metropolitan broadcasts, television, and especially the advent of long-playing records.

After living with the uncertainties of the nuclear age for over a decade —a decade of tension and cold war, suspicion and McCarthyism, misunderstanding and racial violence, unrest and delinquency—Chicagoans, like most Americans, longed for something to cling to, a pillar in a sea of turbulence. For some the affluence of the age served as a barometer, giving life at least a partial meaning. For others technology appeared the one constant amid a world of variables, the one definite and immutable progress. Others sensed that the only certainty was uncertainty, the only absolute, relativity. For a minority, those capable of Freud's "higher and finer" pleasure, a pleasure obtained from mental and intellectual activity, happiness and stability could be derived in part from cultural endeavors, an area in which the old ideals of individualism and initiative could remain unchallenged and thus help to soothe the frustrations of a world in transition. In the 1950's the glow of what was to flicker into the cultural boom of the 1960's was already in evidence. All over the country interest in drama, art, and music began an upward surge, aided by improved methods of transportation and communication, an increased concern for higher education, and the feeling, often subconscious, that in an industrial world of chaos and confusion, the arts held much that is beautiful—the classic catharsis, gently purging man of his emotions and leaving him peaceful and serene, imbued with a sense that there is, after all, nobility. And as man became more humble before the arts, opera—in Chicago and elsewhere—was rediscovered.

It began in 1950, when a young, dark-haired, forceful woman scarcely out of the debutante stage, named Carol Fox, daughter of a wealthy Chicago furniture manufacturer, returned home from studying voice in Europe. A group that had been considering the possibility of forming a local opera company shortly approached her, asking if she would be interested in singing in some of their productions. It was hoped her family might be willing to finance the operas in which she appeared. She declined the offer, but began thinking herself about reviving Chicago's opera, as manager rather than singer. A few weeks later she was in New York and stopped by to visit her former vocal coach, Nicola Rescigno. Rescigno was an ambitious young conductor whose specialty was Italian opera. He had once studied with Giorgio Polacco and had conducted for Gallo's San Carlo troupe and with the Chicago Opera during the Cleva period. During the course of the conversation, Miss Fox mentioned her thoughts on founding a new Chicago company. Rescigno was interested, but how would they ever get the financial backing?

Returning to Chicago, Carol Fox incorporated her proposed company as the Lyric Theatre of Chicago and began checking into the possibilities for financial support. It was a matter of starting from scratch, for most of the old donors were no longer around. She talked with friends, businessmen, prominent society members, and critics, instilling in them a feeling that perhaps the resident opera *could* be resurrected. In her talks she met Lawrence Kelly, a dynamic, crew-cut young real estate agent and insurance broker who loved opera. Kelly was intensely interested in seeing opera returned to the city, and shortly he was invited to join the organization.

In February, 1952, Fox, Kelly, and Rescigno met one night in Box Eight at the Metropolitan Opera House in New York. After the performance, they adjourned to the Waldorf-Astoria Hotel, to chat for several hours longer and do some figuring. Both Miss Fox and Kelly were from socially prominent families and therefore had important contacts, but aside from that their only ace was a dedicated love for opera combined with a pragmatic view of the business world. It would be tough going, and all three of them knew it.

When their plans were announced, Chicagoans heard them with mixed feelings. Local critics could hardly have been more encouraging. Officials of the Opera House building, controlled now by the Kemper Insurance Company, were no less enthusiastic, as they would receive a considerable tax advantage if opera were regularly being staged there. Many individuals eagerly agreed to help in any way they could, beginning with a generous donation. But there were others who frankly hesitated to turn over five million dollars' worth of sets and seven million dollars' worth of costumes to three "kids" whose combined ages would scarcely have totaled a hundred.

To convince their skeptical elders that they knew what they were about, the three decided to stage a "calling card" performance. After months of work and planning, a production of *Don Giovanni* was announced for February 5, 1954, with a repeat two days later. It turned out to be an absolute delight! Nicola Rossi-Lemeni, now an international star, was the Don. Eleanor Steber was the Donna Anna, her first on any stage. Irene Jordan was Donna Elvira, Leopold Simoneau Don Ottavio, and Bidu Sayao Zerlina. Rescigno conducted, the orchestra being composed mostly of members of the Chicago Symphony. "*Don Giovanni* takes talent, carloads of flesh and blood talent," Claudia Cassidy said, "and a touch of genius helps. And there it was a wonderful *Don Giovanni*.... It seemed to have been conjured out of thin air, that extraordinary performance, and in a sense it was, the heady air of hopes and dreams." Roger Dettmer of the Chicago *American* wrote, "*Don Giovanni* brooks no compromise: either its production is notably good, or it cannot be endured. Last evening's mounting... was notably good." The public was equally enthusiastic. The cast was new to Chicago, as only Bidu Sayao had sung her role there before. The old Chicago Opera scenery was ugly and dated, but the performance was good enough to make even that seem unimportant. "With this, their 'Calling Card,'" the program said, "the Lyric Theatre hopes you will invite them to call again this November." With the success of *Don Giovanni*, the invitation was extended.

Carol Fox immediately left for Europe to line up artists for a regular fall season. She visited Tito Gobbi, La Scala's leading baritone, at his home in Rome. The two of them walked together in Gobbi's garden, while the young American girl told of the plans for reviving Chicago's opera. Gobbi was interested—and entranced by the fact that a woman was to be directing things. Would he sing with the Lyric that fall? He would indeed. Fox also talked with Giuseppe di Stefano, one of Italy's most noted tenors, and before she was through, she had convinced him to sign with her company. Giulietta Simionato, the great Italian mezzo, whose only previous American performances had been in San Francisco in 1953, became enthusiastic about the Chicago plans and agreed to join the Lyric in the fall.

The idea of Simionato, di Stefano, and Gobbi all on the same roster was enough to make Chicago, and the entire musical world, shake its head in disbelief. But Carol Fox was not through. She wanted soprano Maria Callas, who, following her 1947 debut in *La Gioconda* at Verona, and a slimming-down process, had become the *prima donna absoluta* of Europe. Born in New York of Greek parents, Callas was taken to Greece when she was thirteen, spent the war there, and sang first with the Royal Opera of Athens. Shortly after her successful appearances at Verona, she married wealthy Italian industrialist Giovanni Battista Meneghini, who helped direct her career. In 1948 at Venice's La Fenice she shocked opera enthusiasts the world over by singing Brünnhilde in *Walküre* one night and Elvira in *I Puritani* two evenings later. She made her La Scala debut in 1950 as Aida, shortly becoming an international celebrity. In addition to her European appearances, she had sung in Mexico and South America, but never in the United States. Carol Fox hoped to talk her into making a long-awaited American debut.

Fox went to see Callas in Verona. The two got along well, and the soprano seemed to enjoy talking business with a young woman so close to her own age. The diva insisted on choosing her repertoire, but it was finally agreed she would do two performances each of three operas. For the six appearances she would be paid a total of twelve thousand dollars, plus travel expenses for herself and her husband.

The young Chicago impresario returned home, having scored the operatic coup of the decade. But unlike so many other efforts at rejuvenating the golden age of Chicago Opera, the Lyric gave out little advance publicity at first, making few high-sounding promises. All three of the company's officials realized the uncertainties involved, and they did not want to overplay their hand. They operated on a small basis with little folderol. Carol Fox, as a matter of fact, typed the company's first press releases and drove them to the four local newspapers in her mother's car.

There were still plenty of people who doubted the project would ever come off. "They'll never get the curtain up," more than one pessimist was heard to say. Others were convinced that Chicagoans really no longer cared for opera and that getting an audience together was going to be as hard as rounding up guarantors. But neither Carol Fox nor Lawrence Kelly believed this for a moment, and filled with the idealism of youth, they plodded on. "Their necks were out so far they must at times have thought the chopping block inevitable," Claudia Cassidy wrote, and Kelly, thinking back on that first season nearly a decade later, shook his head in disbelief. It was launched, he said, with "eighty-seven sets in the warehouse from the Insull regime, a great deal of hope, and even more guts."

One gray morning toward the end of October, Maria Callas landed at the Chicago airport, met by a bevy of photographers and reporters. The legendary Callas temperament was nowhere in evidence. She chatted with newspapermen, cleared herself through customs, and was busily amusing herself when Fox and Kelly, unavoidably detained, arrived to meet her. "Where is the maestro?" were her first words. "When can we get to work?"

A consummate artist, Callas was excited about helping to revive opera in Chicago, and no one worked any harder on stage and off than she. She gave helpful suggestions and listened attentively to the views of others. She considered herself a member of a team and worked accordingly. To achieve the proper balance in the "*Casta Diva*," she sang the long, difficult aria nine times during rehearsals of *Norma*. To the public she was every inch the glamorous prima donna, poised, smartly dressed, her then blonde hair worn in a chignon. Thirty at the time, she had amazed the operatic world by mysteriously losing seventy-five pounds. Her figure was now streamlined, her bearing classic. How did she get so thin? "I didn't," was her answer. "I had a tape worm, and I no longer have it." She granted interviews freely, was natural and candid, and revealed a charming, subtle sense of humor. Her high salary she regarded as a matter of principle. "I really don't care about money," she told reporters. "Nobody can eat two steaks at the same time." A homespun touch was added when her father, George Callas, came to town to hear his daughter sing. Then news leaked out that she had set up housekeeping at her suite at the Ambassador West Hotel. She made frequent shopping trips to the supermarket, and on evenings when she was not singing, cooked her husband's favorite dishes for him. All this caught the public imagination as had nothing since Mary Garden left the scene. By the time opening night arrived, Chicago had taken Maria Callas to its heart and was pleased to be the city to welcome home an American girl who had made good.

Meanwhile ticket orders poured in from all over the country, including Alaska. Largely because of the Callas debut, coupled with the fact that the Chicagoans were offering fresh talent in productions that bore little resemblance to what the Metropolitan was doing at the time, the season drew national and even international attention. All the leading music and news magazines sent reporters to cover the opening, while the major New York and California newspapers dispatched their chief critics. Dario Soria, president of Angel Records, for whom Callas, Gobbi, and di Stefano all recorded, was on hand to trumpet the affair, and excitement began to mount.

On November 1, the three-week season opened with *Norma*, featuring Callas, Simionato, Rossi-Lemeni, and Mirto Picchi. Rescigno conducted. The Civic Opera House, just shy of capacity, "blazed with an electricity that had not been felt since Samuel Insull opened it in 1929." As the *Tribune* reported it, "Diamonds, real or ersatz, sparkled; white mink jostled white ermine and white fox; jewel toned frocks gleamed against men's dinner jackets. And there were many young pretty faces." There were some familiar faces too, among them Giorgio Polacco, Rosa Raisa, Eva Turner, Giovanni Martinelli, and Edith Mason. "We have now what we need," Miss Mason told reporters, "youth and enthusiasm."

On stage was a *Norma* that surpassed even the wildest hopes, worthy of anything the city had heard in its golden age. Said Claudia Cassidy, "This would have been an extraordinary performance in any opera house. It was serenely, handsomely staged, its musical pulse was so warmly secure you could quickly take it for granted, and it was magnificently sung." Callas proved not only a remarkable singer, but a formidable actress as well. "She molds a line as deftly as she tosses off cruelly difficult ornamentations in the highest register," *Musical America* reported. "And she brings to everything a passion, a profile of character and a youthful beauty that are rare in our lyric theater." René Devries, writing for *Musical Courier*, said Callas "guides her voice as a great cellist uses his instrument to achieve a fine legato, and reaches high C's with noble simplicity and astounding effects." "For my money," Cassidy concluded, "she was not only up to specifications, she surpassed them. So did Giulietta Simionato, the Adalgisa, who with her made the great duet, '*Mira, O Norma*,' something to tell your grandchildren about. As for Rossi-Lemeni . . . his Arch-Druid had the magnificence of Michelangelo's Moses." "It was a great night for Chicago," *Musical America* proclaimed. "It may prove an even greater night for opera in America." And the Chicago *Sun-Times* said, "Once more this city has raised an operatic voice which deserves to be heard around the world."

Following the performance, Angel Records held a grand ball for first-nighters at the Hilton Hotel, adding to the social luster. Callas and her husband attended, as did Maestro Rescigno, Rossi-Lemeni, Gobbi, Simionato, Angel's Walter Legge and his wife, soprano Elisabeth Schwarzkopf. And in the wee hours of the morning Chicagoans went home at last convinced that opera had indeed returned to their city.

On November 3, Giannini's *The Taming of the Shrew* received its first full-scale staging, its only other presentation having been a shortened version shown on NBC television. The *Sun-Times* called it "the first really expert operatic score by an American that ever has been heard in the city." Here was a work with no tradition behind it, one the young company had to work out from scratch, and it did so with beautiful results. The cast, headed by Irene Jordan as Katharina, was young and almost wholly American. After the final curtain Giannini was brought on stage, while the audience gave him a hearty round of *bravos.*

The next day E. Richard Bagarozy, who had become Maria Callas' agent when the United States Opera Company collapsed in 1947, filed suit against the soprano for breach of contract. He claimed that his wife had coached Callas for eighteen months, that he had spent $85,000 on her career, and that he had a contract making him her sole representative, entitling him to 10 per cent of her earnings. Callas insisted the contract had been obtained under duress and that Bagarozy had done nothing to promote her career. That his wife had taught her, the singer said was "an enormous, preposterous, and ridiculous lie." And so began the long vigil for the process server that was to underlie Lyric's first two seasons and end in tempest.

Tito Gobbi made his debut on November 6 in *The Barber of Seville.* Said Cassidy, "There is a Figaro. Young, handsome, debonair, with a streak of wit, a touch of malice, a flair for movement. Not the greatest baritone in the world for pure sound, but an accomplished singer who tossed off the '*Largo*' with a tip of the tongue brilliance, and had the quality to take an audience into his confidence and make a huge theater shrink to conversational size." Giulietta Simionato, the Rosina, sang her music in the original mezzo key and proved Gobbi's match. The ensembles bordered on perfection. "There seem to be two kinds of people in town right now," Cassidy wrote, "those a touch intoxicated with operatic song, and those who think them mad.... The era of singers is with us again."

La Bohème resulted in another highly integrated, well-balanced production. Rosanna Carteri was the Mimi, Giacinto Prandelli the Rodolfo, and Gian Giacomo Guelfi (in his American debut) the Marcello. Jonel Perlea conducted. The Chicago *American* found it superior to the Metropolitan's production "note for note, role for role, act for act." When Maria Callas was recognized in the audience, she was given a thunderous ovation. By now word had gotten around that what was happening at the Civic Opera House could not be matched anywhere in America, resulting in a run on the box office. The last two weeks were complete sell-outs. The social whirl died down considerably after opening night, but mink and cocktail dresses still remained plentiful.

Callas appeared next in *La Traviata,* one of the most telling Violettas in Chicago's history. The musical conversation in Act I was more than a collection of sung phrases, it was an almost perfect fusion of music and drama. Callas' acting proved even more astonishing than in *Norma*, the impact of the other singers' lines registering in her large expressive eyes. She sang the first-act arias "with a dazzling brilliance not matched in decades," but sang them in character. Her second act, as the *Sun-Times* recorded it, "was the more poignant in that it was quiet—a woman's suffering too deep to be expressed with the large gestures and emotions of tragic passion." Tito Gobbi's Germont "veritably hushed the listener's breath." René Devries said the Callas death scene recalled "the Duse and Bernhardt tradition."

During the third-act curtain calls, the season's first show of temperament was noted. One of the dancers curtseyed ballet style, causing Callas to glare and mutter, while the male singers pretended to look the other way. "I wouldn't mention names in such a situation as that," the *Tribune's* Seymour Raven wrote, "but hurrah for the good old days of opera. They're back."

The Callas zenith was not reached, however, until the final week, when she sang *Lucia di Lammermoor* and sang it as Chicago had never heard it before. She made Lucia a human being, not just a vehicle for coloratura display, as so many others had done. Her characterization was filled with heartrending poignance, and her anguish in the scene with Enrico was a theatrical marvel. Vocally, she was exquisite, her first act "spun like warm silk, sometimes with an edge of steel." "The most exciting soprano in the world," the Chicago *Daily News* wrote, "sang as she —or anybody else—may never have sung before and may never sing again." After the first division of the "Mad Scene," the house went into a prolonged ovation, while the singer, never stepping out of character, waited for the clapping and shouting to subside. It was a "Mad Scene" in which every phrase had dramatic and musical meaning. At its conclusion, "near pandemonium broke out," Claudia Cassidy wrote. "There was an avalanche of applause, a roar of cheers growing steadily hoarser, a standing ovation, and the aisles were full of men pushing as close to the stage as possible. I am sure they wished for bouquets to throw, and a carriage to pull in the streets. Myself, I wish they had had both. For this creature called Callas is something special." Meanwhile the soprano tried in vain to call attention to the flutist who had accompanied her. But the audience would have none of that. It wanted Callas, calling her before the curtain twenty-two times in an ovation that lasted seventeen minutes. "Let's have just one more," an enthusiast was overheard to say. "Who knows, we might not see her again."

Immediately after her second *Lucia*, Callas left Chicago for Italy, where she was to open the La Scala season three weeks later in Spontini's *La Vestale*. She might return next year, she said, if the right repertoire could be agreed upon. She "came, sang, and conquered," Cassidy said, and she left behind an adoring public, still just a little stunned by it all. Callas "convinced most Chicagoans they were confronted with one of the greatest singers of all time," *Musical America* said. "Certainly she can be likened to no other singer of the immediate past. Her voice is an instrument she uses for dramatic purposes at all times. It is capable of some of the most beautiful sound imaginable, but Miss Callas does not shrink from distorting it when the dramatic occasion requires." Every Callas performance had been different, and she gave a spontaneous quality to each interpretation, making the slightest move and gesture absorbing. René Devries maintained she "has opened a new era in Grand Opera." And without doubt, she had done more than her share to put Chicago back on the opera map.

Meanwhile the Lyric's season had two more productions to go, *Carmen* and *Tosca*. The Bizet was the one serious miscalculation of the season. The orchestra, under the direction of Perlea, was erratic, and Simionato's Carmen, one critic said, was more like a forlorn Santuzza. But the Lyric was leading a charmed life. One man, who had donated ten dollars earlier to the fund-raising drive, sent the management a note saying, "I was beginning to think you were infallible when I saw your *Carmen*. Thank God you're not. Here's another $5." *Tosca* was far better. Eleanor Steber was good in the title role, though not ideal. Giuseppe di Stefano rose to vocal heights as Cavaradossi, but from the moment he entered, it was Tito Gobbi who dominated the performance. "Mr. Gobbi," Cassidy said, "had the obsidian elegance of the self-centered tyrant, silky cruel and enjoying it. He knows make-up, he has his stage timing figured out to the last beat, and he can handle that voice." After the performance Sam Lesner asked in the *Daily News*, "How can it be that opera should have languished so long in Chicago and then suddenly burst forth on a level of total artistic perfection, stunning in its dramatic impact, dazzling in its vocal purity?"

The season closed with a deficit of $13,958; attendance had been 84 per cent of capacity. The company had shown itself well in practically every respect. The chorus was well chosen and well trained. The orchestra had been adequate or better, and Ruth Page's ballet became one of Lyric's immediate assets. The criticisms were primarily two. First, the singers in smaller roles often fell below the standard set by the principals, and, second, the physical productions, dating back to the Civic Opera days or before, showed their age and occasionally looked downright shabby.

And yet these eight productions regained for Chicago an undeniable place among the leading opera centers of the world. The coalition of Carol Fox (general manager), Lawrence Kelly (managing director), and Nicola Rescigno (musical director) had proved explosive, combining high musical values with sound administrative know-how. With Callas there to add a desirable touch of glamour, and Callas, Gobbi, Simionato, di Stefano, Rossi-Lemeni, Carteri, and Steber conferring the necessary vocal weight, success was assured. It was Chicago's first really new look in opera in over twenty years.

The big question now was whether Callas would be back in 1955. To find the answer, Kelly and Miss Fox left for Europe right after Christmas. Joined by Maestro Rescigno, they followed the diva over half the continent trying to get her signature on a contract. After repeated sessions of talking repertoire, casting, and terms, she agreed to sign. Then she turned to Kelly and matter-of-factly said, "You should sign up Renata Tebaldi. Then your audiences will have the opportunity to compare us, and your season will be even more successful."

Tebaldi was Callas' most serious rival, and their lack of cordiality had been discussed the world over. Besides, the prospects of having both Callas and Tebaldi on the roster was pretty heady thinking even for a dreamer like Kelly. Nevertheless, the Lyric began negotiations with Tebaldi, and before long she had signed too. Upon hearing of this latest Fox-Kelly coup, one critic smiled and said, "They're incredible. They don't know these things can't be done, so they do them." And when Broadway's Mary Martin heard the news, she could only gasp, "You've got *both!*"

The two prima donnas arrived in the fall amid a buzz of excitement. Their performances had been sold out for a month. Callas seemed more glamorous than ever, bringing with her a number of Dior originals, her hair now dark. She was again cooperative, willing to attend social functions, and eager to extol the opera management. Tebaldi, though less forceful a personality, was no less willing to assist, and Gobbi, Rossi-Lemeni, di Stefano, and Carteri were all back to help kindle interest.

The season opened on October 31 with Callas in Bellini's *I Puritani*, a work that had not been heard in this country for over thirty years. When Callas appeared on stage, she was greeted by an ovation that stopped the show. One critic found *Puritani* "dead weight," another "a let-down," but for Maria Callas it was a personal triumph. "It was fantastic," Cassidy said, "to see Callas make Elvira a totally different creature from her Lucia. Where Lucia was a normal girl gone mad for love, Elvira is a fey, unstable creature who is off and on again like Finnegan. The glint in her eyes, the dark hair, the lovely hands—you can't take your eyes off her. And her singing is magnificent." Howard Talley wrote for *Musical America*, "Her acting in song, movement, and gesture was memorable; the pathetic droop of her figure during her 'mad' intervals is still vivid in the mind's eye. No mistake about it, she is the premier singing actress of today." Giuseppe di Stefano made an excellent Arthur, Ettore Bastianini a fine Richard. Rescigno conducted, *Musical America* said, "with enthusiasm but not always with discretion." The sets, which were borrowed from Rome, in their old-fashioned way were stunning.

The audience was made up mostly of young men and women, stylishly attired. As the *Tribune* reported it, "Cameramen grumbled as they fought for room to shoot their subjects. Long gowns were trampled on and corsages were swept awry as top hatted box holders pushed past eager spectators who clogged the entrance foyer to watch the parade of gowns, furs, and jewels." Mrs. John Orndorff cheated a bit this year, coming as a "Rococo Puritan." She wore a silver brocade gown with a tall headdress of white egret feathers, which her grandfather supposedly had gotten from a Seminole Indian. Following the performance, another "Angel Ball" was given at the Hilton, with many of the opera stars in attendance. Callas herself made a dramatic entrance, wearing a gown of emerald green and gold. The skirt was green velvet, the top gold and silver brocade, accented by a stole of the green.

The next evening Renata Tebaldi made her local debut as Aida. The *Tribune* said, "The audience kept roaring as if Notre Dame had just made a touchdown." Tebaldi's victory was complete, her voice big and rich. "Warm and lustrous, with a World Series aim, it had her audience in ecstasies of delight," Cassidy wrote. Even Maria Callas was there for the occasion, applauding politely and telling a friend, "Renata is in very good voice tonight." Astrid Varnay made a magnificent Amneris and Tito Gobbi's Amonasro, according to *Musical Courier*, was "one of the strongest and ... most moving characterizations we have ever encountered." On the podium was a seventy-seven-year-old Tullio Serafin, who worked wonders with the Lyric's orchestra.

But the fever pitch was carried even higher a few nights later when Callas, Bjoerling, Bastianini, and Ebe Stignani teamed for *Il Trovatore*. "Not in many a long year," Cassidy held, "has Chicago had a *Trovatore* to rival the Lyric Theatre's in the Civic Opera house Saturday night. ... The applause was so roof-shattering it's nice to know the theater is in a position to carry plenty of insurance." Callas emerged as a distinctly Spanish Leonora, and her fourth act particularly was "a wonder of the western world." "Her Leonora was perfection," Jussi Bjoerling said. "I have heard the role sung often, but never was there a better one than hers." The tenor himself was a virtual sensation, and Cassidy said, "His '*Di Quella Pira*' glitters like his flashing sword." Ebe Stignani walked off with her share of the honors, making an "unforgettable Azucena" and winning a four-minute ovation in the second act. It was the most exciting evening so far.

Again it was Tebaldi's turn, now in *La Bohème*. Together she and Giuseppe di Stefano did "some of the most beautiful singing imaginable," and René Devries called it "as fine a performance as this reviewer has heard in the past thirty years." Rounding out the quartet of Bohemians were Gobbi, Rossi-Lemeni, and Richard Torigi. Gloria Lind was Musetta. The audience seemed to catch the mood of the opera as audiences rarely do. "The finest tribute to last night's *La Bohème*, perhaps to the cumulative effect of the entire Lyric season so far, came . . . in the little flutter of protest that silenced applause after the last act duet for tenor and baritone until Tullio Serafin's orchestra had sung the postlude."

Callas still had one more role to go, *Madama Butterfly*. Since it was her first Butterfly anywhere, much of the international opera set had descended upon Chicago for the event. Staged by Hizi Koyke, a Butterfly of considerable merit herself at one time, the production aimed at creating the atmosphere of the Kabuki Theater. Callas tried to give the impression of childishness in the first act, but her movements seemed overstudied and contrived, many of the Japanese touches exaggerated. The consensus was that it was her least satisfying Chicago role. "This was charming make believe," Cassidy felt, "but it was not Cio-Cio-San, nor was it the ultimate Callas." Giuseppe di Stefano, on the other hand, was an almost perfect Pinkerton.

Although it was not her best role, Chicagoans flocked to hear the Callas Butterfly, for it was her last opera of the season, and the announcement had already been made that she would not be back the next year. On November 8, just before her second *Trovatore*, she had signed a contract with the Metropolitan to open the 1956 season there. The Met's manager, Rudolf Bing, had flown out from New York to woo her, and when at last the agreement was reached, Bing planted a courtly buss on the diva's hand, much to the delight of photographers. Chicagoans were less enchanted, for because of conflicting dates in New York, their angel would not be able to return to the city the next year. So Chicago was making the most of the opportunities it had, using the *Butterfly* appearances as a chance to say farewell. When a third performance was added, patrons lined up for blocks waiting for the box office to open. The house was sold out in an hour and thirty-eight minutes. "The Town, we all know," Roger Dettmer wrote in the Chicago *American*, "has been Callas-crazy for more than a year, and none has been more demented than I. In the proper role and in good voice, I adore the woman; I am a slave in her spell." Her departure for the Metropolitan had brought protests, eulogies, and poems:

> Oh, Maria Meneghini Callas! Of me myself, I sing.
> For I shook the hand that took the kiss from the lips
> of Rudolf Bing.

The final *Butterfly* was one of wanton sentimentality, off stage more than on. Time and again Callas was called before the curtain, while the house paid her homage in every way it knew how. At last physically exhausted, with tears in her eyes, she waved a last good-by and left the stage.

Then the real drama of that day took place. All season long the Bagarozy suit had been hanging fire, resulting in a cloak-and-dagger sort of chase by process servers. The Lyric management had kept up a twenty-four-hour-a-day watch to protect their star, as they had agreed to do in her contract, but there had been close calls. After one performance Carol Fox, Dario Soria, and Walter Legge had sneaked the singer down the freight elevator and out the back exit, down by the river. With the company's stagehands standing guard, Soria and Legge, Angel Records' bosses, carried madame's mound of luggage up to a waiting car. She spent the night at Carol Fox's mother's apartment. Another time the summons was so close the soprano spent the whole day locked in her room. Now, on the day of the final *Butterfly*, the process servers had been after her since morning. They approached her as she was leaving her Oak Street apartment for the theater, but were pushed back by a group of admirers. Then, as Callas came off the stage, in the excitement of her final Chicago performance for at least two years, the guard was momentarily dropped. On her way back to her dressing room, the summons was forced into her kimono, achieving the bodily contact required by law.

The renowned Callas temperament was unleashed in all its fury, as Carol Fox and Lawrence Kelly looked on in amazement. It was an unfortunate ending to a two-year love affair. Callas had felt she was surrounded by friends, but somehow Lyric's best defenses had failed. There is some indication that disgruntled factions who were unhappy about the singer's deserting Chicago for the Metropolitan had actually helped set the trap. "Chicago will be sorry for this!" Callas shrieked. Then, her wrath spent, she broke into sobs. The dressing room, which had been barred to photographers and reporters, was empty, and she sat there in seclusion. The next day she left for Canada and thence flew to Italy, saying simply, "Chicago is fed up with Callas."

The next few days saw the question of Callas' art, her personality, and even her moral fiber thrown open to a heated public scrutiny. Over the back fence and cocktail table, in the barber shop and supermarket, the details of the incident were discussed and embroidered. But amid the emotional outpouring, as Callas' supporters vied with her accusers, Claudia Cassidy kept perspective: "Callas is still a star. The Lyric is still the best thing this town has had since the arrival of Fritz Reiner in the Orchestra hall. Skip the rest. It's not worth the trouble of denying."

For two weeks the Lyric had offered Callas and Tebaldi on alternate nights, a record no other company anywhere could match. The more established opera houses fairly trembled at the thought of the two divas in such close proximity. "The feeling exists," *Newsweek* said, "that what has thus far developed as a full blown prima donna feud at hissing range might degenerate into hair-pulling at close quarters." And yet the two had shared the same dressing room in Chicago without incident, managing to avoid each other completely.

With such a sensational beginning, the last three weeks of the season, with both luminaries gone, were almost destined to be anticlimactic. Attendance did drop appreciably, although repeat performances of operas brought out larger crowds than opening nights, as word spread that there was still plenty of excitement at the Opera House. Tito Gobbi sang a remarkable Rigoletto, probing the character with an intelligence few artists have been able to give. His Gilda was Teresa Stich-Randall, making her American opera debut. She sang the music just as Verdi wrote it, and her tones were "pure and effortless." Jussi Bjoerling was the Duke, the role he had sung here nearly twenty years before when he made his American debut. Bjoerling, Rossi-Lemeni, and Carteri teamed for an uneven *Faust*, with Tullio Serafin conducting. The production included the rarely staged ballet, the dancers headed by young Carol Lawrence, who two years later would achieve Broadway success as Maria in Leonard Bernstein's *West Side Story*.

The first of two interesting triple bills combined Puccini's *Il Tabarro*, Monteverdi's *Il Ballo delle Ingrate*, and a ballet adapted by Ruth Page from Lehár's *The Merry Widow*. *Tabarro* had not been heard in Chicago since 1919, and it proved a real thriller, with Tito Gobbi as Michele and Carlo Bergonzi making his American debut as Luigi. *Il Ballo delle Ingrate* is a masque, first performed in 1608 in Mantua to celebrate a ducal wedding and staged by the Lyric for the first time in America. The singers, who included Stignani and Stich-Randall, sang from the orchestra pit, while the ballet, headed by Vera Zorina, held the boards.

The second triple bill began with *Cavalleria Rusticana*, starring Stignani as Santuzza and di Stefano and Bergonzi alternating as Turiddu. Then came Rafaello de Banfield's *Lord Byron's Love Letter*, staged in Chicago just a few months after its premiere in New Orleans, the production underwritten in part by the American Opera Society. It is one of the finest things the Lyric has ever done. The story, based on a text by Tennessee Williams, tells of a spinster and her grandmother, who live in seclusion in their old home in New Orleans, supporting themselves by showing tourists an old love letter Lord Byron had written the grandmother when she was a young girl. Astrid Varnay was the grandmother, Gertrude Ribla the spinster, and both were excellent. Cassidy found the score "a lovely, lyrical thing," while *Musical America* said it "had its own authentic accent, the kind of music that spells Grand Opera." The evening closed with a ballet entitled *Revanche*, based on Verdi's *Il Trovatore*.

Donizetti's *L'Elisir d'Amore* was given a sterling production with Carteri, Leopold Simoneau, and Rossi-Lemeni, under Serafin's direction. Rossi-Lemeni almost stole the show as the quack doctor, making his entrance in a gaudy carriage drawn by two horses. Montemezzi's *L'Amore dei Tre Re* featured Dorothy Kirsten as Fiora, Carlo Bergonzi as Avito, and Rossi-Lemeni as Archibaldo. The orchestra under Serafin gave its finest performance to date. Rosa Raisa attended, with the composer's widow. Finally, there was *Un Ballo in Maschera*, introducing Anita Cerquetti in her American debut. "Trailing black draperies with all the dignity of an experienced diva," *Musical America* wrote, "Miss Cerquetti amazed the audience with a dramatic soprano, huge, dark, evenly scaled, wanting only a top range with the projection which will surely come with time." Jussi Bjoerling was the Riccardo, Tito Gobbi a capital Renato. The first performance played to an audience about two-thirds of capacity, but the reviews were so glowing, particularly Cerquetti's, that the final night found the house packed.

Audiences nowadays did not seem to be composed of the upper social stratum. "This group," Howard Talley wrote for *The Nation*, "has died off, moved to the suburbs, or its younger members are no longer much interested in cultural enterprises, except that they go to the symphony as regularly as their forebears went to church." The main floor consisted largely of prosperous middle-class business and professional people, great numbers of whom came from surrounding towns and cities like Milwaukee, Madison, Minneapolis, and Detroit. "A good percentage of them seemed to be hearing opera in the flesh for the first time," Talley said. "Their enthusiasm was genuine but undiscriminating. They applauded the rise of the curtain on an act, the first appearance of a well-known singer whether or not he was singing, any retained high note, whether in the middle or at the end of an aria.... A new audience has discovered opera and likes it."

And Lyric was building a new audience, along with a new operatic tradition, and a new base of financial support. For the most part the company had to operate without the assistance of the wealthy who had once played such an important role in underwriting Chicago's opera, underwritten instead by a multitude of smaller donations. The 1955 fund-raising drive had secured approximately one hundred thousand dollars from private and corporate sources, gifts varying from over one thousand dollars down to one dollar. The business and professional people who now attended the Opera, and contributed to its support, were simply incapable of the huge donations that a select group had made during the McCormick days. Further tax revisions had made this impossible. Businesses were gradually becoming aware that the Lyric was good for Chicago and good for them, but even here the size of the contribution was limited, although generous by modern standards.

For the Lyric the box office receipts played a much more important role than they ever had for Campanini or Polacco. Therefore, the repertoire and artistic roster had to have popular appeal. The age when an expensive production could be mounted once and then forgotten was over, as were the days when a single production could be given anything like the twenty-seven orchestra rehearsals *Salome* had received in 1910. The coming of effective musicians' unions and the resulting salary increases had relegated such practices to the realm of fantasy. The Lyric, just as the Metropolitan or any other American opera company, was caught between rising costs on the one hand and limited guarantor support on the other, causing the box office to loom far larger than in countries where opera benefited from government subsidy.

These were considerations which underlay a dispute that had been building all during Lyric's second season. It began when Maestro Rescigno drew up a contract in which he, as artistic director, would be given the right to veto any artistic decision made by the company. Carol Fox and, at first, Lawrence Kelly refused. Eventually Kelly was drawn over to Rescigno's side. Two things were involved: first, a simple struggle over power, and second, a question of what could be accomplished artistically while still keeping the company solvent. All three took an idealistic position, feeling that the company must maintain high artistic standards and production dynamism. Rather than accept a pedestrian, "safe" repertoire, Kelly said: "I would go back to the real-estate business. I love music too much to be satisfied with that familiar old routine." While agreeing that high artistic standards were of the utmost importance, Carol Foz was aware of the past history of Chicago opera, with its fantastic extravagances and huge deficits, and she maintained that the company must be kept on a solid financial footing. The simple facts of life were that the box office demanded a moderately conservative policy in repertoire and casting. Cables from the artists supported her position.

The schism eventually degenerated into a long, involved court battle which found both factions struggling for control. The company's six-man board of directors was evenly divided between the two. After a stalemate of several months, during which neither side could negotiate for the coming season, Carol Fox secured the necessary financial backing and was authorized to go ahead. Kelly shortly received an offer to become general manager of the newly formed Dallas Civic Opera, and Rescigno went with him as artistic director. Meanwhile Carol Fox's organization was revamped, its name changed to the Lyric Opera of Chicago, and it assumed the contracts with artists held by the former Lyric Theatre as well as a large deficit accumulated over the latter's brief two-year life.

Although its career had ended so stormily, the Lyric Theatre's record had been phenomenal by any standards, its productions, for the most part, well mounted, well cast, and well rehearsed. In two short seasons it had reclaimed for Chicago its operatic heritage, exposing a whole new generation to the joy of catching opera fever.

Chapter 14

SHE SHALL HAVE MUSIC WHEREVER SHE GOES

By the time the smoke of battle cleared in February, Carol Fox was left with precious little time for putting together a 1956 season. A repertoire had to be decided upon; casting holes had to be filled; and a subscription campaign, already five months late, was yet to be waged. In addition, the Lyric had lost its number-one box office attraction and its artistic director, making the immediate future even more precarious. In July, Emerson Buckley, formerly of the New York City Opera and currently director of the Central City Opera Festival, was chosen musical administrator. Twenty-five performances of eleven operas were scheduled.

Considering the handicaps, the season came off remarkably well. It opened on October 10 with Puccini's *The Girl of the Golden West*, not heard in Chicago since Rosa Raisa sang it in 1922. "The Lyric's luck held," Claudia Cassidy wrote, "and what luck it had to be to get that 1956 curtain up on schedule." Eleanor Steber made an adorable Minnie, although the vocal honors of the evening went to Mario Del Monaco and Tito Gobbi. "Mario Del Monaco, a power hitter who knocks his high notes right out of the park, was also a handsome charmer as the masquerading bandit," Cassidy said. "Tito Gobbi, a Mephistophelean sheriff more Scarpia than 'Gunsmoke,' played the sonorous villain to the point of being hissed." In the third act, five spirited horses raced across the stage and up an incline to the rear, generating applause from the first-nighters and causing Roger Dettmer of the Chicago *American* to say, "This four-horse relic of an earlier lyric era was given a five-horse staging. . . . Surely such eye-rolling and lurching hasn't been seen since Billy Bryant's Showboat quit the rivers." Steber sang fetchingly despite a somewhat stage-shy mount, but

William Wilderman, the Ashby, was less fortunate. His faithless steed, apparently having important business elsewhere, trotted off the stage before his rider finished his aria. But the laughter was friendly, the production commendable. "Bravo, Carol Fox," René Devries shouted, "and *viva tutti quanti!*"

The audience came "in best bib and tucker," dressing now not only for the first-nighters and the crowd which traditionally gathered outside the Opera House entrance, but for the television cameras as well. Mrs. John Orndorff temporarily departed from her custom of dressing as the opera's heroine, because, she told a reporter, "I didn't want to attend the opening as a barmaid." Mrs. Tito Gobbi was on hand, insisting that American audiences are among the most enthusiastic in the world. "You enjoy things tremendously," she observed. Perhaps part of the audience enjoyed itself more than the performance on stage, for stragglers returned to their seats so late and so noisily for Act III that conductor Dimitri Mitropoulos ordered the curtain closed and began all over again.

Following the performance, a guarantor ball was held in the Opera House foyer. For what must have been the first time in history, the *Tribune's* review of the opening night social scene began with a discussion of finances, indicating something of the company's lack of affluence. "Music to the ears of the women's board of the Lyric Opera," the society columnist said, "was not so much the arias which floated from the stage during the opera as a happy ringing in their eyes of cash registers."

Andrea Chénier, again teaming Del Monaco, Steber, and Gobbi, resulted in some excellent singing and one of the best productions of that opera Chicago had heard. Buckley conducted. Del Monaco repeatedly roused his audience to lusty ovations, causing one observer to ask, "Who says we don't like opera in this town?" *Salome,* featuring Inge Borkh in the title role, saw the American opera debut of conductor Georg Solti. Although Solti was superb, the production itself was rather curious. Borkh's Salome was one of the most active on record, never still for a minute, and most reviewers considered it sadly disappointing. Three nights later, however, Lyric really came of age, when *Die Walküre* was given with Solti conducting and Birgit Nilsson singing Brünnhilde, three years before her debut at the Metropolitan. "The young singer," *Musical America* reported, "had a fresh, evenly-scaled soprano, audible in the middle register, with a by-no-means unpleasant cutting edge in the upper register." And Roger Dettmer said, "This fine trim figure of a Valkyrie is yet very young, but her voice has been schooled impressively, her musicianship attended to and her lustrous driving soprano made strong for such rigors as *The Ring* imposes."

Il Trovatore was repeated with Bjoerling, his Leonoras now Herva

Nelli and Gertrude Ribla, both called in to replace an indisposed Anita Cerquetti. *La Traviata* was given with Steber, Simoneau, and Bastianini, the sets partially imported from Palermo's Teatro Massimo. *Don Giovanni* found Solti conducting, and Rossi-Lemeni, Steber, and Simoneau repeating the roles they had sung in the Lyric's "Calling Card" performance. On October 30, Renata Tebaldi sang her first Chicago *Tosca*. She proved one of the great Toscas of all time, her "*Vissi d'Arte*" stopping the show cold. "Pounds thinner, radiantly beautiful, and in voice so opulent it was both sumptuous and dangerous, she set the wonderful old thriller blazing," Cassidy wrote in her review.

But the season's undisputed pinnacle was reached on November 8, with the company's initial mounting of Verdi's *La Forza del Destino*. Conductor Georg Solti opened so many cuts in the score that the performance had to begin a half hour early. Tebaldi, as Leonora, looked gorgeous, moved with dignity, and sang beautifully. Simionato's Preziosilla was saucy and charming. Richard Tucker was the Alvaro, Ettore Bastianini the Don Carlo, and Nicola Rossi-Lemeni the Padre Guardiano—all three excellent. But Cassidy assured, "The young company so justly Chicago's pride had something more indigenous to offer than an array of distinguished guests. It had a production of quality on stage and in the pit." Both performances were sold out far in advance, and hundreds more were turned away at the box office.

The Gobbi-Simionato *Barber of Seville* was revived, and *La Bohème* was given for the third year in succession, again with Tebaldi. Although the principals sang well enough, neither production came off as well as before, both suffering from deficient staging. Of the *Bohème* Cassidy said, "What we were subjected to this time was an undisciplined muddle with just about every man for himself." The operatic gala on November 10, in which Tebaldi, Simionato, Tucker, Bastianini, and Solti participated, was recorded by London Records and distributed in an album called "An Evening with the Chicago Lyric."

The season closed with gross receipts totaling $449,349, as compared with the 1955 gross of $428,426 for the same number of performances. "Another season of Chicago grand opera is over," *Musical America* wrote. "It ended with no display of Greek fireworks, no outbreaks of temperament, no threats of dissolution. . . . But this is not to say that it was a tame and static affair. Far from it. This time the emphasis was on producing music and drama in full view of the audience, not behind the scenes." Carol Fox was decorated that year by the Italian government in recognition of her "outstanding services to the field of grand opera."

The next year the Lyric extended its season to seven weeks, its repertoire to fourteen productions. *Otello* opened, with a cast headed by Mario

Del Monaco, Renata Tebaldi, and Tito Gobbi, under the direction of Tullio Serafin. Del Monaco made a handsome, imperious Moor, with a voice to match. "It is a big, beautiful voice," Cassidy reported, "with the ring of steel, the hurt of anguish, the spectacular range, and the noble style of declamation." Nevertheless, until the final act it was Tito Gobbi who dominated the scene whenever he was present. René Devries said his "incomparable characterization of Iago stands among the most powerful portrayals ever projected from our operatic stage." The last act belonged to Tebaldi—"the Desdemona of our dreams." Slimmer than before and stunningly made up, she sang like a goddess. "The beauty of the Tebaldi voice is a wonder of our time," Cassidy wrote, "but I think it was never more beautiful than this opening night when it poured out in all its splendor." And for Don Henahan of the Chicago *Daily News*, "the rich cream of Renata Tebaldi's soprano voice made up for some half and half and skimmed milk at other spots in the cast."

Although uneven at times, *Otello* held its own with the first-night social whirl better than any opening production since the Callas-Simionato *Norma*. Chinchilla, ermine, and mink were all present, but bright-colored evening coats were also becoming stylish. Mrs. Orndorff, if not quite Desdemona, came in an Italian Renaissance gown of green velvet with slashed gold sleeves. The young man renting opera glasses attested to the audience's elegance. He had rented only five pairs all evening. "They're all coming in with their own," he said, "inlaid with mother-of-pearl. They'd rather spend a hundred dollars and buy a pair than fifty cents to rent a pair! Oh, well," and he gave a shrug, "there are all kinds of people." With the press rushing around to interview and photograph socialites and other dignitaries, one bystander was heard to comment, "I feel as though I weren't even here!"

A post-opera party was held on stage, tickets selling for one hundred dollars a couple, the funds going to bolster the company's deficit fund. After drinking their champagne, guests walked down a ramp over the orchestra pit, up the main aisle to the foyer, where they ate dinner and danced until three in the morning.

Pennsylvania-born Anna Moffo, after a successful European career, made her American debut with the company that season as Mimi, amid mixed reviews. Jussi Bjoerling was her Rodolfo, his voice fresher than it had sounded in years. Giulietta Simionato was heard as Mignon, with Moffo as Philine and Alvinio Misciano, replacing an ailing Leopold Simoneau, as Wilhelm Meister. Since Misciano knew his part only in Italian, the cast sang in French except when the tenor was on stage, then switched to Italian, marring an otherwise good production. Fortunately Simionato knew her role in both languages and alternated back and forth as the occasion demanded with apparent ease. She was rewarded with the first standing ovation since Callas. Of Moffo, Devries wrote, "A few seasons on her native soil may bring her to stardom, but as yet she is a starlet of the soubrette type, with beauty and a sense of the theatre."

She was heard to much better advantage in *Lucia di Lammermoor* and as Susanna in *The Marriage of Figaro*, although neither production was a notable success. The latter combined Moffo with Steber, Gobbi, Simionato, and Walter Berry—Berry making his American debut. Solti conducted. Neither Gobbi nor Simionato was quite in his element, and a number of the ensembles were pretty ragged. The sets and costumes were new, Lyric's first new production. The *Lucia* was haphazardly staged and uneven vocally. Cassidy claimed, "It was a barnstorming performance with little taste and less style."

On a completely different plane was Puccini's *Manon Lescaut*, with Tebaldi and Bjoerling doing some of the most sumptuous singing of the season, under Serafin's direction. "Miss Tebaldi," Roger Dettmer wrote, "in complete command of her splendid voice, managed to give it as many different colors and textures as Dior's spring collection. It ranged from a celloing richness to the bright cold purity of a flute; in a sense she gestures with it, as effortlessly as an actor uses his hands." *Andrea Chénier*, featuring Tebaldi, Del Monaco, and Gobbi, was even better, each artist seeming to stimulate the other. "Never before . . . has Mme. Tebaldi either sung so majestically or acted so convincingly," Dettmer said, "especially in the tribunal scene when she hears Chenier's sentence and goes screaming through the crowd to clutch him." It was one of those nights when everything seemed to come off just right, leaving the audience exhilarated. "Opera is a wonderfully incendiary business," said Claudia Cassidy. "True, it sometimes sets out smudge pots and smokes you right out of the house. But on a good night spurts of operatic fire flicker vividly, and on a great Italian night you would swear the place is going up in flames. It was like that at *Andrea Chenier*."

Cilèa's *Adriana Lecouvreur*, not staged in the United States since Lina Cavalieri and Caruso sang it at the Metropolitan a half century before, was mounted by the Lyric in 1957 expressly for Tebaldi. The score proved to be made of slight stuff ("Rest easy, Mozart," Don Henahan wrote), but the title role offers good possibilities for the soprano, and Tebaldi had labeled it her favorite role. The Lyric not only agreed to stage *Adriana* for her, but gave her di Stefano, Simionato, Gobbi, and Serafin as colleagues. Among the five of them, they came remarkably close to making it a success. For the first time Chicago saw Tebaldi convincingly suggest a woman of the world. Ulric Kaskell, writing for *Saturday Review*, said she seemed to live the part and sang it "in a particularly glorious voice, giving the most trenchant and memorable portrayal of her American career." Don Henahan said she sang so well and looked so beautiful one wondered if she were real. Simionato had sprained her ankle during rehearsals and had to move slowly to keep from limping, but she sang and acted with her usual finesse. Although no one seemed to feel that *Adriana* was destined for a place in the standard repertoire, the consensus was that Lyric had staged and cast it lavishly and that hearing it once had been fun.

That was also the year Chicago heard Verdi's *Don Carlo* for the first time. The work was staged in a new production and conducted by Solti; its cast included Cerquetti, Nell Rankin, Brian Sullivan (later Bjoerling), Gobbi, and Boris Christoff, the latter in his local debut. Ponchielli's *La Gioconda* brought the first Chicago appearances in opera of Eileen Farrell. Although her acting was tentative and her voice a little tired from too much rehearsal, her performance was a good one, the "*Sucidio*" bordering on magnificent. *Un Ballo in Maschera* found Cerquetti in a far less happy vocal estate than when she conquered the city in the same role two years before, but Bjoerling's Riccardo remained positively matchless. Mario Del Monaco achieved what was probably his greatest Chicago triumph as Canio, which together with Gobbi's Tonio made for a *Pagliacci* which fell only slightly short of the ideal blending of music and drama critics dream of. *Cavalleria Rusticana*, on the other hand, despite the presence of Simionato, never quite managed to catch fire.

The season played to 92 per cent of capacity, with seventeen of the twenty-nine performances sold out. Artistically, critics found the season decisively uneven, and with the company's roots more firmly planted, they became less protective in their attitude—a sure sign that the Lyric was growing up. Cassidy felt that the company "often seemed to have lost sight of its gleaming goal and to have settled for the very kind of opera it was organized to protest." Most reviewers agreed that the greatest single weakness was in secondary casting. Also, the lighting was poor (which seems to have been the case since the Campanini days), and the stagings were often perfunctory. "Adept comprimarios fancied themselves stars," Cassidy said, "bit players developed a mania for putty noses in a gallery of grotesques, and provincialism engulfed the curtain calls until it was possible to see solo bows by the bass who sang Silvano in *The Masked Ball* . . . and by the soprano who sang Alice in *Lucia*." But even the severest critics agreed that, with few exceptions, the principals had been excellent, that the chorus was a definite asset, that the orchestra had been generally good, and that the new sets and many of the old ones were commendable, sometimes superb. Cassidy felt that the company's major shortcoming was its lack of an artistic director. "What the Lyric needs and needs fast," she wrote in *Theatre Arts*, "is not only the right person to say yes, but the person who knows when and how to say no and make it stick." The following summer Pino Donati, a conductor with a considerable reputation in Europe, was brought into the company as musical assistant to the general manager, solving some, though certainly not all, of these production problems.

Opening night, 1958, found the Opera House foyer more crowded than ever before. The opera, *Falstaff*, was broadcast over Station CBS-WBBM, and it was preceded by a commentary from a roped-off area on the main floor. Instead of the audience's going to their seats as usual, almost everyone wanted to pause to listen in on the broadcast. The *Tribune* found the opening "one of the giddiest in history." One young man wore a red velvet waistcoat, while one of the ladies wore a jewel in the middle of her forehead. Another woman sported a yellow coat, cut like a monkey suit in front and falling to the floor in back. Wigs were becoming fashionable, along with "bubble" skirts. Mrs. James McGrath caused some excitement when she entered in a black wool opera cape lined with satin. For the most part, however, it was a season of gay colors. Mrs. Charles Frey, for instance, wore a floor-length emerald chiffon gown with a floating panel embroidered in gold. Former Illinois governor and twice Democratic Presidential candidate Adlai Stevenson was present, and Carol Fox, now Mrs. C. Larkin Flanagan, shuttled between backstage and the foyer, escorted by her doctor husband.

The cocktail lounge adjoining the Opera House had become a popular place to meet and chat with friends before the performance and during intermissions. Although opera would probably be the topic of discussion at most tables, a casual passer-through in the fall of 1958 would likely have heard talk of racial troubles in Little Rock, the growing concern over financial recession, how we were catching up with the Russians in space, and the feats of the current contestants on the popular television quiz program "The $64,000 Question." The national production of Lerner and Loewe's *My Fair Lady* was in town and causing talk; Mary Martin was visiting in what was practically a one-woman revue; and *Gigi* was the big screen attraction. A question which was frequently being asked these days in musical circles was: "Will stereo replace concerts?"—a question which had been asked earlier of the phonograph and radio and even the movies.

Falstaff was another of those all-star productions for which Lyric by now had become noted. Gobbi was Sir John; Tebaldi, Alice Ford; Cornell MacNeil, Ford; Simionato, Dame Quickly; Anna Moffo, Nanetta; Alvinio Misciano, Fenton; and Anna Maria Canali, Mistress Page. Tullio Serafin conducted. Most reviewers, however, agreed with Howard Talley when he wrote in *Musical America* that "this was a good rather than a memorable

Falstaff." There was some miscasting and misdirection which caused the production to fall a mite short of expectations. Gobbi's Falstaff proved another of his expertly drawn characterizations, although not without some controversial moments. Cassidy found Tebaldi "a bewitching Mistress Ford, raven haired, cream skinned, in exquisitely opulent voice, with costumes from some dream book, and that little touch of deviltry Verdi hoped for, if he could get it." Simionato's Dame Quickly was a droll woman "of sonorous obeisance and the walk of a woman whose feet hurt, but not enough to make her scowl." While the critics had reservations, the audience seemed charmed and applauded the production eagerly. When David Shapiro, who had been selling librettos in the Opera House foyer for twenty years, was asked what he thought of it, he confessed he had only taken a peek, then left. "Well, let's be truthful," he said. "I'd rather see a good baseball game!"

Three nights later, October 13, Renata Tebaldi sang her first *Madama Butterfly* in the United States, one of her first performances of the role anywhere. "Not since Elisabeth Rethberg's and Florence Easton's performances of the same role in the 1920's," Howard Talley wrote, "have I heard such exquisitely shaded, opulent, and poignant singing." Making his American debut on the podium was Kiril Kondrashin, who had conducted the Tchaikovsky Piano Concerto for Van Cliburn in Russia. Another exceptionally strong production was *Turandot*, with Nilsson, di Stefano, Moffo, and Serafin. Calaf was one of the finest roles di Stefano had ever sung in Chicago, and Moffo rose to heights previously unapproached. But it was Nilsson who commanded most of the superlatives. *Musical Courier* said she was a marvel to hear, "flinging out one high C after another with ease and amplitude." The chorus and stage direction were both superior, and *Musical America* called Serafin's conducting "masterly." The sets were borrowed from the San Francisco Opera, in exchange for the Lyric's *Don Carlo.*

The high point of the season, however, was a *Tristan und Isolde* conducted by Artur Rodzinski, Chicago's first *Tristan* in eleven years. Back in the city for the first time since his abrupt dismissal as director of the Chicago Symphony, Rodzinski wrought from the Lyric orchestra the best performance it had yet given. Claudia Cassidy felt it was "a miraculous performance," largely because of the warmth and beauty which poured from the pit. "What that orchestra did for Rodzinski," she wrote in her review, "for Wagner, and for the audience was to pour out the molten gold of the score as if mesmerized." Birgit Nilsson the critic pronounced "the next great Nordic Isolde." The whole cast seemed inspired by Rodzinski's presence, almost everyone giving a better performance than was customary. It was without doubt one of the truly great marvels in

Lyric's history, a production whose total impact, Cassidy felt, was far greater than the sum of its parts.

Rodzinski was scheduled to conduct *Boris Godunov* as well, but a severe cold forced him to withdraw. In less than a month, he died in Boston of a heart ailment. His performances with the Lyric were his last anywhere. Without Rodzinski, *Boris* was something of a disappointment, although Boris Christoff, who sang the title role, was favorably compared to Chaliapin. Cassidy found his performance much gentler than Chaliapin's, but nevertheless "quite a Boris." The production was sung in Russian, the chorus giving a particularly good account of itself. The weakness came from the pit; George Sebastian, who stepped in on short notice, was simply not able to hold things together.

Il Trovatore also suffered from weak conducting, coupled with "a neophyte Leonora" in Elinor Ross, who took over when Eileen Farrell became ill. The strong points were Bjoerling's Manrico and Simionato's Azucena. "Miss Simionato sang Azucena," Cassidy said, "as a Spanish gypsy who just happened to have the full Italian opulence of song, with a drifting chromatic scale to drown the ears in delight." *Aida*, however, found the mezzo seemingly miscast as Amneris, wearing unattractive costumes and a curious silky, orange wig. The whole production left much to be desired. Leonie Rysanek, making her local debut in the title role, was vocally uneven, and Bjoerling, the Radames, was far below his usual standard. Only Tito Gobbi seemed really suited to his role both vocally and dramatically. And making matters worse, the sets and costumes were some of the most unfortunate in the warehouse, at times downright laughable.

La Traviata saw more miscasting, particularly in Eleanor Steber's Violetta. According to Cassidy's review, Steber had little real feeling for the role: "She plays a blonde hausfrau who has a bad time of it, sobs a lot, and eventually expires because the script says she must." The staging and costuming were both weak, and *Musical America* complained that "The corps de ballet . . . amused with its mock bullfight, but also indulged in some questionable rock-'n-roll movements." To the other extreme, *The Barber of Seville* with Gobbi and Simionato resulted in a performance in which everything seemed to catch hold. Of Gobbi, Cassidy wrote, "his Figaro is a masterpiece. More than a performance of finger tip brilliance . . . it is a creation so immediate, so personal, and so totally delightful that from his entrance it magnetizes attention. In a kind of quicksilver gaiety streaked with glints of amused malice, he uses that magnetism as a magician uses illusion." Simionato, the critic said, "is a bewitching Rosina, part comedienne, part siren, and all singer."

Gobbi scored another success in Puccini's *Gianni Schicchi*, expertly conducted by Tullio Serafin. Gobbi's Schicchi was droll and sly, a "disarming rascal," as Cassidy put it, who possessed "the lyric baritone to sound precisely the way he means to sound." Anna Moffo, in the small part of Lauretta, was also quite good. *Pagliacci,* which rounded out the double bill, was a success, despite more than its share of pre-curtain problems. To begin with, the Nedda fell ill, and Eva Likova was rushed in to replace her. Then Ettore Bastianini announced that he would not be able to do Tonio. Gobbi said he would take the Bastianini part, but he would not be able to do the prologue—not right after singing *Gianni Schicchi.* So Cornell MacNeil, the Silvio, agreed to do the prologue, giving Gobbi a chance to rest. Still it was one of the best offerings of the season. Di Stefano made an outstanding Canio, although *Musical America* claimed that everyone in the cast "fell into place like the spokes of a wheel around the figure of Mr. Gobbi." In *Rigoletto,* a bit later, Gobbi's voice seemed a little tired, and this, plus a somewhat miscast Anna Moffo, limited the success of that production. Bjoerling's Duke, on the other hand, was undeniably great.

The season of twenty-nine performances closed having played to 90 per cent of capacity. Operating expenses totaled $876,106, while $631,740 was taken in at the box office. Contributions, including a $16,000 subsidy from the Italian government, totaled over $290,000.

The following year opened with a new production of *Carmen,* sets and costumes by Piero Zuffi. Given without the traditional cuts, the production starred Jean Madeira, Giuseppe di Stefano, and Ernest Blanc, in his American debut. The performance, as a whole, was slow-moving, although Madeira gave a good account of herself. Cassidy said, "She is svelte, darkly beautiful, with a mezzo soprano streaked in burnt umber and edged with a threat." At least according to one report, the evening was "wilder than ever" from the social viewpoint. Mrs. Orndorff arrived wearing an embroidered matador cape and a lace mantilla over a gold comb. One man wore a beret, another a black leather cape lined with red velvet. As the crowd poured in, an elderly lady was heard to say to her companion, "Margaret, slow down. No one's stopped us yet to ask our names."

The big novelty that year was Janáček's *Jenufa,* a Czech opera given in English for the first time in America. The production was on loan from the Royal Opera House, Covent Garden, London, and was the first such cargo to arrive in Chicago by way of the St. Lawrence Seaway. Dutch soprano Gré Brouwenstijn made her American debut in the title role. Cassidy found it "one of the dullest operas I have had the misfortune to encounter." The English translation, she thought, was frightful. Others found the work interesting, but little more. Rossini's *La Cenerentola,* staged with sets borrowed from Rome, was something of a disappointment, largely because of the cancellation of Teresa Berganza, who was pregnant. Anna Maria Rota replaced her, but "set off no fireworks." The staging was practically static; *Musical America* called it "a concert with scenery and costumes," but said that musically it "was a joy to hear." Verdi's *Simon Boccanegra*, in its local premiere, was mounted especially for Gobbi, and he made the most of it, assisted by Richard Tucker and Margherita Roberti. Sets again came from Rome.

Turandot was repeated, now even better than the year before. The major new ingredient was Leontyne Price as Liu, one of the loveliest performances of the season. Conductor Gianandrea Gavazzeni, Cassidy said, "had the orchestra playing better than it can play." The television quiz scandals had recently broken, and one of the prize contestants, Charles Van Doren, just a few days before had lost his position at Columbia University as a result of improprieties connected with "The $64,000 Question." All this prompted the *Tribune* to comment, "There were inevitable, not to say quizzical, rumors in the opera house Wednesday night that *Turandot* was rigged, and that Giuseppe di Stefano, who won the Chinese jackpot by guessing the three riddles, had been given the answers in advance."

Two other splendid performances that year were Wagner's *The Flying Dutchman*, with Birgit Nilsson as Senta, and Mozart's *Così Fan Tutte*, which introduced Elisabeth Schwarzkopf in her Chicago opera debut and Christa Ludwig in her first performance in America. The *Così* was remarkably intimate and yet at the same time managed to fill the big opera house. "Schwarzkopf," Cassidy wrote, "looked enchanting and sounded more so. She was in exquisite voice, with the wit to parody the fearful leaps of '*Come Scoglio*.'" Ludwig displayed a "most beautiful mezzo-soprano," which she handled with intelligence and skill. The sets for *The Flying Dutchman* were borrowed from Rome, the ones for *Così* from San Francisco. Both productions were well conducted by Lovro von Matačić, who had been introduced to American audiences in the opening *Carmen*.

Un Ballo in Maschera was repeated, now with Nilsson, di Stefano, and Gobbi heading the cast—all three outstanding. Cassidy felt that with a little more polish Nilsson would become "not just a thrilling singer when her voice goes soaring, but a Verdi soprano to conjure with." Di Stefano gave by far his best performance of the season, and Gobbi almost literally brought down the house. A high degree of rapport was maintained between the audience and the performers throughout the entire production. More uneven was a revival of *La Gioconda*, which brought back Eileen Farrell after a year's absence. Much thinner now and more attractively gowned, the soprano sang well, but seemed prone to overact. While the staging may have left something to be desired, Cassidy felt the old Chicago Opera sets were "handsomer than most of the rented junk imported earlier in the season."

One of the year's bigger fiascos was a mounting of Massenet's *Thaïs*, featuring an unfortunately cast Leontyne Price. Roger Dettmer felt it made no more sense to put Price in *Thaïs* than to star Tebaldi as Salome. "As a courtesan," Cassidy said, "she is decorative and as a penitent she is demure. She has a lovely lyric voice of gleaming range, with the dusk in its shadows that sometimes finds the subtler meanings of French song. But she knows only the surface of the role, and she has been miserably coached. It is often hard to know what she is impersonating, unless it might be the Statue of Liberty." The physical production, just a few months shy of fifty years old, was the same one the Chicago Opera used when Mary Garden sang the part. The one bright spot was Georges Pretre's conducting, although Pretre (in his American debut) had a pretty tough night of it himself. As the *Tribune* reported it, "He had to shush a late and noisy audience, he winced at slammed doors and shrugged at untimely applause. But he finally got used to it. When what sounded like a couple of bass drums and several cymbals clattered to the floor of the orchestra pit at an untactful moment, he took it like a veteran."

The fall of 1960 found Chicago, like the rest of the nation, trying to weigh the relative merits of John Kennedy and Richard Nixon for the presidency. Their "great debates" were by far the biggest television attraction of the season. A look at the theatrical notices that fall would reveal *Fiorello!* playing at the Shubert and Gertrude Berg in *A Majority of One* at the Erlanger. The big movie of the year was William Wyler's *Ben Hur*.

The Lyric's season opened on October 14 with a revival of *Don Carlos*, starring Roberti, Tucker, Simionato, Gobbi, and Christoff. Antonio Votto, in his American debut, conducted. The first-nighters indicated that the ladies were going more and more to evening coats and that the puffed hair-do was fashionable. Mrs. John Orndorff, who had just returned home from a visit to California, managed to stop by on her way from the train station to pick up a green velvet gown with a high standing collar, more or less the garb of Elisabeth de Valois. Another woman wore a black orchid on a gown of blazing red satin. "It's real!" she assured admirers.

Aida returned that year, producing mixed reactions. Roberti substituted for Leontyne Price in the first two performances—"a hapless lamb," Cassidy said, "thrown to the Verdi wolves." Simionato, who had seemed strangely out of place as Amneris two years before, was now superb. Stunningly costumed and wearing an attractive black wig, she sang divinely, her voice "as fresh as a field of daisies." Carlo Bergonzi made a good Radames, but Robert Merrill's Amonasro was "less a proud savage captured than a store keeper gone astray." Cassidy said, "What they all needed and did not get was stage direction, or at least some helpful idea as to what it was all about." The scene in Amneris' chamber, the critic felt, "might have been designed for Mae West." With Price, the later performances went much better. "Miss Price," Cassidy wrote, "turned out to be the most sumptuous Aida we have had in seasons.... She is a beautiful woman with a dark, creamy voice that pours brilliantly from that mutinous red mouth. She has temperament and a sense of mounting excitement in music, her mezzo voice is duskily lovely, and she can spin a pianissimo to melt in the ear."

A well-sung, almost Viennese production of Mozart's *The Marriage of Figaro* was acclaimed one of the most finely integrated performances Lyric has ever given. Magnificently costumed, Schwarzkopf had never seemed more beautiful as the Countess, and she possessed a voice to match. Rita Streich was an excellent Susanna, displaying a pure voice and an adept sense of comedy, while Ludwig "sang like so much mezzo velvet." Walter Berry was a gay, debonair Figaro, and Eberhard Waechter made an auspicious American debut as the Count. "Without using make-up," Cassidy said, "he can look like any role he plays, and in some curious way he can also sound like it. Here was an overprivileged grandee up to his ears in intrigue."

A repeat of *Die Walküre* resulted in the company's best Wagner to date, aside from the Rodzinski *Tristan* of 1958. Nilsson's performance was now that of a mature artist, her voice full of luster, capable of soaring to the heights with purity and ease. Jon Vickers was hailed as the best Siegmund the city had heard since Melchior, and he not only sounded the part, he looked it. Brouwenstijn made a good Sieglinde, and Ludwig's Fricka was nothing short of marvelous, "with the air of a Greek goddess but no airs, and with that lovely warm mezzo soprano taking on the edge of authority a woman must have when she tells a god what he has to do." Cassidy insisted, "It was, I think, the most lyrical *Walküre* I can remember.... But while the scale was huge, the effect was intimate. I felt that I was in a small theater, not in the wide open spaces of the Civic Opera house."

Just as fine was a production of *Tosca* with Tebaldi, di Stefano, and Gobbi. "It was quite an evening," the *Tribune* said. Every seat in the house was sold long in advance. One disappointed patron stood outside the doors, desperately trying to buy a ticket. "Tebaldi is sick," he said, "Gobbi and di Stefano aren't feeling any too well, and the orchestra hasn't even shown up yet." Even with that he failed to drum up a sale. Di Stefano made as much of Cavaradossi as anyone could, and Gobbi's Scarpia "looked so much younger he must have been visiting a spa." Tebaldi was perfectly luscious. "With two such cavaliers," Cassidy wrote,

"Miss Tebaldi was set like the jewel she is. She is a lovely lustrous Tosca with charm to burn and the fire to burn it, and the glowing, dulcet voice to give the love songs their due. There is a quiet dignity about her that holds melodrama in check, yet a sense of theater that knows its value." As an interesting new piece of stage business, Tosca carried a large yellow chiffon scarf in the second act, which Scarpia seized after the stabbing and used to hide his wound. As she fled, Tosca tried to free it from the body but could not, thus being forced to leave behind the evidence to prove her guilt.

Simon Boccanegra was repeated for Gobbi, with Tebaldi now singing Amelia Grimaldi, a role which suited her well and showed her mezzo voice to good advantage. Leontyne Price sang one of her first performances of *Madama Butterfly* anywhere, and did it exceptionally well, though without some of the polish of her later Cio-Cio-Sans. *Carmen* was held over from the year before, Madeira now disturbingly given to overacting. At its worst her portrayal "could have been 'Auntie Mame in Spain,'" Cassidy sniped. But the biggest miscalculation in casting was probably assigning Renata Scotto *La Bohème* for her American debut. Not having the Mimi voice, she made an exceedingly bad initial impression and was little better as Micaela in *Carmen.* Although the men in *Bohème* were good enough, the production as a whole practically fell to pieces. Conductor Gianandrea Gavazzeni, Cassidy wrote, "finally got so desperate for song that he started to sing himself. It sounded fine, comparatively."

The only new work in the repertoire that year was Giordano's *Fedora,* staged because Tebaldi wanted to do it. Lacking the fiery temperament the part requires, the soprano appeared decidedly out of place. Even her singing was disappointing. As Roger Dettmer said in his review, "this banality" must have been revived to give Tebaldi a chance to wear fancy clothes, since "she did not act it credibly and had nary an aria of consequence to sing." Di Stefano contented himself with "*Amor Ti Vieta,*" the most interesting music of the evening, while Gobbi, as De Siriex, wore a monocle and knickers, rode an antique bicycle on loan from the Museum of Science and Industry, and gave every indication of enjoying himself immensely. The opera was far from a success, and Cassidy said, "There were times when it seemed that none of the three [principals] had read the libretto, and I can't really say I blame them, even at those salaries."

The Lyric's 1961 season opened with what on paper looked like a positive sensation—*Lucia di Lammermoor*, with the remarkable Australian coloratura Joan Sutherland in the title role and the brilliant Italian director Franco Zeffirelli doing the staging. The sets and costumes, borrowed from Teatro Massimo, Palermo, were low-budget modifications of Zeffirelli's lauded Covent Garden production, the one that had launched Sutherland to international acclaim. Yet somehow the Chicago *Lucia* never quite got off the ground, at least not until the "Mad Scene." Zeffirelli did not arrive until late, therefore really serving as stage director in name only. Sutherland, perhaps because of an earlier illness, was not the success here she was in Dallas, New York, and San Francisco that same season. Cassidy said, "Her singing was cold, remote and dull until she reached the mad scene, and while once there she had the trill, the range and the fioritura, she created not a ripple of excitement." Roger Dettmer felt the first performance was really "a public rehearsal at benefit prices," and that it laid on the stage "like a dead grenade until Joan Sutherland . . . pulled out the pin in Act III." Her "Mad Scene," he felt was "a notable performance." But for Cassidy, she was "far from anything approaching a great Lucia."

Wigs were now highly popular among the more fashionably dressed Chicagoans, with blondes attending the opening as brunettes and redheads coming as blondes. One woman insisted she could recognize her friends only by looking for their husbands. Satin and brocade wraps were the very height of fashion, diminishing, if not eclipsing, the usual emphasis on fur. Mrs. John Logeman III, president of the American Opera Society, attended the performance, but without her husband. "My husband hates opera," she confessed. "I left him home sitting with his mother-in-law." Most of the men present seemed to enjoy themselves considerably, although their thoughts were not always of opera. "Ohio ran away from Illinois today," one man was heard to say as he pulled off his white gloves. "Yes," his friend agreed. "I thought Northwestern would . . ." and with that they disappeared through a door and down the aisle.

Aside from a disappointing opening, Lyric was plagued that season with illness. Tito Gobbi was forced to miss his first Chicago season since Lyric's inception. Conductor Andre Cluytens, scheduled for *Fidelio*, had to withdraw because of physical exhaustion. When Carlo Bergonzi had to cancel a performance of *La Forza del Destino* because of a respiratory ailment, David Poleri, who had not sung the role in six years, was brought in on twenty-four hours' notice to sing the lead. Lisa Della Casa also flew in on short notice to sing Donna Elvira for Elisabeth Schwarzkopf.

Yet, despite such problems, the season turned out rather well, and several of the productions, even with substitutions in casting, were first-rate. Boito's *Mefistofele* was given with Boris Christoff, one of the most interesting offerings in several years. Christoff for a second time was favorably compared with Chaliapin, and the "Brocken Scene" particularly was an exciting thing to see. As Cassidy described it, "The sky is like flaming forest, the white arms of dancers writhe like snakes from the rocks, and the fury of the witches is right out of Goya." The scenery, designed by Enzo Deho, was all projected, most of it highly effective. Bergonzi, although he looked like an elf as an old man, sang Faust with exceptional beauty, and Ilva Ligabue, in her American debut, won a justly deserved ovation after Marguerite's "L'Altra Notte." Christa Ludwig sang Helen's music magnificently and looked the part, but even she could not save the Greek scene from being static and dull.

Andrea Chénier possessed little of *Mefistofele*'s fire. Jon Vickers sang the title role well, and Mario Zanasi, Gobbi's replacement turned out a creditable performance, but the soprano, Shakeh Vartenissian, was unbelievably bad. As Cassidy reported it, she "is a matronly Madeleine in a mob cap, badly costumed, fearfully made-up, and she sings in what Ashton Stevens once immortally called a bunch of keys." The sets were those used by Campanini in 1916, although they were still surprisingly effective. Eileen Farrell did her first Leonora in *La Forza del Destino* anywhere with the company that year, doing some of her very best singing. In the "Inn Scene," however, she was poorly costumed, dressed in plumes, knee pants, and—of all things—a cutaway coat. Christoff was a strong Padre Guardiano, and Ludwig's Preziosilla was as enchanting as she was beautiful. The rest of the production, however, was variable.

Fidelio, despite an orchestra not up to Beethoven's demands, received a rather good production, with Nilsson and Vickers both turning out remarkable performances. The conductor was Peter Maag. It was a production long on youth, prompting Cassidy to say that for once when "Leonora rescued her Florestan from the clutches of Pizarro they had more to look forward to than a ripe old age together." *Così Fan Tutte* was repeated, again with Schwarzkopf, Ludwig, Simoneau, and Berry, but this time it fell a little flat, lacking much of the cohesiveness which had distinguished the 1959 production. *Don Giovanni* was better. Eberhard Waechter was the Don, Teresa Stich-Randall Donna Anna, Walter Berry Leporello, Irmgard Seefried Zerlina, and Leopold Simoneau Don Ottavio. Della Casa sang the first Donna Elvira in place of Schwarzkopf and was excellent. But Schwarzkopf's interpretation of the role was positively incredible. She swept onto the stage wearing a black wig, gold earrings, and a green mantilla, her eyes dark and tragic. Cassidy said, she was simultaneously "a beautiful virago, a proud, frightened woman, and if not quite mad, at least 'La Pazza.' " *The Barber of Seville* was revived, Simionato again the Rosina—"more brilliant than ever." Sesto Bruscantini made his American debut as Figaro, replacing Gobbi, while Luigi Alva was a capital Almaviva. Some reviewers felt it was the finest *Barber* the company had given yet.

In 1959 the Ford Foundation announced an appropriation of $950,000 to four American opera companies—the Metropolitan, the New York City Center, the San Francisco Opera, and the Lyric Opera of Chicago—for the purpose of stimulating the composition and production of American opera. What the Ford Foundation agreed to do was to cover the deficit on certain new American operas staged by these four companies, operas which the companies themselves would select. Lyric produced its first work under the terms of this grant in 1961. The opera was Vittorio Giannini's *The Harvest*, the composer conducting. The story told of four farmers, a blind father and his three sons. The oldest boy is married to Lora, who in turn loves the middle son and is lusted after by the youngest. The father, realizing Lora's infidelity, waits in the dark for her lover, whom he thinks is the hired man. Not until he has killed his second son does he realize his mistake. Then the father strangles Lora, whom he himself secretly loves. The opera's success was mild at best. "Just about everything happened in the Civic Opera house Saturday night except the great American opera," Cassidy wrote. "In general his [Giannini's] first act is bad Puccini, his second frightful Copland, and his third ghastly Montemezzi." Coming out best in the performance was William Wilderman, who sang the part of the blind man, although Marilyn Horne and Geraint Evans both turned out noteworthy characterizations. Regarding the ballet, Cassidy quipped, "Alas, it was, in the oldest of terms, run of de Mille."

The following season began with a stunning new production of Borodin's *Prince Igor*, sung in Russian, with sets and costumes designed by Nicola Benois. Boris Christoff, who sang two roles, Prince Galitsky and Kontchak, made one of the most dramatic entrances in the city's operatic history with a live, screaming, clawing falcon on his wrist. Aside from that the opera never quite equaled the ballet. For the Polovtsian dances Ruth Page and her troupe outdid themselves, and soloists Sonia Arova and Rudolf Nureyev, in his American opera debut, were an absolute marvel. Nureyev, Cassidy described as "a feral, catlike dancer, who can leap like a fully bent bow, leap in the great style, and pour dynamite into the grand pirouette." It was one of the few times on record of a ballet's stealing an opera.

From the fashion standpoint, it was a great night for the hair stylists. Mrs. Frederick Wacker, Jr., came with her dark hair piled in two round balls atop her head. Sticking out of the top one were two little pointed brushes. Mrs. Edward Byron Smith wore her hair in what looked like two wings shooting back from her brow and curled at the back of the neck. Mrs. Thomas King's coiffure looked like whipped egg whites piled high. "It's all mine!" she assured onlookers. "Lured by advance rumors of Byzantine splendor and czarist opulence," the *Tribune* reported, "Chicago women and visitors outdid themselves in the color and splendor of their gowns." There were very few flowers, but great quantities of feathers—feather trims, ostrich feather boas, one beige feather collar. One woman proved that even in the worldly 1960's feminine attire could cause raised eyebrows. "Feather fans a la Sally Rand," the *Tribune* wrote with something less than approval, "would have been a better cover-up for the woman in the slinky bright red sheath cut away down to *here*. She flirtatiously handled a little black lace fan to cover the exposure, the while surrounded by quite a group of male courtiers." Traffic outside the Opera House had become steadily worse through the years, and parking was an urban nightmare. The younger Henry Spanjers and their guests solved the problem by arriving in the Spanjers' fifty-four-foot cabin cruiser and tying it up in the river in back of the house, after having had refreshments on board. The hustle and bustle of suburban living might prove hectic for some, but not for Madeleine Mackenzie and her fiancé, Christofer Jackson, who picnicked in Jackson's car on their drive down from Winnetka. For the post-opera ball, the Hilton ballroom and entrance were aglitter with jewels and a Byzantine decor. Soldiers in Cossack uniform lined the grand staircase, while a czar-like figure was represented at the top. Guests were served borscht and other Russian delicacies.

The season grew rather frantic when illness forced Renata Tebaldi, scheduled for *La Bohème* and *Tosca*, to cancel. Consuelo Rubio, who had been in *Prince Igor*, and Mietta Sighele, never heard in this country before, filled in for her as Mimi, and Regine Crespin came for Tosca, her American debut. It was one of the most electric *Tosca*'s within memory. Roger Dettmer found Crespin "a singing actress of the first rank. She has what Callas has—intelligence, a born stage presence, subtlety, class, and a big spinto voice of individual timber." Gobbi was again a superlative Scarpia, and Giuseppe Zampieri made an impressive Lyric debut as Cavaradossi. Dettmer was so thrilled with the performance that he ended his review leading the cheer: "Now—all together in chorus—'We want Crespin, we want Zampieri, we love Gobbi.' "

A finely sung, beautifully executed *L'Elisir d'Amore* was given with Alfredo Kraus, Mariella Adani, Mario Zanasi, Fernando Corena, and Joan Marie Moynagh. Kraus and Adani were making their American debut, and both were superb. Cassidy claimed, "There was not really a blot on the whole performance, bubbling with arias and ensembles, never drowned or forced by the orchestra." Nothing Lyric had ever staged had been so consistently lighthearted. *Samson and Delilah*, despite cancellations from both leads, Vickers and Simionato, emerged as the company's best French effort to date. Well staged and well conducted by Pierre Dervaux, the production featured Hans Kaart as Samson and Rita Gorr as Delilah. Gorr particularly was nothing short of sensational. Said Cassidy, "Her voice is an outpouring in the full range, a velvet glory, but it has the resonance of bronze." *The Marriage of Figaro* was less successful. In fact, aside from

Teresa Berganza's Cherubino, it was a pretty dull affair. Gobbi again illustrated that Mozart was not his cup of tea, and even Della Casa was not up to her usual as the Countess. Rita Streich was the Susanna, Renato Capecchi the Figaro.

A revival of *Rigoletto* teamed Bastianini, Tucker, and Gianna D'Angelo in a production that had a few good moments, but little more. Gluck's *Orfeo ed Euridice* fared much better. With sets purchased from London's Royal Opera House, the production was beautifully sung, well balanced, and featured baritone Gabriel Bacquier as Orfeo, Della Casa as Euridice, and Streich as Amore. Maria Tallchief headed the ballet.

The season closed having played to 96.7 per cent of capacity, a new high for opera in Chicago. In April, 1962, a drive was launched to raise $1,000,000. The Montgomery Ward Foundation had agreed to contribute 10 per cent of the amount raised, with a limit of $100,000. The total of $1,100,000 would wipe out the company's existing deficit and furnish a small nest egg for investment. The campaign was successfully completed shortly before the 1963 season began, putting Lyric on a "pay-as-you-go-basis." Still, $425,000, above and beyond ticket sales, would have to be raised annually to keep the company out of debt.

The season opened in 1963 with *Nabucco*, reflecting the current trend toward early Verdi. The Metropolitan had recently staged it; so had San Francisco. Chicago's production featured Gobbi in the title role and Boris Christoff as Zaccaria and used the Metropolitan's sets and costumes. Danica Mastilovic, who made her American debut as Abigaille, was a disappointment, showing a tendency to walk like a female Groucho Marx and an inclination to become shrill vocally. The performance was dedicated to the memory of Rosa Raisa, who had just died. The house was decorated with some 3,700 roses, donated by Medard C. Lange. Pearls were popular that season with the ladies, and much attention was still being paid to the hair. Mrs. James Kimberly caused quite a stir when she made her entrance wearing a floor-length turquoise satin coat, her hair partly falling over her shoulders, the rest wound atop her head and secured by a tiara. Mrs. Orndorff wore an elaborate, high coiffure adorned by a bobbing gilt flower, which she explained was "the hanging gardens of Babylon." One party missed the opening curtain, explaining, "The bridge went up—that's why we're late."

Un Ballo in Maschera was given an interesting revival with Tucker, Crespin, Zanasi, and Grace Bumbry. Cassidy described Bumbry as "a slim-waisted, fascinating creature with a glorious voice born for the opera house. It asks no quarter and dodges no issues, but simply pours out in a flood, a marvelous mezzo all color, life, depth, and excitement." A new production of *Faust* introduced Nicolai Ghiaurov to American audiences as Mephistopheles, and a first-rate one he was, despite the pedestrian quality of the rest of the production. The sets were no more inspired than most of the singing, and Guy Chauvet and Andréa Guiot made Faust and Marguerite frightful bores. *Fidelio*, on the other hand, with Vickers, Crespin, and Christoff, was excellent, well integrated and expertly sung.

Otello, revived with Vickers, Sena Jurinac, and Gobbi, was as strong as *Faust* was weak. Cassidy said, "In its ten seasons the Lyric has seldom come closer to the heart of a great opera than in . . . *Otello*." Gobbi's Iago was more masterly than ever, a subtle portrait matched with intelligent singing. Vickers and Jurinac were both excellent, although neither was quite ideal for his part. "What made this Lyric production so valuable in the history of the young company," Cassidy continued, "was the fused authority of orchestra, chorus, and strong performances in secondary roles."

This is exactly what *Tannhäuser*, staged by the company for the first time a few nights later, lacked. It had the strength of Bumbry's Venus, the role that had catapulted the mezzo to fame when she sang it at Bayreuth, and Crespin's Elisabeth. Looking regally elegant, Crespin sang with power and majesty, although some critics complained that her voice was too white. Dimiter Uzunov was an adequate Tannhäuser, but what crippled the production was a lack of coherence, coupled with routine singing from performers in subordinate roles. *The Barber of Seville* was given for the fifth time in ten years, mainly as a vehicle for Teresa Berganza, and Donizetti's *Don Pasquale* received a lively staging with Adani, Kraus, Bruscantini, and Corena. Sets and costumes for both *Pasquale* and *Tannhäuser* were on loan from the Metropolitan, as part of an exchange program recently worked out among the Metropolitan, Chicago, and San Francisco managements, whereby physical productions could be shared and costs cut.

In 1964 *Il Trovatore* was revived for the opening production. Franco Corelli made his debut with the company as Manrico, and Ilva Ligabue returned for Leonora. Grace Bumbry, who was rehearsing *Carmen* at the time, seemed to have her Verdi confused with Bizet, and her Azucena emerged as something like a decrepit sex-kitten. The whole production was unfortunately, almost laughably, staged, with sets borrowed from the Metropolitan. When *Carmen* was presented a few nights later, Bumbry seemed nearly as tentative in the title role as she had as Azucena, although most critics agreed that with a little more experience she might serve the part well. Corelli, as Done Jose, overdid things. Aside from the usual tenor excesses, he elected to appear with a moustache in Act III ("It must be the mountain air," one patron was heard to comment) and added a five o'clock shadow in Act IV. Nicoletta Panni, the scheduled Micaela, became ill and was replaced in the first performance by Mexican soprano Irma Gonzales. Robert Massard was the Escamillo.

Making up for the two initial miscalculations was a nearly perfect *La Favorita,* meticulously sung by Fiorenza Cossotto, in her American debut, Alfredo Kraus, and Sesto Bruscantini. Intelligently staged, the production turned what might easily have been a bore into a vocal and visual delight, integrated in practically every detail. Donizetti's neglected score seemed well worth reviving. Almost as good was Strauss's *Ariadne auf Naxos,* never given before by a resident Chicago company. Régine Crespin sang her first Ariadne anywhere, revealing unusual wit in the Prologue and her customary vocal lushness in the Opera. Irmgard Seefried, although not in her best voice, made a splendid Composer, while Reri Grist, the Zerbinetta, was a saucy, vivacious charmer who sang as well as she looked. The production, again with sets borrowed from the Metropolitan, was well staged and rehearsed, and the ensemble was superb.

La Cenerentola, despite excellent singing from Berganza and Bruscantini, again proved rather uninteresting, especially visually. *Don Carlo* was repeated in an uneven and badly cut production. Richard Tucker was Carlo; Tito Gobbi added new subtleties to his characterization of Rodrigo; and Leyla Gencer made the most regal, if not the most ear-appealing, Elisabetta in memory. The real honors, however, went to Nicolai Ghiaurov, whose Philip II was called "little short of magnificent" by Harold Rosenthal. Fiorenza Cossotto and Grace Bumbry shared the role of Eboli. Ghiaurov was heard later in *Don Giovanni,* along with Teresa Stich-Randall, Phyllis Curtin, Nicoletta Panni, Alfredo Kraus, and Erich Kunz. The sets, designed by Franco Zeffirelli, were borrowed from Dallas. Josef Krips's conducting was marvellous. "Not only did Krips coax the finest performance from a Lyric orchestra since the late Artur Rodzinski's *Tristan und Isolde* in 1958," Roger Dettmer wrote, "but he paced the most urgent and meticulously sung *Don Giovanni* in a decade."

La Bohème was brought back into the repertoire as a vehicle for the return of Renata Tebaldi, who had not sung in the city for nearly four years. The soprano had just gone through a period of serious vocal difficulty, and there was no little apprehension concerning the status of her voice. Her Mimi indicated that she had reworked her technique considerably, but that, while the voice lacked some of its former sheen, it was still exquisite and had taken on a more dramatic quality. The time of *Bohème* was set forward from the original 1830's to the time of Toulouse-Lautrec, and a number of interesting pieces of stage business were added to give the production a realistic mood. Musetta, for instance, was turned into a prostitute, while the girls at the Cafe Momus smoked cigarettes. The season closed with a repeat of *Tosca* with Crespin, Gobbi, and Tucker—this time seeming a bit over-acted.

In the fall of 1965 the season opened with a staging of Boito's *Mefistofele*, this time with Ghiaurov, Tebaldi, and Kraus in the major roles, and Elena Suliotis making her debut as Helen of Troy. Though the cast was praised, the critical consensus was that the production fell considerably below the 1961 performances with Christoff. *Simon Boccanegra*, on the other hand, was given a splendid revival, with Tito Gobbi doubling as stage director and star. It was Gobbi's American debut as director, and his interpretation emphasized the dramatic, theatrical aspects of the Verdi opera. Particularly successful were his efforts to make the actions of the chorus, minor characters, and supernumeraries purposeful. Another of the season's high points was the double bill of Ravel's *L'Heure Espagnole* and Orff's *Carmina Burana*. The cast of the former, headed by Berganza, Kraus, and Bruscantini, gave a lively, well-integrated performance, with Berganza again enchanting her audience. Orff's work had the benefit of two of Lyric's major assets, its chorus and Ruth Page's ballet. The Chicago premiere of Alban Berg's *Wozzeck*, sung in English with Geraint Evans and Brenda Lewis, marked the year's third triumph. Critics had indicated all season that the Lyric's orchestra was vastly improved, and *Wozzeck* illustrated the point rather decisively.

More routine were productions of *Samson and Delilah* with Bumbry and Vickers, *Rigoletto* with Cornell MacNeil, Renata Scotto, and Alfredo Kraus, and *La Bohème* with Corelli and Mirella Freni. The latter marked Freni's local debut, postponed because of the artist's illness two years before. Although Corelli sang well in the last two acts, it was Freni's performance that stood out, her voice pure and effortless. Leontyne Price returned at her best for *Aida*, in a production that also featured the fiery, opulently sung Amneris of Fiorenza Cossotto. Giorgio Casellato (in his American debut) was the Rhadames, Ettore Bastianini the Amonasro.

At the end of its first decade, Lyric had presented 273 performances of fifty-six different operas, including eight local premieres, one American premiere, and one world premiere. Sixty-two singers, conductors, and designers had made American debuts with the company. More important, Lyric had by then revived a tradition in Chicago, restoring the city to its place as one of the major centers of opera in the United States. In the interim following the collapse of the Cleva organization in 1946, Chicagoans almost forgot their operatic heritage, and the feeling crystallized that opera was old-fashioned and out of keeping with the modern age. Carol Fox has shown this to be untrue, as slowly the pride Chicago once took in its opera has returned. If someone had gotten in a cab in 1953 and wanted to be taken to the opera house, the driver would probably have asked for an address. Today no explanation is necessary. For the new generation, Chicago's operatic greatness includes the era of Callas, Tebaldi, Simionato, Ghiaurov, and Gobbi no less than that of Garden, Raisa, and Galli-Curci. Starting almost from scratch, Lyric has built an artistic reputation, along with a list of loyal guarantors, volunteer workers, and regular patrons—most of whom are dedicated to keeping the new tradition alive.

Times have changed, of course. Today's opera audiences are no more like those of the Insull era than Insull's were like those of Campanini's. In a twentieth-century democracy people do not dress for the opera as they once did, but on the other hand more people attend than ever before. The bulk of Chicago's modern operagoers are not wealthy; they come from the prosperous middle class, most of them professional people. The great wealth of the McCormick era is gone. With today's suburban living, it is difficult for the husband to get home from the office, have dinner, and the couple to get back downtown in time for an eight-o'clock curtain. More often the wife may meet her husband downtown for dinner before the opera, or, if both work, the couple may meet for cocktails without going home to change for the evening. None of this makes formal dress either feasible or practical. Monday night is still dress night at the opera house, but even then business suits and cocktail dresses are common. For the rest of the week, excluding casual wear, one could probably more easily overdress than underdress, as most of the audience wears essentially what they would to a play or a downtown movie. Chicago has always been a business town with an eye toward pragmatism, and the dress of the modern operagoer is no exception.

A few restaurants cater especially to the opera crowd. The Italian Village, a comfortable walk from the opera house, is a notable example. Arriving for dinner, guests climb a staircase lined with autographed pictures of leading Lyric artists. Once seated, one may order a Renata Tebaldi Cocktail, to be followed with beef scaloppini alla Toscanini. In the meantime, waiters, if given half a chance, will chatter with glee about the success of a new soprano or the rumor that this or that artist has promised to return next year. For the singers the Village is a particular favorite, especially for a late supper after a performance.

A certain esprit de corps has developed among the Lyric performers through the years, as many of them have returned season after season. Several of the choristers—none of whom is Italian, incidentally—have performed with the company every year. Of the stars, Tito Gobbi has sung in more productions than anyone else, having returned every year but the one when illness kept him in Italy. Appropriately enough, the baritone's birthday falls during the Chicago season, giving an excuse for festivities. Sometimes a party is given, or, as in 1963, a rehearsal may be interrupted while champagne is rolled on stage and the company drinks the singer's health. For Gobbi, at least, the Lyric is "just a big happy family."

Since her marriage in 1957, Carol Fox has become adept at blending opera with family. Now the mother of a young daughter, Victoria, the energetic lady impresario somehow finds time to run a household as well as an opera company. During the season this may mean nursing a sick child and holding the hand of an ailing tenor at the same time, and even between seasons there are meetings with musicians' unions and fund-raising affairs and endless preparation for the future. A shrewd businesswoman, Carol Fox fits comfortably into the tradition of combining art and commerce set by Crosby, Peck, and Insull, yet she has maintained some of Campanini's experimental dynamism.

When Harold Rosenthal, editor of London's *Opera* magazine, visited the Lyric in 1965, he found the company "run very much like an Italian provincial house." The Italian emphasis, he said, was indicated by the fact that rehearsal schedules gave all terms in Italian—with *Ariadne auf Naxos* even listed as *Arianna!* Rosenthal felt that for Chicago grand opera was synonymous with stars and that the company's two major weaknesses were in the casting of small roles and in the visual productions, points which local critics had been making for years.

Whether or not Chicago has a permanent opera company at last is, of course, impossible to tell, although the future looks bright. Barring some financial or international calamity, the city has reason to be optimistic. How much the company can expand is another question. Lacking the size and cosmopolitan diversity of New York, Chicago's opera public has always been somewhat tentative. While enthusiasts from surrounding cities frequent Lyric's productions with some regularity, visitors from farther distances are not nearly as prone to patronize Chicago's opera as they are the Metropolitan. Despite a rich cultural heritage, Chicago's renown as an art center is limited. For most Americans Chicago means night clubs, or possibly sports; if they are looking for music and theater, they go to New York. Therefore, it is doubtful that the Lyric will ever become the national institution the Metropolitan is. Without national support, Chicago's opera has been and will continue to be more tenuous than New York's. If Lyric can maintain a sound financial foundation and the spirit of adventure with which it was born, its future should prove secure. The loss of either could easily spell ruin, resulting in a drop in support on the one hand, boredom on the other. The Chicago ideal of blending art and business is a delicate balance. History has shown that the scales are sensitive, the equilibrium easily upset. With the era of the McCormicks over, and unless the European custom of government subsidy to the arts becomes accepted, the problem for Chicago's opera, as with American opera everywhere, is essentially one of keeping the weight evenly matched.

Leading Singers in the Operas

1910–11

November 3

Aida

Campanini (c)
King: Berardi
Amneris: de Cisneros
Aida: Korolewicz
Radames: Bassi
Ramfis: de Angelis
Amonasro: Sammarco

November 5 (mat.)

Pelléas et Mélisande

Campanini (c)
Pelléas: Warnery
Golaud: Dufranne
Arkel: Huberdeau
Mélisande: Garden
Geneviève: Bressler-Gianoli

November 5

Il Trovatore

Parelli (c)
Leonora: Korolewicz
Azucena: de Cisneros
Manrico: Zerola
Count di Luna: Costa
Ferrando: Nicolay

November 7

Cavalleria Rusticana

Parelli (c)
Santuzza: White
Lola: Di Angelo
Turiddu: McCormack
Alfio: Beck

I Pagliacci

Perosio (c)
Nedda: Osborn-Hannah
Canio: Bassi
Tonio: Sammarco

November 8

La Bohème

Perosio (c)
Rodolfo: McCormack
Mimi: Grenville
Marcello: Costa
Colline: de Angelis
Musetta: Zeppilli

November 9

Louise

Campanini (c)
Father: Dufranne
Mother: Bressler-Gianoli
Louise: Garden
Julien: Dalmorès
Noctambulist: Warnery
King of Fools: Venturini

November 10

Tosca

Parelli (c)
Tosca: Korolewicz
Cavaradossi: Bassi
Scarpia: Sammarco
Angelotti: Nicolay
Sacristan: Malatesta

November 12 (mat.)

Aida

Same as Nov. 3 except:
Aida: White

November 12

Il Trovatore

Same as Nov. 5 except:
Azucena: Bressler-Gianoli

November 14

Louise

Same as Nov. 9

November 15

Carmen

Campanini (c)
Don José: Dalmorès
Escamillo: Crabbe
Zuniga: Huberdeau
Carmen: Sylva
Micaela: Zeppilli

November 16

La Bohème

Same as Nov. 8 except:
Campanini (c)
Rodolfo: Bassi
Mimi: Melba
Marcello: Sammarco
Colline: Arimondi

November 17

Pelléas et Mélisande

Same as Nov. 5

November 19 (mat.)

La Traviata

Campanini (c)
Violetta: Melba
Alfredo: Bassi
Germont: Sammarco

November 19

Faust

Charlier (c)
Faust: Dalmorès
Méphistophélès: Arimondi
Valentine: Crabbe
Marguerite: Grenville

Siébel: Di Angelo
Martha: Bressler-Gianoli

November 21

Aida
Same as Nov. 3 except:
Aida: White
Radames: Zerola
Amonasro: Dufranne

November 22

Louise
Same as Nov. 9

November 23

Carmen
Same as Nov. 15 except:
Don José: Guardabassi

November 24 (mat.)

Il Trovatore
Same as Nov. 5

November 24

Cavalleria Rusticana
Same as Nov. 7

I Pagliacci
Same as Nov. 7

November 25

Salome
Campanini (c)
Salome: Garden
Herodias: de Cisneros
Herod: Dalmorès
Jokanaan: Dufranne
Narraboth: Warnery
Slave: Dumesnil

November 26 (mat.)

Tosca
Campanini (c)
Same as Nov. 10 except:
Tosca: Farrar
Scarpia: Scotti

November 26

Rigoletto
Perosio (c)
Duke: McCormack
Rigoletto: Sammarco
Gilda: Zeppilli
Sparafucile: Arimondi
Maddalena: Di Angelo

November 28

Salome
Same as Nov. 25

November 29

Madama Butterfly
Campanini (c)
Cio-Cio-San: Farrar
Suzuki: Giaconia
Pinkerton: Bassi
Sharpless: Scotti

November 30

Aida
Same as Nov. 3 except:
Aida: Gadski
Radames: Zerola

December 1

Faust
Same as Nov. 19 except:
Campanini (c)
Méphistophélès: Huberdeau
Valentine: Dufranne
Siébel: Scalfaro

December 3 (mat.)

Lucia di Lammermoor
Perosio (c)
Lucia: Lipkowska
Edgardo: Constantino
Enrico: Sammarco
Raimondo: de Angelis

December 3

Tosca
Same as Nov. 10 except:
Tosca: Grenville
Scarpia: Beck

December 5

Pelléas et Mélisande
Same as Nov. 5

December 6

Thaïs
Campanini (c)
Athanael: Renaud
Nicias: Dalmorès
Palemon: Huberdeau
Thaïs: Garden

December 7

Madama Butterfly
Same as Nov. 29 except:
Cio-Cio-San: Osborn-Hannah
Sharpless: Sammarco

December 8

Rigoletto
Same as Nov. 26 except:
Parelli (c)
Rigoletto: Renaud

December 10 (mat.)

Carmen
Same as Nov. 15 except:
Don José: Guardabassi
Escamillo: Dufranne

December 10

La Bohème
Same as Nov. 8

December 11 (mat.)

I Pagliacci
Same as Nov. 7 except:
Canio: Zerola
Tonio: Costa

Followed by ballet

December 11

Cavalleria Rusticana
Same as Nov. 7 except:
Santuzza: Sylva
Turiddu: Dalmorès

Followed by ballet

December 12

Madama Butterfly
Same as Nov. 29 except:
Cio-Cio-San: Osborn-Hannah
Sharpless: Sammarco

December 13

Faust
Same as Nov. 19 except:
Campanini (c)
Méphistophélès: Huberdeau
Valentine: Dufranne
Marguerite: Garden
Siébel: Scalfaro

December 14

Thaïs
Same as Dec. 6 except:
Nicias: Warnery
Palemon: Nicolay

December 15

The Tales of Hoffmann
Charlier (c)
Guilietta: Sylva
Antonia: Grenville
Olympia: Zeppilli
Niclaus: Di Angelo
Hoffmann: Dalmorès
Coppelius: Renaud
Dapertutto: Renaud
Miracle: Renaud

December 17 (mat.)

Louise
Same as Nov. 9

December 17

La Traviata
Parelli (c)
Violetta: Zeppilli
Alfredo: McCormack
Germont: Beck

December 19

Tosca
Same as Nov. 10 except:
Tosca: Melis
Cavaradossi: McCormack

December 20

The Tales of Hoffmann
Same as Dec. 15

December 21

Pelléas et Mélisande
Same as Nov. 5

December 22

Les Huguenots
Charlier (c)
Valentin: Gadski
Urbain: Riegelman
Marguerite de Valois: Zeppilli
Raoul de Nangis: Zerola
Marcel: Arimondi
Le Comte de Saint Bris: Huberdeau
Le Comte de Nevers: Sammarco

December 24 (mat.)

Rigoletto
Same as Nov. 26 except:
Parelli (c)
Gilda: Lipkowska

December 24

Aida
Same as Nov. 3 except:
Perosio (c)
King: Thormer
Radames: Zerola
Amonasro: Costa

December 26

Thaïs
Same as Dec. 6 except:
Athanael: Dufranne
Palemon: Nicolay

December 27

The Girl of the Golden West
Campanini (c)
Minnie: White
Johnson: Bassi
Rance: Renaud
Nick: Daddi
Ashby: de Angelis
Sonora: Dufranne
Wowkle: Bressler-Gianoli

December 28

The Tales of Hoffmann
Same as Dec. 15 except:
Coppelius: Beck
Dapertutto: Beck
Miracle: Beck

December 29

Thaïs
Same as Dec. 6 except:
Athanael: Dufranne
Palemon: Nicolay

December 31 (mat.)

Thaïs
Same as Dec. 6 except:
Athanael: Dufranne
Palemon: Nicolay

December 31

Cavalleria Rusticana
Same as Nov. 7 except:
Santuzza: Sylva
Turiddu: Venturini

I Pagliacci
Same as Nov. 7 except:
Tonio: Costa

January 5

The Girl of the Golden West
Same as Dec. 27 except:
Rance: Sammarco

January 6—Grand Gala

La Bohème Act III
Campanini (c)
Rodolfo: McCormack
Mimi: Grenville
Musetta: Zeppilli
Marcello: Costa

Romeo and Juliet Act IV
Campanini (c)
Romeo: Guardabassi
Juliet: Garden

Otello Act IV
Campanini (c)
Otello: Zerola
Desdemona: Osborn-Hannah
Emilia: Giaconia
Iago: Sammarco

The Tales of Hoffmann Act II
Campanini (c)
Giulietta: Sylva
Niclaus: Di Angelo
Hoffmann: Dalmorès
Dapertutto: Beck

January 7 (mat.)

The Girl of the Golden West
Same as Dec. 27 except:
Rance: Sammarco

January 7

Rigoletto
Same as Nov. 26 except:
Parelli (c)
Rigoletto: Costa
Gilda: Rabinoff

January 9

The Girl of the Golden West

Same as Dec. 27 except:
Rance: Sammarco

January 10

Thaïs
Same as Dec. 6 except:
Athanael: Dufranne

January 11

Otello
Perosio (c)
Desdemona: Korolewicz
Emilia: Giaconia
Otello: Zerola
Iago: Sammarco
Cassio: Venturini

January 16

The Tales of Hoffmann
Acts I and II
Charlier (c)
Giulietta: Sylva
Olympia: Zeppilli
Niclaus: Di Angelo
Hoffmann: Dalmorès
Coppelius: Beck
Dapertutto: Beck

I Pagliacci
Campanini (c)
Nedda: Sylva
Canio: Caruso
Tonio: Sammarco

January 17

Un Ballo in Maschera
Perosio (c)
Riccardo: Zerola
Renato: Costa
Amelia: Korolewicz
Ulrica: de Cisneros
Oscar: Zeppilli

January 18

The Girl of the Golden West
Same as Dec. 27 except:
Johnson: Caruso
Rance: Sammarco

1911–12

November 22

Samson and Delilah
Campanini (c)
Delilah: Gerville-Réache
Samson: Dalmorès
High Priest: Dufranne
Abimelech: Crabbe
Old Hebrew: Huberdeau

November 23

Carmen
Campanini (c)
Don José: Dalmorès
Escamillo: Dufranne
Zuniga: Scott
Carmen: Garden
Micaela: Zeppilli

November 24

Lucia di Lammermoor
Campanini (c)
Lucia: Tetrazzini
Alisa: Egener
Edgardo: Bassi
Enrico: Sammarco

November 25 (mat.)

The Marriage of Figaro
Campanini (c)
Countess: White
Susanna: Zeppilli
Cherubino: Teyte
Figaro: Huberdeau
Almaviva: Sammarco

November 25

Il Trovatore
Perosio (c)
Leonora: Frease-Green
Azucena: Wittkowska
Manrico: van Hoose
Count di Luna: Costa
Ferrando: Nicolay

November 27

Cendrillon
Campanini (c)
Cendrillon: Teyte
Mme. de la Haltiere: Berat
Prince: Garden
Pandolphe: Dufranne
King: Scott

November 28

La Traviata
Campanini (c)
Violetta: Tetrazzini
Alfredo: Bassi
Germont: Sammarco

November 29

Thaïs
Campanini (c)
Athanael: Dufranne
Nicias: Dalmorès
Palemon: Huberdeau
Thaïs: Garden

November 30 (mat.)

Hänsel und Gretel
Szendrei (c)
Hänsel: Cavan
Gretel: Riegelman
Witch: Wittkowska
Followed by ballet

November 30

Rigoletto
Campanini (c)
Duke: Bassi
Rigoletto: Sammarco
Gilda: Tetrazzini
Sparafucile: Huberdeau
Maddalena: Giaconia

December 1

Samson and Delilah
Same as Nov. 22

December 2 (mat.)

Cendrillon
Same as Nov. 27

December 2

Cavalleria Rusticana
Parelli (c)
Santuzza: White
Lola: Ingram
Turiddu: Venturini
Alfio: Crabbe

I Pagliacci
Perosio (c)
Nedda: Zeppilli
Canio: Guardabassi
Tonio: Costa

December 4

The Barber of Seville
Campanini (c)
Almaviva: Ramella
Bartolo: Malatesta
Rosina: Tetrazzini
Figaro: Sammarco
Basilio: Berardi

December 5

Carmen
Same as Nov. 23

December 6

Lakmé
Campanini (c)
Lakmé: Tetrazzini
Mallika: Giaconia
Gerald: Bassi
Nilakantha: Huberdeau
Frédéric: Crabbe

December 7

The Secret of Suzanne
Campanini (c)
Count Gil: Sammarco
Suzanne: White

Le Jongleur de Notre-Dame
Campanini (c)
Jean: Garden
Boniface: Dufranne
Prior: Huberdeau

December 9 (mat.)

Lucia di Lammermoor
Same as Nov. 24

December 9

Hänsel und Gretel
Same as Nov. 30

Followed by ballet

December 11

Thaïs
Same as Nov. 29 except:
Palemon: Nicolay

December 12

Samson and Delilah
Same as Nov. 22

December 13

Cendrillon
Same as Nov. 27

December 14

Lakmé
Same as Dec. 6 except:
Charlier (c)
Lakmé: Dufau

December 15

Natoma
Campanini (c)
Natoma: Garden
Barbara: White
Lt. Paul Merrill: Hamlin
Don Francisco: Scott
Father Peralta: Dufranne
Juan Bautista Alvarado: Sammarco
Chiquita: Galli

December 16 (mat.)

Faust
Charlier (c)
Faust: Dalmorès
Méphistophélès: Huberdeau
Valentine: Crabbe
Marguerite: Teyte
Siébel: Wittkowska
Martha: Berat

December 16

La Traviata
Parelli (c)
Violetta: Zeppilli
Germont: Costa
Alfredo: Bassi

December 18

The Secret of Suzanne
Same as Dec. 7

Le Jongleur de Notre-Dame
Same as Dec. 7

December 19

Quo Vadis?
Charlier (c)
Lygie: Teyte
Eunice: Zeppilli
Petrone: Whitehill
Nero: Scott
Vinicius: Dalmorès
Chilon: Dufranne
Pierre: Huberdeau

December 20

The Marriage of Figaro
Same as Nov. 25

December 21

Die Walküre
Szendrei (c)
Sieglinde: Osborn-Hannah
Fricka: Schumann-Heink
Brünnhilde: Saltzman-Stevens
Siegmund: Dalmorès
Hunding: Scott
Wotan: Whitehill

December 22

Natoma
Same as Dec. 15

December 23 (mat.)

Quo Vadis?
Same as Dec. 19 except:
Nero: Berardi

December 23

Lucia di Lammermoor
Same as Nov. 24 except:
Parelli (c)
Lucia: Dufau
Enrico: Costa

December 25 (mat.)

Hänsel und Gretel
Same as Nov. 30

Followed by ballet

December 25

The Tales of Hoffmann
Charlier (c)
Olympia: Dufau
Giulietta: White
Antonia: Teyte
Niclaus: Wittkowska
Hoffmann: Dalmorès
Coppelius: Dufranne
Dapertutto: Crabbe
Miracle: Huberdeau

December 26

The Secret of Suzanne
Same as Dec. 7

Le Jongleur de Notre-Dame
Same as Dec. 7

December 27

Quo Vadis?
Same as Dec. 19 except:
Nero: Berardi
Vinicius: Guardabassi

December 28

Natoma
Same as Dec. 15

December 30 (mat.)

Die Walküre
Same as Dec. 21 except:
Fricka: Gerville-Réache
Siegmund: Hensel

December 30

Rigoletto
Same as Nov. 30 except:
Perosio (c)
Rigoletto: Costa
Gilda: Zeppilli
Sparafucile: Berardi

December 31

Cendrillon
Same as Nov. 27

January 1 (mat.)

Hänsel und Gretel
Same as Nov. 30

January 1

Natoma
Same as Dec. 15

January 2

Lohengrin
Szendrei (c)
Henry: Huberdeau
Lohengrin: Dalmorès
Elsa: White
Telramund: Whitehill
Ortrud: Wittkowska

January 3

Carmen
Same as Nov. 23 except:
Charlier (c)
Don José: Bassi
Escamillo: Crabbe

January 4

Quo Vadis?
Same as Dec. 19 except:
Lygie: Dufau
Nero: Berardi
Vinicius: Guardabassi

January 6 (mat.)

The Secret of Suzanne
Same as Dec. 7

Le Jongleur de Notre-Dame
Same as Dec. 7

January 6

Hänsel und Gretel
Same as Nov. 30

Cavalleria Rusticana
Same as Dec. 2 except:
Santuzza: Frease-Green

January 8

Die Walküre
Same as Dec. 21 except:
Fricka: Gerville-Réache

January 9

The Tales of Hoffmann
Same as Dec. 25 except:
Antonia: Zeppilli

January 10 (mat.)

Cendrillon
Same as Nov. 27 except:
Cendrillon: Zeppilli

January 10

Lohengrin
Same as Jan. 2 except:
Elsa: Osborn-Hannah
Ortrud: Schumann-Heink

January 11

Thaïs
Same as Nov. 29 except:
Nicias: Warnery
Palemon: Nicolay

January 13 (mat.)

Lohengrin
Same as Jan. 2 except:
Elsa: Osborn-Hannah

January 13

Carmen
Same as Nov. 23 except:
Charlier (c)
Don José: Guardabassi
Escamillo: Crabbe
Carmen: Gerville-Réache

January 15

Lohengrin
Same as Jan. 2 except:
Elsa: Osborn-Hannah

January 16

The Jewels of the Madonna
Campanini (c)
Gennaro: Bassi
Carmela: Berat
Maliella: White
Rafaele: Sammarco

January 17

Natoma
Same as Dec. 15

January 18

The Jewels of the Madonna
Same as Jan. 16

January 19—Grand Gala

The Tales of Hoffmann
Act I
Charlier (c)
Olympia: Dufau
Niclaus: Wittkowska
Hoffmann: Warnery
Coppelius: Dufranne

The Secret of Suzanne
Campanini (c)
Count Gil: Sammarco
Suzanne: White

Thaïs Act II
Campanini (c)
Athanael: Dufranne
Nicias: Warnery
Thaïs: Garden

Samson and Delilah
Act II
Charlier (c)
Delilah: Gerville-Réache
Samson: Dalmorès

Ballet
Parelli (musical director)

January 20 (mat.)
Thaïs
Same as Nov. 29 except:
Palemon: Nicolay

January 20
The Tales of Hoffmann
Same as Dec. 25 except:
Olympia: Dufau
Giulietta: Dufau
Antonia: Dufau
Hoffmann: Warnery
Miracle: Crabbe
Dapertutto: Crabbe
Coppelius: Crabbe

January 22
The Jewels of the Madonna
Same as Jan. 16

January 23
Die Walküre
Same as Dec. 21 except:
Fricka: Wittkowska
Brünnhilde: Fremstad
Siegmund: Hensel

January 24 (mat)
Carmen
Same as Nov. 23 except:
Charlier (c)

January 24
The Jewels of the Madonna
Same as Jan. 16

January 25
Cendrillon
Same as Nov. 27 except:
Cendrillon: Zeppilli

January 26
Tristan und Isolde
Campanini (c)
Tristan: Dalmorès
King Marke: Scott
Isolde: Fremstad
Kurvenal: Whitehill
Melot: Crabbe
Brangäne: Gerville-Réache
Der Steuermann: Schorr

January 27 (mat.)
The Jewels of the Madonna
Same as Jan. 16

January 27
The Secret of Suzanne
(c) not listed
Count Gil: Costa
Suzanne: Zeppilli

I Pagliacci
Same as Dec. 2 except:
Nedda: Osborn-Hannah

February 1 (special mat.)
The Jewels of the Madonna
Same as Jan. 16

February 1
Tristan und Isolde
Same as Jan. 26 except:
Isolde: Saltzman-Stevens
Brangäne: de Cisneros

1912–13

November 26
Manon Lescaut
Campanini (c)
Manon: White
Lescaut: Sammarco
Des Grieux: Zenatello
Geronte: Trevisan

November 27
Carmen
Charlier (c)
Don José: Dalmorès
Escamillo: Dufranne
Zuniga: Scott
Carmen: Gay
Micaela: Dufau

November 28 (mat.)
Cavalleria Rusticana
Perosio (c)
Santuzza: White
Lola: Legard
Turiddu: Gaudenzi
Alfio: Crabbe

I Pagliacci
Perosio (c)
Nedda: Zeppilli
Canio: Calleja
Tonio: Rossi

November 28
Aida
Campanini (c)
King: Huberdeau
Amneris: Gay
Aida: Gagliardi
Radames: Zenatello
Ramfis: Scott
Amonasro: Sammarco

November 29
Rigoletto
Campanini (c)
Duke: Harrold
Rigoletto: Ruffo
Gilda: Zeppilli
Sparafucile: Huberdeau
Maddalena: Keyes
Giovanna: Berat

November 30 (mat.)
Cendrillon
Charlier (c)
Cendrillon: Teyte
Mme. de la Haltiere: Berat
Prince: Stanley
Pandolphe: Dufranne
King: Huberdeau

November 30
La Traviata
Perosio (c)
Violetta: Zeppilli
Alfredo: Gaudenzi
Germont: Rossi

December 2

Il Trovatore
Campanini (c)
Leonora: Gagliardi
Azucena: Gay
Manrico: Zenatello
Count di Luna: Sammarco
Ferrando: Nicolay

December 3

Hamlet
Campanini (c)
Hamlet: Ruffo
Claudius: Huberdeau
Ghost: Scott
Polonius: Preisch
Gertrude: de Cisneros
Ophelia: Zeppilli

December 4

The Jewels of the Madonna
Campanini (c)
Gennaro: Zenatello
Carmela: Berat
Maliella: White
Rafaele: Sammarco

December 5

Cavalleria Rusticana
Same as Nov. 28 except:
Santuzza: de Cisneros
Lola: Heyl
Turiddu: Venturini

I Pagliacci
Same as Nov. 28 except:
Tonio: Ruffo

December 7 (mat.)

The Cricket on the Hearth
Winternitz (c)
John: Dufranne
Dot: Teyte
May: Darch
Edward Plummer: Hamlin
Tackleton: Scott
Cricket: Riegelman

December 7

Faust
Charlier (c)
Faust: Warnery
Méphistophélès: Huberdeau
Valentine: Mascal
Marguerite: Zeppilli
Siébel: Egener
Martha: Berat

December 9

Rigoletto
Same as Nov. 29 except:
Gilda: Dufau
Sparafucile: Scott

December 10

Aida
Same as Nov. 28 except:
Amneris: de Cisneros
Radames: Calleja

December 11

Cavalleria Rusticana
Campanini (c)
Santuzza: Gay
Lola: Heyl
Turiddu: Venturini
Alfio: Costa

I Pagliacci
Same as Nov. 28 except:
Canio: Zenatello
Tonio: Ruffo

December 12

The Tales of Hoffmann
Charlier (c)
Olympia: Dufau
Giulietta: Cavan
Antonia: Darch
Niclaus: Heyl
Hoffmann: Dalmorès
Coppelius: Dufranne
Dapertutto: Crabbe
Miracle: Huberdeau

December 14 (mat.)

Manon Lescaut
Same as Nov. 26

December 14

The Secret of Suzanne
Perosio (c)
Count Gil: Costa
Suzanne: Dufau

Hänsel und Gretel
Winternitz (c)
Hänsel: Cavan
Gretel: Riegelman
Witch: Legard
Mother: Berat
Father: Crabbe

December 16

Hérodiade
Charlier (c)
Jean: Dalmorès
Herode: Mascal
Phanuel: Huberdeau
Salome: White
Hérodiade: de Cisneros

December 17

The Jewels of the Madonna
Same as Dec. 4

December 18

Cendrillon
Same as Nov. 30 except:
Cendrillon: Zeppilli
King: Scott

December 19

Tristan und Isolde
Campanini (c)
Tristan: Dalmorès
King Marke: Scott
Isolde: Nordica
Kurvenal: Whitehill
Brangäne: Schumann-Heink

December 20

Manon Lescaut
Same as Nov. 26

December 21 (mat.)

Hérodiade
Same as Dec. 16

December 21

Cavalleria Rusticana
Same as Nov. 28 except:
Santuzza: Zeppilli
Lola: Heyl
Turiddu: Venturini
Alfio: Costa

I Pagliacci
Same as Nov. 28 except:
Nedda: Stanley
Tonio: Crabbe

December 23

Mignon
Charlier (c)

Mignon: Teyte
Wilhelm Meister: Dalmorès
Philine: Dufau
Lothario: Huberdeau
Frederick: Heyl

December 24

The Secret of Suzanne
Perosio (c)
Count Gil: Sammarco
Suzanne: White

Le Jongleur de Notre-Dame
Campanini (c)
Jean: Garden
Boniface: Dufranne
Prior: Huberdeau

December 25

The Cricket on the Hearth
Same as Dec. 7

December 26 (mat.)

Cendrillon
Same as Nov. 30 except:
Cendrillon: Zeppilli
King: Scott

December 26

Louise
Campanini (c)
Father: Dufranne
Mother: Berat
Louise: Garden
Julien: Dalmorès
King of Fools: Venturini

December 28 (mat.)

Aida
Same as Nov. 28 except:
King: Nicolay
Amneris: de Cisneros
Aida: White
Radames: Calleja

December 28

The Tales of Hoffmann
Same as Dec. 12 except:
Hoffmann: Warnery

December 30

The Jewels of the Madonna
Same as Dec. 4 except:
Gennaro: Calleja

December 31

Hérodiade
Same as Dec. 16

January 1 (mat.)

Hänsel und Gretel
Same as Dec. 14 except:
Witch: Schumann-Heink

January 1

Lohengrin
Winternitz (c)
Henry: Scott
Lohengrin: Schoenert
Elsa: Osborn-Hannah
Telramund: Dufranne
Ortrud: Claussen

January 2

The Cricket on the Hearth
Same as Dec. 7

January 3

Die Walküre
Winternitz (c)
Sieglinde: Saltzman-Stevens
Fricka: Schumann-Heink
Brünnhilde: Claussen
Siegmund: Dalmorès
Hunding: Scott
Wotan: Whitehill

January 4 (mat.)

Carmen
Same as Nov. 27 except:
Don José: Campagnola
Carmen: Garden
Micaela: Stanley

January 4

Aida
Perosio (c)
King: Nicolay
Amneris: de Cisneros
Aida: Clay
Radames: van Hoose
Amonasro: Costa
Ramfis: Scott

January 6

Louise
Same as Dec. 26

January 7

Lohengrin
Same as Jan. 1 except:
Telramund: Whitehill

January 8

The Secret of Suzanne
Parelli (c)
Count Gil: Sammarco
Suzanne: Zeppilli

Noel
Campanini (c)
Jacques Herblet: Warnery
Madame Herblet: Berat
Madeleine: Saltzman-Stevens
Priest: Dufranne

January 9

Cendrillon
Same as Nov. 30 except:
King: Scott

January 11 (mat.)

Mignon
Same as Dec. 23 except:
Lothario: Dufranne

January 11

The Jewels of the Madonna
Same as Dec. 4 except:
Gennaro: Hamlin
Maliella: Stanley

January 13

Carmen
Same as Nov. 27 except:
Carmen: Garden
Micaela: Zeppilli

January 14

Noel
Same as Jan. 8

The Cricket on the Hearth
Same as Dec. 7

January 15

La Bohème
Parelli (c)
Rodolfo: Giorgini
Mimi: Teyte
Marcello: Sammarco
Colline: Huberdeau
Musetta: Riegelman

January 16

Die Walküre
Same as Jan. 3 except:
Sieglinde: Osborn-Hannah
Fricka: Claussen
Brünnhilde: Saltzman-Stevens
Siegmund: Schoenert

January 17

Tosca
Campanini (c)
Tosca: Garden
Cavaradossi: Dalmorès
Scarpia: Sammarco
Angelotti: Nicolay
Sacristan: Trevisan

January 18 (mat.)

La Traviata
Campanini (c)
Violetta: Tetrazzini
Alfredo: Giorgini
Germont: Sammarco

January 18

Mignon
Same as Dec. 23 except:
Wilhelm Meister: Warnery

January 19 (mat.)

Cavalleria Rusticana
Perosio (c)
Santuzza: Zeppilli
Lola: Heyl
Turiddu: Venturini
Alfio: Mascal

Followed by ballet

January 19

I Pagliacci
Perosio (c)
Nedda: Stanley
Canio: Warnery
Tonio: Mascal

Followed by ballet

January 20

La Bohème
Same as Jan. 15 except:
Rodolfo: Campagnola
Marcello: Polese

January 21

Rigoletto
Same as Nov. 29 except:
Duke: Giorgini
Rigoletto: Sammarco
Gilda: Tetrazzini
Sparafucile: Scott

January 22

Tosca
Same as Jan. 17

January 23 (mat.)

Lucia di Lammermoor
Campanini (c)
Lucia: Tetrazzini
Edgardo: Giorgini
Enrico: Polese
Raimondo: Scott

January 23

Mignon
Same as Dec. 23 except:
Mignon: Riegelman
Wilhelm Meister: Campagnola
Lothario: Dufranne

January 24—Grand Gala

Aida Act IV, Scene 2
Campanini (c)
Amneris: Claussen
Ramfis: Scott

A Lovers' Quarrel
Parelli (c)
Rosaura: Zeppilli
Florindo: Giorgini
Don Fulgenzio: Sammarco
Donna Angelica: Berat

Thaïs Act I, Scene 1
Campanini (c)
Athanael: Dufranne
Nicias: Warnery
Thaïs: Garden

The Barber of Seville
Lesson Scene
Campanini (c)
Rosina: Tetrazzini
Almaviva: Giorgini
Bartolo: Trevisan

January 25 (mat.)

Thaïs
Campanini (c)
Athanael: Dufranne
Nicias: Warnery
Palemon: Huberdeau
Thaïs: Garden

January 25

The Jewels of the Madonna
Same as Dec. 4 except:
Perosio (c)
Gennaro: Hamlin
Maliella: Stanley

January 27

Lucia di Lammermoor
Same as Jan. 23 except:
Enrico: Sammarco

January 28

Thaïs
Same as Jan. 25

January 29

Mignon
Same as Dec. 23 except:
Mignon: Riegelman
Wilhelm Meister: Campagnola
Philine: Tetrazzini
Lothario: Dufranne

January 30 (mat.)

Tosca
Same as Jan. 17 except:
Cavaradossi: Campagnola

January 30

Conchita
Campanini (c)
Conchita: Tarquini
Mateo: Dalmorès
Dolores: Darch
Ruffina: Heyl
Madre di Conchita: Berat
La Gallega: Galli

February 1 (mat.)

Le Jongleur de Notre-Dame
Same as Dec. 24

A Lovers' Quarrel
Same as Jan. 24 except:
Campanini (c)

February 1
Die Walküre
Same as Jan. 3 except:
Sieglinde: Osborn-Hannah
Fricka: Claussen
Brünnhilde: Saltzman-Stevens
Siegmund: Schoenert

1913–14

November 24
Tosca
Campanini (c)
Tosca: Garden
Cavaradossi: Bassi
Scarpia: Vanni Marcoux
Angelotti: Nicolay
Sacristan: Trevisan

November 25
La Gioconda
Sturani (c)
La Gioconda: White
Laura: Claussen
Alvise: Scott
La Cieca: Heyl
Enzo: Giorgini
Barnaba: Ruffo

November 26
Don Quichotte
Campanini (c)
La Belle Dulcinée: Garden
Don Quichotte: Vanni Marcoux
Sancho: Dufranne

November 27 (mat.)
Madama Butterfly
Sturani (c)
Cio-Cio-San: Zeppilli
Suzuki: Keyes
Pinkerton: Bassi
Sharpless: Federici

November 27
Die Walküre
Winternitz (c)
Sieglinde: Osborn-Hannah
Fricka: Keyes
Brünnhilde: Claussen
Siegmund: Dalmorès
Hunding: Scott
Wotan: Whitehill

November 29 (mat.)
Aida
Campanini (c)
King: Huberdeau
Amneris: Van Gordon
Aida: Raisa
Radames: Bassi
Ramfis: Scott
Amonasro: Polese

November 29
Natoma
Herbert (c)
Natoma: Zeppilli
Barbara: Osborn-Hannah
Lt. Paul Merrill: Hamlin
Don Francisco: Scott
Father Peralta: Dufranne
Juan Bautista Alvarado: Crabbe
Chiquita: Galli

December 1
Rigoletto
Perosio (c)
Duke: Giorgini
Rigoletto: Ruffo
Gilda: Zeppilli
Sparafucile: Huberdeau
Maddalena: Keyes

December 2
Samson and Delilah
Charlier (c)
Delilah: Claussen
Samson: Dalmorès
High Priest: Dufranne
Abimelech: Crabbe
Old Hebrew: Huberdeau

December 3
The Girl of the Golden West
Campanini (c)
Minnie: White
Dick Johnson: Bassi
Rance: Polese
Ashby: Scott
Sonora: Dufranne
Wowkle: Wheeler

December 4
Cristoforo Colombo
Campanini (c)
Cristoforo Colombo: Ruffo
Don Fernan Guevra: Bassi
Isabella d'Aragona: Raisa
Don Roldana Ximenes: Huberdeau

December 6 (mat.)
The Jewels of the Madonna
Perosio (c)
Gennaro: Bassi
Carmela: Berat
Maliella: White
Rafaele: Polese

December 6
Carmen
Charlier (c)
Don José: Hamlin
Escamillo: Turner
Zuniga: Scott
Carmen: Wheeler
Micaela: Riegelman

December 8
La Bohème
Sturani (c)
Rodolfo: Giorgini
Mimi: Raisa
Marcello: Polese
Colline: Huberdeau

December 9
Le Ranz des Vaches
Winternitz (c)
Louis XVI: Nicolay
Marquis Massimelle: Huberdeau
Blanchefleur: Dorda
Cleo: Wheeler
Primus Thaller: Dalmorès
Favart: Dufranne

December 10

Cristoforo Colombo
Same as Dec. 4

December 11 (mat.)

Madama Butterfly
Same as Nov. 27 except:
Cio-Cio-San: Osborn-Hannah
Pinkerton: Hamlin

December 11

Hérodiade
Charlier (c)
Jean: Dalmorès
Herode: Crabbe
Phanuel: Huberdeau
Salome: White
Hérodiade: Claussen

December 13 (mat.)

Rigoletto
Same as Dec. 1 except:
Gilda: Dufau
Sparafucile: Scott

December 13

Faust
Charlier (c)
Faust: Bergman
Méphistophélès: Scott
Valentine: Turner
Marguerite: Zeppilli
Siébel: Egener
Martha: Keyes

December 15

The Barber of Seville
Sturani (c)
Almaviva: Giorgini
Bartolo: Trevisan
Rosina: Dufau
Figaro: Ruffo
Basilio: Scott

December 16

Faust
Same as Dec. 13 except:
Faust: Muratore
Méphistophélès: Huberdeau
Valentine: Crabbe
Siébel: Heyl
Martha: Berat

December 17

Samson and Delilah
Same as Dec. 2

December 18

Don Giovanni
Campanini (c)
Don Giovanni: Ruffo
Don Ottavio: Giorgini
Donna Anna: Dorda
Zerlina: Zeppilli
Donna Elvira: White
Leporello: Huberdeau
Masetto: Trevisan
Il Commendatore: Scott

December 19

Zingari
Leoncavallo (c)
Fleana: White
Radu: Bassi
Tamar: Federici
Old Man: Scott

I Pagliacci
Campanini (c)
Nedda: Osborn-Hannah
Canio: Bassi
Tonio: Ruffo

December 20 (mat.)

Fedora
Campanini (c)
Fedora: (Cavalieri)
Conte Loris: Muratore
De Siriex: Polese

December 20

The Cricket on the Hearth
Winternitz (c)
John: Dufranne
Dot: Teyte
May: Evans
Edward Plummer: Hamilton
Tackleton: Scott
Cricket: Riegelman
Followed by ballet

December 22

Le Jongleur de Notre-Dame
Campanini (c)
Jean: Garden
Boniface: Dufranne
Prior: Huberdeau

December 23

Zingari
Same as Dec. 19

I Pagliacci
Same as Dec. 19

December 24

Samson and Delilah
Same as Dec. 2

December 25 (mat.)

Hänsel und Gretel
Parelli (c)
Hänsel: Teyte
Gretel: Riegelman
Witch: Wheeler
Mother: Berat
Father: Crabbe

December 25

Il Trovatore
Sturani (c)
Leonora: Dorda
Azucena: Schumann-Heink
Manrico: Bassi
Count di Luna: Polese
Ferrando: Nicolay

December 26

Thaïs
Campanini (c)
Athanael: Ruffo
Nicias: Dalmorès
Palemon: Huberdeau
Thaïs: Garden

December 27 (mat.)

Le Ranz des Vaches
Same as Dec. 9

December 27

Madama Butterfly
Same as Nov. 27 except:
Cio-Cio-San: Teyte
Pinkerton: Hamlin
Sharpless: Whitehill

December 29

Don Quichotte
Same as Nov. 26

December 30 (mat.)

Thaïs
Same as Dec. 26 except:
Nicias: Warnery

December 30

Die Walküre
Same as Nov. 27 except:
Sieglinde: Saltzmann-Stevens
Fricka: Schumann-Heink

December 31

Aida
Same as Nov. 29

January 1

Tosca
Same as Nov. 24

January 3 (mat.)

Carmen
Charlier (c)
Don José: Muratore
Escamillo: Dufranne
Zuniga: Huberdeau
Carmen: Claussen
Micaela: Zeppilli

January 3

The Tales of Hoffmann
Charlier (c)
Olympia: Dufau
Giulietta: Evans
Antonia: Riegelman
Niclaus: Heyl
Hoffmann: Warnery
Coppelius: Whitehill
Dapertutto: Whitehill
Miracle: Whitehill

January 5

La Traviata
Sturani (c)
Violetta: Hempel
Alfredo: Giorgini
Germont: Polese

January 6

Fedora
Same as Dec. 20 except:
Fedora: White

January 7

Lucia di Lammermoor
Parelli (c)
Lucia: Hempel
Edgardo: Giorgini
Enrico: Federici
Raimondo: Scott

January 8

The Jewels of the Madonna
Same as Dec. 6 except:
Campanini (c)

January 10 (mat.)

Thaïs
Same as Dec. 26 except:
Athanael: Dufranne

January 10

Hänsel und Gretel
Same as Dec. 25

January 11

Parsifal
Campanini (c)
Amfortas: Whitehill
Titurel: Scott
Gurnemanz: Hinckley
Parsifal: Dalmorès
Klingsor: Dufranne
Kundry: Stevens
(Raisa appeared as a Flowermaiden.)

January 12

Carmen
Same as Dec. 6 except:
Don José: Muratore
Escamillo: Dufranne
Zuniga: Huberdeau
Carmen: Claussen
Micaela: Zeppilli

January 13

Le Jongleur de Notre-Dame
Same as Dec. 22

January 14

The Barber of Seville
Same as Dec. 15 except:
Rosina: Macbeth
Figaro: Federici

January 15

La Bohème
Same as Dec. 8 except:
Rodolfo: Bassi
Mimi: Alda

January 16

Manon
Charlier (c)
Manon: Garden
Des Grieux: Muratore
Lescaut: Dufranne
Comte: Huberdeau

January 17 (mat.)

Don Quichotte
Same as Nov. 26

January 17

Madama Butterfly
Same as Nov. 27 except:
Cio-Cio-San: Teyte
Pinkerton: Hamlin
Sharpless: Whitehill

January 18

Parsifal
Same as Jan. 11 except:
Parsifal: Marak
Kundry: Claussen

January 20

Manon
Same as Jan. 16

January 21

The Jewels of the Madonna
Same as Dec. 6 except:
Campanini (c)

January 22

Louise
Campanini (c)
Father: Dufranne
Mother: Berat
Louise: Garden
Julien: Dalmorès
King of Fools: Venturini

January 23

La Bohème
Same as Dec. 8 except:
Campanini (c)
Rodolfo: Bassi

Mimi: Melba
Musetta: Zeppilli

January 24 (mat.)

Fedora
Same as Dec. 20 except:
Fedora: White

January 24

Die Walküre
Same as Nov. 27 except:
Sieglinde: Saltzman-Stevens

January 26

The Jewels of the Madonna
Same as Dec. 6 except:
Campanini (c)

January 27

Don Quichotte
Same as Nov. 26

January 28

Monna Vanna
Campanini (c)
Monna Vanna: Garden
Prinzivalle: Muratore
Guido: Vanni Marcoux
Marco: Huberdeau

January 29 (mat.)

A Lovers' Quarrel
Parelli (c)
Rosaura: Zeppilli
Florindo: Bassi
Don Fulgenzio: Polese
Donna Angelica: Berat

January 29

The Tales of Hoffmann
Charlier (c)
Olympia: Macbeth
Giulietta: White
Antonia: Dufau
Niclaus: Heyl
Hoffmann: Dalmorès
Coppelius: Dufranne
Dapertutto: Crabbe
Miracle: Huberdeau

January 30—Grand Gala

Samson and Delilah Act II
Charlier (c)
Delilah: Claussen
Samson: Dalmorès
High Priest: Dufranne

Lucia di Lammermoor
Mad Scene
Parelli (c)
Lucia: Macbeth

Monna Vanna Act II
Campanini (c)
Monna Vanna: Garden
Trivulzio: Nicolay
Prinzivalle: Muratore

Tannhäuser Overture
Campanini (c)

January 31 (mat.)

Monna Vanna
Same as Jan. 28

January 31

Martha
Winternitz (c)
Lady Harriet: Dufau
Nancy: Keyes
Lionel: Errolle
Plunkett: Scott

1914–15

No season

1915–16

November 15

La Gioconda
Campanini (c)
La Gioconda: Destinn
Laura: de Cisneros
Alvise: Arimondi
La Cieca: Ingram
Enzo: Bassi
Barnaba: Ancona

November 16

Louise
Charlier (c)
Father: Dufranne
Mother: Maubourg
Louise: Edvina
Julien: Dalmorès
King of Fools: Dua

November 17

Tristan und Isolde
Pollak (c)
Tristan: Maclennan
King Marke: Goddard
Isolde: Fremstad
Kurvenal: Whitehill
Brangäne: Claussen

November 18

Werther
Ferrari (c)
Werther: Muratore
Albert: Dufranne
Bailiff: Nicolay
Charlotte: Supervia
Sophia: Sharlow

November 19

La Bohème
Ferrari (c)
Rodolfo: Bassi
Mimi: Melba
Marcello: Ancona
Colline: Journet
Musetta: Pavloska

November 20 (mat.)

Monna Vanna
Campanini (c)
Monna Vanna: Beriza
Prinzivalle: Muratore
Guido: Maguenat
Marco: Journet

November 20

Lucia di Lammermoor
Parelli (c)
Lucia: Macbeth
Edgardo: Moreas
Enrico: Federici
Raimondo: Armondi

November 22

Louise
Same as Nov. 16

November 23

Werther
Same as Nov. 18

November 24

La Traviata
Ferrari (c)
Violetta: Melba
Alfredo: Bassi
Germont: Ancona

November 25

Tannhäuser
Pollak (c)
Hermann: Goddard
Tannhäuser: Maclennan
Wolfram: Whitehill
Elisabeth: van Dresser
Venus: Rose

November 27 (mat.)

La Gioconda
Same as Nov. 15

November 27

La Bohème
Same as Nov. 19 except:
Rodolfo: Vogliotti
Mimi: Sharlow
Marcello: Federici
Musetta: de Phillippe

November 28

Das Rheingold
Pollak (c)
Wotan: Whitehill
Loge: Maclennan
Alberich: Beck
Mime: Dua
Fricka: Claussen
Freia: van Dresser
Erda: Schumann-Heink

November 29

Tannhäuser
Same as Nov. 25

November 30

Tosca
Campanini (c)
Tosca: Farrar
Cavaradossi: Bassi
Scarpia: Ancona
Angelotti: Nicolay
Sacristan: Trevisan

December 1

Monna Vanna
Same as Nov. 20

December 2

Louise
Same as Nov. 16

December 3

Carmen
Campanini (c)
Don José: Muratore
Escamillo: Dufranne
Zuniga: Journet
Carmen: Farrar
Micaela: Alda

December 4 (mat.)

L'Amore dei Tre Re
Ferrari (c)
Archibaldo: Whitehill
Manfredo: Marr
Avito: Fontana
Fiora: Edvina

December 4

Il Trovatore
Parelli (c)
Leonora: Frease-Green
Azucena: de Cisneros
Manrico: Corallo
Count di Luna: Ancona
Ferrando: Nicolay

December 5

Die Walküre
Pollak (c)
Siegmund: Dalmorès
Hunding: Goddard
Wotan: Whitehill
Sieglinde: van Dresser
Brünnhilde: Claussen
Fricka: de Cisneros

December 6

Monna Vanna
Same as Nov. 20

December 7

L'Amore dei Tre Re
Same as Dec. 4

December 8

Tosca
Same as Nov. 30 except:
Scarpia: Scotti

December 9

Déjanire
Campanini (c)
Hercule: Muratore
Philoctète: Maguenat
Iole: Darch
Déjanire: Melis
Phemie: de Cisneros

December 10

Madama Butterfly
Campanini (c)
Cio-Cio-San: Farrar
Suzuki: Ingram
Pinkerton: Bassi
Sharpless: Federici

December 11 (mat.)

Mignon
Charlier (c)
Mignon: Supervia
Wilhelm Meister: Dalmorès
Philine: Verlet
Lothario: Journet
Frederick: Pavloska

December 11

La Gioconda
Same as Nov. 15 except:
Parelli (c)
La Gioconda: Lynbrook
Enzo: Vogliotti

December 12

Siegfried
Pollak (c)
Siegfried: Maclennan
Mime: Reiss
Der Wanderer: Whitehill
Alberich: Beck

Fafner: Arimondi
Erda: Schumann-Heink
Brünnhilde: Easton
Stimme des Waldvogels: Gresham

December 13

Carmen
Same as Dec. 3 except:
Micaela: Sharlow

December 14

Tannhäuser
Same as Nov. 25

December 15

Déjanire
Same as Dec. 9

December 16

Madama Butterfly
Same as Dec. 10

December 18 (mat.)

Carmen
Same as Dec. 3 except:
Micaela: Stanley

December 18

Mignon
Same as Dec. 11

December 19

Götterdämmerung
Pollak (c)
Siegfried: Maclennan
Gunther: Whitehill
Hagen: Hinckley
Alberich: Beck
Brünnhilde: Fremstad
Gutrune: van Dresser
Waltraute: Schumann-Heink
1st Norne: Schumann-Heink
2nd Norne: Van Gordon
3rd Norne: Hall

December 20

The Jewels of the Madonna
Campanini (c)
Gennaro: Bassi
Carmela: Van Gordon
Maliella: Edvina
Rafaele: Ancona

December 21

Monna Vanna
Same as Nov. 20

December 22

L'Amore dei Tre Re
Same as Dec. 4

December 23

Carmen
Same as Dec. 3 except:
Micaela: Stanley

December 25 (mat.)

Madama Butterfly
Same as Dec. 10

December 25

A Lovers' Quarrel
Parelli (c)
Rosaura: Sharlow
Florindo: Hamlin
Don Fulgenzio: Marr
Donna Angelica: Van Gordon

I Pagliacci
Ferrari (c)
Nedda: Melis
Canio: Fontana
Tonio: Ancona

December 26

Parsifal
Pollak (c)
Amfortas: Whitehill
Titurel: Cochems
Gurnemanz: Hinckley
Parsifal: Stiles
Klingsor: Beck
Kundry: Fremstad

December 27

Madama Butterfly
Same as Dec. 10 except:
Parelli (c)
Cio-Cio-San: Melis

December 28

Carmen
Same as Dec. 3
Charlier (c)
Micaela: Stanley

December 29

I Pagliacci
Same as Dec. 25

La Navarraise
Charlier (c)
Anita: Claussen
Araquil: Dalmorès
Garrido: Arimondi

December 30

Tosca
Same as Nov. 30 except:
Parelli (c)
Tosca: Melis
Scarpia: Federici

December 31

La Bohème
Same as Nov. 19 except:
Rodolfo: McCormack
Mimi: Farrar

January 1 (mat.)

The Jewels of the Madonna
Same as Dec. 20

January 1

Rigoletto
Spadoni (c)
Duke: Moreas
Rigoletto: Federici
Gilda: Macbeth
Sparafucile: Arimondi
Maddalena: Pavloska

January 2 (mat.)

Faust
Charlier (c)
Faust: Muratore
Méphistophélès: Journet
Valentine: Maguenat
Marguerite: Farrar
Siébel: Moses
Martha: Shaffer

January 2

Aida
Ferrari (c)
King: Nicolay
Amneris: de Cisneros
Aida: Melis
Radames: Zerola
Ramfis: Goddard
Amonasro: Ancona

January 3

I Pagliacci
Same as Dec. 25

La Navarraise
Same as Dec. 29

January 4

The Jewels of the Madonna
Same as Dec. 20 except:
Carmela: Ingram

January 5

Romeo and Juliet
Charlier (c)
Juliet: Kuznietsov
Romeo: Muratore
Mercutio: Maguenat
Capulet: Dufranne
Friar Lawrence: Journet
Duke of Verona: Arimondi

January 6

Mignon
Same as Dec. 11 except:
Philine: Macbeth

January 8 (mat.)

Faust
Same as Jan. 2 except:
Marguerite: Kuznietsov

January 8

Madama Butterfly
Parelli (c)
Cio-Cio-San: de Phillippe
Suzuki: Moses
Pinkerton: Hamlin
Sharpless: Marr

January 9

Parsifal
Same as Dec. 26 except:
Kundry: Claussen

January 10

Cléopâtre
Campanini (c)
Marc Antoine: Maguenat
Spakos: Dalmorès
Ennius: Journet
Cléopâtre: Kuznietsov

January 11

Aida
Same as Jan. 2 except:
Radames: Bassi

January 12

Carmen
Campanini (c)
Same as Dec. 3 except:
Don José: Dalmorès
Carmen: Supervia
Micaela: Stanley

January 13

Romeo and Juliet
Same as Jan. 5

January 15 (mat.)

Thaïs
Campanini (c)
Athanael: Dufranne
Nicias: Dalmorès
Palemon: Nicolay
Thaïs: Kuznietsov

January 15

A Lovers' Knot
Charlier (c)
Sylvia: Sharlow
Beatrice: Lenska
Walter: Hamlin
Edward: Marr

Tosca
Same as Nov. 30 except:
Parelli (c)
Tosca: Melis
Cavaradossi: Hamlin
Scarpia: Federici

January 16

Die Walküre
Same as Dec. 5

January 17

Zaza
Ferrari (c)
Zaza: Melis
Anaide: Shaffer
Floriana: Peterson
Milio Dufresne: Bassi
Cascart: Maguenat

January 18

Cléopâtre
Same as Jan. 10

January 19

Don Giovanni
Campanini (c)
Don Giovanni: Ancona
Don Ottavio: McCormack
Donna Anna: Rose
Zerlina: Sharlow
Donna Elvira: Stanley
Leporello: Journet
Masetto: Trevisan
Il Commendatore: Goddard

January 20

Thaïs
Same as Jan. 15

January 21—Grand Gala

Aida Act II (Finale)
Ferrari (c)
Aida: Melis
Amneris: de Cisneros
Radames: Bassi
Amonasro: Ancona
Ramfis: Goddard
King: Nicolay

Romeo and Juliet
Balcony Scene
Charlier (c)
Juliet: Kuznietsov
Romeo: Muratore

Spanish Dances
Parelli (c)

Cavalleria Rusticana
Campanini (c)
Santuzza: Melis
Lola: Pawloska
Alfio: Federici
Turiddu: Bassi

Ballet
Spadoni (c)

January 22 (mat.)

Cléopâtre
Same as Jan. 10

January 22

The Jewels of the Madonna
Same as Dec. 20 except:
Gennaro: Hamlin
Maliella: Stanley

1916–17

November 13

Aida
Campanini (c)
King: Arimondi
Amneris: Claussen
Aida: Raisa
Radames: Crimi
Ramfis: Goddard
Amonasro: Rimini

November 14

Hérodiade
Charlier (c)
Jean: Dalmorès
Herode: Beck
Phanuel: Journet
High Priest: Nicolay
Salome: Amsden
Hérodiade: Claessens

November 15

Andrea Chénier
Campanini (c)
Andrea Chénier: Crimi
Gérard: Rimini
Madeleine: Raisa
Madelon: Van Gordon

November 16

Le Prophète
Charlier (c)
John: Dalmorès
Zacharias: Journet
Fidès: Claussen
Bertha: Buckler

November 17

Carmen
Campanini (c)
Don José: Muratore
Escamillo: Dufranne
Zuniga: Journet
Carmen: Farrar
Micaela: Sharlow

November 18 (mat.)

Rigoletto
Sturani (c)
Duke: Nadal
Rigoletto: Rimini
Gilda: Galli-Curci
Sparafucile: Arimondi
Maddalena: Pavloska

November 18

Hänsel und Gretel
Spadoni (c)
Peter: Kreidler
Hänsel: Pavloska
Gretel: de Philippe
Witch: Olitzka

Madeleine
Herbert (c)
Madeleine: Sharlow
Nichette: Eden
Duc d'Esterre: Hamlin
Didier: Kreidler
Chevalier de Monprat: Nicolay

November 19

Das Rheingold
Pollak (c)
Wotan: Whitehill
Loge: Maclennan
Alberich: Beck
Mime: Dua
Fricka: Claussen
Freia: van Dresser
Erda: Van Gordon

November 20

Faust
Charlier (c)
Faust: Muratore
Méphistophélès: Journet
Valentine: Maguenat
Wagner: Defrere
Marguerite: Farrar
Siébel: Moses
Martha: Berat

November 21

Lucia di Lammermoor
Sturani (c)
Lucia: Galli-Curci
Alisa: Eden
Edgardo: Nadal
Enrico: Polese
Raimondo: Arimondi
Arturo: Dua
Normanno: Minerva

November 22

Le Prophète
Same as Nov. 16

November 23

Cavalleria Rusticana
Campanini (c)
Santuzza: Raisa
Lola: Pawloska
Turiddu: Crimi
Alfio: Polese

November 24

Die Königskinder
Pollak (c)
King's Son: Maclennan
Goose Girl: Farrar
Fiddler: Whitehill
Witch: Van Gordon

November 25 (mat.)

Aida
Same as Nov. 13 except:
Amneris: Van Gordon

November 25

Il Trovatore
Campanini (c)
Leonora: Amsden
Azucena: Claessens
Manrico: Kingston
Count di Luna: Polese
Ferrando: Nicolay

November 26

Die Walküre
Pollak (c)
Siegmund: Maclennan
Hunding: Goddard
Wotan: Whitehill
Sieglinde: van Dresser
Brünnhilde: Matzenauer
Fricka: Van Gordon

November 27

Andrea Chénier
Same as Nov. 15

November 28

Carmen
Same as Nov. 17

November 29

Rigoletto
Same as Nov. 18

November 30 (mat.)

Hänsel und Gretel
Pollak (c)
Hänsel: Pavloska
Gretel: de Phillippe
Witch: Olitzka
Mother: Shaffer
Father: Beck

November 30

Die Königskinder
Same as Nov. 24

December 1

La Traviata
Sturani (c)
Violetta: Galli-Curci
Alfredo: Crimi
Germont: Rimini

December 2 (mat.)

Manon
Charlier (c)
Manon: Amsden
Des Grieux: Muratore
Lescaut: Maguenat
Comte: Journet

December 2

Faust
Same as Nov. 20 except:
Faust: Dalmorès
Valentine: Dufranne
Marguerite: Buckler

December 3

Siegfried
Pollak (c)
Siegfried: Maclennan
Mime: Dua
Der Wanderer: Whitehill
Alberich: Beck
Fafner: Arimondi
Erda: Van Gordon
Brünnhilde: Easton
Stimme des Waldvogels: Macbeth

December 4

Lucia di Lammermoor
Same as Nov. 21 except:
Arturo: Venturini

December 5

Andrea Chénier
Same as Nov. 15

December 6

Die Königskinder
Same as Nov. 24

December 7

Manon
Same as Dec. 2

December 8

Madama Butterfly
Sturani (c)
Cio-Cio-San: Farrar
Suzuki: Pavloska
Pinkerton: Nadal
Sharpless: Polese

December 9 (mat.)

Cavalleria Rusticana
Same as Nov. 23

December 9

The Tales of Hoffmann
Charlier (c)
Olympia: Macbeth
Giulietta: Buckler
Antonia: de Phillippe
Niclaus: Pavloska
Hoffmann: Dalmorès
Coppelius: Beck
Dapertutto: Beck
Miracle: Beck

December 10

Götterdämmerung
Pollak (c)
Siegfried: Maclennan
Gunther: Whitehill
Hagen: Hinckley
Alberich: Beck
Brünnhilde: Matzenauer
Gutrune: Easton
Waltraute: Van Gordon

December 11

Manon
Same as Dec. 2

December 12

Die Königskinder
Same as Nov. 24

December 13

Rigoletto
Same as Nov. 18

December 14

Aida
Same as Nov. 13 except:
Amneris: Van Gordon

December 15

Romeo and Juliet
Charlier (c)
Juliet: Galli-Curci
Romeo: Muratore
Mercutio: Maguenat
Capulet: Dufranne
Friar Lawrence: Journet
Duke of Verona: Arimondi

December 16 (mat.)

Tosca
Sturani (c)
Tosca: Farrar
Cavaradossi: Crimi
Scarpia: Rimini
Angelotti: Nicolay
Sacristan: Trevisan

December 16

Madama Butterfly
Same as Dec. 8 except:
Cio-Cio-San: Easton
Sharpless: Kreidler

December 17

Parsifal
Pollak (c)
Amfortas: Whitehill
Titurel: Sargeant
Gurnemanz: Goddard
Parsifal: Maclennan
Klingsor: Beck
Kundry: Fremstad

December 18

Falstaff
Campanini (c)
Falstaff: Rimini
Ford: Polese
Fenton: Nadal
Mistress Ford: Raisa
Anne Ford: Sharlow
Mistress Quickly: Claessens
Mistress Page: Pavloska

December 19

The Tales of Hoffmann
Same as Dec. 9 except:
Giulietta: Amsden
Antonia: Buckler
Dapertutto: Maguenat
Miracle: Dufranne

December 20 (mat.)

Die Königskinder
Same as Nov. 24

December 20

Cavalleria Rusticana
Same as Nov. 23

December 21

La Traviata
Same as Dec. 1 except:
Alfredo: Nadal
Germont: Polese

December 22

La Bohème
Sturani (c)
Rodolfo: Crimi
Mimi: Farrar
Marcello: Rimini
Colline: Journet
Musetta: Pavloska

December 23 (mat.)

Romeo and Juliet
Same as Dec. 15

December 23

Tosca
Same as Dec. 16 except:
Tosca: Amsden
Cavaradossi: Errolle
Scarpia: Beck

December 24

Tannhäuser
Pollak (c)
Hermann: Goddard
Tannhäuser: Maclennan
Wolfram: Whitehill
Elisabeth: Farrar
Venus: van Dresser

December 25

Carmen
Same as Nov. 17 except:
Micaela: Prindville

December 26

Falstaff
Same as Dec. 18

December 27

Lucia di Lammermoor
Same as Nov. 21

December 28

Faust
Same as Nov. 20 except:
Marguerite: Edvina

December 30 (mat.)

Louise
Charlier (c)
Father: Dufranne
Mother: Berat
Louise: Edvina
Julien: Dalmorès
King of Fools: Venturini

December 30

La Bohème
Same as Dec. 22 except:
Rodolfo: Errolle
Mimi: Sharlow
Marcello: Kreidler
Musetta: de Phillippe

December 31 (mat.)

Tristan und Isolde
Pollak (c)
Tristan: Maclennan
King Marke: Goddard
Isolde: Matzenauer
Kurvenal: Whitehill
Melot: Kreidler
Brangäne: Claussen

December 31

Thaïs
Campanini (c)
Athanael: Dufranne
Nicias: Dalmorès
Palemon: Nicolay
Thaïs: Garden

January 1

The Barber of Seville
Campanini (c)
Almaviva: Nadal
Bartolo: Trevisan
Rosina: Galli-Curci
Figaro: Rimini
Basilio: Arimondi

January 2

Le Jongleur de Notre-Dame
Campanini (c)
Jean: Garden
Boniface: Dufranne
Prior: Journet

January 3

Romeo and Juliet
Same as Dec. 15

January 4

Louise
Same as Dec. 30

January 5

Francesca da Rimini
Sturani (c)
Francesca: Raisa
Samaritana: Sharlow
Giovanni: Rimini
Paolo: Crimi

January 6 (mat.)

Carmen
Same as Nov. 17 except:
Escamillo: Maguenat
Carmen: Garden

January 6

Aida
Same as Nov. 13 except:
Spadoni (c)
Amneris: Van Gordon
Aida: Amsden
Radames: Kingston

January 7 (mat.)

Lohengrin
Pollak (c)
Henry: Goddard
Lohengrin: Maclennan
Elsa: van Dresser
Telramund: Whitehill
Ortrud: Van Gordon
King's Herald: Beck

January 7

Lucia di Lammermoor
Same as Nov. 21

January 8

Le Jongleur de Notre-Dame
Same as Jan. 2

January 9

Rigoletto
Same as Nov. 18

January 10

Thaïs
Same as Dec. 31

January 11

Romeo and Juliet
Same as Dec. 15

January 12

Grisélidis
Campanini (c)
Grisélidis: Garden
Bertrade: Berat
Le Diable: Maguenat
Le Marquis de Saluces: Dufranne
Gondebaud: Journet

January 13 (mat.)

Francesca da Rimini
Same as Jan. 5

January 13

Carmen
Charlier (c)
Don José: Hamlin
Escamillo: Kreidler
Zuniga: Sargeant
Carmen: Ingram
Micaela: Prindiville

January 14 (mat.)

The Barber of Seville
Same as Jan. 1

January 15

Francesca da Rimini
Same as Jan. 5

January 16

Thaïs
Same as Dec. 31

January 18

Grisélidis
Same as Jan. 12

January 19–Grand Gala

Francesca da Rimini
Act III
Sturani (c)
Paolo: Crimi
Francesca: Raisa

Le Vieil Aigle
Campanini (c)
Le Kahn: Maguenat
Tolaik: Dalmorès
Zina: Raisa

Grisélidis Act I
Campanini (c)
Grisélidis: Garden
Bertrade: Berat
Le Diable: Maguenat
Le Marquis de Saluces: Dufranne
Gondebaud: Journet

Lucia di Lammermoor
Mad Scene
Sturani (c)
Lucia: Galli-Curci
Raimondo: Arimondi

January 20 (mat.)

Louise
Same as Dec. 30 except:
Louise: Garden

January 20

The Barber of Seville
Same as Jan. 1

January 21

Benefit Performance for the French and Italian War Sufferers
Prologue (M. W. Rice): M. D. Robertson

Francesca da Rimini
Act III
Sturani (c)
Paola: Crimi
Francesca: Raisa

Romeo and Juliet
Balcony Scene
Charlier (c)
Juliet: Galli-Curci
Romeo: Muratore

Thaïs Act II, Scene I
Campanini (c)
Athanael: Dufranne
Nicias: Dalmorès
Thaïs: Garden

"La Marseillaise"
Charlier (c)
Muratore

Italian National Anthem
American National Anthem

The Barber of Seville
Lesson Scene
Campanini (c)
Rosina: Galli-Curci
Almaviva: Nadal
Bartolo: Trevisan
Figaro: Rimini
Basilio: Arimondi

1917–18

November 12

Isabeau
Campanini (c)
King Raimondo: Rimini
Isabeau: Raisa
Giglietta: C. Lazzari
Folco: Crimi

November 13

Lucia di Lammermoor
Sturani (c)
Lucia: Galli-Curci
Edgardo: Crimi
Enrico: Rimini
Raimondo: Arimondi

November 14

Aida
Campanini (c)
Aida: Raisa
Amneris: Van Gordon
Radames: Zinorieff
Amonasro: Rimini

King: Arimondi
Ramfis: Goddard

November 15

Faust
Charlier (c)
Faust: Muratore
Méphistophélès: Baklanoff
Valentine: Maguenat
Marguerite: Melba
Siébel: Swartz
Martha: Berat

November 16

Dinorah
Campanini (c)
Hoël: Rimini
Corentino: Dua
Dinorah: Galli-Curci
Huntsman: Huberdeau

November 17 (mat.)

Isabeau
Same as Nov. 12

November 17

Il Trovatore
Sturani (c)
Leonora: Peralta
Azucena: Claessens
Manrico: Zinorieff
Count di Luna: Hulst
Ferrando: Nicolay

November 18

Romeo and Juliet
Campanini (c)
Juliet: Galli-Curci
Romeo: Muratore
Mercutio: Maguenat
Capulet: Dufranne
Friar Lawrence: Huberdeau
Duke of Verona: Arimondi

November 19

Tosca
Sturani (c)
Tosca: Fitziu
Cavaradossi: Crimi
Scarpia: Baklanoff
Angelotti: Nicolay
Sacristan: Trevisan

November 20

Aida
Same as Nov. 14 except:
Sturani (c)
Radames: Crimi

November 21

Dinorah
Same as Nov. 16

November 22

La Bohème
Sturani (c)
Rodolfo: Crimi
Mimi: Melba
Marcello: Rimini
Colline: Huberdeau
Musetta: Sharlow

November 24 (mat.)

Faust
Same as Nov. 15 except:
Marguerite: Fitziu

November 24

Carmen
Charlier (c)
Don José: Dalmorès
Escamillo: Dufranne
Zuniga: Huberdeau
Carmen: Claessens
Micaela: Peterson

November 25 (mat.)

Rigoletto
Sturani (c)
Duke: Nadal
Rigoletto: Stracciari
Gilda: Galli-Curci
Sparafucile: Arimondi
Maddalena: Claessens

November 26

Les Huguenots
Conti (c)
Valentin: Raisa
Urbain: Sharlow
Marguerite de Valois: Christian
Raoul de Nangis: Crimi
Marcel: Arimondi
Le Comte de Saint Bris: Huberdeau
Le Comte de Nevers: Maguenat

November 27

Romeo and Juliet
Same as Nov. 18 except:
Charlier (c)

November 28

Tosca
Same as Nov. 19

November 29

Rigoletto
Same as Nov. 25

December 1 (mat.)

Manon
Charlier (c)
Manon: Vix
Des Grieux: Muratore
Lescaut: Maguenat
Comte: Huberdeau
Guillot: Dua
De Brétigny: Defrère

December 1

Aida
Same as Nov. 14 except:
Spadoni (c)
Aida: Peralta
Amonasro: Kreidler

December 2 (mat.)

La Traviata
Sturani (c)
Violetta: Galli-Curci
Alfredo: Nadal
Germont: Stracciari

December 3

Romeo and Juliet
Same as Nov. 18 except:
Charlier (c)

December 4

Les Huguenots
Same as Nov. 26

December 5

Le Jongleur de Notre-Dame
Charlier (c)
Jean: Vix
Boniface: Dufranne
Prior: Huberdeau

December 6

Isabeau
Same as Nov. 12 except:
Sturani (c)

December 8 (mat.)

Dinorah
Same as Nov. 16 except:
Conti (c)

December 8

La Bohème
Same as Nov. 22 except:
Rodolfo: Lamont
Mimi: Fitziu
Marcello: Fornari

December 9

The Jewels of the Madonna
Charlier (c)
Gennaro: Crimi
Carmela: Berat
Maliella: Raisa
Rafaele: Rimini

December 10

Cavalleria Rusticana
Sturani (c)
Santuzza: Peralta
Lola: Swartz
Turiddu: Crimi
Alfio: Maguenat

I Pagliacci
Sturani (c)
Nedda: Fitziu
Canio: Muratore
Tonio: Stracciari

December 11

Louise
Charlier (c)
Father: Dufranne
Mother: Berat
Louise: Vix
Julien: Dalmorès
King of Fools: Dua

December 12

Romeo and Juliet
Same as Nov. 18 except:
Charlier (c)

December 13

Le Jongleur de Notre-Dame
Same as Dec. 5

December 15 (mat.)

The Jewels of the Madonna
Same as Dec. 9

December 15

Faust
Same as Nov. 15 except:
Faust: Dalmorès
Valentine: Dufranne
Marguerite: Sharlow

December 16 (mat.)

The Barber of Seville
Sturani (c)
Almaviva: Nadal
Bartolo: Trevisan
Rosina: Galli-Curci
Figaro: Rimini
Basilio: Arimondi

December 17

Louise
Same as Dec. 11

December 18

La Bohème
Same as Nov. 22 except:
Mimi: Fitziu

December 19

La Traviata
Same as Dec. 2

December 20

Louise
Same as Dec. 11

December 21

Lakmé
Charlier (c)
Lakmé: Galli-Curci
Mallika: Swartz
Gerald: Muratore
Nilakantha: Baklanoff
Frédéric: Maguenat

December 22 (mat.)

Tosca
Same as Nov. 19 except:
Scarpia: Stracciari

December 22

Cavalleria Rusticana
Sturani (c)
Santuzza: Hall
Turiddu: Nadal
Alfio: Fornari

I Pagliacci
Sturani (c)
Nedda: Buckler
Canio: Lamont
Tonio: Kreidler

December 23

Manon
Same as Dec. 1

December 24

Dinorah
Same as Nov. 16 except:
Conti (c)

December 25

Faust
Same as Nov. 15 except:
Valentine: Dufranne
Marguerite: Vix

December 26

Azora
Hadley (c)
Azora: Fitziu
Papontzin: Van Gordon
Xalca: Lamont
Ramatzin: Middleton

December 27

La Traviata
Same as Dec. 2

December 29 (mat.)

Ernani
Sturani (c)
Don Carlo: Stracciari
Elvira: Peralta
Silva: Arimondi
Ernani: Crimi

December 29

Tosca
Same as Nov. 19 except:
Cavaradossi: Nadal
Scarpia: Kreidler

December 30 (mat.)

Aida
Same as Nov. 14 except:
Sturani (c)
Radames: Crimi

December 31

Lakmé
Same as Dec. 21

January 1

Ernani
Same as Dec. 29

January 2

Isabeau
Same as Nov. 12

January 3

The Jewels of the Madonna
Same as Dec. 9

January 4

Carmen
Same as Nov. 24 except:
Escamillo: Baklanoff
Carmen: Garden
Micaela: Sharlow

January 5 (mat.)

A Daughter of the Forest
Nevin (c)
Daughter: Peralta
Lover: Lamont
Father: Goddard

Le Jongleur de Notre-Dame
Same as Dec. 5

January 5

La Traviata
Same as Dec. 2 except:
Violetta: Parnell
Germont: Rimini

January 6

Cavalleria Rusticana
Same as Dec. 10

I Pagliacci
Same as Dec. 10

January 7

Azora
Same as Dec. 26

January 8

Dinorah
Same as Nov. 16 except:
Conti (c)

Monna Vanna
Charlier (c)
Monna Vanna: Garden
Prinzivalle: Muratore
Guido: Baklanoff
Marco: Huberdeau

January 10

Sapho
Charlier (c)
Fanny: Vix
Divonne: Berat
Jean: Dalmorès
Caoudal: Dufranne

January 11

La Traviata
Same as Dec. 2 except:
Violetta: Parnell

January 12 (mat.)

Pelléas et Mélisande
Pelléas: Maguenat
Golaud: Dufranne
Arkel: Huberdeau
Mélisande: Garden
Geneviève: Berat

January 12

Azora
Same as Dec. 26

January 13

La Bohème
Same as Nov. 22 except:
Mimi: Galli-Curci

January 14

Sapho
Same as Jan. 10

January 15

Thaïs
Charlier (c)
Athanael: Dufranne
Nicias: Dalmorès
Palemon: Huberdeau
Thaïs: Garden

January 16

Francesca da Rimini
Sturani (c)
Francesca: Raisa
Samaritana: Sharlow
Giovanni: Rimini
Paolo: Crimi

January 17

Pelléas et Mélisande
Same as Jan. 12

January 18—Grand Gala

La Bohème Act III
Sturani (c)
Mimi: Fitziu
Rodolfo: Nadal
Marcello: Rimini
Musetta: Sharlow

Azora Prelude to Act III
Hadley (c)

Thaïs Act II
Charlier (c)
Thaïs: Garden
Nicias: Dalmorès
Athanael: Dufranne

Hymn of the Nations (Verdi): Raisa and chorus

I Pagliacci Prologue
Sturani (c)
Tonio: Stracciari

Manon Act III
Charlier (c)
Manon: Vix
Lescaut: Maguenat
Comte: Huberdeau
Guillot: Dua
De Brétigny: Defrère

Aida Act III
Campanini (c)
Aida: Raisa
Radames: Crimi
Amonasro: Rimini
Amneris: Van Gordon
Ramfis: Goddard

"La Marseillaise"
Charlier (c)
Vix

January 19 (mat.)

Le Sauteriot
S. Lazzari (c)
Arti: Vix
Trine: C. Lazzari
Indrik: Dalmorès
Mikkel: Huberdeau
Le Docteur: Dufranne

January 19

Rigoletto
Same as Nov. 25 except:
Gilda: Redish

1918–19

November 18

La Traviata
Polacco (c)
Violetta: Galli-Curci
Alfredo: Ciccolini
Germont: Stracciari

November 19

Madama Butterfly
Polacco (c)
Cio-Cio-San: Miura
Suzuki: Pavloska
Pinkerton: Lamont
Sharpless: Bouilliez

November 20

Il Trovatore
Sturani (c)
Leonora: Raisa
Count di Luna: Rimini
Manrico: Dolci
Azucena: Van Gordon
Ferrando: V. Lazzari

November 22

Thaïs
Hasselmans (c)
Thaïs: Gall
Nicias: Lamont
Athanael: Journet
Palemon: Huberdeau

November 23 (mat.)

Lucia di Lammermoor
Campanini (c)
Enrico: Stracciari
Lucia: Galli-Curci
Edgardo: Dolci
Raimondo: Arimondi

November 23

Isabeau
Sturani (c)
King Raimondo: Baklanoff
Isabeau: Fitziu
Giglietta: C. Lazzari
Folco: Lamont

November 25

Aida
Polacco (c)
King: Arimondi
Amneris: Van Gordon
Radames: Dolci
Aida: Raisa
Ramfis: V. Lazzari
Amonasro: Rimini

November 26

Carmen
Hasselmans (c)
Zuniga: Huberdeau
Don José: Muratore
Carmen: Sylva
Escamillo: Baklanoff
Micaela: Sharlow

November 27

William Tell
Charlier (c)
Gessler: Huberdeau
Mathilda: Gall
William Tell: Bouilliez
Hedwiga: Berat
Jemmy: Maxwell
Melchthal: Nicolay
Arnold: O'Sullivan
Walther: Journet

November 28

Linda di Chamounix
Sturani (c)
Marquis of Boisfleury: Trevisan
Carlo: Lamont
Parish Priest: V. Lazzari
Antonio: Stracciari
Linda: Galli-Curci
Pierotto: C. Lazzari

November 29

Tosca
Polacco (c)
Tosca: Raisa
Cavaradossi: Dolci
Scarpia: Baklanoff
Angelotti: Nicolay
Sacristan: Trevisan

November 30 (mat.)

Romeo and Juliet
Charlier (c)
Duke of Verona: Arimondi
Capulet: Bouilliez
Juliet: Gall
Romeo: Muratore
Mercutio: Maguenat
Friar Lawrence: Journet

November 30

Madama Butterfly
Same as Nov. 19

December 1 (mat.)

La Bohème
Polacco (c)
Mimi: Galli-Curci
Rodolfo: McCormack
Marcello: Rimini
Colline: Huberdeau
Musetta: Pavloska

December 2

William Tell
Same as Nov. 27

December 3

The Barber of Seville
Campanini (c)
Almaviva: Carpi
Bartolo: Trevisan
Rosina: Galli-Curci
Basilio: Arimondi
Figaro: Stracciari

December 4

Faust
Charlier (c)
Faust: Muratore
Méphistophélès: Journet
Marguerite: Gall

Valentine: Maguenat
Martha: Berat
Siébel: Pavloska

December 6

Carmen
Same as Nov. 26

December 7 (mat.)

La Gioconda
Polacco (c)
La Gioconda: Raisa
La Cieca: C. Lazzari
Alvise: Arimondi
Laura: Van Gordon
Enzo: Dolci
Barnaba: Rimini

December 7

Thaïs
Same as Nov. 22

December 9

Romeo and Juliet
Same as Nov. 30

December 10

Tosca
Same as Nov. 29

December 11

La Traviata
Same as Nov. 18

December 13

Linda di Chamounix
Same as Nov. 28

December 14 (mat.)

Werther
Hasselmans (c)
Werther: Muratore
Bailiff: Huberdeau
Charlotte: Pavloska
Sophia: Sharlow
Albert: Maguenat

December 14

Il Trovatore
Same as Nov. 20

December 16

The Barber of Seville
Same as Dec. 3 except:
Almaviva: Ciccolini

December 17

Samson and Delilah
Hasselmans (c)
Delilah: C. Lazzari
Samson: O'Sullivan
High Priest: Journet
Abimelech: Nicolay
Old Hebrew: Huberdeau

December 18

Cavalleria Rusticana
Polacco (c)
Santuzza: Raisa
Turiddu: Dolci
Alfio: Maguenat
Lola: Pavloska

I Pagliacci
Sturani (c)
Canio: Lamont
Nedda: Fitziu
Tonio: Stracciari

December 20

La Gioconda
Same as Dec. 7 except:
Alvise: V. Lazzari

December 21 (mat.)

Linda di Chamounix
Same as Nov. 28

December 21

Romeo and Juliet
Same as Nov. 30 except:
Romeo: O'Sullivan

December 23

Manon
Hasselmans (c)
Count: Huberdeau
Des Grieux: Fontaine
Manon: Gall
Lescaut: Maguenat
Guillot: Dua
De Brétigny: Defrère

December 24

Cavalleria Rusticana
Same as Dec. 18 except:
Turiddu: Lamont

I Pagliacci
Same as Dec. 18

December 25

Crispino e la Comare
Campanini (c)
Crispino: Trevisan
Annetta: Galli-Curci
Fabrizio: Stracciari
Mirabolano: Arimondi
La Comare: Claessens

December 27

Lucia di Lammermoor
Same as Nov. 23 except:
Enrico: Rimini
Edgardo: Lamont

December 28 (mat.)

Aida
Same as Nov. 25 except:
Amonasro: Baklanoff

December 28

La Bohème
Same as Dec. 1 except:
Sturani (c)
Mimi: Fitziu
Rodolfo: Ciccolini

Hamlet Act IV
Ophelia: Galli-Curci

December 30

Samson and Delilah
Same as Dec. 17

December 31

Dinorah
Campanini (c)
Hoël: Rimini
Dinorah: Galli-Curci
Corentino: Dua
Huntsman: V. Lazzari

January 1

La Gioconda
Same as Dec. 7

January 3

Monna Vanna
Charlier (c)
Guido: Baklanoff
Monna Vanna: Garden
Marco: Huberdeau
Prinzivalle: O'Sullivan

January 4 (mat.)
Faust
Same as Dec. 4 except:
Hasselmans (c)
Faust: Fontaine
Valentine: Bouilliez

January 4
Cavalleria Rusticana
Same as Dec. 18 except:
Santuzza: Gibson
Turiddu: Lamont

I Pagliacci
Same as Dec. 18 except:
Canio: O'Sullivan
Tonio: Baklanoff

January 6
Isabeau
Same as Nov. 23

January 7
Manon
Same as Dec. 23

January 8
Werther
Same as Dec. 14 except:
Werther: O'Sullivan

January 9
Carmen
Same as Nov. 26 except:
Charlier (c)
Don José: Fontaine
Carmen: Garden

January 10
Madama Butterfly
Same as Nov. 19

January 11 (mat.)
Monna Vanna
Same as Jan. 3

January 11
Aida
Same as Nov. 25 except:
Aida: Gibson

January 13
Rigoletto
Polacco (c)
Duke: Ciccolini
Rigoletto: Stracciari
Gilda: Macbeth
Sparafucile: Arimondi
Maddalena: Claessens
Monterone: Nicolay

January 14
Gismonda
Campanini (c)
Gismonda: Garden
Almerio: Fontaine
Zaccaria: Maguenat
Gregorias: Huberdeau
Sophron: Journet

January 15
Samson and Delilah
Same as Dec. 17

January 17
Loreley
Polacco (c)
Rudolfo: V. Lazzari
Anna: Macbeth
Walter: Dolci
Loreley: Fitziu
Hermann: Rimini

January 18 (mat.)
Madama Butterfly
Same as Nov. 19

January 18
Carmen
Same as Nov. 26 except:
Charlier (c)
Don José: Fontaine
Carmen: Garden
Micaela: Namara

January 20
Gismonda
Same as Jan. 14

January 21
Faust
Same as Dec. 4 except:
Faust: O'Sullivan
Valentine: Defrère

January 22
Loreley
Same as Jan. 17

January 23
Cléopâtre
Charlier (c)
Marc Antoine: Maguenat
Spakos: Fontaine
Ennius: Journet
Cléopâtre: Garden

January 24
Rigoletto
Same as Jan. 13

January 25 (mat.)
Le Chemineau
Hasselmans (c)
Toinette: Gall
Aline: Sharlow
Chemineau: Maguenat
François: Baklanoff

January 25
The Barber of Seville
Same as Dec. 3 except
Sturani (c)
Rosina: Macbeth
Figaro: Rimini

1919–20

November 18
La Nave
Montemezzi (c)
Marco Gratico: Dolci
Sergio Gratico: Rimini
Orso Faledro: Arimondi
Basiliola: Raisa

November 19
Madama Butterfly
Hasselmans (c)
Cio-Cio-San: Miura
Suzuki: Pavloska
Pinkerton: Lamont
Sharpless: Baklanoff

November 20
Fedora
de Angelis (c)
Fedora: Jardon
Olga: Namara
Count Loris: Johnson
De Siriex: Rimini

November 21

Un Ballo in Maschera
de Angelis (c)
Riccardo: Bonci
Renato: Galeffi
Amelia: Longaard
Ulrica: Eubank
Oscar: Sharlow

November 22 (mat.)

Norma
de Angelis (c)
Pollione: Dolci
Oroveso: V. Lazzari
Norma: Raisa
Adalgisa: Van Gordon

November 22

Lucia di Lammermoor
de Angelis (c)
Enrico: Rimini
Lucia: Morgana
Edgardo: Lamont
Raimondo: Arimondi

November 24

Madama Butterfly
Same as Nov. 19

November 25

La Bohème
de Angelis (c)
Mimi: Herbert
Rodolfo: Bonci
Marcello: Rimini
Colline: Lazzari
Musetta: Pavloska

Followed by ballet

November 26

Le Chemineau
Hasselmans (c)
Toinette: Gall
Aline: Sharlow
Chemineau: Dufranne
François: Baklanoff

November 27 (mat.)

Madama Butterfly
Same as Nov. 19

November 27

Cléopâtre
Charlier (c)
Marc Antoine: Maguenat
Spakos: Fontaine
Ennius: Huberdeau
Cléopâtre: Garden

November 29 (mat.)

Thaïs
Hasselmans (c)
Thaïs: Garden
Nicias: Fontaine
Athanael: Baklanoff
Palemon: Huberdeau

November 29

Aida
de Angelis (c)
King: Arimondi
Amneris: Van Gordon
Radames: Dolci
Aida: Raisa
Ramfis: V. Lazzari
Amonasro: Rimini

November 30

Un Ballo in Maschera
Same as Nov. 21 except:
Amelia: Eubank
Ulrica: Claessens

December 1

La Nave
Same as Nov. 18

December 2

Le Jongleur de Notre-Dame
Charlier (c)
Jean: Garden
Boniface: Dufranne
Prior: Huberdeau

December 3

La Bohème
Same as Nov. 25

December 4

Rigoletto
Marinuzzi (c)
Duke: Schipa
Rigoletto: Galeffi
Gilda: Galli-Curci
Sparafucile: Cotreuil
Maddalena: Claessens

December 6 (mat.)

Trittico:
Il Tabarro
Marinuzzi (c)
Michele: Galeffi
Luigi: Johnson
Giorgetta: Jardon
La Frugola: Claessens

Suor Angelica
Marinuzzi (c)
Suor Angelica: Raisa
La Principessa: Van Gordon
La Maestra Delle Novizie: Hager

Gianni Schicchi
Marinuzzi (c)
Gianni Schicchi: Galeffi
Lauretta: Herbert
La Vecchia: Claessens
Rinuccio: Johnson

December 6

Carmen
Marinuzzi (c)
Zuniga: Huberdeau
Don José: Fontaine
Carmen: Garden
Escamillo: Baklanoff
Micaela: Morgana

December 7

Lucia di Lammermoor
Same as Nov. 22 except:
Lucia: Galli-Curci
Edgardo: Dolci

December 8

Le Chemineau
Same as Nov. 26

December 9

La Traviata
de Angelis (c)
Violetta: Galli-Curci
Alfredo: Dolci
Germont: Galeffi

December 10

Tosca
Marinuzzi (c)
Tosca: Raisa
Cavaradossi: Schipa

Scarpia: Rimini
Angelotti: Nicolay
Sacristan: Trevisan

December 11

Manon
Marinuzzi (c)
Count: Huberdeau
Des Grieux: Schipa
Manon: Gall
Lescaut: Maguenat
Guillot: Warnery
De Brétigny: Defrère

December 13 (mat.)

The Barber of Seville
Marinuzzi (c)
Almaviva: Schipa
Bartolo: Trevisan
Rosina: Galli-Curci
Basilio: Cotreuil
Figaro: Galeffi

December 13

La Bohème
Same as Nov. 25

December 15

Rigoletto
Same as Dec. 4 except:
Sparafucile: Arimondi

December 16

Norma
Same as Nov. 22 except:
Adalgisa: Sharlow

December 17

La Sonnambula
de Angelis (c)
Count Rodolfo: V. Lazzari
Teresa: Claessens
Amina: Galli-Curci
Elvino: Schipa

December 18

Aida
Same as Nov. 29

December 22

Trittico
Same as Dec. 6

December 23

Ballet: *The Birthday of the Infanta*

La Sonnambula
Same as Dec. 17

December 24

Faust
Charlier (c)
Faust: Fontaine
Méphistophélès: Cotreuil
Marguerite: Gall
Valentine: Defrère
Martha: Claessens
Siébel: Pavloska

December 25

Lucia di Lammermoor
Same as Nov. 22 except:
Lucia: Galli-Curci
Edgardo: Dolci

December 26

Un Ballo in Maschera
Same as Nov. 21 except:
Renato: Rimini
Amelia: Raisa
Ulrica: Claessens
Oscar: Macbeth

December 27 (mat.)

Don Pasquale
Marinuzzi (c)
Don Pasquale: Trevisan
Dr. Malatesta: Rimini
Ernesto: Schipa
Norina: Galli-Curci

December 27

Madama Butterfly
Same as Nov. 19

December 29

La Sonnambula
Same as Dec. 17

Ballet: *The Birthday of the Infanta*
Hasselmans (c)

December 30

Trittico
Same as Dec. 6

December 31

Don Pasquale
Same as Dec. 27

Dinorah Act II, Scene 1
Dinorah: Galli-Curci

January 1

Pelléas et Mélisande
Charlier (c)
Mélisande: Garden
Geneviève: Claessens
Pelléas: Maguenat
Golaud: Dufranne
Arkel: Huberdeau

January 2

Rip Van Winkle
Smallens (c)
Rip Van Winkle: Baklanoff
Hendrick Hudson: Dufranne
Dirck Spuytenduyvil: Cotreuil
Nicholas Vedder: Huberdeau
Peterkee: Herbert

January 3 (mat.)

Hérodiade
Charlier (c)
Jean: O'Sullivan
Herode: Maguenat
Phanuel: Cotreuil
Vitellius: Defrère
Salome: Gall
Hérodiade: D'Alvarez

January 3

Fedora
Same as Nov. 20 except:
Olga: Pavloska

January 5

L'Heure Espagnole
Hasselmans (c)
Torquemada: Defrère
Concepcion: Gall
Ramiro: Maguenat
Don Inigo Gomez: Cotreuil
Gonzalve: Warnery

I Pagliacci
Marinuzzi (c)
Canio: Lamont
Nedda: Sharlow
Tonio: Ruffo

January 6

Monna Vanna
Charlier (c)
Guido: Baklanoff
Monna Vanna: Garden
Marco: Huberdeau
Prinzivalle: O'Sullivan

January 7

Hérodiade
Same as Jan. 3

January 8

Rip Van Winkle
Same as Jan. 2

January 9

L'Amore dei Tre Re
Marinuzzi (c)
Fiora: Garden
Archibaldo: V. Lazzari
Manfredo: Galeffi
Avito: Johnson
Flaminio: Oliviero

January 10 (mat.)

Rigoletto
Same as Dec. 4 except:
Rigoletto: Ruffo
Gilda: Macbeth
Sparafucile: Arimondi

January 10

Tosca
Same as Dec. 10 except:
de Angelis (c)
Cavaradossi: Dolci
Scarpia: Baklanoff

January 11

Carmen
Same as Dec. 6 except:
Don José: O'Sullivan

January 12

Norma
Marinuzzi (c)
Same as Nov. 22 except:
Adalgisa: Sharlow

January 13

Le Vieil Aigle
Charlier (c)
Le Kahn: Baklanoff
Tolaik: Fontaine
An Equerry: Defrère
Zina: Gall

I Pagliacci
Same as Jan. 5

January 14

Louise
Charlier (c)
Father: Dufranne
Mother: Claessens
Louise: Garden
Julien: Fontaine
King of Fools: Warnery

January 15

Hamlet
Charlier (c)
Hamlet: Ruffo
Claudius: V. Lazzari
Gertrude: Van Gordon
Ghost: Cotreuil
Polonius: Trevisan
Ophelia: Macbeth

January 17 (mat.)

L'Amore dei Tre Re
Same as Jan. 9

January 17

Rip Van Winkle
Same as Jan. 2

January 19

Madame Chrysanthème
Hasselmans (c)
Pierre: Fontaine
Yves: Dufranne
Mr. Kangourou: Warnery
Madame Chrysanthème: Miura

January 20

L'Elisir d'Amore
Marinuzzi (c)
Adina: Macbeth
Nemorino: Bonci
Belcore: Rimini
Dulcamara: Blanchat

January 21

L'Elisir d'Amore
Same as Jan. 20

January 22

Hérodiade
Same as Jan. 3 except:
Jean: Fontaine

January 23

Madama Butterfly
Same as Nov. 19

January 24 (mat.)

Madame Chrysanthème
Same as Jan. 19

January 24

The Barber of Seville
Same as Dec. 13 except:
de Angelis (c)
Rosina: Macbeth

1920–21

November 17

Jacquerie
Marinuzzi (c)
Corrado: V. Lazzari
Mazurec: Johnson
Caillet: Galeffi
Isaura: Gall

November 18

The Jewels of the Madonna
Cimini (c)
Gennaro: Lamont
Carmela: Pascova
Maliella: Raisa
Rafaele: Rimini

November 18

The Tales of Hoffmann
Smallens (c)
Olympia: Macbeth
Giulietta: Francis
Antonia: Maxwell
Niclaus: Pascova

Hoffmann: Paillard
Coppelius: Dufranne
Dapertutto: Dufranne
Miracle: Dufranne

November 20

Cavalleria Rusticana
Cimini (c)
Santuzza: Francis
Turiddu: Lamont
Alfio: Defrère
Lola: Paperte

I Pagliacci
Cimini (c)
Canio: Johnson
Nedda: Maxwell
Tonio: Galeffi

November 20 (mat.)

Tosca
Marinuzzi (c)
Tosca: Raisa
Cavaradossi: Hislop
Scarpia: Baklanoff
Angelotti: Nicolay
Sacristan: Trevisan

November 22

Il Trovatore
Cimini (c)
Leonora: Raisa
Count di Luna: Galeffi
Manrico: Lamont
Azucena: Van Gordon
Ferrando: Nicolay

November 23

Le Chemineau
Morin (c)
Toinette: Gall
Aline: Maxwell
Le Chemineau: Dufranne
François: Baklanoff

November 24

Andrea Chénier
Marinuzzi (c)
Andrea Chénier: Johnson
Gérard: Ruffo
Madeleine: Raisa
Madelon: Van Gordon

November 25

La Bohème
Cimini (c)
Mimi: Macbeth
Rodolfo: Hislop
Marcello: Rimini
Colline: V. Lazzari
Musetta: Francis

November 26

The Jewels of the Madonna
Same as Nov. 18

November 27 (mat.)

La Traviata
Smallens (c)
Violetta: Craft
Alfredo: Schipa
Germont: Galeffi

November 27

The Tales of Hoffmann
Same as Nov. 18

November 28 (mat.)

Rigoletto
Marinuzzi (c)
Duke: Hislop
Rigoletto: Ruffo
Gilda: Macbeth
Sparafucile: V. Lazzari
Maddalena: Pascova
Monterone: Nicolay

November 29

Tosca
Same as Nov. 20

November 30

Jacquerie
Marinuzzi (c)
Same as Nov. 17

December 1

Lucia di Lammermoor
Cimini (c)
Enrico: Rimini
Lucia: Galli-Curci
Edgardo: Schipa
Raimondo: V. Lazzari

December 2

Andrea Chénier
Same as Nov. 24

December 4 (mat.)

La Sonnambula
Cimini (c)
Count Rodolfo: V. Lazzari
Teresa: Paperte
Amina: Galli-Curci
Elvino: Schipa

December 4

Il Trovatore
Same as Nov. 22 except:
Leonora: Carrara

December 5 (mat.)

Aida
Marinuzzi (c)
King: Dentale
Amneris: Besanzoni
Radames: Hislop
Aida: Raisa
Ramfis: V. Lazzari
Amonasro: Rimini

December 6

The Jewels of the Madonna
Same as Nov. 18

December 7

The Barber of Seville
Marinuzzi (c)
Almaviva: Schipa
Bartolo: Trevisan
Rosina: Galli-Curci
Basilio: V. Lazzari
Figaro: Galeffi

December 8

Gianni Schicchi
Santini (c)
Gianni Schicchi: Galeffi
Lauretta: Maxwell
La Vecchia: Pascova
Rinuccio: Johnson
Gherardo: Oliviero
La Ciesca: Falco

December 9

Le Chemineau
Same as Nov. 23

December 11 (mat.)

Cavalleria Rusticana
Same as Nov. 20 except:
Santuzza: Raisa

I Pagliacci
Same as Nov. 20

December 11

Aida
Smallens (c)
King: Nicolay

Amneris: Van Gordon
Radames: Martin
Aida: Carrara
Amonasro: Baklanoff
Ramfis: V. Lazzari

December 12 (mat.)

Romeo and Juliet
Morin (c)
Capulet: Dufranne
Juliet: Galli-Curci
Romeo: Hislop
Mercutio: Defrère
Duke: Nicolay
Friar Lawrence: Cotreuil

December 13

Edipo Re
Marinuzzi (c)
Edipo: Ruffo
Creonte: Paillard
Tiresia: Dentale
Giocasta: Francis

December 14

Tosca
Same as Nov. 20 except:
Tosca: Gall

December 15

Falstaff
Marinuzzi (c)
Falstaff: Rimini
Ford: Defrère
Mistress Ford: Raisa
Anne Ford: Maxwell
Mistress Page: Pascova
Mistress Quickly: Claessens
Fenton: Schipa

December 16

Linda di Chamounix
Cimini (c)
Marquis: Trevisan
Carlo: Lamont
Parish Priest: V. Lazzari
Antonio: Rimini
Linda: Galli-Curci
Pierotto: Pascova

December 18 (mat.)

Lakmé
Morin (c)
Gerald: Schipa
Frédéric: Defrère
Nilakantha: Baklanoff
Lakmé: Galli-Curci
Mallika: Diemer

December 18

Rigoletto
Same as Nov. 28 except:
Rigoletto: Galeffi

December 20

La Traviata
Same as Nov. 27 except:
Violetta: Galli-Curci

December 21

Edipo Re
Same as Dec. 13

December 22

Romeo and Juliet
Same as Dec. 12

December 23

L'Elisir d'Amore
Marinuzzi (c)
Adina: Macbeth
Nemorino: Bonci
Belcore: Rimini
Dulcamara: Trevisan

December 24

Lohengrin
Marinuzzi (c)
Henry: Cotreuil
Lohengrin: Johnson
Elsa: Raisa
Telramund: Kreidler
Ortrud: Van Gordon

December 25 (mat.)

Edipo Re
Same as Dec. 13

December 25

The Barber of Seville
Same as Dec. 7 except:
Rosina: Macbeth

December 26

La Bohème
Same as Nov. 25 except:
Mimi: Galli-Curci
Rodolfo: Bonci

December 27

Jacquerie
Same as Nov. 17

December 28

Lakmé
Same as Dec. 18

December 29

Otello
Cimini (c)
Otello: Marshall
Desdemona: Raisa
Iago: Ruffo
Emilia: Claessens
Cassio: Oliviero

December 30

Lucia di Lammermoor
Same as Dec. 1 except:
Edgardo: Bonci

December 31

Aphrodite
Morin (c)
Chrysis: Garden
Demetrios: Johnson
Bacchis: Van Gordon

January 1 (mat.)

Madama Butterfly
Marinuzzi (c)
Cio-Cio-San: Storchio
Suzuki: Francis
Pinkerton: Hislop
Sharpless: Rimini

January 1

The Jewels of the Madonna
Same as Nov. 18

January 3

L'Elisir d'Amore
Same as Dec. 23

January 4

Monna Vanna
Morin (c)
Prinzivalle: Muratore
Guido: Baklanoff
Monna Vanna: Garden
Marco: Cotreuil

January 5

Linda di Chamounix
Same as Dec. 16 except:
Carlo: Schipa
Linda: Storchio
Pierotto: Besanzoni

January 6

Lohengrin
Same as Dec. 24

January 7

L'Amore dei Tre Re
Marinuzzi (c)
Fiora: Carrara
Archibaldo: V. Lazzari
Manfredo: Galeffi
Avito: Johnson

January 8 (mat.)

Manon
Morin (c)
Des Grieux: Muratore
Count: Cotreuil
Manon: Gall
Lescaut: Dufranne
Guillot: Defrère
De Brétigny: Nicolay

January 8

La Traviata
Same as Nov. 27 except:
Violetta: Storchio
Germont: Rimini

January 10

Die Walküre
Marinuzzi (c)
Wotan: Baklanoff
Fricka: Claessens
Hunding: Cotreuil
Sieglinde: Francis
Siegmund: Martin
Brünnhilde: Van Gordon

January 11

Madama Butterfly
Same as Jan. 1

January 12

Carmen
Marinuzzi (c)
Don José: Muratore
Zuniga: Cotreuil
Carmen: Garden
Escamillo: Baklanoff
Micaela: Macbeth

January 13

Lakmé
Same as Dec. 18 except:
Lakmé: Macbeth

January 14

Monna Vanna
Same as Jan. 4

January 15 (mat.)

Lohengrin
Same as Dec. 24

January 15

Tosca
Same as Nov. 20 except:
Santini (c)
Tosca: Gall
Scarpia: Galeffi

January 16 (mat.)

Otello
Same as Dec. 29 except:
Iago: Rimini

January 17

Faust
Cimini (c)
Faust: Muratore
Méphistophélès: Baklanoff
Marguerite: Garden
Valentine: Dufranne
Martha: Claessens
Siébel: Maxwell

January 18

Die Walküre
Same as Jan. 10

January 19

Cavalleria Rusticana
Same as Nov. 20

I Pagliacci
Same as Nov. 20 except:
Tonio: Rimini

January 20

Carmen
Same as Jan. 12

January 21

Mignon
Cimini (c)
Mignon: Besanzoni
Lothario: V. Lazzari
Wilhelm Meister: Schipa
Philine: Macbeth
Frederick: Pascova

January 22 (mat.)

L'Amore dei Tre Re
Same as Jan. 7 except:
Fiora: Garden

January 22

Madama Butterfly
Same as Jan. 1 except:
Sharpless: Baklanoff

1921–22

November 14

Samson and Delilah
Polacco (c)
Samson: Muratore
Delilah: d'Alvarez
High Priest: Dufranne
Abimelech: Defrère
Old Hebrew: Payan

November 15

Tosca
Ferrari (c)
Tosca: Raisa
Cavaradossi: Pattiera
Scarpia: Baklanoff
Angelotti: Nicolay
Sacristan: Trevisan

November 16

Madama Butterfly
Polacco (c)
Cio-Cio-San: Mason
Suzuki: Pavloska
Pinkerton: Johnson
Sharpless: Rimini

November 17

Monna Vanna
Polacco (c)
Prinzivalle: Muratore
Guido: Baklanoff
Monna Vanna: Garden
Marco: Cotreuil

November 19 (mat.)

Aida
Ferrari (c)
King: Cotreuil
Amneris: Reynolds
Radames: Pattiera
Aida: Raisa
Ramfis: V. Lazzari
Amonasro: Rimini

November 19

Le Jongleur de Notre-Dame
Polacco (c)
Jean: Garden
Boniface: Dufranne
Prior: Payan

November 21

Rigoletto
Polacco (c)
Duke: Schipa
Rigoletto: Schwarz
Gilda: Mason
Sparafucile: V. Lazzari
Maddalena: Pavloska
Borsa: Oliviero

November 22

La Bohème
Ferrari (c)
Mimi: Dux
Rodolfo: Pattiera
Marcello: Rimini
Colline: V. Lazzari
Musetta: Pavloska

November 23

Samson and Delilah
Same as Nov. 14

November 24

Tannhäuser
Ferrari (c)
Hermann: Wolf
Elisabeth: Raisa
Tannhäuser: Schubert
Wolfram: Schwarz
Venus: Van Gordon

November 26 (mat.)

Carmen
Polacco (c)
Don José: Muratore
Zuniga: Payan
Carmen: Garden
Escamillo: Baklanoff
Micaela: McCormic

November 26

Madama Butterfly
Same as Nov. 16

November 28

Le Jongleur de Notre-Dame
Same as Nov. 19

November 29

Monna Vanna
Same as Nov. 17

November 30

Tannhäuser
Same as Nov. 24

December 1

La Bohème
Same as Nov. 22

December 3 (mat.)

L'Amore dei Tre Re
Polacco (c)
Fiora: Garden
Archibaldo: V. Lazzari
Manfredo: Baklanoff
Avito: Muratore

December 3

Otello
Cimini (c)
Otello: Marshall
Desdemona: Raisa
Iago: Rimini
Emilia: Claessens
Cassio: Oliviero

December 5

Madama Butterfly
Same as Nov. 16

December 6

Tannhäuser
Same as Nov. 24

December 7

Monna Vanna
Same as Nov. 17

December 8

Tosca
Same as Nov. 15

December 9

Carmen
Same as Nov. 26

December 10 (mat.)

Rigoletto
Same as Nov. 21

December 10

Aida
Same as Nov. 19 except:
King: Nicolay
Amneris: Van Gordon

December 12

Tannhäuser
Same as Nov. 24

December 13

L'Amore dei Tre Re
Same as Dec. 3

December 14

Otello
Same as Dec. 3

December 15

Madama Butterfly
Same as Nov. 16

December 17 (mat.)

Tosca
Same as Nov. 15

December 17

Rigoletto
Same as Nov. 21 except:
Rigoletto: Rimini
Maddalena: Paperte

December 19

Faust
Polacco (c)
Faust: Muratore
Méphistophélès: Baklanoff
Marguerite: Mason
Valentine: Dufranne

Martha: Claessens
Siébel: Pavloska

December 20

La Traviata
Polacco (c)
Violetta: Galli-Curci
Alfredo: Schipa
Germont: Schwarz

December 21

Aida
Same as Nov. 19 except:
Amneris: Van Gordon

December 22

Romeo and Juliet
Polacco (c)
Capulet: Dufranne
Juliet: Mason
Romeo: Muratore
Mercutio: Maguenat
Stephano: Maxwell
Duke of Verona: Nicolay
Friar Lawrence: Payan

December 24 (mat.)

Lucia di Lammermoor
Cimini (c)
Enrico: Rimini
Lucia: Galli-Curci
Edgardo: Schipa
Raimondo: V. Lazzari

December 24

Tosca
Same as Nov. 15

December 26

Manon
Grovlez (c)
Count: Payan
Des Grieux: Muratore
Manon: Mason
Lescaut: Maguenat
Guillot: Dua
De Brétigny: Defrère

December 27

The Jewels of the Madonna
Cimini (c)
Gennaro: Lamont
Carmela: Claessens
Maliella: Raisa
Rafaele: Rimini

December 28

Salome
Polacco (c)
Herod: Muratore
Herodias: Reynolds
Salome: Garden
Jochanaan: Dufranne
Narraboth: Mojica

December 29

The Barber of Seville
Ferrari (c)
Almaviva: Schipa
Bartolo: Trevisan
Rosina: Galli-Curci
Basilio: Lazzari
Figaro: Ballester
Berta: Claessens

December 30

The Love for Three Oranges
Prokofieff (c)
King of Trifle: Cotreuil
Prince: Mojica
Princess Clarice: Pavloska
Leandre: Beck
Trouffaldino: Dua
Pantalon: Defrère
Tchelio: Dufranne
Fata Morgana: Koshetz
Farfarello: Wolf

December 31 (mat.)

Thaïs
Grovlez (c)
Thaïs: Namara
Nicias: Martin
Athanael: Dufranne
Palemon: Nicolay

December 31

Carmen
Same as Nov. 26 except:
Micaela: Mason

January 1 (mat.)

Rigoletto
Same as Nov. 21 except:
Duke: Lamont
Gilda: Galli-Curci

January 2

The Jewels of the Madonna
Same as Dec. 27

January 3

Romeo and Juliet
Same as Dec. 22 except:
Grovlez (c)
Juliet: Galli-Curci

January 4

Le Jongleur de Notre-Dame
Same as Nov. 19

Ballet
Spandoni (c)

January 5

The Love for Three Oranges
Same as Dec. 30

January 6

Salome
Same as Dec. 28

January 7 (mat.)

Madama Butterfly
Same as Nov. 16 except:
Cio-Cio-San: Galli-Curci
Sharpless: Baklanoff

January 7

Tannhäuser
Same as Nov. 24

January 8

Pelléas et Mélisande
Polacco (c)
Mélisande: Garden
Geneviève: Claessens
Pelléas: Maguenat
Golaud: Dufranne
Arkel: Cotreuil

January 9

La Bohème
Same as Nov. 22 except:
Mimi: Galli-Curci
Musetta: McCormic

January 10

Thaïs
Same as Dec. 31 except:
Thaïs: Garden
Athanael: Cotreuil

January 11

Lakmé

Grovlez (c)
Gerald: Schipa
Frédéric: Maguenat
Nilakantha: Baklanoff
Lakmé: Galli-Curci
Mallika: Pavloska

January 12

L'Amore dei Tre Re

Same as Dec. 3

January 13

Tristan und Isolde

Polacco (c)
Tristan: Schubert
King Marke: Lankow
Isolde: Kottlar
Kurvenal: Beck
Melot: Defrère
Brangäne: Reynolds

January 14 (mat.)

I Pagliacci

Cimini (c)
Canio: Muratore
Nedda: Dux
Tonio: Schwarz

Ballet
Grove (c)

January 14

The Barber of Seville

Same as Dec. 29 except:
Rosina: Ivogün

January 16

Pelléas et Mélisande

Same as Jan. 8

January 17

Madama Butterfly

Same as Nov. 16 except:
Ferrari (c)
Cio-Cio-San: Galli-Curci
Sharpless: Baklanoff

January 18

Romeo and Juliet

Same as Dec. 22 except:
Grovlez (c)

January 19

The Girl of the Golden West

Polacco (c)
Minnie: Raisa
Dick Johnson: Lappas
Rance: Rimini
Ashby: Lazzari
Sonora: Dufranne

January 20

La Traviata

Same as Dec. 20

January 21

Louise

Grovlez (c)
Father: Baklanoff
Mother: Claessens
Louise: Garden
Julien: Lappas
King of Fools: Mojica

January 21

Tristan und Isolde

Same as Jan. 13 except:
King Marke: Wolf

1922–23

November 13

Aida

Polacco (c)
King: Cotreuil
Amneris: Bourskaya
Radames: Marshall
Aida: Raisa
Ramfis: V. Lazzari
Amonasro: Formichi

November 14

Carmen

Hageman (c)
Don José: Martin
Zuniga: Cotreuil
Carmen: Garden
Escamillo: Baklanoff
Micaela: McCormic

November 15

La Bohème

Panizza (c)
Mimi: Mason
Rodolfo: Minghetti
Marcello: Rimini
Colline: V. Lazzari
Musetta: Pavloska

November 16

Sniegurotchka

Hageman (c)
Sniegurotchka: Mason
Shepherd Lel: Bourskaya
Spring Fairy: Van Gordon
Czar Berendey: Minghetti
Mizguir: Baklanoff

November 18 (mat.)

L'Amore dei Tre Re

Polacco (c)
Fiora: Garden
Archibaldo: V. Lazzari
Manfredo: Baklanoff
Avito: Crimi
Flaminio: Oliviero

November 18

The Jewels of the Madonna

Cimini (c)
Gennaro: Lamont
Carmela: Claessens
Maliella: Raisa
Rafaele: Rimini

November 19 (mat.)

Parsifal

Panizza (c)
Amfortas: Oster
Titurel: Steschenko
Gurnemanz: Cotreuil
Parsifal: Lamont
Klingsor: Beck
Kundry: Van Gordon

November 20

Tosca

Panizza (c)
Tosca: Raisa
Cavaradossi: Crimi

Scarpia: Formichi
Angelotti: Defrère
Sacristan: Trevisan

November 21

Sniegurotchka
Same as Nov. 16

November 22

Il Trovatore
Polacco (c)
Leonora: Raisa
Count di Luna: Rimini
Manrico: Crimi
Azucena: Homer
Ferrando: V. Lazzari

November 23

Carmen
Same as Nov. 14

November 25 (mat.)

La Bohème
Same as Nov. 15 except:
Colline: Cotreuil

November 25

L'Amore dei Tre Re
Same as Nov. 18

November 27

Madama Butterfly
Polacco (c)
Cio-Cio-San: Mason
Suzuki: Pavloska
Pinkerton: Minghetti
Sharpless: Rimini

November 28

Aida
Same as Nov. 13

November 29

Sniegurotchka
Same as Nov. 16

November 30

Parsifal
Same as Nov. 19 except:
Amfortas: Schwarz

December 2 (mat.)

The Jewels of the Madonna
Same as Nov. 18 except:
Gennaro: Crimi

December 2

Carmen
Same as Nov. 14 except:
Carmen: Bourskaya

December 3 (mat.)

Die Walküre
Polacco (c)
Wotan: Baklanoff
Fricka: Claessens
Hunding: Steschenko
Sieglinde: Holst
Siegmund: Lamont
Brünnhilde: Van Gordon

December 4

Sniegurotchka
Same as Nov. 16

December 5

The Girl of the Golden West
Panizza (c)
Minnie: Raisa
Dick Johnson: Crimi
Rance: Rimini
Ashby: V. Lazzari
Sonora: Defrère

December 6

Rigoletto
Panizza (c)
Duke: Minghetti
Rigoletto: Formichi
Gilda: Mason
Sparafucile: V. Lazzari
Maddalena: Bourskaya

December 7

Aida
Same as Nov. 13 except:
Aida: Muzio

December 8

Il Trovatore
Same as Nov. 22

December 9 (mat.)

Die Walküre
Same as Dec. 3

December 9

Madama Butterfly
Same as Nov. 27 except:
Pinkerton: Crimi

December 11

Il Trovatore
Same as Nov. 22 except:
Leonora: Muzio

December 12

Rigoletto
Same as Dec. 6

December 13

Cavalleria Rusticana
Cimini (c)
Santuzza: McCormic
Turiddu: Lamont
Alfio: Defrère
Lola: Pavloska

I Pagliacci
Cimini (c)
Canio: Marshall
Nedda: Muzio
Tonio: Formichi

December 14

The Jewels of the Madonna
Same as Nov. 18 except:
Gennaro: Crimi

December 15

Lucia di Lammermoor
Cimini (c)
Enrico: Rimini
Lucia: Galli-Curci
Edgardo: Schipa
Raimondo: V. Lazzari

December 16 (mat.)

Rigoletto
Same as Dec. 6 except:
Polacco (c)

December 16

Tosca
Same as Nov. 20 except:
Tosca: Muzio
Scarpia: Baklanoff

December 18

Die Walküre
Same as Dec. 3

December 19

Mefistofele
Polacco (c)
Mefistofele: Chaliapin

Faust: Minghetti
Marguerite: Mason
Martha: Claessens
Helen: Holst
Pantalis: Pavloska

December 20

Aida
Same as Nov. 13 except:
Panizza (c)
Aida: Muzio

December 21

Madama Butterfly
Same as Nov. 27 except:
Panizza (c)
Cio-Cio-San: Galli-Curci
Pinkerton: Crimi

December 22

Mefistofele
Same as Dec. 19

December 23 (mat.)

Il Trovatore
Same as Nov. 22 except:
Panizza (c)
Azucena: Van Gordon

December 23

Cavalleria Rusticana
Same as Dec. 13

I Pagliacci
Same as Dec. 13 except:
Canio: Lamont

December 24 (mat.)

La Traviata
Polacco (c)
Violetta: Galli-Curci
Alfredo: Schipa
Germont: Rimini

December 25

Mefistofele
Same as Dec. 19 except:
Pantalis: Fitzhugh

December 26

La Bohème
Same as Nov. 15 except:
Mimi: Galli-Curci

December 27

Parsifal
Same as Nov. 19

December 28

Mefistofele
Same as Dec. 19

December 29

Manon
Hageman (c)
Count: Cotreuil
Des Grieux: Schipa
Manon: Galli-Curci
Lescaut: Defrère
Guillot: Mojica
De Brétigny: Beck

December 30 (mat.)

Mefistofele
Same as Dec. 19 except:
Pantalis: Fitzhugh

December 30

Lucia di Lammermoor
Same as Dec. 15 except:
Lucia: Macbeth
Edgardo: Lamont

December 31

La Juive
Panizza (c)
Cardinal: V. Lazzari
Léopold: Minghetti
Eudoxia: Passmore
Eléazar: Marshall
Rachel: Raisa

January 1

La Traviata
Same as Dec. 24

January 2

Il Trovatore
Same as Nov. 22 except:
Panizza (c)
Leonora: Muzio
Azucena: Van Gordon

January 3

The Barber of Seville
Cimini (c)
Almaviva: Schipa
Bartolo: Trevisan
Rosina: Galli-Curci
Basilio: Lazzari
Figaro: Rimini

January 4

La Juive
Same as Dec. 31 except:
Eudoxia: Mason

January 5

Samson and Delilah
Polacco (c)
Delilah: Homer
Samson: Marshall
High Priest: Formichi
Abimelech: Defrère
Old Hebrew: Cotreuil

January 6 (mat.)

La Forza del Destino
Panizza (c)
Leonora: Raisa
Carlo: Rimini
Alvaro: Crimi
Abbot: V. Lazzari
Melitone: Defrère
Preziosilla: Pavloska

January 6

Sniegurotchka
Same as Nov. 16

January 7 (mat.)

Rigoletto
Same as Dec. 6 except:
Duke: Schipa
Gilda: Galli-Curci

January 8

Samson and Delilah
Same as Jan. 5

January 9 (mat.)

Manon
Same as Dec. 29

January 10

L'Amore dei Tre Re
Same as Nov. 18

January 11

Martha
Hageman (c)
Lady Harriet: Mason
Nancy: Bourskaya
Lionel: Schipa
Plunkett: Rimini
Sir Tristan: Trevisan

January 12

Tosca
Same as Nov. 20 except:
Tosca: Garden
Scarpia: Baklanoff

January 13 (mat.)

La Traviata
Same as Dec. 24

January 13

Snowbird
Polacco (c)
Snowbird: McCormic
Hermit: Marshall
First Chieftain: Cotreuil

I Pagliacci
Same as Dec. 13 except:
Nedda: McCormic

January 14 (mat.)

Sniegurotchka
Same as Nov. 16

January 15

Carmen
Same as Nov. 14 except:
Polacco (c)
Don José: Crimi

January 16

La Forza del Destino
Same as Jan. 6

January 17

Martha
Same as Jan. 11

January 18

Tosca
Same as Nov. 20 except:
Tosca: Garden
Scarpia: Baklanoff

January 19—Grand Gala

I Pagliacci
Hageman (c)
Canio: Lamont
Nedda: McCormic
Tonio: Rimini
Beppe: Oliviero
Silvio: Defrère

Aida Act III
Panizza (c)
Radames: Marshall
Aida: Raisa
Amneris: Claessens
Amonasro: Formichi
Ramfis: Cotreuil

L'Amore dei Tre Re
Act II
Polacco (c)
Fiora: Garden
Archibaldo: Lazzari
Manfredo: Baklanoff
Avito: Crimi
Flamino: Oliviero

Mefistofele Act IV
Cimini (c)
Faust: Minghetti
Marguerite: Mason
Mefistofele: Steschenko

Die Walküre Act II
Second Half
Polacco (c)
Wotan: Baklanoff
Brünnhilde: Van Gordon

January 20 (mat.)

La Juive
Same as Dec. 31 except:
Eudoxia: Mason

January 20

Carmen
Same as Nov. 14 except:
Polacco (c)
Don José: Crimi

1923–24

November 8

Boris Godunov
Polacco (c)
Boris: Chaliapin
Feodor: Steckiewicz
Xenia: Maxwell
Prince Shuisky: Mojica
Gregory: Lamont
Pimenn: V. Lazzari
Varlaam: Cotreuil
Missail: Oliviero
Marina: Van Gordon
Nurse: Claessens

November 10 (mat.)

Samson and Delilah
Panizza (c)
Delilah: Homer
Samson: Ansseau
High Priest: Formichi
Abimelech: Defrère
Old Hebrew: Cotreuil

November 10

Lucia di Lammermoor
Cimini (c)
Enrico: Gandolfi
Lucia: Macbeth
Edgardo: Crimi
Raimondo: V. Lazzari

November 11

Boris Godunov
Same as Nov. 8

November 12

Faust
Polacco (c)
Faust: Ansseau
Méphistophélès: Baklanoff
Marguerite: Mason
Valentine: Defrère
Martha: Claessens
Siébel: Pavloska

November 13

La Juive
Panizza (c)
Cardinal: V. Lazzari
Léopold: Minghetti
Eudoxia: Macbeth
Eléazar: Marshall
Rachel: Raisa

November 14

Mefistofele
Polacco (c)
Mefistofele: Chaliapin
Faust: Crimi
Marguerite: Mason
Martha: Claessens

Helen: Van Gordon
Pantalis: Browne

November 15

Samson and Delilah
Same as Nov. 10

November 17 (mat.)

Mefistofele
Same as Nov. 14 except:
Faust: Minghetti
Helen: Sharlow

November 17

Il Trovatore
Cimini (c)
Leonora: Raisa
Count di Luna: Rimini
Manrico: Crimi
Azucena: Van Gordon
Ferrando: V. Lazzari

November 18

Siegfried
Stock (c)
Siegfried: Lamont
Mime: Steier
Der Wanderer: Kipnis
Alberich: Beck
Fafner: V. Lazzari
Erda: Meisle
Brünnhilde: Sharlow
Stimme des Waldvogels: Westen

November 19

Boris Godunov
Same as Nov. 8

November 20

Sniegurotchka
Cimini (c)
Spring Fairy: Fernanda
Sniegurotchka: Mason
Czar Berendey: Minghetti
Shepherd Lel: d'Hermanoy
Mizguir: Baklanoff

November 21

La Juive
Same as Nov. 13

November 22

Romeo and Juliet
Polacco (c)
Capulet: Beck
Juliet: Mason
Romeo: Hackett
Mercutio: Defrère
Stephano: Pavloska
Duke of Verona: Gandolfi
Friar Lawrence: Cotreuil

November 23

L'Africana
Panizza (c)
Don Pedro: Kipnis
Don Diego: Beck
Inez: Macbeth
Grand Inquisitor: Cotreuil
Vasco da Gama: Crimi
Selika: Raisa
Nelusco: Formichi
High Priest of Brahma: Kipnis

November 24 (mat.)

Siegfried
Same as Nov. 18

November 24

Mefistofele
Same as Nov. 14 except:
Faust: Minghetti
Helen: Sharlow

November 26

Manon
Panizza (c)
Count: Cotreuil
Des Grieux: Ansseau
Manon: Mason
Lescaut: Defrère
Guillot: Mojica
De Brétigny: Beck

November 27

Andrea Chénier
Polacco (c)
Andrea Chénier: Crimi
Gérard: Rimini
Madeleine: Muzio
Madelon: Meisle
Fleville: Trevisan
Dumas: Kipnis

November 28

Aida
Polacco (c)
King: Kipnis
Amneris: Homer
Radames: Marshall
Aida: Raisa
Ramfis: V. Lazzari
Amonasro: Formichi

November 29

Sniegurotchka
Same as Nov. 20

November 30

Carmen
Panizza (c)
Don José: Ansseau
Zuniga: Cotreuil
Carmen: Gentle
Escamillo: Baklanoff
Micaela: Maxwell

December 1 (mat.)

L'Africana
Same as Nov. 23

December 1

Rigoletto
Cimini (c)
Duke: Minghetti
Rigoletto: Rimini
Gilda: Macbeth
Sparafucile: V. Lazzari
Maddalena: Fernanda

December 3

Lakmé
Panizza (c)
Gerald: Errolle
Frédéric: Defrère
Nilakantha: Baklanoff
Lakmé: Galli-Curci
Mallika: Pavloska

December 4

Aida
Same as Nov. 28 except:
Amneris: Van Gordon

December 5

Manon
Same as Nov. 26

December 6

Andrea Chénier
Same as Nov. 27 except:
Gérard: Formichi

December 7

Dinorah
Panizza (c)
Hoël: Rimini

Dinorah: Galli-Curci
Corentino: Mojica
Huntsman: V. Lazzari

December 8 (mat.)

Hänsel und Gretel
St. Leger (c)
Hänsel: Pavloska
Gretel: Fabian
Witch: Claessens
Mother: Fernanda
Father: Beck

Followed by ballet

December 8

Carmen
Same as Nov. 30

December 9

Martha
Panizza (c)
Lady Harriet: Mason
Nancy: Pavloska
Lionel: Schipa
Plunkett: Rimini
Sir Tristan: Trevisan

December 10

La Juive
Same as Nov. 13

December 11

Monna Vanna
Polacco (c)
Guido: Baklanoff
Monna Vanna: Muzio
Marco: Cotreuil
Prinzivalle: Ansseau

December 12

La Traviata
Polacco (c)
Violetta: Galli-Curci
Alfredo: Schipa
Germont: Rimini

December 13

Otello
Panizza (c)
Otello: Marshall
Desdemona: Raisa
Iago: Rimini
Emilia: Claessens
Cassio: Mojica

December 15 (mat.)

Snowbird
Van Grove (c)
Snowbird: Maxwell
Hermit: Lamont
First Chieftain: Cotreuil

Maestro di Cappella
Van Grove (c)
Maestro: Trevisan
Geltrude: Sherwood

Cavalleria Rusticana
Cimini (c)
Santuzza: Raisa
Lola: Pavloska
Turridu: Crimi
Alfio: Rimini

December 15

Aida
Same as Nov. 28 except:
Amneris: Van Gordon
Radames: Lamont
Aida: Muzio

December 16

Lakmé
Same as Dec. 3 except:
Gerald: Schipa

December 17

L'Africana
Same as Nov. 23 except:
Vasco da Gama: Marshall

December 18

Dinorah
Same as Dec. 7

December 19

La Forza del Destino
Polacco (c)
Marquis: Kipnis
Leonora: Muzio
Don Carlo: Formichi
Alvaro: Crimi
Abbot: V. Lazzari
Melitone: Trevisan
Preziosilla: Meisle

December 20

Hänsel und Gretel
Same as Dec. 8

December 21

The Barber of Seville
Panizza (c)
Almaviva: Schipa
Bartolo: Trevisan
Rosina: Galli-Curci
Basilio: Arimondi
Figaro: Rimini
Bertha: Claessens

December 22 (mat.)

Otello
Same as Dec. 13

December 22

Cavalleria Rusticana
Same as Dec. 15 except:
Santuzza: Muzio
Alfio: Defrère

I Pagliacci
Cimini (c)
Canio: Ansseau
Nedda: Sharlow
Tonio: Formichi

December 23

Lucia di Lammermoor
Same as Nov. 10 except:
Lucia: Galli-Curci
Edgardo: Schipa

December 24

Louise
Polacco (c)
Father: Baklanoff
Mother: Claessens
Louise: Garden
Julien: Ansseau
King of Fools: Mojica

December 25

Die Königskinder
Van Grove (c)
King's Son: C. Hart
Goose Girl: Dux
Fiddler: Gandolfi
Witch: Fernanda
Wood Cutter: Kipnis

December 26 (mat.)

Hänsel und Gretel
Same as Dec. 8

December 26

Monna Vanna
Same as Dec. 11

December 27

La Traviata
Same as Dec. 12

December 28

Cléopâtre
Panizza (c)
Marc Antoine: Baklanoff
Spakos: Defrère
Ennius: Cotreuil
Cléopâtre: Garden

December 29 (mat.)

Dinorah
Same as Dec. 7

December 29

La Juive
Same as Nov. 13 except:
Cardinal: Kipnis
Eudoxia: Westen

December 30

Carmen
Same as Nov. 30 except:
Polacco (c)
Carmen: Garden

December 31

Rigoletto
Same as Dec. 1 except:
Polacco (c)
Duke: Piccaver
Rigoletto: Schwarz
Maddalena: Meisle

January 1

Thaïs
Panizza (c)
Thaïs: Garden
Nicias: Mojica
Athanael: Cotreuil
Palemon: Kipnis

January 2 (mat.)

Sniegurotchka
Same as Nov. 20 except:
Sniegurotchka: Obrassova

January 2

Otello
Same as Dec. 13 except:
Iago: Schwarz

January 3

Louise
Same as Dec. 24

January 4

Romeo and Juliet
Same as Nov. 22 except:
Cimini (c)
Juliet: Galli-Curci

January 5 (mat.)

Le Jongleur de Notre-Dame
Polacco (c)
Jean: Garden
Boniface: Cotreuil
Prior: Kipnis

January 5

Die Königskinder
Same as Dec. 25

January 6

La Forza del Destino
Same as Dec. 19

January 7

La Sonnambula
Cimini (c)
Count Rodolfo: V. Lazzari
Teresa: Claessens
Amina: Pareto
Elvino: Schipa

January 8

Samson and Delilah
Same as Nov. 10 except:
Polacco (c)
Samson: Marshall

January 9 (mat.)

Hänsel und Gretel
Same as Dec. 8 except:
Van Grove (c)

January 9

Cléopâtre
Same as Dec. 28

January 10

Cavalleria Rusticana
Same as Dec. 15 except:
Turridu: Piccaver
Alfio: Defrère

I Pagliacci
Same as Dec. 22 except:
Nedda: Dux

January 11

Aida
Same as Nov. 28 except:
Cimini (c)
Amneris: Van Gordon
Aida: Muzio

January 12 (mat.)

Martha
Same as Dec. 9 except:
Lady Harriet: Pareto

January 12

Thaïs
Same as Jan. 1

January 13

Rigoletto
Same as Dec. 1 except:
Duke: Piccaver
Rigoletto: Baklanoff
Maddalena: Meisle

January 14

La Forza del Destino
Same as Dec. 19

January 15

Lucia di Lammermoor
Same as Nov. 10 except:
Lucia: Paggi
Edgardo: Schipa

January 16 (mat.)

Il Trovatore
Same as Nov. 17 except:
Manrico: Lamont

January 16

Le Jongleur de Notre-Dame
Same as Jan. 5

January 17

Martha
Same as Dec. 9 except:
Lady Harriet: Pareto

January 18

Mefistofele
Same as Nov. 14 except:
Faust: Minghetti
Marguerite: Muzio

January 19 (mat.)

Louise
Same as Dec. 24

January 19

Hänsel und Gretel
Same as Dec. 8

January 20 (mat.)

The Barber of Seville
Same as Dec. 21 except:
Rosina: Pareto
Basilio: Chaliapin

January 21

Cléopâtre
Same as Dec. 28

January 22

Boris Godunov
Same as Nov. 8

January 23 (mat.)

Lucia di Lammermoor
Same as Nov. 10 except:
Lucia: Paggi
Edgardo: Lamont

January 23

Lakmé
Same as Dec. 3 except:
Gerald: Schipa
Lakmé: Pareto

January 24

Carmen
Same as Nov. 30 except:
Carmen: Garden

January 26 (mat.)

La Traviata
Panizza (c)
Violetta: Muzio
Alfredo: Hackett
Germont: Rimini

January 26

Martha
Same as Dec. 9 except:
Cimini (c)
Lady Harriet: Macbeth
Plunkett: V. Lazzari

1924–25

November 5

La Gioconda
Polacco (c)
La Gioconda: Raisa
La Cieca: Meisle
Alvise: Kipnis
Laura: Perini
Enzo: Cortis
Barnaba: Formichi

November 6

Tosca
Moranzoni (c)
Tosca: Muzio
Cavaradossi: Hackett
Scarpia: Stabile
Angelotti: Nicolich

November 7

Le Prophète
Moranzoni (c)
John: Marshall
Fidès: Homer
Bertha: Forrai
Jonas: Dneproff
Matthisen: Cotreuil
Zacharias: Kipnis

November 8 (mat.)

The Pearl Fishers
Polacco (c)
Leila: Pareto
Nadir: Hackett
Zurga: Rimini
Nourabad: Cotreuil

November 8

Aida
Moranzoni (c)
King: Kipnis
Amneris: Lenska
Radames: Marshall
Aida: Raisa
Ramfis: V. Lazzari
Amonasro: Formichi

November 10

Lucia di Lammermoor
Polacco (c)
Enrico: Stabile
Lucia: Dal Monte
Edgardo: Cortis
Raimondo: V. Lazzari

November 11

Tannhäuser
Weber (c)
Hermann: Kipnis
Elizabeth: Raisa
Tannhäuser: Lamont
Wolfram: Schwarz
Walther: Dneproff
Venus: Van Gordon
Young Shepherd: Swarthout

November 12

Samson and Delilah
Polacco (c)
Delilah: Homer
Samson: Marshall
High Priest: Formichi
Abimelech: Defrère
Old Hebrew: Cotreuil

November 13

La Bohème
Moranzoni (c)
Mimi: McCormic
Rudolfo: Cortis
Marcello: Rimini

Colline: V. Lazzari
Musetta: Taylor

November 14

Rigoletto
Polacco (c)
Duke: Hackett
Rigoletto: Schwarz
Gilda: Dal Monte
Sparafucile: V. Lazzari
Maddalena: Perini

November 15 (mat.)

La Gioconda
Same as Nov. 5 except:
Laura: Van Gordon

November 15

Tosca
Same as Nov. 6 except:
Cavaradossi: Lamont

November 16 (mat.)

Cavalleria Rusticana
Cimini (c)
Santuzza: Raisa
Lola: Perini
Turiddu: Lamont
Alfio: Defrère

I Pagliacci
Moranzoni (c)
Canio: Ansseau
Nedda: McCormic
Tonio: Formichi

November 17

Le Prophète
Same as Nov. 7

November 18

The Pearl Fishers
Same as Nov. 8

November 19

Il Trovatore
Cimini (c)
Leonora: Muzio
Count di Luna: Rimini
Manrico: Lamont
Azucena: Homer
Ferrando: V. Lazzari

November 20

Lucia di Lammermoor
Same as Nov. 10

November 22 (mat.)

Madama Butterfly
Polacco (c)
Cio-Cio-San: Mason
Suzuki: Perini
Pinkerton: Hackett
Sharpless: Rimini

November 22

La Bohème
Same as Nov. 13

November 23 (mat.)

Aida
Same as Nov. 8

November 23

Aida
Polacco (c)
King: Nicolich
Amneris: Van Gordon
Radames: Lamont
Aida: Muzio
Ramfis: Cotreuil
Amonasro: Rimini

November 24

Thaïs
Moranzoni (c)
Thaïs: Garden
Nicias: Mojica
Athanael: Schwarz
Palemon: Kipnis

November 25

Cavalleria Rusticana
Same as Nov. 16 except:
Turiddu: Piccaver

I Pagliacci
Same as Nov. 16

November 26

The Pearl Fishers
Same as Nov. 8

November 27

Tannhäuser
Same as Nov. 11 except:
Elizabeth: Forrai

November 28

Werther
Polacco (c)
Werther: Ansseau
Bailiff: Cotreuil
Charlotte: Garden
Sophie: Freund
Albert: Kipnis

November 29 (mat.)

Tosca
Same as Nov. 6 except:
Cavaradossi: Piccaver

November 29

Samson and Delilah
Same as Nov. 12 except:
Van Grove (c)
Delilah: Van Gordon

November 30 (mat.)

La Gioconda
Same as Nov. 5

December 1

Madama Butterfly
Same as Nov. 22

December 2

La Traviata
Cimini (c)
Violetta: Muzio
Alfredo: Schipa
Germont: Schwarz

December 3

Carmen
Polacco (c)
Don José: Ansseau
Zuniga: Cotreuil
Carmen: Garden
Escamillo: Rimini
Micaela: McCormic

December 4

La Juive
Cimini (c)
Cardinal: V. Lazzari
Léopold: Boscacci
Eudoxia: Macbeth
Eléazar: Marshall
Rachel: Raisa

December 5

Faust
St. Leger (c)
Faust: Hackett
Méphistophélès: Chaliapin
Marguerite: McCormic
Valentine: Defrère

Martha: Claessens
Siébel: Swarthout

December 6 (mat.)

Werther
Same as Nov. 28

December 6

Il Trovatore
Same as Nov. 19 except:
Count di Luna: Formichi
Azucena: Lenska

December 7 (mat.)

The Barber of Seville
Cimini (c)
Almaviva: Schipa
Bartolo: Trevisan
Rosina: Pareto
Basilio: Chaliapin
Figaro: Rimini

December 7

Cavalleria Rusticana
Same as Nov. 16 except:
Lola: Swarthout
Turiddu: Piccaver

I Pagliacci
Same as Nov. 16 except:
Canio: Marshall
Nedda: Forrai

December 8

Tannhäuser
Same as Nov. 11 except:
Elizabeth: Forrai

December 9

Mefistofele
Moranzoni (c)
Mefistofele: Chaliapin
Faust: Cortis
Marguerite: Muzio
Martha: Claessens
Helen: Van Gordon
Pantalis: Swarthout
Nereus: Mojica

December 10

Rigoletto
Same as Nov. 14 except:
Weber (c)
Duke: Piccaver
Gilda: Macbeth

December 11

Lakmé
Lauwers (c)
Gerald: Schipa
Frédéric: Defrère
Nilakantha: Cotreuil
Lakmé: Pareto
Mallika: d'Hermanoy

December 12

Carmen
Same as Dec. 3 except:
Micaela: Westen

December 13 (mat.)

The Jewels of the Madonna
Cimini (c)
Gennaro: Lamont
Carmela: Claessens
Maliella: Raisa
Rafaele: Rimini

December 13

La Traviata
Same as Dec. 2 except:
Violetta: Pareto

December 14 (mat.)

Le Jongleur de Notre-Dame
Polacco (c)
Jean: Garden
Boniface: Cotreuil
Prior: Kipnis

December 15

Aida
Same as Nov. 8

December 16

L'Amore dei Tre Re
Polacco (c)
Fiora: Garden
Archibaldo: V. Lazzari
Manfredo: Baklanoff
Avito: Ansseau
Flaminio: Oliviero

December 17

Tosca
Same as Nov. 6 except:
Cavaradossi: Piccaver
Scarpia: Baklanoff

December 18

Thaïs
Same as Nov. 24

December 19

Fra Diavolo
Cimini (c)
Fra Diavolo: Schipa
Roeburg: Cotreuil
Pamela: Perini
Zerlina: Mason

December 20 (mat.)

La Juive
Same as Dec. 4

December 20

The Pearl Fishers
Same as Nov. 8

December 21 (mat.)

Tannhäuser
Same as Nov. 11 except:
Elizabeth: Forrai

December 22

La Traviata
Same as Dec. 2

December 23

Lakmé
Same as Dec. 11 except:
Nilakantha: Baklanoff

December 24

Louise
Polacco (c)
Father: Baklanoff
Mother: Claessens
Louise: Garden
Julien: Ansseau

December 25

The Barber of Seville
Same as Dec. 7 except:
Rosina: Hidalgo

December 26

Otello
Moranzoni (c)
Otello: Marshall
Desdemona: Raisa
Iago: Schwarz
Emilia: Claessens
Cassio: Mojica

December 27 (mat.)

The Barber of Seville
Same as Dec. 7 except:
Rosina: Hidalgo

December 27

Thaïs
Same as Nov. 24 except:
Athanael: Cotreuil
Palemon: Nicolich

December 28 (mat.)

Hänsel und Gretel
St. Leger (c)
Hänsel: Orens
Gretel: Derzbach
Witch: Claessens
Mother: Lenska
Father: Beck

Followed by ballet

December 29

L'Amore dei Tre Re
Same as Dec. 16

December 30 (mat.)

Aida
Same as Nov. 8 except:
Weber (c)
King: Nicolich
Radames: Lamont
Aida: Taylor
Ramfis: Cotreuil

December 30

Fra Diavolo
Same as Dec. 19

Followed by ballet

December 31

Mefistofele
Same as Dec. 9 except:
Pantalis: Perini

January 1

The Jewels of the Madonna
Same as Dec. 13

January 2 (mat.)

Aida
Same as Nov. 8 except:
Van Grove (c)
King: Nicolich
Radames: Lamont
Aida: Taylor
Ramfis: Cotreuil

January 2

The Tales of Hoffmann
Van Grove (c)
Olympia: Macbeth
Giulietta: Forrai
Antonia: Forrai
Niclaus: D'Hermanoy
Hoffmann: Ansseau
Coppelius: Schwarz
Dapertutto: Schwarz
Miracle: Schwarz

January 3 (mat.)

Lakmé
Same as Dec. 11 except:
Nilakantha: Baklanoff
Lakmé: Hidalgo

January 3

La Gioconda
Same as Nov. 5

January 4 (mat.)

Madama Butterfly
Same as Nov. 22

January 5

Tosca
Same as Nov. 6 except:
Cavaradossi: Ansseau
Scarpia: Baklanoff

January 6

La Bohème
Same as Nov. 13 except:
Mimi: Mason
Rudolfo: Hackett
Musetta: Swarthout

January 7 (mat.)

Aida
Same as Nov. 8 except:
Aida: Muzio
Ramfis: Cotreuil

January 7

Lucia di Lammermoor
Cimini (c)
Enrico: Rimini
Lucia: Macbeth
Edgardo: Schipa
Raimondo: V. Lazzari

January 8

Le Jongleur de Notre-Dame
Same as Dec. 14

January 9

La Traviata
Same as Dec. 2 except:
Gaston: Oliviero

January 10 (mat.)

Il Trovatore
Same as Nov. 19

January 10

Rigoletto
Weber (c)
Rigoletto: Formichi
Gilda: Macbeth
Sparafucile: Cotreuil
Maddalena: Meisle
Duke: Hackett

January 11 (mat.)

Louise
Same as Dec. 24

January 12

Samson and Delilah
Same as Nov. 12

January 13

Rigoletto
Same as Jan. 10

January 14 (mat.)

Otello
Same as Dec. 26

January 14

Martha
Moranzoni (c)
Lady Harriet: Mason
Nancy: Perini
Lionel: Schipa
Plunkett: V. Lazzari
Tristan: Trevisan

January 15

Werther
Same as Nov. 28

January 16
Boris Godunov
Polacco (c)
Boris Godunov: Chaliapin
Feodor: Swarthout
Xenia: Kerr
Shuisky: Mojica
Gregory: Cortis
Pimenn: V. Lazzari
Varlaam: Cotreuil
Missail: Oliviero
Marina: Van Gordon
Nurse: Claessens

January 17 (mat.)
L'Amore dei Tre Re
Same as Dec. 16

January 17
Hänsel und Gretel
Same as Dec. 28
Followed by ballet

January 18 (mat.)
Romeo and Juliet
Polacco (c)
Capulet: Formichi
Juliet: Mason
Romeo: Hackett
Mercutio: Defrère
Stephano: Swarthout
Duke: Nicolich
Friar: Cotreuil

January 18
Aida
Same as Nov. 8 except:
Weber (c)
Radames: Lamont
Amonasro: Baklanoff

January 19
Mefistofele
Same as Dec. 9 except:
Helen: Lenska
Pantalis: Perini

January 20
Martha
Same as Jan. 14

January 21
Pelléas et Mélisande
Polacco (c)
Mélisande: Garden
Geneviève: Claessens
Yniold: Freund
Pelléas: Mojica
Golaud: Baklanoff
Arkel: Kipnis

January 22 (mat.)
Lucia di Lammermoor
Same as Nov. 10 except:
Cimini (c)
Enrico: Rimini
Lucia: Hidalgo

January 22
Faust
Same as Dec. 5 except:
Marguerite: Mason

January 23—Grand Gala
La Gioconda Act IV
Moranzoni (c)
Gioconda: Raisa
Laura: Van Gordon
Enzo: Cortis
Barnaba: Formichi

La Traviata Act IV
Cimini (c)
Violetta: Muzio
Alfredo: Schipa
Germont: Beck

Monna Vanna Act II
Polacco (c)
Prinzivalle: Ansseau
Monna Vanna: Garden

Romeo and Juliet Act I
Polacco (c)
Capulet: Formichi
Juliet: Mason
Romeo: Hackett
Mercutio: Defrère

January 24 (mat.)
Boris Godunov
Same as Jan. 16 except:
Marina: Lenska

January 24
The Tales of Hoffmann
Same as Jan. 2 except:
Lauwers (c)

1925–26

November 3
Der Rosenkavalier
Polacco (c)
Princess: Raisa
Baron Ochs: Kipnis
Octavian: Forrai
Faninal: Beck
Sophie: Mason
Marianne: D'Hermanoy
Valzacchi: Oliviero
Annina: Pavloska
Italian Singer: Cortis

November 4
Manon Lescaut
Moranzoni (c)
Manon Lescaut: Muzio
Lescaut: Rimini
Des Grieux: Cortis
Geronte: Cotreuil

November 5
Carmen
Grovlez (c)
Don José: Ansseau
November 5
Zuniga: Cotreuil
Carmen: D'Alvarez
Escamillo: Rimini
Micaela: Kerr

November 7 (mat.)
Un Ballo in Maschera
Polacco (c)
Riccardo: Marshall
Renato: Steel
Amelia: Raisa
Ulrica: Van Gordon
Oscar: Shear

November 7

Rigoletto
Weber (c)
Duke: Hackett
Rigoletto: Formichi
Gilda: Mason
Sparafucile: Cotreuil
Maddalena: Nadworney

November 8

La Traviata
Moranzoni (c)
Violetta: Muzio
Alfredo: Cortis
Germont: Bonelli

November 9

Martha
Moranzoni (c)
Lady Harriet: Mason
Nancy: Pavloska
Lionel: Schipa
Plunkett: V. Lazzari
Tristan: Trevisan

November 10

Aida
Polacco (c)
King: Kipnis
Amneris: Van Gordon
Radames: Marshall
Aida: Raisa
Ramfis: V. Lazzari
Amonasro: Formichi

November 11

Cavalleria Rusticana
Weber (c)
Santuzza: Sawyer
Lola: Pavloska
Turiddu: Lamont
Alfio: Torti

I Pagliacci
Moranzoni (c)
Canio: Ansseau
Nedda: Forrai
Tonio: Steel

November 12

Il Trovatore
Weber (c)
Leonora: Muzio
di Luna: Bonelli
Manrico: Cortis
Azucena: Homer
Ferrando: V. Lazzari

November 13

Der Rosenkavalier
Same as Nov. 3

November 14 (mat.)

La Traviata
Same as Nov. 8 except:
Alfredo: Hackett
Germont: Steel

November 14

Tosca
Moranzoni (c)
Tosca: Fitziu
Cavaradossi: Ansseau
Scarpia: Formichi
Angelotti: Nicolich
Sacristan: Trevisan

November 15 (mat.)

Samson and Delilah
Weber (c)
Delilah: Homer
Samson: Marshall
High Priest: Formichi
Abimelech: Defrère
Old Hebrew: Cotreuil

November 15

Il Trovatore
Same as Nov. 12 except:
Leonora: Raisa
Azucena: Lenska

November 16

Manon Lescaut
Same as Nov. 4

November 17

Faust
Grovlez (c)
Faust: Hackett
Méphistophélès: V. Lazzari
Marguerite: Mason
Valentine: Bonelli
Martha: Claessens
Siébel: Pavloska

November 18

Un Ballo in Maschera
Same as Nov. 7

November 19

Rigoletto
Same as Nov. 7 except:
Gilda: Melius

November 21 (mat.)

Martha
Same as Nov. 9

November 21

Il Trovatore
Same as Nov. 12 except:
Azucena: Lenska

November 22

Carmen
Same as Nov. 5

November 23

Cavalleria Rusticana
Same as Nov. 11

I Pagliacci
Moranzoni (c)
Canio: Cortis
Nedda: Fitziu
Tonio: Steel

November 24

Andrea Chénier
Polacco (c)
Andrea Chénier: Cortis
Gérard: Formichi
Madeleine: Muzio
Madelon: Lenska

November 25

Faust
Same as Nov. 17 except:
Valentine: Defrère

November 26

Otello
Moranzoni (c)
Otello: Marshall
Desdemona: Sawyer
Iago: Bonelli
Emilia: Claessens
Cassio: Mojica

November 27

The Barber of Seville
Moranzoni (c)
Almaviva: Hackett

Bartolo: Trevisan
Rosina: Dal Monte
Basilio: V. Lazzari
Figaro: Rimini

November 28 (mat.)

Der Rosenkavalier
Same as Nov. 3 except:
Italian Singer: Ritch

November 28

La Traviata
Same as Nov. 8 except:
Violetta: Melius
Germont: Steel

November 29 (mat.)

Madama Butterfly
Polacco (c)
Cio-Cio-San: Raisa
Suzuki: Pavloska
Pinkerton: Hackett
Sharpless: Rimini

November 29

Carmen
Same as Nov. 5 except:
Don José: Cortis

November 30

Hérodiade
Grovlez (c)
John: Ansseau
Herod: Bonelli
Phanuel: Cotreuil
Salome: Mason
Hérodiade: Van Gordon

December 1

Samson and Delilah
Same as Nov. 15 except:
Delilah: D'Alvarez

December 2

Tosca
Same as Nov. 14 except:
Tosca: Raisa
Cavaradossi: Hackett
Scarpia: Baklanoff

December 3

Die Walküre
Polacco (c)
Wotan: Kipnis
Fricka: Lenska
Hunding: Cotreuil
Sieglinde: Forrai
Siegmund: Lamont
Brünnhilde: Van Gordon

December 5 (mat.)

Andrea Chénier
Same as Nov. 24 except:
Andrea Chénier: Marshall

December 5

Martha
Same as Nov. 9 except:
Lady Harriet: Macbeth

December 6 (mat.)

Der Rosenkavalier
Same as Nov. 3 except:
Faninal: Preston
Italian Singer: Ritch

December 7

Boris Godunov
Polacco (c)
Boris Godunov: Baklanoff
Feodor: Shear
Xenia: Kerr
Prince Shuisky: Mojica
Gregory: Cortis
Pimenn: V. Lazzari
Varlaam: Cotreuil
Missail: Oliviero
Marina: Van Gordon
Nurse: Claessens

December 8

Lucia di Lammermoor
St. Leger (c)
Enrico: Bonelli
Lucia: Dal Monte
Edgardo: Schipa
Raimondo: V. Lazzari

December 9

La Traviata
Same as Nov. 8 except:
Alfredo: Schipa

December 10

Madama Butterfly
Same as Nov. 29

December 11

I Pagliacci
Same as Nov. 11 except:
Nedda: Muzio
Tonio: Formichi

Namiko-San
Franchetti (c)
Yiro Danyemon: Bonelli
Namiko-San: Miura
Yasui: Ritch
Sato: Trevisan

December 12 (mat.)

Falstaff
Polacco (c)
Falstaff: Rimini
Ford: Steel
Mistress Ford: Raisa
Anne: Mason
Mistress Page: Pavloska
Mistress Quickly: Claessens
Fenton: Hackett

December 12

Aida
Same as Nov. 10 except:
Weber (c)
King: Nicolich
Amneris: Lenska
Aida: Muzio
Ramfis: Cotreuil

December 13 (mat.)

Die Walküre
Same as Dec. 3

December 13

Martha
Same as Nov. 9

December 14

Un Ballo in Maschera
Same as Nov. 7 except:
Ulrica: Lenska

December 15

Werther
Polacco (c)
Werther: Ansseau
Bailiff: Cotreuil
Charlotte: Garden
Sophia: Freund
Albert: Kipnis

December 16

The Barber of Seville
Same as Nov. 27 except:
Rosina: Melius

December 17

Andrea Chénier
Same as Nov. 24 except:
Andrea Chénier: Marshall

December 19 (mat.)

Carmen
Same as Nov. 5 except:
Carmen: Garden
Escamillo: Baklanoff

December 19

Lucia di Lammermoor
Same as Dec. 8 except:
Edgardo: Cortis

December 20

Aida
Same as Nov. 10 except:
Weber (c)
Amneris: Lenska

December 21

Il Trovatore
Same as Nov. 12 except:
Azucena: Van Gordon

December 22

Boris Godunov
Same as Dec. 7

December 23

Werther
Same as Dec. 15

December 24

Cavalleria Rusticana
Same as Nov. 11 except:
Santuzza: Muzio
Alfio: Defrére

Namiko-San
Same as Dec. 11

December 26 (mat.)

A Light from St. Agnes
Harling (c)
Toinette: Raisa
Michel: Baklanoff
Père Bertrand: Lamont

I Pagliacci
Same as Nov. 11 except:
Nedda: Muzio
Tonio: Formichi

December 26

Faust
Same as Nov. 17 except:
Valentine: Defrère

December 27 (mat.)

Namiko-San
Same as Dec. 11

I Pagliacci
Moranzoni (c)
Canio: Cortis
Nedda: Muzio
Tonio: Formichi

December 28

Otello
Same as Nov. 26 except:
Desdemona: Fitziu

December 29

Tosca
Same as Nov. 14 except:
Tosca: Muzio
Cavaradossi: Cortis
Scarpia: Baklanoff

December 30

Aida
Same as Nov. 10

December 31

Resurrection
Moranzoni (c)
Dimitri: Ansseau
Caterina: Garden
Anna: Claessens
Fedia: Freund
Simonson: Baklanoff

January 2 (mat.)

Manon Lescaut
Same as Nov. 4 except:
Lescaut: Defrère

January 2

Madama Butterfly
Same as Nov. 29 except:
Cio-Cio-San: Mason

January 3

Hänsel und Gretel
St. Leger (c)
Hänsel: Pavloska
Gretel: Shear
Witch: Claessens
Mother: Lenska
Father: Preston

Followed by ballet
Grovlez (c)

January 4

Rigoletto
Same as Nov. 7 except:
Gilda: Dal Monte
Sparafucile: V. Lazzari

January 5

Pelléas et Mélisande
Polacco (c)
Mélisande: Garden
Geneviève: Claessens
Yniold: Freund
Pelléas: Mojica
Golaud: Baklanoff
Arkel: Kipnis

January 6

Resurrection
Same as Dec. 31

January 7

Tosca
Same as Nov. 14 except:
Tosca: Raisa
Cavaradossi: Cortis
Scarpia: Baklanoff

January 8

Andrea Chénier
Same as Nov. 24 except:
Andrea Chénier: Marshall

January 9 (mat.)

Hérodiade
Same as Nov. 30

January 9

Hänsel und Gretel
Same as Jan. 3

January 10

Martha
Same as Nov. 9

January 11

Resurrection
Same as Dec. 31

January 12

Lohengrin
Weber (c)
Henry: Kipnis
Lohengrin: Lamont
Elsa: Fitziu
Telramund: Baklanoff
Ortrud: Lenska
King's Herald: Defrère

January 13

Falstaff
Same as Dec. 12

January 14

Louise
Polacco (c)
Father: Baklanoff
Mother: Claessens
Louise: Garden
Julien: Ansseau
King of Fools: Mojica

January 15

La Juive
Weber (c)
Cardinal: Kipnis
Léopold: Mojica
Eudoxia: Mason
Eléazar: Marshall
Rachel: Raisa

January 16 (mat.)

Faust
Same as Nov. 17

January 16

Carmen
Same as Nov. 5 except:
Carmen: Garden
Escamillo: Kipnis
Micaela: Freund

January 17 (mat.)

Lohengrin
Same as Jan. 12 except:
Elsa: Forrai

January 17

Madama Butterfly
Same as Nov. 29

January 18

The Barber of Seville
Same as Nov. 27 except:
Rosina: Garrison

January 19

Resurrection
Same as Dec. 31

January 20

Otello
Same as Nov. 26 except:
Desdemona: Fitziu
Iago: Ruffo

January 21

La Traviata
Same as Nov. 8 except:
Alfredo: Schipa

January 22–Grand Gala

Andrea Chénier Act III
Polacco (c)
Andrea Chénier: Cortis
Gérard: Formichi
Madeleine: Muzio
Madelon: Lenska

Romeo and Juliet Act II
Polacco (c)
Juliet: Garden
Romeo: Ansseau

La Bohème Act I
Moranzoni (c)
Mimi: Mason
Rodolfo: Cortis
Marcello: Rimini
Colline: V. Lazzari

Un Ballo in Maschera Act II
Polacco (c)
Riccardo: Marshall
Renato: Steel
Amelia: Raisa

January 23 (mat.)

Resurrection
Same as Dec. 31

January 23

The Barber of Seville
Same as Nov. 27 except:
Almaviva: Schipa
Rosina: Garrison

1926–27

November 8

Aida
Polacco (c)
King: Kipnis
Amneris: Van Gordon
Radames: Lindi
Aida: Muzio
Ramfis: V. Lazzari
Amonasro: Formichi

November 9

The Jewels of the Madonna
Moranzoni (c)
Gennaro: Lamont
Carmela: Lenska
Maliella: Raisa
Rafaele: Rimini

November 10

La Bohème
Polacco (c)
Mimi: Mason
Rodolfo: Cortis
Marcello: Montesanto
Colline: V. Lazzari
Musetta: Pavloska

November 11

Resurrection
Moranzoni (c)
Dimitri: Ansseau
Caterina: Garden
Anna: Claessens
Fedia: Freund
Simonson: Formichi

November 12

Tristan und Isolde
Polacco (c)
Tristan: Marshall
King Mark: Kipnis
Isolde: Alsen
Kurvenal: Bonelli
Melot: Defrère
Brangäne: Van Gordon

November 13 (mat.)

Rigoletto
Moranzoni (c)
Duke: Hackett
Rigoletto: Montesanto
Gilda: Norena
Sparafucile: V. Lazzari
Maddalena: Jackson

November 13

Il Trovatore
Weber (c)
Leonora: Loring
Count: Polese
Manrico: Lindi
Azucena: Lenska
Ferrando: Nicolich

November 14 (mat.)

Carmen
Polacco (c)
Don José: Ansseau
Zuniga: Cotreuil
Carmen: Garden
Escamillo: Rimini
Micaela: Mason

November 15

Lucia di Lammermoor
St. Leger (c)
Enrico: Bonelli
Lucia: Dal Monte
Edgardo: Cortis
Raimondo: Cotreuil

November 16

Aida
Same as Nov. 8 except:
Radames: Marshall
Aida: Raisa

November 17

L'Amore dei Tre Re
Moranzoni (c)
Fiora: Garden
Archibaldo: V. Lazzari
Manfredo: Rimini
Avito: Ansseau
Flaminio: Oliviero

November 18

Daughter of the Regiment
St. Leger (c)
Maria: Dal Monte
Sulpizio: Cotreuil
Tonio: Hackett
Marchioness: Claessens
Ortensio: Trevisan

Followed by ballet

November 19

La Juive
Weber (c)
Cardinal: Kipnis
Léopold: Mojica
Eudoxia: Norena
Eléazar: Marshall
Rachel: Raisa

November 20 (mat.)

Resurrection
Same as Nov. 11

November 20

Rigoletto
Same as Nov. 13 except:
Weber (c)
Rigoletto: Bonelli
Sparafucile: Cotreuil

November 21

Lucia di Lammermoor
Same as Nov. 15 except:
Enrico: Polese

November 22

Carmen
Same as Nov. 14

November 23

Il Trovatore
Same as Nov. 13 except:
Leonora: Muzio
Count: Bonelli
Ferrando: V. Lazzari

November 24

Daughter of the Regiment
Same as Nov. 18

November 25

Samson and Delilah
Weber (c)
Delilah: Van Gordon
Samson: Marshall
High Priest: Formichi
Abimelech: Polese
Old Hebrew: Cotreuil

November 27 (mat.)

La Cena delle Beffe
Polacco (c)
Giannetto: Cortis
Neri: Montesanto
Gabriello: Ritch
Il Tornaquinci: Polese
Ginevra: Muzio
Lisabetta: Norena

November 27

Resurrection
Same as Nov. 11

November 28 (mat.)

The Jewels of the Madonna
Same as Nov. 9

November 29

Tristan und Isolde
Same as Nov. 12

November 30

L'Amore dei Tre Re
Same as Nov. 17

December 1

La Juive
Same as Nov. 19 except:
Eudoxia: Mason

December 2

The Barber of Seville
Moranzoni (c)
Almaviva: Hackett
Bartolo: Trevisan
Rosina: Dal Monte
Basilio: V. Lazzari
Figaro: Bonelli

December 3

Cavalleria Rusticana
Moranzoni (c)
Santuzza: Raisa
Lola: Jackson
Turiddu: Lindi
Alfio: Defrère

I Pagliacci
Weber (c)
Canio: Ansseau
Nedda: Norena
Tonio: Formichi

December 4 (mat.)

La Bohème
Same as Nov. 10

December 4

Daughter of the Regiment
Same as Nov. 18

December 5 (mat.)

Aida
Same as Nov. 8 except:
Sabino (c)
Ramfis: Cotreuil
Amonasro: Rimini

December 6

La Cena delle Beffe
Same as Nov. 27

December 7

La Sonnambula
Moranzoni (c)
Rodolfo: V. Lazzari
Teresa: Claessens
Amina: Dal Monte
Elvino: Schipa

December 8

A Witch of Salem
Weber (c)
Arnold Talbot: Hackett
Thomas Bowen: Cotreuil
Deacon Fairfield: Mojica
Claris Willoughby: Norena
Elizabeth Willoughby: Freund
Tibudu: Lenska

December 9

The Jewels of the Madonna
Same as Nov. 9

December 11 (mat.)

Aida
Same as Nov. 8 except:
Weber (c)
Amneris: Lenska
Radames: Ansseau

December 11

Lucia di Lammermoor
Same as Nov. 15 except:
Enrico: Polese

December 12 (mat.)

Martha
Moranzoni (c)
Lady Harriet: Mason
Nancy: Pavloska
Lionel: Schipa
Plunkett: V. Lazzari
Tristan: Trevisan

December 13

La Juive
Same as Nov. 19

December 14

Rigoletto
Same as Nov. 13 except:
Duke: Cortis
Rigoletto: Bonelli
Sparafucile: Cotreuil

December 15

La Sonnambula
Same as Dec. 7 except:
Amina: Macbeth

December 16

La Cena delle Beffe
Same as Nov. 27

December 18 (mat.)

L'Elisir d'Amore
Moranzoni (c)
Adina: Macbeth
Nemorino: Schipa
Belcore: Rimini
Dulcamara: Trevisan

December 18

Carmen
Same as Nov. 14 except:
Carmen: Jackson
Escamillo: Kipnis
Micaela: Norena

December 19 (mat.)

Il Trovatore
Same as Nov. 13 except:
Leonora: Muzio
Count di Luna: Bonelli
Ferrando: Cotreuil

December 19

La Bohème
Same as Nov. 10 except:
Rodolfo: Hackett

December 20

A Witch of Salem
Same as Dec. 8

December 21

Otello
Moranzoni (c)
Otello: Marshall
Desdemona: Sawyer
Iago: Montesanto
Emilia: Claessens
Cassio: Mojica

December 22

Martha
Same as Dec. 12 except:
Lionel: Cortis

December 23

Tiefland
Weber (c)
Sebastiano: Rimini
Tomaso: Kipnis
Marta: Alsen
Nuri: Freund
Pedro: Lamont

December 25 (mat.)

La Juive
Same as Nov. 19

December 25

The Barber of Seville
Same as Dec. 2 except:
Rosina: Macbeth
Figaro: Rimini

December 26 (mat.)

La Traviata
Moranzoni (c)
Violetta: Muzio
Alfredo: Schipa
Germont: Bonelli

December 27

Samson and Delilah
Same as Nov. 25 except:
Samson: Ansseau

December 28

La Bohème
Same as Nov. 10 except:

Mimi: Muzio
Rodolfo: Hackett

December 29

Tristan und Isolde
Same as Nov. 12

December 30

Aida
Same as Nov. 8 except:
Weber (c)
Amneris: Lenska
Radames: Ansseau
Ramfis: Cotreuil

December 31

Don Giovanni
Polacco (c)
Don Giovanni: Vanni Marcoux
Don Ottavio: Schipa
Commendatore: Kipnis
Donna Anna: Raisa
Donna Elvira: Loring
Masetto: Trevisan
Zerlina: Mason
Leporello: V. Lazzari

January 1 (mat.)

Tiefland
Same as Dec. 23

January 1

Martha
Same as Dec. 12 except:
Lady Harriet: Macbeth
Lionel: Cortis

January 2 (mat.)

Otello
Same as Dec. 21

January 3

La Traviata
Same as Dec. 26

January 4

Tosca
Moranzoni (c)
Tosca: Garden
Cavaradossi: Ansseau
Scarpia: Vanni Marcoux
Angelotti: Nicolich
Sacristan: Trevisan

January 5

Il Trovatore
Same as Nov. 13 except:
Leonora: Muzio
Count: Bonelli
Manrico: Cortis
Ferrando: Cotreuil

January 6

Der Rosenkavalier
Polacco (c)
Princess: Raisa
Baron Ochs: Kipnis
Octavian: Alsen
Faninal: Polese
Sophia: Mason
Marianne: d'Hermanoy
Valzacchi: Oliviero
Annina: Pavloska
Italian Singer: Ritch

January 8 (mat.)

Samson and Delilah
Same as Nov. 25

January 8

L'Elisir d'Amore
Same as Dec. 18

January 9 (mat.)

La Bohème
Same as Nov. 10 except:
Mimi: Muzio
Rodolfo: Hackett

January 9

Martha
Same as Dec. 12 except:
Lady Harriet: Macbeth
Nancy: Jackson

January 10

The Jewels of the Madonna
Same as Nov. 9

January 11

Tristan und Isolde
Same as Nov. 12

January 12 (mat.)

La Traviata
Same as Dec. 26 except:
Germont: Montesanto

January 12

Carmen
Same as Nov. 14 except:
Micaela: Norena

January 13

Don Giovanni
Same as Dec. 31

January 14

Cavalleria Rusticana
Same as Dec. 3 except:
Santuzza: Muzio
Turiddu: Cortis

I Pagliacci
Same as Dec. 3 except:
Canio: Marshall
Nedda: Mason

January 15 (mat.)

Tosca
Same as Jan. 4 except:
Tosca: Raisa

January 15

Tiefland
Same as Dec. 23

January 16 (mat.)

La Juive
Same as Nov. 19

January 16

La Traviata
Same as Dec. 26 except:
Alfredo: Hackett

January 17

Otello
Same as Dec. 21

January 18

La Cena delle Beffe
Same as Nov. 27 except:
Sabino (c)

January 19 (mat.)

Madama Butterfly
Polacco (c)
Cio-Cio-San: Mason
Suzuki: Pavloska
Pinkerton: Lamont
Sharpless: Rimini

January 19

Boris Godunov
Polacco (c)
Boris Godunov: Vanni Marcoux
Feodor: Shear
Xenia: Hamlin
Prince Shuisky: Mojica
Gregory: Lamont
Pimenn: V. Lazzari
Varlaam: Cotreuil
Missail: Oliviero
Marina: Van Gordon
Nurse: Claessens

January 20

L'Amore dei Tre Re
Same as Nov. 17

January 21

Faust
Polacco (c)
Faust: Hackett
Méphistophélès: Vanni Marcoux
Marguerite: Mason
Valentine: Defrère
Martha: Claessens
Siébel: Pavloska

January 22 (mat.)

Il Trovatore
Same as Nov. 13 except:
Leonora: Muzio
Count di Luna: Bonelli
Manrico: Lamont
Ferrando: Cotreuil

January 22

La Bohème
Same as Nov. 10 except:
Mimi: Norena

January 23 (mat.)

Hänsel und Gretel
St. Leger (c)
Hänsel: Pavloska
Gretel: Shear
Witch: Claessens
Mother: Lenska
Father: Defrère

Followed by ballet

January 23

Carmen
Same as Nov. 14 except:
Micaela: Norena

January 24

Don Giovanni
Same as Dec. 31 except:
Don Ottavio: Hackett

January 25

The Barber of Seville
Same as Dec. 2 except:
Rosina: Kurenko

January 26 (mat.)

Carmen
Same as Nov. 14 except:
Micaela: Norena

January 26

Der Rosenkavalier
Same as Jan. 6 except:
Weber (c)

January 27

Gianni Schicchi
Moranzoni (c)
Gianni Schicchi: Rimini
Lauretta: Norena
La Vecchia: Claessens
Rinuccio: Hackett
Simone: V. Lazzari

Judith
Polacco (c)
Judith: Garden
Holophernes: Formichi
Ozias: Cotreuil
Bagoas: Mojica

January 28—Grand Gala

Martha Act II
Moranzoni (c)
Lady Harriet: Mason
Nancy: Pavloska
Lionel: Cortis
Plunkett: V. Lazzari

Tosca Act II
Polacco (c)
Tosca: Raisa
Cavaradossi: Cortis
Scarpia: Vanni Marcoux

Il Trovatore Act IV
Weber (c)
Leonora: Muzio
Count di Luna: Bonelli
Manrico: Lamont
Azucena: Van Gordon

January 29 (mat.)

Gianni Schicchi
Same as Jan. 27

Judith
Same as Jan. 27

January 29

Un Ballo in Maschera
Sabino (c)
Riccardo: Marshall
Renato: Bonelli
Amelia: Raisa
Ulrica: Lenska
Oscar: Shear

1927–28

November 3

La Traviata
Polacco (c)
Violetta: Muzio
Alfredo: Schipa
Germont: Bonelli

November 4

Tannhäuser
Weber (c)
Hermann: Kipnis
Elisabeth: Kruse
Tannhäuser: Lamont
Wolfram: Schlusnus

November 5 (mat.)

Sniegurotchka
Weber (c)
Sniegurotchka: Mason
Shepherd Lel: Jackson
Fairy Spring: Lenska
Czar Berendey: Hackett

Misguir: Rimini
King Frost: Baromeo

November 5

The Barber of Seville
Moranzoni (c)
Almaviva: Mojica
Bartolo: Trevisan
Rosina: Dal Monte
Basilio: V. Lazzari
Figaro: Bonelli

November 6 (mat.)

Aida
Moranzoni (c)
King: Baromeo
Amneris: Van Gordon
Radames: Marshall
Aida: Raisa
Ramfis: Kipnis
Amonasro: Formichi

November 7

Madama Butterfly
Polacco (c)
Cio-Cio-San: Mason
Suzuki: Pavloska
Pinkerton: Hackett
Sharpless: Rimini

November 8

Loreley
Polacco (c)
Rudolph: Baromeo
Anna: Norena
Walter: Cortis
Loreley: Muzio
Herman: Montesanto

November 9

Otello
Moranzoni (c)
Otello: Marshall
Desdemona: Kruse
Iago: Formichi
Emilia: Claessens
Cassio: Mojica

November 10

Faust
Polacco (c)
Faust: Hackett
Méphistophélès: Kipnis
Marguerite: Mason
Valentine: Defrère
Martha: Claessens
Siébel: Marlo

November 11

La Gioconda
Moranzoni (c)
La Gioconda: Raisa
La Cieca: Lenska
Alvise: Baromeo
Laura: Van Gordon
Grimaldo: Marshall
Barnaba: Formichi

November 12 (mat.)

Lucia di Lammermoor
Polacco (c)
Enrico: Montesanto
Lucia: Dal Monte
Edgardo: Schipa
Raimondo: V. Lazzari

November 12

Aida
Weber (c)
King: Nicolich
Amneris: Lenska
Radames: Sample
Aida: Muzio
Ramfis: Cotreuil
Amonasro: Rimini

November 13 (mat.)

Tannhäuser
Same as Nov. 4

November 13

Faust
Same as Nov. 10 except:
Méphistophélès: V. Lazzari

November 14

Il Trovatore
Weber (c)
Leonora: Raisa
Count di Luna: Bonelli
Manrico: Cortis
Azucena: Lenska
Ferrando: Baromeo

November 15

Martha
Moranzoni (c)
Lady Harriet: Mason
Nancy: Pavloska
Lionel: Schipa
Plunkett: V. Lazzari
Tristan: Trevisan

November 16

Loreley
Same as Nov. 8

November 17

Gianni Schicchi
Moranzoni (c)
Gianni Schicchi: Rimini
Lauretta: Norena
La Vecchia: Claessens
Rinuccio: Hackett

I Pagliacci
Weber (c)
Canio: Marshall
Nedda: Kargau
Tonio: Ringling

Followed by "Hungarian Rhapsody"

November 19 (mat.)

Otello
Same as Nov. 9

November 19

Lucia di Lammermoor
Same as Nov. 12 except:
Edgardo: Cortis

November 20 (mat.)

La Traviata
Same as Nov. 3 except:
Alfredo: Hackett

November 21

Sniegurotchka
Same as Nov. 5

November 22

Un Ballo in Maschera
Sabino (c)
Riccardo: Marshall
Renato: Bonelli
Amelia: Raisa
Ulrica: Lenska
Oscar: Hamlin

November 23

Madama Butterfly
Same as Nov. 7 except:
Pinkerton: Lamont

November 24

La Gioconda
Same as Nov. 11

November 25

Tosca
Polacco (c)
Tosca: Muzio
Cavaradossi: Hackett
Scarpia: Montesanto
Angelotti: Nicolich
Sacristan: Trevisan

Followed by "Hungarian Rhapsody"
Lauwers (c)

November 26 (mat.)

Falstaff
Polacco (c)
Falstaff: Rimini
Ford: Polese
Mistress Ford: Raisa
Anne Ford: Mason
Mistress Page: Pavloska
Mistress Quickly: Claessens
Fenton: Cortis

November 26

Tannhäuser
Same as Nov. 4 except:
Wolfram: Bonelli

November 27 (mat.)

Cavalleria Rusticana
Moranzoni (c)
Santuzza: Muzio
Lola: Jackson
Turiddu: Cortis
Alfio: Defrère

I Pagliacci
Weber (c)
Canio: Marshall
Nedda: Norena
Tonio: Ringling

November 28

Loreley
Same as Nov. 8 except:
Anna: Kargau

November 29

Sniegurotchka
Same as Nov. 5 except:
Sniegurotchka: Norena
Czar Berendey: Mojica
Misguir: Bonelli

November 30

The Jewels of the Madonna
Moranzoni (c)
Gennaro: Lamont
Carmela: Lenska
Maliella: Raisa
Rafaele: Rimini

December 3 (mat.)

Faust
Same as Nov. 10

December 3

Madama Butterfly
Weber (c)
Cio-Cio-San: Norena
Suzuki: Marlo
Pinkerton: Lamont
Sharpless: Polese

December 4 (mat.)

Il Trovatore
Same as Nov. 14 except:
Leonora: Muzio
Azucena: Meisle
Ferrando: V. Lazzari

December 4

La Gioconda
Same as Nov. 11

December 5

The Barber of Seville
Same as Nov. 5 except:
Almaviva: Schipa
Figaro: Rimini

December 6

Monna Vanna
Moranzoni (c)
Guido: Vanni Marcoux
Monna Vanna: Garden
Marco: Cotreuil
Prinzivalle: Ansseau

December 7

Aida
Same as Nov. 6 except:
Weber (c)
Aida: Muzio
Ramfis: Lazzari

December 8

Tannhäuser
Same as Nov. 4 except:
Wolfram: Bonelli

December 9

Carmen
Polacco (c)
Don José: Ansseau
Carmen: Garden
Escamillo: Montesanto
Micaela: Witwer

December 10 (mat.)

Loreley
Same as Nov. 8 except:
Sabino (c)

December 10

The Jewels of the Madonna
Same as Nov. 30

December 11 (mat.)

Martha
Same as Nov. 15

December 12

Tosca
Same as Nov. 25 except:
Scarpia: Vanni Marcoux

December 13

Linda di Chamounix
Moranzoni (c)
Marquis: Trevisan
Carlo: Schipa
Parish Priest: Lazzari
Antonio: Montesanto
Linda: Dal Monte
Pierotto: Jackson

December 14

Louise
Polacco (c)
Father: Vanni Marcoux
Mother: Claessens
Louise: Garden
Julien: Ansseau
King of Fools: Mojica

December 15

Rigoletto
Weber (c)
Duke: Cortis
Rigoletto: Formichi
Gilda: Dal Monte

Sparafucile: Lazzari
Maddalena: Jackson

December 17 (mat.)

Un Ballo in Maschera
Same as Nov. 22

December 17

Cavalleria Rusticana
Same as Nov. 27 except:
Santuzza: Samoiloff
Lola: Marlo
Turiddu: Lamont

Gianni Schicchi
Same as Nov. 17

Followed by "Hungarian Rhapsody"

December 19

Monna Vanna
Same as Dec. 6

December 20

La Traviata
Same as Nov. 3

December 21

Faust
Same as Nov. 10 except:
Faust: Maison
Méphistophélès: Vanni Marcoux

December 22

Le Jongleur de Notre-Dame
Polacco (c)
Jean: Garden
Boniface: Formichi
Prior: Cotreuil

Followed by ballet

December 24 (mat.)

Madama Butterfly
Same as Nov. 7 except:
Pinkerton: Lamont

December 24

Tosca
Same as Nov. 25 except:
Sabino (c)
Tosca: Kruse
Cavaradossi: Ansseau

Followed by ballet

December 25

La Traviata
Same as Nov. 3 except:
Weber (c)

December 26

La Gioconda
Same as Nov. 11 except:
Laura: Jackson

December 27

Louise
Same as Dec. 14

December 28

Linda di Chamounix
Same as Dec. 13

December 29

Lohengrin
Weber (c)
Henry: Kipnis
Lohengrin: Maison
Elsa: Kruse
Telramund: Ringling
Ortrud: Van Gordon
King's Herald: Preston

December 31 (mat.)

Le Jongleur de Notre-Dame
Same as Dec. 22

December 31

Die Fledermaus
Weber (c)
Gabriel: Hackett
Rosalinde: Raisa
Frank: Baromeo
Prince Orlofsky: Mojica
Alfred: Lamont
Dr. Falke: Rimini
Dr. Blind: Oliviero
Adele: Pavloska

January 1 (mat.)

Tosca
Same as Nov. 25 except:
Cavaradossi: Ansseau
Scarpia: Vanni Marcoux

Followed by ballet
Lauwers (c)

January 1

Faust
Same as Nov. 10 except:
Lauwers (c)
Faust: Maison
Marguerite: Norena

January 2 (mat.)

Martha
Same as Nov. 15 except:
Lady Harriet: Kargau
Nancy: Marlo
Lionel: Cortis

January 2

Tannhäuser
Same as Nov. 4 except:
Wolfram: Bonelli

January 3

Lucia di Lammermoor
Same as Nov. 12 except:
Edgardo: Cortis

January 4 (mat.)

Hänsel und Gretel
Weber (c)
Hänsel: Pavloska
Gretel: Meusel
Witch: Claessens
Mother: Lenska
Father: Defrère

Followed by ballet

January 4

Monna Vanna
Same as Dec. 6

January 5

Il Trovatore
Same as Nov. 14 except:
Leonora: Muzio
Manrico: Marshall
Azucena: Van Gordon
Ferrando: Lazzari

January 7 (mat.)

Romeo and Juliet
Polacco (c)
Capulet: Formichi
Juliet: Mason
Romeo: Hackett
Mercutio: Defrère

Duke: Nicolich
Friar: Cotreuil

January 7

Rigoletto
Same as Dec. 15 except:
Rigoletto: Bonelli
Sparafucile: Baromeo

January 8 (mat.)

Carmen
Polacco (c)
Don José: Ansseau
Zuniga: Cotreuil
Carmen: Garden
Escamillo: Vanni Marcoux
Micaela: Witwer

January 9

Die Fledermaus
Same as Dec. 31

January 10

Lohengrin
Same as Dec. 29 except:
Ortrud: Lenska

January 11 (mat.)

Cavalleria Rusticana
Same as Nov. 27 except:
Turiddu: Lamont

I Pagliacci
Same as Nov. 27 except:
Nedda: Kargau
Tonio: Formichi

January 11

Falstaff
Same as Nov. 26

January 12

Sapho
Polacco (c)
Fanny: Garden
Divonne: Claessens
Jean: Ansseau
Caoudal: Defrère
Cesaire: Cotreuil

January 13

Tosca
Same as Nov. 25 except:
Scarpia: Vanni Marcoux

Followed by ballet

January 14 (mat.)

Tannhäuser
Same as Nov. 4 except:
Wolfram: Bonelli

January 14

Il Trovatore
Weber (c)
Leonora: Muzio
Count: Polese
Manrico: Marshall
Azucena: Meisle
Ferrando: Lazzari

January 15 (mat.)

The Jewels of the Madonna
Same as Nov. 30 except:
Gennaro: Cortis

January 15

Louise
Same as Dec. 14

January 16

Faust
Same as Nov. 10 except:
Faust: Maison
Siébel: Pavloska

January 17

La Gioconda
Same as Nov. 11 except:
Laura: Jackson

January 18 (mat.)

Rigoletto
Same as Dec. 15 except:
Moranzoni (c)
Duke: Hackett
Rigoletto: Bonelli
Gilda: Macbeth

January 18

Sapho
Same as Jan. 12

January 19

Die Fledermaus
Same as Dec. 31

January 20

Resurrection
Moranzoni (c)
Dimitri: Maison
Caterina: Garden
Anna: Claessens
Simonson: Formichi

January 21 (mat.)

La Traviata
Same as Nov. 3 except:
Weber (c)
Alfredo: Cortis

January 21

Carmen
Lauwers (c)
Don José: Ansseau
Zuniga: Cotreuil
Carmen: Jackson
Escamillo: Defrère
Micaela: Norena

January 22 (mat.)

Samson and Delilah
Weber (c)
Delilah: Van Gordon
Samson: Marshall
High Priest: Formichi
Abimelech: Polese
Old Hebrew: Cotreuil

January 23

Sapho
Same as Jan. 12 except:
Lauwers (c)
Jean: Maison

January 24

Witch of Salem
Weber (c)
Arnold: Hackett
Thomas: Baromeo
Claris: Mason
Sheila: Pavloska
Anne: Marlo
Tibudu: Lenska

Cavalleria Rusticana
Same as Nov. 27 except:
Lola: Marlo
Turiddu: Lamont

January 25 (mat.)

Il Trovatore
Same as Nov. 14 except:
Sabino (c)
Manrico: Lamont
Ferrando: Lazzari

January 25

Lohengrin
Same as Dec. 29

January 26

Aida
Same as Nov. 6 except:
Weber (c)
Amneris: Lenska
Ramfis: Lazzari
Amonasro: Montesanto

January 27–Grand Gala

Loreley Act I
Sabino (c)
Walter: Cortis
Loreley: Muzio
Hermann: Montesanto

Aida Act III
Moranzoni (c)
Radames: Marshall
Aida: Raisa
Amonasro: Rimini
Amneris: Jackson
Ramfis: Nicolich

I Pagliacci Act I
Weber (c)
Canio: Ansseau
Nedda: Norena
Tonio: Bonelli

Ballet: "Spanish Caprice"
Lauwers (c)

January 28 (mat.)

Louise
Same as Dec. 14 except:
Lauwers (c)
Julien: Maison

January 28

Martha
Same as Nov. 15 except:
Lady Harriet: Macbeth
Lionel: Cortis

1928–29

October 31

Carmen
Polacco (c)
Don José: Maison
Zuniga: Cotreuil
Carmen: Olszewska
Escamillo: Formichi
Micaela: Mock

November 1

La Bohème
Moranzoni (c)
Mimi: Claire
Rodolfo: Cortis
Marcel: Montesanto
Colline: V. Lazzari
Musetta: Pavloska

November 3 (mat.)

Aida
Moranzoni (c)
King: Baromeo
Amneris: Van Gordon
Radames: Lappas
Aida: Turner
Ramfis: V. Lazzari
Amonasro: Formichi

November 3

Rigoletto
Weber (c)
Duke: Cortis
Rigoletto: Bonelli
Gilda: Mock
Sparafucile: Baromeo
Maddalena: Paggi

November 4

Lohengrin
Weber (c)
Henry: Kipnis
Lohengrin: Maison
Elsa: Claire
Telramund: Ringling
Ortrud: Olszewska
King's Herald: Preston

November 5

Romeo and Juliet
Polacco (c)
Capulet: Formichi
Juliet: Mason
Romeo: Hackett
Mercutio: Defrère
Stephano: Pavloska
Duke: Nicolich
Friar: Cotreuil

November 6

Carmen
Same as Oct. 31

November 7

Un Ballo in Maschera
Weber (c)
Riccardo: Marshall
Renato: Bonelli
Amelia: Turner
Ulrica: Van Gordon
Oscar: Mock

November 8

Madama Butterfly
Polacco (c)
Cio-Cio-San: Mason
Suzuki: Pavloska
Pinkerton: Hackett
Sharpless: Montesanto

November 10 (mat.)

La Bohème
Same as Nov. 1

November 10

Aida
Weber (c)
King: Cotreuil
Amneris: Glade
Radames: Marshall
Aida: Burke
Ramfis: Kipnis
Amonasro: Ringling

November 11 (mat.)

Rigoletto
Same as Nov. 3 except:
Duke: Hackett
Sparafucile: Kipnis

November 11

Aida
Same as Nov. 3

November 12

Otello
Moranzoni (c)
Otello: Marshall
Desdemona: Claire
Iago: Formichi
Emilia: Claessens
Cassio: Mojica

November 13

Faust
Polacco (c)
Faust: Hackett
Méphistophélès: Kipnis
Marguerite: Mason
Valentine: Defrère
Martha: Claessens
Siébel: Glade

November 14

Samson and Delilah
Polacco (c)
Delilah: Van Gordon
Samson: Marshall
High Priest: Formichi
Abimelech: Preston
Old Hebrew: Cotreuil

November 15

Cavalleria Rusticana
Moranzoni (c)
Santuzza: Turner
Lola: Paggi
Turiddu: Lamont
Alfio: Montesanto
Lucia: Claessens

I Pagliacci
Weber (c)
Canio: Cortis
Nedda: Claire
Tonio: Bonelli

November 17 (mat.)

Carmen
Same as Oct. 31 except:
Micaela: Kerr

November 17

Un Ballo in Maschera
Same as Nov. 7

November 18 (mat.)

La Bohème
Same as Nov. 1

November 19

Aida
Same as Nov. 3 except:
Amonasro: Montesanto

November 20

Otello
Same as Nov. 12

November 21

Romeo and Juliet
Same as Nov. 5

November 22

Samson and Delilah
Same as Nov. 14

November 24 (mat.)

Boris Godunov
Polacco (c)
Boris Godunov: Vanni Marcoux
Feodor: Paggi
Xenia: Consoli
Prince Shuisky: Mojica
Gregory: Cortis
Pimenn: V. Lazzari
Varlaam: Cotreuil
Missail: Oliviero
Marina: Glade
Nurse: Claessens

November 24

Carmen
Same as Oct. 31 except:
Lauwers (c)
Don José: Lappas

November 25

Madama Butterfly
Same as Nov. 8 except:
Pinkerton: Lamont

November 26

Lohengrin
Same as Nov. 4

November 27

Boris Godunov
Same as Nov. 24

November 28

Rigoletto
Same as Nov. 3 except:
Duke: Hackett
Rigoletto: Montesanto
Sparafucile: V. Lazzari

November 29

Aida
Same as Nov. 3 except:
Radames: Marshall
Amonasro: Bonelli

December 1 (mat.)

Samson and Delilah
Same as Nov. 14

December 1

Cavalleria Rusticana
Moranzoni (c)
Santuzza: Turner
Lola: Paggi
Turiddu: Lamont
Alfio: Montesanto

I Pagliacci
Weber (c)
Canio: Cortis
Nedda: Burke
Tonio: Bonelli

December 2 (mat.)

The Tales of Hoffmann
Weber (c)
Olympia: Freund
Giulietta: Claire
Antonia: Claire
Niclaus: Pavloska
Hoffmann: Maison
Lindorf: Vanni Marcoux
Coppelius: Vanni Marcoux
Dapertutto: Vanni Marcoux
Miracle: Vanni Marcoux

December 2

Rigoletto
Same as Nov. 3 except:
Moranzoni (c)
Duke: Hackett
Sparafucile: V. Lazzari

December 3

La Bohème
Same as Nov. 1 except:
Mimi: Mason

Followed by ballet

December 4

Il Trovatore
Polacco (c)
Leonora: Turner
Count: Bonelli
Manrico: Cortis
Azucena: Van Gordon
Ferrando: V. Lazzari

December 5

Lohengrin
Same as Nov. 4

December 6

The Barber of Seville
Moranzoni (c)
Almaviva: Schipa
Bartolo: Trevisan
Rosina: Salvi
Basilio: V. Lazzari
Figaro: Bonelli

December 8 (mat.)

Die Walküre
Polacco (c)
Wotan: Kipnis
Fricka: Olszewska
Hunding: Cotreuil
Sieglinde: Turner
Siegmund: Lamont
Brünnhilde: Leider

December 8

Faust
Same as Nov. 13 except:
Lauwers (c)
Méphistophélès: Vanni Marcoux
Valentine: Hill
Martha: Eberhart

December 9 (mat.)

Lakmé
Lauwers (c)
Gerald: Schipa
Frédéric: Defrère
Nilakantha: Cotreuil
Lakmé: Mock

December 10

Boris Godunov
Same as Nov. 24

December 11

Cavalleria Rusticana
Same as Dec. 1

I Pagliacci
Same as Dec. 1 except:
Canio: Lappas
Nedda: Claire

December 12

Don Giovanni
Polacco (c)
Don Giovanni: Vanni Marcoux
Don Ottavio: Schipa
Il Commendatore: Baromeo
Donna Anna: Leider
Donna Elvira: Burke
Masetto: Trevisan
Zerlina: Mason
Leporello: Kipnis

December 13

Otello
Same as Nov. 12

December 15 (mat.)

Rigoletto
Same as Nov. 3 except:
Moranzoni (c)
Duke: Hackett
Gilda: Salvi
Sparafucile: V. Lazzari

Followed by ballet

December 15

Samson and Delilah
Same as Nov. 14 except:
Weber (c)

December 16 (mat.)

Die Walküre
Same as Dec. 8

December 17

Lakmé
Same as Dec. 9

December 18

The Tales of Hoffmann
Same as Dec. 2

December 19

La Juive
Weber (c)
Cardinal: Kipnis
Léopold: Mojica
Eudoxia: Mock
Eléazar: Marshall
Rachel: Leider

December 20

Boris Godunov
Same as Nov. 24 except:
Xenia: Meusel

December 22 (mat.)

L'Elisir d'Amore
Moranzoni (c)
Adina: Salvi
Nemorino: Schipa
Belcore: Hill
Dulca: Trevisan

December 22

Il Trovatore
Same as Dec. 4 except:
Weber (c)

December 23 (mat.)

Carmen
Same as Oct. 31 except:
Lauwers (c)
Carmen: Glade

December 23

The Barber of Seville
Same as Dec. 6

December 24

Die Walküre
Same as Dec. 8

December 25

The Barber of Seville
Same as Dec. 6

December 26

The Tales of Hoffmann
Same as Dec. 2

December 27

Der Rosenkavalier
Polacco (c)
Princess: Leider

Baron Ochs: Kipnis
Octavian: Olszewska
Faninal: Ringling
Sophie: Mason
Marianne: d'Hermanoy
Valzacchi: Oliviero
Annina: Pavloska
Italian Singer: Cortis

December 29 (mat.)

La Juive
Same as Dec. 19

December 29

La Bohème
Same as Nov. 1 except:
Rodolfo: Hackett

December 30 (mat.)

L'Elisir d'Amore
Same as Dec. 22

December 30

Cavalleria Rusticana
Same as Dec. 1 except:
Weber (c)
Alfio: Defrère

I Pagliacci
Same as Dec. 1 except:
Tonio: Montesanto

December 31

Norma
Polacco (c)
Pollione: Marshall
Oroveso: V. Lazzari
Norma: Raisa
Adalgisa: Glade

January 1

Don Giovanni
Same as Dec. 12

January 2

Sapho
Polacco (c)
Fanny: Garden
Divonne: Claessens
Jean: Maison

January 3

The Marriage of Figaro
Moranzoni (c)
Figaro: V. Lazzari
Count: Bonelli
Countess: Turner
Susanna: Mason
Cherubino: Claire

January 5 (mat.)

L'Amore dei Tre Re
Polacco (c)
Fiora: Garden
Archibaldo: V. Lazzari
Manfredo: Montesanto
Avito: Maison

January 5

The Barber of Seville
Same as Dec. 6 except:
Almaviva: Hackett
Basilio: Vanni Marcoux
Figaro: Rimini

January 6 (mat.)

Der Rosenkavalier
Same as Dec. 27

January 6

The Barber of Seville
Same as Dec. 6 except:
Almaviva: Mojica
Bartolo: Defrère
Rosina: Mock
Figaro: Rimini

January 7

L'Elisir d'Amore
Same as Dec. 22 except:
Belcore: Rimini

January 8

Sapho
Same as Jan. 2 except:
Lauwers (c)

January 9

The Marriage of Figaro
Same as Jan. 3

January 10

Pelléas et Mélisande
Polacco (c)
Mélisande: Garden
Geneviève: Claessens
Yniold: Freund
Pelléas: Mojica
Golaud: Vanni Marcoux
Arkel: Kipnis

January 11—Grand Gala

Carmen Act II
Polacco (c)
Don José: Cortis
Zuniga: Cotreuil
Carmen: Glade
Escamillo: Formichi

Faust Act II
Polacco (c)
Marguerite: Mason
Faust: Hackett
Méphistophélès: V. Lazzari
Martha: Claessens
Siébel: Pavloska

Samson and Delilah
Act III
Polacco (c)
Delilah: Van Gordon
Samson: Marshall
High Priest: Formichi

January 12 (mat.)

Lohengrin
Same as Nov. 4 except:
Telramund: Schipper
King's Herald: Defrère

January 12

Tosca
Moranzoni (c)
Tosca: Raisa
Cavaradossi: Hackett
Scarpia: Vanni Marcoux
Angelotti: Nicolich
Sacristan: Trevisan

January 13 (mat.)

L'Amore dei Tre Re
Same as Jan. 5

January 13

Un Ballo in Maschera
Same as Nov. 7 except:
Amelia: Leider

January 14

Don Giovanni
Same as Dec. 12 except:
Don Ottavio: Hackett
Anna: Raisa
Leporello: V. Lazzari

January 15

Die Walküre
Same as Dec. 8 except:
Wotan: Schipper

January 16

Thaïs
Moranzoni (c)
Thaïs: Garden
Nicias: Mojica
Athanael: Formichi
Palemon: Nicolich

January 17

Norma
Same as Dec. 31 except:
Oroveso: Baromeo

January 18

Cavalleria Rusticana
Same as Dec. 1 except:
Santuzza: Raisa

Judith
Polacco (c)
Judith: Garden
Holofernes: Formichi
Ozias: Cotreuil
Bagoas: Mojica

January 19 (mat.)

Der Rosenkavalier
Same as Dec. 27 except:
Weber (c)

January 19

The Tales of Hoffmann
Same as Dec. 2 except:
Lauwers (c)

January 20 (mat.)

The Marriage of Figaro
Same as Jan. 3

January 21

Pelléas et Mélisande
Same as Jan. 10

January 22

Don Pasquale
Moranzoni (c)
Don Pasquale: Trevisan
Dr. Malatesta: Rimini
Ernesto: Hackett
Norina: Salvi

Followed by ballet

January 23

Aida
Same as Nov. 3 except:
Radames: Marshall
Aida: Raisa
Amonasro: Bonelli

January 24

Thaïs
Same as Jan. 16

January 25

Die Walküre
Same as Dec. 8 except:
Wotan: Schipper

January 26 (mat.)

Judith
Same as Jan. 18

Cavalleria Rusticana
Same as Dec. 1 except:
Santuzza: Raisa

January 26

Romeo and Juliet
Same as Nov. 5

1929–30

November 4

Aida
Polacco (c)
King: Baromeo
Amneris: Van Gordon
Radames: Marshall
Aida: Raisa
Ramfis: V. Lazzari
Amonasro: Formichi

November 5

Iris
Moranzoni (c)
Cieco: V. Lazzari
Iris: Mason
Osaka: Cortis
Kyoto: Rimini

November 6

La Traviata
Moranzoni (c)
Violetta: Muzio
Alfredo: Hackett
Germont: Bonelli

November 7

Romeo and Juliet
Cooper (c)
Capulet: Formichi
Juliet: McCormic
Romeo: Maison
Mercutio: Defrère
Duke: Nicolich
Friar: Cotreuil

November 9 (mat.)

Tristan und Isolde
Pollak (c)
Tristan: Kipnis
Marke: Leider
Isolde: F. Leider
Kurvenal: Bonelli
Melot: Defrère
Brangäne: Olszewska

November 9

Il Trovatore
Moranzoni (c)
Leonora: Muzio
Count di Luna: Inghilleri
Manrico: Cortis
Azucena: Van Gordon
Ferrando: V. Lazzari

November 10 (mat.)

Norma
Cooper (c)
Pollione: Marshall
Oroveso: Baromeo
Norma: Raisa
Adalgisa: Glade

November 11

Iris
Same as Nov. 5

November 12

Aida
Same as Nov. 4 except:
Aida: Muzio

November 13

Der Rosenkavalier
Pollak (c)
Princess: F. Leider
Baron Ochs: Kipnis
Octavian: Olszewska
Faninal: Ringling
Sophie: Mason
Marianne: d'Hermanoy
Valzacchi: Oliviero
Annina: Pavloska
Italian Singer: Maison

November 14

Falstaff
Polacco (c)
Falstaff: Rimini
Ford: Defrère
Mistress Ford: Raisa
Anne Ford: Mock
Mistress Page: Pavloska
Mistress Quickly: Claessens
Fenton: Cortis

November 16 (mat.)

Romeo and Juliet
Same as Nov. 7

November 16

Norma
Same as Nov. 10

November 17 (mat.)

Tristan und Isolde
Same as Nov. 9 except:
Tristan: Strack
Marke: Kipnis

November 17

Faust
St. Leger (c)
Faust: Hackett
Méphistophélès: V. Lazzari
Marguerite: Mason
Valentine: Defrère
Martha: Claessens
Siébel: Pavloska

November 18

La Traviata
Same as Nov. 6 except:
Alfredo: Cortis
Germont: Inghilleri

November 19

Tosca
Moranzoni (c)
Tosca: Raisa
Cavaradossi: Hackett
Scarpia: Vanni Marcoux
Angelotti: Nicolich
Sacristan: Trevisan

November 20

L'Amore dei Tre Re
Moranzoni (c)
Fiora: Garden
Archibaldo: V. Lazzari
Manfredo: Formichi
Avito: Maison
Flamino: Oliviero

November 21

Die Walküre
Pollak (c)
Wotan: Kipnis
Fricka: Olszewska
Hunding: Cotreuil
Sieglinde: Turner
Siegmund: Strack
Brünnhilde: Leider

November 23 (mat.)

Louise
Polacco (c)
Father: Vanni Marcoux
Mother: Claessens
Louise: Garden
Julien: Maison
King of Fools: Ritch

November 23

Romeo and Juliet
Same as Nov. 7 except:
Capulet: Ringling
Juliet: Mock
Romeo: Hackett

November 24 (mat.)

Otello
Moranzoni (c)
Otello: Marshall
Desdemona: Muzio
Iago: Formichi
Emilia: Claessens
Cassio: Cavadore

November 25

Falstaff
Same as Nov. 14

November 26

Le Jongleur de Notre-Dame
Polacco (c)
Jean: Garden
Boniface: Formichi
Prior: Cotreuil

Followed by ballet
Polacco (c)

November 27

Tristan und Isolde
Same as Nov. 9 except:
Tristan: Strack
Marke: Kipnis

November 28

La Traviata
Same as Nov. 6 except:
Germont: Inghilleri

November 30 (mat.)

Tosca
Same as Nov. 19

November 30

Die Walküre
Same as Nov. 21 except:
Fricka: Eberhart
Hunding: Baromeo

December 1 (mat.)

Il Trovatore
Same as Nov. 9

December 2

Louise
Same as Nov. 23

December 3

Der Rosenkavalier
Same as Nov. 13

December 4

Don Quichotte
Cooper (c)
Dulcinée: Glade

Don Quichotte: Vanni Marcoux
Sancho: Cotreuil

December 5

L'Amore dei Tre Re
Same as Nov. 20

December 7 (mat.)

Tannhäuser
Pollak (c)
Hermann: Kipnis
Elisabeth: Turner
Tannhäuser: Strack
Wolfram: Bonelli
Venus: F. Leider

December 7

Aida
Same as Nov. 4 except:
Amonasro: Inghilleri

December 8 (mat.)

Le Jongleur de Notre-Dame
Same as Nov. 26

December 8

La Traviata
Same as Nov. 6 except:
Alfredo: Cortis
Germont: Inghilleri

December 9

La Juive
Cooper (c)
Cardinal: Kipnis
Léopold: Ritch
Eudoxia: Mock
Eléazar: Marshall
Rachel: Raisa

December 10

Rigoletto
St. Leger (c)
Duke: Hackett
Rigoletto: Bonelli
Gilda: Mason
Sparafucile: V. Lazzari
Maddalena: Paggi

December 11

Falstaff
Same as Nov. 14 except:
Fenton: Hackett

December 12

Don Quichotte
Same as Dec. 4

December 14 (mat.)

La Forza del Destino
Cooper (c)
Leonora: Muzio
Carlo: Formichi
Alvaro: Marshall
Abbot: Baromeo
Melitone: Defrère
Preziosilla: Paggi

December 14

Faust
Same as Nov. 17 except:
Faust: Maison
Siébel: Paggi

December 15 (mat.)

Tannhäuser
Same as Dec. 7

December 16

Der Rosenkavalier
Same as Nov. 13

December 17

La Juive
Same as Dec. 9 except:
Cardinal: Baromeo

December 18

Il Trovatore
Same as Nov. 9

December 19

Lohengrin
Pollak (c)
Henry: Kipnis
Lohengrin: Maison
Elsa: Stiles
Telramund: Ringling
Ortrud: Olszewska

December 21 (mat.)

Iris
Same as Nov. 5

December 21

La Traviata
Same as Nov. 6

December 22 (mat.)

Aida
Same as Nov. 4

December 22

Romeo and Juliet
Same as Nov. 7 except:
Capulet: Ringling
Juliet: Mock

December 23

Tannhäuser
Same as Dec. 7 except:
Venus: Van Gordon

December 24

La Forza del Destino
Same as Dec. 14

December 25

Don Giovanni
Polacco (c)
Don Giovanni: Vanni Marcoux
Don Ottavio: Hackett
Il Commendatore: Baromeo
Donna Anna: Leider
Donna Elvira: Burke
Masetto: Trevisan
Zerlina: Mason
Leporello: V. Lazzari

December 26

Tosca
Same as Nov. 19 except:
Tosca: Muzio
Cavaradossi: Maison

December 28 (mat.)

Otello
Same as Nov. 24

December 28

Rigoletto
Same as Dec. 10 except:
Rigoletto: Inghilleri
Gilda: Salvi
Maddalena: Glade

December 29 (mat.)

Faust
Same as Nov. 17 except:
Faust: Maison

Méphistophélès: Kipnis
Valentine: Bonelli
Martha: Eberhart
Siébel: Paggi

December 29

Falstaff
Same as Nov. 14

December 30

Don Quichotte
Same as Dec. 4

December 31

Conchita
Moranzoni (c)
Conchita: Raisa
Mateo: Cortis
Dolores: Votipka
Rufina: Paggi
Conchita's Mother: Claessens

January 1

The Barber of Seville
Moranzoni (c)
Almaviva: Manuritta
Bartolo: Trevisan
Rosina: Salvi
Basilio: Lazzari
Figaro: Rimini

January 2

Don Giovanni
Same as Dec. 25

January 4 (mat.)

Norma
Same as Nov. 10

January 4

Lohengrin
Same as Dec. 19

January 5 (mat.)

La Forza del Destino
Same as Dec. 14

January 5

Il Trovatore
Same as Nov. 9 except:
Leonora: Turner
Manrico: Lamont

January 6

Le Jongleur de Notre-Dame
Same as Nov. 26

January 7

Lucia di Lammermoor
St. Leger (c)
Enrico: Rimini
Lucia: Salvi
Edgardo: Manuritta
Raimondo: Lazzari

January 8

Conchita
Same as Dec. 31

January 9

Thaïs
Moranzoni (c)
Thaïs: Garden
Nicias: Mojica
Athanael: Vanni Marcoux
Palemon: Nicolich

January 10—Grand Gala

Aida Act II, Scene 2
Polacco (c)
King: Baromeo
Amneris: Van Gordon
Radames: Marshall
Aida: Turner
Ramfis: Lazzari
Amonasro: Rimini

Romeo and Juliet Act II
Cooper (c)
Juliet: Stiles
Romeo: Hackett

Rigoletto Act II
St. Leger (c)
Duke: Manuritta
Rigoletto: Formichi
Gilda: Salvi
Sparafucile: Lazzari

Il Trovatore Act IV, Scenes 1 and 2
Polacco (c)
Leonora: Muzio
Count di Luna: Inghilleri
Azucena: Van Gordon
Manrico: Cortis

January 11 (mat.)

Don Giovanni
Same as Dec. 25

January 11

The Barber of Seville
Same as Jan. 1 except:
Bartolo: Defrère
Basilio: Cotreuil

January 12 (mat.)

La Traviata
Same as Nov. 6 except:
Alfredo: Cortis
Germont: Inghilleri

January 12

Tannhäuser
Same as Dec. 7

January 13

Tosca
Same as Nov. 19 except:
Tosca: Muzio
Scarpia: Formichi

January 14

Louise
Same as Nov. 23

January 15

Otello
Same as Nov. 24

January 16

Conchita
Same as Dec. 31

January 17

Fidelio
Pollak (c)
Pizarro: Ringling
Rocco: Kipnis
Florestan: Maison
Leonore: Leider
Marcellina: Kersting
Fernando: Cotreuil
Jacquino: Cavadore

January 18 (mat.)

Le Jongleur de Notre-Dame
Same as Nov. 26

Followed by ballet
St. Leger (c)

January 18

La Juive
Same as Dec. 9 except:
Cardinal: Baromeo

January 19 (mat.)

Lohengrin
Same as Dec. 19 except:
Lohengrin: Strack
Elsa: Burke

January 20

Lucia di Lammermoor
Same as Jan. 7 except:
Edgardo: Cortis

January 21

Tristan und Isolde
Same as Nov. 9 except:
Tristan: Strack
Marke: Kipnis
Brangäne: Van Gordon

January 22

Pelléas et Mélisande
Polacco (c)
Mélisande: Garden
Geneviève: Claessens
Yniold: Freund
Pelléas: Mojica
Golaud: Vanni Marcoux
Arkel: Cotreuil

January 23

Il Trovatore
Same as Nov. 9 except:
Count di Luna: Bonelli

January 24

La Gioconda
Cooper (c)
La Gioconda: Raisa
La Cieca: Paggi
Alvise: Baromeo
Laura: Glade
Enzo: Marshall
Barnaba: Formichi

January 25 (mat.)

The Barber of Seville
Same as Jan. 1 except:
Almaviva: Schipa

January 25

Don Quichotte
Same as Dec. 4

January 26 (mat.)

Thaïs
Same as Jan. 9 except:
Athanael: Formichi

January 26

Lucia di Lammermoor
Same as Jan. 7 except:
Enrico: Bonelli
Edgardo: Schipa
Raimondo: Baromeo

January 27

La Gioconda
Same as Jan. 24 except:
Laura: Van Gordon

January 28

La Traviata
Same as Nov. 6 except:
Alfredo: Schipa

January 29

Die Walküre
Same as Nov. 21

January 30

Don Pasquale
Moranzoni (c)
Don Pasquale: Trevisan
Malatesta: Rimini
Ernesto: Schipa
Norina: Salvi

January 31

Carmen
Cooper (c)
Don José: Maison
Zuniga: Cotreuil
Carmen: Olszewska
Escamillo: Formichi
Micaela: Stiles

February 1 (mat.)

Pelléas et Mélisande
Same as Jan. 22

February 1

Lucia di Lammermoor
Same as Jan. 7 except:
Enrico: Hill
Edgardo: Lamont

1930–31

October 27

Lorenzaccio
Cooper (c)
Marquise de Cibo: Sharnova
Marie Soderini: Claessens
Catherine Ginori: Votipka
Louise Strozzi: Paggi
First Scholar: Freund
Second Scholar: Tourel
Lorenzo de Medici: Vanni Marcoux
Alexandre de Medici: Hackett
Cardinal Malespina Cibo: Vieuille
Philippe Strozzi: Baromeo
Tebaldeo Freccia: Ritch
Scoronconcolo: Cotreuil
Cardinal Boccio Valori: Preston
Bindo Altovito: Ringling

October 28

Die Walküre
Pollak (c)
Wotan: Nissen
Fricka: Olszewska
Hunding: Baromeo
Sieglinde: Lehmann
Siegmund: Althouse
Brünnhilde: Leider

October 29

La Forza del Destino
Cooper (c)
Leonora: Muzio
Don Carlo: Formichi
Alvaro: Marshall
Abbot: Baromeo
Melitone: Baccaloni

October 30
The Jewels of the Madonna
Moranzoni (c)
Gennaro: Cortis
Carmela: Claessens
Maliella: Raisa
Rafaele: Rimini

November 1 (mat.)
Manon
Cooper (c)
Count: Cotreuil
Des Grieux: Hackett
Manon: McCormic
Lescaut: Vieuille
Guillot: Dua
De Brétigny: Defrère

November 1
Tannhäuser
Pollak (c)
Hermann: Kipnis
Elisabeth: Lehmann
Tannhäuser: Althouse
Wolfram: Nissen
Venus: Van Gordon

November 2 (mat.)
L'Amore dei Tre Re
Moranzoni (c)
Fiora: Muzio
Archibaldo: V. Lazzari
Manfredo: Formichi
Avito: Maison
Flaminio: Oliviero

November 3
Norma
Cooper (c)
Pollione: Marshall
Oroveso: Baromeo
Norma: Raisa
Adalgisa: Glade

November 4
Lorenzaccio
Same as Oct. 27

November 5
Fidelio
Pollak (c)
Pizarro: Nissen
Rocco: Kipnis
Florestan: Maison
Leonora: Leider
Marcellina: Kersting
Fernando: Cotreuil
Jacquino: Cavadore

November 6
Cavalleria Rusticana
Moranzoni (c)
Santuzza: Muzio
Lola: Tourel
Turiddu: Cortis
Alfio: Defrère

I Pagliacci
St. Leger (c)
Canio: Marshall
Nedda: Burke
Tonio: Thomas

November 8 (mat.)
Lohengrin
Pollak (c)
Henry: Kipnis
Lohengrin: Maison
Elsa: Lehmann
Telramund: Nissen
Ortrud: Olszewska
King's Herald: Hill

November 8
The Jewels of the Madonna
Same as Oct. 30

November 9
Manon
Same as Nov. 1 except:
De Brétigny: Ringling

November 9
Cavalleria Rusticana
Same as Nov. 6

I Pagliacci
Same as Nov. 6

November 10
Die Walküre
Same as Oct. 28

November 11
Madama Butterfly
Moranzoni (c)
Cio-Cio-San: McCormic
Suzuki: Pavloska
Pinkerton: Colcaire
Sharpless: Rimini

November 12
Norma
Same as Nov. 3

November 13
Tannhäuser
Same as Nov. 1

November 15 (mat.)
Un Ballo in Maschera
Cooper (c)
Riccardo: Marshall
Renato: Thomas
Amelia: Raisa
Ulrica: Van Gordon
Oscar: Mock

November 15
Manon
Same as Nov. 1 except:
De Brétigny: Ringling

November 17
Cavalleria Rusticana
Same as Nov. 6 except:
Lola: Pavloska

I Pagliacci
Same as Nov. 6

November 18
The Jewels of the Madonna
Same as October 30

November 19
Madama Butterfly
Same as Nov. 11 except:
Pinkerton: Hackett

November 20
Die Meistersinger
Pollak (c)
Hans Sachs: Nissen
Veit Pogner: Kipnis
Sixtus Beckmesser: Habich
Fritz Kothner: Ringling
Walther: Maison
David: Colcaire
Eva: Lehmann
Magdalena: Olszewska

November 22 (mat.)
L'Amore dei Tre Re
Same as Nov. 2

November 22

Lorenzaccio
Same as Oct. 27

November 23

The Jewels of the Madonna
Same as Oct. 30

November 24

Lohengrin
Same as Nov. 8

November 25

Otello
Moranzoni (c)
Otello: Marshall
Desdemona: Muzio
Iago: Vanni Marcoux
Emilia: Claessens
Cassio: Cavadore

November 26

Die Meistersinger
Same as Nov. 20

November 27

Un Ballo in Maschera
Same as Nov. 15 except:
Renato: Bonelli

November 29 (mat.)

Mefistofele
Moranzoni (c)
Mefistofele: Kipnis
Faust: Cortis
Marguerite: Muzio
Martha: Claessens
Helen: Van Gordon
Pantalis: Glade

November 29

Un Ballo in Maschera
Same as Nov. 15 except:
Renato: Bonelli
Ulrica: Sharnova

December 1

Madama Butterfly
Same as Nov. 11

December 2

Tannhäuser
Same as Nov. 1 except:
Elisabeth: Redell
Tannhäuser: Strack

December 3

The Jewels of the Madonna
Same as Oct. 30

December 4

Otello
Same as Nov. 25

December 6 (mat.)

Die Meistersinger
Same as Nov. 20 except:
Eva: Rajdl

December 6

La Traviata
Moranzoni (c)
Violetta: Muzio
Alfredo: Cortis
Germont: Bonelli

December 7

Manon
Same as Nov. 1 except:
De Brétigny: Ringling

December 8

Fidelio
Same as Nov. 5 except:
Florestan: Strack
Marcellina: Rajdl

December 9

Un Ballo in Maschera
Same as Nov. 15 except:
Renato: Bonelli

December 10

Camille
Cooper (c)
Armand: Hackett
Gaston: Ritch
Prudence: Claessens
Marguerite: Garden
Saint-Gaudens: Hill
Julie: Glade
M. Duval: Baromeo

December 11

La Bohème
Moranzoni (c)
Mimi: Muzio
Rodolfo: Cortis
Marcello: Bonelli
Colline: V. Lazzari
Musetta: Pavloska

December 13 (mat.)

Der Rosenkavalier
Pollak (c)
Princess: Leider
Baron Ochs: Kipnis
Octavian: Olszewska
Faninal: Habich
Sophie: Rajdl
Marianne: d'Hermanoy
Valzacchi: Oliviero
Annina: Pavloska
Italian Singer: Colcaire

December 13

Otello
Same as Nov. 25

December 15

La Traviata
Same as Dec. 6 except:
Alfredo: Hackett

December 16

Camille
Same as Dec. 10

December 17

Tannhäuser
Same as Nov. 1 except:
Hermann: Baromeo
Elisabeth: Redell
Tannhäuser: Strack

December 18

Resurrection
Moranzoni (c)
Dimitri: Maison
Caterina: Garden
Anna: Claessens
La Rouge: Tourel
Fedia: Freund
Simonson: Formichi

December 20 (mat.)

Il Trovatore
Moranzoni (c)
Leonora: Muzio
Count di Luna: Bonelli
Manrico: Laurence
Azucena: Van Gordon
Ferrando: V. Lazzari

December 20

Cavalleria Rusticana
Same as Nov. 6 except:
Santuzza: Raisa
Lola: Pavloska

I Pagliacci
Same as Nov. 6 except:
Tonio: Formichi

December 21

Lohengrin
Same as Nov. 8 except:
Elsa: Redell
King's Herald: Habich

December 22

Otello
Same as Nov. 25 except:
Cassio: Ritch

December 23

Lohengrin
Same as Nov. 8 except:
Henry: Baromeo
Lohengrin: Strack
Elsa: Redell
King's Herald: Habich

December 24

Le Jongleur de Notre-Dame
Lauwers (c)
Jean: Garden
Boniface: Formichi
Prior: Baromeo

La Navarraise
Cooper (c)
Anita: Garden
Garrido: Vieuille
Ramon: Ritch
Remigio: Cotreuil
Araquil: Maison

December 25

The Bartered Bride
Pollak (c)
Kruschina: Habich
Katinka: Olszewska
Maria: Rajdl
Micha: Baromeo
Hans: Strack
Kezal: Kipnis
Esmeralda: Burke

December 27 (mat.)

Camille
Same as Dec. 10

December 27

Il Trovatore
Same as Dec. 20 except:
Manrico: Cortis

December 28

Lohengrin
Pollak (c)
Henry: Baromeo
Lohengrin: Strack
Elsa: Burke
Telramund: Ringling
Ortrud: Sharnova
King's Herald: Habich

December 29

Resurrection
Same as Dec. 18

December 30

Don Giovanni
Pollak (c)
Don Giovanni: Vanni Marcoux
Don Ottavio: Hackett
Il Commendatore: Baromeo
Anna: Leider
Elvira: Burke
Masetto: Baccaloni
Zerlina: Rajdl
Leporello: V. Lazzari

December 31

Aida
Moranzoni (c)
King: Baromeo
Amneris: Van Gordon
Radames: Marshall
Aida: Muzio
Ramfis: V. Lazzari
Amonasro: Formichi

January 1

Le Jongleur de Notre-Dame
Same as Dec. 24

La Navarraise
Same as Dec. 24

January 2

Madama Butterfly
Same as Nov. 11 except:
Cio-Cio-San: Burke

January 3 (mat.)

The Bartered Bride
Same as Dec. 25

January 3

Camille
Same as Dec. 10

January 5

Die Meistersinger
Same as Nov. 20 except:
Hans Sachs: Bockelmann
Walter: Strack
Eva: Rajdl

January 6

Resurrection
Same as Dec. 18

January 7

La Bohème
Same as Dec. 11

January 8

Don Giovanni
Same as Dec. 30 except:
Don Ottavio: Schipa

January 9—Grand Gala

I Pagliacci Act I
St. Leger (c)
Canio: Marshall
Nedda: Burke
Tonio: Formichi

Lucia di Lammermoor
Act II, Scene 2
St. Leger (c)
Enrico: Bonelli
Lucia: Salvi
Edgardo: Cortis
Raimondo: Lazzari

L'Amore dei Tre Re
Act II
Moranzoni (c)
Fiora: Muzio
Archibaldo: V. Lazzari
Manfredo: Formichi
Avito: Maison

Die Meistersinger
Act III, Scene 2
Pollak (c)
Hans Sachs: Bockelmann
Veit Pogner: Kipnis
Sixtus Beckmesser: Habich
Fritz Kothner: Ringling
Walter: Strack
David: Colcaire
Eva: Rajdl
Magdalena: Sharnova

January 10 (mat.)

Die Walküre
Same as Oct. 28 except:

Wotan: Bockelmann
Sieglinde: Redell
Siegmund: Strack

January 10

Mefistofele
Same as Nov. 29

January 11

Camille
Same as Dec. 10

January 12

The Bartered Bride
Same as Dec. 25

January 13

Mignon
Cooper (c)
Mignon: Glade
Lothario: Baromeo
Wilheim Meister: Schipa
Philine: Salvi
Frederick: Tourel

January 14

Cavalleria Rusticana
Same as Nov. 6 except:
Santuzza: Raisa
Lola: Pavloska
Alfio: Ringling

Pagliacci
Same as Nov. 6 except:
Tonio: Bonelli

January 15

Tristan und Isolde
Pollak (c)
Tristan: Strack
King Mark: Kipnis
Isolde: Leider
Kurvenal: Bockelmann
Melot: Habich
Brangäne: Olszewska

January 17 (mat.)

Le Jongleur de Notre-Dame
Same as Dec. 24

La Navarraise
Same as Dec. 24

January 17

Lohengrin
Same as Nov. 8 except:
Lohengrin: Strack
Elsa: Redell
Telramund: Bockelmann
King's Herald: Defrère

January 18

Don Giovanni
Same as Dec. 30 except:
Don Ottavio: Schipa

January 19

Camille
Same as Dec. 10

January 20

Die Meistersinger
Same as Nov. 20 except:
Hans Sachs: Bockelmann
Eva: Rajdl

January 21

Mignon
Same as Jan. 13

January 22

Pelléas et Mélisande
Cooper (c)
Mélisande: Garden
Geneviève: Claessens
Yniold: Freund
Pelléas: Hill
Golaud: Vanni Marcoux
Arkel: Cotreuil

January 24 (mat.)

La Traviata
Same as Dec. 6 except:
Alfredo: Schipa

January 24

Le Jongleur de Notre-Dame
Same as Dec. 24

Followed by ballet

1931–32

November 2

Tosca
Moranzoni (c)
Tosca: Muzio
Cavaradossi: Kiepura
Scarpia: Vanni Marcoux
Angelotti: Sandrini
Sacristan: Baccaloni

November 3

The Magic Flute
Pollak (c)
Sarastro: Kipnis
Queen of the Night: Eadie
Pamina: Rajdl
First Lady: Leider
Second Lady: Votipka
Third Lady: Olszewska
Tamino: Marion
Papageno: Habich
Papagena: Freund
Monostatos: Dua

November 4

Aida
Moranzoni (c)
King: Baromeo
Amneris: Van Gordon
Aida: Muzio
Radames: Althouse
Ramfis: Lazzari
Amonasro: Beuf

November 5

Rigoletto
Moranzoni (c)
Duke: Kiepura
Rigoletto: Thomas
Gilda: Eadie
Sparafucile: Lazzari
Maddalena: Glade

November 7 (mat.)

Boris Godunov
Cooper (c)
Boris: Vanni Marcoux

Feodor: Freund
Xenia: Turner
Shuisky: Calcaire
Gregory: Althouse
Pimenn: Baromeo
Varlaam: Baccaloni
Missail: Oliviero
Marina: Glade
Nurse: Sharnova

November 7

Il Trovatore
Moranzoni (c)
Leonora: Di Leo
Azucena: Van Gordon
Manrico: Cortis
Count di Luna: Beuf
Ferrando: Lazzari

November 9

The Magic Flute
Pollak (c)
Same as Nov. 3

November 10

Lucia di Lammermoor
St. Leger (c)
Lucia: Clairbert
Edgardo: Cortis
Enrico: Beuf
Raimondo: Lazzari
Arturo: Cavadore

November 11

The Bartered Bride
Pollak (c)
Maria: Rajdl
Katinka: Olszewska
Hans: Marion
Kruschina: Habich
Springer: Ringling
Kezal: Kipnis
Micha: Baromeo

November 12

Aida
Same as Nov. 4 except:
Aida: Pacetti

November 14 (mat.)

La Bohème
Moranzoni (c)
Rodolfo: Kiepura
Schaunard: Baccaloni
Mimi: Muzio
Marcello: Beuf
Colline: Lazzari
Musetta: Buddy

November 14

Samson and Delilah
Cooper (c)
Delilah: Van Gordon
Samson: Marshall
High Priest: Formichi
Abimelech: Baromeo
Old Hebrew: Benoni

November 16

Il Trovatore
Same as Nov. 7 except:
Leonora: Pacetti
Azucena: Glade

November 17

Tristan und Isolde
Pollak (c)
Tristan: Althouse
King Marke: Kipnis
Isolde: Leider
Kurvenal: Bockelmann
Melot: Habich
Brangäne: Olszewska

November 18

Rigoletto
Same as Nov. 5

November 19

Boris Godunov
Same as Nov. 7

November 21 (mat.)

Mona Lisa
Pollak (c)
Francesco del Giocondo: Bockelmann
Pietro Tumoni: Baromeo
Sandro da Luzzano: Habich
Giovanni de' Salviati: Marion
Mona Fiordalisa: Leider
Mona Ginevra: Votipka
Dianora: Rajdl

November 21

Aida
Same as Nov. 4 except:
Aida: Pacetti
Amonasro: Formichi
King: Benoni

November 23

Samson and Delilah
Same as Nov. 14

November 24

La Bohème
Same as Nov. 14

November 25

Il Trovatore
Same as Nov. 7 except:
Leonora: Pacetti
Azucena: Glade

November 26

Hérodiade
Cooper (c)
Jean: Maison
Herode: Thomas
Phanuel: Baromeo
Vitellius: Defrère
High Priest: Benoni
Salome: McCormic
Hérodiade: Olszewska

November 28 (mat.)

The Magic Flute
Same as Nov. 3

November 28

La Traviata
Moranzoni (c)
Violetta: Muzio
Alfredo: Hackett
Germont: Thomas

November 30

Mona Lisa
Same as Nov. 21

December 1

L'Oracolo
Moranzoni (c)
Win-Shee: Lazzari
Chim-Fen: Vanni Marcoux
Hoo-Tsin: Baccaloni
Win-San-Looee: Cortis
Ah-Yoe: Di Leo
Hoo-Chee: Glade

Gianni Schicchi
Moranzoni (c)
Gianni Schicchi: Vanni Marcoux
Lauretta: McCormic

La Vecchia: Claessens
Rinuccio: Hackett
Nella: Votipka
Simone: Lazzari
Marco: Ringling

Followed by ballet

December 2

Tristan und Isolde
Same as Nov. 17

December 3

Tosca
Same as Nov. 2 except:
Tosca: Pacetti

December 5 (mat.)

Aida
Same as Nov. 4 except:
Amonasro: Formichi

December 5

The Bartered Bride
Same as Nov. 11

December 7

Rigoletto
Same as Nov. 5 except:
Maddalena: Sharnova

December 8

La Traviata
Same as Nov. 28 except:
Alfredo: Schipa
Germont: Beuf

December 9

L'Oracolo
Same as Dec. 1

Gianni Schicchi
Same as Dec. 1

Followed by ballet

December 10

Die Meistersinger
Pollak (c)
Hans Sachs: Bockelmann
Pogner: Kipnis
Eva: Rajdl
Magdalena: Sharnova
David: Colcaire
Beckmesser: Habich
Walther: Maison

December 12 (mat.)

Hérodiade
Same as Nov. 26

December 12

The Magic Flute
Same as Nov. 3 except:
Third Lady: Sharnova
Papagena: Buddy

December 14

The Bartered Bride
Same as Nov. 11

December 15

Martha
St. Leger (c)
Lady Harriet: Turner
Nancy: Glade
Lionel: Schipa
Plunkett: Lazzari
Sir Tristan: Baccaloni

December 16

Samson and Delilah
Same as Nov. 14

December 17

Il Trovatore
Same as Nov. 7 except:
Leonora: Pacetti
Azucena: Glade
Count di Luna: Formichi

December 19 (mat.)

La Traviata
Same as Nov. 28 except:
Germont: Damiani

December 19

Hérodiade
Same as Nov. 26

December 20 (mat.)

Parsifal
Pollak (c)
Amfortas: Nissen
Titurel: Baromeo
Gurnemanz: Kipnis
Parsifal: Maison
Klingsor: Habich
Kundry: Leider

December 21

L'Oracolo
Same as Dec. 1

Gianni Schicchi
Same as Dec. 1

Followed by ballet

December 22

La Juive
Cooper (c)
Cardinal: Baromeo
Eléazar: Marshall
Rachel: Raisa
Léopold: Ritch
Eudoxia: Turner

December 23

Die Meistersinger
Same as Dec. 10

December 24

The Barber of Seville
Moranzoni (c)
Count Almaviva: Schipa
Don Bartolo: Baccaloni
Rosina: Salvi
Don Basilio: Vanni Marcoux
Figaro: Damiani
Bertha: Claessens

December 26 (mat.)

Martha
Same as Dec. 15

December 26

Lucia di Lammermoor
Same as Nov. 10 except:
Lucia: Salvi
Edgardo: Baggiore
Enrico: Damiani
Raimondo: Baromeo

December 28

Boris Godunov
Same as Nov. 7

December 29

Madama Butterfly
Moranzoni (c)
Cio-Cio-San: Pampanini
Suzuki: Ornstein
Pinkerton: Hackett
Sharpless: Damiani

December 30

La Juive
Same as Dec. 22

December 31

Mignon
Cooper (c)
Mignon: Glade
Lothario: Vanni Marcoux
Wilhelm Meister: Schipa
Laerte: Defrère
Philine: Salvi
Frédéric: Ornstein

January 2 (mat.)

Cavalleria Rusticana
Van Grove (c)
Turiddu: Cortis
Santuzza: Raisa
Alfio: Beuf
Lola: Bernhardt

I Pagliacci
St. Leger (c)
Canio: Marshall
Nedda: Muzio
Tonio: Damiani

January 2

Die Meistersinger
Same as Dec. 10

January 3

Martha
Same as Dec. 15

January 4

La Bohème
Same as Nov. 14 except:
Rodolfo: Hackett
Mimi: Pampanini
Marcello: Damiani
Musetta: Salvi

January 5

Barber of Seville
Same as Dec. 24 except:
Figaro: Rimini

January 6

La Traviata
Same as Nov. 28 except:
Alfredo: Schipa
Germont: Damiani

January 7

La Gioconda
Cooper (c)
La Gioconda: Raisa
Laura: Van Gordon
Alvise: Baromeo
La Cieca: Sharnova
Enzo: Cortis
Barnaba: Formichi

January 9 (mat.)

Madama Butterfly
Same as Dec. 29 except:
Sharpless: Rimini

January 9

La Juive
Same as Dec. 22

January 10 (mat.)

Parsifal
Same as Dec. 20

January 11

Mignon
Same as Dec. 31

January 12

Cavalleria Rusticana
Same as Jan. 2 except:
Alfio: Defrère

I Pagliacci
Same as Jan. 2 except:
Tonio: Formichi

January 13

Lohengrin
Pollak (c)
King Henry: Kipnis
Elsa: Lehmann
Telramund: Nissen
Ortrud: Olszewska
Lohengrin: Maison

January 14

La Bohème
Same as Nov. 14 except:
Rodolfo: Hackett
Mimi: Pampanini
Marcello: Damiani
Musetta: Salvi

January 15

Aida
Same as Nov. 4 except:
King: Benoni
Radames: Marshall

January 16 (mat.)

La Gioconda
Same as Jan. 7

January 16

Barber of Seville
Same as Dec. 24

January 18

Carmen
Cooper (c)
Don José: Maison
Carmen: Supervia
Escamillo: Thomas
Micaela: Turner

January 19

Mignon
Same as Dec. 31

January 20

Madama Butterfly
Same as Dec. 29 except:
Sharpless: Rimini

January 21

Lohengrin
Same as Jan. 13 except:
King Henry: Baromeo

January 23 (mat.)

Carmen
Same as Jan. 18

January 23

Cavalleria Rusticana
Same as Jan. 2 except:
Santuzza: Muzio
Lola: Glade

I Pagliacci
Same as Jan. 2 except:
Nedda: Pampanini

January 25

La Gioconda
Same as Jan. 7 except:
Enzo: Marshall

January 26
Die Meistersinger
Same as Dec. 10 except:
Eva: Lehmann

January 27
Carmen
Same as Jan. 18 except:
Don José: Cortis
Escamillo: Formichi

January 28
La Traviata
Same as Nov. 28 except:
Alfredo: Schipa
Germont: Damiani

January 29 (mat.)
Lohengrin
Same as Jan. 13

January 29
Martha
Same as Dec. 15

1932–33

No season

1933–34

December 26
Tosca
Papi (c)
Tosca: Jeritza
Cavaradossi: Borgioli
Scarpia: Amato
Angelotti: Cordon
Sacristan: Trevisan

December 27
Madama Butterfly
Papi (c)
Cio-Cio-San: Rethberg
Suzuki: Paggi
Pinkerton: Chamlee
Sharpless: Frigerio

December 30 (mat.)
La Bohème
Papi (c)
Rodolfo: Borgioli
Mimi: Mason
Marcello: Frigerio
Colline: Baromeo
Musetta: Maxwell

December 30
Aida
Papi (c)
King: Cordon
Amneris: La Mance
Aida: Raisa
Radames: Pane-Gasser
Ramfis: Baromeo
Amonasro: Frigerio

December 31
Rigoletto
Papi (c)
Duke: Borgioli
Rigoletto: Frigerio
Gilda: Talley
Sparafucile: Sjovik
Maddalena: Paggi

January 1
Tosca
Same as Dec. 26 except:
Tosca: Raisa
Cavaradossi: Onofrei
Sacristan: Cavadore

January 2
Carmen
Weber (c)
Don José: Onofrei
Carmen: Glade
Escamillo: Endreze
Micaela: Burke

January 3
Cavalleria Rusticana
Papi (c)
Turiddu: Chamlee
Santuzza: Raisa
Alfio: Defrère
Lola: Paggi

I Pagliacci
Papi (c)
Canio: Lindi
Nedda: Burke
Tonio: Frigerio
Silvio: Jencks

January 6 (mat.)
Aida
Same as Dec. 30 except:
Radames: Lindi
Aida: Burke

January 6
Madama Butterfly
Same as Dec. 27 except:
Cio-Cio-San: Mason
Suzuki: Pavloska
Pinkerton: Onofrei

January 8
La Bohème
Same as Dec. 30

January 9
Faust
Weber (c)
Marguerite: Mason
Martha: Eberhart
Siébel: Ornstein
Faust: Onofrec
Valentine: Defrère
Méphistophélès: Baromeo

January 10
Turandot
Papi (c)
Turandot: Raisa
Timur: Baromeo

Altoum: Laskowsky
Calaf: Lindi
Liu: Claire

January 13 (mat.)

Manon
Weber (c)
Count: Sjovik
Des Grieux: Borgioli
Lescaut: Defrère
Manon Lescaut: Claire
Guillot: Cavadore
De Brétigny: Jencks

January 13

Il Trovatore
Papi (c)
Count Di Luna: Morelli
Leonora: Raisa
Azucena: La Mance
Manrico: Lindi

January 15

Lohengrin
Weber (c)
King Henry: Baromeo
Lohengrin: Onofrei
Elsa: Jeritza
Telramund: Amato
Ortrud: Sharova

January 16

Turandot
Papi (c)
Same as Jan. 10 except:
Calaf: Pane-Gasser

January 17

Rigoletto
Same as Dec. 31 except:
Rigoletto: Morelli
Gilda: Brancato
Sparafucile: Sjovik
Maddalena: Ornstein

January 20 (mat.)

Samson and Delilah
Weber (c)
Samson: Ferrara
Delilah: Onegin
High Priest: Preston
Abimelech: Cordon
Old Hebrew: Baromeo

January 20

La Gioconda
Papi (c)
Barnaba: Morelli
La Gioconda: Raisa
Enzo: Chamlee
Laura: Glade
Alvise: Sjovik
La Cieca: Paggi

January 22

I Pagliacci Act I only
Papi (c)
Canio: Chamlee
Nedda: Diano
Tonio: Morelli

Le Coq d'Or
Kerby (c)
King Dodon: Cordon
General Polkan: Engelman
The Astrologer: Colcaire
Queen of Shemakhan: Meusel
Golden Cockerel: Krakowski

January 23—Grand Gala

I Pagliacci Prologue
Papi (c)
Tonio: Morelli

Aida Acts I and II
Papi (c)
Aida: Raisa
Amneris: Glade
Radames: Pane-Gasser
Amonasro: Morelli
Ramfis: Baromeo
King: Love

Lucia di Lammermoor
Act I—*recitativo* and *cavatina*
Papi (c)
Lucia: Gerber
Alisa: Sanborn

La Gioconda
Act III, Scene 2
La Gioconda: Darlys
Barnaba: Morelli
Enzo: Pane-Gasser
Alvise: Sjovik
La Cieca: Paggi

January 24

Martha
Papi (c)
Lady Harriet: Mason
Nancy: Pavloska
Sir Tristan: Trevisan
Lionel: Schipa

January 25

Il Trovatore
Same as Jan. 13

January 26

La Bohème
Same as Dec. 30 except:
Mimi: Diano
Rodolfo: Chamlee
Colline: Sjovik
Musetta: Vanna

January 27 (mat.)

Turandot
Same as Jan. 10 except:
Timur: Cordon

January 27

Mignon
Weber (c)
Mignon: Glade
Lothario: Baromeo
Wilhelm Meister: Schipa
Laerte: Defrère
Philine: Meusel
Frédéric: Ornstein

1934

November 10

Turandot
Papi (c)
Turandot: Jeritza
Altoum: Laskowsky
Timur: Baromeo
Calaf: Jagel
Liu: Burke
Ping: Frigerio
Pang: Oliviero
Pong: Cavadore

November 12

Andrea Chénier
Papi (c)
Gérard: Morelli
Madeleine: Somigli
Andrea Chénier: Martinelli

November 13

Tosca
Papi (c)
Tosca: Jeritza
Cavaradossi: Bentonelli
Scarpia: Amato
Angelotti: Lovich
Sacristan: Malatesta

November 14

Il Trovatore
Papi (c)
Leonora: Somigli
Count di Luna: Morelli
Manrico: Martinelli
Azucena: La Mance
Ferrando: Guidi

November 17 (mat.)

Turandot
Same as Nov. 10 except:
Liu: L. Turner

November 17

I Pagliacci
Papi (c)
Canio: Martinelli
Tonio: Thomas
Nedda: Burke

Cavalleria Rusticana
Waller (c)
Santuzza: Turkel
Lola: Paggi
Turiddu: Pane-Gasser
Alfio: Royer

November 19

La Traviata
Papi (c)
Violetta: Mason
Alfredo: Bentonelli
Germont: Thomas

November 20

Aida
Papi (c)
King: Guidi
Amneris: La Mance
Aida: Somigli
Amonasro: Morelli
Radames: Martinelli
Ramfis: Baromeo

November 21

Tosca
Same as Nov. 13 except:
Cavaradossi: Duncan
Scarpia: Royer

November 24 (mat.)

La Bohème
Papi (c)
Rodolfo: Bentonelli
Marcello: Frigerio
Colline: Guidi
Mimi: Mason
Musetta: Maxwell

November 24

La Forza del Destino
Papi (c)
Marquis: Belarsky
Leonora: Benni
Carlo: Morelli
Alvaro: Martinelli
Abbot: Baromeo
Melitone: Malatesta
Preziosilla: Paggi

November 26

Lohengrin
Weber (c)
Henry: Baromeo
Elsa: Jeritza
Telramund: Schiffler
Ortrud: La Mance
Lohengrin: Jagel
Herald: Engelman

November 27

Carmen
Van Grove (c)
Don José: Duncan
Zuniga: Belarsky
Carmen: Glade
Escamillo: Royer
Micaela: Burke

November 28

Salome
Van Grove (c)
Herod: Jagel
Herodias: Sharnova
Salome: Jeritza
Jochanaan: Royer
Narraboth: Duncan

I Pagliacci
Kopp (c)
Canio: Pane-Gasser
Tonio: Morelli
Nedda: Diano

December 1 (mat.)

Madama Butterfly
Papi (c)
Cio-Cio-San: Mason
Suzuki: Ornstein
Pinkerton: Bentonelli
Sharpless: Frigerio

December 1

Aida
Same as Nov. 20 except:
Weber (c)
King: Lovich
Aida: Burke
Radames: Jagel
Ramfis: Guidi

December 3

Salome
Same as Nov. 28

Followed by two ballets
Kopp (c)

December 4

Martha
Papi (c)
Tristan: Malatesta
Lady Harriet: Mason
Nancy: Barron
Lionel: Bentonelli
Plunkett: Royer

December 5

Carmen
Same as Nov. 27 except:
Micaela: L. Turner

December 8 (mat.)

Tannhäuser
Weber (c)
Hermann: Baromeo
Elisabeth: Lehmann
Tannhäuser: Althouse
Wolfram: Patton
Venus: Glade

December 8

La Bohème
Same as Nov. 24 except:
Rodolfo: Bentonelli
Mimi: Tennyson

December 10

Manon
Kopp (c)
Chevalier: Bentonelli
Count: Guidi
Manon: Hampton
Lescaut: Royer
Guillot: Cavadore
De Brétigny: Engleman

December 11

Madama Butterfly
Same as Dec. 1 except:
Cio-Cio-San: Burke

December 12

Lohengrin
Same as Nov. 26 except:
Elsa: Rethberg
Herald: Jencks

December 15 (mat.)

Tristan und Isolde
Stock (c)
Tristan: Melchior
Marke: Baromeo
Isolde: Alsen
Kurvenal: Huehn
Melot: Engelman
Brangäne: Olszewska

December 15

Don Giovanni
Van Grove (c)
Commendatore: Guidi
Donna Anna: Turkel
Don Ottavio: Hackett
Don Giovanni: Pinza
Leporello: V. Lazzari
Donna Elvira: Burke
Zerlina: Mason
Masetto: Malatesta

December 17

Faust
Weber (c)
Faust: Bentonelli
Méphistophélès: Pinza
Marguerite: Mason
Valentine: Morelli
Siébel: Ornstein
Martha: Barova

December 18

Tristan und Isolde
Same as Dec. 15

December 19

La Traviata
Same as Nov. 19 except:
Alfredo: Hackett
Germont: Morelli

December 22 (mat.)

Rigoletto
Van Grove (c)
Duke: Bentonelli
Rigoletto: Morelli
Gilda: Morini
Sparafucile: Guidi
Maddalena: Paggi

1935

November 2

Mefistofele
Papi (c)
Mefistofele: Pinza
Faust: Forest
Marguerite: Mason
Martha: Barova
Helen: La Mance
Pantalis: Paggi

November 4

Don Giovanni
Hageman (c)
Don Giovanni: Pinza
Don Ottavio: Bentonelli
Il Commendatore: Rothier
Donna Anna: Leskaya
Donna Elvira: Peters
Masetto: Malatesta
Zerlina: Mason
Leporello: Lazzari

November 5

Carmen
Weber (c)
Don José: Tokatyan
Zuniga: Rothier
Carmen: Glade
Escamillo: Royer
Micaela: Pemberton

November 6

Martha
Papi (c)
Lady Harriet: Mason
Nancy: Barova
Lionel: Chamlee
Plunkett: Lazzari
Tristan: Malatesta

November 9 (mat.)

Cavalleria Rusticana
Papi (c)
Santuzza: Raisa
Lola: Paggi
Turridu: Tokatyan
Alfio: Royer

Followed by ballet
Ganz (c)

November 9

Il Trovatore
Bigalli (c)
Leonora: Leskaya
Count: Morelli

Manrico: Pane-Gasser
Azucena: La Mance
Ferrando: Lazzari

November 11

Thaïs
Hageman (c)
Thaïs: Jepson
Athanael: Thomas
Nicias: Martin
Albine: Barova
Palemon: Cordon

November 12

Lohengrin
Weber (c)
Henry: Baromeo
Lohengrin: Chamlee
Elsa: Lehmann
Telramund: Schiffeler
Ortrud: La Mance
Herald: Jencks

November 13

La Bohème
Papi (c)
Mimi: Tennyson
Rodolfo: Tokatyan
Marcello: Morelli
Colline: Lazzari
Musetta: Fletcher

November 16 (mat.)

Der Rosenkavalier
Weber (c)
Princess: Lehmann
Baron Ochs: List
Octavian: Stueckgold
Faninal: Ringling
Sophie: Claire
Marianne: Peters
Valzacchi: Oliviero
Annina: Paggi
Italian Singer: Martin

November 16

Rigoletto
Bigalli (c)
Duke: Bentonelli
Rigoletto: Thomas
Gilda: Kocova
Sparafucile: V. Lazzari
Maddalena: Paggi

November 18

Der Rosenkavalier
Same as Nov. 16 except:
Sophie: Fletcher

November 19

Rigoletto
Same as Nov. 16 except:
Rigoletto: Morelli

November 20

Turandot
Papi (c)
Turandot: Raisa
Emperor: Laskowsky
Timur: Cordon
Calaf: Tokatyan
Liu: Claire
Ping: Engelman
Pang: Oliviero
Pong: Cavadore

November 22

Aida
Vandsburger (c)
King: Cordon
Amneris: Sharnova
Radames: Pane-Gasser
Aida: Raisa
Amonasro: Morelli
Ramfis: Lazzari

November 23 (mat.)

Tannhäuser
Weber (c)
Hermann: Baromeo
Elisabeth: Stueckgold
Tannhäuser: Rayner
Wolfram: Schiffeler
Venus: La Mance

November 23

Gale (The Haunting)
Leginska (c)
Gale Corlyon: Thomas
Pascoe Corlyon: Forrest
Jenifer Liddicoat: Peters
Morwenna Liddicoat: Bartush

Love Song (ballet)
Ganz (c)

November 25

Il Trovatore
Same as Nov. 9

November 26

La Bohème
Same as Nov. 13 except:
Hageman (c)
Colline: Baromeo

November 27

Aida
Same as Nov. 22 except:
King: Love
Amneris: La Mance
Aida: Leskaya
Amonasro: Fardulli
Ramfis: Cordon

November 28

Lucia di Lammermoor
Bigalli (c)
Enrico: Engelman
Lucia: Gerber
Edgardo: Rayner
Raimondo: Cordon

November 30 (mat.)

La Traviata
Weber (c)
Violetta: Mason
Alfredo: Forrest
Germont: Fardulli

November 30

Madama Butterfly
Vandsburger (c)
Cio-Cio-San: Burke
Suzuki: Paggi
Pinkerton: Bentonelli
Sharpless: Jencks

December 1

Carmen
Same as Nov. 5 except:
Don José: Rayner
Zuniga: Cordon
Escamillo: Fardulli
Micaela: Miller

December 2

La Fiamma
Hageman (c)
Eudossia: Barova
Basilio: Morelli

Donello: Bentonelli
Silvana: Raisa
Agnese: Sharnova
Il Vescovo: Cordon

December 3

Faust
Weber (c)
Faust: Bentonelli
Méphistophélès: Baromeo
Marguerite: Tennyson
Valentine: Fardulli
Siébel: Matyas
Martha: Barova

December 4

La Traviata
Same as Nov. 30 except:
Bigalli (c)
Violetta: Morini

December 7 (mat.)

Thaïs
Same as Nov. 11 except:
Athanael: Fardulli

December 7

La Fiamma
Same as Dec. 2

1936

October 31

La Fiamma
Weber (c)
Eudossia: La Mance
Basilio: Ballarini
Donello: Bentonelli
Silvana: Raisa
Agnese: Sharnova
Il Vescovo: Ruisi

November 2

Thaïs
Hasselmans (c)
Thaïs: Jepson
Athanael: Thomas
Nicias: Martin
Palemon: Ruisi

November 4

Martha
Moranzoni (c)
Lady Harriet: Jepson
Nancy: Barova
Lionel: Schipa
Plunkett: Rimini

November 6

La Fiamma
Same as Oct. 31

November 7 (mat.)

La Traviata
Moranzoni (c)
Violetta: Mason
Alfredo: Tokatyan
Germont: Thomas

November 7

Madama Butterfly
Moranzoni (c)
Cio-Cio-San: Burke
Suzuki: Matyas
Pinkerton: Chamlee
Sharpless: Rimini

November 9

Mignon
Hasselmans (c)
Mignon: Glade
Lothario: Baromeo
Wilhelm Meister: Schipa
Philine: Antoine

November 11

Louise
Hasselmans (c)
Father: Rothier
Mother: Claessens
Louise: Jepson
Julien: Bentonelli
King of Fools: Martin

November 13

Gianni Schicchi
Moranzoni (c)
Gianni Schicchi: Middleton
Lauretta: Burke
La Vecchia: Sharnova
Rinuccio: Bentonelli
Simione: Baromeo

Cavalleria Rusticana
Moranzoni (c)
Santuzza: Raisa
Lola: Brown
Turiddu: Tokatyan
Alfio: Rimini

November 14 (mat.)

Jack and the Beanstalk
Ganz (c)
Jack: Matyas
Old Woman: Diano
Giant: Middleton
Mother: Porter

November 14

Martha
Same as Nov. 4

November 15

La Bohème
Moranzoni (c)
Mimi: Della Chiesa
Rodolfo: Tokatyan
Marcello: Rimini
Colline: Ruisi
Musetta: Fletcher

November 16

Louise
Same as Nov. 11

November 18

L'Elisir d'Amore
Moranzoni (c)
Adina: Della Chiesa
Nemarino: Schipa
Belcore: Rimini
Dulcamara: Trevisan

November 20

Carmen
Hasselmans (c)
Don José: Tokatyan
Zuniga: Ruisi
Carmen: Wettergren
Escamillo: Ballarini
Micaela: Burke

November 21 (mat.)

Faust
Weber (c)
Faust: Bentonelli
Méphistophélès: Pinza
Marguerite: Jepson

Valentine: Morelli
Siébel: Matyas
Martha: Barova

November 21

Mignon
Same as Nov. 9 except:
Lothario: Ruisi

November 23

The Barber of Seville
Moranzoni (c)
Almaviva: Schipa
Bartolo: Trevisan
Rosina: Antoine
Basilio: Ruisi
Figaro: Bonelli

November 24

La Bohème
Same as Nov. 15 except:
Mimi: Galli-Curci

November 25

Aida
Moranzoni (c)
King: Ruisi
Amneris: Wettergren
Radames: Martinelli
Aida: Rethberg
Amonasro: Ballarini
Ramfis: Baromeo

November 27

Otello
Moranzoni (c)
Otello: Martinelli
Desdemona: Mason
Iago: Tibbett
Emilia: Barova
Cassio: Cavadore

November 28 (mat.)

Die Walküre
Weber (c)
Wotan: Schorr
Fricka: Wettergren
Hunding: List
Sieglinde: Leskaya
Siegmund: Melchior
Brünnhilde: Lawrence

November 28

Lakmé
Hasselmans (c)
Gerald: Bentonelli
Frédéric: Cehanovsky
Nilakantha: Baromeo
Lakmé: Pons
Mallika: Matyas

November 30

Mefistofele
Moranzoni (c)
Mefistofele: Pinza
Faust: Tokatyan
Marguerite: Mason
Martha: Barova
Elena: La Mance
Pantalis: Paggi

December 2

La Juive
Weber (c)
Cardinal: Baromeo
Léopold: Martin
Eudoxia: Della Chiesa
Eléazar: Martinelli
Rachel: Raisa

December 3

I Pagliacci
Canarutto (c)
Canio: Pane-Gasser
Nedda: Burke
Tonio: Morelli

Jack and the Beanstalk
Same as Nov. 14

December 4

The Bartered Bride
Weber (c)
Kruschina: Engleman
Katinka: Sharnova
Maria: Burke
Micha: Lovich
Wenzel: Rasely
Hans: Chamlee
Kezal: D'Angelo

December 5 (mat.)

Lohengrin
Kopp (c)
Henry: List
Lohengrin: Melchoir
Elsa: Rethberg
Telramund: Ballarini
Ortrud: La Mance
King's Herald: Love

December 5

Rigoletto
Moranzoni (c)
Duke: Bentonelli
Rigoletto: Tibbett
Gilda: Antoine
Sparafucile: Ruisi
Maddalena: Barova

December 6

La Bohème
Same as Nov. 15 except:
Mimi: Jaynes
Rodolfo: Martinelli

December 7

Die Walküre
Same as Nov. 28 except:
Fricka: Sharnova

December 9

Otello
Same as Nov. 27 except:
Canarutto (c)
Iago: Bonelli

December 10

Il Trovatore
Bigalli (c)
Leonora: Leskaya
Azucena: La Mance
Count di Luna: Morelli
Manrico: Pane-Gasser
Ferrando: Ruisi

December 11

Tannhäuser
Weber (c)
Hermann: Baromeo
Elisabeth: Lawrence
Tannhäuser: Althouse
Wolfram: Bonelli
Venus: La Mance

December 12 (mat.)

Samson and Delilah
Weber (c)
Delilah: Wettergren
Samson: Martinelli
High Priest: Morelli
Abimelech: Ruisi

December 12

The Bartered Bride
Same as Dec. 4

December 13

La Juive
Same as Dec. 2 except:
Rachel: Lawrence

1937

October 30

Aida
Moranzoni (c)
King: Love
Amneris: Wettergren
Radames: Martinelli
Aida: Rethberg
Amonasro: Czaplicki
Ramfis: V. Lazzari

November 1

Samson and Delilah
Weber (c)
Delilah: Wettergren
Samson: Martinelli
High Priest: Morelli
Abimelech: Love
Old Hebrew: Baromeo

November 3

Il Trovatore
Moranzoni (c)
Leonora: Rethberg
Azucena: La Mance
Count di Luna: Morelli
Manrico: Martinelli
Ferrando: Lazzari

November 4

Madama Butterfly
Moranzoni (c)
Cio-Cio-San: Burke
Suzuki: Paggi
Pinkerton: Bentonelli
Sharpless: Engelman

November 5

Manon
Hasselmans (c)
Count: Baromeo
Chevalier: Burdino
Manon: Dosia
Lescaut: Brownlee
Guillot: Cavadore
De Brétigny: Engelman

November 6 (mat.)

The Barber of Seville
Samossoud (c)
Almaviva: Hackett
Bartolo: Trevisan
Rosina: Sack
Basilio: Lazzari
Figaro: Thomas

Followed by ballet
Kopp (c)

November 6

Man Without a Country
Damrosch (c)
Philip Nolan: Carron
Mary Rutledge: Traubel
Harman Blennerhassett: Rasely
Aaron Burr: Dickson

November 8

La Traviata
Moranzoni (c)
Violetta: Jepson
Alfredo: Burdino
Germont: Thomas

November 10

Lucia di Lammermoor
Moranzoni (c)
Enrico: Morelli
Lucia: Sack
Edgardo: Masini
Raimondo: Lazzari

November 11

Aida
Samossoud (c)
Amneris: La Mance
Radames: Pane-Gasser
Aida: Burke
Ramfis: Ruisi
Amonasro: Czaplicki

November 12

Thaïs
Hasselmans (c)
Thaïs: Jepson
Athanael: Thomas
Nicias: Martin
Palemon: Ruisi

November 13 (mat.)

Carmen
Hasselmans (c)
Don José: Luccioni
Zuniga: Ruisi
Carmen: Wettergren
Escamillo: Fardulli
Micaela: Burke

November 13

Tosca
Moranzoni (c)
Tosca: Dosia
Cavaradossi: Masini
Scarpia: Czaplicki
Cesare Angelotti: Ruisi
Sacristan: Trevisan

November 15

L'Amore dei Tre Re
Moranzoni (c)
Fiora: Jepson
Archibaldo: Lazzari
Manfredo: Morelli
Avito: Luccioni
Flaminio: Cavadore

November 17

Manon
Same as Nov. 5 except:
Manon: Moore

November 18

The Barber of Seville
Same as Nov. 6 except:
Almaviva: Bentonelli
Rosina: Brancato
Basilio: Ruisi

November 19

Man Without a Country
Same as Nov. 6 except:
Kopp (c)

November 20 (mat.)

Lohengrin
Weber (c)
Henry: Baromeo
Lohengrin: Maison
Elsa: Stueckgold
Telramund: Czaplicki
Ortrud: La Mance
King's Herald: Love

November 20

Carmen
Same as Nov. 13 except:
Carmen: Glade
Micaela: Ohlin

November 22

Norma
Samossoud (c)
Pollione: Martinelli
Oroveso: Pinza
Norma: Cigna
Adalgisa: Glade

November 24

Tristan und Isolde
Weber (c)
Tristan: Melchoir
Marke: List
Isolde: Flagstad
Kurvenal: Czaplicki
Melot: Schmidt
Brangäne: Wettergren

November 25

Cavalleria Rusticana
Moranzoni (c)
Santuzza: Raisa
Lola: Ross
Turiddu: Sakos
Alfio: Defrère

I Pagliacci
Canarutto (c)
Canio: Luccioni
Tonio: Morelli
Nedda: Burke

November 26

La Gioconda
Moranzoni (c)
La Gioconda: Cigna
La Cieca: Brown
Alvise: Baromeo
Laura: La Mance
Enzo: Masini
Barnaba: Morelli

November 27 (mat.)

Tannhäuser
Weber (c)
Hermann: Baromeo
Elisabeth: Flagstad
Tannhäuser: Melchior
Wolfram: Czaplicki
Venus: La Mance

November 27

Lakmé
Hasselmans (c)
Gerald: Burdino
Frédéric: Engelman
Nilakantha: Baromeo
Lakmé: Pons
Mallika: Matyas

November 29

Otello
Moranzoni (c)
Otello: Martinelli
Desdemona: Mason
Iago: Tibbett
Emilia: Ford
Cassio: Cavadore

November 30

Lakmé
Same as Nov. 27

December 1

Tosca
Same as Nov. 13

December 2

Faust
Samossoud (c)
Faust: Bentonelli
Méphistophélès: Baromeo
Marguerite: Della Chiesa
Valentine: Morelli
Siébel: Matyas
Martha: Barron

December 3

Die Walküre
Weber (c)
Wotan: Hofmann
Fricka: Wettergren
Hunding: List
Sieglinde: Traubel
Siegmund: Melchior
Brünnhilde: Flagstad

December 4 (mat.)

Lucia di Lammermoor
Same as Nov. 10 except:
Lucia: Pons
Raimondo: Ruisi

December 4

La Juive
Kopp (c)
Cardinal: Baromeo
Léopold: Martin
Eudoxia: Della Chiesa
Eléazar: Martinelli
Rachel: Raisa

December 5 (mat.)

Hänsel und Gretel
Kopp (c)
Peter: Love
Gertrude: Barron
Hänsel: Matyas
Gretel: Steen
Witch: Sharnova

December 6

Der Rosenkavalier
Weber (c)
Princess: Lehmann
Ochs: List
Octavian: Stueckgold
Faninal: Schmidt
Sophie: Claire
Marianne: Fletcher
Valzacchi: Oliviero
Annina: Porter
Italian Singer: Martin

December 8

Rigoletto
Moranzoni (c)
Duke: Bjoerling
Rigoletto: Tibbett
Gilda: Lane
Sparafucile: Ruisi
Maddalena: Paggi

December 9

Il Trovatore
Same as Nov. 3 except:
Canarutto (c)
Leonora: Bampton
Manrico: Pane-Gasser
Ferrando: Ruisi

December 10

Martha
Bigalli (c)
Lady Harriet: Mason
Nancy: Glade
Lionel: Schipa
Plunkett: Rimini
Tristan: Trevisan

December 11 (mat.)

La Bohème
Moranzoni (c)
Mimi: Moore
Rodolfo: Masini
Marcello: Morelli
Colline: Ruisi
Musetta: Paull

December 11

Lohengrin
Same as Nov. 20 except:
Kopp (c)
Henry: Gurney
Lohengrin: Laholm
Elsa: Rethberg

December 13

Tristan und Isolde
Same as Nov. 24

December 15

La Bohème
Same as Dec. 11 except:
Mimi: Claire
Rodolfo: Bjoerling
Marcello: Czaplicki

December 16

Mignon
Kopp (c)
Mignon: Glade
Lothario: Ruisi
Wilhelm Meister: Burdino
Philine: Antoine

December 17

La Traviata
Same as Nov. 8

December 18 (mat.)

Der Rosenkavalier
Same as Dec. 6

December 18—Grand Gala

Rigoletto Act II
Weber (c)
Duke: Bentonelli
Rigoletto: Czaplicki
Gilda: Lane

Romeo and Juliet Act II
Samossoud (c)
Romeo: Burdino
Juliet: Dosia

"An American Pattern"
(Chicago City Ballet)

Madama Butterfly Act II
Moranzoni (c)
Cio-Cio-San: Mason
Suzuki: Paggi
Sharpless: Czaplicki

December 19

Rigoletto
Same as Dec. 8 except:
Bigalli (c)
Duke: Bentonelli
Rigoletto: Czaplicki
Gilda: LaPlaca

December 31

Martha
Same as Dec. 10 except:
Lady Harriet: Jepson
Nancy: Barron

1938

October 29

Otello
Moranzoni (c)
Otello: Martinelli
Desdemona: Jepson
Iago: Tibbett
Emilia: Barova
Cassio: Cavadore

October 31

Aida
Moranzoni (c)
King: Love
Amneris: Castagna
Radames: Martinelli
Aida: Giannini
Amonasro: Czaplicki
Ramfis: Lazzari

November 2

Die Meistersinger
Weber (c)
Hans Sachs: Berglund
Veit Pogner: Ernster
Sixtus Beckmesser: Vogel
Fritz Kothner: Schmidt
Walther: Maison
David: Marlow
Eva: Reining
Magdalena: Sharnova

November 3

La Gioconda
Canarutto (c)
La Gioconda: Leskaya
La Cieca: Paggi
Alvise: Lazzari
Laura: La Mance
Enzo: Bentonelli
Barnaba: Morelli

November 4

Rigoletto
Moranzoni (c)
Duke: Tokatyan
Rigoletto: Tibbett
Gilda: Reggiani
Sparafucile: Lazzari
Maddalena: Barova

November 5 (mat.)

Samson and Delilah
Weber (c)
Delilah: Castagna
Samson: Maison
High Priest: Fardulli
Abimelech: Love
Old Hebrew: Beattie

November 5

Madama Butterfly
Moranzoni (c)
Cio-Cio-San: Reining
Suzuki: Paggi
Pinkerton: Melton
Sharpless: Czaplicki

November 7

The Tales of Hoffmann
Hasselmans (c)
Olympia: Antoine
Giuletta: Dosia
Antonia: Dosia
Niclaus: Mayer
Hoffmann: Burdino
Coppelius: Tibbett
Dapertutto: Tibbett
Miracle: Tibbett

November 9

Tosca
Moranzoni (c)
Tosca: Dosia

Cavaradossi: Masini
Scarpia: Czaplicki
Angelotti: Beattie
Sacristan: Trevisan

November 10

Rigoletto
Same as Nov. 4 except:
Canarutto (c)
Rigoletto: Morelli

November 11

La Bohème
Moranzoni (c)
Mimi: Merrell
Rodolfo: Masini
Marcello: Czaplicki
Colline: Lazzari
Musetta: Garrotto

November 12 (mat.)

Die Meistersinger
Same as Nov. 2

November 12

Carmen
Hasselmans (c)
Don José: Tokatyan
Zuniga: Beattie
Carmen: Castagna
Escamillo: Czaplicki
Micaela: Garrotto

November 14

Tosca
Same as Nov. 9

November 16

La Traviata
Moranzoni (c)
Violetta: Jepson
Alfredo: Burdino
Germont: Morelli

November 17

The Tales of Hoffmann
Same as Nov. 7 except:
Olympia: Lane
Coppelius: Brownlee
Dapertutto: Brownlee
Miracle: Brownlee

November 18

Martha
Moranzoni (c)
Lady Harriet: Jepson
Nancy: Barova
Lionel: Gigli
Plunkett: Lazzari
Tristan: Trevisan

November 19 (mat.)

Turandot
Kopp (c)
Turandot: Turner
Altoum: Laskowsky
Timur: Lazzari
Calaf: Masini
Liu: Garrotto
Ping: Harris
Pang: Oliviero
Pong: Cavadore

November 19

Tristan und Isolde
Weber (c)
Tristan: Althouse
Marke: Beattie
Isolde: Flagstad
Kurvenal: Czaplicki
Melot: Schmidt
Brangäne: Glatz

November 21

Lohengrin
McArthur (c)
Henry: Gurney
Lohengrin: Maison
Elsa: Flagstad
Telramund: Czaplicki
Ortrud: La Mance
King's Herald: Harris

November 23

Lucia di Lammermoor
Moranzoni (c)
Enrico: Morelli
Lucia: Pons
Edgardo: Masini
Raimondo: Lazzari

November 24

Carmen
Same as Nov. 12 except:
Carmen: Giannini
Escamillo: Fardulli

November 25

Tristan und Isolde
Same as Nov. 19

November 26 (mat.)

Aida
Same as Oct. 31 except:
King: Beattie
Amneris: La Mance
Radames: Giglio
Aida: Turner
Amonasro: Morelli

November 26

The Barber of Seville
Canarutto (c)
Almaviva: Hackett
Bartolo: Trevisan
Rosina: Pons
Basilio: Lazzari
Figaro: Morelli

Followed by ballet
Canarutto (c)

November 28

Die Walküre
Weber (c)
Wotan: Kipnis
Fricka: Glatz
Hunding: Beattie
Sieglinde: Turner
Siegmund: Maison
Brünnhilde: Manski

November 30

Lakmé
Hasselmans (c)
Gerald: Burdino
Frédéric: Harris
Nilakantha: Love
Lakmé: Pons
Mallika: Mayer

December 1

Tosca
Same as Nov. 9 except:
Canarutto (c)
Tosca: Tennyson
Cavaradossi: Tokatyan
Angelotti: Harris

December 2

Faust
Hasselmans (c)
Faust: Bentonelli
Méphistophélès: Pinza
Marguerite: Jepson
Valentine: Morelli

Siébel: Brown
Martha: Barova

December 3 (mat.)

Manon
Hasselmans (c)
Count: Beattie
Chevalier: Burdino
Manon: Dosia
Lescaut: Royer
Guillot: Cavadore
De Brétigny: Harris

December 3

Lucia di Lammermoor
Same as Nov. 23 except:
Lucia: Reggiani

December 4

Il Trovatore
Bigalli (c)
Leonora: Bampton
Azucena: La Mance
Count di Luna: Morelli
Manrico: Pane-Gasser
Ferrando: Beattie

December 5

La Bohème
Same as Nov. 11 except:
Mimi: Jepson

December 7

The Barber of Seville
Same as Nov. 26 except:
Rosina: Reggiani

December 8

Martha
Same as Nov. 18 except:
Lionel: Bentonelli

December 9 (mat.)

Hänsel und Gretel
Kopp (c)
Peter: Love
Gertrude: Barron
Hänsel: Brown
Gretel: Hoe
Witch: Sharnova

December 9

Turandot
Same as Nov. 19 except:
Calaf: Tokatyan

December 10 (mat.)

Romeo and Juliet
Hasselmans (c)
Capulet: Beattie
Juliet: Dosia
Romeo: Burdino
Mercutio: Royer
Stephano: Mayer
Duke: MacDonald
Friar: Love

December 10

La Traviata
Same as Nov. 16 except:
Alfredo: Melton
Germont: Czaplicki

December 12

Manon
Same as Dec. 3

December 14

Andrea Chénier
Moranzoni (c)
Gérard: Morelli
Madeleine: Bampton
Andrea Chénier: Gigli
Old Woman: Paggi

December 15

La Bohème
Same as Nov. 11 except:
Canarutto (c)
Mimi: Pemberton
Rodolfo: Tokatyan

December 16

Carmen
Same as Nov. 12 except:
Weber (c)
Don José: Burdino
Carmen: Giannini
Micaela: Tennyson

December 17 (mat.)

L'Amore dei Tre Re
Moranzoni (c)
Fiora: Jepson
Archibaldo: Lazzari
Manfredo: Morelli
Avito: Takatyan
Flaminio: Cavadore

December 17

Aida
Same as Oct. 31 except:
King: Beattie
Amneris: La Mance
Aida: Turner
Amonasro: Morelli

January 16—Special Performance

Il Trovatore
Same as Dec. 4 except:
Kopp (c)
Leonora: Leskaya
Azucena: Soderstam
Count: Royer

1939

October 28

Boris Godunov
Weber (c)
Boris Godunov: Pinza
Feodor: Brown
Xenia: Margolyne
Shuisky: Cavadore
Gregory: Tokatyan
Pimenn: Beattie
Varlaam: Lazzari
Missail: Signorelli
Marina: Longone
Nurse: Paggi

October 30

Andrea Chénier
Canarutto (c)
Gérard: Morelli
Madeleine: Bampton
Bersi: Browne
Andrea Chénier: Tokatyan
Old Woman: Paggi

November 1

La Traviata
Weber (c)
Violetta: Jepson

Alfredo: Schipa
Germont: Thomas

November 2

Aida
Alwin (c)
King: Love
Amneris: Longone
Radames: Baum
Aida: Bampton
Amonasro: Czaplicki
Ramfis: Lazzari

November 3

The Barber of Seville
Canarutto (c)
Almaviva: Schipa
Bartolo: Malatesta
Rosina: Reggiani
Basilio: Lazzari
Figaro: Thomas

November 4 (mat.)

Louise
Hasselmans (c)
Louise: Moore
Mother: Claessens
Julien: Kullman
Father: Rothier
King of Fools: Marlowe

November 4

Faust
Hasselmans (c)
Faust: Tokatyan
Méphistophélès: Pinza
Marguerite: Jepson
Valentine: Czaplicki
Siébel: Mayer
Martha: Brown

November 6

Mignon
Hasselmans (c)
Mignon: Swarthout
Lothario: Pinza
Wilhelm Meister: Schipa
Philine: Haskins
Frédéric: Brown
Giarno: Love

November 8

La Bohème
Weber (c)
Mimi: Moore
Rodolfo: Kullman
Marcello: Morelli
Colline: Lazzari
Musetta: Boerner

November 9

Cavalleria Rusticana
Bigalli (c)
Santuzza: Giannini
Lola: Brown
Turiddu: Baroumis
Alfio: Kelso

I Pagliacci
Canarutto (c)
Canio: Pane-Gasser
Tonio: Fardulli
Nedda: Della Chiesa

November 10

La Traviata
Same as Nov. 1 except:
Violetta: Reggiani
Alfredo: Tokatyan

November 11 (mat.)

Boris Godunov
Same as Oct. 28 except:
Gregory: Bentonelli

November 11

Aida
Same as Nov. 2 except:
King: Beattie
Amneris: Branzelli
Aida: Lushanya
Ramfis: Love

November 12

Carmen
Weber (c)
Don José: Tokatyan
Zuniga: Beattie
Carmen: Longone
Escamillo: Czaplicki
Micaela: Della Chiesa

November 13

Louise
Same as Nov. 4 except:
Julien: Burdino

November 15

Mignon
Same as Nov. 6 except:
Mignon: Glade
Lothario: Lazzari
Wilhelm Meister: Burdino

November 16

Lucia di Lammermoor
Kopp (c)
Enrico: Morelli
Lucia: Reggiani
Edgardo: Tokatyan
Raimondo: Lazzari

November 17

Manon
Hasselmans (c)
Count: Rothier
Chevalier: Burdino
Manon: Moore
Lescaut: Czaplicki
Guillot: Cavadore
De Brétigny: Schmidt

November 18 (mat.)

Cavalleria Rusticana
Canarutto (c)
Lola: Mayer
Turiddu: Tokatyan
Alfio: Defrère
Santuzza: Giannini

I Pagliacci
Same as Nov. 9 except:
Canio: Carron
Tonio: Thomas

November 18

Martha
Kopp (c)
Lady Harriet: Jepson
Nancy: Paggi
Lionel: Bentonelli
Plunkett: Lazzari
Tristan: Malatesta

November 20

Otello
Weber (c)
Otello: Martinelli
Desdemona: Jepson
Iago: Morelli
Emilia: Paggi
Cassio: Cavadore

November 22

Madama Butterfly
Weber (c)
Cio-Cio-San: Mason

Suzuki: Paggi
Pinkerton: Bentonelli
Sharpless: Czaplicki

November 23

The Barber of Seville
Same as Nov. 3 except:
Figaro: Morelli

November 24

Tristan und Isolde
McArthur (c)
Tristan: Martinelli
Marke: Beattie
Isolde: Flagstad
Kurvenal: Czaplicki
Melot: Schmidt
Brangäne: Szantho

November 25 (mat.)

Carmen
Same as Nov. 12 except:
Hasselmans (c)
Don José: Kiepura
Carmen: Swarthout

November 25

Lucia di Lammermoor
Same as Nov. 16 except:
Lucia: Pons
Edgardo: Schipa

November 27

Tannhäuser
McArthur (c)
Hermann: Beattie
Elisabeth: Flagstad
Tannhäuser: Althouse
Wolfram: Czaplicki
Venus: Longone

November 29

Lohengrin
McArthur (c)
Henry: Love
Lohengrin: Hartmann
Elsa: Flagstad
Telramund: Czaplicki
Ortrud: Longone
Herald: Schmidt

November 30

The Bartered Bride
Weber (c)
Kruschina: Howell
Maria: Burke
Micha: Macdonald
Wenzel: Marlowe
Hans: Bentonelli
Kezal: Beattie
Springer: Ringling

December 1

Tristan und Isolde
Same as Nov. 24 except:
Tristan: Hartmann

December 2 (mat.)

Aida
Same as Nov. 2 except:
Weber (c)
Radames: Martinelli
Aida: Giannini
Amonasro: Morelli

December 2

Die Walküre
McArthur (c)
Wotan: Huehn
Fricka: Sharnova
Hunding: Beattie
Sieglinde: Bampton
Siegmund: Maison
Brünnhilde: Flagstad

December 4

Madama Butterfly
Same as Nov. 22 except:
Canarutto (c)
Cio-Cio-San: Burke
Pinkerton: Melton

December 6

Manon
Same as Nov. 17 except:
Count: Beattie
Chevalier: Kiepura
Manon: Dosia

December 7

Tosca
Canarutto (c)
Tosca: Giannini
Cavaradossi: Tokatyan
Scarpia: Morelli
Angelotti: Beattie
Sacristan: Malatesta

December 8

Rigoletto
Kopp (c)
Duke: Kiepura
Rigoletto: Weede
Gilda: Reggiani
Sparafucile: Lazzari
Maddalena: Mayer

December 9 (mat.)

Il Trovatore
Weber (c)
Leonora: Rethberg
Azucena: Longone
Count di Luna: Morelli
Manrico: Martinelli
Ferrando: Lazzari

December 9

Romeo and Juliet
Hasselmans (c)
Capulet: Beattie
Juliet: Dosia
Romeo: McChesney
Mercutio: Howell
Stephano: Mayer
Duke: MacDonald
Friar: Love

December 11

Carmen
Same as Nov. 12 except:
Don José: Martinelli
Carmen: Giannini
Micaela: Monroe

December 13

Otello
Same as Nov. 20 except:
Desdemona: Mason

December 14

Rigoletto
Same as Dec. 8 except:
Duke: Bentonelli

December 15

The Bartered Bride
Same as Nov. 30 except:
Hans: Chamlee

December 16 (mat.)

Tosca
Same as Dec. 7 except:
Tosca: Dosia
Cavaradossi: Kiepura
Scarpia: Czaplicki

December 16

Louise
Same as Nov. 4 except:
Mother: Doe
Julien: Burdino

1940

November 2

Aida
Weber (c)
Aida: Milanov
Amneris: Branzell
Radames: Martinelli
Amonasro: Thomas
Ramfis: Lazzari
King: Beattie

November 4

Tristan und Isolde
McArthur (c)
Isolde: Flagstad
Tristan: Melchior
Brangäne: Szantho
Kurvenal: Czaplicki
Marke: Beattie
Melot: Harrell

November 5

La Traviata
Abravanel (c)
Violetta: Jepson
Alfredo: Melton
Germont: Thomas

November 6

Il Trovatore
Weber (c)
Leonora: Bampton
Azucena: Branzell
Manrico: Martinelli
Count di Luna: Morelli
Ferrando: Lazzari

November 7

Madama Butterfly
Canarutto (c)
Cio-Cio-San: Gonzales
Suzuki: Brown
Pinkerton: Melton
Sharpless: Morelli

November 9 (mat.)

Falstaff
Weber (c)
Falstaff: Thomas
Mistress Ford: Giannini
Ford: Harrell
Anne Ford: Haskins
Mistress Page: Summers
Mistress Quickly: Sharnova
Fenton: Mojica

November 9

Manon
Abravanel (c)
Manon: Jepson
Chevalier: Crooks
Lescaut: Czaplicki
Count: Rothier
Poussette: Kirsten
Guillot: Cavadore
De Brétigny: Howell

November 11

Cavalleria Rusticana
Abravanel (c)
Santuzza: Giannini
Lola: Summers
Turiddu: Jagel
Alfio: Morelli

I Pagliacci
Abravanel (c)
Canio: Martinelli
Tonio: Thomas
Nedda: Jepson

November 12

Carmen
Weber (c)
Carmen: Lawrence
Micaela: Kirk
Don José: Kiepura
Escamillo: Czaplicki
Zuniga: Beattie

November 13

Aida
Same as Nov. 2 except:
Breisach (c)
Amneris: Zebranska
Radames: Jagel

November 15

Il Trovatore
Same as Nov. 6 except:
Leonora: Cook
Azucena: Sten
Manrico: Carron
Ferrando: Beattie

November 16

Rigoletto
Kopp (c)
Gilda: Tuminia
Duke: Bjoerling
Rigoletto: Sved
Sparafucile: Beattie
Maddalena: Summers

November 16 (mat.)

Don Giovanni
Breisach (c)
Don Giovanni: Pinza
Donna Anna: Bampton
Donna Elvira: Witwer
Zerlina: Bokor
Don Ottavio: Schipa
Leporello: Lazzari
Commendatore: Destal
Masetto: Alvary

November 18

La Traviata
Abravenel (c)
Violetta: Novotna
Alfredo: Schipa
Germont: Sved

November 19

Madama Butterfly
Canarutto (c)
Cio-Cio-San: Tentoni
Suzuki: Paggi
Pinkerton: Jagel
Sharpless: Czaplicki

November 20

Cavalleria Rusticana
Same as Nov. 11 except:
Turridu: Carron
Alfio: Harrell

I Pagliacci
Same as Nov. 11 except:
Nedda: Bokor
Tonio: Morelli

November 22

Falstaff
Same as Nov. 9

November 23 (mat.)

Manon
Same as Nov. 9 except:
Chevalier: Schipa

November 23

L'Amore dei Tre Re
Montemezzi (c)
Fiora: Moore
Archibaldo: Lazzari
Avito: Kullman
Manfredo: Morelli
Flaminio: Cavadore

November 25

Rigoletto
Same as Nov. 16 except:
Breisach (c)
Gilda: Pons
Duke: Kullman
Sparafucile: Lazzari

November 26

Don Giovanni
Same as Nov. 16

November 27

Carmen
Same as Nov. 12 except:
Breisach (c)
Micaela: Witwer

November 29

La Traviata
Same as Nov. 5 except:
Adler (c)
Alfredo: Melton
Germont: Czaplicki

November 30 (mat.)

Der Rosenkavalier
Reiner (c)
Princess: Hussa
Baron Ochs: List
Octavian: Stevens
Faninal: Destal
Sophie: Bokor
Marianne: Fairbank
Valzacchi: Long
Annina: Sten
Singer: Naya

December 2

Die Walküre
Breisach (c)
Wotan: Destal
Fricka: Zebranska
Hunding: List
Sieglinde: Bampton
Siegmund: Maison
Brünnhilde: Lawrence

December 3

The Jewels of the Madonna
Abravanel (c)
Gennaro: Jagel
Carmela: Paggi
Maliella: Giannini
Rafaele: Czaplicki

December 4

Falstaff
Same as Nov. 9

December 6

Rigoletto
Alwin (c)
Gilda: Haskins
Duke: Peerce
Rigoletto: Morelli
Sparafucile: Lazzari
Maddalena: Summers

December 7

Tosca
Kopp (c)
Tosca: Pauly
Cavaradossi: Kiepura
Scarpia: Thomas
Angelotti: Lawler
Sacristan: Trevisan

December 7 (mat.)

Martha
Adler (c)
Lady Harriet: Jepson
Nancy: Sten
Plunkett: Beattie
Lionel: Melton
Tristan: Alvary

December 9

Aida
Same as Nov. 2 except:
Breisach (c)
Aida: Bampton
Amneris: Zebranska
Amonasro: Czaplicki

December 10

Salome
Alwin (c)
Herod: Jagel
Herodias: Sharnova
Salome: Lawrence
Jochanaan: Destal
Narraboth: Mojica

December 11

Der Rosenkavalier
Same as Nov. 30

December 13

Martha
Same as Dec. 7

December 14 (mat.)

The Jewels of the Madonna
Same as Dec. 3 except:
Rafaele: Morelli

December 14

Die Walküre
Same as Dec. 2 except:
McArthur (c)
Fricka: Sharnova
Sieglinde: Hussa
Siegmund: Melchior
Brünnhilde: Flagstad

December 29 (mat.)

Hänsel und Gretel
Adler (c)
Peter: Beattie
Gertrude: Bartush
Hänsel: Sten
Gretel: Haskins
Witch: Sharnova

December 31

Manon
Kopp (c)
Manon: Moore
Chevalier: Schipa
Lescaut: Czaplicki
Count: Rothier
Guillot: Cavadore
De Brétigny: Howell

1941

November 8

Un Ballo in Maschera
Cooper (c)
Riccardo: Martinelli
Renato: Thomas
Amelia: Rethberg
Ulrica: Kaska
Oscar: Antoine

November 10

Carmen
Peroni (c)
Carmen: Swarthout
Micaela: Albanese
Don José: Jobin
Escamillo: Bonelli
Zuniga: Silva

November 12

Faust
Cooper (c)
Faust: Crooks
Méphistophélès: Pinza
Marguerite: Jepson
Valentine: Morelli
Siébel: Glaz
Martha: Barron

November 14

La Traviata
Peroni (c)
Violetta: Jepson
Alfredo: Bartlett
Germont: Thomas

November 15

Daughter of the Regiment
Papi (c)
Marie: Pons
Marquise: Petina
Sulpice: Baccaloni
Tonio: Jobin
Hortensio: Alvary

November 15 (mat.)

The Barber of Seville
Cooper (c)
Almaviva: Martini
Bartolo: Trevisan
Rosina: Sayao
Basilio: Lazzari
Figaro: Morelli

November 17

Otello
Peroni (c)
Otello: Martinelli
Iago: Tibbett
Cassio: Cavadore
Desdemona: Della Chiesa
Emilia: Paggi

November 19

Aida
Cooper (c)
Aida: Lushanya
Amneris: Branzell
Radames: Baum
Amonasro: Thomas
Ramfis: Lazzari
King: Beattie

November 21

Carmen
Peroni (c)
Carmen: Glade
Micaela: Kirsten
Don José: Rayner
Escamillo: Morelli
Zuniga: Beattie

November 22 (mat.)

Lohengrin
Cooper (c)
Henry: Beattie
Lohengrin: Melchior
Elsa: Bampton
Telramund: Ballarini
Ortrud: Sharnova
Herald: Kozakevich

November 22

Cavalleria Rusticana
Peroni (c)
Santuzza: Giannini
Lola: Bradford
Turiddu: Rayner
Alfio: Morelli

I Pagliacci
Canarutto (c)
Canio: Martinelli
Tonio: Bonelli
Nedda: Turner

November 24

Falstaff
Halasz (c)
Falstaff: Thomas
Mistress Ford: Giannini
Ford: Thompson
Anne Ford: Haskins
Mistress Page: Glaz
Mistress Quickly: Sharnova
Fenton: Knight

November 26

Martha
Peroni (c)
Lady Harriet: Jepson
Nancy: Glade
Plunkett: Beattie
Lionel: Melton
Tristan: Wentworth

November 28

La Bohème
Cooper (c)
Mimi: Mason
Rodolfo: Kiepura
Marcello: Czaplicki
Colline: Lazzari
Musetta: Kirsten

November 29

Il Trovatore
Kopp (c)
Leonora: Lushanya
Azucena: Glade
Manrico: Martinelli
Count: Bonelli
Ferrando: Lazzari

November 29 (mat.)

Carmen
Same as Nov. 10 except:
Carmen: Castagna
Micaela: Turner
Don José: Kiepura
Escamillo: Thomas

December 1

Tosca
Peroni (c)
Tosca: Moore

Cavaradossi: Jagel
Scarpia: Thomas
Angelotti: Beattie
Sacristan: Trevisan

December 3

Madama Butterfly
Bamboschek (c)
Cio-Cio-San: Albanese
Suzuki: Paggi
Pinkerton: Melton
Sharpless: Czaplicki

December 5

Faust
Cooper (c)
Faust: Rayner
Méphistophélès: Silva
Marguerite: Symons
Valentine: Bonelli
Siébel: Mayer
Martha: Barron

December 6

Martha
Same as Nov. 26 except:
Lady Harriet: Antoine

December 6 (mat.)

La Bohème
Same as Nov. 28 except:
Mimi: Moore
Rodolfo: Jagel

December 8

The Barber of Seville
Same as Nov. 15 except:
Rosina: Antoine
Figaro: Bonelli

December 10

Rigoletto
Bojanowski (c)
Gilda: Meusel
Duke: Kiepura
Rigoletto: Bonelli
Sparafucile: Lazzari
Maddalena: Mayer

December 12

Il Trovatore
Same as Nov. 29 except:
Azucena: Wysor
Manrico: Rayner
Count di Luna: Morelli
Ferrando: Silva

December 13 (mat.)

La Traviata
Same as Nov. 14 except:
Germont: Gorin

December 13

Aida
Same as Nov. 19 except:
Aida: Rethberg
Amneris: Glade
Radames: Martinelli
Amonasro: Czaplicki
King: Silva

1942

November 7

Aida
Peroni (c)
Aida: Milanov
Amneris: Kaskas
Radames: Martinelli
Amonasro: Tibbett
Ramfis: Kipnis
King: Love

November 9

Rigoletto
Peroni (c)
Duke: Kiepura
Rigoletto: Thomas
Gilda: Antoine
Sparafucile: Moscona
Maddalena: Kaskas

November 11

Lucia di Lammermoor
Cimara (c)
Lucia: Tuminia
Edgardo: Melton
Enrico: Bonelli
Raimondo: Lazzari

November 13

Martha
Bojanowski (c)
Lady Harriet: Antoine
Nancy: Glade
Tristan: Kozakevich
Lionel: Melton
Plunkett: Beattie
Sheriff: Stack

November 14 (mat.)

Carmen
Peroni (c)
Carmen: Glade
Don José: Jobin
Micaela: Kirsten
Escamillo: Czaplicki

November 14

Faust
Cleva (c)
Faust: Crooks
Méphistophélès: Moscona
Marguerite: Albanese
Valentine: Thomas
Siébel: Mayer

November 16

La Traviata
Cleva (c)
Violetta: Novotna
Alfredo: Melton
Germont: Tibbett

November 18

Mignon
Kepp (c)
Mignon: Tourel
Lothario: Lazzari
Wilhelm Meister: Crooks
Philine: Haskins

November 20

The Barber of Seville
Peroni (c)
Almaviva: Martini
Bartolo: Trevisan
Rosina: Tuminia
Basilio: Lazzari
Figaro: Thomas

November 21 (mat.)

Aida
Peroni (c)
Aida: Giannini

Amneris: Thorborg
Radames: Kiepura
Amonasro: Czaplicki
Ramfis: Lazzari
King: Beattie

November 21

Il Trovatore
Bigalli (c)
Leonora: Bampton
Azucena: Glade
Manrico: Martinelli
Count di Luna: Bonelli
Ferrando: Beattie

November 23

Faust
Cleva (c)
Same as Nov. 14 except:
Faust: Tokatyan
Méphistophélès: Kipnis
Marguerite: Moore
Valentine: Bonelli

November 25

Halka
Bojanowski (c)
Jontek: Kiepura
Halka: Treer
Zofja: Glowacki
Janusz: Czaplicki
Stoinik: Kulpak

November 27

Aida
Peroni (c)
Aida: Bampton
Amneris: Glade
Radames: Raymer
Amonasro: Morelli
Ramfis: Lazzari
King: Beattie

November 28 (mat.)

Manon
Kepp (c)
Count: Beattie
Chevalier: Crooks
Lescaut: Czaplicki
Manon: Jepson

November 28

Otello
Peroni (c)
Otello: Martinelli
Desdemona: Roman
Iago: Tibbett
Cassio: Cavadore

November 30

Cavalleria Rusticana
Lawrence (c)
Turiddu: Raymer
Lucia: Zeiher
Santuzza: Giannini
Alfio: Morelli

I Pagliacci
Bamboschek (c)
Canio: Martinelli
Nedda: Kirsten
Tonio: Thomas

December 2

La Bohème
Cleva (c)
Rodolfo: Tokatyan
Mimi: Moore
Marcello: Czaplicki
Colline: Lazzari
Musetta: Kirsten

December 4

Carmen
Smallens (c)
Carmen: Glade
Don José: Kiepura
Micaela: Symons
Escamillo: Morelli

December 5 (mat.)

Tosca
Cleva (c)
Tosca: Moore
Cavaradossi: Martinelli
Scarpia: Sved
Angelotti: Kozakevich
Sacristan: Trevisan

December 5

Aida
Peroni (c)
Aida: Roman
Amneris: Glade
Radames: Kiepura
Amonasro: Morelli
Ramfis: Lazzari
King: Schmidt

December 7

Martha
Peroni (c)
Same as Nov. 13 except:
Lady Harriet: Jepson
Lionel: Tokatyan

December 9

The Barber of Seville
Halasz (c)
Same as Nov. 20 except:
Almaviva: Knight
Figaro: Morelli

December 11

The Tales of Hoffmann
Peroni (c)
Hoffmann: Conley
Niclaus: Mayer
Olympia: Antoine
Coppelius: Beattie
Giulietta: Lushanya
Antonia: Antoine
Miracle: Beattie

December 12 (mat.)

Rigoletto
Bamboschek (c)
Duke: Kiepura
Rigoletto: Tibbett
Gilda: Tuminia
Sparafucile: Lazzari
Maddalena: Mayer

December 12

La Traviata
Peroni (c)
Violetta: Jepson
Alfredo: Tokatyan
Germont: Thomas

1943

(No season)

1944

October 16

Carmen
Cleva (c)
Don José: Baum
Escamillo: Sved
Zuniga: Love
Carmen: Swarthout
Micaela: Carroll

October 18

La Traviata
Cleva (c)
Violetta: Sayao
Alfredo: Berini
Germont: Weede

October 20

La Bohème
Cleva (c)
Mimi: Hess
Rodolfo: Martini
Marcello: Bonelli
Colline: Lazzari
Musetta: Carroll

October 21 (mat.)

Aida
Cleva (c)
Aida: Milanov
Amneris: Thorborg
Radames: Baum
Amonasro: Sved
Ramfis: Moscona
King: Love

October 21

Die Walküre
McArthur (c)
Siegmund: Darcy
Hunding: Desmarais
Wotan: Janssen
Sieglinde: Varnay
Brünnhilde: Traubel
Fricka: Thorborg

October 23

La Traviata
Same as Oct. 18

October 25

Carmen
Same as Oct. 16 except:
Don José: Martinelli
Zuniga: Kulpak

October 27

Il Trovatore
Bamboschek (c)
Count di Luna: Bonelli
Leonora: Milanov
Azucena: Thorborg
Manrico: Baum
Ferrando: Lazzari

October 28 (mat.)

Otello
Cleva (c)
Otello: Martinelli
Desdemona: Bampton
Iago: Tibbett
Emilia: Brown
Cassio: Cordy

October 28

La Bohème
Same as Oct. 20

October 30

Die Walküre
Same as Oct. 21

November 1

Aida
Same as Oct. 21

November 3

Carmen
Same as Oct. 16 except:
Don José: Martinelli
Zuniga: Kulpak

November 4 (mat.)

Romeo and Juliet
Hasselmans (c)
Capulet: Fardulli
Juliet: MacDonald
Romeo: Bartlett
Mercutio: Ballarini
Stephano: Browning
Duke: Kulpak
Friar: Moscona

November 4

Il Trovatore
Same as Oct. 27

November 6

Otello
Same as Oct. 28 except:
Desdemona: Jessner

November 7

La Traviata
Same as Oct. 18 except:
Germont: Sved

November 8

Pelléas et Mélisande
Goossens (c)
Mélisande: Sayao
Geneviève: Doe
Yniold: Raymondi
Pelléas: Singher
Golaud: Tibbett
Arkel: Moscona

November 10

Faust
Cleva (c)
Faust: Jobin
Méphistophélès: Pinza
Marguerite: Della Chiesa
Valentine: Valentino
Siébel: Browning
Martha: Doe

November 11 (mat.)

Rigoletto
Bamboschek (c)
Gilda: Antoine
Duke: Peerce
Rigoletto: Warren
Sparafucile: Lazzari
Maddalena: Browning

November 11

Romeo and Juliet
Same as Nov. 4

November 13

Pelléas et Mélisande
Same as Nov. 8

November 15

Faust
Same as Nov. 10 except:
Marguerite: MacDonald

November 17

Rigoletto
Same as Nov. 11

November 18 (mat.)

Tosca
Cleva (c)
Tosca: Della Chiesa
Cavaradossi: Jagel
Scarpia: Sved
Angelotti: Brazis
Sacristan: Trevisan

November 18

La Traviata
Same as Oct. 18 except:
Alfredo: Martini

1945

October 8

Manon
Cleva (c)
Manon: Sayao
Des Grieux: Tokatyan
Lescaut: Bonelli
Count: Moscona
Guillot: Oliviero
De Brétigny: Kozakevich

October 10

Rigoletto
Cleva (c)
Duke: J. B. McCormack
Rigoletto: Tibbett
Gilda: Helal
Sparafucile: Lazzari
Maddalena: Nadell
Giovanna: Moser
Monterone: Telasko

October 12

Il Trovatore
Rescigno (c)
Leonora: Kaye
Azucena: Mayer
Manrico: Baum
Count di Luna: Warren
Ferrando: Lazzari

October 13 (mat.)

Carmen
Cleva (c)
Don José: Martinelli
Carmen: Swarthout
Micaela: Helal
Escamillo: Bonelli

October 13

Tosca
Cleva (c)
Tosca: Milanov
Cavaradossi: Tokatyan
Scarpia: Sved
Sacristan: Trevisan

October 15

Rigoletto
Same as Oct. 10

October 17

The Barber of Seville
Rescigno (c)
Almaviva: Martini
Bartolo: Trevisan
Rosina: Antoine
Basilio: Lazzari
Figaro: Brownlee
Bertha: Doe

October 19

Manon
Same as Oct. 8 except:
Lescaut: Brownlee

October 20 (mat.)

Parsifal
Stiedry (c)
Amfortas: Singher
Kundry: Thorborg
Parsifal: Darcy
Titurel: Moscona
Gurnemanz: List
Klingsor: Pechner

October 20

Il Trovatore
Same as Oct. 12

October 22

Tosca
Same as Oct. 13

October 24

Carmen
Same as Oct. 13

October 26

Cavalleria Rusticana
Cleva (c)
Turiddu: Tokatyan
Santuzza: Flesch
Alfio: Ballarini
Lola: Manski

I Pagliacci
Cleva (c)
Canio: Martinelli
Nedda: Stafford
Tonio: Warren

October 27 (mat.)

Faust
Cleva (c)
Faust: Martini
Méphistophélès: Moscona
Marguerite: MacDonald
Valentine: Bonelli
Siébel: Nadell

October 27

Parsifal
Same as Oct. 20

October 29

La Forza del Destino
Walter (c)
Leonora: Roman
Don Carlo: Warren
Don Alvaro: Baum
Padre Guardiano: Moscona
Preziosilla: Nadell
Melitone: Telasko

October 31

Pelléas et Mélisande
Goossens (c)
Arkel: Moscona
Geneviève: Doe
Golaud: Tibbett
Pelléas: Singher
Mélisande: Sayao
Yniold: Tate

November 2

The Barber of Seville
Same as Oct. 17

November 3 (mat.)

La Traviata
Cleva (c)
Violetta: Sayao
Alfredo: Berini
Germont: Bonelli

November 3

Faust
Same as Oct. 27 except:
Valentine: Brownlee

November 5

Pelléas et Mélisande
Same as Oct. 31

November 7

La Forza del Destino
Same as Oct. 29

November 9

La Traviata
Same as Nov. 3

November 10 (mat.)

Aida
Cleva (c)
Aida: Ribla
Amneris: Thorborg
Radames: Jagel
Amonasro: Sved
Ramfis: Moscona
King: Telasko

November 10

The Marriage of Figaro
Walter (c)
Count: Brownlee
Countess: Roman
Susanna: Bokor
Cherubino: Novotna
Figaro: Pinza
Don Basilio: De Paolis
Don Bartolo: Lazzari

November 12

Il Trovatore
Same as Oct. 12 except:
Leonora: Roman
Count di Luna: Sved

November 14

Cavalleria Rusticana
Same as Oct. 26 except:
Turiddu: Berini

I Pagliacci
Same as Oct. 26 except:
Tonio: Bonelli

November 16

Carmen
Same as Oct. 13 except:
Carmen: Djanel

November 17 (mat.)

The Marriage of Figaro
Same as Nov. 10

November 17

Aida
Same as Nov. 10 except:
Amneris: Mayer

1946

September 30

Aida
Cleva (c)
Aida: Milanov
Amneris: Repp
Radames: Baum
Amonasro: Warren
Ramfis: Tajo
King: Telasko

October 2

La Bohème
Cleva (c)
Rodolfo: Tagliavini
Mimi: Kirsten
Marcello: Mascherini
Colline: Lazzari
Schaunard: Engelman
Musetta: Greer

October 4

Amelia Goes to the Ball
Cleva (c)
Amelia: Daum
The Husband: Thompson
The Lover: Tokatyan
The Friend: Doe

The Emperor Jones
Leinsdorf (c)
Brutus Jones: Tibbett
Henry Smithers: Windheim
Old Native Woman: E. Novotna
Congo Witch Doctor: Primus

October 5 (mat.)

Tristan und Isolde
Leinsdorf (c)
King Marke: Ezekiel
Tristan: Svanholm
Isolde: Traubel
Kurvenal: Huehn
Melot: Telasko
Brangäne: Thebom

October 5

Rigoletto
Rescigno (c)
Duke: Bjoerling
Rigoletto: Warren
Gilda: Antoine
Sparafucile: Lazzari
Maddalena: Heckman

October 7

La Bohème
Same as Oct. 2 except:
Rescigno (c)
Rodolfo: Bjoerling

October 9

Lucia di Lammermoor
Rescigno (c)
Lucia: Munsel
Edgardo: Tucker
Enrico: Bonelli
Arturo: Mordino
Raimondo: Lazzari
Alisa: Stafford
Normano: Wolski

October 11

Aida
Same as Sept. 30

October 12 (mat.)

Rigoletto
Same as Oct. 5 except:
Duke: Tucker

October 12

Madama Butterfly
Cleva (c)
Cio-Cio-San: Kirsten
Suzuki: Sachs
Pinkerton: Tagliavini
Sharpless: Bonelli

October 14

Amelia Goes to the Ball
Same as Oct. 4

The Emperor Jones
Same as Oct. 4

October 16

Tristan und Isolde
Same as Oct. 5

October 18

Tosca
Moranzoni (c)
Tosca: Castellani
Cavaradossi: Tagliavini
Scarpia: Guelfi
Angelotti: Brazis
Sacristan: Trevisan

October 19 (mat.)

La Bohème
Same as Oct. 2 except:
Marcello: Bonelli

October 19

Carmen
Leinsdorf (c)
Don José: Vinay
Carmen: Swarthout
Escamillo: Huehn
Micaela: Micheau

October 21

Madama Butterfly
Same as Oct. 12

October 23

La Gioconda
Cleva (c)
La Gioconda: Milanov
La Cieca: Sachs
Laura: Castagna
Enzo: Baum
Barnaba: Guelfi
Alvise: Tajo

October 25

Lucia di Lammermoor
Same as Oct. 9

October 26 (mat.)

Samson and Delilah
Cleva (c)
Delilah: Thorborg
Samson: Jobin
High Priest: Sved
Abimelech: Telasko
An Old Hebrew: Tajo

October 26

Tosca
Same as Oct. 18

October 28

Lohengrin
Stiedry (c)
King Henry: Ezekiel
Lohengrin: Ralf
Elsa: Bampton
Telramund: Sved
Ortrud: Thorborg

October 30

Mignon
Cleva (c)
Mignon: Swarthout
Lothario: Lazzari
Wilhelm Meister: Martini
Philine: Antoine
Frédéric: Pabst
Laerte: Windheim

November 1

La Traviata
Moranzoni (c)
Violetta: Micheau
Alfredo: Tokatyan
Germont: Tibbett

November 2 (mat.)

Madama Butterfly
Same as Oct. 12

November 2

La Gioconda
Same as Oct. 23

November 4

Carmen
Same as Oct. 19

November 6

Lohengrin
Same as Oct. 28

November 8

Samson and Delilah
Same as Oct. 26

November 9 (mat.)

La Traviata
Same as Nov. 1

November 9

Mignon
Same as Oct. 30

1947–1953

No seasons

1954

February 5

Don Giovanni
Rescigno (c)
Commendatore: Sgarro
Donna Anna: Steber
Don Ottavio: Simoneau
Don Giovanni: Rossi-Lemeni
Leporello: Brownlee
Donna Elvira: Jordan
Zerlina: Sayao
Masetto: Alvary

February 7

Don Giovanni
Same as Feb. 5

November 1

Norma
Rescigno (c)
Pollione: Picchi
Oroveso: Rossi-Lemeni
Norma: Callas
Adalgisa: Simionato

November 3

The Taming of the Shrew
Rescigno (c)
Baptista: Stewart
Katharina: Jordan
Bianca: Lind
Petruchio: Thompson
Lucentio: White
Tranio: Tyers
Biondello: Foldi
Hortensio: Gramm

November 5

Norma
Same as Nov. 1

November 6 (mat.)

La Bohème
Perlea (c)
Rodolfo: Prandelli
Marcello: Guelfi
Colline: Alvary
Musetta: Lind
Mimi: Carteri

November 6

The Barber of Seville
Rescigno (c)
Almaviva: Simoneau
Bartolo: Badioli
Basilio: Rossi-Lemeni
Figaro: Gobbi
Rosina: Simionato

November 8

La Traviata
Rescigno (c)
Alfredo: Simoneau
Germont: Gobbi
Violetta: Callas

November 10

The Barber of Seville
Same as Nov. 6

November 12

La Traviata
Same as Nov. 8

November 13 (mat.)

La Bohème
Same as Nov. 6

November 13

The Taming of the Shrew
Same as Nov. 3

November 15

Lucia di Lammermoor
Rescigno (c)
Enrico: Guelfi
Lucia: Callas
Edgardo: di Stefano
Raimondo: Stewart

November 16

Carmen
Perlea (c)
Don José: Picchi
Escamillo: Guelfi
Zuniga: Foldi
Micaela: Jordan
Carmen: Simionato

November 17

Lucia di Lammermoor
Same as Nov. 15

November 18

Tosca
Rescigno (c)
Tosca: Steber
Cavaradossi: di Stefano
Scarpia: Gobbi
Angelotti: Stewart
Sacristan: Badioli

November 20 (mat.)

Carmen
Same as Nov. 16

November 20

Tosca
Same as Nov. 18

1955

October 31

I Puritani
Rescigno (c)
Gaultiers Walton: Wilderman
George Walton: Rossi-Lemeni
Talbot: di Stefano
Forth: Bastianini
Elvira: Callas

November 1

Aida
Serafin (c)
Aida: Tebaldi
Amneris: Varnay
Amonasro: Gobbi
Radames: Antonioli
Ramfis: Wilderman
King: Smith

November 2

I Puritani
Same as Oct. 31

November 4

Aida
Same as Nov. 1

November 5

Il Trovatore
Rescigno (c)
Count: Bastianini
Ferrando: Wildermann
Manrico: Bjoerling
Leonora: Callas
Azucena: Stignani

November 7

La Bohème
Serafin (c)
Rodolfo: di Stefano
Marcello: Gobbi
Colline: Rossi-Lemeni
Musetta: Lind
Mimi: Tebaldi

November 8

Il Trovatore
Same as Nov. 5 except:
Count: Weede
Azucena: Turner

November 9

La Bohème
Same as Nov. 7

November 11

Madama Butterfly
Rescigno (c)
Cio-Cio-San: Callas
Suzuki: Alberts
Pinkerton: di Stefano
Sharpless: Weede

November 12

Rigoletto
Rescigno (c)
Duke: Bjoerling
Rigoletto: Gobbi
Sparafucile: Wilderman
Gilda: Stich-Randall
Maddalena: Dunn

November 14

Madama Butterfly
Same as Nov. 11

November 15

Faust
Serafin (c)
Faust: Bjoerling
Méphistophélès: Rossi-Lemeni
Marguerite: Carteri
Valentine: Weede
Siébel: Dunn
Martha: Alberts

November 16

Il Tabarro
Rescigno (c)
Michele: Gobbi
Luigi: Bergonzi
Giorgetta: Ribla
Frugola: Turner

Il Ballo delle Ingrate
Rescigno (c)
Singers:
Venus: Stignani
Amore: Stich-Randall
Pluto: Smith
Dancers:
Venus: Zorina
Amore: Bockman

The Merry Widow (ballet)
Rescigno (c)
Sonia: Markova
Danilo: Briansky
Popoff: Stone
Baroness Popoff: Arova

November 17

Madama Butterfly
Same as Nov. 11

November 18

Faust
Same as Nov. 15

November 19

Il Tabarro
Same as Nov. 16

Il Ballo delle Ingrate
Same as Nov. 16

The Merry Widow
Same as Nov. 16

November 21

Cavalleria Rusticana
Rescigno (c)
Turiddu: di Stefano
Alfio: Bardelli
Lola: Dunn
Santuzza: Stignani

Lord Byron's Love Letter
Rescigno (c)
Spinster: Ribla
Grandmother: Varnay
Matron: Turner

Revanche (ballet)
Rescigno (c)
Leonora: Markova

Azucena: Arova
Manrico: Briansky
di Luna: Stone

November 22

L'Elisir d'Amore
Serafin (c)
Nemorino: Simoneau
Adina: Carteri
Belcore: Thompson
Dulcamara: Rossi-Lemeni

November 25

Rigoletto
Same as Nov. 12

November 26

Cavalleria Rusticana
Same as Nov. 21 except:
Turiddu: Bergonzi

Lord Byron's Love Letter
Same as Nov. 21

Revanche
Same as Nov. 21

November 28

L'Amore dei Tre Re
Serafin (c)
Archibaldo: Rossi-Lemeni
Manfredo: Weede
Avito: Bergonzi
Flaminio: Caruso
Fiora: Kirsten

November 29

Un Ballo in Maschera
Rescigno (c)
Riccardo: Bjoerling
Amelia: Cerquetti
Renato: Gobbi
Oscar: Bonini
Ulrica: Turner

November 30

L'Elisir d'Amore
Same as Nov. 22

December 2

L'Amore dei Tre Re
Same as Nov. 28

December 3

Un Ballo in Maschera
Same as Nov. 29

1956

October 10

The Girl of the Golden West
Mitropoulos (c)
Minnie: Steber
Jack Rance: Gobbi
Dick Johnson: Del Monaco
Ashby: Wilderman
Sonora: Noel

October 13

The Girl of the Golden West
Same as Oct. 10

October 16

Andrea Chénier
Buckley (c)
Gérard: Gobbi
Madeleine: Steber
Bersi: Lind
Andrea Chénier: Del Monaco

October 17

Salome
Solti (c)
Herod: Vinay
Herodias: Lipton
Salome: Borkh
Jochanaan: Welitsch
Narraboth: Alexander

October 19

Andrea Chénier
Same as Oct. 16 except:
Bersi: Winston

October 20

Die Walküre
Solti (c)
Siegmund: Suthaus
Hunding: Wilderman
Wotan: Schoeffler
Sieglinde: Borkh
Brünnhilde: Nilsson
Fricka: Turner

October 22

Die Walküre
Same as Oct. 20

October 23

Il Trovatore
Bartoletti (c)
Count di Luna: Bastianini
Leonora: Nelli
Manrico: Bjoerling
Ferrando: Wilderman
Azucena: Turner

October 26

La Traviata
Bartoletti (c)
Alfredo: Simoneau
Germont: Bastianini
Violetta: Steber

October 27

Il Trovatore
Same as Oct. 23 except:
Leonora: Ribla

October 29

Don Giovanni
Solti (c)
Commendatore: Schoeffler
Donna Anna: Steber
Don Ottavio: Simoneau
Don Giovanni: Rossi-Lemeni
Leporello: Corena
Donna Elvira: Likova
Zerlina: Wilson
Masetto: Foldi

October 30

Tosca
Bartoletti (c)
Tosca: Tebaldi
Cavaradossi: Bjoerling

Scarpia: Gobbi
Angelotti: Rollman
Sacristan: Badioli

October 31

La Traviata
Same as Oct. 26

November 2

Tosca
Same as Oct. 30 except:
Kopp (c)

November 3

Salome
Same as Oct. 17

November 5

Tosca
Same as Oct. 30

November 8

La Forza del Destino
Solti (c)
Leonora: Tebaldi
Preziosilla: Simionato
Alvaro: Tucker
Don Carlo: Bastianini
Padre Guardiano: Rossi-Lemeni
Melitone: Badioli

November 9

The Barber of Seville
Buckley (c)
Almaviva: Simoneau
Bartolo: Badioli
Basilio: Rossi-Lemeni
Figaro: Gobbi
Fiorello: Nekolny
Rosina: Simionato

November 12

La Forza del Destino
Same as Nov. 8

November 13

Don Giovanni
Same as Oct. 29 except:
Donna Elvira: Lind

November 14

La Bohème
Bartoletti (c)
Rodolfo: Morrell
Marcello: Bastianini
Colline: Cangalovich
Musetta: Wilson
Mimi: Tebaldi

November 15

The Barber of Seville
Same as Nov. 9

November 16

La Bohème
Same as Nov. 14 except:
Rodolfo: Bjoerling

November 17

The Barber of Seville
Same as Nov. 9

1957

October 11

Otello
Serafin (c)
Otello: Del Monaco
Iago: Gobbi
Cassio: Chabay
Desdemona: Tebaldi
Emilia: Kramarich

October 14

Otello
Same as Oct. 11 except:
Desdemona: Koehn

October 16

La Bohème
Gavazzeni (c)
Rodolfo: Bjoerling
Marcello: Protti
Schaunard: Noel
Musetta: Likova
Mimi: Moffo

October 18

Otello
Same as Oct. 11

October 19

Mignon
Gavazzeni (c)
Mignon: Simionato
Philine: Moffo
Frederick: Nadell
Wilhelm Meister: Misciano
Lothario: Wilderman

October 21

Manon Lescaut
Serafin (c)
Manon: Tebaldi
Lescaut: MacNeil
Des Grieux: Bjoerling
Geronte: Badioli
Edmondo: Chabay
Musician: Nadell

October 23

Cavalleria Rusticana
Kopp (c)
Turiddu: Sullivan
Alfio: MacNeil
Lola: Nadell
Santuzza: Simionato

I Pagliacci
Bartoletti (c)
Canio: Del Monaco
Nedda: Likova
Tonio: Gobbi
Silvio: MacNeil

October 25

Manon Lescaut
Same as Oct. 21

October 26

Cavalleria Rusticana
Same as Oct. 23

I Pagliacci
Same as Oct. 23

October 28

Mignon
Same as Oct. 19

October 30

Andrea Chénier
Gavazzeni (c)
Gérard: Gobbi
Madeleine: Tebaldi

Bersi: Nadell
Andrea Chénier:
Del Monaco
Madelon: Kramarich

November 1

La Gioconda
Serafin (c)
La Gioconda: Farrell
La Cieca: Kramarich
Alvise: Wilderman
Laura: Simionato
Enzo: Tucker
Barnaba: Protti

November 2

Andrea Chénier
Same as Oct. 30

November 4

La Bohème
Same as Oct. 16

November 6

La Gioconda
Same as Nov. 1 except:
Enzo: di Stefano

November 8

The Marriage of Figaro
Solti (c)
Almaviva: Gobbi
Figaro: Berry
Cherubino: Simionato
Countess: Steber
Susanna: Moffo
Marcellina: Nadell

November 9

Manon Lescaut
Same as Oct. 21

November 11

The Marriage of Figaro
Same as Nov. 8

November 13

Adriana Lecouvreur
Serafin (c)
Maurizio: di Stefano
Prince de Bouillon: Badioli
Michonnet: Gobbi
Adriana Lecouvreur:
Tebaldi
Princess de Bouillon:
Simionato

November 15

Un Ballo in Maschera
Solti (c)
Riccardo: Bjoerling
Amelia: Cerquetti
Renato: Protti
Oscar: Stahlman
Ulrica: Turner

November 16

Adriana Lecouvreur
Same as Nov. 13

November 18

Un Ballo in Maschera
Same as Nov. 15

November 20

Tosca
Bartoletti (c)
Tosca: Steber
Cavaradossi: di Stefano
Scarpia: Gobbi
Angelotti: Smith
Spoletta: Caruso

November 22

Don Carlo
Solti (c)
Elisabetta di Valois:
Cerquetti
Principessa Eboli: Rankin
Don Carlo: Sullivan
Rodrigo: Gobbi
Filippo II: Christoff
Grand Inquisitor:
Wilderman
Heavenly Voice: Stahlman

November 23

Lucia di Lammermoor
Bartoletti (c)
Ashton: Protti
Lucia: Moffo
Edgardo: di Stefano
Raimondo: Smith

November 25

Don Carlo
Same as Nov. 22

November 27

Lucia di Lammermoor
Same as Nov. 23 except:
Edgardo: Sullivan

November 29

Tosca
Same as Nov. 20 except:
Cavaradossi: Bjoerling

November 30

Don Carlo
Same as Nov. 22 except:
Don Carlo: Bjoerling

1958

October 10

Falstaff
Serafin (c)
Falstaff: Gobbi
Fenton: Misciano
Ford: MacNeil
Mistress Ford: Tebaldi
Nanetta: Moffo
Mistress Page: Canali
Mistress Quickly:
Simionato

October 13

Madama Butterfly
Kondrashin (c)
Cio-Cio-San: Tebaldi
Suzuki: Canali
Pinkerton: di Stefano
Sharpless: MacNeil

October 15

Madama Butterfly
Same as Oct. 13

October 17

Falstaff
Same as Oct. 10

October 18

Turandot
Serafin (c)
Turandot: Nilsson
Altoum: Quinlin
Timur: Wilderman
Calaf: di Stefano

Liu: Moffo
Ping: Torigi
Pang: Caruso
Pong: Vellucci

October 20

Il Trovatore
Schaenen (c)
Count di Luna: Bastianini
Ferrando: Wilderman
Manrico: Bjoerling
Leonora: Ross
Azucena: Simionato

October 22

Turandot
Same as Oct. 18

October 24

Il Trovatore
Same as Oct. 20

October 25

Gianni Schicchi
Serafin (c)
Gianni Schicchi: Gobbi
Lauretta: Moffo
Zita: Canali
Rinuccio: Misciano
Simone: Wildermann

I Pagliacci
Serafin (c)
Prologue: MacNeil
Canio: di Stefano
Nedda: Likova
Tonio: Gobbi
Silvio: MacNeil

October 27

Turandot
Same as Oct. 18

October 29

Il Trovatore
Same as Oct. 20

October 31

Gianni Schicchi
Same as Oct. 25

I Pagliacci
Same as Oct. 25

November 1

Tristan und Isolde
Rodzinski (c)
Tristan: Liebl
Marke: Wilderman
Isolde: Nilsson
Kurvenal: Cassel
Brangäne: Hoffman

November 3

Gianni Schicchi
Same as Oct. 25

I Pagliacci
Same as Oct. 25

November 5

La Traviata
Serafin (c)
Alfredo: Simoneau
Germont: Bastianini
Violetta: Steber

November 7

Tristan und Isolde
Same as Nov. 1

November 8

La Traviata
Same as Nov. 5

November 10

Tristan und Isolde
Same as Nov. 1

November 12

The Barber of Seville
Schaenen (c)
Almaviva: Misciano
Bartolo: Corena
Basilio: Montarsolo
Figaro: Gobbi
Rosina: Simionato

November 14

La Traviata
Same as Nov. 5

November 15

Rigoletto
Sebastian (c)
Duke: Bjoerling
Rigoletto: Gobbi
Sparafucile: Wilderman
Gilda: Moffo
Maddalena: Steffan

November 17

Boris Godunov
Sebastian (c)
Boris Godunov: Christoff
Feodor: Steffan
Xenia: Diamond
Nurse: Bering
Prince Shuisky: Caruso
Pimen: Wilderman
Dimitri: Sullivan
Marina: Hoffman

November 19

Rigoletto
Same as Nov. 15 except:
Rigoletto: MacNeil

November 21

The Barber of Seville
Same as Nov. 12

November 22

Boris Godunov
Same as Nov. 17

November 24

Aida
Sebastian (c)
Aida: Rysanek
Amneris: Simionato
Amonasro: Gobbi
Radames: Bjoerling
Ramfis: Wilderman
King: Smith

November 26

Aida
Same as Nov. 24

November 28

Boris Godunov
Same as Nov. 17

November 29

Aida
Same as Nov. 24

1959

October 12

Carmen
Von Matacic (c)
Don José: di Stefano
Escamillo: Blanc
Zuniga: Harrower
Micaela: Warenskjold
Carmen: Madeira

October 14

La Cenerentola
Gavazzeni (c)
Ramiro: Monti
Dandini: Gramm
Magnifico: Corena
Clorinda: Callaway
Thisbe: Vozza
Angelina: Rota
Alidoro: Foldi

October 16

Carmen
Same as Oct. 12

October 17

La Cenerentola
Same as Oct. 14

October 19

La Cenerentola
Same as Oct. 14

October 21

Carmen
Same as Oct. 12

October 23

Simon Boccanegra
Gavazzeni (c)
Amelia: Roberti
Adorno: Tucker
Simon Boccanegra: Gobbi
Fiesco: Mazzoli
Albiani: Maero
Pietro: Harrower

October 24

Carmen
Same as Oct. 12

October 26

Simon Boccanegra
Same as Oct. 23

October 28

Turandot
Gavazzeni (c)
Turandot: Nilsson
Altoum: Nielsen
Timur: Mazzoli
Calaf: di Stefano
Liu: Price
Ping: Corena
Pang: Caruso
Pong: Vellucci

October 29

Simon Boccanegra
Same as Oct. 23

October 30

Turandot
Same as Oct. 28

November 2

Jenufa
Von Matacic (c)
Jenufa: Brouwenstijn
Grandmother Buryja: Kramarich
Laca Klemen: Cassilly
Kostelnicka Buryja: Fisher
Steva Buryja: Charlebois

November 4

Un Ballo in Maschera
Bartoletti (c)
Riccardo: di Stefano
Amelia: Nilsson
Renato: Gobbi
Oscar: Stahlman
Ulrica: Kramarich

November 6

Jenufa
Same as Nov. 2

November 7

Un Ballo in Maschera
Same as Nov. 4

November 9

Cosi Fan Tutte
Krips (c)
Fiordiligi: Schwarzkopf
Dorabella: Ludwig
Ferrando: Simoneau
Guglielmo: Berry
Alfonso: Corena
Despina: Stahlman

November 11

Cosi Fan Tutte
Same as Nov. 9 except:
Von Matacic (c)

November 13

The Flying Dutchman
Von Matacic (c)
Daland: Greindl
Senta: Nilsson
Eric: Tobin
Mary: MacKenzie
Daland's Steersman: Curzi
Flying Dutchman: Neralic

November 14

Cosi Fan Tutte
Same as Nov. 9 except:
Von Matacic (c)

November 16

The Flying Dutchman
Same as Nov. 13

November 18

La Gioconda
Bartoletti (c)
La Gioconda: Farrell
La Cieca: Kramarich
Alvise: Greindl
Laura: Dalis
Enzo: Tucker
Barnaba: Taddei

November 20

La Gioconda
Same as Nov. 18

November 21

The Flying Dutchman
Same as Nov. 13

November 23

Thaïs
Pretre (c)
Athanael: Roux
Nicias: Simoneau
Palemon: Corena
Thaïs: Price

November 25

Thaïs
Same as Nov. 23

November 27

Thaïs
Same as Nov. 23

November 28

La Gioconda
Same as Nov. 18

1960

October 14

Don Carlo
Votto (c)
Elisabetta: Roberti
Eboli: Simionato
Don Carlo: Tucker
Rodrigo: Gobbi
Filippo II: Christoff
Grand Inquisitor: Mazzoli

October 17

Aida
Votto (c)
Aida: Roberti
Amneris: Simionato
Amonasro: Merrill
Radames: Bergonzi
Ramfis: Mazzoli
King: Ventriglia

October 19

Aida
Same as Oct. 17

October 21

Don Carlo
Same as Oct. 14

October 22

Aida
Same as Oct. 17 except:
Aida: Price
Radames: Ottolini

October 24

Don Carlo
Same as Oct. 14

October 26

The Marriage of Figaro
Krips (c)
Almaviva: Waechter
Bartolo: Corena
Figaro: Berry
Cherubino: Ludwig
Countess: Schwarzkopf
Susanna: Streich
Marcellina: Lipton

October 28

Aida
Same as Oct. 17 except:
Aida: Price
Radames: Ottolini

October 29

The Marriage of Figaro
Same as Oct. 26

October 31

The Marriage of Figaro
Same as Oct. 26

November 2

La Bohème
Gavazzeni (c)
Rodolfo: Tucker
Marcello: Cesari
Colline: Mazzoli
Musetta: Yarick
Mimi: Scotto

November 4

Carmen
Von Matacic (c)
Don José: di Stefano
Escamillo: Merrill
Zuniga: Ventriglia
Micaela: Scotto
Carmen: Madeira

November 5

La Bohème
Same as Nov. 2

November 7

La Bohème
Same as Nov. 2

November 9

Carmen
Same as Nov. 4

November 11

Tosca
Gavazzeni (c)
Tosca: Tebaldi
Cavaradossi: di Stefano
Scarpia: Gobbi
Angelotti: Ventriglia
Sacristan: Pechner

November 12

Carmen
Same as Nov. 4 except:
Don José: Cassilly

November 14

Tosca
Same as Nov. 11

November 16

Die Walküre
Von Matacic (c)
Siegmund: Vickers
Hunding: Wilderman
Wotan: Hotter
Sieglinde: Brouwenstijn
Brünnhilde: Nilsson
Fricka: Ludwig

November 18

Die Walküre
Same as Nov. 16

November 19

Tosca
Same as Nov. 11

November 21

Die Walküre
Same as Nov. 16

November 23

Fedora
Von Matacic (c)
Fedora: Tebaldi
Ipanov: di Stefano
De Siriex: Gobbi
Olga: Scovotti
Rouvel: Schmorr

November 25

Fedora
Same as Nov. 23

November 26

Madama Butterfly
Gavazzeni (c)
Cio-Cio-San: Price
Suzuki: Miller
Pinkerton: Casilly
Sharpless: Cesari

November 28

Madama Butterfly
Same as Nov. 26

November 30

Simon Boccanegra
Gavazzeni (c)
Amelia: Tebaldi
Adorno: Tucker
Simon Boccanegra: Gobbi
Fiesco: Mazzoli
Albiani: Cesari
Pietro: Watson

December 2

Madama Butterfly
Same as Nov. 26

December 3

Simon Boccanegra
Same as Nov. 30

1961

October 14

Lucia di Lammermoor
Votto (c)
Ashton: Zanasi
Lucia: Sutherland
Edgardo: Tucker
Raimondo: Wilderman

October 16

Lucia di Lammermoor
Same as Oct. 14

October 18

Lucia di Lammermoor
Same as Oct. 14 except:
Edgardo: Bergonzi

October 20

Andrea Chénier
Votto (c)
Gérard: Zanasi
Madeleine: Vartenissian
Bersi: Magrini
Andrea Chénier: Vickers
Madelon: MacKenzie

October 21

Mefistofele
Votto (c)
Mefistofele: Christoff
Faust: Bergonzi
Margherita: Ligabue
Martha: Magrini
Elena: Ludwig
Pantalis: MacKenzie

October 23

Mefistofele
Same as Oct. 21

October 25

Andrea Chénier
Same as Oct. 20

October 27

Mefistofele
Same as Oct. 21

October 28

Andrea Chénier
Same as Oct. 20

October 30

La Forza del Destino
Cillario (c)
Leonora: Farrell
Preziosilla: Ludwig
Alvaro: Bergonzi
Carlo: Guelfi
Padre Guardiano: Christoff
Marchese di Calatrava: Warner
Melitone: Cesari

November 1

Cosi Fan Tutte
Maag (c)
Fiordiligi: Schwarzkopf
Dorabella: Ludwig
Ferrando: Simoneau
Guglielmo: Berry
Alfonso: Cesari
Despina: Stahlman

November 3

Cosi Fan Tutte
Same as Nov. 1

November 4

La Forza del Destino
Same as Oct. 30 except:
Alvaro: Poleri

November 6

Don Giovanni
Maag (c)
Commendatore: Wilderman
Donna Anna: Stich-Randall
Don Ottávio: Simoneau
Don Giovanni: Waechter
Leporello: Berry
Donna Elvira: Della Casa
Zerlina: Seefried
Masetto: Cesari

November 8

Don Giovanni
Same as Nov. 6 except:
Donna Elvira: Schwarzkopf

November 10

La Forza del Destino
Same as Oct. 30

November 11

Don Giovanni
Same as Nov. 6 except:
Donna Elvira: Schwarzkopf

November 13

Fidelio
Maag (c)
Florestan: Vickers
Leonora: Nilsson
Fernando: Berry
Pizarro: Hotter
Rocco: Wilderman
Marcellina: Seefried
Jacquino: Knoll

November 15

The Barber of Seville
Cillario (c)
Almaviva: Alva
Bartolo: Corena
Basilio: Christoff
Figaro: Bruscantini
Rosina: Simionato

November 17

Fidelio
Same as Nov. 13

November 18

The Barber of Seville
Same as Nov. 15

November 20

The Barber of Seville
Same as Nov. 15

November 22

Fidelio
Same as Nov. 13

November 24

The Barber of Seville
Same as Nov. 15

November 25

The Harvest
Giannini (c)
Sam: Wilderman
Lora: Horne
Lem: Evans
Jesse: Knoll
Mark: Morell

November 27

The Harvest
Same as Nov. 25

November 29

The Harvest
Same as Nov. 25

December 1

The Harvest
Same as Nov. 25

1962

October 12

Prince Igor
Danon (c)
Igor: Gorin
Jaroslavna: Rubio
Vladimir: Poleri
Galitsky: Christoff
Kontchak: Christoff
Kontchakovna: Smith
Ovlour: Knoll

October 15

Prince Igor
Same as Oct. 12

October 17

La Bohème
Cillario (c)
Rodolfo: Tucker
Marcello: Zanasi
Colline: Wilderman
Benoit: Corena
Alcindoro: Corena
Mimi: Rubio
Musetta: Moynagh

October 19

La Bohème
Same as Oct. 17 except:
Mimi: Sighele

October 20

Prince Igor
Same as Oct. 12

October 22

La Bohème
Same as Oct. 17 except:
Colline: Christoff
Mimi: Sighele

October 24

Prince Igor
Same as Oct. 12

October 26

Tosca
Cillario (c)
Tosca: Crespin
Cavaradossi: Zampieri
Scarpia: Gobbi
Angelotti: Cesari
Sacristan: Corena

October 27

La Bohème
Same as Oct. 17 except:
Colline: Christoff

October 29

Tosca
Same as Oct. 26

October 31

L'Elisir d'Amore
Cillario (c)
Nemorino: Kraus
Adina: Adani
Belcore: Zanasi
Dulcamara: Corena

November 2

L'Elisir d'Amore
Same as Oct. 31

November 3

Tosca
Same as Oct. 26

November 5

L'Elisir d'Amore
Same as Oct. 31

November 7

The Marriage of Figaro
Maag (c)
Almaviva: Gobbi
Figaro: Capecchi
Bartolo: Corena
Cherubino: Berganza
Countess: Della Casa
Susanna: Streich
Marcellina: Evans

November 9

The Marriage of Figaro
Same as Nov. 7

November 10

Samson and Delilah
Dervaux (c)
Delilah: Gorr
Samson: Kaart
High Priest: Bacquier
Abimelech: Wilderman
Old Hebrew: Corena

November 12

The Marriage of Figaro
Same as Nov. 7

November 14

Samson and Delilah
Same as Nov. 10

November 16

Samson and Delilah
Same as Nov. 10

November 17

Rigoletto
Dervaux (c)
Duke: Tucker
Rigoletto: Bastianini
Sparafucile: Wilderman
Gilda: D'Angelo
Maddalena: Smith

November 19

Samson and Delilah
Same as Nov. 10

November 21

Rigoletto
Same as Nov. 17

November 23

Rigoletto
Same as Nov. 17

November 24

Orfeo ed Euridice
Dervaux (c)
Orfeo: Bacquier
Euridice: Della Casa
Amore: Streich

November 26

Rigoletto
Same as Nov. 17

November 28

Orfeo ed Euridice
Same as Nov. 24

November 30

Orfeo ed Euridice
Same as Nov. 24

1963

October 4

Nabucco
Bartoletti (c)
Abigaille: Mastilovic
Fenena: Rota
Ismaele: Morena
Nabucco: Gobbi
Zaccaria: Christoff

October 5

Un Ballo in Maschera
Dervaux (c)
Riccardo: Tucker
Amelia: Crespin
Renato: Zanasi
Tomaso: Smith
Oscar: Kailer
Ulrica: Bumbry

October 7

Nabucco
Same as Oct. 4

October 9

Un Ballo in Maschera
Same as Oct. 5

October 11

Nabucco
Same as Oct. 4

October 12

Faust
Dervaux (c)
Faust: Chauvet
Méphistophélès: Ghiaurov
Marguerite: Guiot
Valentine: Massard
Siébel: Rota
Martha: Vozza

October 14

Un Ballo in Maschera
Same as Oct. 5

October 16

Faust
Same as Oct. 12

October 18

Un Ballo in Maschera
Same as Oct. 5

October 19

Nabucco
Same as Oct. 4

October 21

Faust
Same as Oct. 12

October 23

Fidelio
Rieger (c)
Florestan: Vickers
Leonora: Crespin

Fernando: Cesari
Pizarro: Christoff
Rocco: Wilderman
Marcellina: Steffek
Jacquino: Knoll

October 25

Faust
Same as Oct. 12

October 26

Fidelio
Same as Oct. 23

October 28

Fidelio
Same as Oct. 23 except:
Florestan: Feiersinger

November 1

Fidelio
Same as Oct. 28

November 2

Otello
Bartoletti (c)
Otello: Vickers
Desdemona: Jurinac
Iago: Gobbi
Cassio: Cossutta
Emilia: Vozza

November 4

Otello
Same as Nov. 2 except:
Otello: Uzunov

November 6

The Barber of Seville
Cillario (c)
Almaviva: A. Kraus
Bartolo: Corena
Basilio: Christoff
Figaro: Zanasi
Rosina: Berganza

November 8

Otello
Same as Nov. 2

November 9

The Barber of Seville
Same as Nov. 6

November 11

The Barber of Seville
Same as Nov. 6

November 13

Otello
Same as Nov. 2

November 15

The Barber of Seville
Same as Nov. 6

November 16

Tannhäuser
Danon (c)
Hermann: Wilderman
Tannhäuser: Uzunov
Wolfram: Wolansky
Walter Cossutta
Elisabeth: Crespin
Venus: Bumbry

November 18

Tannhäuser
Same as Nov. 16

November 20

Don Pasquale
Cillario (c)
Don Pasquale: Corena
Dr. Malatesta: Bruscantini
Ernesto: A. Kraus
Norina: Adani

November 22

Tannhäuser
Same as Nov. 16

November 23

Tannhäuser
Same as Nov. 16

November 25

Don Pasquale
Same as Nov. 20

November 27

Don Pasquale
Same as Nov. 20

November 29

Don Pasquale
Same as Nov. 20

1964

October 9

Il Trovatore
Bartoletti (c)
Count di Luna: Zanasi
Ferrando: Vinco
Manrico: Corelli
Leonora: Ligabue
Azucena: Bumbry
Balthazar: Vinco
Leonora: Cossotto
Inez: De Sett

October 12

La Favorita
Cillario (c)
Alfonso XI: Bruscantini
Ferdinand: A. Kraus
Don Gaspar: Deis

October 14

Il Trovatore
Same as Oct. 9

October 16

La Favorita
Same as Oct. 12

October 17

Il Trovatore
Same as Oct. 9

October 19

Il Trovatore
Same as Oct. 9

October 21

La Favorita
Same as Oct. 12

October 23

Carmen
Dervaux (c)
Don José: Corelli
Escamillo: Massard
Zuniga: Meredith

Micaela: Gonzales
Carmen: Bumbry

October 24

La Favorita
Same as Oct. 12

October 26

Carmen
Same as Oct. 23 except:
Micaela: Panni

October 28

Don Carlo
Bartoletti (c)
Elisabetta: Gencer
Eboli: Cossotto
Don Carlo: Tucker
Rodrigo: Gobbi
Filippo II: Ghiaurov
Grand Inquisitor: Marangoni

October 30

Don Carlo
Same as Oct. 28

October 31

Carmen
Same as Oct. 26

November 2

Don Carlo
Same as Oct. 28 except:
Eboli: Bumbry

November 4

Carmen
Same as Oct. 26

November 6

Ariadne auf Naxos
Jochum (c)
Major-Domo: Meredith
Music Master: Uppman
Composer: Seefried
Tenor (later Bacchus): Cox
Zerbinetta: Grist
Prima Donna (later Ariadne): Crespin
Harlequin: Kunz
Scaramuccio: Kraus
Truffaldino: Tadeo
Brighella: Unger

November 7

Don Carlo
Same as Nov. 2

November 8

La Bohème
Dervaux (c)
Rodolfo: Cioni
Marcello: Bruscantini
Colline: Marangoni
Mimi: Tebaldi
Musetta: De Sett

November 9

Ariadne auf Naxos
Same as Nov. 6

November 11

La Cenerentola
Cillario (c)
Ramiro: Casellato
Dandini: Bruscantini
Magnifico: Tadeo
Clorinda: De Sett
Thisbe: Mannion
Angelina: Berganza
Alidoro: Cesari

November 12

La Bohème
Same as Nov. 8

November 13

La Cenerentola
Same as Nov. 11

November 14

Ariadne auf Naxos
Same as Nov. 6

November 16

Don Giovanni
Krips (c)
Commendatore: Marangoni
Donna Anna: Stich-Randall
Don Ottavio: Kraus
Don Giovanni: Ghiaurov
Leporello: Kunz
Donna Elvira: Curtin
Zerlina: Panni
Masetto: Uppman

November 17

La Bohème
Same as Nov. 8

November 18

Ariadne auf Naxos
Same as Nov. 6

November 19

La Cenerentola
Same as Nov. 11

November 20

Don Giovanni
Same as Nov. 16

November 21

La Cenerentola
Same as Nov. 11

November 22

Don Giovanni
Same as Nov. 16

November 23

La Cenerentola
Same as Nov. 11

November 24

La Bohème
Same as Nov. 8

November 25

Don Giovanni
Same as Nov. 16

November 27

Tosca
Bartoletti (c)
Tosca: Crespin
Cavaradossi: Tucker
Scarpia: Gobbi
Angelotti: Cesari
Spoletta: Schmorr

November 30

Tosca
Same as Nov. 27

December 2

Tosca
Same as Nov. 27

December 5

Tosca
Same as Nov. 27

1965

October 8

Mefistofele
Sanzogno (c)
Mefistofele: Ghiaurov
Faust: A. Kraus
Marguerite: Tebaldi
Martha: MacKenzie
Helen: Suliotis
Pantalis: Roggero

October 11

Simon Boccanegra
Bartoletti (c)
Simon Boccanegra: Gobbi
Amelia: Ligabue
Fiesco: Arie
Paolo: Cesari
Pietro: Michalski
Gabriele: Cioni

October 13

Mefistofele
Same as Oct. 8

October 15

Simon Boccanegra
Same as Oct. 11

October 16

Mefistofele
Same as Oct. 8

October 18

Mefistofele
Same as Oct. 8

October 20

Simon Boccanegra
Same as Oct. 11

October 22

La Bohème
Cillario (c)
Rodolfo: Corelli
Marcello: Bruscantini
Colline: Aria
Mimi: Freni
Musetta: Martelli

October 23

Simon Boccanegra
Same as Oct. 11

October 25

La Bohème
Same as Oct. 22

October 27

La Bohème
Same as Oct. 22

October 29

Madama Butterfly
Cillario (c)
Cio-Cio-San: Scotto
Suzuki: Casei
Pinkerton: Cioni
Sharpless: Bruscantini

October 30

La Bohème
Same as Oct. 22

November 1

Madama Butterfly
Same as Oct. 29

November 4

Madama Butterfly
Same as Oct. 29

November 6

Madama Butterfly
Same as Oct. 29

November 10

Madama Butterfly
Same as Oct. 29

November 12

Carmina Burana
Fournet (c)
Lady: Martelli
Drinker: A. Kraus
Poet: Bruscantini

L'Heure Espagnole
Fournet (c)
Concepcion: Berganza
Gonzalve: Alfredo Kraus
Torquemada: Herbert Kraus
Ramiro: Bruscantini
Don Inigo: Tadeo

November 15

Carmina Burana and ***L'Heure Espagnole***
Same as Nov. 12

November 17

Carmina Burana and ***L'Heure Espagnole***
Same as Nov. 12

November 20

Carmina Burana and ***L'Heure Espagnole***
Same as Nov. 12

November 24

Aida
Cillario (c)
Aida: Price
Amneris: Cossotto
Amonasro: Bastianini
Radames: Casellato
Ramfis: Vinco
King: Michalski

November 26

Rigoletto
Bartoletti (c)
Duke: Kraus
Rigoletto: MacNeil
Sparafucile: Vinco
Gilda: Scotto
Maddalena: Casei

November 27

Aida
Same as Nov. 24

November 29

Rigoletto
Same as Nov. 26

November 30

Aida
Same as Nov. 24

December 2

Rigoletto
Same as Nov. 26

December 3

Aida
Same as Nov. 24 except:
Amonasro: Colzani

December 4

Rigoletto
Same as Nov. 26 except:
Rigoletto: Bruscantini

December 6 (mat.)

Rigoletto
Same as Dec. 4

December 6

Aida
Same as Nov. 24 except:
Aida: Lee

December 8

Rigoletto
Same as Dec. 4

INDEX